Collins COBUILD

English/Español
GLOSSARY

HEINLE
CENGAGE Learning

Australia • Brazil • Japan • Korea • Mexico • Singapore • Spain • United Kingdom • United States

HEINLE
CENGAGE Learning

Collins | COBUILD

Collins COBUILD English/Español Glossary

Heinle Cengage Learning

President: Dennis Hogan
Publisher: Sherrise Roehr
Development Editor: Katherine Carroll
Director of Global Marketing: Ian Martin
Director of U.S. Marketing: Jim McDonough
Product Marketing Manager: Katie Kelley
Director of Content and Media Production: Michael Burggren
Content Project Manager: Dawn Marie Elwell
Sr. Frontlist Buyer: Mary Beth Hennebury
Cover Layout: Lisa Mezikofsky

Collins

Publisher: Elaine Higgleton
Project Manager: James Flockhart
Contributors: Patrick Goldsmith, Liliana Andrade Llanas, Guillermina del Carmen Cuevas Mesa, Magdalena Palencia Castro, Mario Alfonso Zamudio Vega
Computing Support: Thomas Callan
Typeset: Wordcraft

Copyright © HarperCollins Publishers 2009

Collins™, COBUILD™, and Bank of English™ are registered trademarks of HarperCollins Publishers Limited.

Harper Collins Publishers
Westerhill Road
Bishopbriggs
Glasgow
G64 2QT
Great Britain

www.collins.co.uk

Heinle
25 Thomson Place
Boston, MA 02210
USA

Cengage Learning products are represented in Canada by Nelson Education, Ltd.

Visit Heinle online at **elt.heinle.com**

Visit our corporate website at **www.cengage.com**

Library of Congress Control Number: 2008930323

ISBN 13: 978-1-4240-1964-9
ISBN 10: 1-4240-1964-8

Printed in China by China Translation & Printing Services Limited
5 6 7 13 12 11

Contents

How to use this Glossary

The *Collins COBUILD English/Español Glossary* is especially designed for Spanish-speaking students who need a quick and easy-to-use English/Spanish reference.

English-Spanish

Guide word
At the top of every right-hand page the guide word is the same as the last entry on that page. On left-hand pages the guide word is the same as the first complete entry on that page. This helps you find the word you are looking for quickly and easily.

Compound Headwords
The stress pattern for compound headwords is shown by underlining the letters that are stressed.

Headword
Every entry begins with a blue headword. Words which are closely related are also printed in blue, with a blue circle (•) before them.

English phrase
Phrases (groups of words which have a particular meaning when they are used together) are printed in blue, with a blue triangle (▶) before them.

93   **geology**

gen|er|al|ly generalmente, en general
gen|er|al store tienda de abarrotes, miscelánea

ge|ner|ic genérico, general, no de marca
gen|er|ous generoso, amplio • gen|er|os|ity

gen|er|al general, en general, generalizado

gen|er|al|ize generalizar • gen|er|al|iza|tion generalización

gela|tin *también* gelatine gelatina

▶ gear up prepararse, orientarse

gauge calcular, medir, ponderar, evaluar, valorar, estimar, juzgar, medidor, indicio

Hyphenation Points
These blue lines show where you can use a hyphen to split a word over two lines.

Letter tab
At the side of each page there is a blue letter tab making it easy to see at a glance where the entries on each page are featured in the A-Z. Left-hand pages show capital letters, while right-hand pages show small letters.

g

Alternative spelling
Where there are alternative spellings or forms of the headword, these are given in blue after the headword.

Spanish translations
Spanish translations appear after English headwords, related words and phrases. Translations are grouped by part of speech, and are listed in order of frequency.

Spanish-English

In addition to the English A-Z, the *Collins COBUILD English/Español Glossary* features a Spanish-English section. Here you will find Spanish words and phrases listed alphabetically, followed by English translations. Below is a section showing how the Spanish to English is arranged.

Guide word
At the top of every right-hand page the guide word is the same as the last entry on that page. On left-hand pages the guide word is the same as the first complete entry on that page. This helps you find the word you are looking for quickly and easily.

gesto

gelatina: gelatin
gélido: bitter
gelifracción: ice wedging

Spanish words or phrases
are listed alphabetically and printed in blue, helping them to stand out on the page.

globo aerostático: balloon
globo ocular: eyeball
globo terráqueo: globe
glóbulo blanco: white blood cell

English translations
are printed in black. These are listed in alphabetical order following the Spanish word or phrase.

gente: crowd, folk, people, public
gentío: crowd
genuino: authentic, genuine, pure, true

The Bank of English

This book has been compiled by referring to the Bank of English ™, a unique database of the English language with examples of over 650 million words enabling Collins lexicographers to analyze how English is actually used and how it is changing. This is the evidence on which the material in this book is based.

The Bank of English ™ is the largest and most current computerized corpus of authentic American English. It contains a very wide range of material from websites, books, newspapers, radio, TV, magazines, letters, and talks reflecting the whole spectrum of American English today. Its size and range make it an unequalled resource.

This ensures that Collins Dictionaries accurately reflect English as it is used today in a way that is most helpful to the user.

English-Spanish

Aa

a *también* an un, una, por

AB dos partes

ABA tres partes

aban|don abandonar, suspender, renunciar, desenfreno • **aban|doned** abandonado • **aban|don|ment** abandono, suspensión

ab|bey abadía

ab|bre|vi|ate abreviar

ab|bre|via|tion abreviatura

ABC's *también* **ABCs** ABC, abecedario

ab|do|men abdomen • **ab|domi|nal** abdominal

abil|ity habilidad

abiot|ic abiótico

able hábil • **ably** hábilmente ▶ **be able to** ser capaz de, poder

ab|nor|mal anómalo • **ab|nor|mal|ly** anormalmente

aboard a bordo

abol|ish abolir • **abo|li|tion** abolición

abor|tion aborto

about sobre, acerca de, en, alrededor de, a punto de

above sobre, de lo alto, arriba de, arriba, por encima de, lo anterior, los anteriores, anterior

abra|sion abrasión

abroad al extranjero, en el extranjero

ab|rupt abrupto, brusco, cortante • **ab|rupt|ly** abruptamente

ab|sence ausencia ▶ **in the absence of** a falta de

ab|sent faltar, ausente • **ab|sent|ly** de manera ausente

ab|sen|tee ausente

absent-minded distraído • **absent-mindedly** distraídamente

ab|so|lute absoluto

ab|so|lute da|ting datación absoluta

ab|so|lute|ly absolutamente, definitivamente

ab|so|lute mag|ni|tude magnitud absoluta

ab|so|lute value valor absoluto

ab|so|lute zero cero absoluto

ab|sorb absorber, integrarse, asimilar • **ab|sorp|tion** absorción, integración

ab|stract abstracto, pintura abstracta ▶ **in the abstract** en teoría

ab|surd absurdo • **ab|surd|ly** absurdamente • **ab|surd|ity** lo absurdo

abun|dant abundante

abuse abuso, insultos, abusar de

abu|sive abusivo, grosero

abys|sal plain plano abisal

a/c *también* **A/C** A/C (aire acondicionado)

aca|dem|ic académico • **aca|dem|ical|ly** académicamente

acad|emy academia

ac|cel|er|ate acelerar • **ac|cel|era|tion** aceleración

ac|cel|era|tion aceleración

ac|cel|era|tor acelerador

ac|cent acento

ac|cept aceptar • **ac|cept|ance** aceptación, aprobación

ac|cept|able aceptable, admisible • **ac|cept|abil|ity** aceptabilidad • **ac|cept|ably** de forma aceptable

ac|cept|ed aceptado

A

ac|cess acceso, entrada, paso, entrar en, tener acceso a, acceder a

ac|ces|sible accesible, acequible, asequible • **ac|ces|sibil|ity** accesibilidad

ac|ces|so|ry accesorio, cómplice • **ac|ces|so|ries** accesorios

ac|ci|dent accidente
▸ **by accident** por accidente, accidentalmente, sin querer

ac|ci|den|tal accidental, por accidente • **ac|ci|den|tal|ly** accidentalmente

ac|claim aclamar, aplaudir, vitorear, aplauso, ovación, aclamación • **ac|claimed** aplaudido

ac|cli|mate también **ac|cli|ma|tize** aclimatar(se), adaptar(se) • **ac|cli|ma|tion** aclimatación

ac|com|mo|date tener cabida, albergar, dar cabida, alojar, hospedar

ac|com|mo|da|tion alojamiento, hospedaje, instalaciones

ac|com|pa|ny acompañar

ac|com|plish lograr, conseguir, llevar a cabo

ac|com|plished consumado

ac|com|plish|ment logro

ac|cord acuerdo, convenio, arreglo, conceder, otorgar, conferir
▸ **of its own accord** por sí solo
▸ **of one's own accord** voluntariamente

ac|cord|ing|ly en la debida forma

ac|cord|ing to de acuerdo con, según, conforme a

ac|count cuenta, cuentas, informe, explicación
▸ **on someone's account** por cuenta propia
▸ **on no account** de ninguna manera
▸ **take into account/take**

account of considerar, tomar en consideración
▸ **account for** representar, constituir, explicar

ac|count|able responsable ante • **ac|count|abil|ity** responsabilidad

ac|count|ant contador o contadora

ac|count|ing contabilidad

ac|cu|mu|late acumular(se), amontonar(se), atesorar • **ac|cu|mu|la|tion** acumulación

ac|cu|rate exacto, preciso, fiel • **ac|cu|ra|cy** exactitud • **ac|cu|rate|ly** exactamente

ac|cu|sa|tion acusación

ac|cuse acusar, culpar, incriminar

ac|cused acusado o acusada

ace as, prominente

ache doler, dolor

achieve lograr, conseguir

achieve|ment logro, éxito, triunfo, consecución

achoo achú

acid ácido • **acid|ity** acidez

acid rain también **acid precipitation** lluvia ácida

ac|knowl|edge admitir, reconocer, acusar recibo de, responder a

ac|knowl|edg|ment también **acknowledgement** reconocimiento, agradecimientos

acne acné, barros

acous|tic acústico • **acous|tics** acústica

ac|quaint|ance conocido o conocida, conocimiento

ac|quire adquirir, obtener

ac|qui|si|tion adquisición, compra

ac|quit absolver, exculpar

acre acre

ac|ro|nym acrónimo, sigla

across a través, de un lado a otro, hacia, de ancho

act actuar, tomar medidas, comportarse, hacer las veces

de, fingir, hecho, acción, acto, ley, decreto

act|ing actuación, suplente, interino

act|ing area zona de actores

ac|tion acción, medida
▸ **out of action** fuera de circulación
▸ **put into action** poner en práctica

ac|ti|vate activar

ac|ti|va|tion en|er|gy energía de activación

ac|tive activo • **ac|tive|ly** activamente

ac|tive duty servicio activo

ac|tive so|lar heat|ing calentamiento solar activo

ac|tive trans|port transporte activo

ac|tive voice voz activa

ac|tiv|ist activista

ac|tiv|ity actividad, actividades

ac|tor actor o actriz

ac|tor's po|si|tion posición del actor

ac|tress actriz

ac|tual real, en realidad, en sí

ac|tu|al|ly de hecho, hasta

acute agudo • **acute|ly** sumamente, plenamente

ad anuncio

AD dC.

ad agen|cy agencia de publicidad

a|dapt adaptar

ad|ap|ta|tion adaptación

ad cam|paign campaña publicitaria

add agregar, añadir, sumar
• **add|ed** más
▸ **add in** agregar
▸ **add on** agregar
▸ **add up** sumar, cuadrar, acumularse
▸ **add up to** ascender a

ad|dict adicto

ad|dict|ed adicto o adicta

ad|dic|tion adicción

ad|dic|tive adictivo

ad|di|tion adición, anexo, suma • **ad|di|tion|al** adicional
▸ **in addition** además

ad|di|tive aditivo
▸ **additive sculpture** escultura aditiva

ad|dress dirección, discurso, dirigir, dirigirse a

ad|enine adenina

ad|equate adecuado
• **ad|equa|cy** aceptabilidad
• **ad|equate|ly** suficientemente

ad|he|sive adhesivo, pegamento

ad ho|mi|nem ad hominem

ad|jec|tive adjetivo

ad|jec|tive phrase frase adjetival

ad|just adaptarse, ajustar, arreglar • **ad|just|ment** cambio, ajuste, arreglo

ad|min|is|ter administrar

ad|min|is|tra|tion administración

ad|min|is|tra|tive administrativo

ad|min|is|tra|tor administrador o administradora

ad|mi|rable admirable
• **ad|mi|rably** admirablemente

ad|mi|ral almirante

ad|mi|ra|tion admiración

ad|mire admirar • **ad|mir|er** admirador o admiradora

ad|mis|sion admisión, reconocimiento, entrada, de admisión

ad|mit admitir

ado|les|cent adolescente
• **ado|les|cence** adolescencia

adopt adoptar • **adop|tion** adopción

adore adorar • **ado|ra|tion** adoración

adult adulto o adulta

ad|vance avanzar, anticipar, adelantar, anticipo, avance,

progreso, previo, anticipado
▸ **in advance** con anticipación

ad|vanced avanzado, desarrollado

ad|van|tage ventaja, superioridad
▸ **take advantage of something** aprovechar algo
▸ **take advantage of someone** aprovecharse de alguien
▸ **to one's advantage** para el provecho de uno

ad|ven|ture aventura
• **ad|ven|tur|er** aventurero o aventurera

ad|verb adverbio

ad|verb phrase frase adverbial

ad|verse adverso
• **ad|verse|ly** adversamente

ad|ver|tise anunciar
• **ad|ver|tis|er** anunciante

ad|ver|tise|ment anuncio

ad|ver|tis|ing publicidad

ad|vice consejo

ad|vice col|umn consultorio sentimental

ad|vice col|umn|ist consejero o consejera sentimental

ad|vise aconsejar

ad|vis|er también **advisor** consejero o consejera

ad|vi|so|ry advertencia, consultivo

ad|vo|cate promocionar, abogar por, defensor o defensora, abogado o abogada

aer|ial aéreo

aer|ial per|spec|tive perspectiva aérea

aero|bics aerobics

aero|phone aerófono

aes|thet|ic también **esthetic** estética • **aes|theti|cal|ly** estéticamente

aes|thet|ic cri|teria criterios estéticos

aes|thet|ics también

esthetics estética

af|fair asunto, amorío

af|fect afectar

af|fec|tion afecto, sentimientos de afecto

af|fili|ate filial, compañía afiliada, afiliarse con, asociarse con • **af|filia|tion** afiliación

af|firm afirmar
• **af|fir|ma|tion** afirmación

af|firma|tive ac|tion acción afirmativa

af|fix afijo

af|ford darse el lujo de

af|ford|able accesible (económicamente)
• **af|ford|abil|ity** viabilidad (financiera)

afloat a flote, solvente, sin deudas

afraid preocupado
▸ **be afraid** tener miedo
▸ **be afraid (that)** temer que

Af|ri|can africano o africana

African-American afroamericano o afroamericana

African-Caribbean afrocaribeño o afrocaribeña

af|ter después de, tras, después, en busca de, como, en honor a, pasadas
▸ **after you** pase usted, adelante

after|math consecuencia, secuela

after|noon tarde

after|ward también **afterwards** después

again de nuevo, otra vez, de nueva cuenta
▸ **again/time and again** una y otra vez

against en, sobre, contra, en contra de, en contra, a pesar de

age edad, época, era, los años, el paso del tiempo, envejecer • **aging** envejecimiento

aged que tiene (edad), de

(edad), anciano, viejo
▸ **the aged** los ancianos

agen|cy agencia, entidad

agen|da plan, orden del día

agent representante, agente, espía

ag|gres|sion agresión

ag|gres|sive agresivo
● **ag|gres|sive|ly** agresivamente

ag|ile ágil ● **agil|ity** agilidad

ago hace

ago|ny agonía

agree estar de acuerdo, concordar
▸ **agree on** convenir en
▸ **agree to** consentir en

agree|ment acuerdo, convenio, coincidencia
▸ **in agreement (with)** de acuerdo (con)

ag|ri|cul|ture agricultura, agronomía ● **ag|ri|cul|tur|al** agrícola

ahead adelante, delante, adelantado, venidero

ahead of adelante de, delante de, antes de

ahold
▸ **get/grab ahold of** encontrar a, conseguir a, ponerse en contacto con
▸ **get ahold of oneself** controlarse

aid ayuda, apoyo, auxilio, ayudar, apoyar, facilitar, auxiliar
▸ **come/go to someone's aid** ir/venir en auxilio de alguien

aide asistente o asistenta

AIDS SIDA

aim aspirar a, querer, proponerse, apuntar, dirigir, enfocar, objeto, meta, puntería
▸ **take aim** apuntar

air aire, transmitir, emitir, airear, ventilar ● **air|ing** transmisión
▸ **by air** en avión
▸ **clear the air** despejar el

ambiente
▸ **on the air** al aire

air|borne aerotransportado, transportado por aire, aéreo, en el aire

air-conditioned con aire acondicionado

air-condition|ing aire acondicionado, acondicionamiento del aire

air|craft avión, aeronave

air force fuerza aérea

air|lift puente aéreo, transportar por aire

air|line línea aérea, aerolínea

air mass masa de aire

air|plane avión, aeroplano

air|port puerto aéreo, aeropuerto

air pres|sure presión del aire

air sac bolsa de aire

air|space *también* **air space** espacio aéreo

aisle corredor, pasillo

à la mode *también* **a la mode** à la mode, a la moda

alarm gran preocupación, alarma, despertador, reloj despertador, preocupar, alarmar ● **alarmed** alarmado ● **alarm|ing** alarmante ● **alarm|ing|ly** de manera alarmante

alarm clock despertador, reloj despertador

al|be|it aunque, no obstante, bien que

al|bum álbum

al|co|hol bebida alcohólica, alcohol

al|co|hol|ic alcohólico o alcohólica, enfermo alcohólico o enferma alcohólica ● **al|co|hol|ism** alcoholismo

alert atento, alerta, vigilante, prevenido, alertar, poner sobre aviso
● **alert|ness** estado de alerta
▸ **on alert** sobre aviso, en guardia

al|gae algas

al|ge|bra álgebra

al|go|rithm algoritmo

al|ien extranjero o extranjera, ajeno, extraterrestre, alienígena

al|ien|ate alejar(se), distanciar(se), alejar
• **alienated** alejado
• **alienation** alejamiento

align|ment alineación

alike igual, semejante, del mismo modo

A-list lista de personajes importantes

alive vivo, activo, enérgico, animado, vigente, en uso
▸ **come alive** cobrar vida

al|ka|li met|al metal alcalino

alkaline-earth met|al también **alkaline earth** metal de tierra alcalina

all todo, completo, iguales
▸ **in all** en total
▸ **all in all** en general
▸ **above all** ante todo
▸ **at all** en absoluto
▸ **of all** antes que nada
▸ **after all** al fin y al cabo, después de todo
▸ **for all** con todo

all-around completo

al|le|ga|tion acusación, imputación

al|lege sostener, pretender
• **al|leg|ed|ly** supuestamente

al|le|giance lealtad, fidelidad

al|lele alelo

al|ler|gic alérgico

al|ler|gy alergia

al|ley callejón

al|li|ance alianza

al|lied aliado, relacionado

al|li|ga|tor caimán

all-in-one todo en uno

al|lit|era|tion aliteración

al|lo|cate asignar
• **al|lo|ca|tion** asignación

all-over todo, completo, integral

al|low permitir, considerar
▸ **allow for** tomar en consideración

al|low|ance mensualidad, mesada
▸ **make allowances for something** tomar algo en consideración
▸ **make allowances for somebody** ser indulgente con alguien

al|loy aleación

all-points bul|letin boletín general

all right bien, adecuado, bueno

all-time de todos los tiempos, sin precedentes

al|lu|vial fan también **alluvial cone** abanico aluvial

al|lu|vium aluvión

ally aliado o aliada, aliarse

al|most casi

alone solo, a solas, sólo

along a lo largo de, a lo largo, avanzar
▸ **take/bring along with you** llevar consigo
▸ **along with** junto con
▸ **all along** todo el tiempo

along|side al lado de, junto a, junto con, codo con codo

aloud alto, en voz alta

al|pha|bet alfabeto

al|pha|beti|cal alfabético

al|pha|bet|ic prin|ci|ple principio alfabético

al|pha par|ti|cle partícula alfa

al|ready ya

also también

al|ter alterar • **al|tera|tion** alteración

al|ter|nate alternar, alterno • **al|ter|nate|ly** alternativamente, alternativo, suplente

al|ter|na|tive alternativa, alternativo

al|ter|na|tive|ly alternativamente

al|though aunque

al|ti|tude altitud

al|to|geth|er totalmente,

a

en total
al|to|stra|tus altoestrato
altricial altricial
alum estudiante, alumno o alumna
alu|mi|num aluminio
alum|nus alumno o alumna
al|veo|lus alveolo
al|ways siempre
am *ver* be
AM A.M.
a.m. a.m.
ama|teur aficionado o aficionada
amaze asombrar • **amazed** asombrado
amaz|ing increíble • **amaz|ing|ly** increíblemente
am|bas|sa|dor embajador o embajadora
am|bigu|ous ambiguo • **am|bigu|ous|ly** ambiguamente, con ambigüedad
am|bi|tion ambición
am|bi|tious ambicioso
am|bu|lance ambulancia
am|bush emboscar, emboscada
amend enmendar
▶ **make amends** dar satisfacciones
amend|ment enmienda
amen|ity atractivo
Ameri|can estadounidense, americano o americana
Ameri|cas Continente Americano
Amish amish
am|mu|ni|tion munición, bala, cartucho, arma
am|nes|ty amnistía
am|ni|on amnios
amoe|ba amiba
among entre
amount cantidad, sumar
▶ **amount to** equivaler
am|per|sand et
am|phib|ian anfibio
am|phi|thea|ter anfiteatro

am|ple abundante, mucho • **am|ply** ampliamente
am|pli|tude amplitud
amu unidad de masa atómica
amuse divertir, entretener
amused divertido
amuse|ment diversión
amuse|ment park parque de diversiones
amus|ing divertido, entretenido • **amus|ing|ly** de manera muy divertida o entretenida
an un, una, por
an|aero|bic anaeróbico
ana|log *también* **analogue** análogo
analo|gous semejante
analy|sis análisis
ana|lyst analista, psicoanalista
ana|lyze analizar
ana|phase anafase
anato|my anatomía • **ana|tomi|cal** anatómico
an|ces|tor antepasado o antepasada • **an|ces|tral** ancestral
an|chor ancla, anclar, fijar, presentador o presentadora
an|cient antiguo
and y
an|ec|do|tal script|ing glosa, nota al margen
an|ec|dote anécdota
anemia anemia
anemic anémico
an|emom|eter anemómetro
an|es|thesi|olo|gist anestesista, anestesiólogo o anestesióloga
an|es|thet|ic anestesia
an|gel ángel
an|ger ira, enfado, enfurecer
anger man|age|ment control de la ira
an|gio|sperm angiosperma
an|gle ángulo
▶ **at an angle** en ángulo
an|glo|phone anglófono o anglófona, anglohablante

A

an|gry enojado, airado
• **an|gri|ly** airadamente
an|guish angustia
ani|mal animal, bestia
Ani|ma|lia reino animal
ani|ma|tion animación
ani|ma|tor animador o animadora
an|kle tobillo
an|ni|ver|sa|ry aniversario
an|no|ta|ted bib|li|og|ra|phy bibliografía anotada
an|nounce anunciar
an|nounce|ment declaración, anuncio
an|noy molestar
an|noy|ance molestia
an|noyed irritado, enojado
an|noy|ing irritante
an|nual anual • **an|nual|ly** anualmente
an|nual ring anillo anual
an|nu|lar eclipse eclipse anular
anony|mous anónimo
• **ano|nym|ity** anonimato
• **anony|mous|ly** anónimamente
an|oth|er otro
▸ **one another** uno al otro
▸ **one thing after another** una cosa tras otra
an|swer contestar, respuesta
▸ **answer for** responder por
an|swer|ing ma|chine contestador automático
ant hormiga
ante|ced|ent antecedente
an|ten|na antena
an|them himno
an|ther antera
an|thro|pol|ogy antropología
• **an|thro|polo|gist** antropólogo o antropóloga
anti|bi|ot|ic antibiótico
anti|body anticuerpo
an|tici|pate prever, anticipar, predecir
anti|cline anticlinal
anti|per|spi|rant antitranspirante, desodorante
an|tique antigüedad
anti|sep|tic antiséptico
anti-virus también **antivirus** antivirus
anxi|ety ansiedad
anx|ious ansioso, preocupado, nervioso
• **anx|ious|ly** ansiosamente
any ninguno, nada, algún, algo, alguno, cualquier, en absoluto
▸ **any more/longer** ya no, ya no...más (tiempo)
any|body cualquiera, nadie, alguien, aquellos
any|how de cualquier modo, en cualquier forma
any|more también **any more** ya no
any|one nadie, alguien, aquellos, cualquiera
any|place lugar alguno, algún lugar
any|thing nada, algo, cualquier, lo que sea
▸ **anything like/close to** algo como, algo parecido a
any|time en cualquier momento, en cuanto
any|way de cualquier modo, no importa, de todos modos, claro, en todo caso
any|where algún lado, ningún lugar, dondequiera
apart alejado, de distancia, separado
▸ **take apart** desarmar, desbaratar
▸ **apart from** además de, salvo por
apart|heid apartheid, segregación racial
apart|ment departamento
apart|ment build|ing también **apartment house** edificio de departamentos
apart|ment com|plex multifamiliar, desarrollo habitacional
ape mono, primate, simio,

imitar
aphe|li|on afelio
aphid afídido, áfido
apolo|gize disculparse, ofrecer una disculpa
apol|ogy disculpa
apos|tro|phe apóstrofe
ap|pall *también* **ap|pal** espantar
ap|pal|ling espantoso
• **ap|pal|ling|ly** espantosamente
ap|par|ent aparente, patente
ap|par|ent|ly aparentemente
ap|par|ent mag|ni|tude magnitud aparente
ap|peal hacer un llamamiento, apelar, atraer, súplica, apelación, encanto
ap|peals court corte de apelaciones
ap|peal to author|ity argumento de autoridad
ap|peal to emo|tion argumento emocional
ap|peal to pa|thos *también* **appeal to pity** argumento emocional
ap|peal to rea|son argumento racional
ap|pear parecer, aparecer, comparecer
ap|pear|ance aparición, apariencia
ap|pel|late court tribunal de apelaciones
ap|pen|dix apéndice
ap|pe|tite apetito
ap|plaud aplaudir
ap|plause aplauso
ap|ple manzana
ap|pli|ance electrodoméstico, aparato
ap|pli|cant aspirante
ap|pli|ca|tion solicitud, aplicación
ap|ply solicitar, dedicarse, hacer uso de, aplicar
ap|point nombrar, designar
ap|point|ment nombramiento,

designación, cita
▸ **by appointment** previa cita
ap|posi|tive en aposición, aposición
ap|prais|al evaluación, avalúo
ap|pre|ci|ate apreciar, reconocer, alcanzar a reconocer, agradecer, subir de precio • **ap|pre|cia|tion** apreciación, reconocimiento, agradecimiento, aumento de precio
ap|proach acercarse a, hacer propuestas a, abordar, acercar, acercamiento, propuesta, cercanía, acceso, enfoque, camino
ap|pro|pri|ate adecuado
• **ap|pro|pri|ate|ly** adecuadamente
ap|prov|al aprobación
ap|prove dar su aprobación, aprobar
ap|proved probado
ap|proxi|mate aproximado, parecer, aproximar
• **ap|proxi|mate|ly** aproximadamente
apri|cot albaricoque, chabacano
April abril
apron delantal
apt adecuado, apropiado, propenso • **apt|ly** adecuadamente
aqui|fer acuífero
arach|nid arácnido
ar|bi|trary arbitrario
• **ar|bi|trari|ly** arbitrariamente
ar|bi|trary col|or color caprichoso
arch arco, arquear
Ar|chae|bac|te|ria arquebacteria
ar|che|ol|ogy arqueología
• **ar|cheo|logi|cal** arqueológico
• **ar|che|olo|gist** arqueólogo

A

o arqueóloga

ar|che|typ|al criti|cism crítica arquetípica

ar|che|type arquetipo
• **ar|che|typ|al** arquetípico

Archimedes' prin|ci|ple Principio de Arquímedes

archi|tect arquitecto *o* arquitecta, artífice

archi|tec|ture arquitectura
• **archi|tec|tur|al** arquitectónico
• **archi|tec|tur|al|ly** desde el punto de vista arquitectónico

ar|chive archivo

are *ver* be

area área

area code código de zona

arena estadio, palestra

aren't = are not

arête arista, cresta, cresta peñascosa

ar|gue discutir, argumentar

ar|gu|ment argumento, razón, discusión

arise presentarse, surgir

arith|me|tic aritmética

ar|ith|met|ic se|quence *también* **arithmetic progression** progresión aritmética

arm brazo, manga, arma, armar

arm|chair sillón

armed armado

armed forces fuerzas armadas

ar|mor armadura, blindaje

ar|mored blindado

arm|pit axila, sobaco

army ejército

aro|ma aroma

arose *ver* arise

around alrededor, a la vuelta, en, en todo, a todas partes, de un lado a otro, por aquí, aproximadamente

arouse despertar, suscitar

ar|range concertar, quedar en, encargarse de, arreglar

ar|range|ment preparativo, arreglo

ar|ray despliegue, selección

ar|rest detener, arrestar, detención, arresto

ar|ri|val llegada, recién llegado *o* recién llegada

ar|rive llegar

ar|ro|gant arrogante
• **ar|ro|gance** arrogancia
• **ar|ro|gant|ly** con arrogancia

ar|row flecha

ar|son incendio provocado

art arte, las bellas artes, letras

art criti|cism crítica de arte

art el|ement elemento artístico

ar|tery arteria

ar|te|sian spring pozo artesiano, aguas artesianas

ar|thri|tis artritis • **ar|thrit|ic** artrítico

ar|ti|choke alcachofa

ar|ti|cle artículo, prenda

ar|ticu|late expresarse bien *o* muy bien, expresarse con claridad

ar|ticu|la|tion articulación

ar|ti|fact objeto

ar|ti|fi|cial artificial, afectado, forzado
• **ar|ti|fi|cial|ly** artificialmente

ar|ti|fi|cial light luz artificial

ar|til|lery artillería

art|ist artista

ar|tis|tic artístico
• **ar|tis|ti|cal|ly** con dotes artísticas

as cuando, al, como, porque, tan...como, hasta, en cuanto a, respecto a, a partir de, como si

asexu|al re|pro|duc|tion reproducción asexual

ash ceniza, fresno

ashamed avergonzado

Asian asiático *o* asiática

aside a un lado, aparte

▶ **aside from** con excepción de, salvo por, aparte de, además de

ask preguntar, pedir, solicitar, preguntar por, invitar
▶ **if you ask me** si me preguntas a mí, si quieres saber

asleep dormido
▶ **fall asleep** quedarse dormido
▶ **fast asleep** profundamente dormido

as|para|gus espárrago

as|pect aspecto, vista

as|pi|ra|tion aspiración

as|pi|rin aspirina

as|sas|si|nate asesinar
● **as|sas|si|na|tion** asesinato

as|sault asalto, agresión, agredir, atacar

as|sem|blage montaje

as|sem|ble reunirse, armar

as|sem|bly asamblea, ensamblaje

as|sem|bly line línea de ensamblaje/montaje/armado

as|sert afirmar, hacer(se) valer, imponer, infundir respeto ● **as|ser|tion** afirmación

as|ser|tive asertivo, confiado, agresivo
● **as|ser|tive|ness** asertividad

as|sess evaluar
● **as|sess|ment** evaluación

as|set bien, activos

as|sign asignar

as|sign|ment tarea, trabajo

as|simi|late integrar(se), asimilar, adoptar
● **as|simi|la|tion** integración, asimilación

as|sist ayudar, asistir

as|sis|tance ayuda, asistencia
▶ **be of assistance** ser de ayuda, ser útil

as|sis|tant asistente, dependiente

as|sis|tant pro|fes|sor profesor asistente o profesora asistente

as|sis|ted liv|ing hogar de convalecencia

as|so|ci|ate asociar(se), juntarse, colega

as|so|ci|ate de|gree diploma técnico de dos años

as|so|ci|ate pro|fes|sor profesor adjunto o profesora adjunta

as|so|cia|tion asociación, relación con
▶ **in association with** junto con, en asociación con

as|sort|ment colección

as|sume suponer, asumir, adoptar

as|sum|ing tomar en cuenta

as|sump|tion suposición

as|sur|ance garantía, certeza

as|sure asegurar

as|sured confiado

as|ter|isk asterisco

as|ter|oid asteroide

as|ter|oid belt cinturón de asteroides

as|theno|sphere astenósfera, astenosfera

asth|ma asma

astig|ma|tism astigmatismo

aston|ish asombrar
● **aston|ished** asombrado

aston|ish|ing sorprendente
● **aston|ish|ing|ly** sorprendentemente

as|trol|ogy astrología
● **as|trolo|ger** astrólogo o astróloga

as|tro|naut astronauta

as|tro|nomi|cal unit unidad astronómica

as|trono|my astronomía
● **as|trono|mer** astrónomo o astrónoma

A-student también **A student** estudiante de puros dieces, sobresaliente

asy|lum asilo

A

asym|met|ri|cal asimétrico

asym|me|try asimetría

as|ymp|tote asíntota

at a, al, a la, a las/los, en, hacia, por

ate *ver* eat

ath|lete atleta

ath|let|ic atlético

ath|let|ics deportes, atletismo

at|las atlas

ATM cajero automático

at|mos|phere atmósfera, ambiente • **at|mos|pher|ic** atmosférico

at|mos|pher|ic per|spec|tive perspectiva aérea

atmos|pher|ic pres|sure presión atmosférica

atom átomo

atom|ic atómico

atom|ic mass masa atómica

atom|ic mass unit unidad de masa atómica

atom|ic num|ber número atómico

aton|al atonal

ATP ATP

atrium aurícula

atroc|ity atrocidad, monstruosidad

at|tach pegar, atar, adjuntar, anexar

at|tached apegado

at|tach|ment cariño, apego, lazo, vínculo, relación, accesorio, anexo

at|tack atacar, agredir, asaltar, criticar, abordar, ataque, agresión, asalto, crítica • **at|tack|er** atacante

at|tain conseguir, alcanzar, lograr • **at|tain|ment** logro

at|tempt intentar, tratar, probar, intento, prueba, tentativa, ataque • **at|tempt|ed** intentado, atentado

at|tend asistir, ir, atender, cuidar • **at|tend|ance** asistencia

attendance asistencia, concurrencia

at|tend|ant asistente *o* asistenta, encargado *o* encargada, padrino *o* madrina

at|tend|ee participante, asistente

at|ten|tion atención ▶ **pay attention** prestar atención

at|tic ático, desván

at|ti|tude actitud

at|tor|ney abogado *o* abogada, procurador *o* procuradora, agente legal

at|tract atraer, captar • **at|tract|ed** atraído

at|trac|tion atracción, atractivo

at|trac|tive atractivo, atrayente, interesante • **at|trac|tive|ness** atractivo

at|trib|ute atribuir, asignar, imputar, atributo, cualidad, característica

AU unidad astronómica, AU

auc|tion subasta, remate, subastar, rematar ▶ **auction off** subastar

audible audible, perceptible • **audibly** de modo audible

audi|ence audiencia, público, auditorio

audio audio, sonido

audit auditar, hacer una auditoría, auditoría • **audi|tor** auditor *o* auditora

audi|tion audición, prueba, audicionar, hacer una audición

audi|to|rium auditorio

aug|ment|ed in|ter|val intervalo aumentado

August agosto

aunt tía

Aus|tra|lo|pithe|cine *también* australopithecine australopithecine

authen|tic auténtico, genuino, verosímil, realista, legítimo, fidedigno ● au|then|tic|ity autenticidad

author autor o autora, creador o creadora, escritor o escritora

authori|ta|tive autoritario, autorizado, fidedigno

author|ity autoridad, experto o experta, autorización, permiso, licencia

author|ize autorizar, facultar, legalizar ● **authori|za|tion** autorización

auto|bi|og|ra|phy autobiografía ● **auto|bio|graphi|cal** autobiográfico

auto|graph autógrafo, autografiar, firmar

auto|maker fabricante de automotores

auto|mat|ic automático, automática ● **auto|mati|cal|ly** automáticamente

auto|mo|bile automóvil, carro, coche, auto

autono|my autonomía ● **autono|mous** autónomo

auto|worker trabajador de la industria automotriz o trabajadora de la industria automotriz

autumn otoño

aux|ilia|ry auxiliar, accesorio, adicional, verbo auxiliar

avail|able disponible ● **avail|abil|ity** disponibilidad

ava|lanche avalancha

avenge vengar(se)

av|enue avenida, Av., Ave., calle, boulevard

av|er|age promedio, lo normal, promediar ▶ **on average/on an average** en promedio

av|er|age speed velocidad promedio

avert desviar, evitar, prevenir, apartar

aviary aviario, pajarera

avia|tion aviación

avo|ca|do aguacate

avoid evitar, esquivar

aw eh, oh

await aguardar, esperar

awake despierto ▶ **wide awake** completamente despierto

awak|en despertar ● **awak|en|ing** despertar

award premio, indemnización, otorgar, dar

aware consciente ● **aware|ness** conciencia

away lejos, fuera, guardar, faltar, visitante, fuera de casa, lejos de, alejado

awe|some formidable, impresionante

aw|ful horrible, repugnante, enorme ● **aw|ful|ly** muy, tremendamente

awk|ward incómodo, torpe ● **awk|ward|ly** incómodo, difícil, torpemente

awoke *ver* awake

awok|en despertado

ax hacha, suprimir

ax|ial move|ment movimiento axial

axi|om axioma

axis eje

axle eje

axon axón

azi|muth|al pro|jec|tion proyección acimutal

Bb

bab|ble balbucear, gruñir, parlotear, murmullo

babe nene *o* nena

baby bebé, nene *o* nena

baby car|riage cochecito, carriola

baby|sit cuidar niños
• **baby|sitter** niñera *o* muchacho que cuida niños

baby tooth diente de leche

bach|elor soltero

bach|elor|ette soltera

bach|elor|ette par|ty despedida de soltera

bach|elor par|ty despedida de soltero

back espalda, atrás, parte posterior, trasero, de atrás, respaldo, afuera, dar marcha atrás, poner en reversa, respaldar, apoyar
▸ **back and forth** de un lado a otro, de atrás para adelante
▸ **back away** retroceder
▸ **back down** dar marcha atrás, echarse para atrás
▸ **back off** retroceder
▸ **back onto** dar a, estar frente a
▸ **back out** dar marcha atrás, abandonar
▸ **back up** apoyar, respaldar, hacer una copia, ir en reversa
▸ **behind somebody's back** a espaldas de alguien
▸ **give/put back** devolver
▸ **go back** regresar, volver
▸ **keep back** alejarse
▸ **move back** apartar(se)
▸ **write/call back** contestar, responder

back|board tablero

back|bone columna vertebral, espina dorsal, fibra, valor, coraje

back|court parte trasera de la cancha, defensa

back|er patrocinador *o* patrocinadora

back|fire fracasar, fallar, producir explosiones

back|ground antecedente, ambiente, fondo

back|hoe excavadora

back|ing respaldo, apoyo, refuerzo

back|lash reacción violenta

back|stage entre bastidores, entre bambalinas

back talk *también* **backtalk** impertinencia

back|up *también* **back-up** respaldo, apoyo, embotellamiento

back|ward hacia atrás, al revés
▸ **backward and forward** vaivén, de atrás para adelante, atrasado

back|yard *también* **back yard** patio trasero

ba|con tocino, panceta

bac|te|ria bacteria
• **bac|te|rial** bacteriano

bad mal, malo

bad check cheque inservible (si hay error en él), cheque sin fondos

badge placa, chapa

bad|ly mal, gravemente, con desesperación

bad|min|ton bádminton

bad off mal, pobre

bad-tempered malhumorado

bag bolsa, ojera
▸ **in the bag** en la bolsa
▸ **be left holding the bag** cargar (con) el muerto

bag|gage equipaje, maleta, carga

bag|gage car furgón, vagón

de equipaje

bag|gage claim recolección de equipaje

bag|ger empaquetador, empaquetadora, cerillo

bail fianza, achicar
▸ **make bail** pagar la fianza
▸ **bail out** sacar de apuros

bail|out rescate

bait cebo, carnada, cebar, picar, provocar
▸ **bait and switch** atraer a posibles clientes con la oferta de bienes a precios bajos, cuya existencia es reducida, e inducirlos a comprar otros de mayor precio

bake hornear ● **bak|ing** hornear

bake-off concurso de horneado

bak|er panadero o panadera, pastelero o pastelera

bak|ery panadería, pastelería

bala|cla|va pasamontañas

bal|ance equilibrar, sostener en equilibrio, equilibrio, compensar, sopesar, saldo, balanza
▸ **on balance** en resumidas cuentas, a fin de cuentas

bal|anced equilibrado, ponderado

bal|anced forces fuerzas equilibradas

bal|co|ny balcón, anfiteatro, galería

bald calvo, gastado, liso, puro ● **bald|ness** calvicie ● **bald|ly** sin rodeos

ball pelota, bola, base de los dedos del pie, base del pulgar, baile
▸ **have a ball** divertirse mucho, pasarla bien, pasar un buen rato

bal|let ballet

ball game juego de pelota, juego de béisbol, juego, jugada

bal|loon globo, globo aerostático, hincharse, aumentar rápidamente

bal|lot votación

ball|player también **ball player** jugador de béisbol o jugadora de béisbol, beisbolista

ball|room danc|ing baile de salón

ba|lo|ney tonterías

bam|boo bambú

ban prohibir, vedar, prohibición

ba|na|na plátano, banana

band banda, conjunto, pandilla, cinta, brazalete, abrazadera, fleje
▸ **band together** unirse, hacer causa común

band|age venda, vendaje, vendar

band|width ancho (amplitud, anchura) de banda

bang detonación, estallido, cerrar de golpe, dar golpes, golpearse, golpear, golpe, fleco

bang-up también **bang up** súper

bank banco, ribera, orilla, talud, masa
▸ **bank on** contar con

bank card también **ATM card** tarjeta de crédito, tarjeta bancaria

bank check cheque

bank|er banquero o banquera

bank|ing banca

bank|rupt en quiebra, en bancarrota, hacer quebrar, arruinar

bank|rupt|cy quiebra, bancarrota

ban|ner pancarta

ban|ner ad báner

bar bar, barra, tableta, obstáculo, abogacía, cuerpo de abogados, compás, bloquear, prohibir

▶ **behind bars** tras las rejas

bar|becue *también* **barbeque, Bar-B-Q** asador, asado, parrillada, asar

bar|bell barra de pesas

bar|ber peluquero *o* peluquera, barbero

bare desnudo, descalzo, vacío, escueto, mostrar
▶ **the bare minimum/ essentials** lo estrictamente mínimo, necesario *o* esencial
▶ **with one's bare hands** con las manos

bare-bones esencial

bare|ly apenas

barf vomitar

bar|gain ganga, trato, negociación, regatear
• **bar|gain|ing** negociar
▶ **into the bargain/in the bargain** encima
▶ **not bargain for** *o* **not bargain on** no tener en cuenta

barge barcaza
▶ **barge into/through** entrar sin llamar, abrirse paso con los codos, abrirse paso a empujones

bar graph gráfica de barras

bark ladrar, ladrido, corteza

barn establo, granero

barn|yard corral, patio

ba|rom|eter barómetro

baro|met|ric barométrico

bar|racks cuartel

bar|rel barril, tonel, cañón

barrel-chested fornido

bar|ren estéril, desierto

bar|rette broche

bar|ri|cade barricada, cerrar con barricadas, atrincherar

bar|ri|er barrera, valla

bar|rio barrio de hablantes del español en una ciudad estadounidense, barrio

bar|ris|ter abogado *o* abogada habilitado para llevar casos ante un tribunal superior

bar|tender camarero *o* camarera, cantinero *o* cantinera, barman

bar|ter hacer trueque, cambiar

bas|alt basalto

base base, basar, domicilio principal
▶ **be off base** estar equivocado, andar errado

base|ball béisbol

base|ball cap gorra de béisbol

base|ment sótano

bases *ver* base, basis

base word lexema

bash juerga, parranda, golpear, pegar, aporrear

ba|sic básico, fundamental

ba|si|cal|ly fundamentalmente

ba|sin cuenco, palangana, bol, lavabo, cuenca

ba|sis base
▶ **on the basis of** de acuerdo con

bas|ket canasta, canasto, cesta, cesto

basket|ball básquetbol

bas|ket sponge esponja, cesta de Venus, regadera de Filipinas

bass bajo

bass clef clave de fa

bat bate, batear, murciélago

batch grupo, montón, hornada, tanda

bath baño (de tina), baño

bathe bañar(se), lavar

bath|room baño, cuarto de baño, baño(s) (edificio público)

bath salts sales de baño

bath|tub bañera, tina

bats|man bateador *o* bateadora

bat|tal|ion batallón

bat|ter apalear, aporrear, azotar, masa, bateador *o* bateadora

bat|tery pila, batería, lesión,

bat|tle batalla, combate, lucha, luchar, pelear, combatir

battle|field campo de batalla

battle|ship acorazado

bay bahía, corral, plataforma, clamar
▸ **keep/hold at bay** mantener a raya, acorralar

BB gun escopeta de aire comprimido

BC *también* **B.C.** antes de Jesucristo, a de J.C.

BCE *también* **B.C.E.** antes de nuestra era

be estar, ser, deber de + *inf.*, ir a + *inf.*, deber + *inf.*, hacer, haber, tener

beach playa

beach chair silla de playa, tumbona

bead cuenta, gota

beak pico

beak|er vaso (de precipitados)

beam sonreír radiante, rayo (de luz), viga, transmitir(se)

bean frijol, poroto, grano

bear oso, cargar, llevar, soportar, resistir, aguantar
▸ **bear out** confirmar
▸ **bear with** aguantar, tener paciencia

beard barba

bear|ing influencia
▸ **get/find one's bearings** orientar(se)
▸ **lose one's bearings** desorientar(se)

beast fiera

beat golpear, latir, palpitar, latir, batir, vencer, derrotar, ganar, latido, ritmo, sacudida ● **beat|ing** golpiza
▸ **beat up** golpear

beau|ti|ful hermoso, bello, lindo, magnífico ● **beau|ti|ful|ly** maravillosamente

beau|ty belleza, bella, hermosura, bello, lo bueno

beau|ty mark lunar

beau|ty pag|eant concurso de belleza

beau|ty shop *también* **beauty parlor** salón de belleza

be|came *ver* become

be|cause porque, por
▸ **because of** debido a, a causa de

be|come convertirse en, empezar a, haber sido

bed cama, arriate, lecho

bed|ding ropa de cama

bed|room cuarto, recámara, ciudad dormitorio

bed|sore úlcera (por decúbito)

bee abeja

beef carne de res
▸ **beef up** reforzar, fortalecer

been *ver* be

beer cerveza

beet remolacha, betabel

bee|tle escarabajo

be|fore antes, ante, frente a, delante de

beg rogar, suplicar, mendigar

be|gan *ver* begin

beg|gar mendigo *o* mendiga, limosnero *o* limosnera

be|gin empezar, comenzar, iniciar
▸ **to begin with** al principio, para empezar

be|gin|ner principiante *o* principianta

be|gin|ning principio, inicio, comienzo

be|gun *ver* begin

be|half
▸ **on somebody's behalf/ on behalf of somebody** en nombre de alguien

be|have comportarse, portarse, actuar, portarse bien

be|hav|ior comportamiento, conducta, funcionamiento

be|hav|ior|ism conductismo ● **be|hav|ior|ist** conductista

b

be|hind atrás, trasero, atrasado
▸ **be behind somebody** respaldar alguien, apoyar alguien
▸ **leave behind** abandonar, dejar atrás
▸ **stay behind** quedarse

beige beige, ocre

be|ing siendo, estando, ser, ente, existencia, vida

be|jew|eled *también* **bejewelled** enjoyado, tachonado de joyas

be|la|bor elaborar, extenderse

be|lief creencia

be|lieve creer, creer a

bell timbre, campana

bell|hop botones

bell pep|per pimiento dulce

bell|wether barómetro

bel|ly vientre, barriga, panza

be|long pertenecer, ser socio

be|long|ings pertenencias

be|lov|ed querido, amado

be|low abajo, debajo, por debajo de, bajo

belt cinturón, correa, banda, región, franja, trancazo, dar trancazos a
▸ **tighten one's belt** apretarse el cinturón
▸ **under one's belt** en el haber de uno

bench banca, mesa de trabajo, estrado

bend inclinarse, agacharse, doblar, curvar, torcer, dar vuelta, curva, codo ● **bent** doblado, torcido

be|neath bajo, abajo

ben|efi|cial beneficioso

ben|efit beneficio, en beneficio de, beneficiar(se), prestación
▸ **the benefit of the doubt** el beneficio de la duda

bent *ver* **bend**, empeñado en, aptitud

ben|thic en|vir|on|ment *también* **benthic zone** medio ambiente béntico

ben|thos bentos

be|ret boina

Bernoulli's prin|ci|ple principio de Bernoulli

ber|ry baya

be|side junto a
▸ **be beside oneself** estar fuera de sí, no caber en sí

be|sides además, también

be|siege sitiar, asediar, cercar

best mejor, lo mejor, mejor momento, más
▸ **at best** cuando mucho

best man padrino de bodas

best-selling *también* **bestselling** de mayor venta, de gran éxito

bet apostar, apuesta
● **bet|ting** apuestas

beta par|ti|cle partícula beta

be|tray traicionar, traslucir, revelar, delatar

bet|ter mejor, más, más que
▸ **for the better** para bien
▸ **to get the better of** poder más que
▸ **had better** es mejor que, más vale que

be|tween entre

bev|er|age bebida

be|ware tener cuidado, poner atención

be|yond más allá, a lo lejos, después de, después, superar, fuera de

B-grade de segunda

bias parcialidad

bi|ased tendencioso, parcial, predispuesto

Bible Biblia ● **biblical** bíblico

bib|li|og|ra|phy bibliografía

bi|cen|ten|nial bicentenario

bi|coas|tal aplicado a alguien o algo que vive u ocurre tanto en la costa este como en la oeste de Estados Unidos

bi|cy|cle bicicleta

bid intento, oferta, pugnar, pujar, ofrecer • **bid|der** postor

big grande

big bang theo|ry teoría del big bang, teoría de la gran explosión

big-box supertienda, megatienda

big bucks un dineral

big busi|ness un gran negocio

big-ticket caro, costoso

big time muchísimo, de veras

bike bici, bicla, cicla, moto

bike path ciclopista

bik|er motociclista, ciclista

bi|lat|er|al sym|met|ry simetría bilateral

bi|lin|gual bilingüe

bill cuenta, factura, facturar, pasar la cuenta, billete (de banco), proyecto de ley

bill|fold cartera, billetera

bil|lion mil millones • **bil|lions** miles de millones

bil|lion|aire multimillonario o multimillonaria

bi|me|tal|lic strip lámina bimetálica, plancha bimetálica

bin cajón

bi|na|ry fis|sion fisión binaria

bind unir, comprometer, obligar, atar, amarrar, encuadernar, empastar

bind|er carpeta

bind|ing obligatorio, encuadernación, tapa, cubierta

bin|go lotería, bingo

bin|ocu|lars binoculares, gemelos

bi|no|mial binomio

bi|no|mial dis|tri|bu|tion distribución binómica

bi|no|mial no|men|cla|ture nomenclatura binómica

bi|no|mial theo|rem teorema binomio

bio|chemi|cal bioquímico, sustancia bioquímica

bio|chem|is|try bioquímica • **bio|chem|ist** bioquímico o bioquímica

bio|degrad|able biodegradable

bio|di|ver|sity biodiversidad

bi|og|raph|er biógrafo o biógrafa

bi|og|ra|phy biografía • **bio|graphi|cal** biográfico

bio|logi|cal biológico • **bio|logi|cal|ly** basado en la biología, de la biología

bio|logi|cal clock reloj biológico

bi|ol|ogy biología • **bi|olo|gist** biólogo o bióloga

bio|mass biomasa

bi|ome bioma

bio|sphere biosfera

bio|tech|nol|ogy biotecnología

bi|ot|ic biótico

bio|weap|on arma biológica

bi|po|lar dis|or|der desorden bipolar

bird ave, pájaro

bird feed|er *también* **birdfeeder** comedero para pájaros

bird flu gripe aviar

bird|seed alpiste

birth nacimiento
  ▸ **give birth** parir, dar a luz

birth con|trol control de la natalidad

birth|day cumpleaños

birth|place lugar de nacimiento, suelo natal, cuna

birth rate *también* **birth-rate** índice de natalidad, tasa de natalidad

bish|op obispo, alfil

bit bit, bocado, *ver* **bite**
  ▸ **a bit** un poquito, un pedacito, un cachito, un poco

B

▸ **a bit of a** poquito
▸ **quite a bit** bastante
▸ **(for) a bit** un poquito
▸ **a bit much** un exceso
▸ **every bit as** tan ...como

bitch perra

bite morder, mordida, picar, piquete, afectar
▸ **bite one's lip/tongue** morderse los labios/la lengua

bit|ten mordido

bit|ter encarnizado, amargado, amargo, penoso, gélido, severo ● **bit|ter|ly** amargamente, severamente ● **bit|ter|ness** amargura

bi|week|ly quincenal

bi|zarre raro, extraño ● **bi|zarre|ly** de modo extraño

black negro, obscuro ● **black|ness** obscuridad ▸ **black out** desmayar

black and white también **black-and-white** blanco y negro
▸ **in black and white** impreso como prueba, papelito habla, lo hablado vuela, lo escrito permanece

black eye ojo morado

black-eyed pea frijol carita

black hole hoyo negro

black|jack blackjack, cachiporra

black|mail chantaje, chantajear ● **black|mail|er** chantajista

black rhi|no también **black rhinoceros** rinoceronte negro

black|top concreto asfáltico

blade cuchilla, hoja, pala, paleta

blame culpar, culpa
▸ **to blame** el/la culpable

bland insulso, insípido

blank en blanco, vacío, desconcertado ● **blank|ly** con desconcierto

▸ **go blank** ponerse en blanco

blank check cheque en blanco

blan|ket manta, manto, cubrir, general

blast explosión, disparar, abrir un hueco, volar, explotar, lo máximo
▸ **blast off** despegar

blaze arder, resplandecer, incendio, esplendor, despliegue

bleach blanquear, decolorar, cloro

bleach|ers gradería, tendido de sol

bleak sombrío, desolado, crudo, triste, desolador ● **bleak|ness** desolación ● **bleak|ly** tristemente

bleed sangrar ● **bleed|ing** sangrado

blend mezclar, armonizar, mezcla, combinación

bless bendecir
▸ **bless you** salud

bless|ing bendición

blew *ver* **blow**

blind ciego, cegar, ofuscar, ceguera, persiana ● **blind|ness** ceguera
▸ **turn a blind eye** hacer la vista gorda

blind|ers anteojera

blind|side sacar de onda

bling también **bling-bling** bisutería o ropa vistosa

blink parpadear, parpadeo

bliz|zard tormenta de nieve

bloc bloque

block bloque, cuadra, manzana, bloquear, tapar
▸ **block out** tratar de no pensar en

block|ade bloqueo, bloquear

block and tackle aparejo de poleas

block|bust|er éxito

blocked también **blocked up** tapado

b

block|ing marcar posiciones

block par|ty fiesta del barrio

blog blog • **blog|ger** bloguero o bloguera • **blog|ging** blogueo

blogo|sphere *también* **blogsphere** blogósfera

blonde rubio, rubia

blood sangre
> **in cold blood** a sangre fría
> **new/fresh/young blood** sangre nueva

blood pres|sure presión arterial, tensión arterial

bloody ensangrentado, sangriento

bloom flor, florecer
> **in bloom** en flor

bloop|er error

blos|som flor, florecer

blouse blusa

blow soplar, volar con el viento, soplar(se), sonar, sonarse, destrozar, echar a perder, gastar(se)
> **blow off** hacer a un lado
> **blow out** apagar
> **blow over** caer en el olvido
> **blow up** explotar, inflar, golpe

blown *ver* blow

blue azul

blue-collar obrero

blunt franco, desafilado, reducir • **blunt|ly** francamente • **blunt|ness** franqueza

blur algo borroso, volver(se) algo borroso, borrar • **blurred** borroso

blush sonrojarse, sonrojo

BMI IMC

board tabla, tablero, pizarrón, consejo, alimentos, abordar, embarcar(se)
> **across the board** en general, para todos
> **on board** a bordo
> **take on board** asumir
> **board up** tapiar

board|ing pass pase

de abordar, tarjeta de embarque

board|walk malecón

boast presumir, presunción

boat bote, barco

bob menearse

bob|ble perder el control de

bob|by pin pasador

bob|sled trineo

bo|da|cious increíble

body cuerpo, tronco, fuselaje, carrocería

body|guard guardaespaldas

body image imagen corporal

body mass in|dex índice de masa corporal

body odor olor corporal

body position posición corporal

bog ciénaga, pantano

boil hervir, poner a hervir, cocer, forúnculo
> **bring to a boil** romper el hervor
> **boil down to** se reduce a
> **boil over** derramarse

boil|ing hirviendo

boil|ing point punto de ebullición

bold audaz • **bold|ly** con audacia • **bold|ness** audacia, llamativo, vigoroso

bo|lo|gna tipo de salchicha ahumada

bol|ster reafirmar

bolt tornillo, atornillar, cerrojo, echar el cerrojo, salir disparado

bomb bomba, bombardear • **bomb|ing** bombardeo

bomb|er terrorista, bombardero

bond vínculo, lazo de union, bono, establecer lazos de unión, adherirse

bone hueso, deshuesar

bon|net gorro, sombrero

bo|nus prima, bonificación, ganancia

boo-boo metida de pata, machucón

B

book libro, libreta, talonario, libro (de contabilidad), reservar
▶ **booked up/fully booked/booked solid** agotado, completo

book|case librero, estante

book group grupo de reseña literaria

book|let folleto

book|mark marcador, señalador, favorito, marcar

book|store librería

boom auge, retumbar, trueno

boom box grabadora portátil, reproductor portátil

boost estimular, elevar, estímulo

boot bota, botín, inmovilizar, arrancar, encender
▶ **give somebody the boot** poner a alguien de patitas en la calle

boot camp campamento militar

booth cabina, reservado, puesto

booze bebida, trago, beber, empinar el codo

bor|der frontera, borde, cenefa, limitar con, lindar con, bordear

bore aburrir, perforar, taladrar, hacer un agujero, aburrido o aburrida, lata, ver bear

bored aburrido

bore|dom aburrimiento

bor|ing aburrido

born nacer, nato, innato

bor|ough municipio, distrito

bor|row tomar prestado, pedir prestado ● **bor|row|ing** endeudamiento

bor|row|er prestatario o prestataria

boss jefe, mandonear, ordenar

bota|ny botánica
● **bo|tani|cal** botánico
● **bota|nist** botánico o botánica

both ambos, dos, tanto... como

both|er preocuparse, molestarse, preocupar, molestar, molestia
● **both|ered** preocupado
▶ **can't be bothered** dar pereza, dar flojera, no tener ganas

bot|tle botella, embotellar

bot|tom pie, fondo, inferior, final, último
▶ **get to the bottom of** ir al fondo de

bought ver buy

bouil|lon cube cubito para caldo

boul|der roca

bounce botar, rebotar, balancear, brincar, devolver, bote

bound saltar, ver bind
● **bounds** límites
▶ **be bound to happen** tener que suceder, estar destinado a algo
▶ **bound for** con rumbo a, con destino a
▶ **out of bounds** restringido

bounda|ry límite, lindero, linde, frontera

bou|quet ramo, ramillete

bout ataque, racha

bow hacer una reverencia, reverencia, inclinar, ceder, moño, lazo, arco
▶ **bow out** retirar(se)

bowed arqueado, encorvado

bow|el intestino

bowl tazón, taza, inodoro, lanzar

bow|ler jugador de bolos o petanca o jugadora de bolos o petanca

bowl|ing bolos, boliche, petanca (inglesa)

box caja, rectángulo, casilla, palco, boxear ● **box|er**

boxeador o boxeadora, pugilista
▶ **box in** cerrar el paso
box|ing box, boxeo
box lunch lunch, almuerzo, refrigerio, box lunch
box of|fice también **box-office** taquilla, boletería
box plot también **box-and-whisker plot**, **box-and-whisker chart** gráfica de caja
box spring box spring, box, cama
boy niño, chico, chamaco, muchacho, escuincle
boy band boy band, banda
boy|cott boicotear, hacer un boicot, boicot, boicoteo
boy|friend novio, galán
Boyle's law ley de Boyle
bra brasier, brassiere, sostén, sujetador, bra
brace preparar(se), apoyarse, sujetarse, aparato ortopédico ● **braces** frenos, brackets
brace|let pulsera, brazalete
braid gallon, trenza, trenzar, hacer trenzas
brain cerebro, encéfalo, sesos, inteligencia, intelecto, autor intelectual o autora intelectual
brain|storm idea brillante, inspiración súbita
brake freno, frenar
branch rama, sucursal, agencia, delegación
▶ **branch off** bifurcarse
▶ **branch out** diversificar(se), ampliar las actividades
brand marca, etiquetar a, tachar de, tildar de, marcar, estigmatizar, marcar (con hierro candente)
brand-name prod|uct producto de marca (registrada)
brand-new flamante, nuevo
brass latón, metales,

bronces, alto mando, espadón
brave valiente, bravo, valeroso, encarar, afrontar, hacer frente a, arrostrar, enfrentar(se) ● **brave|ly** valerosamente
brav|ery valentía, valor, coraje
breach infringir, violar, quebrantar, romper, poner en peligro, violación, infracción, contravención, rompimiento
bread pan
break romper(se), quebrar(se), fracturarse, descomponer(se), averiar(se), interrumpir, parar, infringir, violar, escapar, disminuir, decir, informar, amanecer, salir, descifrar, cambiar, hacer una pausa, fractura, rompimiento, pausa, break, descanso, intermedio, recreo, oportunidad, coyuntura feliz, chiripa
▶ **break down** descomponer(se), averiar(se), estropear(se), fracasar, perder la compostura, derribar, tumbar
▶ **break in** meterse, entrar por la fuerza
▶ **break into** entrar por la fuerza, empezar, entrar, introducirse
▶ **break off** partir(se), romper(se), desprender(se), parar repentinamente
▶ **break out** empezar, desarrollar(se), aparecer
▶ **break through** penetrar
▶ **break up** dividir, separar, separarse, disolver
break|down rompimiento, interrupción, breakdown, crisis nerviosa, descompostura, falla, avería, desglose, análisis detallado
breaker zone línea de

rompimiento de las olas

break|fast desayuno

break-in robo

break|ing point límite, colmo

break|through gran avance

break|up ruptura, rompimiento

breast seno, pecho, mama, tórax, pechuga

breath aliento, respiración, hálito
▸ **breath of fresh air** soplo de aire fresco
▸ **out of breath** sin aliento
▸ **say something under one's breath** susurrar algo

breathe respirar • **breath|ing** respiración
▸ **breathe in** inspirar, tomar aire
▸ **breathe out** expirar, sacar el aire

breath|less falto de aliento • **breath|less|ly** entrecortadamente
• **breath|less|ness** dificultad para respirar

breed raza, clase, especie, criar, procrear, producir, engendrar • **breed|er** criador o criadora
• **breed|ing** cría

breeze brisa
▸ **breeze in(to)** entrar tranquilamente

brew preparar, variedad, infusión, fabricar, avecinarse

brew|ery fábrica de cerveza

bribe soborno, sobornar

brick ladrillo

bride novia • **brid|al** nupcial

bride|groom novio

brides|maid dama de honor

bridge puente, salvar, tender un puente, bridge

bridge loan préstamo puente

brief breve, conciso, fugaz, poner al día • **briefs** calzones

brief|case portafolios

brief|ing reunión informativa

brief|ly fugazmente, en síntesis

bri|gade brigada

bright vivo, inteligente, brillante, animado, luminoso • **bright|ly** vivamente, claramente, radiantemente • **bright|ness** brillo
▸ **brights** luces altas

bright|en iluminársele, animarse, alegrar

bril|liant brillante
• **bril|liant|ly** brillantemente, espléndidamente
• **bril|liance** talento, esplendor

bring traer, llevar, provocar, dar, tener fuerzas para
▸ **bring about** provocar
▸ **bring along** traer
▸ **bring back** recordar, revivir
▸ **bring down** derrocar
▸ **bring forward** adelantar
▸ **bring in** introducir, redituar
▸ **bring out** sacar, sacar a relucir
▸ **bring up** criar, plantear

brink
▸ **on the brink of** a punto de, al borde de

brisk rápido y enérgico, frío, expeditivo • **brisk|ly** rápida y enérgicamente, enérgicamente

Brit|ish británico

Brit|on británico o británica

bro carnal

broad ancho, amplio, diverso
• **broad|ly** ampliamente, diversamente, en un sentido amplio, generalizado, en general

broad|band banda ancha

broad|cast programa, transmitir • **broad|cast|ing** transmisión

broad|cast|er conductor o conductora, locutor o locutora

broad|ly en términos generales

broad-minded también **broadminded** de mentalidad abierta

broc|co|li brócoli

bro|chure folleto

broil rostizar

broil|er parrilla superior del horno

broke ver break, quebrado
▶ **to go broke** irse a la quiebra

bro|ken ver break, discontinuo, fracasado, chapurreado

bro|ker corredor, concertar

bron|chi bronquios

Bronx cheer abucheo

bronze bronce

brooch broche, prendedor

broom escoba

broth|er hermano

brother-in-law cuñado

brought ver bring

brown café, integral, tostar

brown-bag llevar un lunch al trabajo o a la escuela, lunch

brownie pastel de chocolate y nueces, niña guía exploradora, alita

brown sugar azúcar morena

brows|er navegador

bruise moretón, lastimarse
• **bruised** amoratado

brush brocha, pincel, cepillo, cepillar, cepillada, sacudir, alisar, rozar
▶ **brush aside** o **brush away** descartar
▶ **brush up on** repasar

brus|sels sprout también **Brussels sprout** col de Bruselas

bru|tal brutal, crudo
• **bru|tal|ly** brutalmente, crudamente

BSE EEB, encefalopatía espongiforme bovina, enfermedad de las vacas locas

BTW PC

bub|ble burbuja, burbujear, hacer burbujas

buck dólar, macho, corcovear
▶ **pass the buck** pasar la bolita, no aceptar la responsabilidad de algo, hacer responsable a alguien

buck|et cubeta, cubo

buck|le hebilla, abrochar, abrocharse, torcerse, doblarse las piernas o las rodillas
▶ **buckle up** ponerse el cinturón, abrocharse el cinturón

bud capullo, amigo
▶ **nip in the bud** cortar por lo sano

Bud|dhism budismo

Bud|dhist budista

bud|dy cuate
▶ **buddy buddy** muy cuate

budg|et presupuesto, presupuestar, hacer presupuestos, para presupuestos reducidos
• **budg|et|ing** presupuesto

buf|fa|lo búfalo

buf|fet buffet, sacudir, zarandear

bug bicho, infección, falla, error, ocultar micrófonos, fastidiar

build construir, empotrar, crear, formar, incorporar, complexión • **build|ing** construcción • **built** construido
▶ **build on** basarse en
▶ **build up** hacer crecer, fortalecer a, darle fuerzas a

build|er albañil

build|ing edificio

build-up también **buildup**, **build up** acumulación, preparativos

built ver build, que tiene

b

cierta complexión

built-up urbanizado

bulb foco, bulbo

bulk masa, mayor parte, grueso
▸ **in bulk** al mayoreo, al por mayor

bull toro, macho

bull|doze demoler

bul|let bala

bul|letin boletín

bul|letin board tablero de anuncios

bul|let point inciso

bullet|proof también **bullet-proof** a prueba de balas

bull|horn altavoz

bull|pen bullpen

bull ses|sion charla

bul|ly bravucón o bravucona, acosador o acosadora, acosar
• **bul|ly|ing** acoso
▸ **bully somebody into something** obligar a alguien a hacer algo

bumble|bee también **bumble bee** abejorro

bump chocar, golpear, dar tumbos, golpe, chichón, chipote
▸ **bump into** toparse con

bump|er defensa, récord

bumpy lleno de baches, incómodo

bun bollo, chongo

bunch montón, ramo, racimo, bonche
▸ **bunch up** o **bunch together** amontonar(se)

bun|dle paquete, abundancia
▸ **bundle somebody somewhere** echar a alguien hacia algún lado, aventar

bun|ga|low casa de una planta

bun|ker búnker, depósito para combustibles, trampa de arena

bunt tocar, tocar la bola, toque de bola

buoy boya, mantenerse a flote

buoy|ant force fuerza de flotación

'burbs también **burbs** suburbios

bur|den carga, preocupar, agobiar

bu|reau instituto, centro, oficina, cómoda

bu|reau|cra|cy burocracia

bu|reau|crat burócrata

bu|reau|crat|ic burocrático

burg|er hamburguesa

bur|glar ladrón o ladrona de casas

bur|glar|ize robar

bur|gla|ry robo

burka ver burqa

burn arder, estar en llamas, quemar, quema, quemadura • **burn|ing** quemazón
▸ **burn down** quedar reducido a cenizas

burn|er quemador

burn|ing ardiente, ardiendo

burnt ver burn

burqa también **burka** túnica

bur|ri|to taco

burst explotar, reventar(se), irrumpir en, salir de, arranque, estallido
▸ **burst into** echarse a
▸ **burst out** estallar

bury enterrar, cubrir

bus autobús, limpiar

bus boy garrotero, ayudante de mesero

bush arbusto, monte, área silvestre

busi|ness negocio, ventas, empresa, organización, asunto, situación
▸ **have no business** no tener nada que ver

business|man hombre de negocios

business|woman mujer de negocios

bust romper, busto
▸ **go bust** quebrar

busy ocupado, ajetreado
▸ **busy oneself** entretenerse

busy sig|nal ocupado

busy|work trabajo innecesario para mantenerse ocupado

but pero, excepto, menos, sólo
▸ **but for** salvo por

butch|er carnicero o carnicera, descuartizar

butt trasero, culata, colilla, blanco
▸ **butt in** entrometerse
▸ **butt out** largarse

but|ter mantequilla, untar mantequilla

butter|fly mariposa

but|tock nalga

but|ton botón, broche, abotonar, abrochar

button|hole ojal

buy comprar, ganar, compra

● **buy|er** comprador o compradora
▸ **buy into** adquirir propiedad accionaria
▸ **buy out** comprar acciones de socios
▸ **buy up** comprar todo lo posible

buzz zumbar, sonar, bullir, zumbido, bullicio de rumores

buzz cut corte de pelo estilo militar

buzz|saw sierra eléctrica

by por, de, en, junto a, por ahí, al lado de, cerca, antes de, a
▸ **by oneself** solo

bye también **bye-bye** adiós

by|law reglamento

by|pass evitar, cirugía de puente coronario, libramiento

byte byte

b

Cc

cab taxi, cabina
cab|bage col
cab|in cabaña, camarote, cabina
cabi|net gabinete, vitrina
ca|ble cable
ca|ble car teleférico, funicular
ca|boose cabús, furgón de cola
cab stand *también* **cabstand** parada de taxi
cac|tus cactus
café *también* **cafe** café
caf|eteria cafetería
caf|feine cafeína
cage jaula
cake pastel • **-cakes** tortitas
  ▸ **take the cake** ser el colmo, no medirse
cake pan molde para pastel
cake|walk pan comido
cal|cium calcio
cal|cu|late calcular, evaluar
  • **cal|cu|la|tion** cálculo
cal|cu|lat|ed calculado
cal|cu|la|tor calculadora
cal|de|ra caldera
cal|en|dar calendario, agenda
call nombrar, llamar, gritar, convocar, suspender, requerimiento, hacer una visita corta, visita, llamada
  ▸ **on call** de turno
  ▸ **call collect** llamar por cobrar
  ▸ **call back** regresar la llamada
  ▸ **call for** requerir, pasar por, exigir
  ▸ **call in** llamar
  ▸ **call off** cancelar
  ▸ **call on** *o* **call upon** hacer un llamado, pasar a ver
  ▸ **call out** hacer venir

  ▸ **call up** llamar, llamar a filas
  ▸ **call upon** *ver* **call on**
call cen|ter centro de atención telefónica
call|er persona que hace una llamada telefónica, visita
call|er ID identificador de llamadas
calm tranquilo, tranquilidad, calma, calmar
  • **calm|ly** tranquilamente, en calma, sin viento
  • **calm|ing** calmante
  ▸ **calm down** calmar(se)
calo|rie caloría
calo|rim|eter calorímetro
came *ver* **come**
cam|el camello
cam|era cámara
  ▸ **on camera** en cámara
cam|era phone celular (que también toma fotografías)
camp campamento, acampar • **camp|ing** de campamento
cam|paign campaña, hacer campaña • **cam|paign|er** militante
camp|fire hoguera, fogata
camp|ground camping
camp|site campamento
cam|pus ciudad universitaria
can poder, lata, enlatar
ca|nal canal
can|cel cancelar
  • **can|cel|la|tion** cancelación
  ▸ **cancel out** anular
can|cer cáncer • **can|cer|ous** canceroso
can|di|date candidato *o* candidata
can|dle vela
can|dy dulce

can|dy apple manzana acaramelada

can|dy bar chocolatina

candy cane bastón de dulce

cane caña, mimbre, bastón

can|non cañón

can|not no poder

ca|noe canoa

ca|no|la canola

cano|py dosel, baldaquín

can't = cannot

can|teen comedor

can|vas lona, lienzo

can|yon cañón

cap gorra, tapa, coronar

ca|pable capaz
 ● **ca|pa|bil|ity** capacidad, competente ● **ca|pably** competentemente

ca|pac|ity capacidad, calidad
 ▶ **capacity crowd** lleno completo

cape cabo, capa

ca|pil|lary capilar

capi|tal capital, mayúscula

capi|tal|ism capitalismo
 ● **capi|tal|ist** capitalista

capi|tal pun|ish|ment pena capital

capi|tol también **Capitol** capitolio
 ▶ **The Capitol** El Capitolio

cap|let comprimido

cap|sule cápsula

cap|tain capitán, capitanear

cap|tion subtítulo

cap|tive cautivo o cautiva
 ▶ **take/hold captive** tomar prisionero

cap|ture capturar, captura

car carro, coche, vagón

car|bo|hy|drate carbohidrato

car|bon carbono

car|bon|at|ed carbonatado, gaseoso

car|bon di|ox|ide bióxido de carbono

car|bon mon|ox|ide monóxido de carbono

car|bu|re|tor carburador

card tarjeta, credencial, carta, cartón, cartulina, pedir identificación

card|board cartón

car|di|ac cardiaco

car|di|ac mus|cle músculo cardiaco

car|di|nal cardenal, fundamental

car|di|nal di|rec|tion dirección cardinal

car|dio|vas|cu|lar sys|tem sistema cardiovascular

care preocuparse, querer, cuidar, importar, cuidado, preocupación

ca|reen ir a toda velocidad

ca|reer carrera, ir a toda velocidad

care|free despreocupado

care|ful cuidadoso
 ● **care|ful|ly** con cuidado, cuidadosamente

care|giv|er también **care giver** persona que tiene a su cuidado a un incapacitado

care|less descuidado
 ● **care|less|ly** sin cuidado
 ● **care|less|ness** descuido

car|go cargamento

car|go pants pantalones cargo

car|ing bondadoso, afectuoso

car|ni|val carnaval, feria

car|ni|vore carnívoro o carnívora

car|pen|ter carpintero o carpintera

car|pet alfombra

carpet|bag|ger político oportunista que pretende representar una localidad que no es la suya

car|pool también **car pool**, **car-pool** trasladarse en grupo al trabajo, en un sólo automóvil

car rel cubículo

car|riage carruaje, vagón

car|ri|er portaaviones, compañía de

C

telecomunicaciones, línea aérea

car|rot zanahoria, incentivo

car|ry cargar, llevar, portar, conllevar, aprobar, llegar
▸ **get/be carried away** dejarse llevar
▸ **carry on** continuar, mantener
▸ **carry out** llevar a cabo
▸ **carry through** sostener

car|ry|ing ca|pac|ity capacidad de persistencia

car|ry-on bolsas de mano

car|ry|over algo que viene desde

car|sick mareado

cart carreta, carrito, transportar con dificultad

car|tel cártel

car|ti|lage cartílago

car|ton cartón, caja

car|toon caricatura

car|tridge cartucho

carve tallar, grabar, cortar
▸ **carve out** forjar
▸ **carve up** dividir

case caso, estuche, caja, argumentos a favor, argumentos en contra
▸ **in any case** en cualquier caso, de todas formas
▸ **in case/just in case** si acaso/por si acaso, por si las dudas
▸ **in that/which case** en ese caso, en cuyo caso
▸ **a case of** cuestión de

case-sensitive que distingue mayúsculas y minúsculas

cash dinero en efectivo, cobrar
▸ **cash in** aprovecharse de

cash bar barra

cash|ier cajero o cajera

cash|ier's check cheque de caja

cash on de|liv|ery entrega contra reembolso

ca|si|no casino

cas|ket ataúd

cas|se|role guiso, cazuela

cas|sette cassette

cast elenco, reparto, asignar, dar el papel de, proyectar, emitir, fundir
▸ **cast aside** hacer a un lado
▸ **cast doubt on something** poner en duda algo
▸ **cast your eyes/a look** echar un vistazo

caste casta

cas|tle castillo

cas|ual despreocupado, casual, fortuito, ocasional, informal ● **casu|al|ly** con toda tranquilidad, informalmente

casu|al Fri|day también **Casual Friday** viernes informal

casu|al|ty víctima, baja, herido

cat gato, felino

cata|log también **catalogue** catálogo, serie

cata|lyze catalizar

ca|tas|tro|phe catástrofe

catch atrapar, cachar, atrapada, pegar, atorarse, tomar, descubrir, escuchar, llamar, contagiarse de, contraer, reflejar, pasador, pestillo, cierre, problema del sistema
▸ **catch on** entender, captar, ponerse de moda
▸ **catch up** alcanzar, ponerse al día, verse envuelto en
▸ **catch up with** atrapar, poder más que uno

catch|er cátcher, receptor o receptora

catch-up
▸ **play catch-up** jugar para tratar de igualar a

catch|word también **catch phrase** eslogan

cat|ego|ry categoría

ca|ter ofrecer servicios

cat|er|ing catering

cat|er|pil|lar oruga

ca|thar|sis catarsis

ca|thedral catedral

Catho|lic católico o católica
● Ca|tholi|cism catolicismo

cat|nip nébeda

cat|tle ganado

catty-corner *también* kitty-
corner en diagonal

caught *ver* catch

cau|li|flow|er coliflor

caulk enmasillar, calafatear
● caulk|ing calafatear,
calafateado

cause causa, motivo, razón,
causar

cau|tion precaución, cautela,
advertencia, advertir

cau|tious cauteloso,
prudente ● cau|tious|ly
cautelosamente

cav|al|ry caballería

cave cueva
▶ cave in derrumbarse,
ceder

cav|ity cavidad

cc cc, cm³, centímetros
cúbicos

CCTV televisión de circuito
cerrado

CD CD

CD burn|er quemador de CDs

CD play|er reproductor de
CDs

CD-ROM CD-ROM

CD writ|er quemador de CDs

cease dejar de

cease|fire cese al fuego

ceil|ing techo, límite, tope

cel|ebrate celebrar
● cel|ebra|tion celebración

cel|ebrat|ed célebre, famoso

ce|leb|rity celebridad

cel|ery apio

ce|les|tial celestial

cell célula, celda

cell cy|cle ciclo celular

cell di|vi|sion división celular

cell mem|brane membrana
celular

cel|lo violoncelo,

violonchelo, chelo ● cel|list
violoncelista

cell|phone teléfono celular,
teléfono móvil, celular

cell theo|ry teoría celular

cel|lu|lar celular

cel|lu|lar phone teléfono
celular, teléfono móvil,
celular

cel|lu|lar res|pi|ra|tion
respiración celular

cell wall pared celular, pared
de la célula

Celsius Celsius, centígrados

ce|ment cemento,
consolidar, pegar

cem|etery cementerio,
panteón

Ce|no|zo|ic era era cenozoica

cen|sus censo

cent centavo

cen|ten|nial centenario

cen|ter centro, centro de
atención, centrar(se) en
● centered centrado en
▶ center oneself centrarse,
concentrarse

cen|ter stage centro del
escenario

cen|ti|li|ter centilitro

cen|time|ter centímetro

cen|ti|pede ciempiés

cen|tral central, clave,
principal ● cen|tral|ly
céntrico, centralmente

cen|tral nerv|ous sys|tem
sistema nervioso central

cen|trip|etal ac|cel|era|tion
aceleración centrípeta

cen|tro|mere centrómero

cen|tu|ry siglo, centuria

cephalo|tho|rax cefalotórax

ce|ram|ic cerámica
▶ ceramics objetos de
cerámica

ce|real cereal, cereales

cer|ebel|lum cerebelo

cer|ebrum cerebro

cer|emo ny ceremonia,
pompa

C

C

cer|tain seguro, cierto, alguno
▸ **for certain** con certeza, a ciencia cierta, con seguridad
▸ **make certain** asegurarse de

cer|tain|ly seguro, desde luego, sin duda, no hay duda de, por supuesto

cer|tain|ty certeza, seguridad, cosa segura, algo seguro

cer|tifi|cate certificado, acta, constancia

cer|ti|fied check cheque certificado

cer|ti|fied mail correo certificado

cer|ti|fied pub|lic ac|count|ant contador público titulado o contadora pública titulada, CPT

CFC CFC

CGI CGI

chain cadena, serie
▸ **be chained to something** estar encadenado a algo

chair silla, cátedra, presidencia, presidente o presidenta, presidir

chair|man presidente

chair|person presidente o presidenta

chair|woman presidenta

chalk tiza, piedra caliza, gis
▸ **chalk up** anotarse, apuntarse

chalk|board pizarrón, pizarra

chal|lenge desafío, reto, cuestionar, poner en tela de juicio, poner en duda, cuestionamiento, retar, desafiar
▸ **rise to the challenge** estar a la altura, aceptar el reto

chal|leng|er contendiente, rival

chal|leng|ing desafiante, retador

cham|ber sala, cámara

cham|pagne champaña

cham|pi|on campeón o campeona, paladín, defensor o defensora, abogar por, defender

cham|pi|on|ship campeonato

chance posibilidad, oportunidad, chance
▸ **by chance** por casualidad
▸ **stand a chance of** tener la oportunidad de
▸ **take a chance** correr el riesgo, arriesgarse

chan|cel|lor canciller, rector o rectora, ministro o ministra de hacienda/ economía, secretario o secretaria de hacienda/ economía

change cambio, monedas, morralla, ser un cambio, ser diferente, cambiar, cambiarse, cambiar de, convertirse, transbordar
▸ **for a change** para variar
▸ **change of state** cambio de estado
▸ **change over** cambiar

chan|nel canal de televisión, canal, canalizar

channel-surfing navegar entre canales

chant canto, cántico, consigna, cantar, recitar monótonamente, repetir una y otra vez • **chant|ing** consignas

cha|os caos

chap|el capilla

chap|ter capítulo

char|ac|ter carácter, personaje, tipo, reputación

char|ac|ter|is|tic característica, característico • **char|ac|ter|is|ti|cal|ly** de manera característica

char|ac|ter|is|tic prop|er|ty propiedad característica

char|ac|teri|za|tion caracterización

char|ac|ter|ize caracterizar, calificar

• **char|ac|teri|za|tion** descripción

char|broiled también **char-grilled** a las brasas, al carbón

char|coal carbón (vegetal)

charge cobrar, cargar, inculpar, cargar contra, abalanzarse, hacerse cargo de, ser responsable de, carga, precio, acusación
▶ **free of charge** gratis, gratuitamente

charge card tarjeta de crédito

chari|table de beneficencia, benéfico, caritativo, benevolente

char|ity institución de beneficencia, caridad

Charles's law también **Charles' law** ley de Gay-Lussac

charm encanto, amuleto, encantar

charm|ing encantador
• **charm|ing|ly** encantadoramente

chart gráfico, gráfica, carta, mapa, trazar, registrar

char|ter carta, alquilado, fletado, alquilar, fletar

char|ter mem|ber socio fundador o socia fundadora

chase perseguir, echar, expulsar, andar en busca, andar detrás de, andar a la caza de, persecución
▶ **chase down** perseguir y atrapar

chat platicar, conversar, charlar, plática, conversación, charla

chat room también **chatroom** tertulia digital, charla digital

chat|ter parlotear, cotorrear, hablar por los codos, castañetear, parloteo, cotorreo, charla

cheap barato, de pacotilla, corriente, vil, de mal gusto, tacaño, agarrado, codo
• **cheap|ly** barato

cheat hacer trampa, tramposo o tramposa
• **cheat|ing** hacer trampa, estafar, timar
▶ **cheat on** engañar, burlar

cheat|er tramposo o tramposa, embustero o embustera, estafador o estafadora

check comprobar, verificar, revisión, verificación, marcar, detener, parar, frenar, registrar, cuenta, a cuadros, de cuadros, cheque
▶ **hold/keep in check** tener a raya, contener
▶ **check in** registrar(se), internar(se)
▶ **check out** pagar la cuenta, investigar
▶ **check up** investigar

checked a cuadros, de cuadros

checker|board tablero de damas, tablero de ajedrez, de cuadros

check|ers damas

check|ing ac|count cuenta de cheques, cuenta corriente

check mark marca, palomita

check|out caja

check|up revisión médica, examen médico

cheek mejilla, cachete

cheer vitorear, aclamar, ovacionar, levantar el ánimo, ovación • **cheer|ing** alentador
▶ **cheer on** animar, alentar
▶ **cheer up** animar

cheer|ful alegre
• **cheer|ful|ly** alegremente
• **cheer|ful|ness** alegría

cheese queso

cheese|cake pastel de queso, tarta de queso

chef cocinero o cocinera, jefe o jefa de cocina, chef

chef's sal|ad ensalada del chef

chemi|cal químico
• **chemi|cal|ly** químicamente, substancia química, producto químico
chemi|cal bond enlace químico
chemi|cal bond|ing enlace químico
chemi|cal change cambio químico
chemi|cal en|er|gy energía química
chemi|cal equa|tion ecuación química
chemi|cal for|mu|la fórmula química
chemi|cal prop|er|ty propiedad química
chemi|cal re|ac|tion reacción química
chemi|cal weath|er|ing descomposición química a la intemperie
chem|ist químico o química
chem|is|try química
cher|ry cereza, cerezo
chess ajedrez
chest pecho, tórax, cofre
chew masticar, mordisquear
Chi|ca|na chicana
Chi|ca|no chicano
chick pollo, polluelo, muchacha bonita
chicka|dee paro carbonero
chick|en pollo
▶ **chicken out** acobardarse, rajarse
chick flick película para mujeres
chief jefe o jefa, principal, en jefe
chief jus|tice presidente o presidenta de la corte, presidente o presidenta del tribunal
chief of staff jefe o jefa del estado mayor
child niño o niña, hijo o hija
child|hood niñez, infancia
child|ish infantil, pueril
chil|dren ver child

child sup|port pensión para el mantenimiento de los hijos
chili chile, chile con carne, chile con frijoles
chil|i con car|ne chile con carne
chill enfriar, poner a enfriar, escalofrío, enfriamiento
▶ **chill out** relajarse
chil|ly frío
chime sonar, campanada
▶ **chime in** hacerle eco a
chim|ney chimenea
chim|pan|zee chimpancé
chin mentón, barbilla
chi|na porcelana, loza
chip circuito integrado, pedacito, trocito, despostillar, desportillar
• **chipped** descascarillado
• **chips** papas fritas
▶ **chip in** cooperarse, contribuir
chlo|ro|phyll clorofila
chlo|ro|plast cloroplasto
choco|late chocolate
choice selección, variedad, decisión, elección, selecto
▶ **have no/little choice** no tener más alternativa/opción
▶ **of choice** preferido
choir coro
choke ahogar(se), asfixiar(se), atragantar(se), estrangular, atascar, embotellar, congestionar
chol|era cólera (m.)
cho|les|ter|ol colesterol
choose elegir, escoger, decidir, optar
chop cortar, costilla, chuleta
▶ **chop down** cortar
▶ **chop off** cercenar
▶ **chop up** picar
cho|rale coral, coro
chord acorde
chor|do|phone instrumento de cuerda
chore lata

cho|rus estribillo, coro, decir a una voz

chose *ver* choose

cho|sen *ver* choose

Christian cristiano *o* cristiana

Chris|ti|an|ity cristianismo

Christ|mas Navidad

Christ|mas Eve Nochebuena

Christ|mas tree árbol de Navidad, árbol de Pascua

chro|ma|tid cromátide

chro|mo|sphere cromosfera

chron|ic crónico • **chroni|cal|ly** crónicamente, permanentemente

chroni|cle reseñar, reseña, crónica

chrysa|lis crisálida

chuck tirar, botar

chunk pedazo, trozo

church iglesia

ci|der sidra

ci|gar puro

ciga|rette cigarrillo, cigarro

ci|lan|tro cilantro

cilia cilio

cin|der ceniza, rescoldo

cin|der block *también* **cinderblock** ladrillo de cenizas, bloque de concreto de cenizas

cin|der cone *también* **cinder cone volcano** cono volcánico

cin|ema cine • **cin|emat|ic** cinematográfico

cin|na|mon canela

cir|ca alrededor de, cerca de

cir|ca|dian rhythm ritmo circadiano

cir|cle círculo, dar vueltas, volar en círculo

cir|cuit circuito, recorrido

cir|cu|lar circular

cir|cu|late circular, correr

cir|cu|la|tion circulación, tirada

cir|cu|la|tory circulatorio

cir|cum|cise circuncidar • **cir|cum|ci|sion** circuncisión

cir|cum|fer|ence circunferencia

cir|cum|stance circunstancia

cir|cus circo

cir|rus cirro

cite citar, mencionar, emplazar

citi|zen ciudadano *o* ciudadana, habitante

citi|zen's ar|rest detención o aprehensión llevada a cabo por un ciudadano común

citi|zens band banda ciudadana

citi|zen|ship ciudadanía

cit|rus cítrico

city ciudad

city cen|ter centro de la ciudad

city plan|ning urbanismo

city|wide que abarca toda la ciudad

civ|ic cívico, municipal, de la ciudad, del ayuntamiento

civic cen|ter edificios municipales

civ|ics civismo

civ|il civil, cortés • **ci|vil|ity** civismo

civ|il de|fense defensa civil

ci|vil|ian civil

civi|li|za|tion civilización

civi|lized civilizado, educado

civ|il rights derechos civiles

civ|il serv|ant servidor público *o* servidora pública, funcionario público *o* funcionaria pública

civ|il ser|vice servicio público, administración pública, servicio civil

civ|il war guerra civil

claim afirmar, reivindicar, hacerse responsable, reclamar, cobrar, reclamo, reivindicación, afirmación, reclamación, exigencia

clam almeja

clam|bake merienda campestre, especialmente en la playa, donde se sirven almejas y otros alimentos

clam|or clamar

clamp abrazadera, sujetar, afianzar, cerrar
  ▶ **clamp down** ponerse severo, tomar medidas drásticas, apretar las clavijas

clan clan

clang|or estrépito, estruendo

clap aplaudir, dar una palmada, trueno

clari|fy aclarar, clarificar
  • **clari|fi|ca|tion** aclaración

clari|net clarinete

clar|ity claridad

clash entrar en conflicto, discordar, desentonar, chocar, choque, disparidad

class clase, grupo, promoción, clasificar, considerar

class act de primera

clas|sic clásico • **clas|sics** estudios clásicos

clas|si|cal clásico
  • **clas|si|cal|ly** clásicamente

clas|si|fied confidencial, secreto

clas|si|fy clasificar
  • **clas|si|fi|ca|tion** clasificación

class|mate compañero o compañera de clase

class|room salón de clases

class sched|ule horario de clases

classy con estilo, con clase

clause cláusula, oración

claw garra, arañar, aferrar(se)

clay arcilla, barro

clean limpio, apropiado, sin tacha, limpiar • **clean|ing** limpieza
  ▶ **clean out** vaciar y limpiar, hacer una limpieza concienzuda
  ▶ **clean up** limpiar concienzudamente, limpiar a conciencia

clean|er limpiador o limpiadora, afanador o afanadora, quitamanchas, purificador, tintorería

cleanse limpiar

clear claro, despejado, transparente, limpio, sin obstáculos, sin inconvenientes, salir, dejar atrás, limpiar, aclarar, levantar, autorizar, absolver, exculpar • **clear|ly** claramente, obviamente
  ▶ **be clear about** tener en claro
  ▶ **clear away** recoger
  ▶ **clear out** irse, largarse, limpiar y ordenar
  ▶ **clear up** recoger

clear|ance despeje, desmonte, autorización

clear-cut también **clear cut** inequívoco

clear|ing claro

cleav|age despegue

clef clave

cler|gy clero

clerk empleado o empleada, oficinista, dependiente o dependienta, vendedor o vendedora, trabajar

clev|er inteligente, ingenioso, listo • **clev|er|ly** inteligentemente
  • **clev|er|ness** inteligencia

click hacer click, click, dar click, captar, caer en la cuenta

cli|ent cliente

cliff precipicio, acantilado

cli|mate clima

cli|max clímax, culminar

climb escalar, subir, trepar, ascender, subida, ascenso

climb|ing alpinismo, montañismo

clinch ganar

cling aferrarse a

clin|ic clínica

clini|cal clínico, frío
- clini|cal|ly clínicamente

clip clip, broche, pasador, sujetar (con un clip), cortar

clock reloj
▸ around/round the clock día y noche

clock|wise en el sentido de las agujas del reloj, de las agujas del reloj

clog obstruir, zueco

clone clon, clonar

close cerrar, terminar, concluir, cercano, próximo, allegado, estrecho, directo, detenido, detallado, reñido, muy reñido, bochornoso • clos|ing cierre
- close|ly estrechamente, detenidamente • close|ness cercanía
▸ close down cerrar
▸ close by/at hand cerca
▸ close to/on cerca de
▸ close up de cerca
▸ be closing on acercarse a
▸ close in cercar

closed cerrado

closed-circuit circuito cerrado

closed cir|cu|la|tory sys|tem sistema circulatorio cerrado

closed sys|tem sistema cerrado

close-mouthed hermético

close|out liquidación

clos|et clóset, armario, de clóset

clos|ing ar|gu|ment conclusiones finales

clos|ing date fecha límite, fecha tope

clo|sure cierre

cloth tela, trapo

clothed vestido

clothes ropa

cloth|ing ropa

cloud nube, nublar, ofuscar, confundir

cloudy nublado, turbio

clove clavo, diente

clo|ver trébol

clover|leaf trébol

clown payaso o payasa, hacer payasadas, payasear, hacerse el payaso

club club, discoteca, palo de golf, garrotte, basto, trébol, dar garrotazos

club|house casa club

club soda agua mineral

clue pista
▸ not have a clue no tener idea

clum|sy torpe, burdo
- clum|si|ly torpemente
- clum|si|ness torpeza

clung ver cling

clunk|er carcacha, cacharro

clus|ter grupo, agruparse, concentrarse

clus|ter|ing estrategias de agrupamiento, clustering

clutch agarrar con fuerza, apretar, clutch
▸ in somebody's clutches en las garras de alguien

cm cm, centímetro(s)

coach entrenador o entrenadora, carruaje, coche, autobús, vagón, entrenar, preparar, darle clases a

coal carbón

coa|li|tion coalición

coarse burdo, grosero, ordinario • coarse|ly en trozos grandes, de manera ordinaria

coarse ad|just|ment ajuste grueso, ajuste aproximativo

coast costa • coast|al costero

Coast Guard servicio costanero, guardacostas, resguardo marítimo

coast|line costa

coast-to-coast transcontinental, de una costa a (la) otra

coat abrigo, piel, pelo, pelaje, lana, capa, mano,

dar una capa o mano, cubrir, enharinar

coat check *también* **coat-check** guardarropa(s)

coat|room *también* **coat room** guardarropa(s)

co|caine cocaína

coch|lea cóclea, caracol

cock|pit cabina

cock|roach cucaracha

cock|tail coctel, aperitivo, combinación

co|coa cacao en polvo, cocoa, chocolate

coco|nut coco

cod bacalao

C.O.D. contra reembolso, pago contra entrega, COD

code código, clave

co|ed mixto

co|ef|fi|cient coeficiente, factor, índice

coe|lom celoma

co|evo|lu|tion coevolución

cof|fee café

cof|fee shop cafetería

cof|fin ataúd, féretro, caja, cajón

coin moneda, acuñar

co|in|cide coincidir

co|in|ci|dence coincidencia

coke coque, coca

cola refresco de cola

col|an|der coladera, colador, escurridor, escurridora

cold frío, resfriado, catarro, resfrío ● **cold|ness** frialdad ● **cold|ly** fríamente ▶ **catch (a) cold** resfriarse

cold-blooded de sangre fría

cold cuts fiambres, carnes frías

cold read|ing lectura sin preparación

col|labo|rate colaborar ● **col|labo|ra|tion** colaboración ● **col|labo|ra|tor** colaborador o colaboradora

col|lapse derrumbarse, desplomarse, quebrar, fracasar, sufrir un colapso, derrumbe, desmoronamiento, fracaso, ruina, colapso, postración

col|lar cuello, collar

col|league colega, compañero o compañera de trabajo

col|lect recolectar, recoger, reunir, coleccionar, acumularse, recaudar ● **col|lect|ing** colección ● **col|lec|tor** coleccionista

col|lect call llamada por cobrar, llamada a cobro revertido

col|lec|tion colección, recopilación, recaudación

col|lec|tion agen|cy agencia de cobro

col|lec|tive colectivo, cooperativa ● **col|lec|tive|ly** colectivamente

col|lec|tor cobrador o cobradora, recaudador o recaudadora, recolector o recolectora

col|lege universidad, colegio, escuela

col|legi|ate universitario

col|lide chocar

col|li|sion colisión, choque

col|loid coloide

co|lon dos puntos, colon

colo|nel coronel

co|lo|nial colonial

co|lo|ni|al|ism colonialismo

colo|nist colonizador o colonizadora, colono o colona

colo|nize colonizar

colo|ny colonia

col|or color, de color, a color, colorido, pintar, colorear, teñir, empañar, influir ▶ **color in** pintar

color-blind daltónico, daltoniano, imparcial, sin prejuicios ● **color-blindness** daltonismo

color-coded codificado con colores

col|ored de color

col|or|ful colorido, vistoso, interesante, original, pintoresco

col|or|ing book libro para colorear, cuaderno para colorear

col|or re|la|tion|ship *también* **color harmony, color scheme** relación de los colores

col|or scheme combinación (de colores)

col|or the|ory teoría de los colores

col|umn columna

col|um|nist columnista

comb peine, peinar, rastrear

com|bat combate, combatir

com|bi|na|tion combinación

com|bine combinar, mezclar
• **com|bined** combinado

com|bus|tion combustión

come venir, llegar, ir
▸ **come about** suceder, ocurrir
▸ **come across** encontrar(se), dar una impresión
▸ **come along** ir
▸ **come around** venir, aceptar, llegar de nuevo, volver en sí
▸ **come at** venirse encima
▸ **come back** regresar, volver, recordar, volver a estar de moda
▸ **come by** conseguir
▸ **come down** bajar, caer
▸ **come down on** estar a favor de, ponerse de parte de, tratar con mano dura
▸ **come down to** ser cuestión de, reducirse a
▸ **come down with** contraer
▸ **come for** buscar
▸ **come forward** presentarse
▸ **come in** recibir, ganar, entrar, ponerse de moda
▸ **come in for** ser objeto de
▸ **come into** heredar, tener

un papel en
▸ **come off** tener éxito
▸ **come on** vamos, ándale, dar, avanzar, encenderse
▸ **come out** salir, salir a la luz, revelarse
▸ **come out for/against** declararse a favor/en contra
▸ **come over** invadir, parecer
▸ **come round** *ver* come around
▸ **come through** sobrevivir
▸ **come to** volver en sí
▸ **come under** estar bajo
▸ **come up** acercarse a, surgir, acercarse
▸ **come up against** tener que enfrentar

come|back retorno, vuelta

co|median cómico *o* cómica

com|edy comedia

com|et cometa

com|fort comodidad, confort, consuelo, consolar
▸ **live in comfort** vivir desahogadamente

com|fort|able cómodo, a gusto • **com|fort|ably** cómodamente, de posición acomodada, holgadamente

com|fort|er edredón

com|ic cómico *o* cómica

comi|cal cómico

com|ic book cómic

com|ing próximo, llegada

com|ma coma

com|mand ordenar, mandar, imponer, infundir, inspirar, estar al mando de, orden, mando, dominio

com|mand|er comandante, capitán de fragata

com|mand mod|ule módulo de maniobra y mando

com|media dell'ar|te comedia del arte

com|memo|rate conmemorar
• **com|memo|ra|tion** conmemoración

com|men|sal|ism

C

comensalismo

com|ment comentar, comentario

com|men|tary crónica, comentario

com|men|ta|tor comentarista

com|merce comercio

com|mer|cial comercial
• **com|mer|cial|ly** comercialmente

com|mis|sion encargarle, comisionar, encargo, comisión, nombramiento, cargo de oficial

com|mis|sion|er también **Commissioner** comisionado o comisionada

com|mit cometer, asignar, comprometerse a, internar

com|mit|ment compromiso, responsabilidad

com|mit|tee comité

com|mod|ity producto, artículo, mercancía

com|mon común, tierra comunal aledaña a una población • **com|mon|ly** comúnmente
▶ **in common** en común

com|mon an|ces|tor antepasado común

com|mon sense también **commonsense** sentido común

com|mon stock acciones ordinarias

com|mu|nal comunitario

com|mu|ni|cate comunicar(se)

com|mu|ni|ca|tion comunicaciones, comunicación

com|mun|ism también **Communism** comunismo
• **com|mun|ist** también **Communist** comunista

com|mu|nity comunidad, colonia

com|mu|nity col|lege escuela comunitaria

com|mu|nity ser|vice servicio comunitario, trabajo comunitario

com|mute viajar todos los días (de la casa al trabajo)
• **com|mut|er** persona que viaja a diario una distancia considerable de su casa al trabajo

comp compensación, indemnización, invitar

com|pact compacto

com|pact bone hueso compacto

com|pact disc también **compact disk** disco compacto

com|pact|ed compactado

com|pan|ion compañero o compañera

com|pa|ny compañía
▶ **keep somebody company** acompañar a alguien

com|pa|rable comparable, equiparable

com|para|tive relativo
• **com|para|tive|ly** relativamente, comparativo

com|pare comparar

com|pared
▶ **compared with/to** comparado con

com|pari|son comparación

com|part|ment compartimento

com|pass brújula

com|pas|sion compasión

com|pat|ible compatible
• **com|pat|ibil|ity** compatibilidad

com|pel obligar a, forzar a

com|pel|ling convincente, persuasivo

com|pen|sate indemnizar, compensar, resarcir

com|pen|sa|tion indemnización, compensación

com|pete competir

com|pe|tence competencia, capacidad

com|pe|tent competente

• com|pe|tent|ly
competentemente

com|pe|ti|tion competencia

com|peti|tive competitivo
• com|peti|tive|ly
competitivamente
• com|peti|tive|ness
competitividad

com|peti|tor competidor o
competidora, concursante,
participante

com|pile compilar

com|plain quejarse

com|plaint queja, afección

com|ple|ment
complementar,
complemento, atributo

com|plete completo, total,
absoluto, terminado,
concluido, completar,
acabar, terminar, llenar,
rellenar • com|plete|ly
completamente
• com|ple|tion terminación
▸ come complete with
incluir

com|plex complejo

com|plex|ion tez

com|plex|ity complejidad

com|plex num|ber número
complejo

com|pli|cate complicar

com|pli|cat|ed complicado

com|pli|ca|tion complicación

com|pli|ment cumplido,
elogiar

com|pli|men|tary elogioso,
de obsequio

com|ply cumplir

com|po|nent componente

com|pose componer

com|pos|er compositor o
compositora

com|po|site compuesto,
amalgama

com|pos|ite vol|ca|no
estratovolcán, volcán cónico

com|po|si|tion composición,
mezcla

com|post composta

com|pound complejo,

compuesto, oración
compuesta, agravar

com|pound eye ojo
compuesto

com|pound light
micro|scope microscopio
compuesto

com|pound ma|chine
máquina compuesta

com|pound me|ter compás
compuesto

com|pre|hen|sion
comprensión

com|pre|hen|sive exhaustivo
• com|pre|hen|sive|ly
exhaustivamente

com|prise constar

com|pro|mise arreglo, llegar
a un arreglo, comprometer

comp time tiempo libre
dado a los empleados en
compensación por horas
extras trabajadas

com|pul|so|ry obligatorio

com|put|er computadora,
ordenador

com|put|er|ize computarizar
• com|put|er|ized
computarizado

com|put|ing computación

con estafar, timar, estafa

con|cave cóncavo

con|cave lens lente cóncavo

con|ceal ocultar
• con|ceal|ment
ocultamiento

con|cede reconocer

con|ceive concebir

con|cen|trate concentrarse
en, concentrar

con|cen|trat|ed concentrado,
intenso

con|cen|tra|tion
concentración

con|cept concepto
• con|cep|tual conceptual

con|cep|tion concepción,
noción

con|cern inquietud,
preocupación, negocio,
interés, asunto, inquietar,

interesarse, tratar, concernir • **con|cerned** inquieto, involucrado

con|cern|ing con respecto a, acerca de

con|cert concierto

con|cer|to concierto

con|ces|sion concesión, franquicia

con|clude llegar a la conclusión, concluir

con|clu|sion conclusión
▸ **in conclusion** en conclusión

con|crete concreto

con|demn condenar, declarar en ruinas
• **con|dem|na|tion** condena

con|den|sa|tion condensación

con|den|sa|tion point punto de condensación

con|dense condensar, resumir, condensarse

con|di|tion condición, afección, condicionar
• **con|di|tion|ing** condicionamiento
▸ **on condition that** a condición de

con|di|tion|al condicional

con|dom preservativo, condón

con|do|min|ium condominio

con|duct llevar a cabo, conducirse, dirigir, conducir, conducción, conducta

con|duc|tion conducción

con|duc|tor director o directora, revisor o revisora, cobrador o cobradora, conductor

cone cono, piña

con|fec|tion|ers' sug|ar azúcar glas(é)

con|fed|era|tion confederación

con|fer|ence congreso

con|fess confesar

con|fes|sion confesión

con|fi|dence confianza
▸ **in confidence** en confianza

con|fi|dent seguro, que tiene confianza en uno mismo • **con|fi|dent|ly** con confianza

con|fi|den|tial confidencial
• **con|fi|den|tial|ly** con confidencialidad
• **con|fi|den|ti|al|ity** confidencialidad

con|fine confinar, limitar(se), restrigir(se)
• **con|fine|ment** confinamiento

con|fined confinado, limitado, reducido

con|firm confirmar
• **con|fir|ma|tion** confirmación

con|flict conflicto, discrepar

con|form ajustarse, cumplir, someterse, acatar, avenirse

con|front enfrentarse, hacer frente, encarar, confrontar

con|fron|ta|tion confrontación
• **con|fron|ta|tion|al** polémico

con|fuse confundir, complicar, enredar

con|fused confundido, confuso

con|fus|ing confuso

con|fu|sion confusión

con|gratu|late felicitar
• **con|gratu|la|tion** felicitación

con|gratu|la|tions felicidades, felicitaciones

con|gre|ga|tion fieles, feligreses, miembros de la iglesia

con|gress congreso

Con|gress congreso
• **con|gres|sion|al** también **Congressional** del congreso

congress|man congresista

congress|person congresista

congress|woman congresista

con|gru|ent congruente

con|ic pro|jec|tion proyección cónica

co|ni|fer conífera

con|junc|tion conjunción
▶ **in conjunction with** en conjunción con

con|nect conectar, conectar, enlazar, relacionar

con|nect|ed relacionado

con|nec|tion relación, conexión

con|nec|tive tis|sue tejido conjuntivo

con|quer conquistar, vencer, superar, resolver
● **con|quer|or** conquistador o conquistadora

con|science conciencia

con|scious consciente, deliberado ● **con|scious|ly** conscientemente

con|scious|ness conciencia
▶ **lose consciousness** perder la conciencia
▶ **regain consciousness** recobrar la conciencia

con|secu|tive consecutivo

con|sen|sus consenso

con|sent consentimiento, consentir, aceptar

con|se|quence consecuencia
▶ **in consequence/ as a consequence** en consecuencia

con|se|quent|ly consecuentemente, en consecuencia

con|ser|va|tion protección, conservación, ahorro

con|ser|va|tion of en|er|gy conservación de la energía

con|ser|va|tion of mass *también* **conservation of matter** conservación de la masa

con|serva|tive conservador o conservadora
● **con|serva|tism** conservadurismo,

tradicionalismo
● **con|serva|tive|ly** conservadoramente

con|serve ahorrar, conservar, preservar

con|sid|er considerar, tomar en consideración, analizar ● **con|sid|era|tion** consideración

con|sid|er|able considerable, sustancial ● **con|sid|er|ably** considerablemente

con|sid|er|ate considerado, atento

con|sid|era|tion consideración, preocupación, factor
▶ **take into consideration** tomar en consideración, tomar en cuenta, tener en cuenta
▶ **under consideration** en proceso de análisis, en estudio

con|sid|er|ing considerando

con|sist consistir, constar

con|sist|ent constante, coherente, consistente, que concuerda ● **con|sist|en|cy** regularidad ● **con|sist|ent|ly** sistemáticamente

con|sole consolar
● **con|so|la|tion** consuelo, consola

con|soli|date consolidar

con|so|nant consonante

con|so|nant dou|bling doble consonante

con|sor|tium consorcio

con|spira|cy conspiración

con|sta|ble alguacil, agente de policía

con|stant constante
● **con|stant|ly** constantemente

con|stel|la|tion constelación

con|stitu|en|cy electores potenciales, grupo de votantes, distrito electoral

con|stitu|ent elector o electora, componente, elemento constitutivo, constituyente, constitutivo

con|sti|tute constituir, representar

con|sti|tu|tion constitución

• **con|sti|tu|tion|al** constitucional, complexión

con|straint restricción, limitación, coacción

con|struct construir

con|struc|tion construcción, creación

con|struc|tion pa|per cartón, cartulina

con|struc|tive constructivo

con|sult consultar a, consultar con

• **con|sul|ta|tion** consulta

con|sult|ant consultor o consultora, asesor o asesora, especialista

con|sul|ta|tion junta, reunión

con|sume consumir, comerse, beberse

con|sum|er consumidor o consumidora, parásito, depredador

con|sum|er con|fi|dence confianza del consumidor

Con|sum|er Price In|dex índice de precios al consumidor, IPC

con|sum|ing absorbente

con|sump|tion consumo

con|tact contacto, contactar, ponerse en contacto (con)
▶ **in contact with** en contacto con

con|tact lens lente de contacto

con|ta|gious contagioso

con|tain contener, haber, tener, detener

con|tain|er recipiente, contenedor

con|tain|er ship buque/barco portacontenedores

con|tami|nate contaminar

• **con|tami|na|tion** contaminación

con|tem|plate contemplar, considerar, pensar

• **con|tem|pla|tion** contemplación

con|tem|po|rary contemporáneo, actual

con|tempt desprecio

con|tend lidiar con, enfrentar, enfrentarse a, argüir, sostener, argumentar, afirmar, competir • **con|tend|er** aspirante

con|tent contenido, índice, contento, satisfecho, conforme, feliz
▶ **contents** tabla de contenidos

con|ten|tion argumento, punto de vista, opinión, discusión, disputa

con|test competencia, contienda, refutar, impugnar

con|test|ant competidor o competidora, concursante

con|text contexto

con|text clue clave contextual

con|ti|nent continente

con|ti|nen|tal continental

con|ti|nen|tal break|fast desayuno continental

con|ti|nen|tal drift deriva de los continentes

con|ti|nen|tal mar|gin margen continental

con|ti|nen|tal rise cuesta continental

con|ti|nen|tal shelf plataforma continental

con|ti|nen|tal slope declive continental

con|tin|gent contingente

con|tin|ual continuo

• **con|tin|ual|ly** continuamente

con|tin|ue continuar, seguir, proseguir

con|tinu|ous continuo

• **con|tinu|ous|ly** constantemente

con|tour draw|ing dibujo perfilado

con|tour feath|er pluma de contorno

con|tour in|ter|val distancia vertical

con|tour line cota, curva de nivel

contra|cep|tion anticoncepción, contracepción

contra|cep|tive anticonceptivo

con|tract contrato, contratar, contraer(se), contagiarse ● **con|trac|tion** contracción

con|trac|tor contratista

contra|dict contradecir

contra|dic|tion contradicción

contra|dic|tory contradictorio

con|tra|ry contrario
▶ **on the contrary** al contrario
▶ **to the contrary** en contrario

con|trast contraste, comparar, contrastar, diferir
▶ **by contrast/in contrast/in contrast to** por el contrario, a diferencia de

con|trib|ute contribuir, aportar, colaborar

con|tribu|tor donante, donador o donadora, que contribuye

con|tri|bu|tion contribución, aportación, donación

con|trol control, controlar(se), grupo de control
▶ **in control** tener el control
▶ **under one's control** bajo el control ● **con|trol|ler** controlador o controladora
▶ **out of control** fuera de control
▶ **under control** bajo control, controlado ● **con|trolled** controlado

con|trolled ex|peri|ment experimento controlado

con|tro|ver|sial controvertido, polémico

con|tro|ver|sy controversia

con|vec|tion convección

con|vec|tion cur|rent corriente de convección

con|vec|tive zone zona de convección

con|vene convocar, reunirse

con|veni|ence conveniencia, comodidad

con|veni|ent conveniente, práctico, cómodo, muy a mano, oportuno ● **con|veni|ence** conveniencia ● **con|veni|ent|ly** convenientemente

con|ven|tion convención, convencionalismo, congreso

con|ven|tion|al convencional, tradicional ● **con|ven|tion|al|ly** convencionalmente

con|ver|gent bounda|ry límite convergente

con|ver|sa|tion conversación ● **con|ver|sa|tion|al** familiar

con|vert convertir(se), converso o conversa ● **con|ver|sion** conversión

con|vert|ible convertible, descapotable, canjeable

con|vex lens lente convexa

con|vey transmitir

con|vict condenar, declarar culpable, recluso o reclusa, presidiario o presidiaria, preso o presa, reo

con|vic|tion convicción, condena

con|vince convencer ● **con|vinced** convencido

con|vinc|ing convincente ● **con|vinc|ing|ly** convincentemente

con|voy convoy

cook cocinar, guisar,

preparar comida, cocinero o cocinera • **cook|ing** cocinar
▶ **cook up** tramar

cook|book libro de cocina, libro de recetas, recetario

cookie galleta, galletita, cookie

cookie cut|ter *también* **cookie-cutter** molde para galletas, con molde

cookie sheet charola metálica para hornear

cook|ing comida, cocina, cocinar, hacer la comida, preparar la comida

cook|out asado, parrillada

cool fresco, tranquilo, hostil, frío, cool, a la moda, en la onda, moderno, relajado, enfriar(se) • **cool|ly** tranquilamente, fríamente
▶ **cool down** calmar(se), tranquilizar(se)
▶ **cool off** refrescarse

co|oper|ate cooperar
• **co|opera|tion** cooperación

col|or|di|nate coordinar
• **col|or|di|nat|ed** coordinado
• **col|or|di|na|tion** coordinación
• **col|or|di|na|tor** coordinador o coordinadora
▶ **coordinates** coordenadas

col|or|di|nate sys|tem sistema de coordenadas

cootie piojo

cop poli
▶ **cop to** confesar

cope afrontar, enfrentar, sobrellevar, arreglárselas

copi|er copiadora

cop|per cobre

cop|per wire alambre de cobre

copy copia, ejemplar, copiar

copy ma|chine copiadora

copy|right derechos, derechos de autor, copyright

cord cuerda, cable

core corazón, centro, núcleo

Coriolis ef|fect efecto Coriolis

cork|screw sacacorcho, sacacorchos

corn maíz

cor|nea córnea

cor|ner rincón, esquina, acorralar, acaparar, monopolizar
▶ **around/round the corner** a la vuelta de la esquina, a punto de que algo suceda

corn|row *también* **corn row** trencita

corn|starch *también* **corn starch** maicena

co|ro|na corona

cor|po|ral pun|ish|ment castigos corporales

cor|po|rate corporativo

cor|po|ra|tion compañía

corps cuerpo

corpse cadáver

cor|ral corral, acorralar

cor|rect correcto, corregir, tener razón • **cor|rect|ly** correctamente, con corrección • **cor|rect|ness** corrección

cor|rec|tion corrección
• **cor|rec|tion|al** correccional, correctivo

cor|rec|tion|al fa|cil|ity reformatorio

cor|rec|tions of|fic|er guardia de la prisión

cor|re|la|tion|al de|sign diseño correlacionado

cor|re|spond corresponder, mantener correspondencia
• **cor|re|spond|ing** correspondiente
• **cor|re|spond|ing|ly** en proporción

cor|re|spond|ence correspondencia

cor|re|spond|ent corresponsal

cor|rupt corrupto, corromper(se)

cor|rup|tion corrupción

co|sine coseno

cos|met|ic cosmético, superficial

cos|mic back|ground ra|dia|tion radiación del fondo cósmico

cos|mol|ogy cosmología

cost costo, costar
▸ **at a/the cost of** a costa de
▸ **at all costs** a toda costa

co|star coestrella, coprotagonizar

cost-effective reditable

cost|ly costoso

cos|tume traje

cos|tume par|ty *también* **costume ball** fiesta de disfraces

cot|tage casita de campo

cot|ton algodón

cot|ton can|dy algodón de azúcar

cot|ton swab cotonete

cotton|tail conejo de cola de algodón, Sylvilagus, tapetí

coty|ledon cotiledón

couch sofá

cou|gar puma

cough toser, tos • **cough|ing** tos
▸ **cough up** soltar, aflojar

could podía, podías, podíamos, podían, podría, podrías, podríamos, podrían, pudiera, pudieras, pudiéramos, pudieran
▸ **could have** pude haber, pudiste haber, pudo haber, pudimos haber, pudieron haber

couldn't = could not

could've = could have

coun|cil ayuntamiento

coun|ci|lor consejero *o* consejera

coun|sel consejo, aconsejar, orientar • **coun|sel|ing** *también* **counselling** orientación

coun|se|lor *también* **counsellor** consejero *o* consejera, orientador *u* orientadora, abogado *o* abogada

count contar, cuenta, conde
▸ **keep count** llevar la cuenta
▸ **lose count** perder la cuenta
▸ **count against** perjudicar
▸ **count on** *o* **count upon** contar con
▸ **count out** contar uno por uno
▸ **count up** contar
▸ **count upon** *ver* count on

count|able noun sustantivo contable, nombre contable

count|down cuenta regresiva

coun|ter mostrador, contador, ficha, contraatacar
▸ **counter to** contrario a

counter|bal|ance contrapeso

counter|clockwise en sentido contrario a las manecillas del reloj

counter|feit falso, falsificación, falsificar

counter|of|fer contraoferta

counter|part contraparte

counter|top cubierta de cocina

count|less incontable

count noun sustantivo contable, nombre contable

coun|try país, campo, terreno
▸ **country music** música country

coun|try and west|ern *también* **country-and-western** música country

country|side campiña

coun|ty condado

coup golpe de estado, golpe maestro

cou|ple par, pareja, combinar

cou|pon cupón, vale

cour|age valor

cou|ra|geous valiente

C

cou|ri|er mensajero *o* mensajera, mandar por mensajería

course rumbo, camino, curso, tratamiento, plato, campo, cancha
▶ **of course** claro
▶ **on course for** en camino de

court tribunal, cancha, corte, buscar, atraer
▶ **have/want one's day in court** tener/querer su audiencia

cour|teous cortés
• **cour|teous|ly** cortésmente

cour|tesy cortesía

court|house juzgado

Court of Ap|peals tribunal de apelaciones

court|room sala de justica, tribunal

court|yard patio

cous|in primo *o* prima

co|va|lent bond enlace covalente

co|va|lent com|pound compuesto covalente

cov|er cubrir, recorrer, cubierta, tapa, portada, refugio, cobijas
▶ **cover up** tapar, ocultar

cov|er|age cobertura

cover|alls overol

cov|er|ing capa

cov|er let|ter carta adjunta

cow vaca, hembra, intimidar
• **cowed** intimidado

cow|ard cobarde

cow|boy vaquero

cow|boy boots botas vaqueras

cozy acogedor, íntimo y agradable

CPA C.P.

CPI IPC

CPR RCP

crab cangrejo

crack resquebrajar, partir, descifrar, sufrir una crisis nerviosa, quebrarse, contra, rendija, rajadura, estallido, de primera, comentario socarrón, crack
▶ **crack down** tomar medidas enérgicas contra
▶ **crack up** sufrir un ataque de nervios

crack|down medidas enérgicas

crack|er galleta

crack-up ataque de nervios, accidente automovilístico

cra|dle cuna, acunar

craft nave, embarcación, artesanía, hacer con cuidado

cram atiborrar

cramp calambre

crane grúa, grulla, estirar

cranky cascarrabias

crap|shoot volado

crash choque, estrépito, crac, crack, chocar, derrumbarse, quebrar, caerse

cra|ter cráter

craw|fish *también* **crayfish** cangrejo de río

crawl gatear, arrastrarse, paso de tortuga, crol
▶ **be crawling with** estar lleno de

crawl space espacio estrecho bajo el techo o piso que permite el acceso a la plomería o a los cables

cray|on crayón

cra|zy loco *o* loca • **cra|zi|ly** como loco
▶ **crazy about** loco por

cream crema

cream|er cremera

cre|ate crear, causar, provocar • **crea|tion** creación • **crea|tor** creador *o* creadora

crea|tion creación

crea|tive creativo
• **crea|tiv|ity** creatividad

crea|tive dra|ma teatro, arte dramático

crea|tive writ|ing escritura creativa

crea|ture criatura

cred|ible creíble, verosímil, plausible, viable
• **cred|ibil|ity** credibilidad

cred|it crédito, mérito, reconocer, atribuir el crédito
▶ **be to somebody's credit** decir mucho de alguien

cred|it card tarjeta de crédito

cred|it hour crédito, materia

cred|it lim|it límite de crédito

cred|it line línea de crédito

credi|tor acreedor o acreedora

cred|it trans|fer transferencia de créditos

cred|it un|ion unión de crédito

creep moverse sigilosamente, subrepticiamente, deslizamiento lento, movimiento paulatino del terreno

creepy escalofriante, repulsivo

crept ver creep

cres|cent media luna, creciente

crest cima, cresta, emblema, divisa

cre|vasse grieta

crew tripulación, equipo

crib cuna

crick|et cricket, críquet, grillo

crime crimen, delito

crimi|nal criminal, delincuente, penal

crip|ple quedar lisiado, quedar inválido

cri|sis crisis

crisp crujiente, despejado, frío

cri|teri|on criterio

crit|ic crítico o crítica

criti|cal crítico, fundamental
• **criti|cal|ly** críticamente, de manera crítica

criti|cism crítica

criti|cize criticar

croco|dile cocodrilo

crois|sant cuerno, medialuna, croissant

Cro-Magnon Cromañón, Cro-Magnon

crook pillo, sinvergüenza, pliegue, corva

crook|ed torcido, chueco, deshonesto

crop cosecha, cultivo, montón, lote, cortar al ras
▶ **crop up** surgir

crop dust|ing también **crop-dusting** fumigar

cross cruzar(se), atravesar(se), cruz, tache, cruza, mezcla, enojado, enfadado • **cross|ly** con enojo
▶ **cross out** tachar

cross-country cross-country, campo traviesa, de extremo a extremo, a través del país

cross-examine contrainterrogar, repreguntar • **cross-examination** contrainterrogatorio

cross|ing crucero, travesía, cruce

cross|ing over cruzamiento

cross|roads cruce, encrucijada

cross|town también **cross-town** que cruza, que atraviesa, atravesando

cross|walk cruce de peatones

cross|word crucigrama

crouch acuclillarse, agazaparse, agacharse, estar agachado, en cuclillas

crow cuervo, cantar

crowd gentío, multitud, muchedumbre, gente, grupo, aglomerarse, amontonarse

crowd|ed abarrotado, lleno

crown corona, coronilla, coronar

cru|cial crucial, clave • **cru|cial|ly** muy importante

crud porquería

crude ordinario, común, vulgar, rudimentario, burdo, crudo • **crude|ly** de forma rudimentaria, vulgarmente

crude oil petróleo crudo

cru|el cruel • **cru|el|ly** cruelmente • **cru|el|ty** crueldad

cruise crucero, hacer un crucero, desplazarse, circular

cruise con|trol control de crucero

crumb miga, migaja, morona, borona

crum|ble desmoronar(se), desintegrarse, caerse, venirse abajo, derrumbarse

crunch triturar, masticar haciendo ruido, (hacer) crujir, crujido

crush aplastar, apachurrar, triturar, acallar, prensar, apretujar, aglomeración, tumulto, enamoramiento • **crush|ing** represión

crust costra, corteza, corteza terrestre

cry llorar, llanto, gritar, exclamar, grito, chillido • **cry|ing** llanto ▶ **cry out** gritar ▶ **cry out for** clamar, exigir, pedir a gritos

crys|tal cristal, cristal cortado

crys|tal lat|tice red cristalina, retículo cristalino, estructura reticular del cristal

CST CST

cube cubo

cu|bic cúbico

cu|bi|cle cubículo

cu|cum|ber pepino

cue entrada, pie, indicación, señal, taco

cuff puño, bastilla, dobladillo, valenciana ▶ **off the cuff** improvisado

cui|sine cocina

cult secta, de culto

cul|ti|vate cultivar, adoptar • **cul|ti|va|tion** cultivo

cul|tur|al cultural • **cul|tur|al|ly** culturalmente

cul|ture cultura, cultivo

cum laude cum laude, con honores

cu|mu|lo|nim|bus también **cumulo-nimbus** cúmulonimbo

cu|mu|lus cúmulo

cup taza, cáliz, copa, trofeo ▶ **cup one's hands** ahuecar las manos, hacer una bocina con las manos ▶ **cup something in one's hands** tomar/coger algo con delicadeza

cup|board alacena, aparador, armario, clóset

curb frenar, refrenar, contener, control, acera, banqueta, cuneta

curb|stone borde de la acera, borde de la banqueta

cure curar(se), remediar, poner remedio, solucionar, cura

cur|few toque de queda

cu|ri|os|ity curiosidad, objeto curioso

cu|ri|ous curioso, extraño • **cu|ri|ous|ly** curiosamente

curl rizo, chino, bucle, espiral, enchinar, enchinarse, rizarse, ondularse, serpentear ▶ **curl up** acurrucarse, enroscarse

curly chino, rizado, enroscado

cur|ren|cy moneda, divisas

cur|rent corriente, vigente, actual • **cur|rent|ly** actualmente

cur|rent af|fairs también **current events** ver **current events**

cur|rent elec|tric|ity electricidad dinámica

cur|rent ev|ents *también* **current affairs** sucesos de actualidad

cur|ricu|lum plan de estudios, programa de una materia

cur|ry curry

curse maldecir, insultar, insulto, lacra, maldición
▸ **be cursed** estar maldito

cur|sor cursor

cur|tain cortina, telón

cur|tain rod cortinero

cur|va|ture curvatura

curve curva, torcerse, curvearse, desviarse, hacer una curva ● **curved** curvo

cur|vi|lin|ear curvilíneo

cush|ion cojín, amortiguar

cus|tard natilla

cus|to|dy custodia
▸ **in custody** detenido

cus|tom costumbre

cus|tom|er cliente

cus|tom|er ser|vice servicio al cliente

cus|toms aduana

cut cortar(se), corte, cortada, reducción, recorte, achicar, reducir, omitir, recortar, tomar un atajo, interrumpir
▸ **cut across** trascender, rebasar
▸ **cut back** recortar
▸ **cut down** reducir, disminuir, acortar, talar
▸ **cut off** cortar, separarse, cortarse la línea, cortarse la comunicación, interrumpirse la comunicación
▸ **cut out** recortar, eliminar, suprimir, tapar, no dejar pasar, pararse, apagarse
▸ **cut up** cortar en pedazos, picar

cute mono, lindo

cu|ti|cle cutícula

cut|off límite, corte
● **cut|offs** shorts

cut|ting gajo, esqueje, hiriente, cortante

cut|ting board tabla de picar

cut|ting edge a la vanguardia

cuz *también* **'cuz** porque

cyano|bac|te|ria cianobacteria

cy|ber|space cyberespacio, ciberespacio

cy|cle ciclo, motocicleta, moto, bici, bicicleta, bicla, cicla, andar en bici, andar en bicicleta ● **cy|cling** ciclismo

cy|clist ciclista

cy|clone ciclón

cyl|in|der cilindro, tanque

cyni|cal cínico, escéptico, amargado ● **cyni|cal|ly** cínicamente ● **cyni|cism** cinismo

cy|to|ki|nesis citocinesis

cyto|plasm citoplasma

cyto|sine citosina

C

Dd

D.A. fiscal de distrito, procurador general *o* procuradora general

dad papá

dad|dy papi, papito

daf|fo|dil narciso

dag|ger daga, puñal

dai|ly diariamente, a diario, todos los días, diario
  ▸ **daily life** vida cotidiana

dairy lechería, lácteo, vacuno, lechero

dam dique, presa, represa

dam|age dañar, perjudicar, daño ● **dam|ag|ing** dañino, perjudicial
  ▸ **damages** daños y perjuicios

dame tía, vieja

damn criticar severamente

damp húmedo ● **damp|ness** humedad

dance bailar ● **danc|ing** baile, danza

dance form estilo de baile

dance phrase segmento de baile, segmento de danza

danc|er bailarín *o* bailarina

dance se|quence secuencia de pasos de baile

dance struc|ture estructura del baile

dance study estudio de baile, ejercicio de baile

dan|ger peligro, riesgo

dan|ger|ous peligroso
  ● **dan|ger|ous|ly** peligrosamente, arriesgadamente, gravemente

dare osar, atreverse, arriesgarse, animarse, retar, desafiar, reto, desafío
  ▸ **how dare you** cómo te atreves/se atreve/se atreven

dar|ing osado, audaz, temerario, atrevido, audacia, osadía, arrojo

dark oscuro, sombrío
  ● **dark|ness** oscuridad
  ● **dark|ly** oscuramente, misteriosamente
  ▸ **be in the dark** estar a oscuras

dark choco|late chocolate amargo, chocolate oscuro, chocolate sin leche

dark|room cuarto oscuro

dar|ling amor, cariño, querido *o* querida, precioso

dart (salir, correr, lanzarse) como una flecha, lanzar rápidamente, dardo

dash lanzarse, carrera, vuelta, hacer añicos, pizca, guión
  ▸ **dash off** irse corriendo, salir corriendo, escribir a la carrera

dash|board tablero de instrumentos

da|ta datos, dato

da|ta|base *también* **data base** base de datos

da|ta en|try ingreso de datos, entrada de datos, captura de datos

da|ta ta|ble gráfica de datos

date fecha, cita, pareja, compañero *o* compañera, dátil, salir con, fechar, determinar la antigüedad de, pasar de moda ● **dat|ed** pasado de moda, anticuado
  ▸ **to date** hasta la fecha, hasta el momento
  ▸ **date back** remontarse

date rape violación (cometida durante una cita)

daugh|ter hija

daugh|ter cell célula hija

daughter-in-law nuera

dawn amanecer, alba,

crepúsculo, aurora, nacer, alborear • **dawn|ing** albor
▸ **dawn on** o **dawn upon** caer en la cuenta

day día, época
▸ **call it a day** dejar las cosas para otro día o para el día siguiente
▸ **one day/some day/one of these days** un día/algún día/uno de estos días

day care también **daycare** servicio de guardería infantil, centro de atención diurna para ancianos o minusválidos

day|dream soñar despierto, fantasear, ilusionarse, hacerse ilusiones, fantasía

day|light luz de día, luz natural
▸ **in broad daylight** a plena luz del día

day|light sav|ing time también **daylight savings time, daylight savings** horario (hora) de verano

day|time día

day-to-day cotidiano, diario, de cada día

dead muerto, desconectado, cortado, absoluto, total, justo
▸ **stop somebody dead** parar a alguien en seco

dead end callejón sin salida
▸ **dead-end** sin porvenir, sin futuro

dead|line fecha límite, plazo

dead|ly mortal, mortífero, letal, funesto

deaf sordo • **deaf|ness** sordera

deal trato, arreglo, convenio, acuerdo, comerciar en, dedicarse a (la compraventa), repartir, dar • **deal|er** comerciante, corredor o corredora
▸ **a great deal of** mucho
▸ **deal out** dictar, aplicar, imponer
▸ **deal with** ocuparse de,

responder a, tratar de, tratar con

deal|ings relación, trato

dean director, decano, deán

dear querido o querida, estimado, cariño
▸ **dear to** caro a

death muerte
▸ **life and/or death** de vida o muerte
▸ **put (somebody) to death** ejecutar
▸ **to death** muerto de

death row pabellón de los condenados a muerte

death toll también **death-toll** número de víctimas, número de muertos

de|bate discusión, deliberación, debate, discutir, considerar, dar vueltas a

deb|it cargar, hacer un cargo, débito, pasivo, debe

deb|it card tarjeta de débito

de|bris escombros

debt deuda
▸ **in debt** en deuda
▸ **get into debt** endeudarse

de|but debut

dec|ade década, decenio

de|cal calcomanía

de|cay descomponerse, pudrirse, decaer, declinar, descomposición, caries, decadencia, deterioro
• **de|cayed** descompuesto

de|ceased difunto o difunta, fallecido o fallecida

de|ceit engaño

de|ceive engañar, defraudar

De|cem|ber diciembre

de|cent decente, respetable, apropiado • **de|cent|ly** decentemente

de|cen|tral|ize descentralizar(se)
• **de|cen|trali|za|tion** descentralización

de|cep|tion engaño

de|cide decidir, definir, determinar

▶ **decide on** decidir(se)

de|cidu|ous de hoja caduca, caducifolio

deci|mal decimal

deci|mal point punto decimal

de|ci|sion decisión, resolución, determinación

de|ci|sive decisivo, contundente, resuelto • **de|ci|sive|ly** decisivamente, resueltamente
• **de|ci|sive|ness** resolución

deck cubierta, tarima, mazo, baraja

dec|la|ration declaración

de|clara|tive enunciativo, aseverativo

de|clare declarar, manifestar, anunciar

de|cline disminuir, declinar, rehusar, disminución
▶ **in decline/on the decline** en declive, en decadencia, en disminución
▶ **go into decline** entrar en decadencia

de|cod|ing descodificar

de|com|pos|er descomponedor

de|com|po|si|tion re|ac|tion reacción de descomposición

deco|rate adornar, decorar, empapelar, pintar
• **deco|rat|ing** decorado
• **deco|ra|tor** decorador o decoradora

deco|ra|tion decoración, adorno

deco|ra|tive decorativo

de|crease disminuir, disminución

de|cree decreto, sentencia, decretar

dedi|cate dedicar(se), consagrarse • **dedi|cat|ed** dedicado • **dedi|ca|tion** dedicación, dedicatoria

de|duct deducir, restar

de|duct|ible deducible

de|duc|tion deducción

deed acto, hecho, acción, hazaña, escritura

dee|jay disc-jockey, trabajar de/como disc-jockey

deem considerar, juzgar

deep profundo, hondo, grave, intenso, subido
• **deep|ly** profundamente
▶ **go/run deep** venir de lo profundo de uno

deep cur|rent corriente (oceánica) de aguas profundas

deep|en profundizar, estrechar, hacer más grave, ahondar

deep ocean ba|sin cuenca abisal (oceánica)

deep-water zone zona de aguas profundas

deer venado, ciervo

de|fault faltar, dejar de cumplir, incurrir en mora, falta, incumplimiento, mora, preestablecido
▶ **by default** por omisión

de|feat derrotar, vencer, frustrar, derrota

de|fect defecto, desertar
• **de|fec|tion** deserción
• **de|fec|tor** desertor o desertora

de|fec|tive defectuoso

de|fend defender, abogar, refrendar, retener

de|fend|ant acusado o acusada, demandado o demandada

de|fend|er defensor o defensora, abogado o abogada, defensa

de|fense defensa, protección

de|fense mecha|nism mecanismo de defensa

de|fen|sive defensivo, a la defensiva • **de|fen|sive|ly** a la defensiva
▶ **on the defensive** a la defensiva

de|fi|ance desafío, rebeldía

de|fi|ant desafiante, rebelde
• **de|fi|ant|ly** con actitud

desafiante

de|fi|cien|cy deficiencia

defi|cit déficit
> **in deficit** en déficit, en descubierto

defi|cit spend|ing uso de fondos obtenidos en préstamo

de|fine definir

defi|nite definitivo

defi|nite ar|ti|cle artículo definido, artículo determinado

defi|nite|ly definitivamente, sin duda alguna

defi|ni|tion definición, claridad
> **by definition** definición

de|fini|tive definitivo, decisivo, trascendental
• **de|fini|tive|ly** definitivamente

de|fla|tion deflación

de|fog|ger desempañador

de|fores|ta|tion deforestación

de|for|ma|tion deformación

defy desobedecer, desacatar, desafiar, retar

de|gree grado, título

de|lay retrasar, demorar, posponer, entretener, retraso

del|egate delegado o delegada, delegar
• **del|ega|tion** delegación

del|ega|tion delegación

de|lete suprimir, eliminar, borrar

deli delicatessen

de|lib|er|ate a propósito, adrede, intencional, deliberar, considerar, meditar • **de|lib|er|ate|ly** deliberadamente, cuidadoso, pausadamente

deli|cate delicado, fino, frágil • **deli|ca|cy** delicadeza
• **deli|cate|ly** sutilmente, delicadamente, con delicadeza

deli|ca|tes|sen delicatessen

de|li|cious delicioso
• **de|li|cious|ly** deliciosamente

de|light deleite, placer
> **take delight in/take a delight in** disfrutar, deleitar

de|light|ed encantado
• **de|light|ed|ly** con gran alegría

de|light|ful agradable, delicioso, encantador
• **de|light|ful|ly** deliciosamente

de|lin|quent delincuente
• **de|lin|quen|cy** delincuencia

de|liv|er entregar, dar, pronunciar, asistir en el parto, ayudar en el parto, propinar, asestar

de|liv|ery entrega, remesa, parto, alumbramiento, expresión oral

de|liv|ery charge gastos de envío

del|ta delta

deluxe de lujo

de|mand exigir, requerir, demanda, exigencia
> **in (great) demand** de (gran) demanda, solicitado, popular
> **on demand** a solicitud, de libre acceso

de|mand|ing exigente

de|mise fallecimiento, deceso

de|moc|ra|cy democracia

demo|crat demócrata

demo|crat|ic democrático
• **demo|crati|cal|ly** democráticamente

de|mol|ish derribar, demolir, echar por tierra
• **demo|li|tion** demolición

dem|on|strate demostrar, manifestarse
• **dem|on|stra|tion** demostración, manifestación
• **de|mon|stra|tor** manifestante

den|drite dendrita

de|ni|al desmentido, denegación

den|im mezclilla, tela vaquera

de|noue|ment *también* **dénouement** desenlace

de|noue|ment de|sign desenlace

de|nounce denunciar

dense denso, compacto
• **dense|ly** densamente

den|sity densidad

dent abollar, hacer mella, herir, abolladura

den|tal dental

den|tist dentista

den|tist's of|fice consultorio dental

den|tures dentadura (postiza), prótesis dental

deny negar, denegar

de|odor|ant desodorante

de|part partir, salir, irse

de|part|ment departamento, ministerio, secretaría
• **de|part|men|tal** departamental

de|part|ment store gran almacén, tienda de departamentos

de|par|ture partida, salida, desviación, alejamiento

de|par|tures partida, salida

de|pend depender (de), contar con

de|pend|able digno de confianza

de|pend|ent *también* **dependant** dependiente, persona a cargo
• **de|pend|ence** dependencia
• **de|pend|en|cy** dependencia

de|pict describir, representar
• **de|pic|tion** descripción

de|plete reducir, agotar
• **de|plet|ed** agotado
• **de|ple|tion** reducción

de|ploy desplegar
• **de|ploy|ment** despliegue

de|port deportar
• **de|por|ta|tion** deportación

de|pos|it depósito, entrega/pago inicial, enganche, sedimento, yacimiento, depositar

depo|si|tion depósito, sedimento

de|press deprimir, reducir

de|pressed deprimido, en crisis

de|press|ing deprimente
• **de|press|ing|ly** que es deprimente

de|pres|sion depresión, crisis

de|prive privar
• **dep|ri|va|tion** privación
• **de|prived** desposeído

depth profundidad, fondo, profundo
▶ **in the depths** en lo más hondo
▶ **in depth** en profundidad
▶ **be out of one's depth** no saber en qué terreno se pisa

depu|ty segundo, asistente, vice-, ayudante (de la policía)

der|by clásico, competencia, derby, bombín, (sombrero) hongo

de|rive obtener, derivar

der|ma|tolo|gist dermatólogo *o* dermatóloga
• **der|ma|tol|ogy** dermatología

der|mis dermis

de|sali|na|tion desalinización

des|cant contrapunto

de|scend descender, invadir, caer, entrar, rebajarse

de|scribe describir

de|scrip|tion descripción

de|scrip|tive descriptivo

de|scrip|tive de|sign diseño descriptivo

des|ert desierto, abandonar, desertar • **de|sert|ed** desierto • **de|ser|tion** abandono, deserción
• **de|sert|er** desertor *o* desertora

de|serve merecer

de|sign diseñar, diseño

des|ig|nate designar, declarar • **des|ig|na|tion** clasificación
▸ **designated** designado

de|sign|er diseñador o diseñadora, de diseño (exclusivo)

de|sir|able deseable, atractivo, conveniente • **de|sir|abil|ity** conveniencia

de|sire deseo, anhelo, desear, anhelar • **de|sired** deseado

desk escritorio, mostrador

desk|top también **desk-top** de escritorio, computadora de escritorio, escritorio, pantalla

des|pair desesperación, desesperar, perder la esperanza

des|per|ate desesperado • **des|per|ate|ly** desesperadamente

de|spite a pesar de

des|sert postre

des|ti|na|tion destino

des|tined destinado

des|ti|ny destino

de|stroy destruir, arruinar • **de|struc|tion** destrucción

de|struc|tive destructivo

de|tach separar(se)

de|tail detalle, detallar
▸ **in detail** en detalle

de|tailed detallado

de|tain detener, demorar

de|tainee detenido o detenida, preso o presa

de|tect detectar, notar, advertir • **de|tec|tion** detección

de|tec|tive detective

de|ten|tion detención, castigo

de|ten|tion cen|ter centro de detención

de|ter disuadir

de|ter|gent detergente

de|terio|rate deteriorar, degenerar • **de|terio|ra|tion** deterioro

de|ter|mi|na|tion determinación

de|ter|mine determinar

de|ter|mined determinado, decidido, resuelto

de|ter|min|er determinante

de|tour rodeo, desviación

de|value subestimar, menospreciar, devaluar • **de|valua|tion** devaluación

dev|as|tate devastar, asolar • **dev|as|ta|tion** devastación

dev|as|tat|ing devastador, aniquilador

de|vel|op desarrollar(se), evolucionar, degenerar, surgir, presentarse, progresar, establecer, revelar • **de|vel|oped** desarrollado, urbanizado • **de|vel|op|ment** desarrollo, fraccionamiento, urbanización, complejo habitacional • **de|vel|op|er** promotor inmobiliario o promotora inmobiliaria, diseñador o diseñadora

de|vel|op|ing en vías de desarrollo

de|vel op|ment crecimiento, suceso, acontecimiento, avance

de|vice aparato, artefacto, dispositivo

dev|il diablo

de|vise idear, concebir

de|vote dedicar, consagrar, destinar

de|vot|ed devoto, dedicado

de|vo|tion devoción

dew point punto de rocío, punto de condensación, punto de saturación

dia|be|tes diabetes

dia|bet|ic diabético o diabética

di|ag|nose diagnosticar

di|ag|no|sis diagnóstico

di|ago|nal diagonal • **di|ago|nal|ly** diagonalmente

d

diagram 58

dia|gram diagrama, hacer un diagrama

dial esfera, cuadrante, botón regulador, sintonizador, marcar, discar

dia|lect dialecto

dia|log box cuadro de diálogo

dia|logue *también* **dialog** diálogo

dial tone tono de marcar, tono de discado

dial-up de acceso telefónico

di|am|eter diámetro

dia|mond diamante, rombo, carta de diamantes

dia|per pañal

dia|phragm diafragma

di|ar|rhea diarrea

dia|ry diario

dia|ton|ic scale escala diatónica

dice dado, cortar en cubitos, picar en cubitos

di|choto|mous key clave dicotómica

dic|tate dictar, imponer, determinar

dic|ta|tion dictado

dic|ta|tor dictador *o* dictadora

dic|ta|tor|ship dictadura

dic|tion dicción

dic|tion|ary diccionario

did *ver* do .

didn't = did not

die morir, morirse, extinguirse, apagarse, amainar
▶ **die out** caer en desuso

die|sel diesel, (vehículo) diesel

diet régimen (alimenticio), dieta, hacer dieta, ponerse a dieta ● **di|et|er** persona que hace o se pone a dieta o sigue un régimen alimenticio

dif|fer diferir, discrepar, ser diferente, ser distinto

dif|fer|ence diferencia
▶ **make a/no difference** influir/no influir

dif|fer|ent diferente, distinto ● **dif|fer|ent|ly** diferentemente

dif|fer|en|ti|ate diferenciar, distinguir ● **dif|fer|en|tia|tion** diferenciación

dif|fi|cult difícil

dif|fi|cul|ty dificultad
▶ **in difficulty** en dificultades

dif|frac|tion difracción

dif|fuse difundir, esparcir ● **dif|fu|sion** difusión

dig excavar, cavar, escarbar, clavar, meter, comentario, indirecta
▶ **dig out** desempolvar

di|gest digerir, asimilar ● **di|ges|tion** digestión

di|ges|tive digestivo, gástrico

dig|it dígito

digi|tal digital

digi|tal cam|era cámara digital

digi|tal ra|dio radio digital

digi|tal tele|vi|sion televisión digital, televisor digital

dig|nity dignidad

di|graph dígrafo

di|la|tion dilatación

di|lem|ma dilema

di|lute diluir

dim tenue, débil, borroso, vago, atenuar, bajar ● **dim|ly** tenuemente, vagamente

dime moneda estadounidense de diez centavos, daim

di|men|sion dimensión, aspecto

di|men|sion|al analy|sis análisis dimensional

di|min|ish disminuir, reducirse, empañar

di|min|ished in|ter|val intervalo disminuido

dim sum dim sum

dine cenar

ding|bat menso, tonto

din|ing room comedor

din|ner cena, comida

dino|flag|el|late dinoflagelado

di|no|saur dinosaurio

dio|ra|ma diorama

dip meter, bañar, mojar, descender, hundirse, salsa (espesa), declive

di|plo|ma diploma

di|plo|ma|cy diplomacia

dip|lo|mat diplomático *o* diplomática

diplo|mat|ic diplomático • **dip|lo|mati|cal|ly** diplomáticamente

di|rect directo, directamente, franco, dirigir, indicar el camino • **di|rect|ly** directamente, de primera mano • **di|rect|ness** franqueza

di|rect dis|course estilo directo

di|rect|ing dirección

di|rec|tion dirección, indicación

di|rec|tive orden, mandato, disposición

di|rect ob|ject objeto directo, complemento directo

di|rec|tor directivo *o* directiva, director *o* directora

di|rec|tor gen|er|al director general *o* directora general

di|rec|tor's cut versión del director

di|rec|tory directorio, guía

di|rec|tory as|sis|tance servicio de información telefónica

dirt suciedad, mugre, tierra

dirty sucio, colorado, pícaro, con un lenguaje vulgar, ensuciar

dis|abil|ity invalidez, incapacidad

dis|able dejar lisiado, inutilizar

dis|abled lisiado, inválido, incapacitado, descapacitado, discapacitado, minusválido

dis|ad|van|tage desventaja ▸ **at a disadvantage** en desventaja

dis|agree discrepar, no estar de acuerdo con, estar en desacuerdo con, discrepar de

dis|agree|ment desacuerdo, discrepancia

dis|ap|pear desaparecer • **dis|ap|pear|ance** desaparición, desvanecerse

dis|ap|point decepcionar • **dis|ap|point|ing** decepcionante • **dis|ap|point|ing|ly** de manera decepcionante

dis|ap|point|ed decepcionado

dis|ap|point|ment decepción

dis|ap|prove desaprobar • **dis|ap|prov|ing** desaprobatorio • **dis|ap|prov|ing|ly** con desaprobación

dis|as|ter desastre, catástrofe

dis|as|trous desastroso, catastrófico • **dis|as|trous|ly** desastrosamente

dis|band disolver, dispersar

dis|be|lief incredulidad, escepticismo

disc *ver* disk

dis|card desechar

dis|charge dar de alta (hospital), liberar (prisión) poner en libertad (prisión), dar de baja (ejército), cumplir con, descargar, vaciar, alta, liberación, baja, descarga, secreción, caudal (volumétrico)

dis|ci|pli|nary disciplinario

dis|ci|pline disciplina, disciplinar, sancionar

disc jock|ey *también* **disk jockey** disc-jockey

dis|close revelar

dis|clo|sure revelación

dis|co discoteca

d

D

dis|com|fort incomodidad, malestar, inquietud, desasosiego

dis|con|nect desconectar

dis|count descuento, rebaja, descartar, desechar

dis|count store tienda de descuento

dis|cour|age desalentar, desanimar, disuadir
• **dis|cour|aged** desalentado
• **dis|cour|ag|ing** desalentador
• **dis|cour|age|ment** desaliento

dis|cov|er descubrir

dis|cov|ery descubrimiento

dis|cred|it desacreditar, desprestigiar, desautorizar
• **dis|cred|it|ed** desacreditado

dis|creet discreto
• **dis|creet|ly** discretamente

dis|cre|tion discreción

dis|crimi|nate discriminar, distinguir

dis|crimi|na|tion discriminación, discernimiento

dis|cuss discutir

dis|cus|sion discusión
▶ **be under discussion** estar discutiéndose

dis|ease enfermedad

dis|grace desgracia, vergüenza, deshonrar

dis|guise hacerse pasar, disfrazar(se), ocultar, disimular • **dis|guised** disfrazado, disimulado

dis|gust indignación, repugnancia, indignar

dis|gust|ed indignado
• **dis|gust|ed|ly** con indignación

dis|gust|ing repugnante, asqueroso, vergonzoso

dish plato, antena parabólica
▶ **dish out** repartir
▶ **dish up** servir, dar

di|shev|eled también **dishevelled** desmelenado, desarreglado

dis|hon|est deshonesto, fraudulento • **dis|hon|est|ly** fraudulentamente

dis|hon|or deshonrar, incumplir, faltar a, quebrantar, deshonor, deshonra

dis|hon|or|able deshonroso, vergonzoso, indecoroso
• **dis|hon|or|ably** deshonrosamente

dish|rag estropajo, fregón, fregador

dish|washer lavaplatos, lavavajillas

dish|washing liq|uid líquido para lavaplatos/lavavajillas, detergente para lavaplatos/lavavajillas

dis|in|fect desinfectar

dis|in|fect|ant desinfectante

dis|in|te|grate desintegrarse
• **dis|in|te|gra|tion** desintegración

disk también **disc** disco, disco (compacto)

disk drive unidad de disco

dis|like disgustar, aversión

dis|man|tle desmantelar, desmontar, desarmar

dis|may consternación, desánimo, desaliento
• **dis|mayed** consternado, desanimado, desalentado

dis|miss descartar, desechar, desestimar, despedir

dis|mis|sal despido, desestimación, desprecio

dis|obedi|ence desobediencia

dis|obey desobedecer

dis|or|der afección, desorden, disturbio

dis|or|der|ly con|duct alteración del orden público

dis|patch despachar, enviar, mandar, despacho, envío, expedición

dis|patch|er despachador o despachadora

dis|perse dispersar(se),

diseminar

dis|place desplazar
● **dis|place|ment** desplazamiento

dis|play exhibir, mostrar, exteriorizar, manifestar, exhibición, exposición, muestra, demostración, despliegue

dis|pos|able desechable

dis|pos|al disposición, eliminación
▸ **at one's disposal** a su disposición

dis|pose
▸ **dispose of** deshacerse de

dis|prove desmentir, rebatir, refutar

dis|pute disputa, litigio, negociación, disputar, refutar, rebatir
▸ **in dispute** en disputa, en litigio

dis|quali|fy descalificar
● **dis|quali|fi|ca|tion** descalificación

dis|rupt perturbar, afectar
● **dis|rup|tion** perturbación

dis|sent disensión, desacuerdo, discrepar, disentir, estar en desacuerdo ● **dis|sent|er** disidente ● **dis|sent|ing** disidente

dis|ser|ta|tion disertación, tesis

dis|si|dent disidente

dis|solve disolver
● **dis|so|lu|tion** disolución

dis|tance distancia, distanciamiento, distanciarse ● **dis|tanced** distanciado
▸ **at/from a distance** a distancia, desde lejos

dis|tant distante, remoto, lejano, ausente ● **dis|tant|ly** en lontananza, vagamente, con ensimismamiento

dis|tinct distinto, claro, inconfundible, obvio
● **dis|tinct|ly** claramente

dis|tinc|tion distinción

▸ **draw/make a distinction** hacer una distinción, establecer una distinción

dis|tinc|tive característico
● **dis|tinc|tive|ly** característicamente

dis|tin|guish distinguir(se)

dis|tin|guished distinguido

dis|tort distorsionar, deformar ● **dis|tort|ed** distorsionado ● **dis|tor|tion** distorsión

dis|tress angustia, aflicción, peligro, afligir, angustiar
● **dis|tressed** afligido
● **dis|tress|ing** angustiante
● **dis|tress|ing|ly** penosamente

dis|trib|ute distribuir, repartir ● **dis|tri|bu|tion** distribución ● **dis|tribu|tor** distribuidor o distribuidora

dis|tri|bu|tion distribución

dis|trict distrito

dis|trict at|tor|ney fiscal de distrito, procurador general o procuradora general

dis|trict court tribunal de distrito

dis|turb perturbar, molestar, tocar

dis|turb|ance disturbio, perturbación

dis|turbed perturbado, trastornado

dis|turb|ing perturbador, inquietante, alarmante
● **dis|turb|ing|ly** perturbadoramente

ditch zanja, botar

dive tirarse al agua, echarse un clavado, bucear, zambullirse, sumergirse, abalanzarse, precipitarse, arrojarse, movimiento rápido ● **div|ing** clavado, buceo ● **div|er** buzo, buceador o buceadora

di|ver|gent bounda|ry límite divergente

di|verse diverso, variado

di|ver|si|fy diversificar(se)

d

- di|ver|si|fi|ca|tion diversificación

di|ver|sity diversidad

di|vert desviar, derivar, distraer ● di|ver|sion desvío

di|vide dividir, división, (línea) divisoria, separar ● di|vid|ed dividido
▸ divide up dividir

di|vid|ed high|way carretera de dos carriles separados

divi|dend dividendo
▸ pay dividends pagar dividendos, rendir frutos

di|vine divino ● di|vine|ly divinamente ● di|vin|ity divinidad

di|vi|sion división
● di|vi|sion|al divisional

di|vorce divorcio, divorciarse, divorciar

di|vor|cé divorciado

di|vorced divorciado

di|vor|cée divorciada

DIY práctica de hacer las cosas uno mismo

diz|zy mareado ● diz|zi|ness mareo

diz|zy|ing vertiginoso

DJ también D.J., dj disc-jockey

DNA ADN

DNA finger|print|ing análisis de muestras de ADN

do hacer, causar, bastar, ser suficiente
▸ do well/badly ir bien/mal, salir bien/mal
▸ could do with caer bien
▸ have/be to do with tener que ver con
▸ do away with eliminar
▸ do over volver a hacer
▸ do up abrochar, abotonar
▸ do without prescindir de, arreglárselas sin

DOB también d.o.b. fecha de nacimiento

dock muelle, puerto, plataforma, atracadero, banquillo de los acusados, atracar, fondear, descontar, acoplarse

dock|et lista de casos, registro de procedimientos

doc|tor médico o médica, dentista, veterinario o veterinaria, doctor o doctora, adulterar, falsificar, alterar

doc|tor|ate doctorado

doc|tor of phi|loso|phy doctor en filosofía

doc|tor's of|fice consultorio (médico)

doc|trine doctrina
● doc|tri|nal doctrinal

docu|ment documento, documentar

docu|men|tary documental

docu|men|ta|tion documentación

dodge esquivar, apartarse, eludir

dodo dodo

does ver do

doesn't = does not

dog perro, perseguir

dog days canícula, días de mucho calor, época más calurosa del verano

dog|gone maldito, de los mil diablos, infernal

dog|house perrera, casucha del perro

doh también d'oh ¡oye!

doll muñeca, muñeco

dol|lar dólar

doll|house casa de muñecas

dol|phin delfín

do|main dominio, terreno, campo

dome domo, cúpula

do|mes|tic nacional, doméstico, del hogar

domi|nant dominante
● domi|nance dominio

domi|nate dominar, predominar ● domi|na|tion dominación ● domi|nat|ing dominante, dominación

do|nate donar ● do|na|tion donación

done ver do, terminado, listo, cocido

don|key burro, asno

do|nor donador *o* donadora, donante

don't = do not

do|nut

doomed condenado, sentenciado, predestinado

door puerta, entrada
▸ **answer the door** abrir la puerta
▸ **(from) door to door** de puerta en puerta
▸ **out of doors** al aire libre

do-or-die de vida o muerte, a vencer o morir

door|step umbral
▸ **on your doorstep** a la vuelta de la esquina

door|way quicio

dope droga, poner droga, drogar

dor|mi|tory dormitorio, residencia

dor|sal dorsal

dose dosis

dot punto

dot-com *también* dotcom empresa punto com

dot|ted punteado, de puntos, salpicado, esparcido
▸ **sign on the dotted line** firmar sobre la línea punteada

dou|ble doble, matrimonial, de matrimonio, duplicar(se), funcionar también como
▸ **double over** doblarse (de dolor), desternillarse (de risa), morirse (de la risa)

double-barreled de dos cañones, compuesto

dou|ble bass *también* double-bass contrabajo

double-click hacer doble clic

double-header dos encuentros consecutivos

dou|ble he|lix doble hélice

dou|ble-re|place|ment re|ac|tion reacción de doble substitución

double-space *también* double space escribir a doble espacio ● **double-spaced** a doble espacio ● **dou|ble spac|ing** doble espacio

doubt duda, dudar, dudar de
▸ **beyond doubt** fuera de duda
▸ **in doubt** en duda
▸ **no doubt** sin duda
▸ **without (a) doubt** sin duda alguna

doubt|ful dudoso ● **doubt|ful|ly** dubitativamente

dough masa

dough|nut *también* donut dona, rosquilla

down abajo, deprimido, descompuesto, plumón
▸ **put down** dejar, depositar
▸ **go down** bajar, descender
▸ **be down for** tener arreglado
▸ **down on paper** por escrito, anotado

down|draft corriente descendente

down|fall ruina, perdición

down feath|er plumón

down|grade reducir

down|load descargar, trasvasar

down|load|able descargable, trasvasable

down scale barato, de segunda

down|stage proscenio, principal

down|stairs escaleras abajo, abajo

Down's syn|drome síndrome de Down

down|time tiempo muerto, tiempo de inactividad, período de descanso

down|town del centro, en el centro

down|ward descendente, hacia abajo, a la baja, al descenso

doze dormitar
▸ **doze off** adormecerse,

d

quedarse dormido

doz|en docena, decenas

Dr. Dr.

draft borrador, corriente, llamado a filas, redactar un borrador de, reclutar, llamar a filas, asignar

draft dodg|er alguien que rehúye el servicio militar obligatorio

drag arrastrar, arrancar de/a, dragar, volverse pesado (conversación, trabajo), hacerse largo (película, espectáculo, tiempo), eternizarse/hacerse eterno (tiempo), resistencia al avance
▸ **drag your feet** arrastrar los pies, dar largas
▸ **in drag** travestí/travesti
▸ **drag out** alargar, sacar

drag and drop *también* **drag-and-drop** arrastrar y soltar, que se arrastra y suelta

drag|on dragón

dragon|fly libélula, caballito del diablo

drain drenar, desaguar, escurrir, agotar, drenaje, sangría • **drained** agotado • **drain|ing** agotador
▸ **go down the drain** irse al caño, esfumarse

drain|age drenaje

drain|age ba|sin cuenca (fluvial)

dra|ma obra dramática, drama

dra|mat|ic espectacular, drástico, dramático
• **dra|mati|cal|ly** dramáticamente

dra|mat|ic play juego dramático infantil

dra|mat|ic struc|ture trama

drama|turg *también* **dramaturge** dramaturgo o dramaturga

drank *ver* **drink**

dras|tic drástico, radical
• **dras|ti|cal|ly** radicalmente

draw dibujar, irse, alejarse, arrimar, acercar, correr, desenfundar, sacar, aspirar, respirar, extraer, retirar, establecer, llegar a, atraer, provocar
▸ **draw to an end/draw to a close** llegar a su fin
▸ **draw in** involucrar, hacer participar
▸ **draw on** recurrir a, hacer uso de, inspirarse en
▸ **draw up** redactar
▸ **draw upon** *ver* **draw on**

draw|back inconveniente, desventaja

drawer cajón

draw|ing dibujo

drawn *ver* **draw**, demacrado

drawn-out interminable

dread tener terror, temer, horrorizar, terror, horror

dread|ful horrible, espantoso, terrible
• **dread|fully** terriblemente

dream sueño, sonar
▸ **would not dream of** ni en sueños
▸ **dream up** idear

dress vestido, traje, vestir(se)
▸ **dress down** vestir informalmente
▸ **dress up** vestirse elegante, ponerse elegante

dressed vestido

dress|er tocador

dress|ing aderezo, aliño, apósito, vendaje, relleno

dress re|hears|al ensayo general

dress-up disfraces, elegante, formal

drew *ver* **draw**

dried seco

dri|er *ver* **dry**, dryer

drift ir a la deriva, ir sin rumbo fijo, dirigirse poco a poco, éxodo, ventisquero
▸ **drift off** quedarse dormido

drill taladro, taladradora, ejercicio, simulacro,

taladrar, perforar

drink beber, tomar, trago, vaso, copa • **drink|er** bebedor o bebedora, bebedor empedernido o bebedora empedernida • **drink|ing** bebida
▶ **drink to** brindar

drip gotear, chorrear, escurrir, gota, lágrima, gotero

drive manejar, conducir, llevar, mover, hacer funcionar, clavar, hincar, arrear, expulsar, obligar a, llevar a, impulsar a, paseo, camino de entrada, unidad de disco, empuje, búsqueda • **driv|ing** manejo
▶ **drive away** alejar, distanciar

drive-by tiroteo desde un vehículo en movimiento

driv|er chofer, controlador, conductor o conductora

driv|er's li|cense licencia de manejo, permiso para conducir

drive-through también **drive-thru** servicio para automovilistas

drive|way camino de entrada

driv|ing impulsor

driz|zle llovizna, lloviznar

drop bajar, descender, reducir, dejar(se) caer, tirar, caer, meter, soltar, desplomarse, dejar, llevar, abandonar, renunciar a, descenso, reducción, gota, caída • **drop|ping** lanzamiento
▶ **drop by** pasar
▶ **drop in** pasar
▶ **drop off** dormirse, quedarse dormido
▶ **drop out** abandonar

drop-down menu desplegable

drop kick patada a botepronto

drop|let gotita

drop-off disminución

drought sequía

drove ver **drive**

drown ahogar(se)

drug droga, medicamento, estupefaciente, drogar

drug ad|dict toxicómano o toxicómana, drogadicto o drogadicta

drug|store farmacia, botica

drum tambor, barril, bidón, tamborilear, golpetear • **drum|mer** tambor, baterista
▶ **drum into** machacar, repetir
▶ **drum up** conseguir, obtener

drum|beat machaqueo

drum ma|jor tambor mayor

drum ma|jor|ette bastonera

drunk borracho o borracha, ebrio, ver **drink**

drunk driv|er conductor ebrio o conductora ebria • **drunk driv|ing** conducir ebrio

dry seco, secar(se) • **dry|ness** sequedad, árido, mordaz • **dry|ly** mordazmente
▶ **dry out** secar(se)
▶ **dry up** secarse, agotarse

dry-clean lavar en seco, limpiar en seco

dry|er también **drier** secadora

dry goods artículos de confección, comestibles no perecederos

dry ice hielo seco

dry run simulacro, ensayo

DSL DSL

dual dual, doble

dub apodar, llamar, doblar

du|bi|ous dudoso • **du|bi|ous|ly** sospechosamente, con recelo
▶ **be dubious** tener dudas o reservas

duck pato, agacharse, esquivar, eludir, bajar, sacar la vuelta a
▶ **duck out** escurrirse

duct conducto

duc|til|ity ductilidad

duct tape cinta adhesiva

dude cuate

due debido, vencido
▶ **in due course** a su debido tiempo
▶ **with due respect** con todo respeto
▶ **due at a particular time** que debe ocurrir o hacerse en determinado momento

due pro|cess procedimiento debido

dug *ver* dig

DUI conducir bajo la influencia del alcohol

dull aburrido, soso, opaco, mate, pálido, apagado, sordo, opacar • **dull|ness** monotonía • **dul|ly** pálidamente, débilmente

dumb mudo, tonto, bobo
▶ **dumb down** simplificar
• **dumb|ing down** reducción del nivel intelectual

dump tirar, botar • **dump|ing** vertido, basurero, vertedero, tiradero, muladar

dune duna

du|ple me|ter compás binario

du|plex casa dúplex

du|pli|cate duplicar, repetir, copiar, duplicado, repetición • **du|pli|ca|tion** duplicación

du|rable durable
• **du|rabil|ity** durabilidad

du|ra|tion duración

dur|ing durante

dusk anochecer

dust polvo, polvareda, sacudir el polvo
▶ **when the dust settles** cuando pasa la tormenta

dust bowl *también* **dustbowl** terreno semidesértico expuesto a la erosión causada por el viento

dusty polvoriento

duty deber, trabajo, obligación, impuesto, derecho de aduana
▶ **off duty** libre de servicio, franco

DVD disco de video

DVD burn|er *también* **DVD writer** grabadora de discos de video

dwarf eclipsar, empequeñecer, enano

dwarf planet planeta enano

dwelt *ver* dwell

DWI conducir bajo la influencia del alcohol

dye teñir, tinte

dy|ing agonizante, moribundo, en extinción

dy|nam|ic dinámico
• **dy|nami|cal|ly** con dinamismo, enérgicamente, vívidamente • **dy|na|mism** dinamismo
▶ **dynamics** dinámica

dy|nam|ic mark|ing marca dinámica

dyn|as|ty dinastía

dys|lexia dislexia

Ee

each cada, cada uno, uno a otro, mutuamente

eager impaciente, ansioso
• eager|ly ansiosamente
• eager|ness deseo

eagle águila

ear oreja, oído, espiga, mazorca

ear|drum *también* ear drum tímpano

ear|li|er más temprano, antes, a principios, previo, anterior

ear|li|est lo más temprano
▸ at the earliest no antes de

ear|lobe *también* ear lobe lóbulo de la oreja

ear|ly temprano, primero, al principio

ear|mark destinar

earn ganar, recibir, producir, devengar, ganarse, hacerse de

ear|nest en serio, serio
• ear|nest|ly con seriedad

earn|ings ingresos

ear|phone audífono

ear|ring arete, pendiente, zarcillo

earth la Tierra, tierra, suelo
▸ on earth demonios, diablos
▸ come back/down to earth bajar de las nubes, poner los pies en la tierra

earth|quake temblor, terremoto

earth sci|ence *también* Earth science ciencias de la Tierra

earth|worm lombriz (de tierra)

ease facilidad, facilitar, disminuir, reducirse, aliviar
▸ with ease fácilmente, con facilidad, sin problema, con cuidado
▸ at ease cómodo, a gusto
▸ ill at ease incómodo
▸ ease up disminuir, aminorar, calmar, calmarse, aflojar, bajar el ritmo

easel caballete

easi|ly por lo menos, fácilmente, con facilidad

east *también* East este, oriente, al este, al oriente, del este

East|er Pascua

east|ern oriental, de oriente

east|ward en dirección este, hacia el este

easy fácil • easi|ly fácilmente
▸ take it easy tomarlo con calma, tomárselo con calma, tomar las cosas con calma

easy|going sin complicaciones

eat comer(se)
▸ eat away corroer, roer, desgastar, comerse
▸ eat into comerse, ocupar

eat|ing dis|or|der trastorno alimenticio, trastorno de la alimentación, desorden alimenticio

eaves|drop escuchar a escondidas, espiar

ebb bajar, marea baja, reflujo, decaer, disminuir
▸ at a low ebb o at one's lowest ebb de capa caída, decaído

Ebola *también* Ebola virus ébola, virus ébola

ec|cen|tric excéntrico o excéntrica, extraño
• ec|cen|tri|city excentricidad

echo eco, resonar, retumbar, repetir, hacerse eco

ec|lec|tic ecléctico

eclipse eclipse, eclipsar, desmerecer

eco-friendly inocuo para el ambiente, amigable con el ambiente, que no daña el ambiente

eco|logi|cal suc|ces|sion sucesión ecológica

ecol|ogy ecología • ecolo|gist ecologista • eco|logi|cal ecológico • eco|logi|cal|ly ecológicamente

eco|nom|ic económico • eco|nomi|cal|ly económicamente, rentable

eco|nomi|cal económico, ahorrativo

eco|nom|ics economía

econo|mist economista

econo|my economía

eco|sys|tem ecosistema

ec|sta|sy éxtasis

ec|to|therm ectotérmico

edge orilla, borde, extremo, filo, ventaja, acercarse
  ▸ on edge estar los nervios de punta, tener los nervios de punta
  ▸ edge out sacar ventaja

edge|wise
  ▸ get a word in edgewise lograr decir una palabra

ed|ible comestible

edit revisar, corregir, editar

edi|tion edición

edi|tor editor o editora, corrector o correctora, revisor o revisora

edi|to|rial editorial

edu|cate educar(se), concientizar, informar

edu|cat|ed culto, educado

edu|ca|tion educación • edu|ca|tion|al educativo

edu|ca|tor educador o educadora, pedagogo o pedagoga

eel anguila

ef|fect efecto, llevar a cabo, efectuar, lograr
  ▸ in effect de hecho
  ▸ take effect o come into effect o be put into effect entrar en vigor, hacer efecto
  ▸ to (good) effect con (buenos) resultados
  ▸ to this/that effect en este/ese sentido

ef|fec|tive efectivo, en vigor • ef|fec|tive|ly de manera efectiva • ef|fec|tive|ness efectividad

ef|fec|tive|ly en efecto

ef|fi|cient eficiente • ef|fi|cien|cy eficiencia • ef|fi|cient|ly de manera eficiente

ef|fort esfuerzo
  ▸ with effort con esfuerzo, con trabajos

ef|fort force fuerza de esfuerzo

EFL EFL, inglés como lengua extranjera

e.g. por ejemplo

egg huevo, óvulo
  ▸ egg on incitar, azuzar

egg|plant berenjena

ego ego, yo

eight ocho

eight|een dieciocho

eight|eenth decimoctavo, dieciochoavo

eighth octavo, octava parte

eighth note octava

eighti|eth octagésimo, ochentavo

eighty ochenta
  ▸ the eighties arriba de ochenta, los (años) ochenta

either o...o, ni...ni, ni, ninguno, o, alguno, cualquier, cualquiera, tampoco, cada, uno y otro

eject expulsar, echar, sacar • ejec|tion expulsión

elabo|rate complicado, complejo, ampliar, entrar en detalles, explicar, elaborado • elabo|rate|ly minuciosamente

elapse transcurrir, pasar

elas|tic liga, elástico
elas|tic re|bound recuperación de la deformación elástica
elat|ed eufórico • **ela|tion** euforia
el|bow codo, dar codazos, empujar con los codos
el|der mayor, anciano
el|der|ly anciano, de la tercera edad
▸ **the elderly** personas de la tercera edad
eld|est mayor
elect elegir, nombrar, decidir
elec|tion elección
elec|tive optativo
elec|tor elector o electora
elec|tor|al electoral
• **elec|tor|al|ly** en términos electorales
elec|tor|al col|lege colegio electoral
elec|tor|ate electorado
elec|tric eléctrico, electrizante, cargado de electricidad
elec|tri|cal eléctrico
• **elec|tri|cal|ly** eléctricamente
elec|tri|cal charge carga eléctrica
elec|tri|cal en|er|gy energía eléctrica
elec|tric force fuerza eléctrica
elec|tric gen|era|tor generador de energía eléctrica, generador de electricidad
elec|tri|cian electricista
elec|tric|ity electricidad, energía eléctrica
elec|tric pow|er energía eléctrica
elec|tric shock descarga eléctrica, toque
elec|tro|cute electrocutar(se)
• **elec|tro|cu|tion** electrocución

elec|tro|mag|net electroimán
elec|tro|mag|net|ic spec|trum espectro electromagnético
elec|tro|mag|net|ic wave onda electromagnética
elec|tron electrón
elec|tron cloud nube de electrones
elec|tron|ic electrónico
• **elec|troni|cal|ly** electrónicamente
elec|tron|ic me|dia medios electrónicos
elec|tron|ics electrónica
elec|tron micro|scope microscopio electrónico, microscopio de electrones
elec|tro|stat|ic dis|charge descarga electrostática
el|egant elegante • **el|egance** elegancia • **el|egant|ly** elegantemente
el|ement elemento, parte, algo, resistencia
▸ **in one's element** en su elemento, como pez en el agua
el|emen|ta|ry básico, elemental
el|emen|ta|ry school escuela primaria, escuela elemental
el|ements of art elementos artísticos
el|ements of mu|sic elementos musicales
el|ephant elefante
el|evate elevar, incrementar, subir, levantar
el|eva|tion altitud, ascenso
el|eva|tor elevador, ascensor
elev|en once
elev|enth undécimo, onceavo
elic|it provocar, suscitar, obtener
eli|gible elegible • **eli|gibil|ity** elegibilidad
elimi|nate eliminar, acabar con • **elimi|na|tion** eliminación

e

elite élite, selecto, de élite

Eliza|bethan thea|ter teatro isabelino

el|lipse elipse

el|lip|ti|cal gal|axy galaxia elíptica

El Niño El niño

elo|quent elocuente
● **elo|quence** elocuencia
● **elo|quent|ly** elocuentemente

else más, los demás, otra cosa, otro lugar, otra parte, si no, de lo contrario, o, o...o
▸ **if nothing else** aparte de eso, además de eso, más que eso

else|where en otro lugar, en otra parte, de otra parte

e-mail *también* **E-mail, email** e-mail, correo electrónico, correo, mandar un e-mail, mandar un correo electrónico

em|bar|go embargo, prohibición

em|bark embarcarse, emprender

em|bar|rass avergonzar, hacer pasar vergüenza
● **em|bar|rass|ing** embarazoso, incómodo
● **em|bar|rass|ing|ly** penosamente

em|bar|rassed avergonzado, apenado

em|bar|rass|ment vergüenza, pena

em|bas|sy embajada

em|bel|lish|ment floritura

em|brace abrazar(se), adoptar, aceptar, incluir, abarcar, comprender, abrazo, adopción, aceptación

em|broi|dery bordado

em|bryo embrión

em|cee presentador *o* presentadora, maestro de ceremonias *o* maestra de ceremonias, presentar, hacer de maestro *o* maestra de ceremonias, ser el maestro *o* la maestra de ceremonias

emerge salir, aparecer, surgir, revelarse, emerger
● **emer|gence** salida

emer|gen|cy emergencia, de emergencia

emer|gen|cy brake freno de mano, freno de emergencia

emer|gen|cy room sala de urgencias, urgencias

emi|grate emigrar
● **emi|gra|tion** emigración

emi|nent eminente, ilustre, prestigioso, prestigiado
● **emi|nence** eminencia

emis|sion emisión

emit emitir

emo|tion emoción

emo|tion|al emocional, emotivo ● **emo|tion|al|ly** emocionalmente

em|pa|thy empatía

em|per|or emperador

em|pha|sis énfasis, importancia, acento

em|pha|size hacer énfasis, poner énfasis, subrayar, recalcar, hacer hincapié

em|phat|ic enfático, categórico, enérgico, rotundo, contundente
● **em|phati|cal|ly** enfáticamente

em|pire imperio

em|piri|cal empírico
● **em|piri|cal|ly** de una manera empírica

em|ploy emplear, dar trabajo, dar empleo, contratar, utilizar, usar

em|ployee empleado *o* empleada

em|ploy|er patrón *o* patrona, empleador *o* empleadora, jefe *o* jefa

em|ploy|ment trabajo, empleo

em|power empoderar,

dar poder, conferir poder • **em|pow|er|ment** empoderamiento

em|press emperatriz

emp|ty vacío, desocupado, hueco, falso, vaciar(se) • **emp|ti|ness** vacío

empty-handed con las manos vacías

en|able permitir, hacer posible

en|act promulgar, aprobar • **en|act|ment** promulgación, representar

enam|el esmalte

en|close envolver, envasar, adjuntar, anexar

en|coun|ter encontrar(se), enfrentar(se), toparse, encuentro

en|cour|age animar, alentar, dar aliento, estimular, entusiasmar, impulsar, fomentar • **en|cour|aged** animado

en|cour|age|ment ánimo, aliento

en|cour|ag|ing alentador, esperanzador • **en|cour|ag|ing|ly** alentadoramente

en|cy|clo|pedia *también* **encyclopaedia** enciclopedia

end fin, final, punta, extremo, objetivo, terminar, acabar • **end|ing** final
▶ **make ends meet** tener apenas lo suficiente para vivir
▶ **on end** sin interrupción, sin parar
▶ **end up** terminar en, acabar en

en|dan|ger poner en peligro, poner en riesgo

en|deav|or intentar, esforzarse, esfuerzo, intento, tentativa

end|ing final, desenlace, conclusión

en|dive endivia, endibia

end|less interminable, eterno, infinito • **end|less|ly** interminablemente

endo|crine endocrino

endo|cy|to|sis endocitosis

endo|plas|mic re|ticu|lum retículo endoplásmico

en|dorse aprobar, refrendar, respaldar, promocionar • **en|dorse|ment** aprobación, promoción

endo|skel|eton endoesqueleto

endo|therm endotermo

endo|ther|mic endotérmico

en|dow|ment donación, legado, fideicomiso

en|dure soportar, aguantar, tolerar, perdurar • **en|dur|ing** duradero

end user usuario final

en|emy enemigo *o* enemiga

en|er|get|ic lleno de energía • **en|er|geti|cal|ly** con energía

en|er|gy energía

en|er|gy con|ver|sion conversión de energía

en|er|gy ef|fi|cien|cy eficiencia energética

energy-efficient *también* **energy efficient** de gran rendimiento energético

en|er|gy pyra|mid pirámide energética

en|er|gy re|source recurso energético

en|er|gy source fuente de energía, fuente energética

en|force hacer cumplir, hacer respetar, hacer obedecer • **en|force|ment** cumplimiento

en|gage dedicarse, captar, atraer, entablar, contratar

en|gaged dedicado, comprometido

en|gage|ment compromiso, cita, combate

en|gine motor, máquina, locomotora

e

en|gi|neer ingeniero *o* ingeniera, construir, planear, tramar

en|gi|neer|ing ingeniería

Eng|lish inglés
▶ **the English** los ingleses

Eng|lish muf|fin bollo inglés

en|hance realzar, mejorar
• **en|hance|ment** mejora

en|joy disfrutar, gozar, disfrutar de

en|joy|able agradable, placentero

en|joy|ment placer

en|large agrandar(se), abundar, extenderse, ampliar • **en|large|ment** ampliación

en|list alistarse, enrolarse, conseguir

enor|mous enorme, grande • **enor|mous|ly** enormemente

enough suficiente, suficientemente, bastante

en|rich enriquecer
• **en|rich|ment** enriquecimiento

en|roll inscribir(se)
• **en|roll|ment** inscripción

en route *ver* route

en|sem|ble conjunto, ensamble

en|sure asegurar(se)

en|ter entrar, ingresar, llevar, inscribirse, introducir, registrar
▶ **enter into** participar, establecer, iniciar

en|ter|prise empresa, proyecto, iniciativa
• **en|ter|pris|ing** emprendedor

en|ter|tain entretener, divertir, agasajar, tener invitados, invitar, recibir invitados, contemplar, considerar • **en|ter|tain|ing** entretenido

en|ter|tain|er artista, animador *o* animadora

en|ter|tain|ment entretenimiento, espectáculo

en|thu|si|asm entusiasmo, gusto

en|thu|si|ast entusiasta, aficionado *o* aficionada

en|thu|si|as|tic entusiasta, entusiasmado
• **en|thu|si|as|ti|cal|ly** con entusiasmo

en|tire todo, entero

en|tire|ly totalmente, completamente

en|ti|tle tener derecho, dar derecho • **en|ti|tle|ment** derecho, titulado, intitulado

en|ti|ty entidad

en|trance entrada, llegada, ingreso, fascinar
• **en|tranced** fascinado

en|tre|pre|neur empresario *o* empresaria
• **en|tre|pre|neur|ial** empresarial

en|try entrada, acceso, ingreso, anotación, participante
▶ **no entry** prohibida la entrada

en|vel|op envolver, rodear

en|ve|lope sobre

en|vi|ous envidioso
• **en|vi|ous|ly** envidiosamente

en|vi|ron|ment ambiente, entorno, medio ambiente
• **en|vi|ron|men|tal** ambiental
• **en|vi|ron|men|tal|ly** ambientalmente

en|vi|ron|men|tal|ist ecologista, ambientalista

en|vis|age pensar, considerar, imaginar

en|vi|sion imaginar(se)

en|voy enviado *o* enviada, enviado plenipotenciario *o* enviada plenipotenciaria

envy envidiar, envidia

en|zyme enzima

epic epopeya, épico, heroico,

legendario
epi|cen|ter epicentro
epic thea|ter teatro épico
epi|dem|ic epidemia
epi|der|mis epidermis
epi|di|dy|mis epidídimo
epi|sode episodio, capítulo
epi|thelial tis|sue tejido epitelial
equal igual, mismo, igualar
▶ equal to capaz de, adecuado para, a la altura de
equali|ty igualdad
equal|ly igualmente, de igual modo, de todas maneras, aun así
equal op|por|tu|nity oportunidades iguales
equal op|por|tu|nity em|ploy|er empresa que ofrece las mismas oportunidades
equate equivaler, equiparar, corresponder, identificar
equa|tion ecuación
equa|tor ecuador
equi|lat|eral equilátero
equip equipar, preparar
equip|ment equipo
equiva|lent equivalente
er mmm, este
ER departamento de urgencias, urgencias
era era, época, periodo
eradi|cate erradicar
• eradi|ca|tion erradicación
erase borrar
eras|er borrador, goma, goma de borrar
erect levantar, erigir, construir, erecto, derecho, erguido • erec|tion construcción
erode erosionar(se), afectar, reducir • ero|sion erosión, deterioro
erot|ic erótico
err errar, equivocarse, cometer un error
▶ to err on the side of pecar de, exagerar

er|rand mandado, recado
er|ro|neous erróneo, equivocado • er|ro|neous|ly erróneamente
er|ror error, equivocación
erupt hacer erupción, estallar • erup|tion erupción, brote
es|ca|late intensificar(se), aumentar, empeorar(se) • es|ca|la|tion intensificación
es|ca|la|tor escalera eléctrica
es|cape escapar(se), fugarse, salvarse, escape, huida, fuga
es|cort escoltar, acompañar, llevar, escolta, guardaespaldas, guarura, acompañante
▶ under escort escoltado
es|pe|cial|ly especialmente, sobre todo, particularmente
es|say ensayo, composición, trabajo
es|sence esencia
▶ in essence en esencia, esencialmente
▶ of the essence esencial
es|sen|tial esencial, indispensable, fundamentos, lo esencial, lo básico
es|sen|tial|ly esencialmente, básicamente, en lo esencial, en esencia
es|tab|lish establecer, crear, formar, demostrar, definir • es|tab|lish|ment establecimiento
• es|tab|lished comprobado
es|tab|lished establecido, de prestigio, de tradición
es|tab|lish|ment establecimiento, clase dirigente
es|tate propiedad, rancho, legado
es|teem estima, aprecio
es|ti|mate estimar, calcular, estimado, estimación, cálculo, juicio, valoración,

evaluación • es|ti|mat|ed estimado

es|ti|va|tion *también* aestivation estivación, letargo estival

es|tranged distanciado, separado • es|trange|ment distanciamiento

etc. etc., etcétera

et|cet|era *también* et cetera *ver* etc.

eter|nal eterno • eter|nal|ly eternamente

eth|ic ética

ethi|cal ético • ethi|cal|ly éticamente

eth|nic étnico • eth|ni|cal|ly étnicamente

ety|mol|ogy etimología

EU UE

eu|bac|te|ria eubacteria

eu|glena euglena

eu|karyot|ic cell célula eucariota

eulo|gize hacer una apología, elogiar

eulogy apología

euphemism eufemismo

euro euro

Euro|pean europeo *o* europea

Euro|pean Un|ion Unión Europea

evacu|ate evacuar • evacu|ation evacuación

evalu|ate evaluar • evalu|ation evaluación

evapo|rate evaporar(se) • evapo|ra|tion evaporación

eve víspera

even incluso, inclusive, aun, todavía, aún, aun si, aun cuando, parejo, regular, uniforme, par • even|ly regularmente, igual, equitativamente
▶ even so de todos modos, de cualquier forma, de cualquier modo, aun así
▶ break even recuperar los costos
▶ even out emparejar

eve|ning tarde

event suceso, evento
▶ in the event of en caso de
▶ in the event that en caso de que

even|tual final

even|tu|al|ly finalmente, con el tiempo, a la larga

ever nunca, jamás, alguna vez
▶ as ever como siempre
▶ ever since desde que, desde entonces

ever|green de hoja perenne, siempre verde

every cada, todo, mucho
▶ every now and then de vez en cuando, de vez en vez
▶ every other day cada tercer día, cada quince días, un día/semana sí y otro/otra no

every|body todos, todo el mundo

every|day diario

every|one todos, todo el mundo

every|place *ver* everywhere

every|thing todo

every|where *también* everyplace en/a/por todas partes, en/a/por todos lados

evi|dence prueba
▶ give evidence dar testimonio
▶ be in evidence ser evidente, ser notorio

evi|dent evidente

evi|dent|ly evidentemente

evil el mal, lo nocivo, malvado

evoke evocar

evo|lu|tion evolución, desarrollo

evolve evolucionar, convertirse, desarrollar, transformarse

ex|act exacto, arrancar

ex|act|ly exactamente, exacto
▶ not exactly no exactamente

ex|ag|ger|ate exagerar
• ex|ag|gera|tion exageración

ex|ag|ger|at|ed exagerado

exam examen, estudio, análisis

ex|ami|na|tion examen, inspección

ex|am|ine examinar

ex|am|ple ejemplo
▶ for example por ejemplo
▶ follow someone's example seguir el ejemplo de alguien
▶ set an example poner el ejemplo, sentar un parámetro

ex|ceed exceder

ex|cel sobresalir, destacar

ex|cel|lence excelencia

ex|cel|lent excelente
• ex|cel|lent|ly excelentemente

ex|cept excepto, salvo

ex|cep|tion excepción
▶ take exception to something objetar, criticar

ex|cep|tion|al excepcional, extraordinario
• ex|cep|tion|al|ly excepcionalmente, extraordinariamente

ex|cerpt resumen, extracto

ex|cess exceso, excesivo, sobrante
▶ in excess of más que
▶ to excess en exceso

ex|ces|sive excesivo, desmedido • ex|ces|sive|ly excesivamente

ex|change intercambiar, canjear, intercambio
▶ in exchange for a cambio de

ex|change rate tipo de cambio

ex|cite emocionar, despertar

ex|cit|ed entusiasmado, emocionado • ex|cit|ed|ly agitadamente

ex|cite|ment entusiasmo, emoción

ex|cit|ing emocionante

ex|claim exclamar

ex|cla|ma|tion point también exclamation mark signo de admiración

ex|cla|ma|to|ry exclamativo

ex|clude excluir, descartar
• ex|clu|sion exclusión

ex|clud|ing con excepción de

ex|clu|sive exclusivo
▶ mutually exclusive mutuamente excluyente

ex|clu|sive|ly exclusivamente

ex|cuse pretexto, justificar(se), disculpar, exculpar, exentar, despedirse
▶ excuse me disculpe, perdón

ex|ecute ejecutar, llevar a cabo, realizar • ex|ecu|tion ejecución • ex|ecu|tion|er verdugo

ex|ecu|tive ejecutivo o ejecutiva, (la) directiva, (poder) ejecutivo

ex|ecu|tive or|der orden ejecutiva

ex|empt exento, exentar
• ex|emp|tion exención

ex|er|cise ejercer, hacer ejercicio, ejercicio

ex|ert ejercer, hacer un gran esfuerzo • ex|er|tion esfuerzo

ex|hale exhalar

ex|haust agotar, gases
• ex|haust|ed exhausto
• ex|haust|ing agotador
• ex|haus|tion agotamiento

ex|haust pipe escape, mofle

ex|hib|it presentar, mostrar, exhibir, exponer, pieza en exposición, prueba

ex|hi|bi|tion exposición, espectáculo

ex|hi|bi|tion game juego de exhibición

ex|ile exiliar, exilio, exiliado o exiliada

ex|ist existir

e

ex|ist|ence existencia

ex|ist|ing existente

exit salida, salir, cerrar

exit poll encuesta de salida

exit strat|egy estrategia de salida

exo|cy|to|sis exocitosis

exo|skel|eton exoesqueleto

exo|sphere exosfera

exo|ther|mic exotérmico

ex|ot|ic exótico • ex|oti|cal|ly exóticamente

ex|pand expandir(se), aumentar • ex|pan|sion expansión
▶ expand on o expand upon ahondar en

ex|pand|ed form forma desarrollada

ex|pect creer, esperar
▶ be expecting esperar (un bebé)

ex|pec|ta|tion expectativa

ex|pedi|tion expedición

ex|pel expulsar

ex|pendi|ture gasto

ex|pense gasto
▶ at someone's expense a expensas de alguien, a costa de alguien

ex|pen|sive caro
• ex|pen|sive|ly ostentosamente

ex|peri|ence experiencia, experimentar
• ex|pe|ri|enced experimentado

ex|peri|ment experimento, experimentar
• ex|peri|men|ta|tion experimentación

ex|peri|men|tal experimental
• ex|peri|men|tal|ly de manera experimental

ex|peri|men|tal de|sign diseño experimental

ex|pert experto o experta
• ex|pert|ly con pericia

ex|per|tise experiencia, conocimientos, pericia

ex|pert wit|ness testigo experto

ex|pi|ra|tion date fecha de caducidad

ex|pire caducar

ex|plain explicar, dar explicaciones
▶ explain away justificar

ex|pla|na|tion explicación

ex|plana|tory explicativo

ex|plic|it explícito, claro
• ex|plic|it|ly explícitamente

ex|plode explotar, estallar

ex|ploit explotar, aprovecharse de, proeza, hazaña • ex|ploi|ta|tion explotación, aprovechamiento, utilización

ex|plore explorar, sondear, examinar, ir en busca de
• ex|plo|ra|tion exploración, sondeo, búsqueda
• ex|plor|er explorador o exploradora

ex|plo|sion explosión, aumento dramático

ex|plo|sive explosivo

ex|po|nen|tial func|tion función exponencial

ex|port exportar, exportación, artículo de exportación • ex|port|er exportador o exportadora

ex|pose exponer, desenmascarar, poner en peligro

ex|po|sure exposición, hipotermia, revelación, presencia, publicidad, tiempo aire

ex|press expresar, expreso, preciso, express, rápido
• ex|press|ly expresamente

ex|pres|sion expresión, manifestación, aspecto, frase

ex|pres|sive con|tent contenido emocional

ex|pres|sive writ|ing escritura emocional

ex|pul|sion expulsión

ex|quis|ite exquisito
• **ex|quis|ite|ly** exquisitamente

ex|tend extender(se), ampliar

ex|ten|sion anexo, ampliación, extensión

ex|ten|sive extensivo, extenso • **ex|ten|sive|ly** extensivamente, extensamente

ex|ten|sor extensor

ex|tent alcance, extensión
▸ **to a certain extent** hasta cierto punto

ex|te|ri|or exterior, aspecto, apariencia

ex|ter|nal externo, exterior
• **ex|ter|nal|ly** externamente

ex|ter|nal com|bus|tion en|gine motor de combustión externa

ex|ter|nal fer|ti|li|za|tion fertilización externa

ex|ter|nal fuel tank tanque de combustible externo

ex|tinct extinto

ex|tra adicional, suplementario, extra, recargo, cargo extra, sobreprecio, extremadamente

ex|tract extraer, sacar, extracto, fragmento, selección • **ex|trac|tion** extracción

extra|dite extraditar
• **extra|di|tion** extradición

extraor|di|nary extraordinario
• **extraor|di|nari|ly** extraordinariamente

ex|trava|gant extravagante, carísimo • **ex|trava|gance** extravagancia
• **ex|trava|gant|ly** de modo extravagante, extravagantemente

ex|treme extremo, fin, final • **ex|treme|ly** extremadamente

ex|trem|ist extremista, radical • **ex|trem|ism** extremismo

extro|vert extrovertido

extro|vert|ed extrovertido

ex|tru|sive eruptivo, volcánico

eye ojo, ojal, echar un ojo/vistazo, contemplar, observar, mirada
▸ **before/in front of/under your eyes** ante (sus/los/mis propios) ojos
▸ **catch someone's eye** llamar la atención de alguien, atraer la atención de alguien
▸ **keep your eyes open, keep an eye out** mantener ojos abiertos, vigilar, no perder de vista
▸ **have your eye on something** tener los ojos puestos en algo

eye|ball globo ocular

eye|brow ceja
▸ **raise an eyebrow** levantar la ceja/las cejas, subir la ceja/las cejas

eye can|dy *también* **eye-candy** simple decoración

eye|glasses lentes, anteojos

eye|lash pestaña

eye|lid párpado

eye|liner delineador (de ojos)

eye|piece ocular

eye-popping impactante

eye shad|ow *también* **eye-shadow, eyeshadow** sombra de ojos

eye|sight vista

eye|witness testigo ocular, testigo presencial

Ff

fab|ric tela, estructura
fabu|lous fabuloso
face cara, rostro, ladera, lado, carátula, aspecto, prestigio, estar de frente, enfrentar, no atreverse a
▸ **face to face** cara a cara, de frente
▸ **fly in the face of** ignorar, hacer caso omiso de
▸ **in the face of** ante
▸ **make/pull a face** poner mala cara
▸ **keep a straight face** aguantarse la risa
face card figura
face mask mascarilla, máscara
face-off enfrentamiento
face value valor nominal
▸ **at face value** en sentido literal
fa|cial facial
fa|cili|tate facilitar
fa|cil|ity instalación, medio, sistema
fact hecho, hecho real
▸ **the fact that** el hecho de que
▸ **in fact** de hecho
fac|tion facción ● **fac|tion|al** entre facciones
fac|tor factor
▸ **factor in** tomar en cuenta
fac|to|ry fábrica
fac|ul|ty facultad, cuerpo docente, profesorado
fad moda pasajera
fade decolorar(se), apagar(se), perder color o intensidad, desvanecerse ● **fad|ed** apagado
Fahr|en|heit Fahrenheit
fail no hacer, no lograr, fracasar, no cumplir con, fallar, reprobar

▸ **without fail** sin falta
fail|ure fracaso, falla
▸ **fail to do something** no hacer algo
faint débil, tenue, ligero, desmayarse ● **faint|ly** apenas, mareado
fair justo, considerable, rubio, blanco, despejado, feria, exposición, bazar ● **fair|ness** justicia
▸ **fair enough** bueno, está bien
fair|ly bastante, más o menos, limpiamente
fairy hada
fairy tale *también* **fairytale** cuento de hadas
faith fe, confianza, creencia
▸ **in good faith** de buena fe
faith|ful fiel
▸ **the faithful** los incondicionales
faith|ful|ly fielmente
▸ **Yours faithfully** Atentamente
fa|ji|ta fajita
fake falso, falsificación, imitación, falsea, falsificar, simular
fall caer(se), caída, descenso, otoño, bajar, disminuir, descender
▸ **falls** cascada, caída de agua, catarata(s)
▸ **fall into** clasificar, cubrir
▸ **fall apart** deshacerse, desmoronarse, venirse abajo
▸ **fall back on** recurrir a, echar mano de
▸ **fall behind** rezagarse, quedarse a la zaga
▸ **fall for** enamorarse de, tragarse
▸ **fall off** caerse, soltarse
▸ **fall out** caerse, pelearse

▶ **fall through** no concretarse
▶ **fall to** tocarle, corresponderle
fall|en ver fall
fall|lo|pian tube trompa de Falopio
fall|out lluvia radiactiva
false falso, postizo, fingido
• **false|ly** falsamente, fingidamente
false alarm falsa alarma
false cau|sal|ity causalidad falsa
fame fama
fa|mili|ar familiar, familiarizado, con demasiada confianza
• **fa|mili|ar|ity** familiaridad, confianza • **fa|mili|ar|ly** confianzudamente
fami|ly familia
fami|ly room cuarto de la tele, cuarto de televisión
fami|ly values valores familiares, valores tradicionales
fam|ine hambruna
fa|mous famoso, muy conocido
fan aficionado o aficionada, admirador o admiradora, fanático o fanática, ventilador, abanico, abanicar(se)
▶ **fan out** desplegar(se)
fa|nat|ic fanático o fanática, aficionado o aficionada
• **fa|nati|cal** fanático, aficionado
fan base también **fanbase** admiradores o admiradoras
fan|cy estrambótico, extravagante, caprichoso, lujoso, elegante, muy chic
▶ **fancy (that)!** ¡mira nada más!, ¡qué barbaridad!, ¡imagínate!
▶ **take somebody's fancy** encantar a alguien, fascinar a alguien, gustar a alguien, llamar la atención a alguien
fan mail cartas a una

personalidad
fan|ny pack cangurera
fan|ta|size fantasear, soñar
fan|tas|tic fantástico
• **fan|tas|ti|cal|ly** fantásticamente
fan|ta|sy fantasía
FAQ preguntas frecuentes
far lejos, lejano, a más de, extremo, mucho
▶ **how far** a qué distancia, qué tan lejos, hasta, hasta dónde, hasta qué punto
▶ **go too far** pasarse de la raya, ir demasiado lejos
▶ **so far** hasta ahora, hasta el momento, hasta este momento
▶ **by far** por mucho, con mucho
▶ **far from** lejos de, al contrario, ni mucho menos
far|away lejano, remoto
fare boleto, pasaje, billete
▶ **fare well/badly** irle bien/mal
Far East Lejano Oriente, Extremo Oriente
far-fetched exagerado
farm rancho, granja, hacienda, finca, cultivar, trabajar la tierra, criar animales, sembrar
farm|er ranchero o ranchera, granjero o granjera, agricultor o agricultora
farm|ing agricultura, crianza de animales, cultivo, labranza
far off remoto, lejano, distante, alejado, a lo lejos
Farsi lengua persa, dari
far-sighted présbite, miope
farther más lejos
far|thest lo más lejos, lejísimos
fas|ci|nate fascinar(se)
fas|ci|nat|ing fascinante
fas|cist fascista • **fas|cism** fascismo
fash|ion moda, manera, forma

f

F

▸ **in fashion** de moda, en boga

fash|ion|able a la moda, de moda ● **fash|ion|ably** a la moda

fast rápido, veloz, firme, rápidamente, velozmente, inmediatamente, adelantado, de inmediato, con firmeza, firmemente, ayunar, ayuno
▸ **fast asleep** profundamente dormido

fas|ten asegurar(se), abrochar(se), cerrar(se), sujetar(se), pegar, fijar

fast food comida rápida

fast lane carril de alta velocidad
▸ **live in the fast lane** vivir a tope

fat gordo, obeso, grasa, grueso ● **fat|ness** gordura

fa|tal fatal, mortal, desastroso ● **fa|tal|ly** fatalmente

fa|tal|ity muerto, víctima mortal, fatalidad

fate suerte, destino

fa|ther padre, papá, progenitor, engendrar, ser el padre

father-in-law suegro

fa|tigue fatiga, cansancio, uniforme de faena

fat|so gordo o gorda, gordinflón o gordinflona

fat|ty grasoso, graso

fau|cet llave, grifo, canilla

fault culpa, responsabilidad, defecto, falla, criticar, encontrar defectos, censurar
▸ **at fault** ser culpable, tener la culpa
▸ **find fault** criticar, desaprobar

fault block roca de dislocación

fault-block moun|tain bloque fallado, bloque de falla

fava bean haba

fa|vor aprecio, estimación, gusto, favor, preferir, estar a favor de, favorecer, privilegiar
▸ **in favor** a favor, en el favor
▸ **in somebody's favor** en favor de alguien
▸ **in favor of** en pro de

fa|vor|able favorable

fa|vor|ite favorito, favorita

fa|vor|it|ism favoritismo

fax fax, mandar por fax, enviar por fax

FDA FDA

fear miedo, temor, temer, sentir temor
▸ **for fear of** por miedo de

fear|ful temeroso, miedoso, espantoso, horrible

feast banquete, festín, festejar, agasajarse, darse un festín

feat hazaña, proeza

feath|er pluma

fea|ture característica, rasgo distintivo, artículo, programa especial, película, facción, rasgo, incluir, destacar, participar, actuar, aparecer

Feb|ru|ary febrero

fed ver feed
▸ **the Fed** Reserva Federal
▸ **feds** agentes federales, agentes del FBI

fed|er|al federal, nacional ● **fed|er|al|ly** a escala federal

Fed|er|al Re|serve la Reserva Federal

fed|era|tion federación

fe|do|ra sombrero de fieltro de ala ancha

fed up harto, hasta el copete, hasta el gorro

fee derechos, cuota, honorarios

feed alimentar(se), dar de comer, comer, amamantar, dar de mamar, dar el biberón, dar la mamila, proveer, llevar ● **feed|ing**

alimento, alimentación

feed|back retroalimentación

feed|back con|trol control de retroalimentación

feel sentir(se), hacer sentir, dejar una sensación, sensación, tocar, sentir, palpar, pensar, creer, pensar sobre, opinar, tacto
▸ **feel for** palpar, buscar(se), compadecer(se), sentir lástima por, dar lástima
▸ **feel like** antojarse, querer algo, tener ganas, apetecer

feel|ing sensación, sentimiento, impresión, opinión, sentir afecto
▸ **bad feeling/ill feeling** resentimiento

feet *ver* **foot**

feld|spar feldespato

fell *ver* **fall**, derribar, talar

fel|low colega, compañero, correligionario, miembro

felo|ny delito grave

fel|sic félsico

felt *ver* **feel**, fieltro

fe|male mujer, hembra, de sexo femenino, de mujeres, femenino, del sexo femenino

femi|nine femenino
• **femi|nin|ity** feminidad

femi|nist feminista

fence cerca, valla, cercar
▸ **sit on the fence** no definirse, mirar los toros desde la barrera, no tomar partido

fenc|ing esgrima, material para cercas

fend valerse por sí mismo, arreglárselas solo
▸ **fend off** eludir, evadir, esquivar

fend|er defensa

fer|ment agitación, conmoción, fermentar
• **fer|men|ta|tion** fermentación

Fer|ris wheel *también* **ferris wheel** rueda de la fortuna

fer|ry ferry, transbordador, transportar, llevar

fer|tile fértile, fecundo
• **fer|til|ity** fertilidad

fer|ti|lize fertilizar
• **fer|ti|li|za|tion** fertilización

fer|ti|liz|er fertilizante

fes|ti|val festival, fiesta, celebración

fe|tal po|si|tion posición fetal

fetch buscar, recoger, ir por, traer, vender

fe|tus feto

fe|ver fiebre, temperatura, calentura

fe|ver blis|ter boquera, fuego

few algunos, unos cuantos, poco, alguno, algún
▸ **as few as** apenas
▸ **few and far between** muy de cuando en cuando, muy de vez en cuando, muy rara vez
▸ **no fewer than** no menos de

fi|an|cé prometido, novio

fi|an|cée prometida, novia

fi|ber fibra

fiber|glass fibra de vidrio

fi|ber op|tics por fibra óptica, de fibra óptica

fi|brous root raíces fibrosas

fic|tion ficción, narrativa
• **fictional** ficticio

fid|dle jugar, juguetear, violín

field campo, sembradío, potrero, cancha, terreno de juego, yacimiento, especialidad, campo visual, de campo, fildear • **field|er** fildeador

field goal gol de campo

field hand bracero *o* bracera, jornalero *o* jornalera, peón de campo

field hock|ey hockey, hockey sobre pasto

field trip viaje de estudio

fierce feroz, fiero, violento

● **fierce|ly** violentamente, ferozmente

fif|teen quince

fif|teenth décimoquinto, quince, quinceavo

fifth quinto

Fifth Amend|ment la Quinta Enmienda

fif|ti|eth quincuagésimo, cincuentavo

fif|ty cincuenta
  ▸ **the fifties** los (años) cincuenta

fig higo

fight luchar, combatir, pelear(se), emprender, participar, tratar de contener, discutir, discusión, combate, lucha, pelea ● **fight|ing** lucha
  ▸ **fight back** defenderse, oponerse, reprimir
  ▸ **fight off** combatir, resistir(se), lograr, rechazar
  ▸ **fight one's way to/ through** abrirse camino a, abrirse paso entre

fight|er caza, avión de combate, luchador o luchadora, boxeador o boxeadora, peleador o peleadora, púgil

fight|ing chance posibilidades de algo, la oportunidad de algo

fig|ura|tive figurado, metafórico, figurativo
  ● **fig|ura|tive|ly** metafóricamente

fig|ure cifra, número, guarismo, silueta, figura, personaje, personalidad, dígito, figurar(se), imaginarse, aparecer
  ▸ **figure out** entender
  ▸ **figure up** sumar, calcular

fig|ure eight ocho

file expediente, archivo, lima, archivar, clasificar, presentar, entablar, limar(se)
  ▸ **single file** en fila, en fila india

file|name nombre del archivo

file-sharing *también* **file sharing** compartir archivos

fil|et filete

fili|bus|ter maniobra dilatoria, obstruccionismo

fil|ings expediente judicial

fill llenar(se), atiborrar, rellenar, ocupar, desempeñar(se) ● **filled** lleno
  ▸ **fill in** llenar, poner al corriente, informar, cubrir, sustituir, reemplazar
  ▸ **fill out** llenar
  ▸ **fill up** llenar

fill|ing tapadura, incrustación, empaste, relleno, llenador

film película, film, filme, capa, filmar, rodar ● **film|ing** filmación

fil|ter filtrar(se), esparcirse, filtro

filthy sucio, mugroso, asqueroso, cochino

fin aleta, alerón

fi|nal último, final, definitiva, inapelable

fi|nal|ize terminar, finalizar, concluir, acabar

fi|nal|ly finalmente, por fin, por último, al final

fi|nance financiar(se), costear(se), financiamiento, financiación, finanzas

fi|nance charge cargo financiero

fi|nan|cial financiero
  ● **fi|nan|cial|ly** en lo financiero

fi|nan|cial ad|vis|er asesor financiero o asesora financiera

fi|nan|cial ser|vices servicio financiero

find encontrar(se), descubrir, percatarse, darse cuenta, declarar, hallar, parecer, resultar, hallazgo
  ▸ **find one's way** encontrar el camino, orientarse

▸ **find out** descubrir, averiguar, saber, enterarse

find|ing resultado, hallazgo

fine magnífico, excelente, fino, bien, delgado, preciso, sutil, pequeño, bueno, multa, multar, imponer una multa, poner una multa
• **fine|ly** magníficamente, delicadamente, finamente

fine ad|just|ment ajuste fino

fine-tune afinar, ajustar, poner a punto

fin|ger dedo, palpar, tentar, tocar
▸ **cross one's fingers** o **keep one's fingers crossed** cruzar los dedos, poner changuitos
▸ **point the finger at** o **point an accusing finger at** señalar con el dedo, acusar
▸ **put one's finger on something** dar con algo, acertar algo

finger|nail uña

finger|print huella digital
▸ **take fingerprints** tomar las huellas digitales

fin|ish terminar, acabar, concluir, fin, final, toque, terminado, acabado
▸ **the finishing touch** toque final, último toque
▸ **finish off** terminar(se), acabar(se)

fin|ished acabado
▸ **be finished** haber acabado, estar harto

fin|ish line meta, línea de llegada

fire fuego, lumbre, incendio, fogata, hoguera, calentador, calentón, calefactor, disparo, disparar, hacer fuego, despedir, correr
• **fir|ing** balacera
▸ **fire questions** preguntar, hacer preguntas
▸ **catch fire** incendiarse
▸ **be on fire** quemarse
▸ **set fire to** o **set on fire** prender fuego, encender, incendiar

fire alarm alarma contra incendio

fire|arm arma de fuego

fire blan|ket manta contra incendios

fire de|part|ment departamento de bomberos

fire en|gine camión de bomberos, carro de bomberos

fire ex|tin|guish|er también **fire-extinguisher** extintor de incendios, extinguidor de incendios

fire|fight|er bombero o bombera

fire|place chimenea, hogar

fire|storm tormenta

fire truck carro de bomberos, camión de bomberos

fire|works fuegos artificiales, fuegos pirotécnicos, fuegos de artificio

firm empresa, compañía, despacho, firme, fuerte, enérgico, definitiva, sólido
• **firm|ly** firmemente
▸ **stand firm** mantenerse firme

first primero, primer, principal, para empezar, al principio, acontecimiento sin precedentes, lo primero
▸ **first of all** en primer lugar, antes que nada
▸ **at first** al principio

first aid primeros auxilios

first aid kit equipo de primeros auxilios, botiquín

First Amend|ment Primera Enmienda a la Constitución de los Estados Unidos

First Fami|ly la familia del presidente

first floor planta baja

First Lady Primera Dama

first name nombre, nombre de pila

fis|cal fiscal

fish pez, pescado, pescar

fish and chips pescado

capeado con papas fritas

fish|bowl *también* **fish bowl** pecera
▶ **be in a fishbowl** estar en un aparador, estar a la vista de todo el mundo

fisher|man pescador *o* pescadora

fish|ing pesca

fish stick dedo de pescado, palito de pescado

fish|tail colear(se)

fist puño

fist|fight *también* **fist fight** pelea a puñetazos, pleito a puñetazos

fit ajustar, quedar bien, caber, poner, colocar, instalar, adecuado, capacitado, digno, en forma, ataque ● **fit|ness** capacidad, buena forma física
▶ **see fit** parecer conveniente, parecer adecuado, parecer apropiado
▶ **fit in** acomodar, cuadrar, encajar
▶ **fit out** proveer de algo, equipar

fit|ting adecuado, digno, accesorio ● **fit|ting|ly** adecuadamente
▶ **fittings** accesorios, aditamentos

five cinco

fix arreglar, reparar, fijar, concretar, decidir, instalar, amañar, comprar, arreglo, chanchullo
▶ **fix up** conseguir

fixed fijo

fixed pul|ley polea fija

fix|tures aditamentos

flag bandera, banderín, flaquear, disminuir, decaer

fla|gella flagelo

flame flama, llama
▶ **burst into flames** estallar en llamas
▶ **in flames** en llamas

fla|min|go flamenco

flank costado, flanco, flanquear

flap ondear, agitar(se), batir las alas, aletear, colgajo, faldón

flare bengala, llamear, flamear, encenderse, enardecer(se), estallar, recrudecer(se)

flash chispazo, destello, fogonazo, linterna, flash, flashazo, brillar, destellar, hacer señales con una luz, pasar como rayo, pasar volando
▶ **in a flash** de repente

flash drive unidad de disco portátil, USB

flash flood inundación repentina, torrente

flash|light linterna

flask frasco, termo

flat plano, llano, desinflado, ponchado, bajo, descargado, en sólo, en apenas, fijo, bemol, desafinado, categórico, rotundo, terminante ● **flat|ly** de plano
▶ **fall flat** fracasar, no ser bien recibido
▶ **flat out** lo más rápidamente, a toda velocidad, a todo vapor

flat|lands llano, llanura

flat|ten aplanar(se), aplastar, agachar, pegar(se)

flat|ter halagar, adular, considerarse

flat|ware cubiertos

fla|vor sabor, sazonar, dar sabor

fla|vored sazonado

fla|vor|ful sabroso, rico

fla|vor|ing sazonador, saborizante, condimento

fla|vor|less insípido, soso, sin sabor

fled *ver* flee

flee escapar, huir, darse a la fuga, echar(se) a correr

fleet flota, flotilla

flesh carne, cuerpo, pulpa

▶ **own flesh and blood** pariente, familiar, consanguíneo

▶ **in the flesh** en persona

▶ **flesh out** desarrollar, dar cuerpo

flesh-colored color carne

flew ver fly

flex|ible flexible • **flexi|bil|ity** flexibilidad

flex|or flexor

flex|time también **flexitime** horario flexible

flick quitar, chasquear, sacudir, chasquido, sacudida, trazo rápido, hojear

▶ **flick a switch** accionar un interruptor

flight vuelo, tramo, huida, fuga, a salto de mata, volar

flight deck cubierta de vuelo, cabina de mando

fling lanzar, arrojar, aventar, aventura

flip hojear, volcar(se), voltear(se)

flip-flop chancla, dar virajes

flirt coquetear, flirtear, coqueto o coqueta • **flir|ta|tion** coqueteo

float flotar, emitir acciones, cotizar en bolsa, colocar en bolsa, flotador

flock bandada, rebaño, multitud, tropel, acudir en tropel, ir en tropel

flood inundación, raudal, inundar(se), anegar(se), saturar(se) • **flood|ing** inundación

flood plain también **floodplain** terreno aluvial, terreno de aluvión

floor piso, suelo, fondo, dejar helado

floor lamp lámpara de pie

flop dejarse caer, desplomarse, caer de golpe, fracasar estrepitosamente, fracaso, fiasco

flop|py flexible, blando, aguado

flop|py disk disqueta, disquete, disco flexible, flopy

flo|rist florista, florería

floun|der tambalearse, fallar, dar tumbos, perder pie

flour harina

flour|ish florecer, prosperar, darse, crecer bien, gesto ceremonioso • **flour|ish|ing** próspero, floreciente

flow fluir, manar, correr, salir, flujo

flow chart diagrama de flujo

flow|er flor, florecer

flow|er|ing en flor, florido, florecimiento

flown ver fly

flu gripa, gripe

flub fallar, echar a perder, meter la pata, metida de pata, error

flu|ent fluido, elocuente • **flu|en|cy** fluidez • **flu|ent|ly** fluidamente, con fluidez

▶ **be fluent in a language** hablar con fluidez una lengua, tener dominio de una lengua, dominar una lengua

flu|id fluido, líquido

flung ver fling

flunk reprobar, tronar

fluo|res|cent fluorescente

▶ **fluorescent light** tubo fluorescente, lámpara fluorescente

flush sonrojarse, ponerse rojo, ponerse colorado, ruborizarse, hacer salir, jalarle al baño, jalar la cadena, jalar, ruido del baño al jalarle, sonrojo, rubor, bochorno • **flushed** rojo

flute flauta

flut|ist flautista

fly mosca, bragueta, volar, mandar en avión, ondear, flotar en el aire • **fly|er** aviador

f

▶ **fly into a rage** montar en cólera, ponerse hecho una furia

fly ball *también* **flyball** globo

fly|er *también* **flier** folleto, volante

fly|ing volador, viajar en avión
▶ **get off to a flying start** empezar con el pie derecho, arrancar bien

fo|cus concentrar(se), enfocar(se), centro, foco, atención, interés, epicentro
▶ **in focus** enfocado, en foco
▶ **out of focus** fuera de foco, desenfocado

fo|cus group grupo de sondeo

fog niebla, neblina

fog|gy brumoso, nebuloso

foil papel aluminio, frustrar

fold doblar(se), plegar(se), cruzar, pliegue, doblez
● **fold|ing** plegable
▶ **fold up** doblar, plegar

fold|ed moun|tain montaña de plegamiento

fold|er fólder, carpeta

fo|li|at|ed
▶ **foliated rock** roca lamelar

folk gente, música popular, música folklórica, popular
● **folks** padres, papás

folk|lore folklor, tradición

fol|li|cle folículo

fol|low seguir, perseguir, alcanzar, deducir(se), tener interés en, interesarse por, entender
▶ **as follows** siguiente, como sigue
▶ **followed by** seguido de
▶ **follow through** continuar, seguir adelante con algo

fol|low|er seguidor *o* seguidora, discípulo *o* discípula

fol|low|ing siguiente, lo siguiente, el siguiente, la siguiente, lo que sigue, después de
▶ **have a following** tener seguidores *o* tener admiradores

follow-up seguimiento, continuación

fond buen, bueno, cariñoso, complaciente ● **fond|ness** cariño, afición, gusto
● **fond|ly** cariñosamente, con cariño
▶ **be fond of someone** estar encariñado con alguien, estar aficionado de alguien
▶ **be fond of something** ser aficionado a algo, gustarle mucho algo a uno

food comida, alimento
▶ **give food for thought** hacer reflexionar

Food and Drug Ad|min|is|tra|tion Dirección de Alimentos y Medicinas

food bank banco de alimentos

food chain cadena alimenticia, cadena alimentaria, cadena trófica

food court zona de restaurantes de comida rápida, zona de alimentos

food web red de cadenas alimenticias, trama alimentaria

fool idiota, tonto *o* tonta, engañar, hacer creer
▶ **make a fool of someone** poner a alguien en ridículo
▶ **fool around** bromear, tontear, hacerse guaje, hacerse el tonto

fool|ish insensato, estúpido, tonto ● **fool|ish|ly** tontamente ● **fool|ish|ness** insensatez

foot pie
▶ **on foot** a pie, caminando
▶ **on one's feet** de pie, parado
▶ **get back on one's feet** recuperarse, levantarse
▶ **put one's foot down** no ceder, mantenerse firme
▶ **put one's feet up** descansar con los pies en alto

▶ **get/rise to one's feet** levantarse, pararse, ponerse de pie

foot|age metraje, secuencia

foot|ball futbol americano *o* fútbol americano, fútbol, futbol soccer, futbol, soccer, balón de futbol, pelota de futbol

foot|ball field cancha de futbol *o* cancha de fútbol, campo de futbol *o* campo de fútbol

foot|ing base, fundamento, equilibrio

foot|locker *también* **foot locker** baúl

foot|note nota de pie de página, nota a pie de página, nota al pie

foot|print huella, pisada

foot|step paso
▶ **follow in somebody's footsteps** seguir los pasos de alguien

foot|wall pared baja de una falla inclinada

for para, por, durante, a favor de, en favor de, en honor de

for|bid prohibir, impedir

for|bid|den prohibido

force forzar, obligar, meter a fuerza, fuerza, poder, figura, personalidad
▶ **in force** vigente
▶ **join forces** unir fuerzas

force field campo de fuerza

fore|arm antebrazo

fore|cast pronóstico, previsión, pronosticar, prever, predecir
● **fore|cast|er** analista

fore|head frente

for|eign extranjero, exterior, extraño

for|eign|er extranjero *o* extranjera

for|eign ex|change mercado de divisas, divisas

for|eign ser|vice servicio exterior, servicio

diplomático

fore|man capataz

fore|see prever

for|est bosque, selva

for|est land *también* **forestland** superficie forestal, terreno forestal

for|est|ry silvicultura

for|ever siempre, por siempre, para siempre, permanentemente, eternamente

for|gave *ver* forgive

forge forjar, fraguar, falsificar, seguir ● **forg|er** falsificador
▶ **forge ahead** seguir adelante

for|gery falsificación

for|get olvidar(se)

for|get|ful olvidadizo

for|give perdonar(se)
● **for|giv|ing** indulgente
● **for|give|ness** perdón

for|got *ver* forget

for|got|ten *ver* forget

fork tenedor, y griega, bifurcación, horqueta, horca, bifurcarse, dividirse
▶ **fork out** gastar(se), desembolsar

form forma, tipo, formulario, formar(se), constituir, crear

for|mal formal ● **for|mal|ly** formalmente ● **for|mal|ity** formalidad

for|mal thea|ter teatro convencional

for|mat formato, estilo, formatear

for|ma|tion formación, creación

for|mer ex, antiguo, anterior, el primero, lo primero

for|mer|ly antes, anteriormente

form-fitting pegado, ceñido, ajustado

for|mi|dable extraordinario, monumental

f

form let|ter circular

for|mu|la fórmula, receta

for|mu|late formular, idear, concebir, expresar • **for|mu|la|tion** formulación

for-profit lucrativo, comercial, con fines de lucro

fort fuerte

forth
▸ **go forth** salir a, marchar a, ir a
▸ **bring forth** producir, provocar, suscitar, llevar a

forth|com|ing próximo, futuro, que está por llegar, comunicativo

for|ti|eth cuadragésimo, cuarentavo

for|tu|nate afortunado, suertudo

for|tu|nate|ly afortunadamente, por fortuna, por suerte

for|tune fortuna, suerte, trayectoria, vicisitudes

for|ty cuarenta
▸ **the forties** los (años) cuarenta

fo|rum foro

for|ward hacia adelante, adelante, adelantado, presentar(se), proponer(se), enviar, reenviar, transmitir, mandar, remitir

for|ward slash barra oblicua, barra diagonal, diagonal

fos|sil fósil

fos|sil fuel *también* **fossil-fuel** combustible fósil

fos|sil rec|ord registro fósil

fos|ter de acogida, sustituto, acoger, fomentar, promover

fought *ver* **fight**

foul nauseabundo, fétido, repugnante, mal, malo, falta, faul
▸ **foul language** lenguaje obsceno
▸ **run/fall foul of someone** tener problemas con alguien

foul line línea de faul

found *ver* **find**, fundar, crear, establecer • **found|ing** fundación

foun|da|tion base, fundamento, fundación, cimientos

found|er fallar, fracasar, zozobrar, fundador *o* fundadora, creador *o* creadora

found|ing mem|ber miembro fundador

foun|tain fuente, manantial, chorro, surtidor

four cuatro
▸ **on all fours** en cuatro patas, a gatas

four|teen catorce

four|teenth decimocuarto, catorceavo

fourth cuarto, cuarta parte

four-wheel drive transmisión en las cuatro ruedas, tracción integral, propulsión total

fowl ave de corral

fox zorro

foxy sexy

frac|tion fracción

frac|ture fractura, fracturar(se)

frag|ile frágil • **fra|gil|ity** fragilidad

frag|ment fragmento, trozo, fragmentar(se), abrirse • **frag|men|ta|tion** fragmentación

frag|men|ta|tion escisión, fragmentación

fra|grance fragancia, aroma

fra|grant fragante

frame marco, armazón, cuadro, enmarcar, incriminar, cuerpo

frame|work marco de referencia, parámetro, marco, estructura, armazón

fran|chise franquicia, concesión, sufragio, derecho de voto

frank franco, sincero • **frank|ly** francamente • **frank|ness** franqueza

fran|tic desesperado, frenético, furioso, desequilibrado
• **fran|ti|cal|ly** desesperadamente

fra|ter|ni|ty fraternidad, hermandad, asociación, organización, apoyo fraterno, asociación estudiantil masculina, club estudiantil masculino

fraud fraude, impostor o impostora, simulador o simuladora

fraudu|lent fraudulento
• **fraudu|lent|ly** fraudulentamente

fraz|zle
▶ **wear yourself/be worn to a frazzle** estar hecho polvo, estar agotado, estar muerto de cansancio

fraz|zled hecho polvo, rendido, agotado

freak raro, inesperado, inusitado, insólito, fenómeno, monstruo, bicho raro, fenómeno de circo, freak

free gratis, libre, abierto, sin costo, en libertad, desocupado, suelto, soltar, liberar(se), poner en libertad, dejar en libertad, dejar libre • **free|ly** libremente
▶ **free of** libre de, exento de, sin
▶ **feel free** con confianza

free agent agente libre

free as|so|cia|tion asociación libre

free|dom libertad, inmunidad

free|dom of speech libertad de expresión

free fall también **free-fall** caída libre

freely profusamente, a manos llenas, libremente, voluntariamente, de buen grado, sin restricciones

free ride
▶ **get a free ride** aprovechar(se) de la situación

free speech libertad de expresión

free trade libre comercio

free|way autopista

freeze congelar(se), helarse, quedarse inmóvil, paralizarse, inmovilizar, congelamiento

freez|er congelador o congeladora

freez|ing congelado, helado, congelación

freez|ing point también **freezing-point** punto de congelación

freight carga, flete

freight car vagón de carga, carro de carga

French fries papas fritas, papas a la francesa

French toast torreja, pan francés

fre|quen|cy frecuencia

fre|quent frecuente
• **fre|quent|ly** frecuentemente

fresh nuevo, adicional, otro, fresco, fresca, reciente
• **fresh|ly** recién

fresh|man novato o novata, estudiante de primer año de universidad

fresh|water agua dulce

fric|tion fricción

Fri|day viernes

fridge refrigerador, refri, heladera

friend amigo o amiga, cuate o cuata
▶ **friends** amigos, partidarios, aliados, favorecedores
▶ **be friends** estar en buenos términos, ser amigos
▶ **make friends** hacer amistad, hacer amigos, trabar amistad

friend|ly amistoso, amable,

f

simpático, cordial
• **friend|li|ness** afabilidad, de exhibición
friend|ly fire fuego amigo
friend|ship amistad
fries papas fritas, papas a la francesa
fright miedo, susto
fright|en asustar, espantar, atemorizar
▸ **frighten away** o **frighten off** asustar, alejar
fright|ened asustado
▸ **be frightened** estar asustado, tener miedo
fright|en|ing espantoso, aterrador, alarmante
• **fright|en|ing|ly** de manera alarmante
fringe fleco, cenefa, margen, en las afueras, en la periferia
frog rana
from de, a través de, por, desde, a partir de
front frente, campo, cara, pantalla
▸ **in front** adelante, al frente
▸ **in front of** frente a, en frente de
front and cen|ter centro de la atención
front desk recepción
fron|tier frontera, límite
front line también **front-line** primera línea
front of|fice oficina de atención al público
front-page primera plana
frost escarcha, helada, embetunar, cubrir con azúcar glaseada
frost|ing betún
frosty helado, con escarcha, cubierto de escarcha
frown fruncir el ceño, fruncir el entrecejo, ceño fruncido, cara de enojo/concentración
▸ **frown upon** o **frown on** estar mal visto, desaprobar
froze ver **freeze**
fro|zen ver **freeze**, congelado,

helado
fruit fruta, fruto
▸ **bear fruit** dar fruto, fructificar
frus|trate frustrar(se)
• **frus|trat|ed** frustrado
• **frus|trat|ing** frustrante
• **frus|tra|tion** frustración
fry freír
fry|ing pan sartén
fuel combustible, carburante
fuel cell célula electroquímica, célula de combustible, celda de combustible
fueled también **fuelled** alimentado
fu|gi|tive fugitivo o fugitiva
fugue fuga
ful|crum fulcro, punto de apoyo
ful|fill cumplir, hacer realidad, llevar a cabo, desempeñar, realizar, satisfacer, llenar • **ful|filled** satisfecho • **ful|fil|ling** pleno
• **ful|fill|ment** satisfacción
full lleno, satisfecho, completo, total, todo, pleno, intenso, concentrado
• **full|ness** plenitud
▸ **in full** completamente, íntegramente, en detalle
▸ **to the full** al máximo
full-blown verdadero, auténtico, en toda la extensión de la palabra, todo
full-flavored de sabor intenso
full-length de largo normal, completo, largo, de cuerpo entero, cuan largo es
full-scale declarado, de gran envergadura, de tamaño natural
full-time también **full time** de tiempo completo, tiempo completo
ful|ly completamente, totalmente, del todo, por completo, en detalle, de lleno

fun diversión, divertido
▸ **in fun** de chiste
▸ **make fun of** burlarse, reírse de

func|tion función, recepción, ceremonia, funcionar, hacer las veces

func|tion|al funcional, práctico, en buen estado

fund fondos, dinero, fondo, financiar

fun|da|men|tal fundamental ● **fun|da|men|tal|ly** fundamentalmente

fun|da|men|tal|ism fundamentalismo ● **fun|da|men|tal|ist** fundamentalista

fun|da|men|tals fundamento, principio, base

fund|ing financiación, financiamiento, fondos, recursos

fund man|ag|er administrador financiero o administradora financiera

fund|rais|er también **fund-raiser** evento para recaudar fondos, recaudador de fondos o recaudadora de fondos

fund-raising también **fundraising** recaudación de fondos

fu|ner|al funeral

fu|ner|al home funeraria

fu|ner|al par|lor funeraria

fun|gus hongo ● **fun|gal** micótico

funky en la onda, original

fun|ny divertido, chistoso, cómico, gracioso, raro, extraño, curioso, ocurrente, medio mal

fur piel, pelo, pelaje, pieles

fu|ri|ous furioso, furibundo, febril, feroz, frenético ● **fu|ri|ous|ly** furiosamente, febrilmente

fur|nace horno, caldera, alto horno

fur|nish amueblar, amoblar, proveer, surtir, proporcionar ● **fur|nished** amueblado

fur|ni|ture muebles

fur|ther más, aún más, todavía más, más allá, más adelante, más lejos, otro, adicional, remontarse, retroceder, adelantarse, anticiparse, adelantar, favorecer, fomentar

fur|ther edu|ca|tion educación continua, educación para adultos, programas de extensión universitaria

further|more además, por otra parte

fur|thest aún más, todavía más, más lejano, extremo

fury furia, ira, furor

fuse fusible, tapón, fundir(se), fusionar(se), amalgamar(se)

fu|sion fusión

fuss alboroto, escándalo, agitación, preocupar(se), inquietar(se), ir de aquí para allá, complicar(se) la existencia
▸ **fuss over** mimar, consentir, hacer fiestas

fu|ture futuro, porvenir
▸ **in (the) future** en el futuro, en un futuro

fuzzy chino, rizado, crespo, borroso, confuso

FYI para su información

f

Gg

gadg|et instrumento, artefacto, artilugio, aparato, chisme

gag or|der orden mordaza

gag rule ley mordaza

gain ganar, adquirir, salir ganando, subir, cobrar, aumentar, conseguir, lograr, ganancia, incremento
▸ **gain ground** ganar terreno

gal|axy *también* **Galaxy** galaxia

gale vendaval

gal|lery galería

gal|lon galón

gam|ble apuesta, riesgo, jugársela, apostar

gam|bling juego

game juego, deporte, juego de azar, caza, animal de caza, estar dispuesto
▸ **beat somebody at their own game** ganarle a alguien con sus propias armas
▸ **give the game away** abrir las cartas, descubrir el pastel, delatarse

ga|meto|phyte gametofito

gam|ing juego

gam|ma rays rayos gamma

gang pandilla, banda, grupo, grupito, cuadrilla, brigada
▸ **gang up** confabularse contra, tomarla contra

gan|gli|on ganglio

gang|ster gángster, pandillero *o* pandillera, pistolero *o* pistolera

gap espacio, abertura, brecha, separación, intervalo, hueco

gap hy|poth|esis hipótesis de la falla

gar|age garage, garaje, taller

gar|age sale venta de garage

gar|bage basura, porquería

gar|bage can bote de basura, basurero

gar|bage col|lec|tor basurero

gar|bage dis|pos|al triturador, trituradora

gar|bage dump basurero, relleno sanitario, tiradero

gar|bage man basurero

gar|bage truck carro de la basura, camión de la basura

gar|den jardín, trabajar en el jardín, jardinear, hacer el jardín ● **gar|den|er** jardinero ● **gar|den|ing** jardinería

garden-variety lugar común, común y corriente, casero

gar|lic ajo

gar|ment prenda de vestir, ropa

gas gas, gasolina, gasear, asfixiar con gas, matar en la cámara de gases
▸ **step on the gas** pisar el acelerador, acelerar

gas ex|change intercambio de gases, respiración

gas gi|ant gigante gaseoso

gas guz|zler *también* **gas-guzzler** tragón de gasolina

gaso|hol gasohol

gaso|line gasolina

gasp resuello, suspiro, exclamación, suspirar, jadear, respirar con dificultad
▸ **last gasp** último suspiro, últimos momentos

gas pe|dal acelerador

gas sta|tion gasolinera, estación de gasolina

gas tank tanque de gasolina

gate reja, portón, puerta, puerta de embarque

gat|ed com|mu|nity fraccionamiento cerrado

gath|er reunir(se), juntar(se), recoger, acumular, cobrar, tener entendido, deducir
▸ **gather up** juntar, reunir, recoger, acumular

gath|er|ing reunión, asamblea

gator *también* **'gator** caimán, lagarto, cocodrilo

gauge calcular, medir, ponderar, evaluar, valorar, estimar, juzgar, medidor, indicio

gave *ver* **give**

gay gay, homosexual

gaze mirar fijamente, fijar la mirada, quedarse mirando, mirada fija, mirada penetrante

gear transmisión de velocidad, caja de transmisión, velocidad, equipo, herramienta, ropa, uniforme, avíos, orientar, preparar
▸ **gear up** prepararse, orientarse

gear|shift palanca de velocidades

GED GED

geese *ver* **goose**

gel ser compatible, compaginar, cuajar, gel

gela|tin *también* **gelatine** gelatina

gen|der género, sexo

gene gen

gen|er|al general, en general, generalizado
▸ **in general** en general, la generalidad de

gen|er|al elec|tion elecciones generales

gen|er|al hos|pi|tal hospital general

gen|er|al|ize generalizar
● **gen|er|ali|za|tion** generalización

gen|er|al|ly generalmente, en general

gen|er|al store tienda de abarrotes, miscelánea

gen|er|ate generar, producir, provocar

gen|era|tion generación

gen|era|tion time periodo generacional

gen|era|tor generador

ge|ner|ic genérico, general, no de marca

gen|er|ous generoso, amplio ● **gen|er|os|ity** generosidad ● **gen|er|ous|ly** generosamente

ge|net|ic genético
● **ge|neti|cal|ly** genéticamente

ge|neti|cal|ly-modi|fied modificado genéticamente

ge|net|ic en|gi|neer|ing ingeniería genética

ge|net|ics genética

ge|ni|us genio, genialidad, don

geno|cide genocidio

geno|type genotipo

gen|re género

gen|tle suave, moderado, discreto, tierno, cortés, caballeroso, bajo ● **gen|tly** suavemente, cortésmente
● **gen|tle|ness** suavidad

gentle|man caballero, señor

genu|ine genuino, verdadero, auténtico, legítimo, sincero, honesto
● **genu|ine|ly** realmente

geo|graphi|cal *también* **geographic** geográfico
● **geo|graphi|cal|ly** geográficamente

ge|og|ra|phy geografía

geo|logi|cal time scale *también* **geological timescale** escala del tiempo geológico

ge|ol|ogy geología
● **geo|logi|cal** geológico
● **ge|olo|gist** geólogo *o* geóloga

g

geo|met|ric se|quence *también* geometric progression secuencia geométrica

ge|om|etry geometría

geo|sta|tion|ary *también* geosynchronous geoestacionario

geo|ther|mal en|er|gy energía geotérmico

germ germen, microbio, origen

Ger|man shep|herd pastor alemán

ger|mi|nate germinar, tomar forma • ger|mi|na|tion germinación

ges|ta|tion pe|ri|od periodo de gestación, gestación

ges|ture ademán, seña, gesto, hacer gestos, hacer señas, señalar

ges|ture draw|ing dibujo gestual

get conseguir, sacar, obtener, recibir, llegar a ser, llegar a estar, preparar(se), empezar a, lograr, convencer, persuadir, poner(se), poder, hacer, afectar, dar, traer, vender, sentir, tener la sensación, entender, contraer, tomar
▸ get across hacer(se) entender
▸ get along llevarse bien
▸ get around sortear, evitar, sacarle la vuelta a, eludir, circular, viajar, desplazarse, caminar
▸ get around to encontrar el momento para
▸ get at llegar, descubrir, querer decir, querer llegar
▸ get away irse, alejarse, salir de vacaciones, escapar(se)
▸ get away with salirse con la suya, escaparse
▸ get back recuperar
▸ get back to regresar, volver, volver a ponerse en contacto, llamar

▸ get by arreglárselas
▸ get down deprimir, agacharse, ponerse en el piso
▸ get down to empezar, ponerse a
▸ get in ser electo, resultar electo, ganar
▸ get into entrar en, participar, meterse, ser aceptado, ser admitido
▸ get off librar(se), salir(se)
▸ get on seguir adelante
▸ get on to llegar a, pasar a
▸ get out irse, saberse, hacerse público
▸ get out of librarse de, salvarse de
▸ get over recuperarse, superar, resolver
▸ get through terminar, sobrevivir, lograr comunicarse, conseguir comunicarse
▸ get together reunir(se), juntarse, formar, organizar, juntar
▸ get up levantarse, pararse

get-go
▸ from the get-go desde el principio

ghet|to gueto

ghost fantasma

GI soldado estadounidense, GI

gi|ant gigante, gigantesco

gi|ant pan|da panda, panda gigante

gift regalo, presente, obsequio, don, talento

gift cer|tifi|cate certificado de regalo

gift|ed de talento, talentoso

gig tocada, performance

gi|ga|byte gigabyte

gi|gan|tic gigantesco

gig|gle reírse nerviosamente, risa nerviosa

gill branquia

gilt dorado, enchapado en oro

gin|ger jengibre, anaranjado, pelirrojo

gi|raffe jirafa

girl niña, muchacha

girl|friend novia, amiga

give dar, hacer, donar, otorgar, dar de sí, ceder, doblarse
  ▶ **be given to** dar a entender, hacer creer
  ▶ **give thought/attention (to)** pensar en, prestar atención
  ▶ **give and take** concesiones mutuas, toma y daca
  ▶ **give or take** más o menos
  ▶ **give away** pasar, regalar, revelar, translucir
  ▶ **give back** devolver, regresar
  ▶ **give in** rendirse, acceder
  ▶ **give off** o **give out** despedir
  ▶ **give/hand out** repartir
  ▶ **give over to** o **give up to** dedicar, reservar
  ▶ **give up** abandonar, darse por vencido, renunciar
  ▶ **give up to** ver **give over to**

giv|en ver **give**, dado, determinado, de tener

gla|cial glacial

gla|cial drift morena

glaci|er glaciar

glad contento ● **glad|ly** gustosamente, con gusto

glam|or ver **glamour**

glam|or|ous glamoroso

glam|our también **glamor** glamour

glance echar un vistazo, ojear, hojear, mirada
  ▶ **at first glance** a primera vista

gland glándula

glare mirar furiosamente, deslumbrar, resplandor, mirada furiosa, bajo los reflectores

glar|ing flagrante
  ● **glar|ing|ly** flagrantemente

glass vidrio, vaso, objetos de vidrio
  ▶ **glasses** lentes, anteojos

glass slide ver **slide**

glazed vidrioso, vidriado, con vidrio

gleam resplandecer, atisbo

glid|er planeador

glimpse vistazo, vislumbrar, divisar, probadita

glit|ter destellar, brillo

glob|al global ● **glob|al|ly** globalmente

glob|al po|si|tion|ing sys|tem sistema de posicionamiento global

glob|al vil|lage aldea global

glob|al warm|ing calentamiento global

globe Tierra, globo, mundo, globo terráqueo

globu|lar clus|ter cúmulo globular

gloom penumbra, desaliento

gloomy sombrío, tétrico, desalentado ● **gloomi|ly** con tristeza, desalentador

glo|ri|ous espléndido, magnífico, soberbio
  ● **glo|ri|ous|ly** magníficamente, glorioso

glo|ry gloria

glove guante

glow resplandor, rubor, oleada, brillar con luz tenue, enrojecer, resplandecer

glu|cose glucosa

glue pegamento, pegar(se), clavar(se)

GM transgénico

GM-free no transgénicos

GMO organismo transgénico

GMT hora (media) de Greenwich

go ir(se), avanzar, salir, andar, deshacerse, perderse, descomponerse, fundirse, corresponder, quedar bien, volverse, intento, prueba, turno
  ▶ **make a go of** salir adelante, sacar adelante
  ▶ **on the go** no parar, no descansar

g

▸ to go faltar, para llevar
▸ go about abordar, emprender, empezar, estar ocupado en
▸ go after ir por
▸ go against ir en contra de
▸ go ahead seguir adelante, llevarse a cabo
▸ go along with secundar, estar de acuerdo
▸ go around ir, alcanzar
▸ go away irse
▸ go back on no cumplir con
▸ go back to regresar a
▸ go before presentar ante
▸ go by pasar
▸ go down bajar, ponerse, hundirse, caerse
▸ go for decidirse por, optar por, irse sobre
▸ go in meterse
▸ go in for practicar
▸ go into entrar en, entrar, llevar
▸ go off explotar, activarse, apagarse
▸ go on seguir, suceder, transcurrir, continuar, encender
▸ go out salir
▸ go over revisar
▸ go round ver go around atravesar, pasar por
▸ go through with llevar a cabo, cumplir
▸ go under hundirse, quebrar
▸ go up subir, estallar, incendiarse
▸ go with ir acompañado de, acompañar
▸ go without arreglárselas sin

go-ahead visto bueno, luz verde, emprendedor, decidido, con empuje
goal portería, gol, meta
goalie portero o portera
goal|keeper portero o portera
goal|post también goal post poste de la portería
goat chivo, cabra

gob pedazo, montón
go-cart también go-kart go kart
god Dios, dios
god|dess diosa
GOES satélites meteorológicos geoestacionarios
gog|gles goggles, gafas
going actual
▸ the going las cosas
▸ be going to ir a
▸ have something/a lot going for you tener algo/mucho a su favor
▸ get going moverse
▸ keep going seguir adelante
goings-on tejemanejes
gold oro, objeto de oro, dorado
gold|en dorado, de oro, excelente
gold|fish pez dorado
gold med|al medalla de oro
golf golf • golf|er golfista • golf|ing golf
golf club palo de golf, club de golf
Golgi com|plex también Golgi body, Golgi apparatus aparato de Golgi
gone ver go, retirado, ausente
gong gong
gon|na ir a
good bueno, bien, considerado
▸ as good as a punto
▸ be no good no sirve de nada
▸ for good para siempre
▸ good at bueno en
▸ make good cumplir
good after|noon buenas tardes
good|bye también good-bye adiós, despedida
good guy bueno
good-humored de buen humor, alegre, jovial,

amistoso

good-looking guapo

good-natured de buen carácter

good|ness bondad
▸ **goodness/my goodness** válgame Dios, Dios mío

goods productos, bienes

good|will buena voluntad

goody bag muestra gratis, bolsita de dulces

goof
▸ **goof off** flojear

goose ganso

gore cornear, sangre coagulada

gorge desfiladero, hartarse de

gor|geous guapísimo, magnífico

go|ril|la gorila

gos|pel evangelio, gospel, pura verdad

gos|sip chisme, chismear, chismoso o chismosa

got ver get
▸ **have got** tener
▸ **have got to** tener que, deber

got|ta tener que

got|ten ver get

gov|ern gobernar, regir

gov|ern|ment gobierno
● **gov|ern|men|tal** gubernamental

gov|er|nor gobernador o gobernadora, consejero o consejera

gown vestido de gala, toga

GP también **G.P.** médico familiar o médica familiar, médico de cabecera o médica de cabecera

GPA promedio

GPS GPS

grab agarrar, alcanzar, intento de agarrar
▸ **up for grabs** libre, disponible

grab bag bolsa de sorpresas, caja de sorpresas, montón

de cosas varias

grace gracia, adornar, dar las gracias

grace|ful elegante
● **grace|ful|ly** graciosamente

grad licenciado o licenciada, graduado o graduada

grade calificar, calidad, calificación, grado, categoría, pendiente
▸ **make the grade** dar la talla, tener éxito

grade point av|er|age también **grade-point average** promedio

grad|ual gradual
● **gradu|al|ly** gradualmente

gradu|ate licenciado o licenciada, egresado o egresada, graduado o graduada, graduarse, ascender

gradu|at|ed graduado

gradu|ate stu|dent estudiante de posgrado

gradua|tion graduación

graf|fi|ti grafiti

gra|ham crack|er galleta de harina de trigo integral

grain grano, pizca, veta
▸ **go against the grain** ir a contracorriente, ir contra

gram gramo

gram|mar gramática, redacción, expresión

gram|mati|cal gramatical, correcto

gramme ver gram

grand majestuoso, grande, gran, que se cree superior, creído, mil dólares o mil libras

grand|child nieto o nieta

grand|dad abuelito

grand|daughter nieta

grand|father abuelo

grand jury jurado de acusación

grand|ma abuelita

grand|mother abuela

grand|pa abuelito

grand|parent abuelo o abuela

grand slam gran slam, jonrón con las bases llenas

grand|son nieto

gran|ny *también* **grannie** abuelita

gra|no|la granola

grant subsidio, beca, otorgar, reconocer
▶ **take for granted** no valorar, dar por sentado o dar por descontado

grape uva
▶ **sour grapes** inalcanzable, carente de valor

grape|fruit toronja

grape|vine
▶ **on the grapevine** por vía secreta, contado por un pajarito

graph gráfica

graph|ic gráfico
● **graphi|cal|ly** gráficamente
● **graphics** gráficas, diseño gráfico

grasp agarrar, comprender, apretón, comprensión
▶ **be in one's grasp** tener en las manos
▶ **slip from one's grasp** perder de las manos
▶ **within grasp** al alcance

grass pasto

grass|land pastizal, pradera

grass|roots bases

grate chimenea, rallar, chirriar, irritar

grate|ful agradecido
● **grate|ful|ly** con agradecimiento

grat|er rallador

grati|fy satisfacer
● **grati|fy|ing** satisfactorio
● **grati|fi|ca|tion** satisfacción

grati|tude gratitud

grave tumba, grave, serio
● **grave|ly** gravemente

grav|eled de grava

grave|yard shift turno de noche, turno nocturno

gravi|ta|tion|al gravitacional

gravi|ta|tion|al po|ten|tial en|er|gy energía potencial gravitacional

gra|vit|ro|pism gravitropismo

grav|ity gravedad

gra|vy salsa (hecha con el jugo de la carne asada)

gray gris

gray area terreno o materia poco definidos

gray mat|ter materia gris

graze pastar, rasparse, arañarse, rozar, rasguño

grease grasa, engrasar

great grande, maravilloso, qué bien ● **great|ly** muy
● **great|ness** grandeza

Great Red Spot La Gran Mancha Roja

greed codicia

greedy codicioso ● **greedi|ly** avaramente

Greek thea|ter teatro griego

green verde, hoyo
● **green|ness** verdor

green|house invernadero

green|house ef|fect efecto invernadero

green|house gas gas invernadero

green on|ion cebollita, cebolla cambray, cebollino

green plant planta verde

green tea té verde

greet saludar, acoger, recibir

greet|ing saludo

greet|ing card tarjeta de felicitación

grew *ver* **grow**

grid|lock paralización del tráfico, punto muerto

grief pena, dolor
▶ **come to grief** irse al traste

grieve estar de luto por alguien, llorar a alguien

grill parrilla, asar a la parrilla, acribillar a preguntas ● **grill|ing**

interrogatorio

grim desalentador, sombrío, lúgubre

grin sonreír, sonrisa

grind moler, incrustar, meter, talacha
▸ **grind to a halt** estancarse, detenerse con gran chirrido de frenos
▸ **grind down** avasallar

grip agarrar, acto de sujetar algo con fuerza, control, atrapado ● **grip|ping** que lo atrapa a uno
▸ **come to grips with** enfrentarse a
▸ **get a grip** dominarse

groan gemir, gemido

gro|cer tendero o tendera, tienda de abarrotes

gro|cery tienda de abarrotes, abarrotes, comestibles

groin ingle, entrepierna

groom novio, mozo de cuadra, cepillar, preparar

groove ranura

gross extremo, asqueroso, bruto, en bruto ● **gross|ly** escandalosamente

ground suelo, tierra, terreno, lugar, área, razón, molido, fundamentar, detener en tierra, *ver* grind
● **grounds** jardines
▸ **off the ground** despegar
▸ **stand one's ground/ hold one's ground** no ceder terreno, mantenerse firme
▸ **middle ground** medio plano

grounds|keeper encargado o encargada

ground|water aguas freáticas, agua subterránea, agua del subsuelo

ground zero *también* **Ground Zero** zona cero

group grupo, agrupar

grove arboleda

grow crecer, cultivar, dejarse crecer, volverse, aumentar
● **grow|er** cultivador o cultivadora

▸ **grow apart** distanciarse
▸ **grow into** ajustar, ir bien
▸ **grow on** empezar a gustar
▸ **grow out of** pasar una etapa, dejar algo atrás, dejar de quedar
▸ **grow up** criarse, madurar, surgir

grown adulto

grown-up adulto o adulta, mayor

growth crecimiento, tumor

grudge rencor

grudg|ing con renuencia, a regañadientes ● **grudg|ing|ly** a regañadientes

grunge grunge, mugre ● **grungy** mugroso

grunt work trabajo pesado, talacha

gua|nine guanina

guar|an|tee garantizar, garantía

guard vigilar, custodiar, proteger, vigilante, custodio, guardia, barbiquejo, barboquejo
▸ **catch somebody off guard** coger a alguien desprevenido
▸ **on one's guard** en guardia
▸ **guard against** prevenir

guard cell célula oclusiva, célula de guarda

guard|ian tutor o tutora, defensor o defensora

guer|ril|la *también* **guerilla** guerrillero o guerrillera

guess adivinar, pensar, cálculo, intento de calcular algo
▸ **I guess** supongo

guest invitado o invitada, huésped

guest house casa de huéspedes

guest of hon|or invitado de honor o invitada de honor

GUI Interfaz Gráfica de Usuario

guid|ance orientación, consejos

g

guid|ance coun|se|lor orientador vocacional u orientadora vocacional

guide guía, guiar, idea, conducir

guide|line pauta

guild gremio

guilt culpa, culpabilidad

guilty culpable • **guilti|ly** con aire de culpabilidad, vergonzoso

gui|tar guitarra • **gui|tar|ist** guitarrista

G

gulch barranco

gulf abismo, golfo

gul|ly también **gulley** barranco, hondonada

gum chicle, encía

gum|ball bolita de chicle

gun arma
▶ **stick to one's guns** mantenerse firme
▶ **gun down** tumbar a tiros, matar a tiros

gun|fire disparos

gun|man pistolero

gun|point
▶ **at gunpoint** a punta de pistola

gur|ney camilla

gut vísceras, tripas, intestino, agallas, destripar, limpiar (pescado), destruir (interior de edificio)
▶ **gut reaction** reacción instintiva, reacción visceral

guy tipo, chavo

gym gimnasio, gimnasia

gym|na|sium gimnasio

gym|no|sperm gimnosperma

gyro giroscopio

gyro|scope giroscopio

Hh

H alta presión

hab|it hábito, drogadicción
▸ **be in the habit of/get into the habit of/make a habit of** hacerse el hábito

habi|tat hábitat

hack cortar, hackear, escritor mercenario o escritora mercenaria ● **hack|er** hacker ● **hack|ing** hackear

had ver have

hadn't = had not

hail ser aclamado, hacerle señas a, granizo

hair cabello, pelo, vello

hair|cut corte de pelo

hairy peludo, escalofriante

half medio, media, mitad, tiempo (en deportes)

half-hour media hora

half-life también **half life** vida media

half note blanca, mitad

half|time medio tiempo

half|way a la mitad, a la mitad de, a medio

hall vestíbulo, pasillo, corredor, salón, sala

Hal|ley's com|et cometa Halley

Hal|low|een también **Hallowe'en** noche de brujas, Halloween

hall|way pasillo, recibidor

halo|gen halógeno

halo|phile halófila

halt detener(se), parar(se), interrumpir

halve reducir a la mitad, partir en dos, dividir en dos, ver half

ham jamón

ham|burg|er hamburguesa

ham|mer martillo, clavar, golpear, castigar

▸ **hammer out** negociar

ham|per dificultar, canasta, cesto

hand mano, juego, manecilla, (echar la) mano, dar (con la mano)
▸ **at hand** a la mano
▸ **by hand** a mano
▸ **change hands** pasar de mano en mano
▸ **a free hand** entera libertad
▸ **hand in hand** ir (tomado) de la mano
▸ **have a hand in something** tener que ver con
▸ **in hand** bajo control
▸ **live hand to mouth** vivir al día
▸ **on hand** a la mano
▸ **on the one hand** por una parte
▸ **on the other hand** sin embargo
▸ **get out of hand** salir(se) de control, fuera de control
▸ **try your hand** probar suerte
▸ **wash one's hands of somebody/something** lavarse las manos de alguien/algo
▸ **hand down** transmitir
▸ **hand in** entregar
▸ **hand on** ver hand down
▸ **hand out** repartir
▸ **hand over** dar, transferir

hand|bag bolsa (de mano)

hand|ful (unos) cuantos, puñado, travieso o traviesa

handi|cap impedimento, desventaja, (poner en) desventaja

handi|capped impedido

hand|ker|chief pañuelo

han|dle manija, mango, asa, manejar, poder (manejar una situación), ocuparse (de algo), encargarse (de algo), manipular • han|dling manejo

hand|made *también* hand-made hecho a mano

hand-me-down ropa heredada

hand|out dádiva, folleto informativo, notas

hands-free manos libres

hand|shake apretón de manos

hands-off de no intromisión

hand|some guapo, bueno, generoso

hand|writing letra

hand|written escrito a mano, manuscrito

handy práctico, a la mano

hang colgar, caerle a alguien, ahorcar(se), amenazar
▸ get the hang of something agarrarle la onda (a algo)
▸ hang back hacer(se) para atrás
▸ hang on esperar, aguantar, mantener, aferrarse a, depender de
▸ hang out tender, pasar el rato
▸ hang up colgar

hang|er colgador, gancho

hang|ing val|ley valle pendiente

hang|ing wall pared colgante

hap|pen suceder, ocurrir
▸ as it happens sucede que

hap|pi|ly afortunadamente

hap|py feliz, contento, con gusto • hap|pi|ly felizmente
• hap|pi|ness felicidad

har|bor puerto, guardar, albergar

har|bor|master *también* harbor master capitán *o* capitana de puerto

hard duro, difícil, fuerte, concreto, definitivo, con dureza • hard|ness dureza
▸ hard going muy difícil

hard|ball
▸ play hardball ser despiadado

hard ci|der sidra

hard core *también* hard-core de hueso colorado

hard|cover libro de pasta dura

hard disk disco duro

hard drive disco duro

hard-earned ganado con dificultad

hard|en endurecer(se)
• hard|en|ing endurecimiento

hard la|bor trabajos forzados

hard-line *también* hardline de línea dura

hard|ly apenas, casi

hard|ship apuro, privación

hard|ware hardware, ferretería

har|dy resistente

harm daño, hacer daño, lastimar

harm|ful dañino

harm|less inofensivo

har|mon|ic pro|gres|sion progresión armónica

har|mo|ny armonía

harp arpa
▸ harp on insistir en, machacar acerca de

har|row|ing espeluznante

harsh áspero, duro
• harsh|ness aspereza, dureza • harsh|ly duramente

har|vest cosecha, cosechar

has *ver* have

hasn't = has not

has|ty apresurado • has|ti|ly apresuradamente

hat sombrero

hatch salir del cascarón (las crías), romperse (el cascarón), tramar, escotilla

hate odiar, odio

ha|tred odio

haul arrastrar
▸ long haul viaje largo y cansado

haunt perseguir, rondar, lugar favorito

have haber, tener, tomar
▶ **have a baby** dar a luz, estar embarazada
▶ **have something done** mandar hacer
▶ **have something happen** suceder
▶ **have to do** tener que hacer algo
▶ **rumour/legend/tradition has it** se dice

ha|ven refugio

haven't = have not

hawk halcón

hay heno

haz|ard peligro, riesgo, aventurar

haz|ing novatada

hazy brumoso, vago, incierto

HDTV HDTV

he él

head cabeza, mente, jefe *o* jefa, cabecera, principio, cara, sol, encabezar, ir al frente, dirigir(se), estar a la cabeza, ir(se), ir hacia, cabecear
▶ **heads up!** ¡cuidado!
▶ **a/per head** cada uno, por cabeza, por persona
▶ **come to a head/bring something to a head** hacer crisis
▶ **get something into one's head** meterse algo en la cabeza
▶ **go to one's head** subírsele a la cabeza, subírsele a la cabeza
▶ **keep one's head** mantener la calma
▶ **lose one's head** perder la calma, perder la cabeza
▶ **be over somebody's head** no entender

head|ache dolor de cabeza, cefalea, problema, preocupación, quebradero de cabeza

head|light faro

head|line encabezado, encabezamiento, resumen de noticias
▶ **hit/grab the headlines**

ser noticia, aparecer en las noticias

head|master director (de escuela), rector (de escuela)

head of state jefe de estado *o* jefa de estado

head-on de frente, frontal, frontalmente

head|phones audífonos, auriculares

head|quarters oficina central, cuartel general, jefatura de policía

heads-up aviso

head|waters *también* head-waters, head waters naciente, cabecera

heal curar, sanar, cicatrizar, soldar, remediar(se), componer(se), corregir

health salud, bienestar, prosperidad

health care *también* healthcare atención de la salud, política sanitaria

health cen|ter centro de salud, centro médico

health main|te|nance or|gani|za|tion servicios médicos exclusivos para un grupo específico

healthy saludable, sano, robusto, floreciente, abundante ● **healthi|ly** saludablemente

heap montón, pila, amontonar, apilar, acumular, colmar de, prodigar(se) ● **heaps** montones, muchos

heap|ing colmado

hear oír, escuchar
▶ **hear from** saber de, oír de
▶ **hear of** llegar a saber
▶ **won't/wouldn't hear of something** no querer saber nada de algo

hear|ing oído, audición, audiencia, vista, sesión, juicio
▶ **give a fair hearing** escuchar con imparcialidad

heart corazón, miocardio, espíritu, generosidad, centro, núcleo
▸ **at heart** en el fondo
▸ **break somebody's heart** romper el corazón a alguien, arrancar el alma a alguien
▸ **by heart** de memoria
▸ **have a change of heart** cambiar de opinión
▸ **close to one's heart/ near to one's heart** muy importante
▸ **from the heart/from the bottom of one's heart** con toda sinceridad
▸ **take heart** tomar aliento
▸ **take something to heart** tomar algo a pecho
▸ **with all one's heart** profundamente

heart at|tack ataque al corazón, ataque cardíaco

heart-stopping *también* **heartstopping** impresionante, que quita el aliento, emocionante

heart|worm gusano del corazón

hearty sincero, cordial, enérgico, espontáneo, abundante • **hearti|ly** con entusiasmo, completamente, abundantemente

heat calor, calentar
▸ **heat up** calentar(se), recalentar

heat|ed acalorado, caldeado • **heat|ed|ly** acaloradamente

heat en|gine máquina térmica, termomotor, motor térmico

heat|er calentador, calefactor, calentón

heav|en cielo, paraíso
▸ **(good) heavens** ¡por Dios!, ¡Dios mío!
▸ **heaven knows** no saber nadie

heavy pesado, intenso, fuerte, profundo, cargado, duro, difícil

• **heavi|ness** peso
• **heavi|ly** intensamente, pesadamente

heavy cream doble crema

heavy-duty muy resistente

heavy|weight peso pesado, pez gordo

he'd = he had *o* he would

hedge seto, cubrirse, protegerse
▸ **hedge one's bets** cubrirse

hedge|hog cac|tus cactus erizo

heel talón, tacón, taco

height altura, estatura, altitude
▸ **at its height** en la cima, en la cumbre
▸ **the height of** lo más alto

height|en aumentar, acrecentar, incrementar(se)

heir heredero *o* heredera

held *ver* hold

heli|cop|ter helicóptero

he|lix hélice

hell infierno, lo peor

he'll = he will

hel|lo *también* **hullo** saludo, bueno, diga

hel|met casco, yelmo, careta (de esgrima)

help ayudar, socorrer, asistir, colaborar, favorecer, servir(se), ayuda, asistencia, auxilio, socorro
▸ **be of help** ayudar, ser útil
▸ **help out** ayudar, echar una mano

help desk help desk, centro de ayuda (remota)

help|er ayudante, asistente *o* asistenta

help|ful útil, servicial, conveniente, beneficioso • **help|ful|ly** con amabilidad

help|less impotente, sin recursos, desvalido • **help|less|ly** con impotencia • **help|less|ness** indefensión

hema|tol|ogy hematología

hemi|sphere hemisferio

hen gallina

hence por lo tanto

her la/le/se/ella, su/sus

her|ald anunciar, presagiar, proclamar, portavoz, precursor o precursora, heraldo

herb hierba, yerba • **herb|al** de hierbas

her|bi|vore herbívoro

herbivorous herbívoro

herd hato, rebaño, manada, agrupar, arriar

here aquí, en este punto

he|red|ity herencia

her|it|age patrimonio, legado

hero héroe o heroína, protagonista

he|ro|ic heroico, colosal • **he|roi|cal|ly** heroicamente

hero|in heroína

hero|ine heroína, protagonista

hers de ella

her|self ella misma, se

Hertz|sprung-Rus|sell dia|gram diagrama de Hertzsprung-Russell, diagrama HR

he's = he is o he has

hesi|tate dudar, vacilar • **hesi|ta|tion** duda

hetero|geneous heterogéneo, mixto

hetero|geneous mix|ture mezcla heterogénea

hetero|sex|ual heterosexual • **hetero|sexu|al|ity** heterosexualidad

hexa|gon hexágono

hey ¡eh!, ¡oye!, ¡oiga!, hola

hi hola

hi|ber|nate hibernar, invernar

hi|ber|na|tion hibernación

hicko|ry nogal americano

hid ver hide

hid|den ver hide, oculto, secreto, escondido

hide esconder(se), ocultar, piel, pellejo

hid|eous espantoso, horrible, monstruoso, horroroso, horrendo • **hid|eous|ly** espantosamente

hid|ing escondido

hi|er|ar|chy jerarquía • **hi|er|ar|chi|cal** jerárquico

high alto, elevado, arriba, en alto, por encima, fuerte, intenso, violento, rico, abundante, importante, gran, muy bueno, agudo, animado, contento, lo más alto
  ▸ **high up** en lo alto, muy arriba
  ▸ **high priority** prioritario, lo más importante

high beams luces altas

high-class de gran clase

high|er edu|ca|tion educación superior

high fi|del|ity también **high-fidelity** alta fidelidad

high-frequency word palabra de uso frecuente

high-impact de alto impacto

high|lands tierras altas, altiplanicie

high|light destacar, sacar a relucir, evento más importante

high|light|er marcador, rotulador, sombra clara de ojos

high|ly sumamente, alto
  ▸ **think highly of** tener un gran concepto de

high-maintenance también **high maintenance** de mucho mantenimiento

high power lens objetivo de gran aumento

high road camino del éxito, el mejor camino

high school bachillerato, preparatoria, liceo

high-stakes Hay mucho en juego

high-strung muy nervioso

h

high-tech *también* **high tech, hi tech** de alta tecnología

high tech|nol|ogy alta tecnología

high tide marea alta

high|way carretera

high|way pa|trol policía de caminos

hike caminata, excursión, ir de caminata, ir de excursión, subir, incrementar • **hik|er** caminante • **hik|ing** ir de caminata

hi|lari|ous comiquísimo, muy cómico • **hi|lari|ous|ly** de manera muy cómica

hill colina

hilly accidentado

him él, lo, le

him|self se, sí mismo, él mismo, en persona

Hin|du hindú

hint indirecta, insinuación, consejo, tip, dejo, insinuar

hip cadera, in, en la onda

hire contratar
▶ **hire out** ofrecer un servicio

his su, suyo

His|pan|ic latino, hispano

his|to|gram histograma, gráfica de barras

his|to|rian historiador *o* historiadora

his|tor|ic histórico

his|tori|cal histórico
• **his|tori|cal|ly** históricamente

his|to|ry historia, historial, antecedentes
▶ **make history** hacer historia
▶ **go down in history** pasar a la historia

hit golpear, afectar, darse cuenta, atinar, golpe, éxito, visita
▶ **hit it off** congeniar
▶ **hit on** *o* **hit upon** dar con
▶ **hit up** pedir

hit-and-miss *también* **hit and miss** un volado, una lotería

hit-and-run accidente en el que el conductor se da a la fuga

HIV VIH
▶ **HIV positive/negative** VIH positivo/negativo

HMO servicios médicos exclusivos para un grupo específico

hoarse ronco • **hoarse|ly** de manera ronca

hob|by pasatiempo, hobby

hobo vagabundo *o* vagabunda, trabajador *o* trabajadora itinerante

hock|ey hockey

hoe azadón

hog puerco, acaparar

hold sujetar, tomar, mantener, tener, guardar, contener, causar, celebrar, llevar a cabo, esperar, control, bodega • **holder** poseedor
▶ **get hold of (something)** conseguir algo
▶ **get/grab hold of (something)** agarrar algo, asir algo
▶ **get hold of (somebody)** encontrar a alguien
▶ **hold an opinion** tener una opinión
▶ **hold it!** ¡espere!, ¡alto!
▶ **hold one's own** saber defenderse
▶ **put something on hold** posponer algo
▶ **take hold** apoderarse
▶ **hold against** guardar rencor a
▶ **hold back** contenerse, inhibir(se), ocultar
▶ **hold down** mantener
▶ **hold off** posponer
▶ **hold on** *o* **hold onto** aferrarse, mantener la ventaja
▶ **hold out** tender la mano, aguantar
▶ **hold up** retrasar, asaltar

hold|er contenedor

hold|ing inversión

hold|ing pat|tern vuelo en círculos, estancado

hold|over miembro veterano, resto, vestigio

hole hoyo
▸ in the hole en números rojos

holi|day día feriado

hol|low hueco, hundido, hondonada, vano, falso
• hol|low|ness falsedad

holy sagrado

Holy Land Tierra Santa

holy war guerra santa

home casa, hogar, asilo, tierra, en casa, local
▸ at home en casa
▸ drive/hammer something home hacer entender algo

home|body hogareño u hogareña

home field campo local

home front frente interno

home|land patria

home|less sin hogar
• home|less|ness falta de vivienda
▸ the homeless los que no tienen hogar

home|made casero

home|maker ama de casa

homeo|sta|sis homeostasis
• homeo|stat|ic homeostático

home plate base del bateador, home

home|room aula del curso

home run jonrón

home school|ing también home-schooling educación en casa

home|sick
▸ be homesick for sentir nostalgia por, añorar

home|sick|ness añoranza

home|work tarea
▸ do one's homework prepararse, investigar

homey acogedor

homi|nid homínido

homo|geneous mixture mezcla homogénea

homo|graph homógrafo

ho|molo|gous homólogo

homo|pho|bia homofobia
• ho|mo|pho|bic homofóbico

homo|phone homófono

homo sa|pi|ens Homo sapiens

homo|sex|ual homosexual
• homo|sex|ual|ity homosexualidad

hon|est honesto, te lo juro
• hon|est|ly honestamente

hon|est|ly ¡por favor!

hon|es|ty honestidad

hon|ey miel, cariño

honey|moon luna de miel, ir de luna de miel

hon|or honor, honrar, cumplir (con)
▸ your/his/her honor su Señoría
▸ in honor of en honor de

hon|or|able men|tion mención honorífica

hon|or roll cuadro de honor

hon|or sys|tem atendiendo sólo a la palabra

hood capucha, cofre, cubierta

hoof casco, pezuña

hook gancho, enganchar
▸ be off the hook librarse, descolgar
▸ ringing off the hook sonar constantemente
▸ hook up engancharse, relacionarse, ligar(se), hacer buenas migas, unirse, conectar(se)

hoop|la con bombo y platillo

hooves ver hoof

hop saltar con un pie, saltar en un pie, brincar de cojito, dar saltitos, ir rápidamente, salto con un pie, saltito, vuelo corto

hope esperar, esperanza
▸ hope for the best esperar que (alguien) tenga suerte
▸ in the hope of/that con la esperanza de

hope|ful esperanzado, optimista, esperanzador

hope|ful|ly con suerte

hope|less desesperado, sin esperanzas, no tener remedio, un desastre • **hope|less|ly** sin esperanzas • **hope|less|ness** desesperanza

ho|ri|zon horizonte
▸ **on the horizon** en puerta

hori|zon|tal horizontal • **hori|zon|tal|ly** horizontalmente

hor|mone hormona • **hor|mo|nal** hormonal

horn claxon, cuerno, pico piramidal

hor|ri|ble horrible • **hor|ri|bly** horriblemente

hor|ri|fy horrorizar • **hor|ri|fy|ing** horroroso

hor|ror horror, de horror

horse caballo

horse|back rid|ing equitación, montar

hose manguera, regar

hos|pice residencia para enfermos desahuciados

hos|pi|tal hospital

hos|pi|tal|ity hospitalidad

host anfitrión o anfitriona, ofrecer, ser la sede de, presentar, sede, presentador o presentadora, gran cantidad, huésped

hos|tage rehén
▸ **take/hold somebody hostage** tomar a alguien como rehén

host|ess anfitriona

hos|tile opuesto a, hostil • **hos|til|ity** hostilidad

hos|til|ities hostilidades

hot caliente, caluroso, picoso, popular, de actualidad, tener calor

hot but|ton punto caliente

hot dog hot dog

ho|tel hotel

hot spot también **hotspot** punto caliente

hound sabueso, acosar

hour hora
▸ **on the hour** a la hora en punto

house casa, los de la casa, Cámara, alojar, albergar

house|hold casa, familia, hogar, personal, conocido

house-sit cuidar la casa

house|wife ama de casa

house|work tareas domésticas

hous|ing viviendas

hous|ing proj|ect complejo de viviendas

hov|er mantenerse inmóvil en el aire, vacilar

how cómo, cuánto, qué tal, qué tan, qué tanto

how|dy hola

how|ever sin embargo, sin importar, como sea, cómo

howl aullar, dar alaridos, estallar de risa, carcajearse, aullido, alarido, ataque de risa

how-to con información práctica

HQ oficina central

hr = hour

H-R dia|gram también **HRD** diagrama H-R

HTML html

hug abrazar, llevar en los brazos, ir pegado a, abrazo

huge enorme • **huge|ly** enormemente

hull casco

hum zumbar, tararear, zumbido

hu|man humano

hu|man be|ing ser humano

Hu|man Ge|nome Proj|ect Proyecto del Genoma Humano

hu|mani|tar|ian humanitario

hu|man|ity humanidad

hu|man na|ture naturaleza humana

hu|man rights derechos humanos

hum|ble humilde, modesto, dar una lección de humildad
• **hum|bly** con humildad
• **hum|bling** lección de humildad

hu|mid húmedo

hu|mid|ity humedad

hu|mili|ate humillar
• **hu|mili|at|ed** humillado
• **hu|mili|at|ing** humillante

hu|milia|tion humillación

hu|mil|ity humildad

hu|mor humor, seguir la corriente
▶ **in a good/bad humor** de buen/mal humor

hu|mor|less sin sentido del humor

hu|mor|ous divertido, gracioso • **hu|mor|ous|ly** con humor

hump montículo, joroba

hump|back whale ballena jorobada

hu|mus humus

hun|dred cien • **hundreds** cientos, centenares, montones
▶ **a hundred percent/one hundred percent** cien por ciento, totalmente, absolutamente

hun|dredth centésimo, centésima parte

hung ver **hang**, jurado en desacuerdo

hun|ger hambre, ansias, deseo, desear, anhelar, ansiar

hun|gry ansioso, deseoso
▶ **be hungry** estar hambriento, tener hambre
• **hun|gri|ly** ávidamente
▶ **go hungry** pasar hambre

hunker
▶ **hunker down** agacharse, ponerse en cuclillas

hunt buscar, cazar, búsqueda, caza, cacería
• **hunt|ing** búsqueda, caza, cacería

▶ **hunt down** acorralar, capturar, dar caza

hunt|er cazador, cazadora, buscador o buscadora

hur|dle obstáculo, vallas, carrera de obstáculos

hurl lanzar, arrojar

hur|ri|cane huracán

hur|ry apurarse, darse prisa, apresurar(se), apurar, apremiar, prisa, premura
▶ **hurry along o hurry up** apurarse, ir de prisa

hurt lastimar(se), herir(se), hacer(se) daño, doler, tener dolor, hacer sufrir, dañar, estropear, herido, lastimado, ofendido

hus|band esposo, marido

hut cabaña, choza, casucha

hy|brid híbrido

hydro|car|bon hidrocarburo

hydro|elec|tric también **hydro-electric** hidroeléctrico

hydro|elec|tric|ity hidroelectricidad

hydro|gen hidrógeno

hydro|log|ic cy|cle ciclo hidrológico, ciclo del agua

hydro|pon|ics hidroponia, hidroponía
• **hydro|pon|ic** hidropónico
• **hydro|poni|cal|ly** de manera hidropónica

hydro|power energía hidroeléctrica, fuerza hidroeléctrica

hype promoción intensa, promocionar intensamente

hyper|link hipervínculo

hyper|son|ic hipersónico

hy|phen guión

hypo|thala|mus hipotálamo

hy|poth|esis

hys|teri|cal histérico, incontrolable, muy gracioso, muy divertido
• **hys|teri|cal|ly** de forma histérica, histéricamente

hys|ter|ics histeria, histerismo, ataque de risa

h

I i

I yo

ice hielo
▶ **break the ice** romper el hielo

Ice Age glaciación, edad de hielo, periodo glaciar

ice|berg iceberg, témpano de hielo

ice cream helado, nieve

iced helado

ice wa|ter agua fría, agua helada, agua con hielo

ice wedg|ing gelifracción, crioclastia

ici|cle carámbano

icky empalagoso, pegajoso

ID identificación, ID

I'd = I had o I would

ID card identificación, credencial, carné de identidad, carnet de identidad, documento de identificación

idea idea, opinión, concepto, noción, objetivo

ideal ideal ● **ideal|ly** idealmente

ideal|is|tic idealista

ideal|ly lo ideal, de preferencia, lo recomendable

ideal ma|chine máquina ideal

iden|ti|cal idéntico, igual, mismo ● **iden|ti|cal|ly** idénticamente

iden|ti|fi|ca|tion identificación

iden|ti|fi|ca|tion card identificación, credencial, carné de identidad, carnet de identidad, documento de identificación

iden|ti|fy identificar(se), reconocer ● **iden|ti|fi|ca|tion** identificación

iden|tity identidad

iden|tity card identificación, carné de identidad, credencial, cédula de identidad, identificación personal, documento de identificación

iden|tity cri|sis crisis de identidad

iden|tity theft robo de identidad

ideol|ogy ideología
● **ideo|logi|cal** ideológico
● **ideo|logi|cal|ly** ideológicamente

idi|om modismo, expresión idiomática, locución idiomática

idio|phone idiófono

idi|ot idiota, imbécil, necio o necia

idle inactivo, desocupado, sin trabajo, en paro, parado, ocioso, perezoso, flojo, haragán, sin importancia, fútil ● **idly** despreocupadamente, ociosamente

if si, aunque, como si, si es que
▶ **if not** si no es, por no decir

ig|ne|ous ígneo

ig|no|rant ignorante, maleducado ● **ig|no|rance** ignorancia

ig|nore ignorar, no hacer caso

ill enfermo, malo, indispuesto, mal, infortunio, negativo, adverso, desgracia

I'll = I will o I shall

il|legal ilegal, contra las reglas, contra la ley
● **il|legal|ly** ilegalmente

il|legiti|mate ilegítimo

il|lit|er|ate analfabeto

ill|ness enfermedad, mal, padecimiento

il|lu|sion ilusión, impresión

il|lus|trate ilustrar, ejemplificar, mostrar, demostrar, aclarar
• il|lus|tra|tion ejemplo, ilustración

IM mensaje instantáneo, IM

I'm = I am

im|age imagen, idea, representación

im|agi|nary imaginario

im|agi|na|tion imaginación, fantasía

im|agi|na|tive imaginativo
• im|agi|na|tive|ly imaginativamente

im|ag|ine imaginar(se), suponer, figurarse

im|bal|ance desequilibrio, desproporción

imi|tate imitar, copiar, remedar • imi|ta|tor imitador

im|ma|ture inmaduro

im|medi|ate inmediato, urgente, cercano
• im|medi|ate|ly inmediatamente

im|medi|ate|ly inmediatamente, de inmediato

im|mense inmenso, enorme, grandísimo

im|merse sumergir(se), enfrascarse • im|mersed inmerso

im|mi|grant inmigrante

im|mi|gra|tion inmigración, migración

im|mi|nent inminente

im|mor|al inmoral

im|mune inmune
• im|mun|ity inmunidad

im|mune sys|tem sistema inmunitario, sistema inmune

im|mun|ize vacunar, inmunizar

• im|mun|iza|tion inmunización

im|mu|no|de|fi|cien|cy inmunodeficiencia

im|pact impacto, repercusión, efecto, choque, colisión, impactar, afectar

im|pa|tient impaciente, intolerante, ansioso
• im|pa|tient|ly impacientemente
• im|pa|tience impaciencia

im|pede dificultar, obstaculizar, impedir

im|pend|ing inminente

im|pen|etrable impenetrable, incomprensible, inescrutable

im|perial imperial
▸ imperial system (of measurement) sistema inglés de pesos y medidas

im|peri|al|ism imperialismo
• im|peri|al|ist imperialista

im|per|son|al impersonal

im|per|son|ate hacerse pasar, fingir ser, imitar
• im|per|sona|tion suplantación

im|ple|ment implementar, instrumentar, poner en práctica, ejecutar, implemento, utensilio, herramienta, instrumento
• im|ple|men|ta|tion implementación

im|pli|ca|tion implicación, consecuencia, repercusión

im|plic|it implícito, tácito, sobrentendido, incondicional, total, absoluto • im|plic|it|ly implícitamente, incondicionalmente

im|ply sugerir, insinuar, dar a entender

im|port importar, importación • im|por|ta|tion importación • im|port|er importador o importadora
• imports productos

importados

im|por|tant importante, significativo, valioso
● **im|por|tance** importancia

im|pose imponer(se), hacerse aceptar
● **im|po|si|tion** imposición

im|pos|ing imponente, impresionante

im|pos|sible imposible, lo imposible, intolerable, insoportable ● **im|pos|sibly** extremadamente
● **im|pos|sibil|ity** imposibilidad

im|po|tent impotente, inerme, desvalido
● **im|po|tence** impotencia

im|prac|ti|cal poco práctico, impráctico

im|press impresionar, impactar, recalcar, subrayar, inculcar
● **im|pressed** impresionado

im|pres|sion impresión, efecto, imitación, huella, marca, señal
▶ **make a good/bad impression** causar buena/mala impresión
▶ **be under the impression** tener la impresión

im|pres|sive impresionante, emocionante, notable, admirable, digno de admiración, imponente
● **im|pres|sive|ly** admirablemente

im|pris|on encarcelar, encerrar, meter en la cárcel, meter a la cárcel ● **im|pris|on|ment** encarcelamiento

im|prop|er indebido, incorrecto, erróneo, impropio, inadecuado, indecoroso, deshonesto
● **im|prop|er|ly** indebidamente, impropiamente

im|prove mejorar(se), hacer mejoras, perfeccionar(se), superar ● **im|prove|ment** mejora

im|pro|vise improvisar
● **im|provi|sa|tion** improvisación

im|pulse impulso, arranque
▶ **on impulse** por un impulso, en un arranque

im|pul|sive impulsivo
● **im|pul|sive|ly** impulsivamente

in en, de, por, con, dentro, adentro, a la moda, in
▶ **be in** estar en algún lugar, haber llegado
▶ **be in for something** esperar algo
▶ **come in** entrar, llegar, subir (la marea)
▶ **have it in for somebody** estar enojado con alguien
▶ **be in on** participar en, ser parte de
▶ **in that** en el sentido de, porque, ya que

in|abil|ity incapacidad, ineptitud

in|ac|cu|rate inexacto, incorrecto, erróneo
● **in|ac|cu|ra|cy** inexactitud

in|ac|tive inactivo
● **in|ac|tiv|ity** inactividad

in|ad|equate insuficiente, inadecuado, incompetente, no preparado ● **in|ad|equa|cy** insuficiencia, ineptitud
● **in|ad|equate|ly** inadecuadamente

in|ap|pro|pri|ate inadecuado, inoportuno, poco apropiado

in|box también **in-box** bandeja de entrada

Inc. Inc.

in|ca|pable inútil, incapaz, incompetente

in|cen|tive incentivo, estímulo

in|cest incesto

inch pulgada, (mover) lentamente, (mover) paso a paso

in|ci|dent incidente, lo que

pasó

in|ci|den|tal secundario, incidental

in|ci|den|tal|ly a propósito, por cierto

in|cin|er|ate incinerar, quemar • **in|cin|era|tion** incineración

in|ci|sor incisivo

in|cline pendiente, cuesta, declive, inclinar(se), predisponer

in|clined proclive, dispuesto, con la inclinación, con aptitud

in|clined plane plano inclinado

in|clude incluir, abarcar, contener

in|clud|ing incluido, incluso

in|come ingreso

in|come tax impuesto sobre la renta

in|com|ing entrante, que llega

in|com|pe|tent incompetente, inepto • **in|com|pe|tence** incompetencia

in|com|plete incompleto, inconcluso

in|con|ven|ient poco conveniente, inoportuno, inconveniente

in|cor|po|rate incluir, incorporar algo

In|cor|po|rated constituido legalmente, Incorporated

in|cor|rect incorrecto, equivocado, erróneo • **in|cor|rect|ly** incorrectamente

in|crease aumentar, incrementar, crecer, incremento, aumento ▶ **be on the increase** ir en aumento

in|creas|ing|ly cada vez más, en aumento

in|cred|ible increíble • **in|cred|ibly** increíblemente

in|cum|bent funcionario o funcionaria, titular

in|cur incurrir en, acarrear

in|cur|able incurable, incorregible • **in|cur|ably** incurablemente

in|debt|ed en deuda

in|de|cent obsceno, indecente, indecoroso • **in|de|cen|cy** indecencia • **in|de|cent|ly** indecorosamente

in|deed efectivamente, claro está, de hecho, ¡no me digas!, de veras, en serio

in|defi|nite indefinido, indeterminado, incierto, vago, impreciso • **in|defi|nite|ly** indefinidamente

in|defi|nite ar|ti|cle artículo indefinido

in|defi|nite pro|noun pronombre indefinido

in|de|pend|ent independiente • **in|de|pen|dent|ly** de manera independiente • **in|de|pend|ence** independencia

in-depth a fondo, exhaustivo

in|dex índice, índice analítico, hacer un índice, poner en un índice, indexar

in|dex con|tour también index contour line curva de nivel

in|di|cate indicar, señalar, denotar, dar indicios, dar a entender

in|di|ca|tion indicio, idea, pauta

in|di|ca|tor indicador

in|di|ces ver index

in|dif|fer|ent indiferente, insensible, mediocre, regular, del montón • **in|dif|fer|ence** indiferencia • **in|dif|fer|ent|ly** indiferentemente

in|dig|enous indígena, autóctono

in|di|ges|tion indigestión

in|dig|nant indignado
• in|dig|nant|ly de manera indignante

in|di|rect indirecto • in|di|rect|ly indirectamente

in|di|rect dis|course estilo indirecto

in|di|rect ob|ject objeto indirecto

in|di|rect speech estilo indirecto

in|dis|pen|sable indispensable, imprescindible, esencial

in|di|vid|ual individual, cada, personal, individuo, persona, tipo • in|di|vid|ual|ly individualmente

in|door dentro, adentro, en el interior, bajo techo

in|doors en el interior, bajo techo, adentro, dentro

in|duce inducir, provocar, producir, convencer, persuadir

in|duct reclutar

in|dulge consentir, consentirse, darse un gusto, ser complaciente, disfrutar, mimar

in|dul|gent indulgente, consentidor, complaciente, condescendiente
• in|dul|gence indulgencia
• in|dul|gent|ly con indulgencia

in|dus|trial industrial, industrializado

in|dus|tri|al|ist industrial, industrialista

in|dus|tri|al|ize industrializar(se)
• in|dus|tri|ali|za|tion industrialización

in|dus|trial park parque industrial, zona industrial

in|dus|try industria, sector

in|ed|ible incomestible, incomible

in|ef|fec|tual inútil,
incapaz • in|ef|fec|tu|al|ly ineficazmente

in|ef|fi|cient ineficiente, incompetente
• in|ef|fi|cien|cy ineficiencia
• in|ef|fi|cient|ly de manera ineficiente

in|er|tia apatía, inercia

in|evi|table inevitable, ineludible, lo inevitable
• in|evi|tabil|ity inevitabilidad • in|evi|tably inevitablemente

in|ex|pen|sive barato, económico, poco costoso

in|ex|pe|ri|enced inexperto, sin experiencia, novato

in|fa|mous de triste memoria, de mala reputación, infame

in|fan|cy infancia, niñez
▶ in its infancy en pañales

in|fant bebé, criatura

in|fan|try infantería

in|fect infectar, contagiar, contaminar • in|fec|tion infección

in|fec|tion infección, enfermedad

in|fec|tious infeccioso, contagioso

in|fer deducir

in|fe|ri|or inferior, mediocre, subordinado • in|fe|ri|or|ity inferioridad

in|fer|tile infértil, estéril, infecundo • in|fer|til|ity infertilidad

in|fi|del|ity infidelidad

in|field diamante, centro

in|fil|trate infiltrar(se)
• in|fil|tra|tion infiltración

in|fi|nite infinito, ilimitado, inmenso • in|fi|nite|ly infinitamente

in|fini|tive infinitivo

in|fin|ity infinito

in|flam|ma|tion inflamación

in|flat|able inflable, que se infla

in|flate inflar(se),

hinchar(se)

in|fla|tion inflación

in|flec|tion inflexión, entonación, modulación

in|flict infligir, imponer, causar

in|flu|ence influencia, ascendiente, autoridad, influir, inducir, persuadir, influenciar

in|flu|en|tial influyente

info información

in|form informar, comunicar, enterar

in|for|mal informal, sin ceremonias • **in|for|mal|ly** informalmente

in|for|mal thea|ter teatro informal

in|for|ma|tion información, datos

in|for|ma|tion tech|nol|ogy tecnología de la información, TI, IT

in|forma|tive informativo, instructivo

in|formed informado, sabedor, al corriente, fundamentado

in|frac|tion infracción, transgresión, violación

infra|red infrarrojo

infra|struc|ture infraestructura

in|furi|ate enfurecer, poner furioso • **in|furi|at|ing** exasperante

in|grained arraigado

in|gre|di|ent ingrediente, elemento

in|hab|it habitar, vivir en

in|hab|it|ant habitante

in|hale inhalar, aspirar • **inhalation** inhalación

in|her|ent inmanente, inherente, intrínseco • **in|her|ent|ly** intrínsecamente

in|her|it heredar, recibir una herencia

in|hib|it inhibir, impedir,

detener

in|hi|bi|tion inhibición

in|hibi|tor inhibidor, retardador

in|hu|man inhumano, cruel

ini|tial inicial, primero, poner sus iniciales, firmar con sus iniciales, inicialar

ini|tial con|so|nant también **initial blend** consonante inicial

ini|tial|ly inicialmente, en un principio, al principio

ini|ti|ate iniciar, empezar, principiar • **ini|tia|tion** inicio, iniciación

ini|tia|tive iniciativa
▸ **take the initiative** tomar la iniciativa

in|ject inyectar(se)

in|jec|tion inyección

in|jure herir, lastimar, lesionar

in|jured herido, lesionado, ofendido, agraviado
▸ **the injured** los heridos

in|ju|ry herida, lesión

in|jus|tice injusticia, arbitrariedad

ink tinta

in|land tierra adentro, interior de un país

in-laws parientes políticos, familia política

in|let ensenada

in-line skates patines en línea

in|mate interno, preso, recluso, enfermo

inn hotel, posada, hostería, taberna, inn

in|ner interno, interior, íntimo

in|ner city zonas urbanas deprimidas

in|ner core centro de la tierra

in|no|cence inocencia

in|no|cent inocente • **in|no|cent|ly** inocentemente

in|no|va|tion innovación,

novedad

in|no|va|tive innovador

in|put aportación, input, entrada, información introducida, introducir, capturar

in|put force potencia de entrada

in|quire preguntar, informarse, averiguar, inquirir, investigar

in|quiry pregunta, averiguación, investigación, indagación

in|quisi|tive inquisitivo, preguntón, curioso

in|roads
▸ **make inroads** afectar, adentrarse

in|sane loco, demente, chiflado, insensato, descabellado • **in|san|ity** locura, insensatez
• **in|sane|ly** locamente

in|sa|tiable insaciable

in|scrip|tion inscripción, letrero, dedicatoria

in|sect insecto

in|sec|ti|cide insecticida

in|secure inseguro
• **in|secu|rity** inseguridad

in|sen|si|tive insensible, duro • **in|sen|si|tiv|ity** insensibilidad

in|sepa|rable inseparable

in|sert insertar, introducir, meter, agregar, añadir
• **in|ser|tion** inserción

in|side dentro, adentro, en, en el interior, interior, interno, de dentro, de adentro, confidencial
• **insides** entrañas, órganos internos, vísceras
▸ **inside out** al revés

in|sid|er persona informada, miembro de un grupo

in|sight conocimiento

in|sig|nifi|cant insignificante, pequeño, sin importancia
• **in|sig|nifi|cance**

insignificancia

in|sist insistir, obstinarse, persistir • **in|sist|ence** insistencia

in|sist|ent insistente, obstinado • **in|sist|ent|ly** insistentemente

in|som|nia insomnio

in|spect inspeccionar, revisar, examinar
• **in|spec|tion** inspección

in|spec|tor inspector o inspectora, revisor o revisora

in|spi|ra|tion inspiración

in|spire inspirar(se), influir
• **in|spir|ing** inspirador

in|stabil|ity inestabilidad

in|stall instalar, colocar, montar • **in|stal|la|tion** instalación, tomar posesión

in|stal|la|tion art instalación

in|stall|ment capítulo, entrega, fascículo
▸ **by installments** a plazos

in|stall|ment plan plan de pagos, facilidades de pago, con financiamiento

in|stance caso, ejemplo
▸ **for instance** por ejemplo, como
▸ **in the first instance** en primer lugar, en primer término

in|stant instante, momento, instantáneo, inmediato • **in|stant|ly** instantáneamente

in|stant mes|sage mensaje instantáneo, IM, mandar un mensaje instantáneo

in|stant mes|sag|ing mandar mensajes instantáneos, mensajería instantánea

in|stant re|play repetición instantánea

in|stead
▸ **instead of** en lugar de, en vez de, más bien

in|stinct instinto, intuición,

presentimiento

in|stinc|tive instintivo
• **in|stinc|tive|ly** instintivamente

in|sti|tute instituto, instituir, establecer

in|sti|tu|tion institución, asilo, manicomio, orfanatorio

in-store dentro de una tienda, adentro de la tienda

in|struct instruir, ordenar, dar instrucciones, enseñar, mandar

in|struc|tion instrucción, orden, educación, enseñanza

in|struc|tive instructivo, educativo, didáctico

in|struc|tor instructor *o* instructora, profesor auxiliar *o* profesora auxiliar

in|stru|ment instrumento, herramienta, utensilio

in|stru|men|tal decisivo, instrumental, música instrumental

in|suf|fi|cient insuficiente, escaso • **in|suf|fi|cient|ly** insuficientemente

in|su|late aislar

in|su|la|tion aislante, aislamiento

in|su|la|tor aislante

in|su|lin insulina

in|sult insultar, offender, insulto, ofensa, injuria
• **in|sult|ed** insultado
• **in|sult|ing** insultante
▸ **to add insult to injury** por si fuera poco, para acabarla de amolar, para colmo, para colmo de males

in|sur|ance seguro

in|sure asegurar(se), comprar un seguro

in|sur|er aseguradora, compañía de seguros

in|sur|rec|tion insurrección, rebelión, levantamiento

in|tact intacto, entero, íntegro

in|take ingestión, consumo

in|te|ger entero, número entero

in|te|grate integrar(se), combinar, mezclar
• **in|te|grat|ed** integrado
• **in|te|gra|tion** integración

in|teg|rity integridad
▸ **of integrity** íntegro

in|tegu|men|tary sys|tem sistema integumentario, sistema tegumentario

in|tel|lect inteligencia, intelecto

in|tel|lec|tual intellectual, inteligente
• **in|tel lec|tual|ly** intelectualmente

in|tel|lec|tual prop|er|ty propiedad intelectual

in|tel|li gence inteligencia, información

in|tel|li|gent inteligente
• **in|tel|li|gent|ly** inteligentemente

in|tend proponerse, pensar (en), querer (hacer)
▸ **be intended for** estar destinado a, estar dedicado a, ser para

in|tense intenso, profundo, apasionado • **in|tense|ly** intensamente, vehemente
• **in|ten|sity** intensidad

in|ten|si|fy intensificar, agudizar, recrudecer

in|ten|sity intensidad, fuerza

in|ten|sive intenso, intensivo • **in|ten|sive|ly** intensamente

in|ten|sive care cuidados intensivos, terapia intensiva

in|tent decidido, resuelto, intento • **in|tent|ly** atentamente
▸ **for all intents and purposes** prácticamente, en el fondo, para efectos prácticos

in|ten|tion intención,

propósito
▸ **have every intention of** tener la intención de
▸ **have no intention of** no tener intenciones de

inter|act interactuar, relacionarse • **inter|ac|tion** interacción

inter|ac|tive interactivo • **inter|ac|tiv|ity** interactividad

inter|cept interceptar • **inter|cep|tion** intercepción

inter|col|legi|ate intercolegial

inter|course coito, acto sexual, relaciones sexuales

in|ter|est interés, gusto, beneficio, provecho, intereses, negocios, interesar(se)
▸ **have an interest in** convenir algo
▸ **in the interest(s) of** en pro de

in|ter|est|ed interesado

in|ter|est|ing interesante, de interés • **in|ter|est|ing|ly** de modo interesante

inter|face interfaz, interfase

inter|fere interferir, entrometerse, inmiscuirse
▸ **interfere with** afectar

inter|fer|ence interferencia, intromisión

in|ter|im interino, provisional
▸ **in the interim** en el ínterin, entretanto

in|te|ri|or interior, parte interna

inter|lude intervalo, paréntesis, intermedio

inter|medi|ate intermedio

inter|mit|tent intermitente, recurrente • **inter|mit|tent|ly** de manera intermitente

in|tern internar, recluir, interno

in|ter|nal interno • **in|ter|nal|ly** internamente

in|ter|nal com|bus|tion en|gine motor de combustión interna

in|ter|nal fer|ti|li|za|tion fertilización interna

In|ter|nal Rev|enue Ser|vice IRS, agencia de impuestos interiores estadounidense

inter|na|tion|al internacional • **inter|na|tion|al|ly** internacionalmente

In|ter|net *también* **internet** Internet

In|ter|net café café internet, cibercafé, cybercafé

in|tern|ist internista

in|tern|ship internado

in|ter|pret interpretar • **in|ter|pret|er** intérprete

in|ter|pre|ta|tion interpretación

in|ter|rupt interrumpir • **in|ter|rup|tion** interrupción

inter|state interestatal, carretera interestatal

in|ter|val intervalo, interrupción
▸ **at intervals** a intervalos

inter|vene intervenir • **inter|ven|tion** intervención

inter|view entrevista, entrevistar • **inter|view|er** entrevistador *o* entrevistadora

in|tes|tine intestino • **in|tes|ti|nal** intestinal

in|ti|mate íntimo, profundo, insinuar • **in|ti|mate|ly** a profundidad, íntimamente

in|timi|date intimidar • **in|timi|dat|ed** intimidado • **in|timi|dat|ing** intimidatorio • **in|timi|da|tion** intimidación

into en, dentro, contra, sobre
▸ **change into** transformar
▸ **get into** ponerse (algo de

ropa)
▶ **talk into** convencer de

intra|mu|ral intramuros

in|tra|net intranet, red interna

in|tran|si|tive intransitivo

intra|venous intravenoso
• **intra|venous|ly** por vía intravenosa

in|tri|cate intrincado, complejo, delicado
• **in|tri|ca|cy** complejidad
• **in|tri|cate|ly** delicadamente

in|trigue intriga, intrigar
• **in|trigued** intrigado

in|tri|guing fascinante
• **in|tri|guing|ly** de manera intrigante

intro|duce introducir, presentar • **introductions** presentaciones

intro|duc|tion introducción

in|tui|tion intuición

in|vade invadir • **in|vad|er** invasor o invasora

in|va|lid inválido o inválida

in|valu|able invaluable

in|vari|ably invariablemente

in|va|sion invasión, intromisión

in|vent inventar • **in|ven|tor** inventor o inventora

in|ven|tion invento, invención

in|ven|tory inventario

in|vert invertir, voltear

in|ver|te|brate invertebrado

in|vest invertir, investir
• **in|ves|tor** inversionista

in|ves|ti|gate investigar
• **in|ves|ti|ga|tion** investigación

in|ves|ti|ga|tor investigador o investigadora, detective

in|vest|ment inversión

in|vis|ible invisible
• **in|vis|ibil|ity** invisibilidad

in|vi|ta|tion invitación

in|vi|ta|tion|al por invitación, evento al que

sólo se puede asistir con invitación

in|vite invitar, atraer, invitación

in|vo|ca|tion invocación

in|voice factura, pasarle factura a

in|vol|un|tary involuntario
• **in|vol|un|tari|ly** involuntariamente

in|volve involucrar

in|volved involucrado, comprometido, implicado, complejo

in|volve|ment participación

in|ward interno • **in|ward|ly** por dentro, hacia adentro

ion ión

ion|ic bond enlace iónico

ion|ic com|pound compuesto iónico

IP ad|dress dirección IP

IQ IQ, coeficiente intelectual

iris iris

iron hierro, plancha, acero, planchar • **iron|ing** planchado
▶ **iron out** resolver, superar

iron|ic también **ironical** irónico • **ironi|cal|ly** irónicamente

iro|ny ironía

ir|ra|tion|al irracional, irrazonable, absurdo
• **ir|ra|tion|al|ly** irracionalmente
• **ir|ra|tion|al|ity** irracionalidad

ir|ra|tion|al num|ber número irracional

ir|regu|lar irregular, discontinuo, inadmisible
• **ir|regu|lar|ly** irregularmente
• **ir|regu|lar|ity** irregularidad

ir|regu|lar gal|axy galaxia irregular

ir|rel|evant irrelevante, intrascendente, no pertinente • **ir|rel|evance**

irrelevancia

ir|re|sist|ible irresistible
● ir|re|sist|ibly
irresistiblemente

ir|re|spon|sible irresponsable
● ir|re|spon|sibly
irresponsablemente
● ir|re|spon|sibil|ity
irresponsabilidad

ir|re|vers|ible irreversible,
irrevocable

ir|ri|gate irrigar, regar
● ir|ri|ga|tion irrigación

ir|ri|tate irritar, molestar,
enojar ● ir|ri|tat|ed
irritado ● ir|ri|tat|ing
irritante ● ir|ri|tat|ing|ly
insufriblemente

ir|ri|ta|tion irritación,
molestia, enfado, enojo

Is|lam islam, islamismo
● Is|lam|ic islámico

is|land isla

isle isla

isn't = is not

iso|bar isobara

iso|late aislar, separar,
apartar

iso|lat|ed aislado, apartado,
único

iso|la|tion aislamiento
▶ in isolation por sí solo,
solo

iso|tope isótopo

ISP proveedor de servicios de
internet

is|sue problema, cuestión,
asunto, tema, número,
reparto, expedición,
entrega, emitir, expedir,
publicar, entregar
▶ (question/point) at
issue de lo que se trata, en
cuestión
▶ the issue lo más
importante

it él, ella, ello, lo, la, le

ital|ic itálica, cursiva,
bastardilla, itálico

itch picar, tener comezón,
arder, picor, picazón,
comezón, prurito, ansia,
impaciencia ● itch|ing
irritación ● itchy irritado,
ansioso, impaciente

it'd = it would o it had

item artículo, objeto, pieza,
tema, punto

it'll = it will

its su(s)

it's = it is o it has

it|self a sí mismo, por
sí solo, mismo, en sí,
personificación

IV vía intravenosa, sistema
intravenoso, IV

I've = I have

IVF FIV

ivo|ry marfil

Ivy League Ivy League, tipo
Ivy League

Jj

jack gato, jota

jack|et chamarra, cubierta

jack|ham|mer martillo neumático

jack-o'-lantern *también* **jack o'lantern** calabaza de Halloween

jade jade

jag|ged dentado, escarpado

jail cárcel, mandar a la cárcel

jail|house cárcel (local)

jam meter a presión, atorar(se), trabar(se), abarrotar, bloquear, embotellamiento, mermelada •**jammed** repleto •**jam|ming** interferencia

Jane Doe Juana N

jani|tor conserje

Janu|ary enero

jar frasco, bote, crispar (los nervios) •**jar|ring** discordante

java café

jaw quijada, mandíbulas, fauces

jazz jazz

jazz dance danza jazz

jeal|ous celoso, envidioso •**jeal|ous|ly** celosamente, con envidia

jeal|ousy celos, envidia

jeans jeans

jel|ly mermelada

jelly|fish aguamala, medusa, aguaviva

jel|ly roll brazo de gitano

jerk mover (bruscamente), mover (repentinamente), sacudida, imbécil

jer|sey tejido de punto

Jesus Jesús, Jesucristo

jet jet, avión a reacción, chorro, viajar en jet

jet en|gine motor de reacción

jet|liner avión de pasajeros

jet stream corriente en chorro

jet|ty embarcadero, malecón, muelle

Jew judío *o* judía

jew|el joya

jew|el|er joyero *o* joyera, joyería

jew|el|ry joyería

Jew|ish judío

jin|gle tintinear, jingle, canción publicitaria

jive jive, jerga jive

job empleo, trabajo, tarea

job|less desempleado

job sat|is|fac|tion satisfacción con el empleo

job share alternar (el trabajo)

jock|ey jinete

jog correr (lentamente), mover, vuelta corriendo •**jog|ger** corredor *o* corredora •**jog|ging** correr

John Doe Juan N

join acompañar, afiliarse a, alistarse en, integrarse, participar en, formarse, unir
▸ **join in** participar en, unirse a
▸ **join up** alistarse

joint conjunto, articulación, junta •**joint|ly** conjuntamente

joint ven|ture alianza estratégica, empresa conjunta

joke chiste, burla, bromear
▸ **no joke** no es un chiste
▸ **you're/you must be/ you've got to be joking** ¡Estás bromeando!, ¡Debes estar bromeando!

j

jok|er comodín

jol|ly alegre, jovial

joule julio

jour|nal revista, periódico, diario

jour|nal|ist periodista •**jour|nal|ism** periodismo

jour|ney viaje, viajar

joy júbilo, alegría

judge juez, arbitrar, juzgar

judg|ment opinión, buen juicio, criterio, fallo

ju|di|cial judicial

ju|di|ci|ary judicatura

jug|gle balancear, abarcar, hacer malabares •**jug|gler** malabarista •**jug|gl|ing** malabarismo

juice jugo

juicy jugoso, sabroso

July julio

jum|bo enorme, jumbo jet

jump saltar, brincar, sobresaltar, dispararse, subir repentinamente, salto, alza abrupta
  ▸ **jump at** aceptar inmediatamente

jump|er jumper, suéter

jump|er ca|bles cables de arranque

jump rope cuerda de saltar

June junio

jun|gle selva, maraña

jun|ior subalterno, auxiliar, menor, estudiante de tercer año

jun|ior col|lege escuela técnica, escuela semisuperior

jun|ior high school *también* **junior high** escuela secundaria

junk chatarra, remates

Ju|pi|ter Júpiter

ju|ror miembro del jurado

jury jurado

just justo, exactamente, justamente, en este momento, solamente, apenas, simplemente, sólo
  •**just|ly** con justicia
  ▸ **just about** prácticamente
  ▸ **have just** acabar de

jus|tice justicia, legitimidad, sistema judicial, juez
  ▸ **bring to justice** capturar y enjuiciar
  ▸ **do justice** hacer justicia

jus|ti|fi|ca|tion justificación

jus|ti|fied justificado

jus|ti|fy justificar

ju|ve|nile joven

Kk

K-12 sistema escolar, que consta de doce años, desde la educación elemental hasta la pre-universitaria
Ka|bu|ki kabuki
kan|ga|roo canguro
kan|ga|roo rat rata canguro
kar|at quilate
ka|ra|te karate
karst to|pog|r|aphy topografía kárstica
Kb *también* **kb** Kb, kilobit
KB *también* **K** KB, kilobyte
Kbps *también* **kbps** kilobits por segundo
keel
  ▶ **on an even keel** con estabilidad
  ▶ **keel over** desplomarse
keen con mucha visión, con un olfato agudo, gran, aguda • **keen|ly** con entusiasmo, profundamente
keep mantener, guardar, seguir, cumplir, llevar, impedir, detener, ocultar, sustento
  ▶ **keep doing something** hacer algo repetidamente, continuar haciendo algo
  ▶ **in keeping with** de acuerdo con
  ▶ **keep something to yourself** callarse algo
  ▶ **keep to yourself** ser muy reservado
  ▶ **keep down** mantener bajo, limitar
  ▶ **keep someone on** mantener a alguien como empleado
  ▶ **keep to** respetar, limitar
  ▶ **keep up** mantener
keep|er guardia
ken|nel criadero, pensión, guardería (de perros)
kept *ver* **keep**
kero|sene queroseno, petróleo
ket|tle cafetera (para hervir agua), pava, olla
key llave, tecla, tono, clave
key|board teclado
key card tarjeta que funciona como llave electrónica
key|stone piedra angular, sillar de clave
key|word *también* **key word** palabra clave
kg kg, kilogramo
kha|ki caqui
kick patear, patalear, dejar (un mal hábito), patada, gusto
  ▶ **kick in** surtir efecto, aportar
  ▶ **kick off** comenzar
  ▶ **kick out** correr, echar
kick|er pateador o pateadora
kick|off patada inicial, patada
kick|stand pie de bicicleta/motocicleta que sirve para mantenerla derecha
kick-start *también* **kickstart** arrancar
kid niño o niña, cabrito, bromear, hacerse tontos
kiddo amigo
kid|nap secuestrar
  • **kid|nap|per** secuestrador o secuestradora • **kid|nap|ping** secuestro
kid|ney riñón
kid|ney bean frijol
kill matar, acabar con
  • **kill|ing** homicidio
  ▶ **kill off** matar, exterminar
kill|er homicida, asesino o

k

asesina, causa de muerte

kilo kilo

kilo|bit kilobit

kilo|byte kilobyte

kilo|calo|rie kilocaloría

kilo|gram kilogramo

kilo|meter kilómetro

kin
  ▶ **next of kin** pariente

kind estilo, tipo, amable
  ▶ **kind of** algo
  ▶ **in kind** en especie • **kind|ly** amablemente • **kind|ness** amabilidad

kin|der|gar|ten jardín de niños

kind|ly amable

kin|es|thet|ic *también* **kinaesthetic** cinestético

ki|net|ic en|er|gy energía cinética

king rey

king|dom reino

ki|osk kiosko

kiss besar, beso

kit equipo, juego, maqueta

kitch|en cocina

kite papalote, cometa

kitsch ostentoso y de mal gusto, cursi

kit|ten gatito

kit|ty caja de ahorros, gatito

kitty-corner *ver* catty-corner

kiwi kiwi

kiwi fruit kiwi

klutz desmañado, torpe

km kilómetro

knack habilidad de hacer algo difícil

knead amasar

knee rodilla
  ▶ **bring to its knees** aniquilar, destruir
  ▶ **on one's knees** arodillado
  ▶ **have something on one's knees** tener algo en las piernas

K

kneel arrodillarse, hincarse

knew *ver* know

knife cuchillo, acuchillar

knight caballero, caballo, armar caballero

knit tejer

knit|ting el tejido

knives *ver* knife

knob perilla, interruptor

knock golpe, tocar, golpear, pegar, aventar, hablar mal, criticar • **knock|ing** golpes
  ▶ **knock down** derribar, demoler, destruir, rebajar, disminuir
  ▶ **knock off** rebajar, reducir
  ▶ **knock out** noquear, poner fuera de combate, derrotar

knock|out *también* **knock-out** nocaut, golpe de nocaut

knot anudar, hacerse nudos, nudo

know saber, conocer(se)
  ▶ **get to know somebody** conocerse
  ▶ **in the know** al tanto

know-how conocimiento

know|ing|ly a sabiendas

know-it-all sabelotodo

knowl|edge conocimiento
  ▶ **to (the best of) somebody's knowledge** hasta donde se sabe

knowl|edge|able *también* **knowledgable** conocedor

known *ver* know, conocido
  ▶ **let it be known** hacer saber

knuck|le nudillo de la mano

kook loquito o loquita

Ko|ran Corán

Kuiper belt cinturón de Kuiper

Kurd kurdo o kurda

Kur|dish kurdo

kvetch quejarse constantemente/de un modo malhumorado

kW *también* **KW** KW, kilovatio

Ll

L baja presión
lab laboratorio, lab, labo
laba|no|ta|tion labanotación
lab apron bata de laboratorio
la|bel etiqueta, rótulo, etiquetar, rotular, poner una etiqueta, catalogar, calificar
la|bor gran esfuerzo, trabajo duro, faena, mano de obra, trabajadores, fuerza laboral, parto, trabajar con las manos, trabajar incansablemente, esforzarse, luchar
la|bora|tory laboratorio
la|bor camp campo de trabajos forzados
la|bored trabajoso, difícil, fatigoso, forzado, torpe
la|bor|er obrero *u* obrera, trabajador *o* trabajadora, trabajador agrícola *o* trabajadora agrícola, peón
la|bor force fuerza laboral, mano de obra, trabajadores
labor-intensive intensivo en mano de obra
la|bor mar|ket mercado laboral
la|bor re|la|tions relación laboral
labor-saving que ahorra esfuerzo, economizador de trabajo
la|bor un|ion sindicato, gremio
lace encaje, agujeta, cordón, amarrar(se), rociar
lack falta, carencia, faltar, carecer • **lack|ing** falta ▶ **no lack of something** no faltar
lad|der escalera, escalera de mano
la|dle cucharón, servir (con cucharón)
lady dama, señora
lady|bug mariquita, catarina
lag quedarse atrás, rezagarse, atrasarse, intervalo, demora, lapso, retraso
laid *ver* lay
lain *ver* lie
lake lago
lake|front *también* **lake front**, **lake-front** orilla del lago, ribera del lago
lamb cordero, borrego
lame cojo, rengo, renco, inválido, pobre, malo, débil • **lame|ly** débilmente
lamp lámpara
land tierra, terreno, campo, país, aterrizar, caer, ir a parar, atracar, ir a dar • **land|ing** aterrizaje ▶ **land in (a bad situation)** meter en problemas, meter en líos
land|fill vertedero, relleno sanitario
land|form *también* **land form** accidente geográfico
land|ing rellano, descanso, descansillo, pasillo
land|lord casero, dueño, arrendador, propietario
land|mark hito, edificio representativo, acontecimiento importante, característica
land mass *también* **landmass** masa continental
land|scape paisaje, vista, panorama, ajardinar, construir un jardín, arreglar un jardín, enjardinar • **land|scap|ing** paisajismo
land|slide victoria arrolladora, derrumbamiento,

derrumbe, deslizamiento de tierra

lane camino, sendero, carril, ruta de navegación

lan|guage lengua, idioma, lenguaje, vocabulario, palabra, expresión

lan|tern linterna, farol

lap regazo, vuelta, sacar ventaja, chapalear, bañar, lamer, dar lengüetazos
- **lap|ping** chapaleo
▸ **lap up** deleitarse

lap|top lap, laptop, computadora portátil

large grande, amplio, vasto, importante, abundante, grave
▸ **at large** en general

large|ly en buena parte, en gran medida, mayormente, sobre todo, principalmente

large-scale *también* **large scale** en grande, en gran escala, a gran escala

lar|va larva

lar|ynx laringe

la|ser láser, rayo láser

lash pestaña, latigazo, azote, amarrar, atar, azotar
▸ **lash out** atacar, arremeter contra, atacar verbalmente

Lasik *también* **LASIK** Lasik

last pasado, último, anterior, lo último, lo que queda, durar
▸ **at last/at long last** por fin, al fin, finalmente

last|ing duradero, perdurable, durable

last-minute *ver* minute

late tarde, tardío, a finales, al final, atraso, demora, retraso, difunto, fallecido
- **late|ness** lo tarde, tardanza, atraso, demora
▸ **too late** demasiado tarde

late|ly últimamente, recientemente, a últimas fechas

lat|er más tarde, después, posterior, más adelante, último

lat|er|al line sys|tem línea lateral

lat|est último, más reciente
▸ **at the latest** a más tardar, cuando mucho

La|ti|na latina

Lat|in Ameri|can latinoamericano

La|ti|no *también* **latino** latino

lati|tude latitud, libertad, laxitud

lat|ter último, segundo

laugh reír(se), risa
▸ **laugh off** tomar a broma, reírse de algo

laugh|ter risotada, carcajada

launch lanzar, botar, iniciar, emprender, lanzamiento, botadura, principio
▸ **launch into** embarcarse en, lanzarse en

launch|er lanzador

launch pad plataforma de lanzamiento

launch ve|hi|cle lanzacohetes

laun|dro|mat lavandería automática pública

laun|dry ropa lavada, ropa para lavar, lavandería

lava lava

lav|ish suntuoso, espléndido, derrochador, generoso, extravagante, derrochar, no escatimar, desvivirse
- **lav|ish|ly** espléndidamente

law ley, leyes, abogacía, derecho

law and or|der orden público

law enforcement aplicación de la ley, ejecución de la ley

law|maker legislador *o* legisladora

lawn prado, césped, pasto

lawn bowl|ing lawn bowling

lawn chair silla para jardín

lawn|mow|er podadora de pasto, cortadora de pasto

law|suit pleito, juicio, litigio, proceso

law|yer abogado o abogada, licenciado o licenciada

lay poner, colocar, depositar, instalar, poner (huevos), desovar, sentar las bases, hacer (planes), preparar, culpar, lego, laico, seglar, no especialista
▶ **lay aside** dejar de lado, apartar
▶ **lay down** imponer, determinar
▶ **lay off** despedir o suspender (a un empleado)
▶ **lay out** preparar, disponer, exhibir, plantear, exponer

lay|er capa, estrato, interpretación, acomodar en capas

lay|over parada, escala

lazy flojo, perezoso, holgazán, relajado, descansado ● **la|zi|ness** flojera ● **la|zi|ly** perezosamente

lb. libra

lead encabezar, guiar, dirigir, llevar, conducir, ir a la cabeza, llevar la delantera, provocar, pista, cable, papel principal, primer actor o primera actriz, protagonista, plomo, punta, mina
▶ **lead up to** preceder, culminar en, preparar el terreno para, llevar gradualmente a

lead|er líder, dirigente, jefe, cabecilla, guía, puntero o puntera

lead|er|ship liderazgo, conducción, autoridad, mando, dirección

lead|ing principal, destacado, importante
▶ **leading role** protagonista
▶ **leading man** primer actor
▶ **leading lady** primera actriz

leaf hoja
▶ **leaf through** hojear

leaf|let folleto

league liga, asociación, federación, nivel, categoría
▶ **in league with** confabulado con

leak filtrar(se), gotear, filtración, fuga

lean inclinarse, doblarse, ladearse, encorvarse, apoyar(se), delgado, atlético, musculoso, magro, de escasez, de vacas flacas
▶ **lean on** o **lean upon** depender de, apoyarse en

leap saltar, brincar, moverse rápidamente, salto, brinco

leap year año bisiesto

learn aprender(se), estudiar, instruirse, enterarse, saber, conocer, memorizar
● **learn|er** estudiante
● **learn|ing** aprendizaje

learn|ed culto, sabio, erudito, ilustrado

learned be|hav|ior comportamiento aprendido

learn|er's per|mit permiso para conducir

lease arrendamiento, alquiler, arrendar, rentar, alquilar

least lo menos, lo mínimo, menos, menor
▶ **at least** cuando menos, al menos, por lo menos
▶ **in the least** en lo más mínimo, de ninguna manera
▶ **not least** hasta, incluido
▶ **to say the least** por no decir más, para decir lo menos

leath|er piel

leave dejar, irse, salir, abandonar, heredar, olvidar, permiso
▶ **be left behind** quedarse atrás
▶ **leave behind** abandonar, dejar atrás, irse sin, rezagarse
▶ **leave off** dejar fuera, no incluir
▶ **leave out** dejar fuera, exluir

I

leav|ened hecho con levadura

leaves ver leaf

lec|ture conferencia, disertación, sermón, cátedra, plática, enseñar sobre, dictar cátedra sobre, sermonear, dar sermones

lec|tur|er conferencista, catedrático, conferenciante, profesor universitario

left ver leave, lo que sobra, lo que queda, izquierda, hacia la izquierda, izquierdo

left-hand izquierda

left-of-center centro izquierda

left-wing también **left wing** de izquierda, izquierdista, izquierda

lefty zurdo

leg pata, pierna, pernera, etapa, trecho, tramo

lega|cy legado, herencia

le|gal legal, jurídico
 • **le|gal|ly** legalmente
 • **le|gal|ity** legalidad

leg|end leyenda, mito

leg|end|ary legendario

leg|gings leggings, leotardos, mallas, mallones

leg|is|la|tion legislación

leg|is|la|tive legislativo

leg|is|la|ture legislatura, poder legislativo, cuerpo legislativo

le|giti|mate legítimo, legal, válido, auténtico, justificado • **le|giti|ma|cy** legitimidad, justificación
 • **le|giti|mate|ly** legítimamente, justificadamente

leg|work trabajo preliminar, trabajo de campo, talacha

lei|sure ratos de ocio, tiempo libre
 ▶ **at leisure/at somebody's leisure** cuando uno quiere, cuando se tiene tiempo, al gusto de cada quien

lem|on limón

lem|on|ade limonada

lend prestar, proporcionar, ayudar, apoyar • **lend|er** prestamista • **lend|ing** préstamo

length longitud, largo, duración, tramo, pedazo, tiempo, lapso
 ▶ **at length** extensamente, detalladamente, con detenimiento
 ▶ **go to great lengths** hacer todo lo posible

lengthy largo, prolongado

lens lente, cristalino

lent ver lend

len|til lenteja

lep|re|chaun duende, gnomo

les|bian lesbiana

less menos
 ▶ **less than** menos de, menos que

less|er menor, inferior, menos

les|son clase, lección
 ▶ **teach somebody a lesson** darle una lección a alguien

let dejar, permitir(se), dar permiso, sugerir
 ▶ **let alone** menos aún, mucho menos
 ▶ **let go of** soltar, liberar
 ▶ **let somebody know** hacer saber, informar, comunicar
 ▶ **let down** desilusionar, fallar, decepcionar
 ▶ **let in** dejar entrar, dejar pasar
 ▶ **let off** perdonar, no castigar, hacer estallar, disparar
 ▶ **let out** dejar salir
 ▶ **let up** amainar, disminuir, parar

le|thal letal, mortal, mortífero

let's = let us

let|ter carta, letra, ser seleccionado

let|ter car|ri|er cartero o cartera

levee dique

lev|el nivel, piso, altura, plano, horizontal, igual, a nivel, parejo, alcanzar, arrasar, criticar, acusar
▶ **level off** o **level out** nivelarse, estabilizarse
▶ **level with** al mismo nivel de, a la misma altura de

lev|el|er también **leveller** nivelador, igualador

lev|er|age influencia, poder

levy gravamen, impuesto, recaudar, imponer

lia|bil|ity desventaja, riesgo, pasivo, deuda

lia|ble susceptible, responsable
▶ **liable to** propenso a, tendencia a, susceptible de
▶ **liable for** ser sujeto de
● **lia|bil|ity** responsabilidad

li|bel libelo, escrito difamatorio, difamar, calumniar

li|bel|ous también **libellous** difamatorio, injurioso

lib|er|al liberal, tolerante, generoso, abundante
● **lib|er|al|ly** liberalmente

lib|er|al arts humanidades

lib|er|al|ize liberalizar
● **lib|er|ali|za|tion** liberalización

lib|er|ate liberar, libertar
● **lib|era|tion** liberación
● **lib|er|at|ing** liberador

lib|er|at|ed liberado

lib|er|ty libertad
▶ **be at liberty to** ser libre de, tener permiso para, estar autorizado para, tener la libertad de

li|brar|ian bibliotecario o bibliotecaria

li|brary biblioteca

lice ver **louse**

li|cense licencia, permiso, autorización, autorizar, otorgar un permiso, otorgar una licencia

li|censed autorizado, registrado

li|cense num|ber número de placa

li|cense plate placa, chapa

lick lamer, lamedura, lamida

lickety-split a toda mecha, de volada, rapidísimo

lid tapa, tapadera

lie echarse, acostarse, estar situado, extenderse, estar, situarse, encontrarse, radicar, estribar, tener por delante, mentir, decir mentiras, mentira
▶ **lie around** dejar botado, dejar tirado
▶ **lie behind** haber detrás de
▶ **lie down** acostarse, tumbarse ● **ly|ing** mentiras

lieu|ten|ant teniente

lieu|ten|ant gov|er|nor vicegobernador o vicegobernadora, lugarteniente del gobernador, lugarteniente de la gobernadora

life vida, existencia, forma de vida, vitalidad, de por vida, prisión perpetua, duración
▶ **fight for one's life** luchar por la vida

life pre|serv|er salvavidas

life sci|ence ciencias de la vida, ciencias biológicas

life style también **life-style**, **life style** estilo de vida, tren de vida

life support respirador artificial, máquina corazón-pulmón, equipo para mantener la vida

life|time vida, curso de la vida

lift levantar, recoger, alzar, cargar, revocar, suprimir, fuerza ascensional
▶ **give somebody a lift somewhere** dar un aventón, dar un "ride", llevar

light luz, claridad, iluminación, aspecto,

claro, pálido, ligero, escaso, poco, liviano, frívolo, superficial, iluminar, prender, encender • **light|ly** ligeramente, a la ligera, poco, apenas • **light|ness** luminosidad, ligereza
▸ **be light** tener luz, estar iluminado
▸ **be (day)light** ser de día, haber luz, haber sol, estar claro el día
▸ **come/bring to light** salir a la luz, sacar a la luz, revelar
▸ **in the light of** a la luz de, en vista de
▸ **shed/throw/cast light on** echar luz, arrojar luz, aclarar
▸ **light up** iluminarse, encenderse la luz, prenderse
light bulb foco, bombilla
light cream crema ligera
light en|er|gy energía de luz
light|ing iluminación
light min|ute minuto luz
light|ning rayo, relámpago
▸ **at lightning speed** como rayo, como de rayo, a gran velocidad
light|ning rod pararrayos
▸ **be a lightning rod for** atraer
light source fuente luminosa
light|weight *también* **light-weight** ligero, de poco peso, superficial, poco serio, peso ligero
light year año luz
like como, a la manera de, similar a, igual que, por ejemplo, gustar, querer, preferencia
▸ **if you like** si quieres
▸ **like that/this/so** así, de cierto modo
▸ **something like** más o menos, aproximado
like|li|hood probabilidad, posibilidad
like|ly probable, posible, probablemente, lo probable

like|wise asimismo, así mismo, de la misma manera, lo mismo, otro tanto
lily lirio, azucena
limb miembro, extremidad
▸ **go out on a limb** aventurarse
lime limón (verde), cal
lim|it límite, limitar(se), restringir • **limi|ta|tion** limitación • **lim|it|ing** limitante
▸ **off limits** de acceso prohibido
lim|i|ta|tion limitación, restricción
lim|it|ed limitado, restringido
lim|it|ing fac|tor factor limitante
limp cojear, caminar con dificultad, cojera, flácido, flojo, aguado • **limp|ly** sin fuerza
line línea, raya, arruga, cola, fila, papel, parte, cuerda, cable, línea divisoria, límite, postura, línea de negocio, llenar, ocupar, forrar, recubrir
▸ **draw the line** no ir más allá, poner un límite, pintar su raya
▸ **in/into line** de acuerdo con, de conformidad con
▸ **on line** en línea
▸ **stand/wait in line** hacer cola, formarse
▸ **line up** poner(se) en fila, organizar, planear
lin|ear equa|tion ecuación lineal
lin|ear ex|pres|sion expresión lineal
lin|ear per|spec|tive perspectiva lineal
line di|rec|tion dirección lineal
line drive recta
line graph gráfica lineal
line|man delantero

L

lin|en lino

line of credit línea de crédito

line of scrim|mage línea de scrimmage

line qual|ity características de la línea

lin|er barco de pasajeros

lin|er note comentarios de la funda del CD

line|up integrantes

lin|ger quedarse, persistir, tardar en irse

lin|gui|ne *también* **linguini** linguine

lin|guis|tics lingüística
• **lin|guis|tic** lingüístico

lin|ing forro, revestimiento, pared interior

link vínculo, relación, eslabón, connexion, unión, link, enlace, vincular, conectar, relacionar, unir, enlazar
▶ **link up** reunirse, encontrarse

lint pelusa, hilacho

lion león

lip labio

lip|id lípidos

lip|stick bilé, pintura de labios, lápiz de labios, labial, pintalabios, barra de labios

liq|uid líquido

liq|uor bebida alcohólica, alcohol, bebida, bebida espirituosa

liq|uor store licorería, tienda de vinos y licores

list lista, relación, hacer una lista, enumerar

lis|ten oír, escuchar, estar atento, prestar atención, hacer caso, oír razones
• **lis|ten|er** oyente
▶ **listen in** escuchar a escondidas, espiar una conversación

lis|ten|er radioescucha, oyente

list|serv listserv, lista de correo

li|ter litro

lit|er|al|ly literalmente

lit|er|ary literario

lit|er|ary analy|sis análisis literario

lit|er|ary criti|cism crítica literaria

lit|era|ture literatura, impresos, información

litho|sphere litosfera, litósfera

lit|ter basura, tiradero, ensuciar, tirar basura
• **lit|tered** desordenado, lleno

litter|bug alguien que tira basura en la calle

lit|tle poco, escaso, algo, corto, pequeño, chico, sin importancia, insignificante

lit|to|ral zone litoral

live vivir, habitar, estar vivo, vivo, en vivo, en directo, con corriente, cargado
▶ **live it up** darse la gran vida
▶ **live down** hacer olvidar
▶ **live off (somebody)** vivir de
▶ **live on** *o* **live off (an amount)** vivir con
▶ **live up to** estar a la altura de, cumplir con

live|ly vivaz, animado, bullicioso, vigoroso
• **live|li|ness** vivacidad

liv|er hígado

liv|er|wort hepática, empeine

lives *ver* **life, live**

live|stock ganado, ganadería, res

liv|ing sustento, medios de vida, forma de vida

liv|ing room *también* **living-room** sala

liz|ard lagartija, lagarto

load cargar, llenar, carga, peso, gran número
▶ **a load of** mucho

load|ed tendencioso, cargado, lleno, inclinado

I

loaf hogaza, barra, baguette

loam tierra negra

loan préstamo, crédito, empréstito, prestar
▸ **on loan** prestado

loaves ver **loaf**

lob|by cabildear, buscar aprobación, presionar, cabilderos, grupo de pesión, vestíbulo, hall, entrada

lobe lóbulo

lob|ster langosta

lo|cal local • **locals** vecinos del lugar, habitantes • **lo|cal|ly** localmente

lo|cal col|or color local

lo|cal gov|ern|ment gobierno local

lo|cate localizar, ubicar(se), situar(se) • **lo|cat|ed** situado

lo|ca|tion posición, ubicación
▸ **on location** en locación, en exteriores

lock cerrar con llave, echar llave, guardar bajo llave, inmovilizar, bloquear, chapa, cerradura, cerrojo, esclusa, mechón
▸ **lock away** guardar bajo llave, encerrar
▸ **lock up** encarcelar, asegurar

lock|smith cerrajero o cerrajera

lock-up también **lockup** prisión

lo|co|mo|tive locomotora

lo|co|mo|tor locomotor, locomotriz

lodge casa de campo, hotel campestre, denunciar, interponer, poner, alojar(se), hospedar(se), atorarse • **lodg|er** inquilino o inquilina, huésped

lo|ess loes, loess

log tronco, leña, bitácora, diario de navegación, registrar, anotar, tomar nota
▸ **log in** o **log on** entrar al sistema
▸ **log out** o **log off** salir del sistema, cerrar el sistema

loga|rithm logaritmo

log|ger leñador, maderero, explotador forestal

log|ger|head tur|tle tortuga mordedora, tortuga boba

log|ic lógica

logi|cal lógico, razonable, lógica • **logi|cal|ly** lógicamente

lo|gis|tics logística

logo logo, logotipo

LOL LOL

lone solitario

lone|ly solo, solitario, aislado, triste • **lone|li|ness** soledad

lone|some solitario, triste, alejado

long largo, mucho, mucho tiempo, prolongado, grande, echar de menos, extrañar, añorar • **long|ing** nostalgia
▸ **as long as/so long as** siempre que, con tal que
▸ **before long** dentro de poco
▸ **no longer/any longer** no más

long-distance larga distancia, de larga distancia

lon|gi|tu|di|nal wave onda longitudinal

long-lost perdido de vista

long-range de largo plazo

long|shore cur|rent corriente litoral, corriente costera longitudinal, corriente longitudinal de la costa

long|shore|man estibador, cargador

long-standing de años atrás, duradero

long-time de siempre, de tiempo atrás

look ver, mirar, fijarse, observar, buscar, analizar, examinar, parecer, dar hacia, mirada, ojeada,

vistazo, aspecto, apariencia, aspecto físico, mira
▸ **look out** ¡cuidado!
▸ **look after** cuidar de, atender, ocuparse de
▸ **look around** ver
▸ **look back** mirar atrás, recordar, reflexionar
▸ **look down on** menospreciar
▸ **look forward to** desear, esperar con ansias
▸ **look into** considerar
▸ **look on** contemplar
▸ **look on** o **look upon** considerar como, estimar
▸ **look out for** buscar, estar atento a
▸ **look round** ver **look around**
▸ **look through** revisar, echar un vistazo
▸ **look to** esperar, confiar
▸ **look up** buscar, visitar, ir a ver
▸ **look up to** admirar, respetar
▸ **by the look of/by the looks of** según parece
▸ **not like the look of something/somebody** desconfiar

loom aparecer algo amenazador, asomarse algo vagamente, amenazar, avecinarse, telar

loop vuelta, lazo, lazada, enrollar, enlazar, dar la vuelta
▸ **be in the loop** estar enterado, formar parte de algo

loose suelto, flojo, holgado, flexible ● **loose|ly** sin apretar, sin rigidez, sin cohesión
▸ **break loose** soltarse
▸ **on the loose** en libertad

loos|en relajar, aflojar(se) ● **loos|en|ing** distensión
▸ **loosen up** relajar(se), estirar

loot saquear, pillar, robar ● **loot|ing** saqueo ● **loot|er** saqueador o saqueadora

lord lord, señor, noble

lose perder, ser derrotado
▸ **lose one's way** perderse
▸ **lose out** salir perdiendo
▸ **lose weight** bajar de peso, adelgazar

los|er perdedor o perdedora
▸ **be a good loser** saber perder
▸ **be a bad loser** no saber perder

loss pérdida
▸ **be at a loss** sentirse perdido

lost perdido, extraviado, confundido, desorientado

lost and found objetos perdidos, objeto perdido

lot lote, grupo, terreno, solar
▸ **a lot of** cantidad sustancial de, mucho, montón de
▸ **draw lots** echar suertes, echar un volado, rifarse

lot|tery lotería, volado

loud alto, fuerte, intenso, chillón, llamativo, escandaloso ● **loud|ly** fuertemente
▸ **out loud** en voz alta

lounge salón, sala de estar, sala de espera, no hacer nada, relajarse

louse piojo

love querer, amar, gustar, tener cariño por, gustar mucho (algo), desear (algo), amor, cero (en tenis)
▸ **love/love from/all my love** con todo cariño, besos, TQM
▸ **fall in love** enamorarse

love|ly bonito, lindo, encantador, adorable

lov|er amante, querido, novio, aficionado o aficionada

lov|ing afectuoso, cariñoso, amoroso ● **lov|ing|ly** cariñosamente, amorosamente

low bajo, de poca altura,

mínimo, más bajo, malo, opaco, deprimido, desanimado, desganado

low-end low-end, chafa, de baja calidad, económico

low|er inferior, de abajo, bajar, reducir • **low|er|ing** reducción

low|er class *también* **lower-class** de clase baja, clase baja

low|er man|tle corteza inferior

low-impact bajo impacto

low-maintenance *también* **low maintenance** fácil de mantener

low-rise de poca altura, bajo, edificio de poca altura

low tide marea baja

loy|al leal, fiel • **loy|al|ly** lealmente

loy|al|ty lealtad, fidelidad

LP LP, disco de larga duración

LPN ayudante de enfermería, ayudante de enfermera

LSAT examen de admisión a la escuela de derecho

lub|ri|cant lubricante

luck suerte
▸ **bad luck** mala suerte
▸ **good luck/best of luck** buena suerte
▸ **be in luck** estar de suerte, tener suerte
▸ **luck out** estar de suerte

lucky afortunado, suertudo, que trae suerte • **luckily** con suerte, por suerte, por casualidad
▸ **be lucky** tener suerte

lu|cra|tive lucrativo, provechoso

lug|gage equipaje, maletas

lug|gage rack portaequipaje, portaequipajes

lum|ber madera, avanzar pesadamente

lumber|man leñador

lumber|yard *también* **lumber yard** maderería, depósito de madera

lump trozo, bulto, protuberancia, chichón, chipote
▸ **lump together** agrupar, englobar

lu|nar lunar

lu|nar eclipse eclipse de luna, eclipse lunar

lun|ar mod|ule módulo lunar

lunch comida, almuerzo, comer

lunch meat carnes frías, embutido, fiambre

lunch|room *también* **lunch room** comedor, refectorio

lunch|time *también* **lunch time** hora de la comida, hora de comer

lung pulmón

lure atraer, seducir, tentar, tentación, atractivo, señuelo

lus|ter lustre, brillo, fulgor

Lu|ther|an luterano *o* luterana

luxu|ry lujo, pompa, suntuosidad, lujoso, suntuoso

lymph linfa

lym|phat|ic sys|tem sistema linfático

lym|phat|ic ves|sel vaso capilar

lymph ca|pil|lary capilar linfático

lymph node nódulo linfático

lym|pho|cyte linfocito

lynch linchar

lyr|ic lírico, letra

lyso|some lisosoma

Mm

ma'am señora

maca|ro|ni and cheese macarrones con queso

ma|chine máquina, maquinaria

ma|chine gun ametralladora

ma|chin|ery maquinaria

macho macho

macro|eco|nom|ics *también* **macro-economics** macroeconomía • **macro|eco|nom|ic** macroeconómico

mad furioso, loco, desenfrenado, alocado • **mad|ness** locura • **mad|ly** desenfrenadamente
  ▸ **drive mad** volver loco
  ▸ **like mad** como loco
  ▸ **be mad about** estar loco por, volver loco

mad|am *también* **Madam** señora

made *ver* make, hecho

made to or|der *también* **made-to-order** a la medida, de/por encargo, sobre pedido

Mafia *también* **mafia** mafia

maf|ic fémico (máfico)

mag revista

maga|zine revista, recámara, cargador

mag|got cresa, larva, gusano

mag|ic magia, mágico

magi|cal mágico, maravilloso • **magi|cal|ly** como por arte de magia

ma|gi|cian mago *o* maga

mag|is|trate juez *o* jueza

mag|ma magma

mag|net imán

mag|net|ic magnético, con magnetismo

mag|net|ic dec|li|na|tion declinación magnética

mag|net|ic field campo magnético

mag|net|ic pole polo magnético

mag|net|ic re|ver|sal inversión magnética

mag|net|ize imantar, magnetizar

mag|nifi|cent magnífico, espléndido • **mag|nifi|cence** magnificencia • **mag|nifi|cent|ly** magníficamente

mag|ni|fy agrandar, aumentar, amplificar • **mag|ni|fi|ca|tion** aumento

maid recamarera, sirvienta, mucama

maid|en doncella, inaugural

maid of hon|or dama de honor

mail correo, mensaje, correspondencia, enviar/mandar por correo, enviar/mandar por correo electrónico
  ▸ **mail out** enviar por correo

mail|box buzón

mail|er sobre, paquete, folleto publicitario enviado por correo, remitente

mail|man cartero

mail or|der compraventa por correo

main principal
  ▸ **in the main** por lo general, en general • **mains** tubería principal, red de suministro, cañería principal

main clause oración principal

main drag calle principal

main frame computadora central

main idea idea central

main|land tierra firme,

m

continente, territorio
continental
main|ly principalmente
main-sequence star estrella
de secuencia principal
main|stream corriente
principal
Main Street Calle Mayor,
Calle Principal, provincia,
ciudad pequeña
main|tain mantener,
sostener, afirmar
main|te|nance
mantenimiento, pensión
alimenticia
mai|tre d' jefe de comedor,
capitán de meseros
ma|jes|tic majestuoso
• **ma|jes|ti|cal|ly**
majestuosamente
maj|es|ty majestad,
majestuosidad
ma|jor muy importante,
mayor, comandante,
materia principal, liga
mayor, especializarse
ma|jor|ity mayoría
▶ **in a majority/in the
majority**
ma|jor key si/do mayor
ma|jor league gran liga, de
primera línea
make hacer(se), obligar,
convertir, establecer, ganar,
ser, formar parte, lograr,
alcanzar, marca
▶ **make a note/list** escribir
▶ **make do** conformarse
▶ **make for** dirigirse a
▶ **make it** lograr llegar,
lograr
▶ **make of** pensar de
▶ **make off** escapar, salir
corriendo
▶ **make out** distinguir,
comprender, entender, dar
a entender
▶ **make up** representar,
constituir, inventar,
reconciliarse
mak|er fabricante
make|up maquillaje,

composición, estructura
mak|ing hechura,
elaboración
▶ **in the making** en ciernes
▶ **be the making of** ser
decisivo para
▶ **have the makings of** tener
el potencial para
▶ **of one's own making**
hechura de uno, obra suya
male macho, varón, hombre,
masculino
ma|lig|nant maligno
mall centro comercial
mal|le|able maleable
• **mal|le|abil|ity** maleabilidad
mal|prac|tice negligencia
profesional
mama *también* **mamma**
mamá
mam|bo mambo
mam|mal mamífero *o*
mamífera
mam|ma|ry mamario
mam|ma|ry glands glándula
mamaria
mam|mog|ra|phy
mamografía
man hombre, manejar,
manipular, ocuparse de
man|age administrar,
arreglárselas
man|aged care asistencia
médica dirigida
man|age|ment
administración, gerencia
man|ag|er gerente,
administrador *o*
administradora, director *o*
directora
mana|tee manatí
man|date mandato, orden,
instrucción, directriz,
estipular, resolver
man|di|ble mandíbula
inferior
mane crin, melena
ma|neu|ver maniobrar,
abrirse paso, maniobra,
estratagema
man|hood madurez

mani|fest manifiesto, patente, evidente, mostrar, hacerse evidente • **mani|fest|ly** manifiestamente

mani|fes|to manifiesto

ma|nipu|late manipular • **ma|nipu|la|tion** manipulación

man|kind humanidad, género humano

man-made también **manmade** artificial, sintético, hecho por el hombre

manned tripulado

man|ner manera, modo, actitud • **-mannered** de ciertas maneras, de ciertos modales
▸ **good manners** buenos modales

man|sion mansión

man|tle manto

manu|al manual • **manu|al|ly** manualmente

manu|fac|ture fabricar, manufacturar, inventar, manufactura, fabricación, elaboración • **manu|fac|tur|ing** manufactura

manu|fac|tured home casa prefabricada

manu|fac|tur|er fabricante

manu|script manuscrito, original

many mucho o mucha, muchos o muchas, cuánto o cuánta, cuántos o cuántas
▸ **as many as** no menos de

map mapa, planisferio
▸ **map out** trazar, planear, planificar

map key explicación (de símbolos, distancias, etcétera)

ma|ple arce, arce (madera de)

ma|quette maqueta

mar estropear

mara|thon maratón, maratónico

mar|ble mármol, canica, bolita

march marchar, hacer marchar, ir, entrar, llevar, marcha, avance, manifestación • **march|er** manifestante

March marzo

mare yegua

mar|gin margen

mar|gin|al secundario, mínimo • **mar|gin|al|ly** ligeramente

mari|achi mariachi

ma|ri|jua|na mariguana, mota, yerba, marihuana, marijuana, de la verde

mari|nate marinar(se)

ma|rine infante de marina, marines, marino, marítimo

mari|tal marital, conyugal, nupcial

mari|time marítimo, náutico

mark marcar(se), señalar, dejar una marca, poner una marca, poner una señal, calificar, mancha, marca, señal, signo, calificación, punto, nota, punto de referencia, hito, indicador, meta, muestra • **mark|er** marcador • **mark|ing** calificar, calificación
▸ **leave one's/a mark** dejar marca, dejar marcado, marcar
▸ **make your/a mark** dejar marca
▸ **wide of the mark** errado, equivocado, no dado en el blanco
▸ **mark down** rebajar, bajar, reducir, anotar, escribir, apuntar
▸ **mark up** incrementar, subir

marked marcado, claro, evidente, notable • **mark|ed|ly** claramente

mar|ket mercado, plaza, tianguis, vender, comercializar,

m

poner a la venta,
distribuir • mar|ket|ing
mercadotecnia
▶ on the market en el
mercado, a la venta

mar|quee carpa,
marquesina, toldo

mar|riage matrimonio, vida
de casado, enlace, boda,
nupcias, casamiento

mar|riage li|cense licencia
de matrimonio, licencia
matrimonial, licencia para
casarse

mar|ried casado

mar|ry casar(se), contraer
matrimonio, contraer
nupcias, unir en
matrimonio

Mars Marte

marsh pantano, ciénaga,
marisma

mar|shal formar, reunir,
organizar, supervisor o
supervisora, vigilante, jefe
de policía, jefe de bomberos

mar|su|pial marsupial

mar|tial marcial

mar|tial art arte marcial

mar|vel|ous maravilloso,
prodigioso, espléndido
• mar|vel|ous|ly
maravillosamente

Marx|ism marxismo

Marx|ist marxista

mas|cara máscara, rímel

mas|cu|line masculino,
varonil • mas|cu|lin|ity
masculinidad

mask máscara, careta,
antifaz, mascarilla,
fachada, disfraz, ocultar,
disimular, disfrazar, cubrir

masked enmascarado,
disfrazado, encubierto

ma|son jar también Mason jar
frasco para conservas

mass montón, masa,
cúmulo, abundancia,
gran cantidad, misa,
masivo, generalizado,
concentrar(se), juntar(se)

• massed concentrado
▶ a mass of mucho
▶ masses of montones de,
mucho

mas|sa|cre masacre,
matanza, carnicería,
masacrar, matar en masa,
asesinar con crueldad

mas|sage masaje,
masajear(se), dar(se) masaje

m|ass ex|tinc|tion extinción
masiva, extinción en masa

mas|sive sólido, masivo,
enorme, cuantioso, muy
grande, grandísimo
• mas|sive|ly enormemente

mass me|dia medios de
comunicación (de masas)

mass move|ment
deslizamiento masivo

mass num|ber número de
masa, número másico

mass-produce producir en
masa, producir en serie,
fabricar en masa, fabricar
en serie • mass-produced
producido en serie

mass trans|it transporte
público

mast mástil, antena

mas|ter amo, patrón, jefe,
maestro, experto, señor,
dueño, dominar

master|piece obra maestra

mat mantel individual,
mantelito, tapete, felpudo

match juego, partido,
cerillo, fósforo, cerilla,
combinar, hacer juego,
casar, equiparar, estar a la
altura, comparar, ser igual
• match|ing que combina,
comparable, similar,
concordado

match|book carterita de
cerillos, cerillos de carterita

matched que hace pareja,
comparable, ser digno rival

mate pareja, aparearse

ma|terial material,
materia, tela, materiales
• ma|teri|al|ly

materialmente

ma|ter|nal maternal, materno

ma|ter|nity maternidad

math matemáticas

math|emati|cal matemático
• math|emati|cal|ly matemáticamente

math|ema|ti|cian matemático o matemática

math|emat|ics matemáticas

mati|nee matiné

ma|tron of hon|or dama de honor, madrina de boda

matte también matt, mat mate

mat|ter asunto, cuestión, cosas, material impreso, impresos, materia, problema, situación, circunstancia, cosa, importar, dar igual
▶ another matter/a different matter otro asunto, otra cosa, diferente
▶ it doesn't matter no importa, no tiene importancia
▶ no matter what sin importar

mat|tress colchón

ma|ture madurar, crecer, desarrollarse, maduro, adulto, desarrollado
• ma|tur|ity madurez

ma|ven experto

maxi|mum máximo, cuando mucho

may poder(se), quizá/quizás, poder, ser posible

May mayo

may|be quizá, posiblemente, tal vez, acaso

may|on|naise mayonesa

mayor alcalde o alcaldesa, presidente o presidenta municipal

me a mí, me, mí

meal comida

mean significar, querer decir, traducirse en, decir en serio, tener la intención, malo, cruel, promedio, media • mean|ness maldad

mean|ing significado, sentido, acepción, intención, propósito

mean|ing|ful significativo, importante, con sentido
• mean|ing|ful|ly significativamente

mean|ing|less sin sentido

means medio, instrumento, manera, recursos, medios, ingresos
▶ by means of por medio de, mediante
▶ by all means ¡cómo no!, por supuesto

meant ver mean
▶ be meant for estar destinado a, ser para
▶ be meant to se supone que

mean|time
▶ (in the) meantime entretanto, mientras, mientras tanto, por lo pronto

mean|while mientras tanto, entretanto

mea|sles sarampión

meas|ure medir, compás, gran medida, indicador
▶ measure up estar a la altura, ponerse a la altura
▶ take measures tomar medidas

meas|ure|ment medida

meat carne

meat|pack|ing también meat-packing, meat packing empacado de carne

me|chan|ic mecánico o mecánica, mecanismo

me|chani|cal mecánico, maquinal, automático
• me|chani|cal|ly mecánicamente

me|chani|cal ad|van|tage rendimiento mecánico

me|chani|cal en|er|gy energía mecánica

me|chani|cal weath|er|ing desgaste mecánico

m

mecha|nism mecanismo

mecha|nize mecanizar, automatizar
• **mecha|ni|za|tion** mecanización

med|al medalla, condecoración

med|al|ist medallista

Med|al of Hon|or Medalla de Honor

me|dia medios de comunicación, *ver* medium

me|dia cir|cus circo mediático

me|dian valor medio, mediana

me|dian strip camellón, mediana

me|dia source fuente de los medios, fuente mediática

me|di|ate mediar, hacer de mediador, actuar como mediador, arbitrar
• **me|dia|tion** mediación
• **me|dia|tor** mediador *o* mediadora

med|ic médico *o* médica, estudiante de medicina

Medi|caid Medicaid, programa estadounidense de asistencia médica para los pobres

medi|cal médico
• **medi|cal|ly** médicamente

medi|cal ex|am|in|er médico *o* médica forense, el forense *o* la forense

Medi|care Medicare, programa estadounidense de asistencia médica para ancianos

medi|ca|tion medicación, medicamento, medicina, remedio

medi|cine medicina, medicamento, remedio, medicación

me|di|eval medieval, de la Edad Media

me|dio|cre mediocre, ordinario • **me|di|oc|rity** mediocridad

medi|tate meditar, reflexionar, cavilar
• **medi|ta|tion** meditación

me|dium mediano, medio, intermedio, instrumento

me|dul|la médula, médula oblonga, bulbo raquídeo

me|du|sa medusa, aguamala, malagua

meet conocer(se), encontrar(se), verse, juntarse, reunirse, recibir, recoger, aceptar, satisfacer, cumplir, resolver, hacer frente, enfrentar, sufragar, correr con, tocarse
▶ **meet up** conocer(se), encontrar(se)

meet|ing reunión, junta, encuentro

mega|byte megabyte

meio|sis meiosis

mela|nin melanina

meld unir, mezclar, fusionar(se), mezcla

melo|dy melodía

mel|on melón

melt derretir(se), fundir(se), desvanecerse, disiparse, desaparecer, derretido
• **melting** fusión

melt|ing point punto de fusión

mem|ber miembro, asociado *o* asociada, socio *o* socia

Mem|ber of Par|lia|ment parlamentario *o* parlamentaria, miembro del parlamento

mem|ber|ship afiliación, calidad de socio, calidad de asociado, nómina de socios

mem|bra|no|phone membranófono

memo memorándum, circular

mem|oirs memorias

memo|rable memorable

me|mo|rial monumento, conmemorativo

memo|rize memorizar

M

memo|ry memoria, recuerdo
 ▸ **from memory** de memoria
memo|ry card tarjeta de
 memoria
men *ver* **man**
mend zurcir, remendar,
 curar(se)
 ▸ **be on the mend** mejorar,
 reponerse
me|nis|cus menisco
Men|no|nite menonita
meno|pause menopausia
 • **meno|pau|sal**
 menopáusico
me|no|rah menorá
men's room baño de
 hombres
men|stru|ate menstruar
 • **men|strua|tion**
 menstruación
men|tal mental • **men|tal|ly**
 mentalmente
men|tion mencionar, decir
men|tor mentor *o* mentora
menu carta, menú
MEP eurodiputado
Mercator pro|jec|tion
 proyección de/conforme a
 Mercator
mer|chan|dise mercancía,
 mercadería
mer|chan|dis|er
 comerciante, minorista
mer|chant comerciante,
 mercante
mer|ci|ful|ly por fortuna,
 felizmente
mer|cu|ry mercurio
Mer|cu|ry Mercurio
mer|cy piedad
 ▸ **at the mercy of** a merced
 de
mere mero, simple, apenas
mere|ly simplemente,
 apenas
 ▸ **not merely** no
 simplemente, no solamente
merge fusionar(se), confluir,
 unir(se)
mer|ger fusión
mer|it mérito, ventaja,

merecer, ameritar
mer|ry alegre, feliz
 • **mer|ri|ly** alegremente
me|sa meseta, mesa
meso|sphere mesosfera
Meso|zo|ic era mesozoico
mess desorden, revoltijo,
 desastre, caos
 ▸ **mess around**
 entretenerse, meterse con
 ▸ **mess up** echar a perder,
 arruinar, desarreglar,
 desordenar
mes|sage mensaje,
 recado, enviar mensajes
 electrónicos
mes|sage board tablero de
 anuncios
mes|sen|ger mensajero
Messiah Mesías
messy desordenado,
 sucio, sucio y descuidado,
 desagradable
met *ver* **meet**
me|tabo|lism metabolismo
met|al metal
me|tal|lic bond enlace
 metálico
met|al|loid metaloide
meta|mor|phic metamórfico
meta|mor|pho|sis
 metamorfosis, conversión
meta|phase metafase
meta|phor metáfora
me|tas|ta|size
 extenderse/diseminarse por
 metástasis
me|teor|oid meteoroide
me|teor|ol|ogy meteorología
me|ter medidor, metro,
 compás
 ▸ **meters per second** metros
 por segundo
metha|done metadona
metha|no|gen bacterias
 productoras de metano
metha|nol metanol
meth|od método
me|thodi|cal metódico
 • **me|thodi|cal|ly**
 metódicamente

m

met|ric métrico

met|ric sys|tem sistema métrico decimal

met|ric ton tonelada (métrica)

met|ro *también* **Metro** metro, metropolitano, tren subterráneo

met|ro|poli|tan metropolitano

mez|za|nine mezzanine, platea, primer balcón

mg miligramo (mg)

MIA desaparecido en acción

mice *ver* **mouse**

micro|chip microcircuito

micro|cli|mate *también* **micro-climate** microclima

micro|eco|nom|ics *también* **micro-economics** microeconomía

• **micro|eco|nom|ic** microeconómico

micro|fiber microfibra

micro|organism microorganismo

micro|phone micrófono

micro|scope microscopio

micro|scop|ic microscópico

micro|wave horno de microondas, calentar/cocinar en horno de microondas

mid-Atlantic mezcla de acento británico y estadounidense

mid|dle centro, medio, en medio/enmedio, de enmedio

▶ **in the middle of** en medio de

mid|dle age madurez, mediana edad

middle-aged de mediana edad, maduro

mid|dle class clase media, de clase media

Mid|dle East Medio Oriente, Oriente Medio

middle|man intermediario

mid|field centro del campo, centro/centrocampista, medio/mediocampista

mid|field|er centro, medio

mid|night medianoche

mid-ocean ridge *también* **mid-oceanic ridge** cordillera océanica central

mid|ship|man guardia marina/guardiamarina

midst

▶ **in the midst of** en medio de, entre

mid|term mitad de un período

mid|town del centro, centro

mid|wife comadrona, partera

might *ver* **may**, poder(se), poderío

mightn't = might not

might've = might have

mighty poderoso, fortísimo, muy, sumamente

mi|graine jaqueca, migraña

mi|grant trabajador extranjero *o* trabajadora extranjera

mi|grate emigrar, migrar

• **mi|gra|tion** emigración, migración

mild ligero, suave • **mild|ly** ligeramente, benigno

mile milla

▶ **miles (away)** lejísimos

mile|age kilometraje, provecho

mili|tant militante, combativo • **mili|tan|cy** militancia

mili|tary militar, ejército • **mili|tari|ly** militarmente

mi|li|tia milicia

milk leche, ordeñar, aprovecharse de • **milk|ing** ordeña

Milky Way Vía Láctea

mill molino, acería/fundición (acero), aserradero (madera), fábrica (algodón)

▶ **mill around** dar vueltas,

arremolinarse

mil|li|gram miligramo

mil|li|meter milímetro

mil|lion millón

mil|lion|aire millonario o millonaria

mil|lionth millonésimo

mince picar

mind mente, cabeza, cerebro, importar, cuidar, atender
▸ **bear/keep in mind** tener en mente, tener presente, tener en cuenta
▸ **change one's mind** cambiar de opinión
▸ **cross one's mind** ocurrirse, pasar(se) por la cabeza
▸ **in one's mind's eye** como estarlo viendo
▸ **make up one's mind** decidirse
▸ **be on one's mind** tener en la cabeza, pensar en
▸ **one's mind is on/have one's mind on** tener la mente puesta en, concentrarse
▸ **have an open mind** tener una actitud abierta
▸ **be out of one's mind** estar loco
▸ **take one's mind off** distraer
▸ **to my mind** en mi opinión
▸ **never mind** ni hablar de, ya no decir para

mind|less insensato, sin sentido, ciego, mecánico ● **mind|less|ly** mecánicamente

mine mí/mío, mina, extraer, explotar ● **min|er** minero o minera ● **min|ing** minería

min|er|al mineral

min|er|al wa|ter agua mineral

minia|ture miniatura
▸ **in miniature** en miniatura

mini|bus *también* **mini-bus** minibús

mini|mal mínimo
● **mini|mal|ly** mínimamente

mini|mal|ism minimalismo

mini|mize reducir al mínimo, desestimar

mini|mum mínimo o mínima

mini|mum se|cu|rity pris|on prisión de baja seguridad, cárcel abierta, cárcel de puertas abiertas

min|is|ter ministro o ministra, pastor o pastora, cónsul, secretario o secretaria

min|is|te|rial ministerial, administrativo, de gabinete

min|is|try ministerio, clero, clerecía, secretaría

mini|van minivan

mi|nor menor, poco importante, menos importante, menor de edad

mi|nor|ity minoría

mi|nor key tono menor

mi|nor league liga menor, de segunda, menor

min|strel show minstrel show

mint menta, pastilla de menta, casa de moneda, casa de la moneda, acuñar ● **mint|ing** acuñación

mi|nus menos, sin, desventaja, deficiencia, contra

mi|nute minuto, rato, instante, momento, minuta, muy pequeño, diminuto, muy poco, poquito ● **mi|nute|ly** mínimamente
▸ **(at) any minute (now)** en cualquier momento, ya
▸ **last minute** de último momento, a ultima hora
▸ **take minutes** levantar acta
▸ **the minute** en el momento, tan pronto como
▸ **wait a minute** un momento

mira|cle milagro, milagroso

mir|ror espejo, reflejar(se)

mis|be|hav|ior mala

m

conducta, mal comportamiento

mis|car|riage aborto espontáneo, aborto no provocado

mis|cel|la|neous mixto, heterogéneo, variado, de todo tipo

mis|chief travesura, diablura, maldad, daño, engorro

mis|con|duct mala conducta, falta de ética profesional, inmoralidad

mis|er|able infeliz, desgraciado, desdichado, pésimo, atroz, lamentable • **mis|er|ably** miserablemente

mis|ery miseria, infelicidad, desdicha, desgracia, sufrimiento

mis|fit inadaptado *o* inadaptada, raro *o* rara

mis|lead engañar, inducir a error

mis|lead|ing engañoso • **mis|lead|ing|ly** engañosamente

mis|led *ver* mislead

mis|per|cep|tion idea falsa, error

mis|placed que no viene al caso, equivocado

mis|read entender mal, interpretar mal, malinterpretar, leer mal • **mis|read|ing** mala interpretación

Miss señorita

miss errar, fallar, pasar por alto, omitir, escapársele a uno algo, írsele a uno algo, extrañar, echar de menos, hacer falta algo, perder, perderse uno algo, faltar, fallo, falla
▶ **miss out** dejar pasar, desaprovechar

mis|sile misil, proyectil

miss|ing perdido, traspapelado, que falta, desaparecido

mis|sion misión, delegación

mis|sion|ary misionero *o* misionera

mis|state exponer mal, exponer falsamente

mis|state|ment declaración tergiversada, relato inexacto, inexactitud, hecho erróneo

mis|step desliz, paso en falso

mist neblina, bruma, empañar(se), cubrir(se) de neblina

mis|take error, equivocación, confundir
▶ **there's no mistaking** ser inconfundible algo, no caber duda

mis|tak|en equivocado, falso • **mis|tak|en|ly** equivocadamente

mis|ter señor

mis|took *ver* mistake

mis|tri|al juicio nulo

mis|trust desconfianza, recelo, desconfiar de, recelar de

mis|under|stand interpretar mal, no entender, no comprender, entender mal, comprender mal

mis|under|stood *ver* misunderstand, incomprendido

mito|chon|drion mitocondria

mi|to|sis mitosis

mix mezclar(se), juntar(se), combinar(se), preparado, mezcla, mixtura, combinación
▶ **mix up** confundir, revolver

mixed encontrado, ambivalente, de todo tipo, diverso, mixto , mezclado

mixed me|dia técnica mixta

mixed me|ter compás mixto

mixed up confundido, confuso, desorientado, enredado, liado, mezclado

mix|ture mezcla, mixtura,

mescolanza

ml ml, mL, mililitro

mm mm, milímetro

moan quejarse, protestar, gemir, quejido, queja, gemido, lamento

mob turba, asediar

mo|bile móvil, ambulante • **mo|bil|ity** movilidad

mo|bi|lize movilizar(se) • **mo|bi|li|za|tion** movilización

mo|cha café moca/moka

mock burlarse de • **mock|ing** burlón, simulado, fingido

mode estilo de vida, modo de vida, estilo, modo

mod|el modelo, maqueta, a escala, en miniatura, inspirar, modelar • **mod|el|ing** modelaje

mod|er|ate moderado o moderada, mediano, moderar • **mod|er|ate|ly** moderadamente • **mod|era|tion** moderación

mod|ern moderno

mod|ern dance danza contemporánea, danza moderna

mod|ern|ize modernizar • **mod|erni|za|tion** modernización

mod|est modesto, moderado • **mod|est|ly** moderadamente, modestamente

mod|es|ty modestia

modi|fi|er modificador

modi|fy modificar • **modi|fi|ca|tion** modificación

Moho *también* **Mohorovicic Discontinuity** Discontinuidad de Mohorovicic

moist húmedo

mois|ture humedad

mold molde, moho, moldear, modelar

mol|ecule molécula

mo|lest abusar sexualmente (de alguien)

mol|ten fundido

molt|ing muda (piel, pelo, plumaje)

mom ma, mamá

mo|ment instante, momento
▸ **at the moment** o **at this moment** o **at the/this present moment** en este momento, por el momento
▸ **for the moment** hasta este momento
▸ **the moment** en cuanto, en el momento

mo|men|tum impulso, momento, momentum

mom|ma mamá

mom|my mami

mon|arch monarca

mon|ar|chy monarquía

mon|as|tery monasterio

Mon|day lunes

mon|etary monetario

mon|ey dinero
▸ **(get your) money's worth** sacarle jugo al dinero, verse recompensado

mon|ey or|der giro postal

moni|tor observar, seguir de cerca, monitor

monk monje

mon|key chango, mono

mon|key bars estructura de barras para juegos infantiles

mono mononucleosis, enfermedad del beso, fiebre glandular

mono|chro|mat|ic monocromático

mono|cline pliegue monoclinal

mono|lith|ic monolítico

mono|logue *también* **monolog** monólogo

mo|no|mial monomio, de un solo término, de un monomio

mono|nu|cleo|sis mononucleosis, fiebre

m

glandular, enfermedad del beso

mo|nopo|lize monopolizar

mo|nopo|ly monopolio

mono|theism monoteísmo

mono|theis|tic monoteístas

mono|to|nous monótono

mono|treme monotrema

mon|soon monzón

mon|ster monstruo, gigante

month mes

month|ly mensual, mensualmente

monu|ment monumento

monu|men|tal monumental

mood humor
▶ be in a mood estar de mal humor

moody voluble, temperamental ● moodi|ly de mal humor ● moodi|ness mal humor

moon luna

moon|light luz de (la) luna, tener un segundo empleo

moon|shine aguardiente casero, tontería, sandez, estupidez

moor atracar, amarrar (un bote, un barco)

mop trapeador, trapear
▶ mop up limpiar, secar
▶ mop one's forehead secarse la frente

mo|ped bicimoto

mo|raine morena

mor|al moralidad, sentido moral, moral, moraleja ● mor|al|ly moralmente
▶ moral support apoyo moral

mo|rale ánimo

mor|al fi|ber carácter

mo|ral|ity moralidad

more más
▶ more and more más y más, cada vez más
▶ more than más que/de
▶ what is more lo que es más

more|over además

morn|ing mañana

▶ in the morning en la mañana

mor|tal mortal ● mor|tal|ity mortalidad ● mor|tal|ly mortalmente

mor|tar mortero, cemento

mor|tar|board birrete

mort|gage hipoteca, hipotecar

mo|sa|ic mosaico

mosque mezquita

mos|qui|to mosquito

moss musgo

most casi todos, la mayoría, la mayor parte, la mayor, lo más, más
▶ most of all más
▶ at most/at the most máximo, como más
▶ make the most of something sacar el mayor provecho

most|ly principalmente, en su mayor parte

mo|tel motel

moth polilla

moth|er madre, proteger

moth|er coun|try madre patria

mother-in-law suegra

mo|tion movimiento, ademán, gesto, moción, indicar con un gesto, indicar con la mano
▶ go through the motions hacer algo sin interés, hacer algo por pura fórmula
▶ in motion en movimiento, en marcha
▶ set the wheels in motion poner en marcha, echar a andar

mo|tion pic|ture película, cine

mo|ti|vate motivar ● mo|ti|vat|ed motivado ● mo|ti|va|tion motivación

mo|ti|va|tion motivación

mo|tive motivo

mo|tor motor, motorizado

motor|cycle motocicleta

M

mo|tor|ist automovilista

mo|tor neu|ron neurona motora

mound montículo, montón

mount montar, realizar, aumentar, acumular, subir, monte

moun|tain montaña, montón

moun|tain bike bicicleta de montaña

moun|tain go|ril|la gorila de montaña

moun|tain lion puma, león de montaña

mount|ed montado
 ▶ mounted police policía montada

mourn llorar, enlutarse, llevar luto, lamentar

mouse ratón, mouse

mouse pad también mousepad mousepad, cojín del mouse, cojín del ratón

mousse mousse

mouth boca, entrada, desembocadura, esbozar con los labios ● -mouthed boqui-

mov|able pul|ley también moveable pulley polea móvil

move mover(se), quitar, cambiar(se), mudar, pasar, mudar/cambiar de opinión, avanzar, desarrollarse, incitar, causar, conmover(se), movimiento, paso, jugada, movida, mudanza, cambio, mudanza/cambio de opinión, avance ● moved conmovido
 ▶ on the move en marcha, en movimiento, de un lado para otro
 ▶ move in cambiarse, mudarse, intervenir
 ▶ move off retirarse, alejarse
 ▶ move on trasladarse
 ▶ move out mudarse

 ▶ move up hacerse a un lado

move|ment movimiento, desplazamiento, avance, actividades

move|ment pat|tern patrón de movimiento

mov|er cargador o cargadora, persona que hace mudanzas

movie película, cine

movie star estrella del cine

movie thea|ter cine

mov|ing conmovedor, movible, móvil ● mov|ing|ly de manera conmovedora

moz|za|rel|la queso mozzarella

MP3 MP3

MP3 play|er reproductor de MP3

mph también m.p.h. mph, millas por hora

Mr. señor (Sr.)

Mrs. señora (Sra.)

Ms. señora (Sra.) o señorita (Srita.)

MS esclerosis múltiple (EM)

m/s m/s, metros por segundo

m/s/s m/s², metros por segundo cuadrado

much mucho, tanto, muy similar, la mayor parte, cuánto
 ▶ not so much no tan... como/no tanto como
 ▶ too much demasiado

mu|cus mucosa

mud lodo, fango

mud|dle lío, confundir, enredar, entreverar
 ● mud|dled up enredado
 ▶ muddle through arreglárselas
 ▶ muddle up confundir

mud|dled confundido, hecho un lío

mud|dy lodoso, enlodar(se), enredar, enmarañar

mud|flow alud de lodo

mud|slide alud de lodo

muf|fin panquecito,

panqueque

mug tarro, asaltar
- **mug|ging** asalto - **mug|ger** asaltante

multi|cel|lu|lar pluricelular, multicelular

multi|col|ored multicolor

multi|lat|er|al multilateral

multi|media multimedia

multi|na|tion|al multinacional, compañía multinacional

multi|ple múltiple, múltiplo

multi|pli|er multiplicador

multi|ply multiplicar
- **multi|pli|ca|tion** multiplicación

multi|pur|pose multiuso

multi|story *también* **multistoried** edificio de varios pisos

multi|vita|min *también* **multi-vitamin** multivitamínico

mu|nici|pal municipal

mu|ni|tions municiones

mu|ral mural

mur|der asesinato, asesinar
- **mur|der|er** asesino *o* asesina

mur|mur susurrar, murmurar, susurro, murmullo

mus|cle músculo, influencia
▶ **flex one's muscles** demostrar poder
▶ **muscle in** meterse por la fuerza, entrometerse

mus|cle tis|sue tejido muscular

mus|cu|lar muscular, musculoso

mus|cu|lar sys|tem sistema muscular

muse cavilar, preguntarse, reflexionar - **mus|ing** cavilación

mu|seum museo

mush|room hongo, crecer como hongo

mu|sic música

mu|si|cal musical, con aptitudes para la música

- **mu|si|cal|ly** musicalmente

mu|si|cal in|stru|ment instrumento musical

mu|si|cal|ity musicalidad

mu|si|cal thea|ter teatro musical

mu|si|cian músico *o* música

Mus|lim musulmán *o* musulmana

muss desordenar, despeinar

mus|sel mejillón

must deber, tener que, cosa imprescindible
▶ **if one must** si uno debe hacer algo

mus|tache bigote

mus|tard mostaza

mustn't = must not

must've = must have

mu|ta|gen mutágeno

mute mudo, disminuir, bajar el sonido o el volumen, bajo - **mut|ed** débil

mut|ter hablar entre dientes, mascullar, murmullo
- **mut|ter|ing** murmullos

mut|ton carne de borrego/carnero

mu|tu|al mutuo - **mu|tu|al|ly** para ambos

mu|tu|al fund fondo de inversión

mu|tu|al|ism mutualismo

muz|zle hocico, bozal, boca, cañón (de un arma), poner un bozal

MVP jugador más valioso *o* jugadora más valiosa

my mi

my|self yo mismo *o* yo misma, a mí mismo *o* a mí misma, por mi parte

mys|teri|ous misterioso
- **mys|teri|ous|ly** misteriosamente

mys|tery misterio, misterioso, novela de misterio/suspenso

myth mito - **mythi|cal** mítico

my|thol|ogy mitología
- **mytho|logi|cal** mitológico

Nn

na|chos totopos
nail clavo, uña, clavar
▶ **nail down** establecer con certeza, concretar
na|ive *también* **naïve** ingenuo
● **na|ive|ly** ingenuamente
● **na|ive|té** ingenuidad
na|ked desnudo, descubierto, manifiesto ● **na|ked|ness** desnudez ● **nakedly** manifiestamente
▶ **to the naked eye** a simple vista
name nombre, nombrar, llamar, identificar, decir
▶ **by name/by the name of** al nombre de
▶ **call somebody names** insultar, decir de todo
▶ **in somebody's name/in the name of somebody** a nombre de
▶ **in the name of something** en nombre de, con pretexto de
▶ **make a name for oneself/ make one's name** hacerse de un nombre, hacerse de fama
▶ **the name of the game** el nombre del juego
name|ly es decir, a saber
nan|ny nana, niñera
nap siesta, dormitar
nap|kin servilleta
nar|ra|tive relato, narración
nar|row angosto, estrecho, intolerante, cerrado, escaso, estrecharse, angostarse, reducir ● **nar|row|ness** estrechez ● **nar|row|ing** reducción ● **nar|row|ly** escasamente
▶ **narrow down** reducir
▶ **have a narrow escape** salvarse de milagro
nas|ty detestable, repugnante, horripilante, cruel, peliagudo, horrible
● **nas|ti|ness** lo repugnante
● **nas|ti|ly** de manera cruel
na|tion nación, país, estado
na|tion|al nacional, ciudadano *o* ciudadana
● **na|tion|al|ly** a escala nacional
na|tion|al debt deuda nacional
na|tion|al holi|day fiesta patria, día de fiesta nacional
na|tion|al|ist nacionalista
● **nationalism** nacionalismo
na|tion|al|ity nacionalidad
na|tion|al se|cu|rity seguridad nacional
nation|wide a escala nacional, en todo el país
na|tive natal, originario de *u* originaria de, materno
natu|ral natural, nato, innato, de nacimiento, talento innato ● **natu|ral|ly** con naturalidad, naturalmente
● **natu|ral|ness** naturalidad
natu|ral food alimento natural
natu|ral gas gas natural
natu|ral light luz natural
natu|ral|ly naturalmente, de manera natural
▶ **come naturally** con toda naturalidad
natu|ral re|sources recursos naturales
natu|ral se|lec|tion selección natural
na|ture naturaleza, carácter, índole
▶ **by its nature** por su naturaleza
▶ **second nature** parte de la naturaleza de

n

naugh|ty travieso

na|val naval, de la marina

navi|gate conducir, navegar, capitanear • **navi|ga|tion** navegación

navy marina de guerra, armada, azul marino

NBA Asociación Nacional de Baloncesto/Basketball, NBA

Ne|an|der|thal Neanderthal, hombre de Neanderthal

neap tide marea muerta

near cerca, cercano, a punto de, al borde de, cerca de, casi
  ▶ **in the near future** en un futuro próximo
  ▶ **nowhere near/not anywhere near** ni siquiera cerca, para nada

near|by cerca, cercano

near|ly casi
  ▶ **not nearly** ni con mucho

near-sighted miope, corto de vista

neat ordenado, ingenioso, a todo dar • **neat|ly** con cuidado, netamente • **neat|ness** pulcritud

nebu|la nebulosa

nec|es|sari|ly necesariamente
  ▶ **not necessarily** no necesariamente

nec|es|sary necesario
  ▶ **necessary evil** mal necesario

ne|ces|sity necesidad
  ▶ **of necessity** por necesidad

neck cuello
  ▶ **neck and neck** a la par

neck|lace collar

nec|tar néctar

need necesitar, necesidad
  ▶ **in need** necesitado
  ▶ **be in need of** necesitar, hacer falta

nee|dle aguja, aguja hipodérmica, aguja de tejer

nega|tive desalentador, negativo, negación
  • **nega|tive|ly** negativamente

• **nega|tiv|ity** negativismo

nega|tive ac|cel|era|tion aceleración negativa, desaceleración

ne|glect descuidar, abandonar, desatender, descuido, abandono, negligencia • **ne|glect|ed** abandonado

ne|go|ti|ate negociar

ne|go|tia|tion negociación

neigh|bor vecino o vecina, persona que está al lado, cosa que está cerca o junto a otra

neigh|bor|hood vecindario, barrio

neigh|bor|ing vecino

neigh|bor|ly amable, con amabilidad

nei|ther ni, ninguno o ninguna, ni uno ni otro, tampoco

nek|ton necton

neph|ew sobrino

Nep|tune Neptuno

nerve nervio, valor, coraje, frescura, desvergüenza, descaro
  ▶ **get on somebody's nerves** poner los nervios de punta, crispar los nervios, sacar de quicio

nerv|ous nervioso
  • **nerv|ous|ly** nerviosamente
  • **nerv|ous|ness** nerviosismo

nerv|ous sys|tem sistema nervioso

nerv|ous tis|sue tejido nervioso

nerv|y valiente

nest nido, colmena, avispero, hormiguero, ratonera, anidar

net red, net, Internet, neto, producir, ganar

net force fuerza neta

net|work red, cadena, grupo, establecer contacto

net|work card también **network interface card**

tarjeta de red

neu|ron neurona

neu|tral neutral, neutro, punto muerto • **neu|tral|ity** neutralidad

neu|tron neutrón

neu|tron star estrella de neutrones

nev|er nunca
▸ **never ever** nunca jamás

never|the|less no obstante, sin embargo

new nuevo

new|comer recién llegado

new|ly recientemente, recién

news noticia, nueva, noticias
▸ **bad news/good news** buenas/malas nuevas
▸ **be news to (somebody)** ser nuevo para

news agen|cy agencia de noticias

news|cast noticiario (formal), noticiero (informal)

news|caster locutor o locutora, presentador o presentadora

news con|fer|ence rueda de prensa, conferencia de prensa

news|paper periódico, diario, papel periódico

news re|lease comunicado de prensa

new|ton newton

New Year's Año Nuevo

next siguiente, próximo, de al lado, ahora
▸ **next best** segundo mejor
▸ **next to** junto a, casi, prácticamente

NFL Liga Nacional de Fútbol

NHL Liga Nacional de Hockey sobre hielo

nice sabroso, rico, bueno, amable • **nice|ly** hermosamente, amablemente, muy bien

nick hacer una muesca,

cortar(se), muesca, corte, rasguño
▸ **in the nick of time** justo a tiempo, muy a tiempo

nick|el níquel, centavo, céntimo

nick|name apodo, sobrenombre, mote, apodar, poner (un apodo)

niece sobrina

night noche
▸ **at night** de la noche
▸ **day and night/night and day** noche y día, día y noche
▸ **have an early/late night** acostarse temprano/tarde
▸ **anoche** last night

night|club club nocturno

night|gown camisón

night|mare pesadilla

night|stick macana, porra

nil nada, cero, nulo

nim|bus nimbo

NIMBY también **Nimby** comodino

nine nueve

nine-eleven también **nine eleven, 9/11** once de septiembre

nine|teen diecinueve

nine|teenth décimonono, décimonoveno

nine|ti|eth nonagésimo

nine-to-five de nueve a cinco

nine|ty noventa
▸ **the nineties** los (años) noventa

ninth noveno

nite noche

ni|trate nitrato

ni|tro|gen nitrógeno

nix rechazar

no no, ninguno o ninguna
▸ **there is no** no hay

No. No.

no|ble noble, aristócrata
• **no|bly** generosamente

no|ble gas gas noble, gas inerte, gas raro

no|body nadie, don nadie

no-brain|er algo muy fácil de

hacer, entender o responder
noc|tur|nal nocturno,
noctívago
nod asentir con la cabeza,
hacer un gesto de
aprobación con la cabeza,
señalar con la cabeza,
saludar con (un gesto de) la
cabeza
▸ **nod off** cabecear, quedarse
dormido
Noh teatro no/nō
noise ruido
noisy ruidoso • **noisi|ly**
ruidosamente
no|mad nómada, nómade
• **no|mad|ic** nómada
nomi|nal nominal
• **nomi|nal|ly** nominalmente
nomi|nate nombrar,
postular, nominar
nomi|na|tion
nombramiento,
postulación, nominación
nomi|nee candidato
none ninguno o ninguna,
nada
▸ **none too** no...mucho/muy
none|the|less no obstante,
sin embargo
non|fo|li|at|ed sin foliación
non|liv|ing también **non-
living** inorgánico
non|met|al también **non-
metal** no metal
non|objec|tive abstracto
nonpoint-source pol|lu|tion
contaminación sin origen
determinado
non|pre|scrip|tion sin
receta, sin necesidad de
receta
non|profit también **not-for-
profit** sin fines de lucro, sin
fines lucrativos
non|re|new|able también
non-renewable no
removable
▸ **non-renewable resources**
recursos no renovables
non|sense tontería,
disparate, desatino

non|sense syl|la|ble sílaba
absurda
non|sili|cate min|er|al
mineral sin silicatos
non|stand|ard unit unidad
no normalizada
non|vas|cu|lar plant también
non-vascular plant planta
sin sistema vascular
non|ver|bal no verbal
noo|dle fideo
noon mediodía
no one nadie
noon|time también **noon-
time, noon time** mediodía
nor ni, tampoco
norm norma
nor|mal normal
nor|mal fault falla normal
nor|mal|ly normalmente
north también **North** norte
north|east noreste/nordeste
north|eastern
noreste/nordeste
north|ern también **Northern**
del norte
north|ern|er norteño
nose nariz, proa
▸ **under somebody's nose**
en las narices
nosh tentempié, bocado
no-show alguien que no se
presenta donde lo esperaban
not no
▸ **not (even)** no...ni
▸ **not at all** claro que no
no|table notable
no|tably especialmente,
particularmente
no|ta|tion notación
note nota, notar, anotar
▸ **compare notes** comparar
notas
▸ **of note** de nota, digno de
nota, notable
▸ **take note** tomar nota
▸ **note down** anotar
note|book cuaderno (de
notas), computadora
portátil
not|ed conocido

noth|ing nada
▶ **nothing but** lo único que, solamente
▶ **be nothing to it** ser muy fácil

no|tice notar, avisar, letrero, aviso
▶ **until further notice** hasta nuevo aviso
▶ **give somebody notice** avisar, despedir
▶ **hand/give in one's notice** presentar la renuncia
▶ **take notice** prestar atención
▶ **take no notice** no hacer caso

no|tice|able perceptible, evidente ● **no|tice|ably** perceptiblemente

no|ti|fy notificar
● **no|ti|fi|ca|tion** notificación

no|tion idea, artículo (de la materia de que se trate)

no|to|ri|ous notorio, de mala fama ● **no|to|ri|ous|ly** notoriamente

noun nombre, sustantivo

nov|el novela, novedoso

nov|el|ist novelista

No|vem|ber noviembre

nov|ice novato o novata, principiante o principianta

now ahora, ya, bueno, vamos
▶ **any day/moment/time now** en cualquier momento
▶ **just now** hace un rato
▶ **now and then/now and again/every now and then/ every now and again** de vez en cuando, alguna que otra vez, de cuando en cuando

nowa|days hoy en día, en la actualidad, actualmente

no|where en ningún lugar, de la nada
▶ **be getting nowhere** no llevar a ninguna

parte/ningún lado
▶ **in the middle of nowhere** en medio de la nada
▶ **nowhere near** ni por asomo, ni con mucho

no-win situa|tion callejón sin salida

nu|clear nuclear

nu|clear en|er|gy energía nuclear

nu|clear fis|sion fisión nuclear

nu|clear fu|sion ver fusion

nu|cleic acid ácido nucleico

nu|cleo|tide nucleótido

null
▶ **null and void** nulo, inválido

numb entumecido, adormecido, petrificado, atontar, entumecer ● **numb|ness** entumecimiento ● **numbed** atontado

num|ber número, vario, tener en total, numerar

nu|mer|ous numeroso

nun monja

nurse enfermero o enfermera, atender, cuidar, abrigar, sufrir

nurse prac|ti|tion|er enfermero especializado o enfermera especializada

nurse|ry semillero, vivero

nurse|ry rhyme canción infantil

nur|ture criar, educar, fomentar

nut nuez, tuerca, fanático o fanática
▶ **nuts (about something/ somebody)** loco, chiflado
▶ **do one's nut/go nuts** estar hecho una fiera

nu|tri|ent nutriente

nu|tri|tion nutrición

nu|tri|tious nutritivo

n

Oo

oak roble, (madera de) roble

oar remo

oasis oasis

oath juramento

oat|meal avena, hojuelas de avena

oats avena

obese obeso • obesity obesidad

obey obedecer

ob/gyn ginecología, ginecólogo o ginecóloga

obi|tu|ary obituario, nota necrológica

object objeto, propósito, objetar, poner objeción
  ▶ money is no object el dinero no preocupa

objec|tion objeción

objec|tive objetivo
  • objec|tive|ly objetivamente
  • objec|tiv|ity objetividad

objec|tive lens objetivo

obli|ga|tion obligación

oblige obligar, ponerse a disposición, complacer

obo ofrezca

ob|scure oscuro, críptico, tapar • ob|scu|rity oscuridad

ob|ser|va|tion observación
  • ob|ser|va|tion|al de observación

ob|serve observar
  • ob|ser|vance observancia

ob|serv|er observador u observadora

ob|sess obsesionar(se)
  • ob|sessed obsesionado

ob|ses|sion obsesión

ob|sta|cle obstáculo

ob|tain obtener

ob|vi|ous obvio

ob|vi|ous|ly obviamente, evidente, claro

oc|ca|sion ocasión

oc|ca|sion|al ocasional
  • oc|ca|sion|al|ly ocasionalmente

oc|cu|pant ocupante, inquilino o inquilina

oc|cu|pa|tion ocupación, trabajo • oc|cu|pa|tion|al profesional

oc|cu|py ocupar(se)
  • oc|cu|pied ocupado

oc|cur ocurrir(se), haber

ocean océano

ocean-going trasatlántico

ocean|og|ra|phy oceanografía

ocean trench fosa océanica, fosa submarina

o'clock en punto

Oc|to|ber octubre

oc|to|pus pulpo

odd raro, extraño, ocasional, uno que otro, y tantos, y tantas, impar, non • odd|ly de manera rara
  ▶ odd one out excepción

odd jobs trabajitos

odds probabilidad
  ▶ at odds en desacuerdo, enfrentado
  ▶ against all odds en contra de todo, a pesar de todo

odom|eter odómetro

odor olor

odor|less inodoro

od|ys|sey odisea

of de, para (la hora)
  ▶ dream of (somebody/something) soñar con

of course claro, desde luego, por supuesto
  ▶ of course not claro que no, desde luego que no, por supuesto que no

off de, hacia afuera, fuera, cancelado, apagado, frente

a, cerca de, a poca distancia de
▸ **a long time/way off** en el futuro, muy lejano
▸ **be off something** sin tomar, sin usar
▸ **go off (somewhere)** alejarse
▸ **have a day off** tener un día libre
▸ **off and on** de vez en cuando, alguna que otra vez, de cuando en cuando

off-center descentrado, de lado, heterodoxo, poco convencional

off-color impropio, atrevido, de color subido

of|fend offender, delinquir, infringir la ley • **of|fend|ed** ofendido • **of|fend|er** delincuente

of|fense delito, infracción, crimen, ofensa, insulto, afrenta, ofensiva
▸ **take offense** ofenderse, sentirse ofendido

of|fen|sive ofensivo, ofensiva
▸ **go on the offensive** tomar la ofensiva

of|fer ofrecer(se), ofrecimiento, oferta

of|fer|ing oferta

of|fice oficina, ministerio, departamento, dirección, consultorio, consulta, cargo

of|fice build|ing edificio de oficinas

of|fic|er oficial, agente, policía, directivo

of|fi|cial oficial, funcionario o funcionaria • **of|fi|cial|ly** oficialmente

off|line fuera de línea, desconectado

off-peak fuera de las horas pico, en las horas de menor demanda

off-ramp vía de salida

off|set compensar

off|shore a distancia de la costa, frente a la costa, marino, a cierta distancia de la costa

off|spring descendencia, progenie

of|ten frecuentemente, con frecuencia, a menudo
▸ **how often** con qué frecuencia, qué tan seguido
▸ **every so often** de vez en cuando
▸ **as often as not** la mitad de las veces, las más de las veces

often|times frecuentemente

oh ah, vaya, este

oil petróleo, aceite, aceitar

oil|field *también* **oil field** yacimiento petrolífero

oil paint color al óleo, pintura al óleo, óleo

oil paint|ing cuadro al óleo, pintura al óleo, óleo

oil plat|form plataforma petrolífera

OJ jugo de naranja

okay *también* **OK, O.K.,** ok bien, de acuerdo, ¿te parece?

okey do|key *también* **okey doke** bien

old anciano, de edad, viejo, antiguo
▸ **any old** cualquier
▸ **the old** los ancianos

old-fashioned anticuado, pasado de moda

Old Glo|ry bandera de Estados Unidos

old-timer viejo

old world *también* **Old World, old-world** pintoresco

ol|ive aceituna, olivo, color aceituna, aceitunado

ol|ive oil aceite de oliva

Olym|pic olímpico
▸ **the Olympics** las olimpiadas, los juegos olímpicos

Olym|pic Games juegos olímpicos, olimpiadas

ome|let *también* **omelette** omelet, tortilla de huevo

o

omit omitir, olvidar

om|ni|vore omnívoro *u* omnívora

om|niv|or|ous omnívoro, voraz

on en, de, con, a, encima, sobre, ahora, en proceso, todavía, encendido
▸ **on (a drug)** tomando

on board *también* **onboard**, **on-board** comprometido

once una vez, antes, en otro tiempo, una vez que
▸ **at once** inmediatamente, ahora mismo
▸ **at once/all at once** al mismo tiempo
▸ **for once** por una vez siquiera
▸ **once and for all** de una vez por todas
▸ **once in a while** de vez en cuando

one un, uno, una, algún, alguno, alguna
▸ **one or other** uno u otro, uno de los dos
▸ **one or two** uno o dos

one-of-a-kind único

one-point per|spec|tive perspectiva con un solo punto de fuga

one's de uno, = **one is** o **one has**

one|self uno mismo, sí mismo

one-shot excepcional

one-time *también* **onetime** antiguo, el que fuera, único

one-way de sentido único, de un solo sentido, de ida, sencillo

on|going en curso

on|ion cebolla

on|line *también* **on-line** en línea

only sólo, solamente, único, tan sólo, pero, más que
▸ **only just** apenas, acabar de

ono|mato|poeia onomatopeya

on-ramp vía de acceso

onto hasta, a, tras, sobre la pista de

on|ward de conexión, adelante, hacia adelante, en adelante

Oort cloud Nube de Oort

op-ed artículos de opinión

open abrir, desplegar, extender, desabrochar, desabotonar, inaugurar, iniciar, dar inicio, abierto, destapado, sincero, franco, expuesto ● **open|ness** sinceridad ● **open|ness** comienzo, inauguración
▸ **in the open** al aire libre, a la intemperie
▸ **(out) in the open** público, a la luz
▸ **open out** abrir, desplegar, extender
▸ **open up** abrirse, hacer surgir, generar

open cir|cu|la|tory sys|tem sistema circulatorio abierto

open clus|ter cúmulo abierto

open|er abridor, destapador

open|ing inicial, primero, introducción, primera escena, obertura, abertura, claro, oportunidad, vacante

open|ly abiertamente, francamente

open-source *también* **open source** código abierto

open-water zone zona de agua superficial

op|era ópera ● **op|er|at|ic** operístico

op|er|ate operar, funcionar, manejar, manipular, intervenir ● **op|era|tion** operación, funcionamiento

op|er|at|ing room sala de operaciones, quirófano

op|era|tion operación, empresa, compañía, funcionamiento

op|era|tion|al en funcionamiento, en servicio, de funcionamiento

• **op|era|tion|al|ly** en lo referente al funcionamiento

op|era|tive en vigor, operario u operaria, agente secreto
▶ **the operative word** la palabra pertinente

op|era|tor operador u operadora, operario u operaria, empresa

opin|ion opinión

opin|ion poll encuesta de opinión, sondeo de opinión

op|po|nent oponente, adversario, contrincante, rival, opositor u opositora

op|por|tu|ni|ty oportunidad

op|pose oponer(se)

op|posed opuesto
▶ **as opposed to** en contraposición a, a diferencia de

op|po|site enfrente de, frente a, enfrente, opuesto, de enfrente, contrario, lo contrario

op|po|site sex sexo opuesto

opos|sum tlacuache, zarigüeya, comadreja

op|po|si|tion oposición

opt optar
▶ **opt out** optar por no hacer algo

op|ti|cal fi|ber fibra óptica

op|tic nerve nervio óptico

op|ti|mism optimismo
• **op|ti|mist** optimista

op|ti|mis|tic optimista
• **op|ti|mis|ti|cal|ly** con optimismo

op|tion opción
▶ **keep/leave one's options open** no descartar opciones

op|tion|al opcional

or o, si no

oral oral, examen oral, bucal, bucodental • **oral|ly** oralmente

oral his|to|ry historia oral

or|ange anaranjado, color naranja, naranja

ora|to|rio oratorio

or|bit órbita, orbitar

or|chard huerto, huerta

or|ches|tra orquesta, platea, butaca de platea, palco de platea • **or|ches|tral** orquestal

or|deal suplicio

or|der ordenar, pedir, orden, pedido, sistema
▶ **under orders** bajo órdenes de
▶ **order around** mandar de acá para allá
▶ **in order to** con el propósito de, para
▶ **in/of the order of something** aproximadamente, del orden de
▶ **be in working order** funcionar bien
▶ **out of order** descompuesto

or|di|nary común, normal
▶ **out of the ordinary** fuera de lo normal

ore mineral

or|gan órgano • **or|gan|ist** organista

or|gan|elle orgánulo

or|gan|ic orgánico
• **or|gani|cal|ly** orgánicamente

or|gan|ic com|pound compuesto orgánico

or|gan|ism organismo

or|gani|za|tion organización, estructura
• **or|gani|za|tion|al** organizativo, orgánico

or|gan|ize organizar
• **or|gan|iz|er** organizador u organizadora

or|gan|ized organizado

or|gan sys|tem sistema de órganos

ori|en|tal oriental

ori|en|ta|tion orientación, brújula, tendencia

ori|ent|ed orientado

ori|gin origen

origi|nal original
• **origi|nal|ly** originalmente

O

origi|nal|ity originalidad
origi|nate originarse
ori|ole oropéndola, oriol
or|nery intratable, de mal genio, de malas pulgas
or|phan huérfano *o* huérfana, dejar huérfano
▶ **quedar huérfano** to be orphaned
ortho|dox ortodoxo
or|thog|ra|phy ortografía
ortho|pedic ortopedista, ortopédico
OS sistema operativo
OSHA Departamento de Salud y Seguridad en el Trabajo, Administración de la Seguridad y Salud Ocupacionales
os|ti|na|to ostinato
OT tiempo suplementario, prórroga
oth|er otro *u* otra
▶ **(the) others** los otros *o* las otras, los demás
▶ **every other day/ week/month** cada dos días/semanas/meses, un día/semana/mes sí, otro no, en días/semanas/meses alternos
▶ **no/nothing other than** nada más que
▶ **other than** excepto por
other|wise de lo contrario, por lo demás, a menos que
ot|to|man otomana, diván, reposapiés, cojín para los pies
ought deber
oughtn't = ought not
ounce onza, pizca
our nuestro
ours nuestro
our|selves nos, nosotros (mismos)
oust expulsar, hacer caer
● **oust|er** destitución
● **oust|ing** destitución
out fuera, apagado, abierto, eliminado, incorrecto, en

flor, a la venta, hacia afuera
▶ **out of** fuera de, por, de cada
▶ **out to (do something)** en busca de
▶ **take/get out** sacar
▶ **be out of something** acabarse, agotarse, no tener
▶ **made out of** de
out|age corte de luz, apagón
out|box *también* **out-box** bandeja de salida
out|break brote
out|come resultado, consecuencia
out|dat|ed anticuado, pasado de moda
out|do superar
out|door al aire libre
out|doors al aire libre, afuera
▶ **the outdoors** la vida al aire libre
out|doors|man persona que gusta de la vida al aire libre
out|er exterior
out|er core núcleo externo
out|er space espacio exterior, espacio sideral
out|fit traje, conjunto, equipo, equipar
out|go|ing de salida, sociable, extrovertido, saliente
out|house excusado exterior
out|ing excursión
out|law prohibir, declarar ilegal
out|let tienda, válvula de escape, salida, enchufe, tomacorriente
out|line bosquejo, bosquejar, recortarse
out|look actitud, panorama
out|ma|neu|ver mostrarse más hábil que
out|num|ber superar en número, ser más numeroso
out-of-court *ver* court
out-of-state forastero, foráneo, fuereño, de fuera del lugar

out|put producción, resultado, salida

out|put force potencia de salida

out|rage indignar, ultrajar, escandalizar, indignación, ultraje, escándalo
• **out|raged** escandalizado

out|ra|geous escandaloso
• **out|ra|geous|ly** escandalosamente

out|right descarado, categórico, rotundo, abiertamente, categóricamente, rotundamente, instantáneamente, en el acto

out|set principio, comienzo

out|side exterior, fuera, afuera, afuera de, fuera de, en las afueras de, externo, externo a

out|sid|er externo, extraño, desconocido

out|skirts las afueras, los alrededores

out|spo|ken directo, categórico
• **out|spo|ken|ness** franqueza

out|stand|ing destacado, extraordinario, pendiente, notable • **out|stand|ing|ly** extraordinariamente

outta fuera de

out|ward aparente, externo, hacia afuera, hacia el exterior, de ida • **out|ward|ly** aparentemente

out|wards ver outward

oval ovalado, oval, óvalo

Oval Of|fice el despacho oval

oven horno

over sobre, encima (de), por encima (de), por sobre, más (de), en exceso de, hacia un lado, al/del otro lado, allá, al revés, otra vez, de nuevo, terminado, acabado, a lo largo de, durante

▶ **over here** acá, aquí
▶ **over there** allí, ahí

over|all general, global, en conjunto, a final de cuentas, overol, pantalones de peto, mameluco

over|came ver overcome

over|coat abrigo, sobretodo

over|come superar, vencer, abrumar

over|do exagerar, excederse

over|dose sobredosis, dosis excesiva, tomar una sobredosis

over|due ya era hora, vencido, atrasado

over easy también **over-easy** frito de los dos lados

over|flow derramarse, desbordarse, rebosante de, repleto de

over|head interior, de arriba, por encima

over|lap superponer, sobreponer, traslapar, coincidir parcialmente, traslape, superposición

over|look tener vista a, pasar por alto, descuidar

over|night durante la noche, nocturno, de la noche a la mañana

over|pass paso elevado, paso a desnivel, paso superior

over|popu|la|tion sobrepoblación

over|ride pasar por encima de, invalidar, anular, anulación • **over|rid|ing** primordial

over|seas extranjero, exterior, en el extranjero

over|see supervisar

over|take sobrecoger

over|throw derrocar, derrocamiento, caída

over|turn volcar, dar una vuelta de campana, anular, invalidar, revocar

over|weight excedido de peso

O

over|whelm abrumar, anonadar, arrollar
• **over|whelmed** abrumado

over|whelm|ing abrumador, inmenso
• **over|whelm|ing|ly** extremadamente, abrumadoramente

ovule óvulo

owe deber, adeudar, estar obligado
▸ **owing to** debido a

owl tecolote, lechuza, búho

own propio, tener, ser dueño de, poseer
▸ **my own, your own, his own, our own** el mío, el tuyo, el suyo, el nuestro
▸ **come into one's/its own** lograr el éxito merecido

▸ **on one's own** solo
▸ **own up** reconocer, admitir, confesar

own|er dueño o dueña, propietario o propietaria

own|er|ship propiedad

ox buey

ox|ford *también* **Oxford** zapato de estilo Oxford, tela de algodón especial para camisas

oxy|gen oxígeno

oys|ter ostra, ostión

oz. onza

ozone ozono

ozone-friendly inocuo para la capa de ozono, que no daña la capa de ozono

ozone lay|er capa de ozono

O

Pp

PAC PAC

pace ritmo, paso, pasearse
▶ keep pace mantenerse al ritmo
▶ at one's own pace al ritmo propio

Pa|cif|ic Rim Cuenca del Pacífico

pac|ing ritmo

pack empacar, embalar, envasar, apiñar(se), paquete, jauría • pack|ing hacer las maletas • packed abarrotado

pack|age paquete, empacar, envasar

pack|ag|ing envase, empaque, presentación

pack|et paquete

pact pacto

pad almohadilla, algodón, fibra, bloc de notas

pad|ded acolchado

pad|dle remo, paleta

pa|gan pagano

page página, hoja, mensajero o mensajera

paid ver pay, a sueldo

pail cubeta, cubo, balde

pain dolor
▶ be in pain dolor, doler
• pained afligido
▶ a pain (in the neck) una lata
▶ take pains to esmerarse

pain|ful adolorido, doloroso
• pain|ful|ly dolorosamente

pain|killer analgésico

paint pintura, pintar

paint|brush pincel, brocha

paint|er pintor o pintora

paint|ing cuadro, pintar

pair par

pais|ley (tejido) de colores y dibujos vistosos, Paisley

pa|jam|as pijama, piyama

pal cuate

pal|ace palacio

pale claro, pálido

pale|on|tol|ogy paleontología
• pale|on|tolo|gist paleontólogo o paleontóloga

Paleo|zo|ic era era paleozoica

pal|ette knife espátula, paleta

palm palmera, palma

pam|phlet folleto

pan sartén, refractario

pan|cake hotcake

pan|da panda

pane hoja

pan|el panel, hoja, tablero

pan|el|ist panelista

pan|el truck camioneta de reparto

Pan|gaea Pangaea

pan|han|dle delgada franja de tierra, mendigar
• pan|han|dler mendigo o mendiga

pan|ic pánico, entrar en pánico

panties calzones

pan|to|mime pantomima

pants pantalones

pant|suit también pants suit traje sastre

pan|ty hose también panty hose medias

pa|pa|raz|zi paparazzi

pa|per papel, periódico, documento, identificación, artículo, ponencia, informe, propuesta, empapelar, tapizar

paper|back edición de tapa blanda, edición en rústica

pa|per clip también paper-

clip, paperclip clip, sujetapapeles

pa|per route reparto de periódicos

pa|per trail expediente

paper|work papeleo burocrático

par
▸ **on a par with** del mismo nivel
▸ **be below par** no estar a la altura

para|chute paracaídas, lanzarse en paracaídas

pa|rade desfile, formación, desfilar, exhibir

para|dise paraíso

para|graph párrafo

para|le|gal asistente de abogado

par|al|lax paralaje

par|al|lel paralelismo, paralelo, asemejarse

par|al|lel cir|cuit circuito en paralelo

par|al|lel|ism paralelismo sintáctico

para|lyze paralizar
● **para|lyzed** paralizado

para|mecium paramecio

para|phrase parafrasear, paráfrasis

para|site parásito
● **para|sit|ic** parásito *o* parásita

para|sit|ism parasitismo

par|cel paquete
▸ **part and parcel** parte de

par|cel post paquete postal

par|don ¿Perdón?, Disculpe, indultar, indulto

par|ent padre, madre
● **pa|ren|tal** de los padres

par|ent cell célula madre

par|ent|hood paternidad

par|ish parroquia, condado

park parque, campo, estacionar(se) ● **parked** estacionado ● **parking** estacionarse

park|ing gar|age estacionamiento

park|ing lot estacionamiento

park|way avenida

par|lia|ment *también* **Parliament** parlamento

par|lia|men|ta|ry parlamentario

pa|ro|chial school escuela religiosa

par|rot perico, repetir como perico

pars|ley perejil

part parte, pieza, papel, participación, raya, separar(se), abrir, hacer la raya ● **part|ing** separación
▸ **play a part** jugar un papel
▸ **take part** tomar parte, participar
▸ **for somebody's part** por mi/su/tu, etc parte
▸ **on somebody's part** de mi/tu/su, etc parte
▸ **in part** en parte
▸ **part with** dejar ir

par|tial parcial ● **par|tial|ly** parcialmente
▸ **be partial to** inclinarse por, tener debilidad por

par|tial eclipse eclipse parcial

par|tici|pant participante

par|tici|pate participar
● **par|tici|pa|tion** participación

par|ti|ci|ple participio

par|ti|cle partícula

par|ticu|lar específico, concreto, en particular, especial, particular
▸ **in particular** en particular

par|ticu|lar|ly particularmente

par|ticu|lars detalles, pormenores

par|ti|san partidario

part|ly en parte

part|ner pareja, socio *o* socia, ser pareja de

part|ner and group skills habilidades para trabajar en

equipo

part|ner|ship sociedad, relación, asociación

part-time medio tiempo

par|ty partido, fiesta, grupo, parte, ir de juerga, fiestear
▸ **be (a) party to** prestarse a

pas|cal pascal

Pascal's prin|ci|ple *también* **Pascal's law** ley de Pascal

pass pasar, atravesar, rebasar, aprobado, pase
• **pass|ing** paso
▸ **pass away** pasar a mejor vida, fallecer
▸ **pass off as** hacer pasar por
▸ **pass on** fallecer
▸ **pass out** perder el conocimiento
▸ **pass over** pasar por alto
▸ **pass up** dejar pasar

pas|sage pasillo, pasaje, paso

pas|sen|ger pasajero *o* pasajera

pass|ing pasajero, al pasar, muerte, fin
▸ **in passing** de pasada

pas|sion pasión

pas|sion|ate apasionado
• **pas|sion|ate|ly** apasionadamente

pas|sive pasivo, pasiva
• **pas|sive|ly** pasivamente

pas|sive so|lar heat|ing calefacción solar pasiva

pas|sive trans|port transporte pasivo

pass|port pasaporte

pass|word clave

past pasado, pasadas, pasando, anterior
▸ **go past** pasar
▸ **half past two** las dos y media

pas|ta pasta

paste pasta, engrudo, pegar

pas|try masa, repostería

pas|ture prado, pastura

pat dar palmaditas, palmada
▸ **stand pat** no cambiar de opinión, no dar su brazo a

torcer

patch porción, parcela, huerto, parche, parchar
▸ **a rough patch** una mala racha
▸ **patch up** hacer las paces, arreglar

pa|tent patente, evidente, patentar • **pa|tent|ly** evidentemente

pa|ter|nal paternal

path sendero, camino

pa|thet|ic patético
• **pa|theti|cal|ly** patéticamente, lastimeramente

path|way camino, sendero

pa|tience paciencia

pa|tient paciente
• **pa|tient|ly** pacientemente

pa|tri|ot patriota

pat|ri|ot|ic patriota
• **pat|ri|ot|ism** patriotismo

pa|trol patrullar, patrulla

patrol|man patrullero

pa|tron patrocinador *o* patrocinadora, mecenas, cliente

pat|tern patrón

pat|ty hamburguesa

pause detenerse, hacer una pausa, pausa

pave pavimentar

pave|ment pavimento

paw pata, tocar con la pata

pawn empeñar, peón, títere

pay pagar, convenir, prestar paga
▸ **pay back** pagar
▸ **pay off** terminar de pagar, valer la pena
▸ **pay out** desembolsar
▸ **pay up** pagar
▸ **pay a visit** hacer una visita

pay|back recuperación

pay|check sueldo

pay|dirt *también* **pay dirt**
▸ **strike paydirt** encontrar una mina de oro

pay|ment pago

pay|off *también* **pay-off**

P

beneficio, soborno, mordida

pay|roll nómina

PBS PBS, cadena independiente de televisión

PC PC (computadora personal)

PDA agenda electrónica

PDF PDF, archivos de computadora

pea chícharo, guisante

peace paz

peace|ful pacífico, tranquilo • **peace|ful|ly** pacíficamente, tranquilamente

peach durazno, color durazno

peachy de perlas

peak apogeo, más alto, cima, cumbre, alcanzar el nivel más alto

pea|nut cacahuate, maní

pear pera

pearl perla

peas|ant campesino

peat turba

peb|ble piedrita, guijarro

pec|to|ral pectoral

pe|cu|liar raro, peculiar, característico • **pe|cu|liar|ly** peculiarmente, típicamente

ped|al pedal, pedalear

pe|des|trian peatón o peatona, pedestre

pe|dia|tri|cian pediatra

pe|dom|eter podómetro

peek mirar a hurtadillas, vistazo

peel cáscara, pelar, despegar

peer mirar detenidamente, escudriñar, igual, par, compañero o compañera

peer press|ure presión del grupo

peeve fastidio

peg espiga, estaquilla, colgador, gancho, vincular

pe|lag|ic en|vi|ron|ment también **pelagic zone** hábitat pelágico, zona

pelágica

pen pluma, redil, corral, redactar, escribir, acorralar, encerrar
▸ **the pen** el tanque

pen|al|ty pena, castigo, multa, penalty, penalti, penal

pen|cil lápiz

pen|cil push|er tinterillo

pen|dant colgante

pend|ing pendiente, en espera de, a reserva de

pen|etrate penetrar, introducirse, infiltrarse
• **pen|etra|tion** penetración, infiltración

pen|guin pingüino

pen|in|su|la península

pe|nis pene

peni|ten|tia|ry penitenciaría

pen|nant gallardete

pen|ni|less pobre, indigente, en la miseria

pen|ny centavo, céntimo

pen|sion pensión

Pen|ta|gon Pentágono

pen|ta|ton|ic scale escala pentatónica, escala de cinco notas

peo|ple gente, personas, pueblo, poblar

pep|per pimienta, pimiento, pimentón, salpicar con, salpicar de, acribillar

pep|per shak|er pimentero

pep|per spray gas pimienta

pep ral|ly reunión de apoyo

per por

per an|num por año

per|ceive percibir, considerar

percent por ciento

per|cent|age porcentaje

per|cent|age point punto porcentual

per|cen|tile percentil

per|cep|tion idea, imagen, perspicacia, percepción

per|cep|tive perspicaz,

inteligente

perch sentarse en el borde de algo, encaramar, colgar, posarse

per|cus|sion percusión

per diem por día, diario

per|en|nial perenne, eterno

per|fect perfecto, redomado, consumado, perfeccionar • **per|fect|ly** perfectamente

per|fec|tion perfección

per|form ejecutar, llevar a cabo, actuar, interpretar, desempeñarse • **per|form|er** actor o actriz, ejecutante, intérprete, empresa cotizada en la bolsa

per|for|mance representación, función, desempeño, rendimiento

per|for|mance art arte de acción

per|fume perfume

per|haps quizá, quizás, tal vez

peri|he|lion perihelio

pe|rim|eter perímetro

pe|ri|od período, periodo, de época, punto
  ▶ **period of revolution** período de revolución
  ▶ **period of rotation** período de rotación

pe|ri|od|i|cal revista, publicación periódica, periódico • **pe|ri|od|i|cal|ly** periódicamente

pe|ri|od|ic law ley de periodicidad

pe|ri|od|ic ta|ble sistema periódico de los elementos, tabla periódica de los elementos

pe|riph|er|al ner|vous sys|tem sistema nervioso periférico

per|ma|frost permafrost

per|ma|nent permanente • **per|ma|nence** permanencia • **per|ma|nent|ly** permanentemente

per|me|able permeable • **permeability** permeabilidad

per|mis|sible permisible, lícito

per|mis|sion permiso

per|mit permitir, permiso

per|mu|ta|tion permutación, combinación, variante

per|pet|ual mo|tion ma|chine máquina de movimiento perpetuo

per|se|cute perseguir • **per|se|cu|tion** persecución • **per|se|cu|tor** perseguidor o perseguidora

per|sist persistir, insistir

per|sis|tent persistente, tenaz • **per|sis|tence** persistencia • **per|sis|tent|ly** persistentemente

per|snick|ety quisquilloso

per|son persona
  ▶ **in person** en persona, personalmente

per|son|al personal

per|son|al com|put|er computadora personal

per|son|al ex|emp|tion exenciones para las personas físicas

per|son|al|ity personalidad

per|son|al|ly personalmente

per|son|al pro|noun pronombre personal

per|son|als anuncios clasificados

per|son|nel personal

per|spec|tive visión, perspectiva
  ▶ **in perspective** objetivamente

per|suade persuadir de, convencer de

per|sua|sion persuasión, insistencia, creencia, convicción, credo

pest plaga, insecto nocivo, fastidio, lata

pes|ter molestar, acosar

pes|ti|cide pesticida

P

pes|tle mano de mortero

pet mascota, favorito, acariciar

pet|al pétalo

pe|ter
▸ peter out decaer, apagarse, agotarse

pe|tite pequeño, menudo

pe|ti|tion petición, presentar una petición, presentar una demanda

Petri dish cápsula o caja de Petri

pe|tro|leum petróleo

pet|ty insignificante, trivial, nimio, mezquino, menor
• pet|ti|ness mezquindad

pH valor pH, potencial de hidrógeno, índice de Sörensen

phar|ma|ceu|ti|cal farmacéutico
• pharmaceuticals productos farmacéuticos

phar|ma|cy farmacia, botica, química farmacéutica

phar|ynx faringe

phase fase, etapa
▸ phase in introducir/aplicar paulatinamente
▸ phase out eliminar paulatinamente, excluir por fases, discontinuar por etapas

Ph.D. también PhD doctorado

phe|nom|enon fenómeno

phe|no|type fenotipo

phero|mone feromona

phi|loso|pher filósofo

philo|sophi|cal filosófico
• philo|sophi|cal|ly filosóficamente
▸ be philosophical tomar (las cosas) con filosofía

phi|loso|phy filosofía

phloem floema

pho|bia fobia

phone teléfono, llamar por teléfono, telefonear
▸ on the phone al teléfono
▸ be on the phone estar hablando por teléfono

phone booth cabina telefónica

phone call llamada telefónica

phone|card también phone card tarjeta telefónica

pho|neme fonema

pho|ne|mic aware|ness conciencia fonémica

phon|ics fonética

pho|no|gram fonograma

pho|ny también phoney falso, farsante, impostor

phos|pho|lip|id fosfolípido

pho|to foto

photo|cell también photoelectric cell fotocélula, célula fotoeléctrica, fotocelda

photo|copi|er fotocopiadora

photo|copy fotocopia, fotocopiar

photo|graph fotografía, fotografiar

pho|tog|ra|pher fotógrafo o fotógrafa

photo|graph|ic fotográfico

pho|tog|ra|phy fotografía

photo|recep|tor fotorreceptor, fotorreceptora

pho|to shoot también photo-shoot sesión de fotos

photo|sphere fotosfera

photo|syn|the|sis fotosíntesis

pho|tot|ro|pism fototropismo

photovoltaic fotovoltaico

phras|al verb frase verbal

phrase frase, frase hecha, expresar, formular, redactar
▸ turn of phrase manera de expresarse

phras|ing fraseo

phy|lum filum, filo

phys ed educación física, deportes

physi|cal físico • physi|cal|ly físicamente

physi|cal change cambio
físico

physi|cal edu|ca|tion
educación física, deportes

physi|cal prop|er|ty
propiedad física

physi|cal sci|ence ciencias
físicas

physi|cal ther|a|py
fisioterapia, kinesiología,
quinesiología, terapia física

phy|si|cian médico o médica

phy|si|cian's as|sis|tant
asociado médico o asociada
médica

physi|cist físico o física

phys|ics física

phy|sique físico

phyto|plank|ton
fitoplancton

pia|nist pianista

pi|ano piano

pick escoger, seleccionar,
elegir, cortar, recoger,
buscar, forzar
▸ **pick on** meterse con,
agarrarla con
▸ **pick out** reconocer,
distinguir
▸ **pick up** recoger, levantar,
ir a buscar, aprender,
adquirir, captar, recibir,
repuntar
▸ **the pick** lo mejor

pick|le encurtido, escabeche,
adobo, encurtidos

pick|led en salmuera

pick|up camioneta, repunte,
mejora, recogida

pic|nic comida en el campo,
picnic, comer

pic|ture pintura, cuadro,
fotografía, imagen,
película, idea, descripción,
situación, circunstancia,
retratar, representarse,
imaginarse
▸ **put somebody in the
picture** poner al tanto

pic|ture mes|sag|ing envío
de fotografías o imágenes de
un teléfono portátil a otro

pie pastel, pay

piece trozo, pedazo, artículo,
pieza, obra, cuadro, parte
▸ **in one piece** sano y salvo
▸ **go to pieces** quedar
deshecho
▸ **piece together**
reconstruir, unir los pedazos
de

pie chart gráfica circular,
gráfico circular

pierce pinchar, agujerear,
perforar ● **pierc|ing** piercing

pig puerco, cerdo, chancho

pi|geon paloma, pichón

pig|ment pigmento

pig|pen *también* **pig pen**
zahúrda, pocilga, chiquero

pig|tail trenza

Pilates pilates

pile montón, pila, pelo,
amontonar, apilar
▸ **pile into/out of** entrar o
salir desordenadamente
▸ **be at the bottom/
top of the pile** ser los
últimos/primeros en la lista
▸ **pile up** apilar(se),
acumularse

pil|grim peregrino

pill píldora

pil|lar pilar

pil|low almohada

pi|lot piloto, pilotear, pilotar,
poner a prueba

pin alfiler, prender con
alfileres, inmovilizar,
atribuir, echar, cifrar,
perno, clavo, broche,
prendedor, botón
▸ **pin down** precisar,
comprometer

pinch pellizcar, birlar,
pellizco, pizca
▸ **feel the pinch** estar
apretado, pasar estrecheces

pinch-hit *también* **pinch hit**
substituir, sustituir, batear
de emergencia

pine pino, (madera de) pino
▸ **pine for** suspirar por,
anhelar, extrañar

P

pine|apple piña

pink rosa, rosado

pink slip aviso de despido

pin|stripe *también* pin-stripe raya

pint medio litro, pinta

pin|to bean frijol pinto, judía pinta

pio|neer precursor *o* precursora, ser el primero en desarrollar • pio|neer|ing innovador, colonizador *o* colonizadora, pionero *o* pionera

pipe tubo, tubería, pipa, tubo de órgano, cañón de órgano, llevar

pipe|line conducto, ducto
▸ be in the pipeline estar proyectado, estar previsto

pipe or|gan órgano de tubos, órgano de cañones

pi|rate pirata, piratear
• pi|rated pirata

pis|til pistilo

pis|tol pistola

pit pozo, mina, galería, hueso, enfrentar
▸ pits (auto racing) pits

pitch lanzar, arrojar, caerse de bruces, irse de bruces, establecer, tono, grado
▸ pitch in echar la mano, arrimar el hombro

pitch|er jarra, lanzador *o* lanzadora, pítcher

pit|ted deshuesado, salpicado, lleno de

pity lástima, pena
▸ take pity on someone compadecerse

piz|za pizza

pjs *también* pj's piyama

pkg. paquete

place lugar, casa, colocar, meter, poner, clasificar
▸ place an order hacer un pedido
▸ fall/click/fit into place aclararse
▸ in place en aplicación
▸ in place of something/

somebody / in something's/ somebody's place en lugar de
▸ in the first place en primer lugar
▸ put (somebody) in their place poner en su lugar
▸ take place tener lugar

place|ment test prueba de aptitud

pla|cen|ta placenta

pla|cen|tal mam|mal mamífero placentario, mamífero placentado

plague plaga, peste (bubónica), atormentado

plaid cuadro

plain liso, simple, sencillo, claro, poco atractivo, planicie, llanura • plain|ly simplemente

plain|tiff demandante

plan plan, plano, planear, programar, hacer planes
▸ plan on planear, pensar en

plane avión, plano, cepillo, garlopa, cepillar, desbastar

plan|et planeta

plan|etary planetario

plan|etesi|mal corpúsculo (del espacio)

plank|ton plancton

plan|ner planificador *o* planificadora

plan|ning planificación, programación, urbanismo

plant planta, vegetal, maquinaria pesada, sembrar, plantar, colocar, colocar (subrepticiamente)
• plant|ing siembra, plantar de

Plan|tae vegetales

plan|ta|tion plantación

plas|ma screen *también* plasma display pantalla de plasma

plas|tered pegado, cubierto

plas|tic plástico

plas|tic wrap plástico adherente, película

adherente

plate plato, placa, ilustración, lámina • **plates** placas, chapas

plate boundary frontera de placas tectónicas

plated (en)chapado, recubierto

platelet plaqueta

plate tectonics tectónica de placas

platform plataforma, andén

platitude tópico, lugar común

platter fuente, platón, bandeja
 ▸ **hand on a platter** servir en bandeja de plata

plausible verosímil, creíble, convincente
 • **plausibly** razonablemente
 • **plausibility** credibilidad

play jugar, jugar a, jugar con, jugar contra, gastar, actuar, representar un papel, tocar, poner, juego, obra
 ▸ **play a part/play a role** influir, tener que ver
 ▸ **play around** juguetear
 ▸ **play at** jugar a
 ▸ **play back** reproducir
 ▸ **play down** restar importancia a
 ▸ **play on** aprovecharse de, explotar

play-by-play comentario jugada a jugada

player jugador o jugadora, ejecutante, músico o música, protagonista

playful juguetón • **playfully** juguetonamente
 • **playfulness** calidad de juguetón

playground patio de recreo

playing card carta, naipe, baraja

playoff final, partida decisiva

playwright dramaturgo o dramaturga, autor o autora

plaza plaza, centro comercial

plea llamado, petición, súplica, alegato

plead suplicar, defender, aducir
 ▸ **plead guilty/innocent** declararse (culpable o inocente), confesarse (culpable)

pleasant agradable
 • **pleasantly** agradablemente

please por favor, complacer, agradar, contentar
 ▸ **as you please/whatever you please** como guste, lo que quiera, lo que le plazca

pleased contento, complacido
 ▸ **pleased to meet you** encantado de conocerlo/conocerla, mucho gusto de conocerlo/conocerla

pleasing agradable
 • **pleasingly** agradablemente

pleasure placer, gusto, ocio, diversión
 ▸ **It's a pleasure/my pleasure** de nada, no hay de qué

pleated plisado, tableado

pledge prometer, comprometerse, compromiso

plenty mucho, de sobra, más que suficiente

pliers alicate(s), pinza(s)

plight apuro, aprieto, situación peligrosa

plot conspirar, solar, trazar, determinar, conspiración, complot, trama, argumento, parcela, terreno
 • **plotter** conspirador o conspiradora

plotline argumento, trama

plow arado, arar

plug clavija, enchufe, tapón, publicidad, tapar, promover

P

▸ **pull the plug** (hacer) cancelar

▸ **plug in** o **plug into** conectar, enchufar

plugged también **plugged up** tapado, obstruido, atorado

plum ciruela

plumb|er plomero o plomera, fontanero o fontanera

plumb|ing cañería, tubería, plomería, fontanería

plunge zambullirse, clavar, hincar, hundir, precipitar, desplomarse, irse a pique, desplome

▸ **to take the plunge** arriesgarse, dar el paso

plung|er desatascador, destapador, bomba (de excusado)

plunk dejar(se) caer, aventar

plu|ral plural

plus más, más de, ventaja, calificación intermedia

Pluto Plutón

p.m. también **pm** la tarde, pasado meridiano

pock|et bolsa, bolsillo, de bolsillo, embolsarse

▸ **out of pocket** corto de dinero

pocket|book bolsa, monedero

pod|cast podcast, archivo de audio

poem poema

poet poeta o poetisa

po|et|ic li|cense licencia poética

po|et|ry poesía

point punto, punta, punto decimal, argumento, opinión, observación, asunto, caso, sentido, aspecto, característica, lugar, momento, señalar (con el dedo), apuntar, indicar

▸ **have a point** tener razón en algo

▸ **make a point of** proponerse

▸ **on the point of** a punto de

▸ **up to a point** hasta cierto punto

▸ **points of the compass** puntos cardinales

▸ **point out** señalar

point|ed acabado en punta, puntiagudo, mordaz • **point|ed|ly** deliberadamente

point|less vano, inútil, sin sentido • **point|less|ly** innecesariamente

point of view punto de vista, opinión

point-source pol|lu|tion fuente puntual de la contaminación

poised listo, preparado, dispuesto, sereno

poi|son veneno, envenenar • **poi|son|ing** envenenamiento

poi|son oak zumaque venenoso

poi|son|ous venenoso

poke meter, asomar, golpe

po|lar polar

po|lar co|or|di|nate coordenada polar

po|lar east|er|lies viento polar de levante

po|lar equa|tion ecuación de coordenadas polares

po|lar zone zona polar

pole poste, polo

po|lice policía, policías, patrullar, vigilar, supervisar

po|lice de|part|ment departamento de policía

po|lice force policía, fuerzas del orden

police|man policía

po|lice of|fic|er oficial de policía

po|lice sta|tion comisaría

police|woman mujer policía

poli|cy política, póliza de seguro

po|lio poliomielitis, polio

pol|ish cera, betún, pulir,

lustrar, sacar brillo, perfeccionar • pol|ished pulido, brillo

po|lite cortés • po|lite|ly cortésmente • po|lite|ness cortesía

po|liti|cal político • po|liti|cal|ly políticamente, referente a la política

po|liti|cal ac|tion com|mit|tee comité de acción política

poli|ti|cian político

poli|tics política, ideas políticas

pol|ka dots lunares

poll encuesta, sondeo, votación, urna

pol|li|nate polinizar • pol|li|na|tion polinización

poll|ing place centro electoral, casilla de votación

pol|lu|tant contaminante

pol|lute contaminar • pol|lut|ed contaminado

pol|lu|tion contaminación

poly|es|ter poliéster

poly|no|mial polinomio

pol|yp pólipo

pom|mel horse caballo con arzones

pond estanque

pon|der ponderar

pony pony
▸ pony up pagar, apoquinar

pony|tail cola de caballo, coleta

pool alberca, piscina, pileta, estanque, charco, cantidad, grupo, juntar, billar

pool hall billar

pooped muerto

poor pobre, mal, bajo • poor|ly pobremente
▸ the poor los pobres

pop pop, música popular, chasquido, pa, estallar, reventar, chasquear, echar de repente
▸ pop off vociferar, clamar
▸ pop up aparecer

pop|corn palomitas

pop|over panecillo

pop|per utensilio para hacer palomitas

popu|lar popular, común, generalizado • popu|lar|ity popularidad

popu|la|tion población

porce|lain porcelana

porch porche

pork cerdo, puerco

pork bar|rel también pork-barrel corrupción, corrupto

po|ros|ity porosidad

po|rous poroso

port puerto, babor, oporto

port|able portátil

por|ter maletero

port|fo|lio carpeta, colección

por|tion porción, parte

por|trait retrato

por|tray representar, retratar

pose plantear, formular, hacerse pasar, posar, pose

po|si|tion posición, colocar, puesto, en posición de

posi|tive positivo, optimista, seguro, cierto, de forma definitva, lo positivo • posi|tive|ly positivamente

posi|tive ac|cel|era|tion aceleración positiva

pos|sess poseer

pos|ses|sion posesión

pos|ses|sive posesivo • pos|ses|sive|ness posesividad

pos|sibil|ity posibilidad

pos|sible posible
▸ as... as possible tan ... como sea posible
▸ the possible lo posible

pos|sibly posiblemente, es posible

post fijar, colgar, subir, poner, asignar a un puesto, puesto, poste

post|age gastos de envío, franqueo

P

post|card *también* **post card** postal

post|er póster, cartel

post|er child *también* **poster boy, poster girl** perfecto ejemplo

post|mod|ern dance *también* **post-modern dance** danza posmoderna

post|mor|tem autopsia

post of|fice correo

post|par|tum de|pres|sion depresión posparto

post|pone posponer, aplazar • **post|pone|ment** posposición

pos|ture postura, posición

post|war de posguerra

pot olla, tetera, cafetera, fondo común, vaca, pozo, barriga, plantar en maceta

po|table potable

po|ta|to papa

po|ta|to chip papa

po|tent potente • **po|ten|cy** potencia

po|ten|tial potencial, possible, posibilidad • **po|ten|tial|ly** potencialmente, posiblemente

po|ten|tial dif|fer|ence diferencia potencial

po|ten|tial en|er|gy energía potencial

pot|tery cerámica, alfarería

pouch bolsa pequeña, bolsa

poul|try aves de corral, carne de ave, volatería, aves

pound libra, libra esterlina, golpear, latir con fuerza

pound cake bizcocho

pour verter, vaciar, servir, brotar, salir a borbotones, diluviar, llegar/salir en cantidades grandes, entrar a montones en, llegar a montones
▶ **pour out** llenar

pov|er|ty pobreza

pow|der polvo

pow|dered en polvo

pow|er poder, capacidad, facultad, potencia, energía, fuerza, dar energía a

pow|er|ful poderoso, potente, fuerte • **pow|er|ful|ly** poderosamente, potentemente

pow|er plant central eléctrica

pow|er sta|tion central eléctrica

pow|er walk|ing *también* **power-walking** caminata rápida

PPO PPO, organización que ofrece descuentos médicos

PR RR.PP.

prac|ti|cal práctico

prac|ti|cal|ly prácticamente, en la práctica

prac|tice práctica, ejercicio, despacho, clientela, practicar, ejercer • **prac|tic|ing** practicante
▶ **in practice** en la práctica
▶ **put into practice** poner en práctica

prac|ticed experto

prac|ti|tion|er médico *o* médica

prai|rie pradera, llanura

praise alabar, elogio

pray rezar

prayer oración, rezos

preach pronunciar un sermón, dar un sermon, predicar, aconsejar • **preach|er** sacerdote

Pre|cam|brian *también* **Pre-Cambrian** precámbrico

pre|cau|tion precaución

pre|cede preceder

prec|e|dent precedente

pre|cious precioso, preciado

pre|cipi|ta|tion precipitación

pre|cise preciso, exacto

pre|cise|ly precisamente

pre|ci|sion precisión

pre|co|cial precocial

preda|tor depredador

pre|de|ces|sor predecesor o predecesora, antecesor

pre|dict predecir

pre|dict|able previsible, predecible • **pre|dict|ably** previsiblemente • **pre|dict|abil|ity** previsibilidad

pre|dic|tion predicción

preen limpiar y arreglar • **preening** limpieza y arreglo

pref|ace prefacio, prologar, escribir un prefacio

pre|fer preferir

prefer|able preferible • **prefer|ably** preferiblemente

prefer|ence predilección, preferencia

pre|fix prefijo

pre|game también **pre-game** previo al juego o al partido, realizado antes del juego o partido

preg|nant embarazada • **preg|nan|cy** embarazo

preju|dice prejuicio, predisponer, perjudicar

pre|limi|nary preliminar

prema|ture prematuro • **prema|ture|ly** prematuramente

pre|med también **pre-med** premédico

prem|ier primer ministro o primera ministro o primera ministra, primero

premi|ere estreno

prem|ise edificio, premisa

pre|mium prima, extra ▶ **be at a premium** escasea

pre|nup también **pre-nup** acuerdo prenupcial

pre|nup|tial agree|ment también **pre-nuptial agreement** acuerdo prenupcial

pre-owned usado

prep preparar

prepa|ra|tion preparación, preparativos

pre|pare preparar ▶ **prepare for** preparar para

pre|pared preparado, listo • **pre|par|ed|ness** preparación ▶ **prepared for** listo para, preparado para

pre-pay también **prepay** pagar por adelantado, prepagar

prepo|si|tion preposición

prep|py fresa

pre|school|er también **pre-schooler** niño en edad preescolar

pre|scribe recetar, prescribir

pre|scrip|tion receta ▶ **by prescription** con receta

pre|sea|son también **pre-season** pretemporada

pres|ence presencia, porte ▶ **in someone's presence** en presencia de

pres|ent actual, presente, regalo, hacer entrega de, presentar, aparentar ▶ **at present** por el momento ▶ **the present day** el día de hoy • **pres|en|ta|tion** entrega

pres|en|ta|tion presentación

pre|serve preservar, conservar, reserva • **pres|er|va|tion** preservación

pre|side presidir

presi|den|cy presidencia

presi|dent presidente

presi|den|tial presidencial

Presi|dents' Day el Día del Presidente

press presionar, empujar, apretar, pisar, pedir, insistir, planchar, presión, prensa, imprenta ▶ **press charges** levantar cargos ▶ **press together** fusionar

press con|fer|ence

conferencia de prensa

pres|sure presión, presionar
• pres|sured presionado

pres|sur|ized presurizado

pres|tige prestigio

pres|tig|ious prestigioso

pre|sum|ably
probablemente,
presumiblemente

pre|sume imaginarse,
suponer, presumir,
atreverse

pre|tend aparentar, fingir,
imaginarse

pret|ty bonito, lindo,
bastante • pret|ti|ly
hermosamente, lindamente

pre|vail prevalecer, existir

pre|vail|ing predominante

pre|vent evitar, impedir
• pre|ven|tion prevención

pre|view avance, preestreno

pre|vi|ous anterior, previo

pre|vi|ous|ly previamente,
antes, hasta entonces

pre|writ|ing también
pre-writing ejercicios
o preparación previa a la
escritura

prey presa
▶ prey on alimentarse de

price precio, costo, costar,
tener precio de • pric|ing
poner precio
▶ at any price a cualquier
precio

pride orgullo
▶ pride oneself
enorgullecerse

priest sacerdote

pri|mari|ly primordialmente

pri|ma|ry primordial,
primaria, elección primaria

pri|ma|ry col|or color
primario

pri|ma|ry pol|lu|tant
principal contaminante

pri|mate primate

prime principal, excelente,
de primera, mejor, preparar,
plenitud, número primo

prime me|rid|ian primer
meridiano

prime min|is|ter primer
ministro o primera ministro
o primera ministra

primi|tive primitivo,
rudimentario

prince príncipe

prin|cess princesa

prin|ci|pal principal, director
o directora

prin|ci|pal parts formas
principales del verbo

prin|ci|ple principio,
principios
▶ in principle en principio
▶ on principle por principio
▶ principles of composition
principios de composición
▶ principles of design
principios de diseño

print imprimir, imprimir en,
publicar, escribir con letra
de molde, texto • print|ing
imprenta
▶ be in print ser publicado
▶ print out imprimir

print|er impresora, imprenta

print|mak|ing estampar,
hacer grabados, grabar

pri|or previo, anterior
▶ prior to antes de

pri|or|ity prioridad
▶ give priority dar prioridad
▶ take/have priority ser
prioritario

prism prisma

pris|on cárcel, prisión

pris|on|er prisionero o
prisionera

pri|va|cy privacidad, privacía

pri|vate privado, particular,
íntimo, soldado raso o
soldado rasa • pri|vate|ly
en privado, íntimamente
▶ private life vida privada
▶ in private en privado

privately held corporation
corporación privada

pri|vat|ize privatizar
• pri|vati|za|tion
privatización

privi|lege privilegio

privi|leged privilegiado

prize premio, premiado, digno de premio, apreciar, forzar

pro profesional
▸ **pros and cons** el pro y contra

prob|ably probablemente

probe investigar, escudriñar, investigación

prob|lem problema

pro|cedure procedimiento

pro|ceed proceder, seguir adelante
▸ **proceeds** ganancias

pro|cess proceso, procesar • **pro|cess|ing** procesamiento
▸ **in the process of** en proceso de
▸ **in the process** mientras, al mismo tiempo

pro|ces|sion procesión

pro|ces|sor procesador

pro|claim proclamar

pro|duce producir, ocasionar, mostrar, presentar, producto agrícola • **pro|duc|er** productor o productora

pro|duc|er productor

prod|uct producto, resultado

pro|duc|tion producción

pro|duc|tion values valores de producción

pro|duc|tive productivo, fructífero

prod|uc|tiv|ity productividad

pro|fes|sion profesión

pro|fes|sion|al professional, con carrera • **pro|fes|sion|al|ly** profesionalmente • **pro|fes|sion|al|ism** profesionalismo

pro|fes|sor profesor universitario o profesora universitaria, catedrático o catedrática, profesor o profesora, doctor o doctora

pro|file perfil
▸ **high profile** papel destacado

prof|it ganancia, utilidad, beneficio
▸ **profit from** sacar provecho de, beneficiarse con algo

prof|it|able rentable, redituable, lucrativo • **prof|it|ably** de manera rentable, provechosamente • **prof|it|abil|ity** rentabilidad

pro|found profundo, intenso • **pro|found|ly** profundamente

pro|grade ro|ta|tion rotación prógrada

pro|gram programa, programar • **pro|gram|ming** programación • **pro|gram|mer** programador o programadora

pro|gress progreso, avance, desarrollo, evolución, progresar, avanzar, desarrollar
▸ **in progress** en proceso

pro|gres|sive progresista, progresivo • **pro|gres|sive|ly** progresivamente

pro|hib|it prohibir • **pro|hi|bi|tion** prohibición

proj|ect proyecto, trabajo, proyectar(se), reflejar

pro|jec|tile mo|tion trayectoria del proyectil

pro|jec|tion proyección, pronóstico, extrapolación, voz y presencia

pro|karyo|tic cell *también* **prokaryote** célula procariota, célula procariótica

pro|lif|er|ate proliferar • **pro|lif|er|a|tion** proliferación

pro|longed prolongado

prom baile de graduación, baile de la escuela

promi|nent destacado, prominente, importante

●**promi|nence** prominencia
●**promi|nent|ly** prominentemente
prom|ise prometer, presagiar, promesa
▶ **show promise** prometer
prom|is|ing prometedor
prom|is|sory note pagaré
pro|mote promover, fomentar, impulsar, ascender ● **pro|mo|tion** promoción, ascenso
pro|mot|er promotor o promotora, hombre de negocios o mujer de negocios
pro|mo|tion|al promocional, publicitario
prompt provocar, inducir, incitar, sugerir, pronto, inmediato ● **prompt|ing** recordatorio
prompt|ly prontamente, sin demora, puntualmente
prone propenso, proclive
pro|noun pronombre
pro|nounce pronunciar(e), declarar
pro|nun|cia|tion pronunciación
proof prueba, acreditación
prop apoyar, puntal, soporte, utilería
▶ **prop up** apoyar
propa|gan|da propaganda
pro|pel|ler hélice, impulsor, propulsor
prop|er apropiado, verdadero, adecuado, correcto, propio
●**prop|er|ly** con propiedad, adecuadamente
prop|er noun nombre propio
prop|er|ty propiedad, inmueble
prop|er|ty tax impuesto predial, impuesto sobre la propiedad inmobiliaria
pro|phase profase
proph|et profeta
pro|por|tion parte,

proporción, porcentaje, tamaño ● **pro|por|tions** dimensiones, proporciones
▶ **in proportion to** respecto de, comparado con
▶ **out of proportion to** desproporcionado a
pro|por|tion|al proporcional
pro|po|sal propuesta, oferta
pro|pose proponer, sugerir, proponer matrimonio
propo|si|tion propuesta, proposición, oferta, argumento
pro|pri|etor propietario o propietaria, dueño o dueña
pro|rate también **pro-rate** prorratear
pro|scenium arco del proscenio, proscenio
prose prosa
pros|ecute procesar, enjuiciar ● **pros|ecu|tion** proceso
pros|ecu|tion parte acusadora
pros|ecu|tor fiscal, querellante, demandante
pro|sim|ian también **pro-simian** prosimio
pros|pect posibilidad, perspectiva, buscar, explorar
pro|spec|tive potencial, posible
pros|per|ity prosperidad
pros|per|ous próspero, floreciente
pros|ti|tute prostituta
pro|tect proteger, defender, custodiar ● **pro|tec|tor** protector o protectora, defensor o defensora
pro|tec|tion protección, resguardo, defensa
pro|tec|tive protector
pro|tein proteína
pro|test protestar, quejarse, protesta, manifestación
●**pro|test|er** también **protestor** manifestante

Prot|es|tant protestante
pro|tist protisto
Pro|tis|ta protista, protoctista
pro|ton protón
proto|type prototipo
proto|zoan protozoario, protozoo
proud orgulloso, satisfecho, ufano, arrogante, altanero
• **proud|ly** orgullosamente
prove resultar, demostrar, probar
prov|erb proverbio, refrán
pro|vide proporcionar, proveer, estipular, disponer
▶ **provide for** mantener, sostener, prever
pro|vid|ed siempre que, siempre y cuando
pro|vince provincia, estado
pro|vin|cial provincial, de la provincia, provinciano, pueblerino
pro|vi|sion provisión, aprovisionamiento, disposición
▶ **provisions** medidas, previsiones
pro|vi|sion|al provisional, transitorio • **pro|vi|sion|al|ly** de manera provisional
pro|voke provocar, irritar, suscitar
pro|vo|lo|ne también **provolone cheese** (queso) provolone
prune ciruela pasa, podar
prun|ing shears tijeras de podar
pry husmear, fisgonear, curiosear, forzar
▶ **pry something out of somebody** sacarle algo a alguien
P.S. también **PS** posdata
pseudo|pod pseudópodo, seudópodo
psy|chic psíquico, síquico, médium
psycho|logi|cal

psicólogico, sicológico
• **psycho|logi|cal|ly** psicológicamente
psy|chol|ogy psicología, sicología • **psy|cholo|gist** psicólogo o psicóloga, sicólogo o sicóloga
psycho|thera|py psicoterapia, sicoterapia
• **psycho|thera|pist** psicoterapeuta
psy|chrom|eter psicrómetro
pub|lic público, gente
• **pub|lic|ly** públicamente
▶ **in public** en público
pub|lic as|sis|tance asistencia pública
pub|li|ca|tion publicación
pub|lic de|fend|er abogado de oficio o abogada de oficio
pub|lic hous|ing vivienda subvencionada
pub|lic|ity publicidad, propaganda
pub|li|cize hacer público, divulgar
pub|lic of|fice puesto público, puesto de elección popular
pub|lic re|la|tions relaciones públicas, PR
pub|lic school escuela pública, escuela de gobierno, escuela oficial, colegio privado, internado privado
pub|lic sec|tor sector público
pub|lic tele|vi|sion también **public TV** televisión oficial
pub|lic trans|por|ta|tion transporte público
pub|lish publicar(se), sacar
pub|lish|er editor o editora
pub|lish|ing edición
pud|ding budín, natilla
pud|dle charco
pudgy gordinflón, rechoncho
pueb|lo aldea de indios
puff dar una fumada, dar una calada, fumar,

P

resoplar, jadear, fumada, calada, bocanada, nube, comentario favorable

Pu|lit|zer Prize Premio Pulitzer

pull jalar, tirar, extraer, arrancar, arrastrar, estirarse, ponerse, jalón, fuerza
▶ **pull away** arrancar(se), separarse, alejarse
▶ **pull back** echarse para atrás, retirarse
▶ **pull down** demoler
▶ **pull in** detenerse
▶ **pull into** estacionarse
▶ **pull off** lograr
▶ **pull out** arrancar, salirse, irse
▶ **pull over** estacionarse
▶ **pull through** reponerse, recuperarse
▶ **pull together** unirse, trabajar en conjunto, calmarse, recobrar la compostura
▶ **pull up** parar

pul|ley polea

Pull|man pullman, carro dormitorio

pul|mo|nary cir|cu|la|tion circulación pulmonar

pul|sar pulsar

pulse pulso, pulsación, impulso

pump bomba, zapatilla escotada, bombear
▶ **have one's stomach pumped** lavar el estómago, hacer un lavado de estómago
▶ **pump out** producir intensivamente
▶ **pump up** inflar

pump|kin calabaza

punch dar puñetazos, dar trompadas, presionar, oprimir, picar, perforar, puñetazo, trompada, perforadora, ponche
▶ **punch in** teclear, marcar

punch|ing bag punching bag, costal (de boxeo)

punc|tu|al puntual

• **punc|tu|al|ly** puntualmente

punc|tu|ate interrumpir

punc|tua|tion puntuación

punc|tua|tion mark signo de puntuación

pun|ish castigar, sancionar

pun|ish|ment castigo, sanción

punk música punk, punk, hooligan, vándalo

Pun|nett square rejilla de Punnett

pu|pil discípulo, alumno o alumna, pupila

pup|pet marioneta, títere, instrumento

pup|pet|ry teatro de títeres, teatro de marionetas

pup|py perrito, cachorro

pur|chase comprar, adquirir, adquisición, compra, lo comprado • **pur|chas|er** comprador o compradora

pure puro, sin mezcla, genuino • **pu|rity** pureza

pure|ly únicamente, estrictamente

pur|ple púrpura, morado, violeta

pur|pose objetivo, propósito, fin
▶ **on purpose** intencionalmente, a propósito

purse bolso, bolsa, cartera, fruncir

pur|sue buscar, luchar por, continuar con, proseguir, perseguir • **pur|su|er** perseguidor o perseguidora

pur|suit búsqueda, actividad, pasatiempo, recreación
▶ **in pursuit of** en persecución de, a la caza de

push empujar, impulsar, luchar, mover, presionar, obligar, promocionar, vender ilegalmente, empujón, impulso, lucha
▶ **push ahead** o **push forward**

seguir adelante
▶ **push on** seguir adelante
▶ **push over** derribar, tumbar
▶ **push through** hacer aprobar
▶ **push your way through** abrirse paso a empujones

push|cart carretilla, carrito

push-up lagartija, plancha, flexión de brazos

put poner(se), colocar, situar, acomodar, internar, encerrar, depositar, dedicar, invertir, expresar(se)
▶ **put across** o **put over** hacer entender
▶ **put aside** guardar, reservar
▶ **put at** estimar, calcular
▶ **put away** guardar
▶ **put back** posponer, retrasar
▶ **put down** anotar, escribir, apuntar, dar (un anticipo), dejar (un depósito), sofocar, aplastar, humillar, rebajar, sacrificar, matar
▶ **put down to** atribuir a
▶ **put forward** presentar, proponer
▶ **put in** dedicar, solicitar
▶ **put off** posponer, postergar, desalentar, provocar rechazo, distraer
▶ **put on** poner(se), montar, organizar, prender, encender
▶ **put on weight** engordar
▶ **put out** sacar, publicar, apagar, extinguir, extender, dar, causar molestia
▶ **put over** ver **put across**
▶ **put through** comunicar, pasar la comunicación, someter
▶ **put together** armar, reunir, hacer, preparar
▶ **put up** construir, levantar, colgar, oponer, elevar, incrementar, alojar
▶ **put up with** aguantar, soportar
▶ **put a question to (somebody)** preguntar a, hacer una pregunta a, interrogar a

putt potear, golpear (la pelota)

putt|er putter, entretenerse

puz|zle confundir, reflexionar, pensar, acertijo, juego, adivinanza, enigma, misterio ● **puz|zled** confundido ● **puz|zling** preocupante

P wave *también* **P-wave** onda (primaria)

pyra|mid pirámide

pyro|clas|tic ma|terial material piroclástico

P

Qq

qt. *ver* quart

quad|rat|ic func|tion función cuadrática

quad|ru|ple cuadruplicar, cuádruple, cuádruplo

quad|ru|plet cuádruple

quag|ga cuaga

quail codorniz

quaint pintoresco, extraño, curioso

quake terremoto, sismo, temblor (de tierra), temblar, estremecerse

quali|fi|ca|tion calificación, requisito, condición, limitación, salvedad, reserva

quali|fied con reservas, con salvedad

quali|fi|er clasificado, eliminatoria

quali|fy clasificar(se), moderar, suavizar, habilitar, capacitar, titularse, recibirse

quali|ta|tive cualitativo

qual|ity calidad, cualidad, característica, naturaleza

qual|ity of life calidad de vida

qualm escrúpulo (de conciencia)

quan|tity cantidad

quan|tum quántum, avance espectacular

quar|an|tine cuarentena

quar|rel pelea, riña, pelearse, reñir
▶ **have no quarrel with** no tener nada contra

quart cuarto (de galón)

quar|ter cuarto, cuarta parte, moneda de veinticinco centavos, trimestre, barrio
▶ **at close quarters** desde cerca

quarter|back mariscal de campo, quarterback

quarter|final cuarto de final

quar|ter|ly trimestral, trimestralmente

quar|ter note negra, semínima

quar|tet cuarteto

qua|sar quasar

queen reina

que|ry duda, preguntar (por), consultar, inquirir

quest búsqueda

ques|tion pregunta, duda, cuestión, preguntar, hacer preguntas, interrogar, dudar de, poner en duda, poner en tela de juicio
● **ques|tion|er** interrogador o interrogadora
● **ques|tion|ing** interrogatorio
▶ **in question** en cuestión, de que se trate
▶ **out of the question** imposible, inaceptable, impensable
▶ **there's no question of** no hay posibilidad de

ques|tion|able discutible, dudoso, sospechoso

ques|tion mark signo de interrogación

ques|tion|naire cuestionario

quick rápido, veloz ● **quick|ly** rápidamente ● **quick|ness** rapidez

quick study perspicaz

qui|et callado, tranquilo, callar(se), tranquilizar, calmar ● **qui|et|ly** calladamente, tranquilamente, silenciosamente
● **qui|et|ness** silencio, tranquilidad
▶ **keep (something) quiet**

callar, guardar silencio
quilt colcha, edredón
quilt|ing acolchar, hacer colchas
quin|tu|plet quíntuple
quit dejar (de)
▸ **call it quits** darse por satisfecho
quite bastante, totalmente, muy, todo

quiz serie de preguntas, concurso, examen, preguntar, interrogar
quo|ta cuota, parte
quo|ta|tion cita, presupuesto, cotización
quo|ta|tion marks comillas
quote citar, presupuestar, cotizar, cita, presupuesto, cotización ● **quotes** comillas

q

Rr

rab|bi rabino

rab|bit conejo

race carrera, contienda, raza, correr, jugar una carrera, echar(se) una carrera, agolparse las ideas (en la cabeza), latir apresuradamente
▸ **a race against time** una carrera contra el tiempo

race|way autódromo, pista de carreras

ra|cial racial • **ra|cial|ly** racialmente

rac|ing carreras

rac|ist racista • **rac|ism** racismo

rack estante, sufrir dolores atroces
▸ **off the rack** de confección

rack|et raqueta, jaleo, bulla, fraude organizado, tinglado, intriga

rac|quet|ball juego parecido al frontenis

ra|dar radar

ra|dial sym|me|try simetría radial

ra|dia|tion radiación

ra|dia|tive zone zona de radiación

radi|cal radical • **radi|cal|ly** radicalmente

ra|dio radio, transmitir por radio, llamar por radio

radio|ac|tive radioactivo • **radio|ac|tiv|ity** radioactividad

radio|act|ive sym|bol símbolo de radioactividad

ra|dio tele|scope radiotelescopio, radiorreceptor

ra|dio wave onda de radio, onda radioeléctrica

ra|dius radio

raft balsa

rag trapo, andrajos, harapos

rage ira, rabia, cólera, rugir, enfurecer, embravecer, expresar ira • **rag|ing** rugiente

raid asaltar, allanar, registrar, asalto, allanamiento, registro

rail riel, barra, cortinero, vía, carril, rail
▸ **by rail** en tren

rail|road ferrocarril, vía

rail|road cross|ing paso a nivel, crucero

rain lluvia, llover
▸ **rain out** suspenderse, cancelarse

rain|bow arco iris

rain check vale por suspensión o cancelación de un espectáculo

rain|drop gota de lluvia

rain|fall precipitación pluvial

rain for|est *también* **rainforest** selva (tropical), bosque (ecuatorial o pluvial)

rainy lluvioso

raise levantar, alzar, llevarse a, aumentar, incrementar, mejorar, recaudar, alimentar, poner, criar, educar, cultivar, aumento

rai|sin pasa

rake rastrillo, rastrillar, recoger con rastrillo
▸ **rake in** forrarse con, embolsarse

ral|ly concentración, carrera, manifestación, unirse (en apoyo de), recuperarse, reponerse
▸ **rally around** acudir en apoyo de

ram|bunc|tious revoltoso

ramp rampa

ran *ver* run

ranch rancho

ranch house casa de una sola planta, casa (principal)

ran|dom aleatorio, fortuito • **ran|dom|ly** al azar ▸ **at random** al azar

ran|dom vari|able variable aleatoria

R&R *también* **R and R** descanso y esparcimiento

range gama, variedad, intervalo, alcance, sierra, cordillera, cadena, campo de tiro, escala ▸ **range from… to** variar de…a, ir de…a

rank grado (militar), categoría, clasificar • **ranks** filas ▸ **break rank** romper filas ▸ **close ranks** cerrar filas

rank|ing de más alto grado, de mayor jerarquía

rap rap, golpetear, llamar, golpe, golpeteo • **rap|per** cantante de rap, intérprete de música rap

rape violar, violación • **rapist** violador *o* violadora

rap|id rápido • **rap|id|ly** rápidamente • **ra|pid|ity** rapidez

rapid-fire rápido, veloz

rap|pel practicar rappel

rap sheet antecedentes penales

rare raro, poco asado, casi crudo, a la inglesa

rar|efac|tion rarefacción, enrarecimiento

rare|ly raramente, pocas veces, raro

rash precipitado, irreflexivo, salpullido, sarpullido, erupción, roncha, proliferación • **rash|ly** imprudentemente

rasp|berry frambuesa

rat rata

rate velocidad, ritmo, tarifa, tasa, considerar, clasificar

▸ **at any rate** en todo caso
▸ **at this rate** a este paso, a este ritmo

ra|ther antes que, más bien que, en lugar de, más bien ▸ **would rather do** preferir hacer

rati|fy ratificar • **rati|fi|ca|tion** ratificación

rat|ing renombre, reputación, índice

ra|tio proporción

ra|tion|al racional, inteligente, razonable, en su (sano) juicio • **ra|tion|al|ity** racionalidad • **ra|tion|al|ly** racionalmente

ra|tion|al num|ber número racional

rat|tle traquetear, inquietar, poner nervioso, traqueteo, ruido, sonaja, sonajero • **rat|tled** inquieto

rat|ty raído, andrajoso

rave desvariar, disparatar, despotricar, fiesta con música electrónica ▸ **rave about** deshacerse en elogios por, hablar de algo con entusiasmo

raw prima, crudo, en carne viva, novato, inexperto, bisoño ▸ **a raw deal** mala pasada, tratamiento severo o injusto

raw|hide cuero crudo o sin curtir

ray rayo

ra|zor rasuradora, rastrillo para rasurarse, navaja para rasurarse

razz tomar el pelo, reírse de, vacilar a

r-controlled sound vocal cuyo sonido varía por influencia de la "r"

reach llegar, alcanzar(se) meter la mano, comunicarse

re|act reaccionar, actuar de manera distinta

re|ac|tant reactivo

re|ac|tion reacción, reflejo

r

re|ac|tor reactor nuclear

read leer, decir, sonar, lectura
▸ **read into** buscar significado
▸ **read out** leer en voz alta
▸ **read up on** estudiar, investigar

read|er lector *o* lectora

read|er's thea|ter teatro de lectura

read|ily inmediatamente, sin dificultad

read|ing lectura, recital

ready listo, preparado, dispuesto, a punto, a la mano, fácil, prepararse
• **readi|ness** preparación, disposición

ready-made de confección, preparado, precocido, tópico

real real, verdadero, realmente, verdaderamente
▸ **for real** en serio, de verdad

real es|tate bien raíz, agente inmobiliario, inmobiliaria

re|al|is|tic realista
• **re|al|is|ti|cal|ly** realistamente

re|al|ity realidad
▸ **in reality** en realidad

re|al|ity check toma de conciencia

re|al|ity show programa de telerrealidad, espectáculo realista

re|al|ity TV telerrealidad, televisión realista

re|al|ize darse cuenta de, comprender, caer en la cuenta de, hacerse realidad, convertirse en realidad, cumplirse, hacer
• **re|ali|za|tion** comprensión, cumplimiento

re|al|ly de veras, de verdad, realmente

realm campo, esfera, terreno

real num|ber número real

real prop|er|ty bien raíz, inmueble

real world realidad, mundo real

rear parte trasera, trasero, criar, encabritarse, empinarse, pararse en dos patas

re|arrange cambiar de orden, volver a arreglar o disponer, reorganizar
• **re|arrange|ment** reorganización

rea|son razón, motivo, causa, razonar, pensar, reflexionar
▸ **by reason of** en virtud de
▸ **reason with** razonar con

rea|son|able razonable, aceptable • **rea|son|ably** sensatamente, razonablemente, aceptablemente, bastante
• **rea|son|able|ness** sensatez
▸ **a reasonable amount of** bastante

re|assure tranquilizar
• **re|assur|ance** seguridad

re|bel rebelde, rebelarse

re|bel|lion rebelión

re|boot reiniciar, reinicio

re|bound rebotar, salir el tiro por la culata

re|build reconstruir, restablecer

re|call recordar, llamar

re|cede retroceder, alejarse, desvanecerse, ceder, tener entradas

re|ceipt recibo, ingreso, entrada, recepción

re|ceive recibir, ser objeto de, acoger

re|ceiv|er auricular, receptor, síndico

re|cent reciente

re|cent|ly recientemente

re|cep|tion recepción, acogida

re|cep|tion|ist recepcionista

re|cep|tor receptor, órgano sensorio

re|ces|sion recesión

re|ces|sive recesivo

reci|pe receta, fórmula

re|cipi|ent destinatario *o* destinataria, receptor *o* receptora, ganador *o* ganadora

re|cite recitar, enumerar

reck|on suponer, calcular, estimar
- ▶ **reckon with** tener *o* tomar en cuenta, contar con
- ▶ **to be reckoned with** vérselas con, habérselas con

re|claim reivindicar, recuperar

rec|la|ma|tion rescate, recuperación

re|cline reclinar(se), recostar(se), apoyar(se), abatir

re|clin|er sillón reclinable

rec|og|ni|tion reconocimiento, aceptación
- ▶ **in recognition of** en reconocimiento por

rec|og|nize reconocer, apreciar

re|com|bi|nant DNA ADN recombinante

rec|om|mend recomendar, aconsejar • **rec|om|mend|ed** recomendado
- • **rec|om|men|da|tion** recomendación

rec|on|cile reconciliar(se), resignarse • **rec|on|cili|a|tion** reconciliación • **rec|on|ciled** resignado

rec|ord registro, disco, marca, récord, registrar, grabar
- ▶ **off the record** extraoficial
- ▶ **on record** en disco

re|cord|er flauta dulce

re|cord|ing grabación

rec|ord play|er tocadiscos, fonógrafo, gramófono

re|cov|er recuperar(se), recobrar

re|cov|ery recuperación, restablecimiento, reactivación

re|cov|ery room sala de recuperación, sala de restablecimiento

rec|rea|tion esparcimiento, diversión, entretenimiento
- • **rec|rea|tion|al** recreativo

rec|rea|tion|al ve|hi|cle caravana, cámper, vehículo de recreo

re|cruit reclutar, recluta
- • **re|cruit|ing** reclutamiento
- • **re|cruit|ment** reclutamiento

rec|tan|gle rectángulo

rec|ti|fy rectificar

rec|ti|lin|ear rectilíneo

re|cu|per|ate recuperarse, recobrarse, restablecerse
- • **re|cu|pera|tion** recuperación

re|cur recurrir, volver a ocurrir, repetirse
- • **re|cur|rence** repetición

re|cuse declinar, eximirse

re|cy|cle reciclar

red rojo, pelirrojo
- ▶ **in the red** en números rojos
- ▶ **see red** enfurecerse, ponerse furioso

red blood cell glóbulo rojo

red card tarjeta roja

red gi|ant gigante roja

red her|ring indicio falso, pista falsa

red-hot al rojo (vivo)

re|dis|trict|ing volver a dividir en distritos

red tape papeleo, burocracia, trámites burocráticos

re|duce reducir, achicar
- ▶ **reduce to** reducir a, sumir en

re|duc|tion reducción, disminución

re|dun|dant redundante, superfluo

reek apestar, oler, hedor, peste

reel carrete, rollo, tambalearse, flaquear, impactarse, aturdirse

r

▸ **reel off** recitar

re|elect *también* **re-elect** reelegir • **re|elec|tion** reelección

re|evalu|ate reconsiderar, volver a evaluar
• **re|evalu|ation** revaluación

re|fer referir, remitir, consultar • **ref|er|ence** referencia
▸ **refer to** referirse a, hacer referencia a

ref|eree árbitro *o* árbitra, réferi, arbitrar, hacer de árbitro

ref|er|ence referencia, recomendación, de referencia
▸ **with/in reference to** respecto de, en relación con

ref|er|ence point punto de referencia

ref|er|en|dum referéndum, referendo, plebiscito

re|fer|ral referencia

re|fine refinar, pulir, mejorar, perfeccionar
• **re|fin|ing** refinación
• **re|fine|ment** refinamiento

re|fin|ery refinería

re|flect reflejar(se), reflexionar, pensar, verse

re|flec|tion reflejo, reflexión, imagen en espejo
▸ **law of reflection** ley de la reflexión de la luz

re|flex reflejo
▸ **reflex (action)** acción refleja, acto reflejo

re|flex|ive pro|noun pronombre reflexivo

re|flex|ive verb verbo reflexivo

re|form reforma, modificar, reformar, reformar(se), corregir(se) • **re|form|er** reformador *o* reformadora
• **re|formed** reformado

re|form school reformatorio, centro de readaptación social para menores

re|fract refractar(se)

▸ **re|frac|tion** refracción

re|fract|ing tele|scope telescopio de refracción

re|frain abstenerse, refrenarse, estribillo

re|fresh refrescar
• **re|freshed** fresco
• **re|fresh|ing** refrescante
▸ **refresh one's memory** ayudar a recordar

re|fresh|ing refrescante, alentador • **re|fresh|ing|ly** refrescantemente

re|fried beans frijoles refritos

re|frig|era|tor refrigerador, nevera

re|fu|el reabastecer, repostar, poner gasolina, llenar el tanque • **re|fu|el|ing** reabastecimiento de combustible

ref|uge refugio

refu|gee refugiado *o* refugiada

re|fund devolución, rembolso, reembolso, devolver, rembolsar, reembolsar

re|fur|bish renovar, retocar • **re|fur|bish|ment** renovación

re|fus|al negativa, rechazo

re|fuse rehusar, negar(se), rechazar, basura, residuos, desperdicio

re|fute refutar, rebatir

re|gain recuperar, recobrar

re|gard considerar, mirar con, respeto, consideración
▸ **(give) regards** saludos
▸ **as regards** en cuanto a, en relación con, respecto de
▸ **in/with regard to** en relación con

re|gard|ing respecto de, en cuanto a, en relación con

re|gard|less
▸ **regardless of** independientemente, a pesar de

reg|gae reggae

re|gime régimen, sistema

regi|ment regimiento
• **regi|men|tal** de regimiento

re|gion región, zona, área
• **re|gion|al** regional
▶ **in the region of** alrededor de

reg|is|ter registro, lista, padrón, registrar(se), inscribirse, demostrar

reg|is|tered nurse enfermera titulada o enfermero titulado

reg|is|trar secretario de admisiones o secretaria de admisiones

reg|is|tra|tion registro, padrón

re|gret arrepentirse, lamentar, pesar, arrepentimiento, remordimiento

regu|lar regular, sistemático, habitual, común, constante, asiduo o asidua, normal • **regu|lar|ly** regularmente • **regu|lar|ity** regularidad

regu|late regular, reglamentar

regu|la|tion regla, reglamento

regu|la|tor regulador o reguladora • **regu|la|tory** regulador

re|ha|bili|tate rehabilitar
• **re|ha|bili|ta|tion** rehabilitación

re|hears|al ensayo

reign reinar, reino

re|im|burse reembolsar
• **re|im|burse|ment** reembolso

rein rienda
▶ **give free rein to** dar rienda suelta, dar carta blanca, dejar las manos libres
▶ **rein in** frenar

re|inforce reforzar, fortalecer
• **re|inforce|ment** refuerzo

re|install reinstalar

re|instate restituir, rehabilitar
• **re|instate|ment** rehabilitación

re|it|er|ate reiterar

re|ject rechazar, producto defectuoso • **re|jec|tion** rechazo

re|late relacionarse

re|lat|ed emparentado, relacionado, pariente de

re|la|tion relación, pariente
▶ **in relation to** en relación con, con relación a

re|la|tion|ship relación

rela|tive pariente, relativo
• **rela|tive|ly** relativamente
▶ **relative to** en relación con, con relación a, en comparación con

rela|tive clause oración adjetiva, oración de relativo

rela|tive da|ting fechamiento relativo, datación relativa

rela|tive hu|mid|ity humedad relativa

rela|tive pro|noun pronombre relativo

re|lax descansar, relajar(se), aflojar • **re|laxa|tion** relajamiento • **re|laxed** informal • **re|lax|ing** relajante

re|lay carrera de relevos, carrera de postas, transmitir por repetidor, retransmitir

re|lease poner en libertad, soltar, liberar, eximir, aliviar, divulgar, despedir, lanzar, poner en circulación, alivio, divulgación, liberación, novedad

rel|egate relegar

re|lent|less incesante
• **re|lent|less|ly** incesantemente

rel|evant importante, relevante • **rel|evance** relevancia

re|li|able confiable, fidedigno • **re|li|ably** confiablemente, de

r

fuente fidedigna

• re|li|abil|ity seguridad de funcionamiento, fiabilidad

re|lief alivio, ayuda, auxilio, relieve

re|lief map mapa en relieve

re|lieve aliviar, tranquilizar, relevar

re|lieved aliviado

re|li|gion religión

re|li|gious religioso

rel|ish saborearse, fruición, deleite, salsa (de frutas o verduras)

re|lo|cate trasladar(se), establecerse en un nuevo lugar • re|lo|ca|tion traslado

re|luc|tant renuente, reacio • re|luc|tant|ly con renuencia • re|luc|tance renuencia

rely
▶ rely on depender de, confiar en, contar con

re|main permanecer, quedar(se), persistir, perdurar, subsistir • re|mains restos

re|main|der resto

re|main|ing restante

re|mark observar, comentar, hacer observaciones, comentario, observación

re|mark|able extraordinario, admirable • re|mark|ably extraordinariamente

re|match partido de desquite, partido de revancha

rem|edy remedio, remediar

re|mem|ber recordar, acordarse de

re|mind recordar a, hacer acordarse a, acordar de

re|mind|er recordatorio

remi|nisce rememorar, recordar

remi|nis|cent que recuerda

re|mold cambiar

re|mote remoto, alejado, distante

re|mote con|trol control remoto

re|mote sens|ing detección a distancia

re|mov|al remoción, extirpación

re|move retirar, sacar, quitarse, remover

re|moved distante

re|nais|sance renacimiento

ren|der hacer

re|new renovar

re|new|al renovación

reno|vate renovar, restaurar • reno|va|tion renovación

re|nowned renombrado, famoso, conocido

rent alquilar, rentar, alquiler, renta

rent|al alquiler, renta, de alquiler

re|or|gan|ize reorganizar • re|or|gani|za|tion reorganización

rep representante comercial, agente comercial, representante

Rep. miembro de la Cámara de Representantes de Estados Unidos

re|pair reparar, reparación

re|pat|ri|ate repatriar • re|pat|ria|tion repatriación

re|pay pagar, corresponder

re|pay|ment pago

re|peat repetir(se), repetición

re|peat|ed repetido, reiterado • re|peat|ed|ly repetidamente

re|pel repugnar, rechazar • re|pelled repulsado

rep|eti|tion repetición

re|place reemplazar, cambiar, volver a poner

re|place|ment reemplazo, substituto

re|play volver a jugar, repetir, repetición

re|ply responder, reponer, contestar, respuesta

R

re|port informar, denunciar, dar parte de, presentarse, noticia, informe

re|port card boleta de calificaciones

re|port|ed|ly según se informa, según se dice

re|port|ed speech discurso indirecto, estilo indirecto

re|port|er reportero o reportera

re|port|ing reportajes, cobertura

re|pos|i|tory depósito, almacén, museo

re|pos|sess recuperar la posesión de

rep|re|sent representar, presentar

rep|re|sen|ta|tion representación

rep|re|sen|ta|tive representante, representativo

re|pro|duce reproducir(se) • **re|pro|duc|tion** reproducción

re|pro|duc|tion reproducción

rep|tile reptil

re|pub|lic república

re|pub|li|can republicano

repu|ta|tion reputación

re|quest solicitar, solicitud, petición
▸ **at somebody's request/at the request of somebody** a petición de alguien
▸ **on request** a solicitud

re|quire requerir, necesitar, obligar

re|quire|ment requisito, necesidad

res|cue rescatar • **res|cu|er** rescatador, rescate
▸ **go to somebody's rescue/ come to somebody's rescue** ir en auxilio de

re|search investigación, investigar • **re|search|er** investigador o investigadora

re|sem|blance parecido

re|sem|ble parecerse

re|sent resentir

re|sent|ment resentimiento

res|er|va|tion reserva, reservación

re|serve reservar, reserva
▸ **in reserve** en reserva

re|served reservado

res|er|voir embalse, presa, represa, reserva

resi|dence residencia
▸ **be in residence** tener su residencia en, residir en

resi|dence hall residencia de estudiantes

resi|den|cy internado, residencia

resi|dent residente, vecino, habitante, médico interno o médica interna

resi|dent al|ien residente extranjero

resi|den|tial residencial, internado

re|sign renunciar, resignarse

res|ig|na|tion renuncia, resignación

re|signed resignado

re|sist resistir(se)

re|sist|ance resistencia

re|sist|ant renuente, resistente

reso|lu|tion resolución, propósito, decisión, solución

re|solve resolver, resolución

reso|nance resonancia

re|sort recurrir, centro vacacional
▸ **as a last resort** como último recurso

re|source recurso

re|source re|cov|ery recuperación de recursos

re|spect respetar, respeto
▸ **pay one's respects** presentar respetos
▸ **in this respect/in many respects** en este sentido/en muchos sentidos
▸ **with respect to** con

r

respecto a

re|spect|able respectable, aceptable, digno
• **re|spect|abil|ity** respetabilidad

re|spect|ed respetado

re|spec|tive|ly respectivamente

res|pi|ra|tion respiración

res|pira|tory respiratorio

res|pira|tory sys|tem vías respiratorias, aparato respiratorio, sistema respiratorio

re|spond responder

re|sponse reacción

re|spon|sibil|ity responsabilidad

re|spon|sible responsable
• **re|spon|sibly** responsablemente

rest resto, descanso, descansar, depender, apoyar(se) • **rest|ed** descansado
▸ **and the rest/all the rest of it** etcétera
▸ **come to rest** detenerse

rest area parada de descanso, área de descanso, área de reposo

res|tau|rant restaurante

rest|less impaciente, inquieto, nervioso
• **rest|less|ness** inquietud
• **rest|less|ly** nerviosamente

re|store restablecer, devolver, restituir, restaurar • **res|to|ra|tion** restablecimiento, restauración

re|strain contener, moderar
• **re|strained** moderado

re|strain|ing or|der orden restrictiva

re|straint restricción, limitación, compostura, circunspección

re|strict restringir, limitar
• **re|strict|ed** restringido
• **re|stric|tion** restricción

restroom *también* **rest room**

baños, sanitarios, servicios

re|struc|ture reestructurar
• **re|struc|tur|ing** reestructuración

rest stop parada de descanso

re|sult resultado, resultar

re|sult|ant ve|loc|ity velocidad resultante

re|sume reasumir, reanudar
• **re|sump|tion** reanudación

ré|su|mé *también* **resume** resumen, reseña, currículum vítae

re|tail por menor, minorista, vender al por menor

re|tail|er minorista

re|tain conservar

re|tali|ate vengarse, desquitarse, tomar represalias • **re|talia|tion** venganza

reti|na retina

re|tire jubilarse • **re|tired** jubilado

re|tiree jubilado

re|tire|ment jubilación

re|tire|ment fund fondo de jubilación, fondo de retiro

re|tire|ment plan plan de jubilación, plan de retiro

re|tort replicar, réplica

re|treat retirarse, retirada, retiro

re|triev|al recuperación

re|trieve ir por

retro|grade inversión

retro|grade or|bit órbita retrógrada

retro|grade ro|ta|tion rotación retrógrada

retro|spect
▸ **in retrospect** en retrospectiva

re|turn volver, regresar, retornar, devolver, emitir, vuelta, regreso, retorno, devolución, recuperación, rendimiento

re|union reunión, reencuentro

re|use reutilizar, volver a

utilizar, reutilización

re|veal revelar, descubrir, dejar ver

re|veal|ing revelador

rev|ela|tion revelación

rev|el|er *también* **reveller** juerguista, parrandero *o* parrandera, jaranero *o* jaranera

re|venge venganza

rev|enue ingreso

rev|enue stream ingreso

Rev|er|end clérigo, religioso, sacerdote

re|verse revocar (legal), anular (legal), cambiar, dar marcha atrás, invertir, en reversa, en marcha atrás, inverso, contrario, opuesto
▶ **in reverse** a la inversa, al revés

re|verse fault falla inversa, falla invertida

re|verse psy|chol|ogy psicología en reversa

re|vert volver, revertir

re|view revisión, estudio, examen, crítica, reseña, repaso, revisar, estudiar, examinar, reseñar, repasar ● **re|view|er** crítico *o* crítica

re|vise reconsiderar, cambiar, revisar ● **re|vi|sion** revisión

re|vis|it volver a visitar

re|viv|al renovación, reposición, reestreno

re|vive reactivar, reponer, reestrenar, reanimar

re|volt revuelta, levantamiento, sublevación, rechazo, sublevarse, rebelarse, alzarse

revo|lu|tion revolución

revo|lu|tion|ary revolucionario *o* revolucionaria

re|volve girar, dar vueltas
▶ **revolve around** girar en torno a

re|volv|er revólver

re|ward premio, prima, recompensa, recompensar, premiar

re|ward|ing gratificante

re|write volver a redactar, volver a dictar

rheto|ric retórica

rhe|tori|cal strat|egy estrategia retórica

rhi|zoid rizoide

rhi|zome rizoma

rhom|bus rombo

rhyme rimar, poema, rima

rhythm ritmo

rib costilla

rib|bon cinta, listón

ribo|some ribosoma

rice arroz

rich rico, grasoso, pesado, indigesto ● **riches** riqueza ● **rich|ness** riqueza
▶ **the rich** los ricos

ri|cot|ta *también* **ricotta cheese** queso ricota, requesón

rid librar
▶ **get rid of** deshacerse de

rid|dle adivinanza, acertijo, enigma, misterio

ride montar, andar, viajar, paseo, vuelta
▶ **a rough ride** mal rato
▶ **ride herd on** supervisar, vigilar

rid|er jinete *o* amazona, ciclista, motociclista

ridge cresta, protuberancia

ri|dicu|lous ridículo

rid|ing monta, equitación

rife extendido

ri|fle rifle, buscar, hojear

rift val|ley valle producto de una fisura o grieta en la superficie de la tierra

rig amañar, arreglar, manipular, plataforma, camión de remolque
● **rig|ging** fraude

right correcto, bien, indicado, justo, verdad, adecuado, derecho, derecha,

r

correctamente, rectificar, enderezar • **right|ness** rectitude
▸ **be right** tener razón
▸ **by rights** por derecho, propiamente
▸ **in one's own right** por derecho propio
▸ **be right there/back** volver enseguida
▸ **right after** justo después
▸ **right away** de inmediato, inmediatamente
▸ **right now** justo ahora, en este preciso momento

right an|gle ángulo recto
▸ **at right angles** en ángulo recto

right|ful legítimo
• **right|ful|ly** legítimamente

right-hand a la derecha, al lado derecho

right-handed diestro, derecho, con la derecha

right-of-center centro-derecha

right of way servidumbre, derecho de paso

right tri|an|gle triángulo rectángulo

right-wing de derecha, derechista, ala derecha
• **right-winger** derechista

rig|id riguroso, rígido
• **ri|gid|ity** severidad, rigidez
• **rig|id|ly** rigurosamente

rig|id mo|tion movimiento rígido

rig|or|ous riguroso
• **rig|or|ous|ly** rigurosamente

rim borde

ring anillo, alianza, sortija, sonido, repique, timbrazo, aro, cuadrilátero, ring, red, banda, sonar, repicar, repiquetear, volver a llamar, colgar, cortar, cercar, rodear
▸ **ring true/ring hollow** suena convincente/hueco

ringtone melodía

rinky-dink de mala muerte

rinse enjuagar, enjuague

riot disturbio, causar disturbios, amotinarse
• **ri|ot|er** alborotador o alborotadora • **ri|ot|ing** disturbio

rip rasgar, romper, arrancar(se), rasgadura
▸ **rip off** timar, tracalear
▸ **rip up** romper en pedazos

ripe maduro, oportuno, propicio

rip|en madurar

rise subir, elevarse, ponerse de pie, levantarse, salir, aumentar, aumentar de volumen, subir de tono, ascender, aumento, ascensión
▸ **give rise to** dar origen a, dar lugar a, ocasionar
▸ **rise above** sobreponerse, superar
▸ **rise up** levantarse, rebelarse, alzarse

ris|ing ac|tion acción creciente

risk riesgo, arriesgarse, arriesgar
▸ **be at risk** correr riesgos
▸ **at one's own risk** por cuenta y riesgo propios
▸ **run a risk** correr el riesgo

risky aventurado, peligroso, riesgoso

rite rito

ritu|al ritual, costumbre

ri|val rival, rivalizar

ri|val|ry rivalidad

riv|er río

RNA ARN

roach cucaracha

road camino, carretera, calle

road|kill también **road kill** restos de animales muertos en las carreteras

road rage violencia vial

road|runner correcaminos

road|side borde del camino, orilla del camino

road test también **road-test** someter a una prueba de

R

carretera, probar, prueba de carretera, prueba

road|work obras viales

roam vagar

roar zumbar, ruido, estrépito, reír(se) a carcajadas, rugir, bramar, rugido

roast asar, asado

rob robar, privar, asaltar
• **rob|ber** ladrón o ladrona

rob|bery robo, asalto

robe toga, bata

rob|in petirrojo, tordo norteamericano

ro|bot robot

ro|bust robusto

rock roca, peñasco, peñón, piedra, rock, mecer(se), sacudir, estremecer

rock cy|cle ciclo de las rocas

rock|et cohete espacial, cohete, misil, dispararse

rock|fall alud de rocas, desprendimiento de rocas

rod barra, varilla, bastoncillo

ro|dent roedor

rogue state estado malhechor

roil arremolinarse, revolverse

role función, papel

role mod|el modelo de conducta

roll rodar, enrollar, hacer bola de, rollo, bolillo, pancito, lista, padrón
▸ **rolled into one** todo en uno
▸ **roll in** entrar a raudales
▸ **roll up** enrollar(se)

roll|back reducción

roll|er rodillo

roll|ing pin rodillo, palote

ROM ROM

Ro|man romano o romana

Ro|man Catho|lic católico romano, católico

ro|mance romance, idilio, romanticismo, novela romántica, novela rosa

ro|man|tic romántico o romántica • **ro|man|ti|cal|ly**

de manera romántica

ron|do rondó

roof techo, tejado, paladar
▸ **go through the roof** irse a las nubes
▸ **hit the roof/go through the roof** poner el grito en el cielo

rookie novato o novata

room cuarto, habitación, sala, lugar, espacio, margen

room and board pensión completa

room|ing house pensión

room|mate compañero de cuarto

roost percha, posarse

roost|er gallo

root raíz, hurgar
▸ **take root** echar raíz
▸ **root out** hacer una limpia de, extirpar, erradicar

root ex|trac|tion extraer la raíz de un número

root hair rizoma, rizoide, pelo absorbente o radical

root sys|tem raíces

root word raíz

rope cuerda, soga, amarrar, atar
▸ **rope in** agarrar

rose ver **rise**, rosa

rose-colored
▸ **look through rose-colored glasses** ver las cosas color de rosa

rosy sonrosado, halagüeño

rot pudrirse, descomponerse, podredumbre, putrefacción

ro|tate girar, rotar(se), turnar(se) • **ro|ta|tion** rotación, giro, turno

ro|ta|tion ver **rotate**

ROTC Centro de Entrenamiento de Oficiales de la Reserva

rot|ten podrido, pésimo

rott|wei|ler también **Rottweiler** rottweiler (raza de perros)

rough áspero, brusco,

r

peligroso, difícil, aproximado • **rough|ness** aspereza • **rough|ly** bruscamente, aproximadamente

round redondo, ronda, ronda eliminatoria, asalto, vuelta, round, recorrido, disparo, andanada, rodear, dar vuelta, doblar, redondear
▸ **round up** hacer una redada de, reunir
▸ **all year round** todo el año

round|about indirecto, con rodeos, con ambages

round trip viaje redondo, viaje de ida y vuelta

round|up rodeo

roust provocar

route ruta, camino, carretera, vía, encaminar, enviar, dirigir
▸ **en route** en camino a, de camino a

rou|tine rutina, rutinario • **rou|tine|ly** rutinariamente

row hilera, fila, remar, bogar
▸ **in a row** seguidos
• **row|ing** remo

row|boat bote de remos

row house *también* **rowhouse** casa adosada

roy|al real

roy|al|ty realeza, regalías

Rte. carretera

rub frotar(se), restregar, borrar
▸ **rub shoulders/elbows with someone** codearse

rub|ber goma, hule, caucho

rub|ber band banda elástica, liga

rub|ber boot bota de hule, bota de goma

rub|bing al|co|hol alcohol para usos médicos

rub|down fricción, friega, masaje

ru|bric rúbrica, reglas impresas en un examen

ruck|us jaleo

rude grosero, maleducado, desagradable • **rude|ly** groseramente, bruscamente • **rude|ness** grosería

ruf|fled encrespado, erizado

rug alfombra, tapete

rug|by rugby

ruin arruinar, ruina
▸ **in ruins** en ruinas

rule regla, norma, gobernar
▸ **as a rule** por regla general, por lo general
▸ **bend/stretch the rules** hacer la vista gorda
▸ **rule out** descartar, impedir, imposibilitar

rul|er gobernante, rey *o* reina, soberano *o* soberana, regla

rul|ing en el poder, fallo, resolución

rum|mage sale venta de artículos donados con fines caritativos

ru|mor rumor

ru|mor mill fábrica de rumores

ru|mor|monger chismoso *o* chismosa

run correr, pasar, presentarse, contender, dirigir, funcionar, hacer, andar, consumir, usar, ir, operar, llevar, correrse, durar, tener validez, carrera, temporada • **run|ning** correr, corriente, dirección
▸ **run late** atrasarse, ir con tiempo
▸ **run (water/faucet/bath)** abrir la llave, abrirle al agua, dejar/hacer correr el agua
▸ **in the long/short run** a la larga/en el corto plazo
▸ **on the run** fugado
▸ **run across** toparse con, tropezarse con, encontrarse con
▸ **run away** huir, escapar(se)
▸ **run away with** dejarse llevar por, dejar correr
▸ **run down** hablar mal de, sobajar(se), atropellar

▶ **run into** tropezar con, encontrarse con, chocar contra, llegar a, alcanzar

▶ **run off** huir, fugarse, sacar

▶ **run out** agotarse, acabarse, vencer, caducar

▶ **run over** atropellar

▶ **run through** leer, repasar, ensayar

▶ **run up** acumular

▶ **run up against** tropezarse con

run|away arrollador, niño o muchacho que se fuga temporal o definitivamente de su casa, fugitivo, que se fuga

run-in roce

run|ner corredor o corredora, guía, riel, patín, estolón

runner-up subcampeón

run|ning interminable, actualizado, consecutivo, seguido

▶ **in the running/out of the running** en/fuera de la carrera

run|ning mate compañero de candidatura o compañera de candidatura

run|ny líquido, que haya perdido consistencia, que gotea, lloroso

run|off escurrimiento, aflujo

run-through ensayo

run|way pista de aterrizaje

rup|ture ruptura, rotura, hernia, herniar(se), romper(se), reventar

ru|ral rural, campestre, del campo

rush correr, acelerar, apresurar(se), precipitar(se), llevar rápidamente, prisa, torrente, torbellino ● **rushed** precipitado, apresurado

rush hour hora pico, hora del tránsito pesado

Rus|sian dress|ing salsa rusa

rust óxido, herrumbre, orín, oxidarse, herrumbrarse

rus|tler abigeo, cuatrero o cuatrera

ru|ta|ba|ga nabo de Suecia, rutabaga

ruth|less despiadado, cruel ● **ruth|less|ly** despiadadamente ● **ruth|less|ness** crueldad

RV caravana, cámper, vehículo de recreo

Rx receta, prescripción

rye centeno, pan de centeno

r

Ss

sa|ber sable

saber-rattling bravuconería, fanfarronada

sack costal

sa|cred sagrado • sac|red|ness lo sagrado

sac|ri|fice sacrificar, sacrificio • sac|ri|fi|cial expiatorio

sad triste • sad|ly con tristeza, tristemente • sad|ness tristeza

sad|dle silla de montar, montura, asiento, ensillar

sa|fa|ri safari

safe seguro, a salvo, sin peligro, seguro, caja fuerte • safe|ly con seguridad
▸ in safe hands / safe in someone's hands en buenas manos
▸ to be on the safe side para mayor seguridad
▸ safe from a salvo de

safe|guard salvaguardar, salvaguarda

safe ha|ven refugio

safe sex sexo seguro

safe|ty seguridad

sag caer, colgar

said ver say

sail vela, navegar, zarpar, navegar a vela, velear
▸ set sail zarpar, hacerse a la mar
▸ sail through something hacer algo muy fácilmente

sail|boat velero

sail|ing veleo, salida

sail|or marinero

saint santo • saint|ly piadoso

sake
▸ for the sake of por el bien de
▸ for the sake of argument pongamos que
▸ for its/their own sake por sí mismo

sal|ad ensalada

sala|man|der salamandra

sala|ry salario, sueldo

sale venta, barata, temporada de rebajas
▸ for sale en venta
▸ on sale a la venta, en rebaja
▸ up for sale en venta

sales clerk también salesclerk vendedor o vendedora

sales|man vendedor

sales slip recibo

sa|lin|ity salinidad

sa|li|va saliva

salm|on salmón

sa|lon salón de belleza, estética

salt sal, salar • salt|ed salado

salt|ta|tion saltación

salt|ine galleta salada

salt shak|er salero

salt|water también salt water agua salada, de agua salada

salty salado

sa|lute saludar, saludo, rendir homenaje a

sal|vage rescatar, salvar, rescate, objetos salvados

sal|va|tion salvación

same igual, mismo
▸ the same lo mismo
▸ all the same/just the same de todas formas

sam|ple muestra, degustar, probar

sanc|tion aprobar, consentir, aprobación, consentimiento • sanc|tions sanciones

sanc|tu|ary santuario, refugio

sand arena, lijar

san|dal sandalias

sand|box arenero

sand dune duna, colina de arena, médano

sand trap trampa de arena

sand|wich sándwich, emparedado, intercalar, insertar

sandy arenoso

sane cuerdo, sensato

sani|tary sanitario

sani|tary nap|kin toalla sanitaria

san|ity cordura, sensatez

sap|py bobo

sar|cas|tic sarcástico
• **sar|cas|ti|cal|ly** de manera sarcástica

sar|gas|sum sargassum

sass hablar con descaro, hablar irrespetuosamente

sas|sa|fras sasafrás

sas|sy fresco, respondón, llamativo y elegante

SAT examen SAT (para entrar a la universidad)

sat|el|lite satélite, por satélite

sat|el|lite dish antena de satélite

sat|in satín

sat|ire sátira

sat|is|fac|tion satisfacción, reparación

sat|is|fac|tory satisfactorio
• **sat|is|fac|to|ri|ly** de manera satisfactoria

sat|is|fied satisfecho

sat|is|fy satisfacer, convencer

sat|is|fy|ing satisfactorio

sat|urat|ed hydro|car|bon hidrocarburo saturado

sat|urat|ed so|lu|tion solución saturada

Sat|ur|day sábado

Sat|urn Saturno

sauce salsa

sauce|pan cacerola

sau|cer platito para la taza

sau|sage salchicha

sav|age salvaje, atacar salvajemente • **sav|age|ly** salvajemente

sa|van|na también **savannah** sabana

save salvar, ahorrar, guardar, ahorrarle a alguien, parar el gol, parada
• **sav|er** ahorrador
▸ **save up** ahorrar

sav|ings ahorros

sav|ings and loan sociedad de ahorro y préstamo

saw ver see, serrucho, sierra, aserrar

say decir, marcar, por ejemplo, oye
▸ **have a say** tener voz y voto
▸ **say to oneself** decirse a sí mismo
▸ **say it all** decir todo
▸ **to be said for** que decir en pro de
▸ **goes without saying** ni falta hace decirlo, es evidente
▸ **that is to say** es decir
▸ **you can say that again** ¡y que lo digas!

say|ing dicho

scaf|fold|ing andamio, andamiaje

sca|lar ma|trix matriz escalar

scale escala, modelo a escala, escama, báscula, escalar
▸ **scale back/down** reducir

scal|lion cebollín, cebollita (cambray)

scal|lop callo de hacha

scalp|er revendedor o revendedora

scan vistazo, ecografía, echar un vistazo, recorrer con la vista, escudriñar, escrutar

scan|dal escándalo

scan|ner escáner, ecógrafo

scape|goat chivo expiatorio

scar cicatriz, marca, huella, marcar, dejar marcado
• **scarred** cubierto de

S

cicatrices

scarce escaso

scarce|ly apenas

scare asustar, susto, temor, amenaza de bomba
 ▸ **scare away/off** ahuyentar

scared tener miedo, temer

scarf bufanda, mascada

scary de miedo, que da miedo

scat|ter esparcir(se)

scat|tered regado, disperso, desparramado, esparcido, desperdigado

scatter|plot scatterplot, gráfica de dispersión

scav|en|ger carroñero

scav|en|ger hunt búsqueda del tesoro, rally

sce|nario escenario, perspectiva

scene escena, escenario, situación, ámbito
 ▸ **behind the scenes** entre bastidores, tras bastidores

scen|ery paisaje, alrededores, panorama, escenografía, decorado

sce|nic pintoresco

scent aroma, fragancia, perfume, olor, rastro, oler, rastrear, olfatear

sched|ule programa, horario, plan, lo programado, lista, catálogo, inventario, programar

scheme esquema, proyecto, plan, programa, conspirar, intrigar, tramar
 ▸ **the (grand) scheme of things** el orden del universo

schlep también **schlepp** cargar con, andar de un lugar a otro

schmooze cotorrear, platicar, chismear

schmuck estúpido o estúpida

schol|ar erudito o erudita, estudioso o estudiosa, sabio o sabia

schol|ar|ship beca,

erudición, saber

school escuela, colegio, facultad, universidad

school board junta de educación

school|boy colegial, estudiante, alumno

school dis|trict distrito escolar

school|girl colegiala, estudiante, alumna

school|house escuela (edificio)

school|ing formación, educación, estudios

schtick sketch, número

sci|ence ciencia

sci|ence fic|tion ciencia ficción

sci|en|tif|ic científico
 • **sci|en|tif|i|cal|ly** científicamente

sci|en|tif|ic meth|od método científico

sci|en|tif|ic no|ta|tion notación científica

sci|en|tist científico o científica

sci-fi ciencia ficción, sci-fi

scis|sors tijeras, tijera

scold regañar, reprender, reñir, reconvenir, sermonear, amonestar

scoop sacar con cuchara, levantar, coger, pala, cuchara, cucharón, primicia, exclusiva
 ▸ **scoop up** levantar, recoger

scope oportunidad, posibilidad, alcance, campo, ámbito

score anotar, marcar, meter, sacar, obtener, lograr, conseguir, hacer cortes, puntuación, marcador, partitura, gran cantidad, score • **scor|er** anotador o anotadora
 ▸ **on that/this score** a ese respecto, en cuanto a eso
 ▸ **settle a score** ajustar cuentas pendientes, saldar

cuentas

scout avanzada, patrulla de reconocimiento, buscar algo, reconocer el terreno

scrag|gly ralo

scram|ble abrirse paso con dificultad, trepar, apresurarse, amontonarse, pelear (por algo), andar a la rebatiña, revolver, batir, rebatiña, relajo, confusión, prisa • **scram|bled** revuelto

scrap pedacito, pizca, descartar, deshacerse de (algo), desechar, abandonar, chatarra, desperdicio
• **scraps** restos, desechos, sobras

scrape rascar, raspar(se), rozar, rayar, arrastrar
▸ **scrape through** pasar de panzazo, pasar a duras penas, pasar apenas
▸ **scrape together** juntar a duras penas, conseguir con trabajos

scratch rascar(se), arañar(se), rasguñar(se), rasguño, arañazo
▸ **from scratch** de cero, desde cero

scratch card *también* **scratchcard** tarjeta para raspar

scream gritar, berrear, dar alaridos, vociferar, grito, alarido, chillido

screen pantalla, pasar, proyectar, tapar, someter a revisión médica, mampara, biombo, ocultar • **screen|ing** proyección, detección

screen|play guión

screw tornillo, atornillar, instalar con tornillos, apretar, enroscar, hacer muecas, torcer el gesto
▸ **screw up** fastidiar algo, echar a perder

screw|driver desarmador, desatornillador

scrim|mage partido, juego, sesión de entrenamiento, partido de práctica

script guión, letra, caligrafía, escritura

scroll bar barra deslizable, scroll bar

scro|tum escroto

scrub restregar, tallar, fregar, tallada, restregada, maleza, matorral, bata

scrub|ber depurador de gases

scrunchie *también* **scrunchy** dona, liga

scru|ti|ny observación

sculp|ture escultura, estatua

scut|tle escabullirse

sea mar, océano • **seas** mares, aguas del mar
▸ **at sea** en el mar, en alta mar

sea-floor spread|ing expansión del fondo del mar, expansión del fondo oceánico

sea|food marisco

sea|gull gaviota

sea|horse *también* **sea horse** caballito de mar, hipocampo, caballo marino

seal sellar, cerrar, sello, sello hermético, foca

sea lev|el *también* **sea-level** nivel del mar

seam costura, filón
▸ **bursting at the seams** estar a punto de estallar, retacado

sea|mount montaña submarina

search buscar, registrar, catear, búsqueda
▸ **in search of** en busca de

search and res|cue *también* **search-and-rescue** búsqueda y rescate

search en|gine máquina de búsqueda, herramienta de búsqueda

sea|side costa, playa, balneario

sea|son estación, estación del año, temporada, sazonar, aderezar,

S

condimentar

sea|son|al de temporada, estacional • **sea|son|al|ly** en cada estación

sea star *también* **seastar** estrella de mar

seat asiento, escaño, curul, sentar(se), tener cupo para
▸ **have a seat on** ser miembro de
▸ **take a back seat** mantenerse al margen
▸ **take a seat** sentar(se)

seat belt cinturón de seguridad

sea tur|tle tortuga marina

sea|weed alga marina, alga

SEC SEC, Comisión Controladora de Acciones y Valores

sec|ond segundo, secundar, apoyar, favorecer • **seconds** segundas (productos)
▸ **second to none** sin comparación, sin par
▸ **second only to** sólo superado por

sec|ond|ary secundario, secundaria, de menor importancia, segunda enseñanza

sec|ond|ary col|or color secundario

sec|ond|ary pol|lu|tant contaminante secundario, contaminante derivado

second-class *también* **second class** de segunda, de menor calidad

second|hand *también* **second-hand** segunda mano, usado, de segunda mano, a través de terceros

second|hand smoke *también* **second-hand smoke** humo de terceros

sec|ond|ly en segundo lugar

se|cre|cy secreto, reserva, sigilo

se|cret secreto • **se|cret|ly** secretamente
▸ **in secret** en secreto

sec|re|tary secretaria *o* secretario, ministro *o* ministra

Sec|re|tary of State Secretario de Estado *o* Secretaria de Estado, Ministro de Relaciones Exteriores *o* Ministra de Relaciones Exteriores

se|cret ser|vice servicio secreto, servicios de inteligencia
▸ **Secret Service** Servicio Secreto

sect secta

sec|tar|ian sectario, confesional

sec|tion sección, parte, porción, sector

sec|tor sector, industria

secu|lar seglar, laico, secular

se|cure asegurar(se), garantizar, proteger, seguro, asegurado, fijo • **se|cure|ly** bien, adecuadamente

se|cu|rity seguridad, certeza, garantía

se|cu|rity cam|era cámara de seguridad

se|dan sedán

sedi|ment sedimento

sedi|men|tary sedimentario

se|duce seducir, atraer • **se|duc|tion** seducción

see ver, visitar, reunirse con, asistir, percatarse, entender, considerar, pensar, pronosticar, imaginarse, experimentar, sufrir, atender, encargarse de, llevar a alguien, ir con alguien, consultar
▸ **I'll/we'll see** ya veremos
▸ **let me/let's see** vamos a ver
▸ **seeing as/that** dado que
▸ **see you** nos vemos
▸ **see about** ocuparse de algo
▸ **see off** despedir(se)
▸ **see through** no dejarse engañar

▶ **see to** ocuparse de

seed semilla, simiente, germen

seed fern pteridosperma

seed|less sin semilla

seek buscar, pedir, tratar, intentar • **seek|er** buscador o buscadora, que busca
▶ **seek out** buscar

seem parecer, dar la impresión, parecer a uno, darle a uno la impresión

seg|ment segmento, sector, sección, parte

seis|mic sísmico, radical

seis|mic gap hiato sísmico

seis|mo|gram sismograma

seis|mo|graph sismógrafo

seis|mol|ogy sismología • **seis|molo|gist** sismólogo o sismóloga

seize agarrar, coger, tomar, asir, capturar, secuestrar, aprovechar
▶ **seize on** aprovechar
▶ **seize up** atorarse, engarrotarse, agarrotarse, paralizarse, atascarse

sel|dom rara vez

se|lect seleccionar, escoger, selecto, escogido, distinguido • **se|lec|tion** selección

se|lec|tion selección, surtido

se|lec|tive selectivo • **se|lec|tive|ly** de manera selectiva, con criterio selectivo

se|lec|tive breed|ing cría selectiva

self persona, personalidad, identidad propia

self-centered egocéntrico, egoísta

self-confident seguro de sí mismo • **self-confidence** confianza en sí mismo

self-conscious tímido, falto de naturalidad

self-control dominio de sí mismo

self-defense defensa propia, legítima defensa

self-determination autodeterminación

self-employed que trabaja por cuenta propia, trabajador independiente o trabajadora independiente

self-esteem amor propio

self-image imagen de sí mismo

self-indulgent indulgente consigo mismo • **self-indulgence** indulgencia consigo mismo

self-interest interés propio, egoísmo

self|ish egoísta • **self|ish|ly** de manera egoísta • **self|ish|ness** egoísmo

self|less desinteresado, desprendido

self-pollinating autopolinizado, autofecundado

self-promotion que se hace promoción a sí mismo

self-respect dignidad, respeto por sí mismo

self-righteous pretencioso • **self-righteousness** con pretensiones

self-rising flour harina que no necesita levadura

self-study autoestudio

self-sufficient autosuficiente • **self-sufficiency** autosuficiencia

sell vender(se)
▶ **sell out** venderse todo, agotarse

sell|er vendedor o vendedora, que se vende

sell-out también **sellout** lleno, éxito de taquilla, traición

selt|zer también **seltzer water** agua mineral, agua de Seltz

se|mes|ter semestre

semiannual semestral

semi|co|lon punto y coma

S

semi|con|duc|tor
semiconductor

semi|fi|nal semifinal

semi|nar seminario

semi|nif|er|ous tu|bule
túbulo seminífero

Se|mit|ic semítico

Sen|ate senado

sena|tor senador o senadora

send mandar, enviar,
remitir, expedir, echar,
despedir, emitir, lanzar
• send|er remitente
▶ send for mandar por, pedir
▶ send off mandar,
despachar
▶ send off for pedir
▶ send out mandar
▶ send out for mandar por,
mandar a por, encargar

se|nile senil • se|nil|ity
senilidad

sen|ior de más alto rango,
superior, mayor, estudiante
del último año

sen|ior citi|zen persona de la
tercera edad

sen|ior high school también
senior high preparatoria,
prepa

sen|ior mo|ment mal
momento

sen|sa|tion sensación,
sensibilidad, éxito

sen|sa|tion|al sensacional,
que causa sensación
• sen|sa|tion|al|ly
sensacionalmente

sense sentido, sensación,
sentido común, sensatez,
significado, sentir, intuir
▶ come to one's senses/
bring somebody to their
senses entrar en razón
▶ make sense tener sentido
▶ make sense of entender
▶ make sense ser razonable
/sensato

sense|less sin sentido,
inconsciente

sense memo|ry memoria
sensorial

sense of hu|mor sentido del
humor

sen|sible sensato • sen|sibly
con sensatez

sen|si|tive sensible,
susceptible, delicado
• sen|si|tive|ly con
sensibilidad • sen|si|tiv|ity
sensibilidad,
susceptibilidad
▶ sensitive subject/issue lo
delicado

sen|sor sensor

sen|so|ry sensorial

sen|so|ry neu|ron neurona
sensorial

sen|tence oración,
sentencia, sentenciar

sen|ti|ment sentimiento,
opinión, sentimentalismo

sen|ti|ment|al sentimental
• sen|ti|men|tal|ly de
manera sentimental
• sen|ti|men|tal|ity
sentimentalismo

se|pal sépalo

sepa|rate diferente,
separado, aparte,
separar(se), distinguir
• sepa|rate|ly por separado
• sepa|ra|tion separación
• sepa|rat|ed separado
▶ separates (clothing)
prendas combinables
▶ go their separate ways
tomar caminos distintos
▶ separate out separar

sepa|ra|tist separatista
• sepa|ra|tism separatismo

Sep|tem|ber septiembre

sep|tic tank fosa séptica

se|quel secuela

se|quence secuencia, orden

se|quined también sequinned
con lentejuelas

se|quoia secoya

ser|geant sargento

ser|geant ma|jor también
sergeant-major sargento
mayor

se|rial serie, serial

se|rial mu|sic música serial

se|ries serie

se|ries cir|cuit circuito en serie

se|ri|ous serio
• **se|ri|ous|ness** seriedad

se|ri|ous|ly en serio, en verdad, seriamente
▸ **take seriously** tomar en serio

ser|mon sermón

serv|ant sirviente o sirvienta

serve servir, cumplir, sacar, servicio, saque
▸ **serve somebody right** se lo tiene bien merecido
▸ **serve up** servir

serv|er servidor, mesero o mesera

ser|vice servicio, fuerzas armadas, oficio religioso, dar servicio, revisar
▸ **in service / out of service** en servicio / fuera de servicio

ser|vice|man militar

ser|vice pro|vid|er proveedor de servicios

serv|ing porción, ración

ses|sion sesión

set conjunto, set, televisión, poner, colocar, dejar, fijar, acordar, establecer, asignar, plantear, desarrollarse, cuajar, fraguar, ponerse, ubicado, fijo, colocado, establecido • **set|ting up** creación
▸ **set to** listo para
▸ **set on** decidido a
▸ **set the scene/stage for** situar la escena
▸ **set aside** apartar, reservar, dejar de lado
▸ **set back** retrasar, costar
▸ **set down** establecer
▸ **set in** llegar
▸ **set off** salir, partir, hacer sonar, hacer explotar
▸ **set out** salir, proponerse, exponer
▸ **set up** crear, abrir, montar, armar, establecerse

set|back contratiempo

set|ting escenario, posición

set|tle resolver, pagar, liquidar, establecerse, asentar, quedarse, decidido, arreglado
▸ **settle down** sentar cabeza, calmarse, arreglarse, ponerse a
▸ **settle for** conformarse con
▸ **settle oneself** ponerse cómodo
▸ **settle in** adaptarse a
▸ **settle on** decidirse por
▸ **settle up** arreglar cuentas

set|tled ordenado, estable

set|tle|ment acuerdo, convenio, asentamiento

set|tler colono, colona

set up también **set-up** sistema, arreglo, organización

sev|en siete

sev|en|teen diecisiete

sev|en|teenth decimoséptimo

sev|enth séptimo, séptima parte

sev|en|ti|eth septuagésimo

sev|en|ty setenta
▸ **the seventies** los (años) setenta

sev|er|al varios

se|vere grave, serio, severo
• **se|vere|ly** gravemente, con severidad • **se|ver|ity** gravedad

sew coser • **sew|ing** costura

sew|age aguas residuales

sew|age treat|ment plant planta de tratamiento de aguas residuales

sew|er alcantarilla

sewn cosido

sex sexo
▸ **have sex** tener relaciones sexuales

sex cell célula sexual

sex chro|mo|some cromosoma sexual

sex|ist sexista • **sex|ism** sexismo

S

sex offender delincuente sexual

sexual sexual • **sexually** sexualmente

sexuality sexualidad

sexually transmitted disease enfermedad de transmisión sexual

sexual reproduction reproducción sexual

sexy sexy, sensual

shabby gastado

shack choza

shade tono, sombra, matiz, persiana, dar sombra

shadow sombra, ensombrecer, dar sombra, seguir de cerca

shadow zone zona de sombra

shaft pozo, árbol, rayo

shaggy enmarañado

shake agitar, sacudir, impresionar, afectar, sacudida
  ▶ **shake one's head** negar con la cabeza
  ▶ **with a shake of the head** negando con la cabeza
  ▶ **shake hands** dar la mano
  ▶ **shake off** deshacerse de
  ▶ **shake out** acabar

shaky precario, tembloroso • **shakily** de manera temblorosa

shall
  ▶ **shall we go?** ¿nos vamos?
  ▶ **we shall go** iremos

shallow poco profundo, superficial

shame vergüenza, pena, deshonrar, avergonzar

shampoo shampoo, champú, lavar el cabello con shampoo

shan't = shall not

shape forma, figura, conformación, forjar, moldear
  ▶ **in (good) shape** en (buena) forma
  ▶ **out of shape** fuera de condición
  ▶ **shape up** tomar forma

shaped con forma de

share acción, parte, compartir
  ▶ **share out** dividir por partes iguales

shareholder accionista

shark tiburón

sharp afilado, cerrado, en curva cerrada, perspicaz, severo, duro, súbito, repentino, claro, nítido, ácido, en punto, sostenido • **sharply** en vuelta cerrada, duramente, súbitamente, nítidamente • **sharpness** agudeza, severidad, nitidez

sharpen agudizar, afilar

shatter hacerse añicos, destrozar, devastador • **shattering** destrozo

shattered devastado

shave rasurar(se), afeitada, rasurada • **shaving** rasurarse
  ▶ **shave off** cepillar

shaver rasuradora

shawl chal, mantón

she ella

shed cobertizo, mudar, perder, despojarse de, derramar

she'd = she had o she would

sheep borrego, oveja

sheer puro, escarpado, vertical, muy fino

sheet sábana, hoja, lámina

sheikh también **sheik** jeque

shelf estante

shell cáscara, concha, conchita, proyectil, pelar, bombardear • **shelling** bombardeo
  ▶ **shell out** soltar, apoquinar

she'll = she will

shellfish marisco

shelter refugio, refugiarse, proteger, dar refugio

shelve dar carpetazo, ver shelf

shepherd pastor o pastora,

S

conducir

sher|bet nieve

sher|iff alguacil

she's = she is o she has

shield proteger, escudo

shield vol|ca|no volcán en escudo

shift mover, cambiar, cambio, turno

Shi|ite también **Shi'ite** chiita

shin espinilla

shine brillar, alumbrar, destacar, brillo

shin|ing magnífico

shiny brillante

ship barco, buque, embarcar, enviar por barco • **ship|ment** embarque

ship|building construcción naval

ship|ment envío, embarque

ship|ping embarque, envío

shirt camisa, blusa

shiv|er temblar, tiritar, escalofrío

shock conmoción, impresión, susto, impacto, choque, electrochoque, descarga eléctrica, escandalizar(se), indignar(se), impresionar • **shocked** conmocionado, horrorizado, escandalizado, impresionado, indignado

shock|ing escandaloso, horroroso, espeluznante • **shock|ing|ly** terriblemente, escandalosamente

shock wave también **shockwave** onda expansiva, conmoción

shoe zapato, herrar ▸ **in somebody's shoes** en el pellejo de, en el lugar de

shoe|string agujeta, cordón ▸ **on a shoestring** con muy pocos recursos, con muy poco dinero

shoo-in seguro y fácil ganador

shook ver shake

shoot brote, retoño, filmación, rodaje, disparar, tirar, salir disparado, filmar, rodar, jugar a, patear, lanzar • **shoot|ing** tiroteo ▸ **shoot down** derribar, abatir

shoot sys|tem parte de una planta expuesta al aire

shop tienda, comprar, hacer las compras, ir de compras • **shop|per** comprador o compradora ▸ **shop around** recorrer tiendas para comparar precios

shop floor también **shop-floor**, **shopfloor** taller, planta de producción, los obreros

shop|keeper tendero o tendera, comerciante

shop|lift robar en tiendas • **shop|lifter** ladrón o ladrona • **shop|lifting** hurto en una tienda

shop|ping compras

shop|ping cart carrito, carrito del súper

shop|ping cen|ter centro comercial

shore costa, ribera, orilla ▸ **shore up** apuntalar, fortalecer

short corto, poco, ligero, bajo, de corta estatura, chaparro, diminutivo, escaso • **shorts** pantalones cortos, cortos, short, calzoncillos, boxer ▸ **cut/stop short** interrumpir(se) bruscamente ▸ **have a short temper** ser irritable, irritarse con facilidad, tener mal genio ▸ **in short** en resumen, en suma, es decir ▸ **stop short of** estar a punto de ▸ **short of** falto de, corto de

S

short|age escasez

short|cake pastel de frutas, shortcake

short|en reducir, acortar, abreviar

short|en|ing mantequilla, manteca, margarina

short|hand taquigrafía

short|ly en breve, dentro de poco
▸ **shortly after** poco después

short-order plato rápido

short-term corto plazo

shot ver **shoot**, disparo, tiro, balazo, patada, lanzamiento, fotografía, toma, oportunidad, inyección
▸ **a good/bad shot** buen/mal tirador o buena/mala tiradora
▸ **give something your best shot** hacer su mejor esfuerzo, lo mejor que se puede
▸ **call the shots** tener la última palabra, ser el que manda
▸ **a long shot** improbable

shot|gun escopeta

should deber
▸ **should think** parecerle a uno, creer que

shoul|der hombro, acotamiento, banquina
▸ **carry (responsibilities/ problems) on one's shoulders** llevar sobre las espaldas, echarse al hombro

shouldn't = should not

should've = should have

shout gritar, grito
● **shout|ing** gritería
▸ **shout out** gritar

shove empujar, dar empujones, empujón

shov|el pala, palear

show indicar, mostrar, demostrar, ilustrar, tratar sobre, enseñar, acompañar, llevar, verse, revelar, dar muestras, presentarse, aparecerse, pasar, proyectar, estar en cartelera, despliegue, demostración, actitud para darse tono, programa, espectáculo, exposición, desfile
▸ **have something to show for something** tener un beneficio
▸ **show off** alardear, presumir, hacer alarde

show and tell también **show-and-tell** exposición

show busi|ness farándula, mundo del espectáculo

show|er ducha, chubasco, chaparrón, lluvia, regadera, baño, fiesta de regalos para la novia o para la mujer que va a tener un hijo, bañarse, ducharse, cubrir de, colmar de

show|er gel gel de baño

shown ver **show**

shrank ver **shrink**

shred destruir, desmenuzar, cortar

shrimp camarón

shrimp cock|tail coctel de camarones

shrink encogerse, reducir(se), retroceder, loquero
▸ **shrink away from** evitar, rehuir

shrub arbusto, mata

shrug encogerse de hombros
▸ **shrug off** hacer caso omiso de

shrunk ver **shrink**

shuck pelar (verduras), abrir (mariscos)
▸ **shucks** ¡caray!, ¡caramba!

shuf|fle arrastrar los pies, andar pesado, revolverse, barajar, revolver

shut cerrar(se), cerrado
▸ **shut down** cerrar
▸ **shut in** encerrar
▸ **shut off** apagar
▸ **shut out** echar, dejar afuera, ahuyentar, ganar

sin conceder puntos en contra
▸ shut up callar(se)

shut|down cierre, paro

shut|out *también* shut-out triunfo o partido en el que el equipo perdedor no marca tantos, derrota en cero

shut|ter contraventana, postigo, obturador

shut|tle transbordador espacial, transbordador, avión, autobús o tren de enlace, ir y venir

shy tímido • shy|ly tímidamente • shy|ness timidez
▸ be/feel shy dar vergüenza, avergonzar
▸ shy away from rehuir

Si|berian ti|ger tigre de Siberia, tigre siberiano

sib|ling hermano

sick enfermo, de muy mal gusto, morboso
▸ feel sick tener náuseas, tener ganas de vomitar
▸ be sick vomitar
▸ sick of harto de, hasta la coronilla de
▸ the sick los enfermos
▸ make somebody sick dar rabia, enfermar
▸ out sick ausente por enfermedad

sick|ness enfermedad, náuseas

side lado, costado, ladera, cara, guarnición, acompañamiento, aspecto, parte, lateral, tomar partido por, ponerse de parte de
▸ from side to side de un lado a(l) otro
▸ on somebody's side del lado de
▸ on the side extra, guarnición
▸ put to/on one side dejar a un lado/dejar de lado
▸ side by side al lado, codo con codo

side|burns patillas

side effect *también* side-effect efecto secundario, efecto colateral

side|line actividad suplementaria, línea lateral, al margen

side road camino secundario

side sal|ad plato de ensalada

side|step *también* side-step eludir, dejar de lado

side street calle lateral

side|walk acera, banqueta

side|ways de reojo, de soslayo

siege sitio

si|er|ra sierra

sigh suspirar, suspiro

sight vista, lugar de interés, ver
▸ at the sight of al ver
▸ catch sight of descubrir
▸ in/within sight a la vista, ver venir
▸ out of sight fuera de la vista
▸ lose sight of perder de vista
▸ on sight a la vista
▸ set one's sights on tener la vista puesta en

sight|see|ing visita a lugares de interés

sight word palabra de fácil reconocimiento para un lector sin análisis de sus partes

sign signo, señal, letrero, muestra, firmar, subscribir, contratar, fichar • sign|ing firma
▸ no sign of no haber señales de
▸ sign for firmar (por algo)
▸ sign in registrarse
▸ sign up contratar

sig|nal señal, hacer señas, sugerir

sig|na|ture firma

sig|nifi|cance importancia

sig|nifi|cant importante, significativo
• sig|nifi|cant|ly

S

considerablemente, significativamente

Sikh sij

si|lence silencio, silenciar, callar

si|lent callado, silencioso •**si|lent|ly** silenciosamente, en silencio

si|lent part|ner socio capitalista

sili|ca sílice

sili|cate min|er|al silicato

sili|con silicio

sili|cone silicona

silk seda

sill antepecho, alféizar

sil|ly tonto •**sil|li|ness** tontería

silt cieno, limo

sil|ver plata, monedas de plata, platería, plateado

SIM card tarjeta sim

simi|lar similar, semejante, parecido

simi|lar|ity parecido, similitud, semejanza

simi|lar|ly de manera parecida, de manera similar/semejante

sim|mer hervir a fuego lento

sim|ple simple •**simp|ly** simplemente, con sencillez

sim|ple ma|chine máquina simple, pieza simple, mecanismo elemental

sim|pli|fy simplificar •**sim|pli|fied** simplificado •**sim|pli|fi|ca|tion** simplificación

simp|ly simplemente, solamente

sim|ul|ta|neous simultáneo •**sim|ul|ta|neous|ly** simultáneamente

sin pecado, pecar •**sin|ner** pecador

since desde, hasta ahora, después, porque

sin|cere sincero •**sin|cer|ity** sinceridad

sin|cere|ly sinceramente, atentamente

sine seno

sing cantar •**sing|ing** canto ▶**sing along** hacer coro, cantar a coro

sing|er cantante

sin|gle solo, soltero, individual, sencillo ▶**single out** señalar, distinguir

single-handed *también* **single-handedly** sin ayuda, solo

single-minded resuelto, con un solo/único propósito •**single-mindedness** resolución

sin|gle par|ent padre soltero, madre soltera

sin|gle-re|place|ment re|ac|tion reacción de desplazamiento, reacción de reemplazo simple

sin|gu|lar singular

sin|is|ter siniestro

sink fregadero (cocina), lavaplatos (cocina), pileta, lavabo (baño), lavamanos (baño), hundir(se), ponerse, caer(se), hincar, hundir ▶**sink in** calar, comprender

sip sorber, tomar/beber a sorbos, sorbo

sir señor, Sir, Estimado Señor

si|ren sirena

sis|ter hermana, sor

sister-in-law cuñada

sit estar sentado, sentar(se), formar parte de, sesionar ▶**sit tight** no moverse ▶**sit back** ponerse cómodo ▶**sit in on** asistir, estar presente ▶**sit on** dar largas ▶**sit out** esperar a que algo termine ▶**sit through** aguantar ▶**sit up** incorporarse, enderezarse, velar, quedarse en vela

site lugar, obra en construcción, sitio,

emplazar • **sit|ing**
emplazamiento
situ|at|ed situado
situa|tion situación
six seis
six king|doms los seis reinos
orgánicos
six|teen dieciséis
six|teenth decimosexto,
dieciseisavo
sixth sexto
six|ti|eth sexagésimo
six|ty sesenta
▸ **the sixties** los (años)
sesenta
siz|able *también* **sizeable**
considerable
size tamaño • **-sized** de cierto
tamaño, magnitud, talla,
número
▸ **size up** medir(se)
skate patinar • **skat|ing**
patinaje • **skat|er** patinador
o patinadora
▸ **ice skates** patines de hielo
▸ **roller skates** patines de
ruedas
ske|dad|dle largarse
skel|etal óseo
skel|etal mus|cle músculo
esquelético
skel|eton esqueleto,
mínimo, básico
skep|ti|cal escéptico
sketch bosquejo, esbozo,
bosquejar, esbozar, hacer
bosquejos, reseñar, resumir,
reseña, escena
ski esquí, esquiar • **ski|er**
esquiador *o* esquiadora
• **ski|ing** esquí
skid patinar, derrapar,
patinazo, derrape
skill habilidad, destreza
skilled hábil, especializado
skill|ful hábil, diestro,
habilidoso • **skill|ful|ly**
hábilmente
skim milk leche descremada,
leche desnatada
skin piel, cáscara, nata,

despellejar, desollar
skin|ny flaco, flacucho
skip saltar(se), brincar,
saltar la cuerda, saltar la
reata, omitir, salto, brinco
• **skip|ping** saltar la cuerda
skip|per capitán, patrón,
patrona
skip rope cuerda para/de
saltar, reata para/de saltar
skirt falda, bordear, eludir,
dar la vuelta
skull cráneo
sky cielo
sky|line horizonte
sky|scraper rascacielos
slam cerrar de golpe, azotar,
golpear, chocar, embestir
slam dunk *también* **slam-
dunk** fácil, clavada
slang jerga, argot
slant inclinar(se), sesgar(se),
presentar con parcialidad,
inclinación, sesgo, declive
slap abofetear, cachetear,
arrojar con violencia,
arrojar violentamente,
bofetada, cachetada
slash acuchillar, tajar,
mechar, rebajar
drásticamente, cuchillada,
tajo, corte
slate pizarra, teja de pizarra
slaugh|ter masacrar, matar,
sacrificar, carnicería,
matanza
slave esclavo *o* esclava
slave la|bor trabajo de
esclavos
slav|ery esclavitud
slaw ensalada de col
slay|ing asesinato
slea|zy sórdido, vil, ruin,
mezquino
sled trineo, ir en trineo,
deslizarse en trineo
sleep sueño, dormida,
siesta, dormir, alojar, tener
espacio para
▸ **lose sleep** perder el sueño
▸ **put to sleep** sacrificar

S

▶ **sleep off** dormir para reponerse

sleep|ing bag bolsa de dormir, saco de dormir

sleep|less en blanco (noche), desvelado, sin poder dormir
• **sleep|less|ness** insomnio

sleepy adormilado, somnoliento, soñoliento
• **sleepi|ly** con/de sueño

sleet aguanieve

sleeve manga
▶ **have up one's sleeve** tener bajo la manga

slice rebanada, parte, rebanar

slick ingenioso, logrado, pulido, hábil, embaucador, derrame de petróleo, marea negra

slick|er impermeable

slide deslizar(se), caer, diapositiva, transparencia, tobogán, resbaladilla, platina, portaobjetos

slight ligero, mínimo, liviano, desprecio, ofensa, desairar • **slight|ly** ligeramente
▶ **be/feel slighted** sentirse ofendido, sentirse desairado
▶ **in the slightest** en lo más mínimo, en absoluto

slight|ly ligeramente

slim delgado, esbelto, escaso
▶ **slim down** adelgazar, reducir el personal

sling|shot honda, resortera

slip resbalar, deslizar(se), pasar, caer, quitarse, desliz, trozo
▶ **slip up** cometer un desliz

slip|cover también **slip cover** funda

slip|per pantufla, chancla

slip|pery resbaladizo, resbaloso
▶ **slippery slope** pendiente resbaladiza

slit cortar, corte, rasgadura, abertura

slo|gan lema, consigna

slope ladera, inclinación, pendiente, descender, inclinarse • **slop|ing** inclinado

slop|py descuidado
• **slop|pi|ness** descuido

slop|py joe sándwich de carne guisada en salsa

slot ranura, intervalo, lapso, meter

slow lento, atrasado, aminorar la velocidad
• **slow|ly** lentamente
• **slow|ness** lentitud
▶ **slow down** aminorar la velocidad, retardar, tomarse las cosas con calma
▶ **slow up** disminuir

slow mo|tion también **slow-motion** cámara lenta

slow|poke torpe

slug|ger bateador o bateadora que golpea fuerte la pelota

slum barriada, barrio bajo

slum|ber par|ty piyamada

slump desplomarse, desplome, depresión

smack dar un manotazo, dar palmadas, palmearse, oler a, manotazo

smack dab exactamente, directamente

small pequeño, chico, insignificante
▶ **small business** pequeña empresa
▶ **small of one's back** región baja

small claims court también **small-claims court** tribunal de causas de poca monta

small po|ta|toes bagatelas, fruslería

small-scale pequeña escala

small town pueblerino

smart listo, escocer, picar, arder, estar resentido

smart aleck también **smart alec** sabiondo

smart growth urbanismo funcional, urbanismo

orgánico

smart phone smartphone, teléfono celular versátil, celular inteligente

smarts madera

smash romper, hacer(se) añicos, abrirse paso a golpes, golpear, hacer pedazos
▸ **smash up** destrozar

smear embadurnar, difamar, mancha, calumnia
● **smeared** embadurnado

smell olor, oler, apestar, olfato

smile sonreír, sonrisa

smog esmog

smoke humo, humear, fumar, ahumar ● **smok|er** fumador o fumadora
● **smok|ing** fumar

smoke de|tec|tor detector de humo

smol|der arder (sin llamas), arder

smooth terso, liso, suave, homogéneo, sin grumos, sin problemas, sin contratiempos, desenvuelto y seguro de sí mismo, alisar
● **smooth|ness** suavidad
● **smooth|ly** suavemente
▸ **smooth out** allanar
▸ **smooth over** suavizar

smooth mus|cle músculo liso, músculo involuntario

smoth|er sofocar, asfixiar, bañar, ahogar

smug|gle contrabandear, meter de contrabando
● **smug|gler** contrabandista
● **smug|gling** contrabando

snack tentempié, refrigerio

sna|fu metedura de pata

snag inconveniente, engancharse

snail caracol

snake culebra, serpiente, serpentear

snap romper(se), quebrar(se), chasquido, cerrar con un chasquido, cerrar con un golpe seco, hablar con brusquedad, tratar de morder, repentino, instantánea, foto
▸ **snap up** no dejar escapar

snap|shot instantánea, foto

snare drum tambor

snatch arrebatar, tomarse, fragmento

sneak escabullir(se), hacer algo a hurtadillas, hacer algo con disimulo

sneak|er tenis, zapatilla de deporte

sneeze estornudar, estornudo

sniff resollar, olfatear, resuello, oler

snippy atrevido

snob presumido, esnob

snore roncar, ronquido

snow nieve, nevar, embaucar

snow|ball bola de nieve, crecer rápidamente, aumentar rápidamente

snow|board snowboard, tabla para deslizarse en la nieve

snow|board|ing hacer snowboard, deslizarse en la nieve en una tabla ● **snow|board|er** snowboarder, deslizador o deslizadora

snow|flake copo de nieve

snow pea chícharo (chino), arveja

snow|plow quitanieve, limpianieve

snowy nevado

snub desairar, desaire

snug cómodo, ceñido
● **snug|ly** cómodamente

so así, eso, lo, también, tan, tan/tanto...que, tan...como para, entonces, así que, por eso, para que
▸ **so (what)?** ¿Y?, ¿Y qué?
▸ **and so on/and so forth** etcétera
▸ **not so much** tanto...como

S

▸ **or so** más o menos
▸ **so much/many** hasta cierto punto, cierta cantidad
soak remojar, dejar en remojo, empapar, filtrarse, bañarse con agua caliente, baño con agua caliente
• **soaked** empapado
• **soak|ing** empapado
▸ **soak up** absorber

soap jabón, telenovela, culebrón, comedia

soap op|era telenovela, culebrón, comedia

soar dispararse, elevarse, remontar el vuelo, planear

sob sollozar • **sob|bing** sollozo

so|ber sobrio, serio
• **so|ber|ly** seriamente, sobriamente
▸ **sober up** pasarse la embriaguez

so-called también **so called** supuesto, llamado

soc|cer fútbol

soc|cer play|er jugador de fútbol o jugadora de fútbol

so|cia|ble sociable

so|cial social • **so|cial|ly** socialmente

so|cial be|hav|ior conducta social

so|cial dance baile social

so|cial|ism socialismo

so|cial|ist socialista

so|cial|ize socializar, alternar

so|cial sci|ence ciencias sociales

So|cial Se|cu|rity seguridad social

So|cial Se|cu|rity num|ber número de la Seguridad Social

so|cial ser|vices servicios sociales

so|cial work trabajo social

so|cial work|er trabajador social o trabajadora social

so|ci|ety sociedad, asociación

so|ci|ol|ogy sociología
• **so|cio|logi|cal** sociológico
• **so|ci|olo|gist** sociólogo o socióloga

sock calcetín, media

sock|et enchufe, tomacorriente, alvéolo, cuenca

soda pop refresco

so|dium sodio

sofa sillón, sofá

soft suave, blando, indulgente • **soft|ness** suavidad • **soft|ly** suavemente

soft|cover también **soft-cover** rústica, pasta blanda

soft drink refresco

sof|ten ablandar, amortiguar, moderar

soft|ware software

soil suelo

so|lar solar

so|lar col|lec|tor panel solar

so|lar eclipse eclipse solar

so|lar neb|ula nebulosa solar

so|lar sys|tem sistema solar

sol|dier soldado

sole único, suela, planta
• **sole|ly** únicamente

sol|emn solemne
• **sol|emn|ly** solemnemente
• **so|lem|nity** solemnidad

sol|fege solfeo

so|lici|tor procurador o procuradora, abogado o abogada

sol|id sólido, serio, bueno, confiable, seguido, sin parar
• **sol|id|ly** sólidamente, firmemente • **so|lid|ity** solidez, constancia

soli|dar|ity solidaridad

soli|taire solitario

solo solista, a solas, solo

sol|stice solsticio

sol|ubil|ity solubilidad

sol|uble soluble

so|lute soluto

S

so|lu|tion solución

solve resolver

some un, uno, una, unos, unas, algún, alguno, alguna, algunos, algunas, un poco (de), algo (de), alrededor de, cierto

some|body alguien

some|how de alguna manera, de algún modo, de una u otra manera

some|one alguien

some|place algún lugar, alguna parte

some|thing algo
▶ something of a un verdadero

some|time algún día

some|times a veces

some|what un tanto

some|where alguna parte, algún lugar, otra parte, alrededor de, aproximadamente
▶ be getting somewhere avanzar, adelantar

son hijo

sonata-allegro form también sonata form sonata-allegro

song canción, canto, trino

song|book cancionero

song form estructura de una canción

son|ic sónico, del sonido

son-in-law yerno

soon pronto
▶ as soon as tan pronto como
▶ would just as soon preferir

soothe calmar, tranquilizar, aliviar • sooth|ing tranquilo, calmante

so|phis|ti|cat|ed complejo, mundano, sofisticado

sopho|more estudiante de segundo año de bachillerato o de universidad

sore adolorido, disgustado, llaga

sor|row pesar

sor|ry lamentable, lastimoso, sentir(lo), disculparse, lamentar, apenar
▶ feel sorry for sentir pena por
▶ I'm sorry (to hear that) qué pena
▶ sorry? ¿Perdón?, ¿Cómo?

sort tipo, clase, género, organizar, clasificar, ordenar, dividir
▶ of sorts/a sort una especie de
▶ sort of en cierto modo
▶ sort out arreglar, separar, resolver, aclarar

soul alma, espíritu, persona, música soul, soul

soul food soul food

soul music soul music, soul

sound sonido, ruido, sonar, tocar, oírse, comportarse, dar la impresión, parecer, impresión, sano, saludable, sólido, estable, sensato, confiable, responsable, profundo
▶ sound out tantear, sondear
▶ sound asleep profundamente dormido

sound en|er|gy energía sonora

sound|track también sound track banda sonora

sound wave también soundwave onda sonora

soup sopa, caldo, consomé

sour ácido, agrio, cortado, acedo, desagradable, amargado, avinagrado, amargar, echar a perder • sour|ly agriamente

source origen, fuente, principio

sour|dough masa fermentada

south también South sur, al sur, del sur

south|east sureste, sudeste, al sureste, al sudeste, del sureste, del sudeste

S

south|eastern (del) sureste, (del) sudeste

south|ern *también* **Southern** del sur, sureño, sureña, meridional

South|ern|er sureño *o* sureña

south|west suroeste, sudoeste, al suroeste, al sudoeste, del suroeste, del sudoeste

south|western (del) suroeste, (del) sudoeste

sou|venir souvenir, recuerdo

sov|er|eign soberano, soberana

sov|er|eign|ty soberanía

sow plantar, sembrar, cerda, puerca, cochina, marrana

soy soya

soy|bean *también* **soy bean** frijol de soya

soy sauce salsa de soya

spa spa, balneario de aguas termales

space espacio, lugar, sitio, lapso, espaciar, separar
• **spac|ing** distancia

space|craft nave espacial

space probe sonda espacial

space|ship nave espacial

space shut|tle transbordador espacial

space sta|tion estación espacial

space suit *también* **space-suit** traje espacial

spa|cious espacioso, amplio

spade pala, espada

spa|ghet|ti spaghetti, espagueti

spam enviar spam, correspondencia electrónica no deseada, spam
• **spam|mer** spammer

span distancia, lapso, periodo, periodo de atención, durar, extenderse, cubrir, abarcar, envergadura, atravesar

spare de más, adicional, repuesto, refacción, reserva, de sobra, sobrar, tener disponible, contar con, evitar algo a alguien

spare part repuesto, refacción

spare time tiempo libre, ratos libres

spare tire llanta de refacción, rueda de recambio, rueda de repuesto, llanta, llantita, lonja

spark chispa, gracia, desatar, desencadenar, provocar

spar|kle brillar, chispear, destellar, destello, brillo, chispa

spark plug bujía

spar|row gorrión

spa|tial espacial • **spa|tial|ly** desde la perspectiva espacial

speak hablar, pronunciar (un discurso) • **speak|er** hablante, el que habla *o* la que habla, orador *u* oradora • **spo|ken** hablado
▸ **be not speaking** dejarse de hablar, retirar la palabra
▸ **speaks for itself** habla por sí mismo/solo
▸ **speak of somebody** hablar de alguien, decir algo de alguien
▸ **so to speak** por así decir
▸ **speak out** dar la propia opinión
▸ **speak up** hablar más fuerte

speak|er presidente, bocina, bafle

spear lanza, arpón, alancear, arponear, pinchar

spe|cia|tion especiación, evolución de las especies

spe|cif|ic grav|ity gravedad específica, peso específico

spe|cif|ic heat ca|pac|ity calor específico

spe|cial especial, específico

spe|cial ef|fects efectos especiales

spe|cial|ist especialista

spe|cial|ize especializarse • **spe|cial|i|za|tion** especialización

spe|cial|ized especializado

spe|cial|ly especialmente, particularmente

spe|cial|ty especialidad

spe|cies especie

spe|cif|ic específico

spe|cif|ical|ly específicamente, concretamente, expresamente

spe|cif|ics detalles (específicos)

speci|fy especificar

speci|men espécimen, muestra

spec|ta|cle espectáculo

spec|tacu|lar espectacular, gran espectáculo • **spec|tacu|lar|ly** espectacularmente

spec|ta|tor espectador

spec|trum espectro, gama

specu|late especular, conjeturar • **specu|la|tion** especulación • **specu|la|tor** especulador o especuladora

speech habla, lenguaje hablado, discurso

speed velocidad, rapidez, ir a gran velocidad, exceder el límite de velocidad • **speed|ing** exceso de velocidad ▶ **speed up** acelerarse, darse prisa

speed bump tope, obstáculo

speed da|ting sesión de contactos rápidos

speed lim|it límite de velocidad

speed|way carrera de motocicletas, pista para carreras de motocicletas

speedy rápido, pronto

spell deletrear, significar, período, encanto, encantamiento, hechizo

▶ **spell out** explicar con detalle

spell-check también **spell check** corregir la ortografía

spell-checker también **spell checker** corrector ortográfico

spell|ing ortografía, deletreo

spell|ing bee concurso de ortografía

spe|lunk|er espeleólogo aficionado o espeleóloga aficionada

spend gastar, dedicar, pasar

sperm espermatozoide, semen, esperma

sperm bank banco de semen, banco de esperma

SPF FPS

sphere esfera, ámbito

spice especia

spicy picante, muy condimentado

spi|der araña

spif|fy elegante

spig|ot llave, canilla, espita

spike punta

spike heels zapatos con tacón de aguja

spill derramar(se), rebosar

spin girar, dar vuelta, hilar, tejer, vuelta, giro ▶ **spin out** alargar

spin|ach espinaca

spi|nal espinal

spi|nal cord médula espinal

spine columna vertebral

spin|ning wheel también **spinning-wheel** rueca

spin|off beneficio indirecto, resultado benéfico

spi|ral espiral, voluta, curva ascendente, en forma de caracol, torcerse en espiral, volar en espiral, dispararse, ascender

spi|ral gal|axy galaxia espiral

spir|it espíritu, temple, estado de ánimo

S

spir|itu|al espiritual
• **spir|itu|al|ly** espiritualmente
• **spir|itu|al|ity** espiritualidad

spit saliva, escupir

spite maldad, molestar
▶ **in spite of** a pesar de
▶ **in spite of oneself** en contra de nuestra voluntad

splash chapotear, salpicar, chapoteo, salpicadura
▶ **make a splash** causar un revuelo

splat|ter salpicar

splen|did espléndido, magnífico • **splen|did|ly** de maravilla

split partir(se), romper(se), cortar, dividir(se), escindir(se), rasgarse, división, escisión, cisma, abismo, dividido
▶ **split up** separar(se), dividir, dispersar

spoil echar a perder, consentir, consentirse

spoke ver speak, rayo

spo|ken ver speak

spokes|man vocero, portavoz

spokes|person vocero o vocera, portavoz

spokes|woman vocera, portavoz

sponge esponja, hule espuma, limpiar con una esponja
▶ **sponge off (others)** vivir a costa de otros

spon|gy bone hueso reticulado, hueso esponjoso

spon|sor patrocinar, apoyar, patrocinador, patrocinadora

spon|sor|ship patrocinio

spon|ta|neous espontáneo
• **spon|ta|neous|ly** espontáneamente

spool carrete

spoon cuchara, cucharear, poner con cuchara

spo|ro|phyte esporofito, esporófito

sport deporte

sport coat también **sports coat** saco deportivo, saco informal

sport|ing deportivo

sport jack|et saco deportivo, saco informal

sports car auto/coche/carro deportivo

sports|cast emisión deportiva

sports|caster comentarista de deportes

sports|man deportista

sports|woman deportista

spot mancha, lugar, notar
▶ **on the spot** de inmediato, sin demora

spot|light reflector, poner de relieve

spot|ty irregular

spous|al marital

spouse esposo o esposa, cónyuge

sprawl despatarrarse, extenderse, expansión

spray rocío, aerosol, rociar, arrojar chorros de agua, esparcirse

spread extender, untar, difundir(se), diseminar(se), diferir, pagar a plazos, distribuir, difusión, distribución, gama
▶ **spread out** dispersarse

spring primavera, resorte, manantial, fuente, saltar, brincar, abrirse de golpe, ser producto de, sorprender
▶ **spring up** surgir

spring-cleaning limpieza completa

spring tide marea viva

sprin|kle rociar, espolvorear, lloviznar, chispear

sprin|kler aspersor, rociador

sprint carrera de velocidad, carrera, correr rápidamente

sprout echar brotes, echar retoños, retoñar, salir, colecita de Bruselas,

S

repollito de Bruselas

spur acicatear, estimular, alentar, estímulo
▶ **on the spur of the moment** impulsivamente, sin pensarlo

spy espía, espiar • **spy|ing** espionaje

sq. cuadrado

squad brigada, equipo

squad|ron escuadrón

squan|der despilfarrar

square cuadro, plaza, cuadrado, elevar al cuadrado, concordar
▶ **square away** arreglar
▶ **square off** alistarse para enfrentarse, alistarse para pelear

square root raíz cuadrada

squash aplastar, apretujar, apiñado, squash

squat ponerse en cuclillas, ocupar un lugar sin derecho, cuclillas, regordete, rechoncho

squeak rechinar, chirriar, crujir, chirrido

squeeze apretar, meter, estar apretado, apretón

squir|rel ardilla

squirt echar un chorrito, salir a chorros, chorrito

stab apuñalar, acuchillar, golpear, agarrar, mover como apuñalando, intento, punzada

sta|bi|lize estabilizar(se) • **sta|bi|li|za|tion** estabilización

sta|ble estable, cuadra, caballeriza • **sta|bil|ity** estabilidad

stack montón, pila, apilar, colocar
▶ **things/the odds are stacked against** ser desfavorables las circunstancias para, tener las probabilidades en contra, llevar las de perder

sta|dium estadio

staff personal, empleados, dotar de personal, pentagrama • **staffed** dotado de personal

staff|er empleado o empleada, funcionario o funcionaria

stage etapa, escenario, platina, portaobjetos, poner en escena, montar, representar, hacer

stage crew tramoyistas

stage left parte del escenario a la izquierda de un actor de cara al público

stage man|ag|er director de escena

stage right parte del escenario a la derecha de un actor de cara al público

stag|ger tambalearse, dejar perplejo, dejar estupefacto, alternar, escalonar
• **stag|gered** perplejo

stag|ger|ing asombroso

stain mancha, manchar
• **stained** manchado

stain|less steel acero inoxidable

stair escalera(s), escalón, peldaño

stair|case escalinata

stair|lift *también* stair lift elevador de escalera

stair|way escalinata

stake apuesta, estaca, interés, apostar, jugar(se), arriesgar
▶ **at stake** en juego, en riesgo, comprometido
▶ **stake a claim** reivindicar un derecho

stale rancio, añejo, viejo, anquilosado

stalk tallo, acechar, acosar, asediar, perseguir • **stalk|er** acosador o acosadora

stall estancar, dar largas, ahogar(se), puesto, tenderete, cubículo, compartimiento, compartimiento

S

sta|men estambre

stam|mer tartamudear, balbucear • **stam|mer|ing** tartamudeo

stamp estampilla, timbre, sello, troquelar, patear, pisotear
▶ **stamp out** erradicar

stam|pede estampida, desbandada, salir en desbandada

stance postura, posición

stand estar de pie, estar parado, ponerse de pie, pararse, alzarse, colocar, poner, tener una postura, tener una posición, seguir en vigor, soportar, resistir, aguantar, puesto, tribuna, base, pedestal, sitio, parada, estrado
▶ **stand aside/back** hacerse a un lado, hacerse para atrás
▶ **stand at** llegar a
▶ **stand by** estar en alerta, mantenerse al margen
▶ **stand down** retirarse
▶ **stand for** significar, defender, tolerar
▶ **stand in** substituir
▶ **stand out** resaltar
▶ **stand to gain** poder ganar
▶ **stand up** admitir
▶ **stand up for** defender
▶ **stand up to** resistir, enfrentar, hacer frente
▶ **make/take a stand** adoptar una actitud firme

stand|ard calidad, norma de conducta, normal

stand|ard Ameri|can Eng|lish inglés estadounidense común

stan|dard de|via|tion desviación normal, desviación tipo, desviación estándar

stand|ard|ize normalizar, uniformar • **stand|ardi|za|tion** uniformación

stand|ard of liv|ing nivel de vida, estándar de vida

stand|by también **stand-by** reserve, sujeto a disponibilidad, de lista de espera, en lista de espera
▶ **on standby** listo, en guardia

stand-in substituto o substituta

stand|ing wave onda estacionaria

stand|off callejón sin salida

stand|point punto de vista, perspectiva

stand|still detención, paralización

stand-up también **standup** (cómico) de micrófono, comedia

sta|ple básico, alimento básico, grapa, engrapar

sta|pler engrapadora

star estrella, astro, protagonizar, tener como protagonista
▶ **the/one's stars** los astros

starch almidón, fécula

stare mirar, mirada

stark duro, marcado
• **stark|ly** crudamente

Star of David estrella de David

start empezar, comenzar, iniciarse, abrir, montar, encender, arrancar, prender, sobresaltarse, comienzo, principio, inicio, sobresalto
▶ **for a start/to start with** para empezar
▶ **start off** empezar por, comenzar por
▶ **start on** empezar con, comenzar con
▶ **start out** empezar como, comenzar como
▶ **start over** empezar de nuevo, comenzar de nuevo
▶ **start up** abrir, montar

star|tle sobresaltar
• **star|tled** asustado

star|tling asombroso, sorprendente

starve pasar hambre, privar de comida, morir(se) de hambre • **star|va|tion** hambre
▸ **be starved of** sufrir por la falta de, morir(se) por la falta de

starv|ing
▸ **be starving** morirse de hambre

state estado, Estado, de estado, exponer, escribir, consignar
▸ **the States** Estados Unidos
▸ **state of matter** estado de la materia

state line límite del estado

state|ment afirmación, declaración, estado de cuenta

state of emer|gen|cy estado de alarma, estado de emergencia

state of mind estado de ánimo

state-of-the-art con tecnología de punto, último modelo, de vanguardia

State of the Un|ion informe sobre el estado de la nación, informe presidencial en los Estados Unidos

state school institución escolar o universitaria pública

states|man hombre de estado, estadista

state trooper policía estatal

state uni|ver|sity universidad pública

stat|ic estático, estacionario, invariable, electricidad estática, interferencia

sta|tion estación del ferrocarril, estación de autobuses, estación de radio o canal de televisión, destacar, apostar

sta|tion|ary estacionario, inmóvil

sta|tion|ery artículos o útiles de escritorio

sta|tion house comisaría

sta|tion mod|el modelo climático, modelo meteorológico

sta|tion wag|on camioneta

sta|tis|tic estadística(s)
• **sta|tis|ti|cal** estadístico
• **sta|tis|ti|cal|ly** estadísticamente

statue estatua

sta|tus categoría, condición

sta|tus quo statu quo

stat|ute ley

stat|ute of limi|ta|tions ley de prescripción

statu|tory reglamentario

stay quedarse, alojarse, estancia, mantenerse, parar, no intervenir
▸ **stay put** quedarse
▸ **stay in** quedarse
▸ **stay on** permanecer
▸ **stay out** pasar fuera cierto tiempo
▸ **stay up** quedarse levantado

steady constante, fijo, firme, fijar, sujetar
• **steadi|ly** regularmente, fijamente
▸ **steady onself** tranquilizarse

steak filete

steal robar(se) • **steal|ing** robo • **sto|len** robado

steam vapor, arrojar vapor, cocinar al vapor, cocer al vapor
▸ **run out of steam** cansarse

steel acero
▸ **steel oneself** armarse de valor

steep escarpado, abrupto, marcado
• **steep|ly** abruptamente, considerablemente

steer conducir, dirigir, gobernar, llevar
▸ **steer clear of** evitar

steer|ing wheel volante, timón

stem provenir, ser producto

S

de, contener, tallo

ste|nog|ra|pher taquígrafo o taquígrafa, estenógrafo o estenógrafa

step paso, escalón, pisar, dar pasos
▸ **one step ahead of** un paso adelante de
▸ **be in step** estar en sintonía
▸ **step by step** paso a paso
▸ **step aside** ver step down
▸ **step back** retroceder, distanciarse, tomar distancia
▸ **step down** o **step aside** hacerse a un lado, renunciar
▸ **step in** intervenir
▸ **step up** aumentar, redoblar

step|family familia con hijastros

step|father también **stepfather** padrastro

step|mother también **stepmother** madrastra

ste|reo estereofónico, estéreo

ste|reo|type estereotipo, catalogar

ster|ile estéril • **ste|ril|ity** esterilidad

steri|lize esterilizar • **steri|li|za|tion** esterilización

ster|ling excelente, libras esterlinas

stern severo • **stern|ly** severamente

ster|oid esteroide

stew estofado, puchero, guisar a fuego lento, cocer a fuego lento, estofar

stew|ard camarero, sobrecargo, auxiliar de vuelo, organizador

stew|ard|ess camarera, sobrecargo, auxiliar de vuelo, organizadora

stick vara, rama, palillo, baqueta, bastón, palo, meter, clavar, pegar, adherirse
▸ **stick around** quedarse
▸ **stick by** no abandonar
▸ **stick out** sacar
▸ **stick it out** soportar
▸ **stick to** atenerse a, cumplir con
▸ **stick together** mantenerse unidos
▸ **stick up for** defender
▸ **stick with** perseverar

stick|er etiqueta engomada, calcomanía

stick|er price precio de lista

stick|er shock sorpresa causada por el precio de algo

stick fig|ure figura esquemática

stick shift palanca de velocidades

sticky pegajoso, húmedo, bochornoso, penoso

stiff rígido, tieso, duro, apretado, entumecido, ceremonioso, afectado, tenaz • **stiff|ly** rígidamente, con rigidez, ceremoniosamente • **stiff|ness** rigidez
▸ **be (bored/worried/scared etc.) stiff** a más no poder

still todavía, aún, de todos modos, quieto, tranquilo • **still|ness** tranquilidad

still life naturaleza muerta, bodegón

stimu|lant estimulante

stimu|late estimular • **stimu|la|tion** estímulo • **stimu|lat|ing** estimulante

stimu|lus estímulo

sting picar(se), cortar, herir profundamente, aguijón, piquete • **sting|ing** hiriente

stink apestar, mal olor

sti|pend estipendio

stir menear, revolver, remover, moverse, agitarse, despertar, revuelo
▸ **stir up** levantar, provocar

stir|rup estribo

stitch coser, bordar, suturar, puntada, punto, punto de

sutura, punzada

stock acción, capital comercial, existencias, reserva, caldo
▶ **be in stock/out of stock** haber/no haber existencias
▶ **take stock** evaluar, estimar
▶ **stock up** abastecerse, aprovisionarse

stock|broker corredor de valores o corredora de valores

stock char|ac|ter personaje estereotipado

stock ex|change bolsa (de valores)

stock|holder accionista

stock|ing media

stock mar|ket mercado de valores, mercado bursátil

stock op|tion opción a la compra de acciones

stock|pile almacenar, hacer acopio, reservas, acopio

stocky fornido, bajo y fornido

stoked emocionado, alborotado

sto|len ver steal

sto|ma estoma

stom|ach estómago, tolerar

stomp pisotear, caminar con paso enérgico

stomp|ing ground territorio personal, lugar predilecto, guarida

stone piedra, piedra (preciosa), gema

Stone Age Edad de Piedra

stool taburete, banco

stop dejar de, detener(se), hacer una pausa, evitar, parada, paradero
▶ **put a stop to** poner fin a
▶ **stop by** o **stop in** pasar a
▶ **stop off** hacer una parada breve

stop|light también **stop light** semáforo

stop|per tapón

stor|age almacenaje, almacenamiento, depósito

store tienda, provisión, reserva, almacén, depósito, bodega, almacenar, guardar
▶ **in store** en reserva
▶ **store away** almacenar, guardar
▶ **store up** hacer acopio

store-bought comprado

store brand marca libre

stored en|er|gy energía acumulada, energía almacenada, energía potencial

store|front fachada de una tienda, tienda que da a la calle, oficina que da a la calle

store|keeper tendero o tendera

storm tormenta, tempestad, escándalo, salir/entrar bramando de cólera, asaltar, tomar por asalto • **storm|ing** toma por asalto
▶ **take something by storm** tomar por asalto

storm surge aumento del nivel del mar a lo largo de la costa a causa de una tempestad

stormy tormentoso, tempestuoso, violento

sto|ry historia, cuento, relato, anécdota, artículo, noticia, piso
▶ **a different story** harina de otro costal, otro cantar
▶ **the same old story** o **the old story** la historia de siempre
▶ **only part of the story** o **not the whole story** sólo parte de la historia
▶ **side of the story** versión de las cosas

stout gordo, sólido, resistente

stove estufa

strad|dle ponerse o sentarse a horcajadas, extenderse sobre, unir, tener un pie

S

en un lugar y el otro en otra parte

straight recto, derecho, lacio, erguido, directo, directamente, inmediatamente, francamente, con franqueza
▶ **get something straight** asegurarse de

straight ar|row muy convencional y correcto

straight|en enderezar(se), ordenar
▶ **straighten out** aclarar
▶ **straighten up** ordenar

straight|forward fácil, sencillo, franco
● **straight|forward|ly** con sencillez, francamente

strain presión, torcedura, esguince, ejercer presión, torcerse, hacer un gran esfuerzo para, colar, escurrir

strait estrecho
▶ **be in dire/desperate straits** estar en apuros, pasar apuros

strand pelo, alambre, hebra
▶ **be stranded** quedarse varado

strange extraño, raro
● **strange|ly** de manera rara
● **strange|ness** rareza

stran|ger extraño, extraña
▶ **be a stranger to something** desconocido algo a alguien
▶ **be no stranger to something** no serle desconocido algo a alguien

stran|gle estrangular

strap correa, tira, sujetar con correa

stra|tegic estratégico
● **stra|tegi|cal|ly** estratégicamente

strat|egy estrategia, plan

strati|fi|ca|tion estratificación

strati|fied drift morena estratificada, derrubio estratificado

stra|tus estrato

straw paja, popote, pajita
▶ **the last straw** el colmo, la gota que derrama el vaso

straw|berry fresa

stray extraviarse, perderse, divagar, distraerse, perdido, callejero, suelto

streak línea, rasgo, veta, filón, vetear, surcar, chorrear, cruzar o pasar velozmente

stream arroyo, riachuelo, torrente, sarta, correr, entrar a raudales

stream|line racionalizar
● **stream|lined** racionalizado

street calle

street|car tranvía

street crime delincuencia callejera

street smart también **street-smart** experimentado en la vida callejera

street smarts experiencia necesaria para vivir en una ciudad difícil

strength fuerza, fortaleza, resistencia, potencia, intensidad, virtud, efectivos
▶ **go from strength to strength** tener un éxito tras otro
▶ **on the strength of** como consecuencia de

strength|en fortalecer

strep también **strep throat** inflamación estreptocócica, inflamación de garganta, infección en la garganta

stress hacer hincapié, subrayar, poner énfasis, acentuar, énfasis, tensión, acento, esfuerzo

stress frac|ture fractura por fatiga

stress|ful estresante

stretch extenderse, alargarse, estirar(se), desperezarse, agotar, tramo, trecho, período, estiramiento ● **stretched**

que no da más de sí
▶ **stretch out** estirarse, alargar, extender

strick|en agobiado

strict estricto, riguroso • **strict|ly** estrictamente, rigurosamente

strict|ly estrictamente

stride dar zancadas, zancada, progreso
▶ **take something in one's stride** tomarse las cosas con calma

strike huelga, ataque, desventaja, hacer huelga, golpear(se), dar golpes, atacar, afectar, parecer, dar la impresión, impresionar, infundir, dar la hora, sonar la hora, encender, encontrar
▶ **strike down** abatir, abolir, derogar, abrogar
▶ **strike out** ponchar(se), actuar por su propia cuenta, hacerse independiente, fracasar
▶ **strike up** entablar

strik|er delantero o delantera, huelguista

strik|ing asombroso, sorprendente, atractivo • **strik|ing|ly** asombrosamente

string cordel, collar, sucesión, cuerda, cuerdas
▶ **no strings/no strings attached** sin condición, incondicionalmente

string bean ejote

strip tira, franja, avenida, desvestirse, desnudar(se), quitar la ropa de, deshacer (una cama), despojar
▶ **strip away** despojar
▶ **strip off** quitarse la ropa

stripe lista, raya

striped listado, rayado

strip mall centro comercial

strip mine mina a tajo abierto

strip min|ing también **strip-mining** explotación a tajo abierto

strive esforzarse

stroke acariciar, ataque de apoplejía, derrame cerebral, trazo, brazada, golpe de remo, estilo, campanada, golpe

stroll caminar tranquilamente, caminar despreocupadamente, paseo, caminata

strong fuerte, sólido, firme, ardiente, convencido, enérgico, fuerza, penetrante • **strong|ly** sólidamente, fuertemente, mucho
▶ **go strong** marchar bien, funcionar bien

strong|hold plaza fuerte, baluarte, bastión

struc|tur|al estructural • **struc|tur|al|ly** estructuralmente

struc|ture estructura, estructurar • **struc|tured** estructurado

strug|gle luchar, forcejear, lucha, refriega

strut pavonearse, farolear, puntal

stub cacho, talón, golpearse un dedo del pie, tropezar
▶ **stub out** apagar

stub|born obstinado, terco, persistente • **stub|born|ly** obstinadamente, persistentemente • **stub|born|ness** obstinación

stuck ver **stick**, atascado, metido, estancado, atorarse

stud tachón, semental

stu|dent estudiante, alumno o alumna

stu|dent body estudiantado, alumnado

stu|dent coun|cil asociación o federación estudiantil

stu|dent loan préstamo estudiantil

stu|dent un|ion centro estudiantil

stu|dio estudio

S

study estudiar, estudio
• **studies** estudios

study hall sala de estudio

stuff cosas, meter, atestar, rellenar, disecar

stuffed animal animal de peluche

stuffing relleno

stuffy viciado (aire)

stumble tropezar
▶ **stumble across** o **stumble on** tropezar con, dar con, encontrar

stumbling block obstáculo, impedimento, escollo

stump tocón, dejar perplejo

stun dejar perplejo, conmocionar • **stunned** perplejo

stung ver **sting**

stun gun arma para aturdir

stunning despampanante
• **stunningly** asombrosamente

stupid estúpido, tonto
• **stupidly** tontamente
• **stupidity** estupidez, tontería

sturdy robusto • **sturdily** sólidamente

stutter tartamudeo, tartamudear • **stuttering** tartamudeo

style estilo, manera, diseñar, peinar

stylish elegante • **stylishly** elegantemente

stylistic nuance matiz estilístico

sub sándwich, maestro suplente o maestra suplente, suplente, submarino

subconscious subconsciente, inconsciente
• **subconsciously** inconscientemente

subculture subcultura

subdue someter, mitigar

subject tema, materia, sujeto, súbdito o súbdita, someter
▶ **subject to** sujeto a, sujeto de

subjective subjetivo
• **subjectively** subjetivamente
• **subjectivity** subjetividad

subject matter contenido, tema

subjunctive subjuntivo, modo subjuntivo

sublimation sublimación

submarine submarino

submerge sumergir(se)

submission sumisión, rendición

submit someterse, presentar, entregar

subordinate subordinado o subordinada, subalterno o subalterna, subordinar
• **subordination** subordinación

subordinate clause oración subordinada

subscribe suscribir, apoyar, estar de acuerdo, suscribirse
• **subscriber** suscriptor o suscriptora

subscript subíndice

subscription suscripción, abono, cuota, de paga

subsequent subsecuente, subsiguiente
• **subsequently** posteriormente

subsidiary subsidiaria, filial, subsidiario, secundario, adicional

subsidize subsidiar
• **subsidized** subsidiado

subsidy subsidio

subspecies también **subspecies** subespecie

substance sustancia, substancia, lo esencial, fundamento, esencia, base

substance abuse abuso de sustancias, toxicomanía

substantial sustancial, considerable, importante
• **substantially**

sustancialmente

sub|sti|tute sustituir, sustituto o sustituta, suplente o sucedáneo • **sub|sti|tu|tion** sustitución

sub|sti|tute teach|er maestro suplente o maestra suplente

sub|ter|ra|nean subterráneo

sub|text trasfondo, subtexto

sub|tle sutil, leve, ligero • **sub|tly** sutilmente

sub|tract restar, sustraer • **sub|trac|tion** resta

sub|trac|tive sculp|ture escultura sustractiva

sub|tropical subtropical

sub|urb suburbio, periferia

sub|ur|ban suburbano

sub|way metro, ferrocarril subterráneo, subte, ferrocarril metropolitano

suc|ceed tener éxito, lograr, dar resultado, suceder

suc|cess logro, éxito, triunfo

suc|cess|ful exitoso, triunfador, de éxito, próspero • **suc|cess|ful|ly** satisfactoriamente

suc|ces|sion sucesión, secuencia, serie

suc|ces|sive sucesivo

suc|ces|sor sucesor o sucesora

suc|cess sto|ry evento exitoso

such tal, así, de cierto tipo, tan, tanto, tal...que
▶ **such and such** tal
▶ **as such** como tal

suck chupar, succionar, aspirar, libar

suck|er imbécil, ventosa
▶ **be a sucker for something** tener debilidad por algo

sud|den repentino, súbito, inesperado • **sud|den|ly** repentinamente
• **sud|den|ness** lo imprevisto
▶ **all of a sudden** de pronto

sue demandar, entablar una demanda

suf|fer sufrir, padecer, ser afectado, resentirse, perjudicarse • **suf|fer|er** el que sufre

suf|fer|ing sufrimiento, dolor

suf|fi|cient suficiente, bastante • **suf|fi|cient|ly** suficientemente

suf|fix sufijo

suf|fo|cate sofocarse, asfixiarse, ahogarse
• **suf|fo|ca|tion** asfixia

suf|fra|gist sufragista

sug|ar azúcar

sug|gest sugerir, proponer, insinuar, indicar

sug|ges|tion sugerencia, propuesta, insinuación

sug|ges|tive indicativo, sugerente

sui|cid|al suicida

sui|cide suicidio

suit traje, terno, traje sastre, demanda, juicio, convenir, venir bien, ser apropiado, quedar bien algo

suit|able adecuado, conveniente • **suit|abil|ity** idoneidad • **suit|ably** adecuadamente

suit|case maleta, petaca, valija

suite suite, piso, departamento, habitaciones, juego

suit|ed apropiado, adecuado

sul|fur azufre

sum suma, cantidad, monto
▶ **sum up** resumir, sintetizar

sum|ma cum lau|de summa cum laude, sobresaliente

sum|ma|rize resumir, sintetizar, hacer un resumen

sum|mary resumen, síntesis
▶ **in summary** en resumen, en síntesis

sum|mer verano

sum|mer camp

campamento de verano

sum|mer school verano, curso de verano

sum|mer squash calabacita fresca

sum|mit cumbre, cima

sum|mon llamar, convocar, mandar llamar, reunir

sum|mons citatorio

sun sol

sun|burned *también* **sunburnt** quemado por el sol, bronceado, asoleado

Sun|day domingo

sun|down puesta de sol, caída de la tarde, atardecer

sun|flower girasol, maravilla

sun|glasses lentes de sol, anteojos de sol

sun|light luz del día, luz del sol, luz solar

Sun|ni suni, sunita

sun|ny soleado, alegre

sun|rise salida del sol, amanecer, alba

sun|screen crema para el sol, protector solar, filtro solar

sun|set puesta del sol, atardecer, crepúsculo

sun|shine luz del sol, rayos del sol, rayos solares, calor del sol

sun|spot peca, mancha solar

sun|tan bronceado, bronceador

sun-up *también* **sunup** amanecer, alba, salida del sol

su|per súper

su|perb soberbio, magnífico, espléndido, excelente • **su|perb|ly** magníficamente

Su|per Bowl *también* **Superbowl** Super Bowl, Super Tazón

super|cell supercelda

super|fi|cial superficial, por encima • **super|fi|cial|ity** superficialidad

• **super|fi|cial|ly** superficialmente

super|gi|ant supergigante

super|high|way supercarretera, supercarretera de la información

super|in|ten|dent superintendente, inspector *o* inspectora, encargado *o* encargada, conserje, portero *o* portera

su|peri|or superior, jefe *o* jefa, arrogante • **su|peri|or|ity** superioridad

su|peri|or court *también* **Superior Court** corte superior, tribunal superior

super|la|tive superlativo

super|mar|ket supermercado, super

super|natu|ral sobrenatural ▶ **the supernaural** lo sobrenatural

super|no|va supernova

super|pow|er superpotencia

super|size extragrande, ofrecer porciones enormes

super|son|ic supersónico

super|sti|tion superstición

super|sti|tious supersticioso

super|vise supervisar, vigilar, inspeccionar • **super|vi|sion** supervisión • **super|vi|sor** supervisor *o* supervisora

sup|per cena, merienda

sup|plement complementar, completar, complemento, suplemento

sup|pli|er proveedor *o* proveedora, abastecedor *o* abastecedora

sup|ply proveer, abastecer, proporcionar, suministrar, aprovisionar, provisiones, víveres, existencias, surtido, inventario ▶ **be in short supply** escasear

sup|ply chain cadena de producción y distribución

sup|port apoyar(se), ayudar,

sostener(se), soportar, sustentar, apoyo, soporte, sostén, respaldo, ayuda
• sup|port|er defensor *o* defensora, partidario *o* partidaria, seguidor *o* seguidora

sup|port|ive que da apoyo

sup|pose suponer, presumir, creer, imaginarse

sup|posed supuesto, presunto, imaginado
• sup|pos|ed|ly supuestamente
▶ be supposed to se supone

sup|press suprimir, reprimir, contener, ocultar
• sup|pres|sion represión, supresión, represión, ocultamiento

su|preme supremo
• su|preme|ly sumamente

sure seguro, sí
▶ sure enough efectivamente
▶ for sure seguro
▶ make sure asegurarse, checar, verificar
▶ sure of oneself seguro de uno mismo
▶ sure thing sin duda

sure|ly seguramente, con seguridad
▶ slowly but surely lento pero seguro

surf oleaje, espuma, resaca, surf, surfear • surf|er el/la que surfea, quien navega en Internet • surf|ing surfear, navegar

sur|face superficie, cara, aspecto superficial, salir a la superficie, emerger

sur|face cur|rent corriente de superficie, corriente superficial

sur|face grav|ity gravedad superficial

sur|face ten|sion tensión superficial

surface-to-volume ra|tio relación superficie-volumen

sur|face wave onda de superficie, onda superficial

surge incremento repentino, aumento repentino, aumentar, avanzar violentamente, penetrar

sur|geon cirujano *o* cirujana

sur|geon gen|er|al *también* Surgeon General inspector general de sanidad *o* inspectora general de sanidad, director general de salud pública *o* directora general de salud pública

sur|gery cirugía, intervención quirúrgica, operación, sala de operaciones, quirófano

sur|gi|cal quirúrgico
• sur|gi|cal|ly quirúrgicamente

sur|name apellido

sur|pass superar, sobrepasar, rebasar

sur|plus excedente, superávit, sobrante

sur|prise sorpresa, sorprender

sur|prised sorprendido

sur|pris|ing sorprendente
• sur|pris|ing|ly sorprendentemente

sur|ren|der rendirse, entregarse, capitular, renunciar, rendición, capitulación, renuncia, entrega

sur|ro|gate suplente, sustituto

sur|round rodear, cercar, rodearse

sur|round|ings ambiente, entorno

sur|veil|lance vigilancia, observación

sur|vey sondeo, encuesta, inspección, peritaje, levantamiento, planimetría, sondear, encuestar, revisar, reconocer, deslindar, medir
• sur|vey|or topógrafo *o* topógrafa, perito *o* perita,

S

deslindador o deslindadora

sur|viv|al supervivencia, sobrevivencia

sur|vive sobrevivir, salir con vida, salvar la vida
• **sur|vi|vor** sobreviviente, familiar

sus|pect sospechar, recelar, tener sospechas, sospechoso o sospechosa

sus|pend suspender, dejar de hacer algo temporalmente, expulsar temporalmente, colgar

sus|pend|ers tirantes, tiradores

sus|pense suspenso, suspense, incertidumbre

sus|pen|sion suspensión

sus|pi|cion sospecha, recelo, desconfianza

sus|pi|cious desconfiado, suspicaz, sospechoso
• **sus|pi|cious|ly** sospechosamente

sus|tain sostener, mantener, apoyar, sufrir

sus|tain|able sustentable, sostenible • **sus|tain|abil|ity** sustentabilidad

SUV vehículo con tracción en las cuatro ruedas, vehículo todo terreno

swal|low tragar(se), ingerir, deglutir, creer, trago, golondrina

swamp ciénaga, pantano, anegar, inundar, sumergir, hundir, abrumar(se), inundar(se)

swap cambiar(se), intercambiar, cambio, intercambio

swarm multitud, montón, enjambre, pulular, enjambrar, irrumpir, amontonarse, aglomerarse, hervir

swathe franja, faja, envolver, cubrir

SWAT team policía de élite, grupo táctico, grupo de

ataque y armas especiales

S-wave onda S

sway balancear(se), mecerse, influir, influenciar
▶ **hold sway** prevalecer, dominar

swear jurar, insultar, maldecir, prometer, prometer solemnemente
▶ **swear by** tener fe ciega en algo
▶ **swear in** prestar juramento, juramentar

sweat sudor, sudar, transpirar • **sweat|ing** sudor, bañado en sudor, empapado en sudor
• **sweats** pants, conjunto deportivo

sweat|er suéter, jersey, pulóver, chompa

sweat gland glándula sudorípara

sweat|shirt también **sweat shirt** sudadera

sweep barrer, empujar, quitar, aventar, extenderse
▶ **sweep under the carpet/ rug** ocultar
▶ **sweep up** barrer

sweet dulce, endulzado, melodioso, azucarado, encantador, amable, amoroso, tierno, mono, lindo, caramelo, postre
• **sweet|ness** dulzura
• **sweet|ly** dulcemente, agradable

sweet|en|er edulcorante, endulzante artificial

sweet|heart querido, amor, vida, cariño

swell hincharse, inflarse, crecer, aumentar, inflamarse, oleaje

swept ver **sweep**

swerve virar bruscamente, desviarse, viraje brusco, volantazo

swift veloz, rápido • **swift|ly** rápidamente • **swift|ness** rapidez

S

swim nadar, flotar, nado, natación • **swim|mer** nadador o nadadora

swim blad|der vejiga natatoria

swim|ming nado, natación

swim|ming pool alberca, piscina, pileta

swim|suit traje de baño, bañador, vestido de baño, malla de baño

swin|dle estafar, timar, transar, estafa, timo, transa • **swind|ler** estafador o estafadora, timador o timadora

swing balancear(se), columpiar(se), girar, dar(se) vuelta, virar, intentar dar un golpe, cambiar, oscilar, balanceo, vaivén, oscilación, cambio, viraje, golpe, columpio, péndulo, hamaca
▶ **in full swing** en plena marcha, en pleno desarrollo

swing vote voto indeciso

swing vot|er votante indeciso

swipe golpear con algo, manotazo

swipe card también **swipecard** tarjeta (de banda magnética)

switch switch, interruptor, apagador, llave de encendido, aguja, cambio, cambiar, intercambiar
▶ **switch off** apagar, desconectarse, dejar de poner atención
▶ **switch on** prender, encender

swol|len hinchado, inflamado, ver swell

sword espada

swum ver swim

swung ver swing

syl|labi|ca|tion también **syllabification** silabeo, división en sílabas

syl|la|ble sílaba

sym|bio|sis simbiosis

sym|bol símbolo

sym|bol|ic simbólico
• **sym|boli|cal|ly** simbólicamente
• **sym|bol|ism** simbolismo

sym|met|ri|cal simétrico
• **sym|met|ri|cal|ly** de manera simétrica

sym|pa|thet|ic favorablemente dispuesto, favorable, receptivo
• **sym|pa|theti|cal|ly** con comprensión

sym|pa|thize compadecer(se), comprender, entender, simpatizar, aprobar
• **sym|pa|thiz|er** simpatizante, partidario o partidaria

sym|pa|thy compasión, lástima, aprobación, afinidad

sym|pho|ny sinfonía

sym|pho|ny or|ches|tra orquesta sinfónica

symp|tom síntoma

syna|gogue sinagoga

syn|cline sinclinal, pliegue sinclinal

syn|co|pa|tion síncopa

syn|di|cate agrupación, agencia de distribución de publicaciones

syn|drome síndrome

syno|nym sinónimo

syn|the|sis re|ac|tion reacción de síntesis

syn|thet|ic sintético

syr|up jarabe, almíbar, sirope

sys|tem sistema, método

sys|tem|at|ic sistemático, metódico • **sys|tem|ati|cal|ly** sistemáticamente

sys|tem|ic sistémico

sys|tem|ic cir|cu|la|tion circulación sistémica, circulación general

S

Tt

ta|ble mesa, tabla, posponer, diferir

tab|leau cuadro vivo

table|spoon cuchara para servir

tab|let tableta, pastilla

tab|loid tabloide, periódico sensacionalista, periódico amarillista

tack chinche, tachuela, chincheta, enfoque, táctica, estrategia, clavar
▸ **tack on** agregar, añadir, pegar

tack|le atacar, enfrentar, abordar, taclear, confrontar, tacleada, aparejos

tac|tic táctica, estrategia

tac|ti|cal táctico
• **tac|ti|cal|ly** tácticamente

tad|pole renacuajo

taf|fy chicloso, caramelo masticable

tag etiqueta, gafete, rótulo, etiquetar, marcar
▸ **tag along** pegársele a alguien, ir con alguien sin ser invitado

tai chi *también* **Tai Chi** tai chi

tai|ga taiga

tail cola, seguir
▸ **tail off** disminuir, mermar

tail|gate par|ty picnic al lado de un coche

tai|lor sastre *o* sastra, adaptar

tail|pipe tubo de escape, escape

tail|spin picada, en picada

take tomar, coger, llevar, transportar, robar, quitar, ocupar, adueñarse, tolerar, necesitar, aceptar, seguir, hacer, usar
▸ **take (a size in shoes/ clothes)** quedarlo algo

▸ **take it or leave it** tómelo o déjelo
▸ **take after** heredar, parecerse a
▸ **take apart** desarmar, deshacer
▸ **take away** llevarse, restar
▸ **take back** regresar, devolver, retractarse
▸ **take down** quitar, desmontar, anotar, apuntar, escribir
▸ **take in** acoger, engañar, registrar, asimilar
▸ **take off** despegar, quitarse, pedir un permiso
▸ **take on** aceptar, hacerse cargo de, adoptar, adquirir, contratar, enfrentar
▸ **take out** solicitar, sacar
▸ **take over** asumir el control, apoderarse, hacerse cargo
▸ **take to** adaptarse, sentirse a gusto, aficionarse
▸ **take up** empezar, emprender, tratar, asumir

tak|en *ver* take, entusiasmado

take|off *también* **take-off** despegue

take|out comida preparada, comida para llevar, tienda de comida para llevar

take|over adquisición, absorción, toma del poder político

tale cuento, relato, historia

tal|ent talento, capacidad

tal|ent|ed talentoso, capaz

talk hablar, conversar, platicar, exponer, cantar, delatar, discutir, plática, conversación, exposición
▸ **talk down** menospreciar, restar importancia a
▸ **talk into** persuadir
▸ **talk out of** disuadir

▶ **talk over** discutir

▶ **talk through** analizar

▶ **talk up** alabar

talk ra|dio estación radiofónica especializada en comentarios, noticieros

tall alto

▶ **tall order** empresa difícil

tam|bou|rine pandero, pandereta

tame domesticado, domado, insípido, domar, domesticar

tam|per manipular indebidamente

tan bronceado, broncearse

• **tanned** bronceado

tan|dem tándem

▶ **in tandem** en tándem

tan|gle maraña, enredar(se), enmarañar(se)

tank tanque, depósito

tank|er camión cisterna, buque/barco cisterna, (barco) petrolero

tank top camiseta sin mangas

tan|ning bed instalación para broncearse con rayos ultravioleta

tap tamborilear, dar golpecitos, intervenir, tamborileo, golpecitos, intervención

tap dance tap, claqué

tape cinta adhesiva, cinta, cinta de llegada, grabar (en cinta), unir con cinta adhesiva, pegar con cinta adhesiva, sujetar con cinta adhesiva

tape meas|ure metro, cinta métrica

tape|worm (lombriz) solitaria, tenia

tap|root también **tap root** raíz primaria

tar|get blanco, objetivo, objeto, dirigir, atraer

▶ **on target** dentro del plazo previsto

tar|iff arancel

tarp lona impermeabilizada

tar|tar sauce también **tartare sauce** salsa tártara

task tarea, misión

task|bar también **task bar** barra de trabajo

taste gusto, prueba, experiencia, sabor, probar, saber, distinguir el sabor de, experimentar

▶ **in bad/poor taste** de mal gusto

taste bud también **tastebud** papila gustativa

taste|less de mal gusto, vulgar, insípido, desabrido

tasty sabroso, apetitoso

tat|too tatuaje, tatuar

tax impuesto, imponer contribuciones, gravar

tax|able gravable

taxa|tion tributación, contribución de impuestos, carga fiscal, contribución

tax break exención fiscal

tax-deferred de impuestos diferidos

tax-exempt exento de impuestos

tax-free libre de impuestos

taxi taxi, coche de alquiler, rodar

taxi|cab también **taxi-cab** taxi, coche de alquiler

tax in|cen|tive incentivo fiscal

taxi stand parada de taxis, paradero de taxis, sitio de taxis

tax|ono|my taxonomía

tax|payer contribuyente

TB tuberculosis

TBA también **tba** será anunciado

T-ball juego infantil similar al béisbol

TCP/IP protocolo de control de transmisión, protocolo de internet (TCP/IP)

tea té

teach enseñar • **teach|er** maestro o maestra, profesor *o* profesora

teach|er's aide ayudante de maestro

teach|ing enseñanza

teach|ing as|sis|tant maestro auxiliar *o* maestra auxiliar, pasante de maestro

tea|kettle *también* **tea kettle** tetera

team equipo
▶ **team up** asociarse con, unirse con

team|mate *también* **team-mate** compañero de equipo *o* compañera de equipo

team|work trabajo en equipo

tea|pot *también* **tea pot** tetera

tear lágrima, desgarradura, rotura, rasgar, arrancar, andar apresuradamente
▶ **tear apart** separar, desgarrar, destrozar
▶ **tear away** arrancar(se)
▶ **tear down** destrozar, derribar
▶ **tear off** arrancar(se)
▶ **tear up** rasgar, romper

tease burlarse

tea|spoon cucharita, cucharilla

tech|ni|cal técnico
● **tech|ni|cal|ly** técnicamente

tech|ni|cian técnico *o* técnica

tech|nique técnica

tech|nol|ogy tecnología
● **tech|no|logi|cal** tecnológico
● **tech|no|logi|cal|ly** tecnológicamente

tec|ton|ic plate placa tectónica

te|di|ous tedioso, aburrido
● **te|di|ous|ly** tediosamente

tee tee, punto de partida
▶ **tee off** molestar, hacer enojar, dar el primer golpe a la pelota de golf

teen adolescencia, adolescente, para adolescentes, juvenil

teen|age adolescente, para adolescentes

teen|ager adolescente

teeth *ver* tooth

tee|to|tal|er abstemio *o* abstemia

TEFL enseñanza del inglés como lengua extranjera

Teja|no tejano-mexicano

tele|cast transmisión por televisión, emisión por televisión

tele|com|mu|ni|ca|tions telecomunicación

tele|mar|ket|ing ventas por teléfono

tele|phone teléfono, telefonear, llamar por teléfono
▶ **on the telephone** al teléfono

tele|phone pole poste de teléfonos

tele|scope telescopio

tele|vise televisar

tele|vi|sion televisor, televisión

tell decir, narrar, saber, indicar, afectar
▶ **tell apart** distinguir
▶ **tell off** regañar

tell|er cajero *o* cajera

telo|phase telofase

tem|per humor, carácter, genio
▶ **lose one's temper** perder la paciencia, perder los estribos

tem|per|ate zone zona templada

tem|pera|ture temperatura, fiebre, calentura
▶ **run/have a temperature** tener calentura, tener fiebre, tener temperatura
▶ **take someone's temperature** tomar la temperatura

tem|ple templo, sien

tem|po|rary temporal, provisional ● **tem|po|rari|ly** temporalmente

T

tempt tentar

temp|ta|tion tentación

tempt|ed tentado
● **tempt|ing** tentador

ten diez

ten|ant inquilino o inquilina

tend tender a, soler, tener tendencias

ten|den|cy tendencia

ten|der tierno, cariñoso, cálido, blando, sensible, licitar, propuesta
● **ten|der|ly** tiernamente
● **ten|der|ness** ternura

ten|don tendón

ten|nis tenis

tense tenso, tensar(se), tiempo verbal

ten|sion tensión

tent tienda

ten|ta|tive provisional, vacilante, indeciso
● **ten|ta|tive|ly** vacilantemente

tenth décimo

term término, trimestre, período, calificar de, llamar
▶ **in terms of** desde el punto de vista de
▶ **come to terms with** aceptar
▶ **on equal terms/on the same terms** en igualdad de condiciones
▶ **be on good terms with** tener buenas relaciones con
▶ **in the long/short/ medium term** a largo/corto/mediano plazo
▶ **think in terms of** pensar en

ter|mi|nal terminal
● **ter|mi|nal|ly** en fase terminal

ter|mi|nal ve|loc|ity velocidad final, velocidad de llegada

ter|mi|nate terminar(se), poner fin a, poner término a, vencer, llegar al final del recorrido ● **ter|mi|na|tion** terminación

ter|mite termita

term pa|per exposición o ensayo que se presenta en la escuela sobre algún tema estudiado durante un trimestre

ter|race terraza

ter|res|trial plan|et planeta similar a la Tierra, planeta terrestre, telúrico o rocoso

ter|ri|ble malísimo, atroz
● **ter|ri|bly** muchísimo, enormemente

ter|rif|ic estupendo

ter|ri|fy aterrar, aterrorizar
● **ter|ri|fied** aterrado

ter|ri|fy|ing aterrador, espantoso, horroroso

ter|ri|to|rial territorial

ter|ri|to|ry territorio, terreno, región

ter|ror terror

ter|ror|ist terrorista
● **ter|ror|ism** terrorismo

ter|ror|ize aterrorizar

test probar, examinar, analizar, prueba, examen, análisis
▶ **put to the test** poner a prueba

test drive también **test-drive** hacer la prueba de carretera, prueba de carretera

tes|ti|fy testificar, declarar, dar testimonio, prestar testimonio

tes|ti|mo|ny testimonio, declaración, prueba de, muestra de

tes|tis testículo

test tube también **test-tube** probeta, tubo de ensayo

Tex-Mex Tex-Mex (tejano-mexicano)

text texto, mensaje de texto, enviar un mensaje de texto, versión impresa

text|book también **text book** libro de texto

tex|tiles productos textiles, industria textil

t

text|ing envío de mensajes de texto

text mes|sage mensaje de texto

text mes|sag|ing envío de mensajes de texto

tex|ture textura

than que, de

thank agradecer, dar las gracias, agradecimiento, gratitud
▸ **thank you** gracias
▸ **thank you very much** muchas gracias
▸ **thank God** gracias a Dios, gracias al cielo
▸ **thanks to** merced a, gracias a

thank|ful agradecido

that que, eso, aquello, aquel, aquella, ese, esa, tan
▸ **that is/that is to say** es decir
▸ **that is that** es todo

that's = that is o that has

thaw derretir(se), fundir(se), deshacer(se), disolver(se), deshielo

the el, la, los, las, lo
▸ **the more... the** mientras más ...más

thea|ter *también* **theatre** teatro, cine, representación teatral, obra de teatro, arte dramático

thea|ter of the ab|surd teatro del absurdo

the|at|ri|cal teatral, dramático, escénico, afectado, artificial, artificioso, histriónico
● **the|at|ri|cal|ly** teatralmente

the|at|ri|cal con|ven|tion convención teatral

the|at|ri|cal ex|peri|ence experiencia teatral

the|at|ri|cal game juego teatral

theft robo, hurto

their su

theirs el suyo

them ellos *o* ellas, los, las, les, le, a ellos, a ellas, a él, a ella

theme tema, asunto, idea principal

theme and vari|ation tema y variación

them|selves ellos mismos, ellas mismas, sí mismos, sí mismas, se, a sí mismo, a sí misma

then entonces, luego, después, antes, pues, por otra parte

theo|reti|cal teórico, hipotético

theo|rize especular, teorizar
● **theo|rist** teórico *o* teórica
● **theo|riz|ing** especulación

theo|ry teoría
▸ **in theory** teóricamente

thera|pist terapeuta

the|rap|sid terápsido

thera|py terapia, tratamiento

there ahí, allí, allá, en eso, ese punto
▸ **there you go / there we are** ahí está
▸ **Is... there? (telephone)** ¿se encuentra...?
▸ **there and then/then and there** de inmediato
▸ **there you are/go** ahí tiene

there|after de ahí en adelante

there|by con lo cual

there|fore por lo tanto, por consiguiente, de modo que

ther|mal térmico

ther|mal en|er|gy energía térmica

ther|mal equi|lib|rium equilibrio térmico

ther|mal ex|pan|sion expansión térmica

ther|mal pol|lu|tion contaminación térmica

ther|mo|cline termoclina

ther|mo|cou|ple termopar, termocupla

ther|mom|eter termómetro

ther|mo|sphere termosfera

these estos, estas
▸ these days en esta época

the|sis argumento, tesis

they ellos, ellas
▸ they say se dice

they'd = they had o they would

they'll = they will

they're = they are

they've = they have

thick grueso, gordo • thick|ly de forma gruesa, de forma espesa • thick|ness grosor, espeso

thick|en espesar(se), dar consistencia

thief ladrón o ladrona, ratero o ratera, caco

thigh muslo

thin delgado, fino, flaco, claro, aguado, escasear(se), disminuir, hacer menos denso • thin|ly delgadamente

thing cosa, eso, cosita
▸ first/last thing lo primero, lo último
▸ for one thing en primer término
▸ the thing is lo importante es

think pensar, creer, considerar, suponer, meditar, reflexionar, ocurrirse, imaginar(se), tener en buen concepto, idear • think|ing idea, pensamiento
▸ I think creo, opino
▸ think nothing of hacer como si nada
▸ think back recordar, hacer memoria
▸ think over pensar
▸ think through pensar detenidamente
▸ think up idear, crear, inventar, imaginar

think|ing ver think

third tercero, tercio, tercera parte

Third World Tercer Mundo

thirst sed

thirsty sediento

thir|teen trece

thir|teenth decimotercero, treceavo

thir|ti|eth trigésimo

thir|ty treinta
▸ the thirties los (años) treinta

this este, esta, esto
▸ this is (telephone/radio/ television) soy, está usted escuchando
▸ this and that/this, that, and the other esto y aquello

thong tanga, hilo dental, chancla, chancla de pata de gallo

thor|ax tórax

thor|ough completo, cuidadoso, concienzudo, riguroso, minucioso, perfecto • thor|ough|ly completamente • thor|ough|ness esmero, rigor, meticulosidad

those aquellos, aquellas, esos, esas, quien, quienes

though aunque, si bien, bien que

thought ver think, pensamiento, idea, opinión, reflexión

thought|ful pensativo, meditabundo, atento, considerado • thought|ful|ly cuidadosamente, consideradamente

thou|sand mil
▸ thousands miles, montones

thread hilo, hebra, secuencia, rosca, filete, tema, ensartar, enhebrar, abrirse paso, abrirse camino

threat riesgo, peligro, amenaza

threat|en amenazar, poner en riesgo, amagar

threat|en|ing amenazador

t

three tres

three-dimensional tridimensional

three-quarters tres cuartos, tres cuartas partes

thresh|old umbral, puerta
▸ **on the threshold of** en el umbral de, a las puertas de

thrift economía, ahorro, frugalidad

thrift shop bazar de cosas usadas

thrill emoción, emocionar, entusiasmar

thrill|er de suspenso

thrill|ing emocionante

thrive prosperar, enriquecerse, tener éxito

throat garganta, cuello
▸ **clear one's throat** aclararse la garganta, carraspear

throne trono

through por, a través de, de un lado a otro, a través, durante, continuamente, de …a, gracias a, merced a, de principio a fin, a la siguiente etapa
▸ **through (with something)** terminado
▸ **be through with (someone)** no querer nada con

through|out durante, todo el tiempo, por todo, por todos lados

throw tirar, lanzar, aventar, arrojar, echar(se), aventar(se), caer, sumir(se), desconcertar, organizar, dar, lanzamiento, tiro, tirada
▸ **throw away** o **throw out** tirar, deshacerse de, desaprovechar, desperdiciar, malgastar
▸ **throw out** rechazar, echar a alguien de algún lugar, expulsar
▸ **throw up** vomitar, devolver, guacarearse
▸ **throw oneself into** something dedicarse a algo intensamente

thrown ver **throw**

throw rug tapete pequeño

thrust empujar, empujón, embestida, propulsión

thru|way también **throughway** autopista

thumb pulgar

thumb|tack chinche, chincheta, tachuela

thun|der trueno, estruendo, fragor, estrépito, tronar
▸ **thunder past** pasar haciendo mucho ruido

thunder|storm tormenta eléctrica

Thurs|day jueves

thus por lo tanto, por consiguiente, por eso, así

thy|mine timina

thy|mus timo

tick hacer tictac, tictac
● **tick|ing** tictac
▸ **tick off** fastidiar, molestar

tick|et boleto, billete, entrada, multa, boleta, papeleta

ticket|less sin boleto

tick|le hacer cosquillas, hormiguear, sentir cosquillas, picar, tener comezón

tic-tac-toe también **tick-tack-toe** gato, tres en línea

tid|al bore macareo

tid|al range amplitud de la marea

tide marea, corriente

tie anudar, atar, amarrar, hacer un nudo, hacer un moño, conectar, relacionar, vincular, empatar, igualar, corbata, vínculo, relación, empate, igualada
▸ **tie up** anudar, atar, amarrar

ti|ger tigre

tight pegado, ajustado, apretado, ceñido, firme, fuerte, estricto,

riguroso, tirante, estirado
• **tight|ly** apretadamente, estrechamente, estrictamente, ajustadamente

tight|en apretar(se), ajustar, tensar, hacer más estricto, restringir

tile baldosa, loza, azulejo, mosaico, loseta

till hasta, caja registradora, depósito glacial, aluvión glaciárico, morrena, acarreo glacial

tilt inclinar(se), ladear(se), inclinación, declive

tim|ber madera de construcción

tim|bre timbre

time tiempo, hora, momento, rato, periodo, época, ocasión, vez, compás, lapso, plazo, programar, cronometrar, medir el tiempo
▸ **times (multiplication)** por
▸ **be about time** ser hora de
▸ **ahead of/before one's time** adelantado
▸ **all the time** todo el tiempo, siempre, continuamente
▸ **at one time** anteriormente
▸ **at the same time** a la vez
▸ **for the time being** por el momento, entretanto
▸ **from time to time** de tiempo en tiempo, de cuando en cuando, de vez en vez
▸ **in/on time** a tiempo
▸ **in time** con el tiempo
▸ **of all time** de todos los tiempos
▸ **to take time** llevar tiempo, tomar tiempo
▸ **to take your time** tomar(se) su tiempo

time-honored tradicional, consagrado

time|line también **time line** cronología, línea cronológica, línea de tiempo, calendario, programa

time|table horario, itinerario

tim|id tímido, huraño
• **ti|mid|ity** timidez
• **tim|id|ly** tímidamente

tim|ing oportunidad, sincronización

tin estaño, hojalata, lata, bote

tiny diminuto, chiquito, minúsculo, menudo

tip punta, extremo, propina, sugerencia, consejo práctico, tip, inclinar, verter, vaciar, servir, dar propina
▸ **tip off** avisar, pasar información, prevenir, poner sobre aviso • **tip-off** pitazo
▸ **tip over** volcar, caerse

tire llanta, neumático, goma, cansar(se), aburrirse

tired cansado, fatigado, aburrido • **tired|ness** cansancio

tire|some tedioso, pesado, molesto

tir|ing agotador, cansado

tis|sue tejido, papel de china, papel de seda, pañuelo desechable

ti|tle título, tratamiento, campeonato

ti|tled que tiene un título nobiliario

TLC cariño, cuidado

to a, en, con, para, hasta

toast pan tostado, tostada, brindis, tostar, brindar

toast|er tostador

to|bac|co tabaco

to|day hoy, actualmente, hoy en día

tod|dler niño que ha empezado a caminar o niña que ha empezado a caminar

toe dedo del pie

to|fu tofu

to|geth|er juntos, uno con otro, junto, a un tiempo,

simultáneamente
▸ **together with** junto con

toi|let excusado, taza, inodoro, retrete

toi|let pa|per *también* **toilet tissue** papel higiénico, papel de baño, papel sanitario, papel confort

toi|let tissue *ver* **toilet paper**

to|ken simbólico, ficha
▸ **by the same token** de igual modo, por la misma razón

told *ver* **tell**
▸ **all told** con todo

tol|er|ate tolerar, aguantar, soportar

toll tañer, tocar, doblar, cuota, peaje, derecho, de cuota, número de víctimas, índice de siniestralidad
▸ **take its toll** cobrar(se)

toll-free gratuito, gratuitamente

to|ma|to jitomate, tomate

to|mor|row mañana

ton tonelada

to|nal|ity tonalidad

tone tono, tonificar, dar tono
▸ **tone down** moderar, atenuar

tone poem poema sinfónico

tongue lengua, idioma, lenguaje
▸ **tongue in cheek** comentario medio en broma

to|night esta noche

ton|sils amígdala

too también, asimismo, además, de veras, demasiado, muy
▸ **all too/only too** de veras

took *ver* **take**

tool herramienta, instrumento, utensilio

tool|bar barra de herramientas

tooth diente, púa

tooth|brush cepillo de dientes

tooth|paste pasta de dientes, dentífrico, pasta dentífrica

top parte superior, parte de arriba, superior, de arriba, tapa, tapón, top, blusa, playera, máximo, tope, cúspide, cumbre, lo mejor, lo más alto, en la cúspide, el primero *o* la primera, mejor
▸ **top out** alcanzar
▸ **be on top of/get on top of** tener el control de
▸ **on top** sobre, arriba
▸ **on top of** además de, encima de

top-down verticalista

top hat sombrero de copa, chistera

top|ic tema, tópico, materia, asunto

top|ical de interés actual, del día

top|ic sen|tence tema, idea principal

topo|graph|ic map mapa topográfico

top|ple caerse, tambalearse, perder el equilibrio, derrocar, derribar

top-shelf de primer nivel

To|rah Torá

torch antorcha

tor|na|do tornado

tor|toise tortuga

tor|ture torturar, atormentar, dar tormento, tortura, tormento, suplicio

toss tirar, lanzar, aventar, arrojar, sacudir, echar un volado, sortear, volado

to|tal total, sumar, hacer un total de, completo ● **to|tal|ly** totalmente
▸ **in total** en total

to|tal eclipse eclipse total

tote bag bolsón, bolsa grande

touch tocar(se), tentar, sentir, estar en contacto, tratar por encima, aludir, referirse, afectar, influir, toque, tacto, contacto,

detalle ● **touched** conmovido ● **touch|ing** enternecedor
▶ **in touch** al corriente
▶ **in touch with** en contacto con, informado
▶ **lose touch** perder contacto
▶ **touch down** aterrizar

tough duro, firme, fuerte, estricto, inflexible, difícil, peliagudo, correoso, resistente ● **tough|ness** dureza

tour hacer una gira, andar de gira, viaje, recorrer, viajar, visitar, recorrido, gira, tour

tour guide guía de turistas

tour|ism turismo

tour|ist turista, viajero o viajera, visitante

tour|na|ment torneo, justa, certamen, competencia

tour of duty servicio

tow remolcar, arrastrar

to|ward *también* **towards** en dirección de, hacia, en relación con, para con, cercano a, próximo, en favor de

tow|el toalla, secar con toalla
▶ **throw in the towel** tirar la toalla

tow|er torre
▶ **tower over** ser mucho más alto que

town ciudad, pueblo, población

town meet|ing consejo municipal de vecinos

town|ship municipio, ayuntamiento, municipalidad, distrito segregado

tox|ic tóxico

toy juguete
▶ **toy with** jugar con, dar(le) vueltas a una idea, considerar, juguetear

trace rastrear, seguir la pista, investigar, localizar, ubicar, calcar, vestigio, indicio

trace gas oligoelemento, microelemento, elemento menor

tra|chea tráquea

track camino, sendero, pista, vía, vía férrea, riel, tema, pieza, huella, pisada, rastrear, seguir(le) la pista
▶ **keep track of** estar al día, mantenerse informado
▶ **lose track of** perder el rastro
▶ **be on the right track** estar bien encaminado
▶ **track down** encontrar, localizar, averiguar

track meet torneo de atletismo

track rec|ord historial, antecedentes

tract espacio, extensión, sistema (de órganos), tracto

trac|tor tractor

tractor-trailer camión con remolque, camión con tráiler

trade comerciar, intercambiar, canjear, comercio, negocio
▶ **be traded** cambiar de equipo, vender, pasar
▶ **trade places with** (inter)cambiar de lugar ● **trad|ing** comercio

trade defi|cit déficit comercial, déficit de la balanza comercial

trade|mark marca de fábrica, marca registrada

trad|er comerciante, vendedor o vendedora, operador de bolsa u operadora de bolsa

trade show feria comercial

trade wind *también* **tradewind** viento alisio

trad|ing card estampa, lámina

tra|di|tion tradición, costumbre ● **tra|di|tion|al** tradicional ● **tra|di|tion|al|ly** por tradición

t

traf|fic tráfico, circulación, tránsito, movimiento, traficar con ● **traf|fick|ing** tráfico ● **traf|fick|er** traficante

traf|fic jam embotellamiento, atascamiento

trag|edy tragedia, situación trágica

trag|ic trágico, dramático, funesto ● **tragi|cal|ly** de manera trágica

trail sendero, senda, vereda, huella, rastro, estela, rastrear, seguir, seguir la pista, arrastrar ▶ **be on the trail of** seguir la pista de

trail|er tráiler, casa rodante, cámper, remolque, avance publicitario, corto, avances

trail|er park tráiler park, campamento para remolques

trail|er truck camión con remolque

train tren, ferrocarril, serie, sucesión, capacitar(se), entrenar(se), preparar(se) ● **train|er** entrenador o entrenadora, instructor o instructora, preparador o preparadora, preparador físico o preparadora física ● **train|ing** capacitación, entrenamiento

trait rasgo

tram tren, tranvía, teleférico

trans|ac|tion transacción, negocio, operación

tran|script transcripción

trans|fer transferir, cambiar de lugar, trasladar(se), pasar, transferencia, traspaso, traslado, cambio

trans|form transformar, convertir, transfigurar ● **trans|for|ma|tion** transformación

trans|form bounda|ry límite de transformación

trans|it tránsito, transporte ▶ **in transit** en tránsito, de tránsito

tran|si|tion transición ● **tran|si|tion|al** de transición

tran|si|tive transitivo

trans|late traducir, convertir ● **trans|la|tor** traductor o traductora

trans|la|tion traducción, traslación

trans|lu|cent translúcido

trans|mis|sion transmisión, emisión

trans|mit transmitir, contagiar

trans|mit|ter transmisor

trans|par|ent transparente, translúcido, claro

tran|spi|ra|tion transpiración

trans|plant trasplante, trasplantar, trasladar

trans|pond|er radiofaro de respuesta, transpondedor

trans|port transportar, acarrear

trans|por|ta|tion transporte

trans|ver|sal transversal

trans|verse wave onda transversa

trap trampa, artimaña, ardid, atrapar, cazar, tender una trampa

trash basura, desecho, desperdicio, porquería

trash can bote de basura, cubo de basura, basurero, tacho de basura

trau|ma trauma

trav|el viajar, hacer un viaje, propagarse, viaje

trav|el agen|cy agencia de viajes

trav|el|er también **traveller** viajero o viajera, viajante, turista

trav|el|er's check cheque de viajero, traveler's check

tray charola, bandeja

tread dibujo, pisar, irse con cuidado

treas|ure tesoro, riqueza, atesorar, apreciar mucho
• **treas|ured** preciado

treas|ur|er tesorero o tesorera

treas|ury bill también **Treasury bill, Treasury Bill** bono del Tesoro

treat tratar, considerar, atender, curar, invitar, convidar, obsequiar, regalo, obsequio, agasajo, gusto

treat|ment tratamiento, terapia, régimen terapéutico, trato

trea|ty tratado, acuerdo, convenio

tre|ble clef clave de sol

tree árbol

trek caminar fatigosamente, hacer senderismo, caminata

trem|ble temblar, estremecerse, vibrar

tre|men|dous tremendo, enorme, formidable, extraordinario, impresionante, increíble
• **tre|men|dous|ly** tremendamente

trend tendencia, inclinación

tri|ad triada, acorde perfecto

tri|al juicio, proceso, experimento, prueba
▶ **trial and error** ensayo y error

tri|an|gle triángulo
• **tri|an|gu|lar** triangular

tribe tribu • **trib|al** tribal

tri|bu|nal tribunal, juzgado, comisión investigadora

tribu|tary tributario

trib|ute tributo, homenaje, resultado

trick engañar, embaucar, ardid, treta, jugarreta, broma, truco
▶ **do the trick** resolver el problema, surtir efecto

tricky difícil, delicado, peliagudo

tri|col|or tricolor

tried de probada calidad

trig|ger gatillo, disparador, hacer estallar, disparar, desencadenar, provocar, desatar

tril|lion billón

trim bonito, pulcro, esbelto, elegante, recortar, arreglar, adornar, decorar, corte, recorte, ribete, adorno

tri|mes|ter trimestre

trio trío, terceto, terna

trip viaje, excursión, tropezar(se), dar un traspié, poner una zancadilla, hacer tropezar

tri|ple triple, triplicar(se)

tri|ple me|ter compás ternario

tri|umph éxito, triunfo, victoria, triunfar, obtener una victoria

trom|bone trombón

troop tropas, soldados, tropa, ejército, escuadrón, apiñarse, agruparse, entrar/salir en tropel

troop|er agente de policía, soldado de caballería

tro|phy trofeo, copa

tropi|cal tropical

tropi|cal de|pres|sion depresión tropical

tropi|cal dis|turb|ance perturbación tropical

tropi|cal storm tormenta tropical

tropi|cal zone zona tropical, región tropical

tro|pism tropismo

tropo|sphere tropósfera, troposfera

trou|ble contratiempo, problema, inconveniencia, trastorno, enfermedad, disturbio, agitación, preocupar, molestar, inquietar, afligir
• **trou|bling** inquietante
▶ **in trouble** en problemas, en aprietos

t

▶ **take the trouble** tomarse la molestia

trou|bled preocupado, atribulado

trou|ble|some penoso, fastidioso, problemático

trough artesa, comedero, abrevadero, depresión, seno

trou|sers pantalones, pantalón

trow|el desplantador, paleta, llana

truce tregua, respiro, pausa

truck camión de carga, camioneta, pick-up

truck|er camionero o camionera, conductor de camión o conductora de camión, transportista

truck stop paradero de camiones

true cierto, válido, verdadero, real, genuine
▶ **true north/south** norte/sur geográfico, norte/sur verdadero
▶ **come true** resultar cierto, realizarse
▶ **hold true** seguir siendo cierto

true-breeding autofertilizante

tru|ly sinceramente, correctamente, de veras, efectivamente
▶ **Yours truly** cordiales saludos, su seguro servidor

trum|pet trompeta

trunk tronco, cajuela, baúl, maletero, trompa

trust confiar, tener confianza, fiar(se), confianza, fe, responsabilidad, fondo de inversiones, fideicomiso
▶ **trust someone to do something** confiar en que alguien hará algo
▶ **trust someone with** confiar(le) a
▶ **not trust** desconfiar

trus|tee fiduciario o

fiduciaria, fideicomisario o fideicomisaria, síndico

truth verdad, veracidad, realidad

try tratar, intentar, procurar, intentar conseguir, probar, someter a juicio, juzgar, procesar, intento, prueba, tentativa
▶ **try on** probar(se)
▶ **try out** probar, poner a prueba
▶ **try out for** presentarse a una prueba

T-shirt *también* **tee-shirt** t-shirt, camiseta, playera

tsu|na|mi tsunami

tub tina, bañera, bañadera, envase, tarrina

tube tubo, conducto

tube worm *también* **tubeworm** poliqueto tubícola

tuck meter, fajar(se)
▶ **tuck away** guardar, ocultar
▶ **tuck in/into (something)** fajar(se), meter(se)
▶ **tuck (someone) in** arropar

Tues|day martes

tug tirar de, jalar, arrastrar, tirón, jalón, remolcador

tui|tion colegiatura, matrícula

tum|ble caerse, desplomarse, caída

tu|mor tumor, bulto, masa, bola

tun|dra tundra

tune melodía, canción, aire, tonada, afinar, sintonizar, poner
▶ **change one's tune** cambiar de parecer, cambiar de idea
▶ **in tune/out of tune** afinado/desafinado
▶ **tune in** sintonizar, ver, oír

tun|nel túnel, abrir un túnel, hacer un túnel

tur|bine turbina

tur|key pavo, guajolote

T

tur|moil agitación, confusión

turn volver(se), dar (media) vuelta, dar(se) vuelta, girar, doblar, ir a, concentrarse en, acudir a, recurrir a, convertir en, ponerse, cumplir, vuelta, giro, turno
▸ **in turn** a la vez de
▸ **take turns** turnarse
▸ **turn against** volverse
▸ **turn around** dar vuelta a
▸ **turn away** rechazar
▸ **turn back** regresar, volver, hacer retroceder
▸ **turn down** rechazar, bajar
▸ **turn off** abandonar, salir, dejar , apagar
▸ **turn on** prender, encender, volverse contra, emprenderla contra
▸ **turn out** resultar, resultar ser/estar
▸ **turn over** dar vuelta, volcarse, dar vueltas a, entregar
▸ **turn up** aparecer, subir

turn|over facturación, renovación, movimiento

turn|pike camino de peaje o cuota

turn sig|nal direccional

tur|tle tortuga

turtle|neck cuello (de) tortuga, cuello alto

tu|tor maestro particular o maestra particular, maestro o maestra de la categoría inferior en algunas universidades o colegios estadounidenses

tu|to|rial clase impartida por un maestro encargado de orientar más de cerca a determinado grupo de alumnos, guía práctica sobre algún tema

TV tele, televisión

twelfth duodécimo, decimosegundo, doceavo

twelve doce

twelve-bar blues blues de doce compases

twelve-tone dodecafónico

twen|ti|eth vigésimo

twen|ty veinte
▸ **the twenties** los (años) veinte

24-7 también **twenty-four seven** de día y de noche, toda la semana

twice dos veces, doble

twin gemelo o gemela, doble, bi-

twist torcer(se), retorcer, poner, volver, dar vuelta, tergiversar, giro

twist|ed retorcido

two dos

two-dimensional también **two dimensional** bidimensional

two-percent milk leche descremada

two-point per|spec|tive perspectiva angular, perspectiva de dos conjuntos

two-thirds también **two thirds** dos tercios, dos terceras partes

two|way doble sentido, bidireccional

type tipo, teclear, escribir a máquina, mecanografiar
• **typ|ing** mecanografía
▸ **type in** o **type into** escribir
▸ **type up** pasar a máquina

type|writ|er máquina de escribir

ty|phoon tifón

typi|cal típico, característico, representativo

typi|cal|ly típicamente, como de costumbre, como es característico

typ|ist mecanógrafo o mecanógrafa, dactilógrafo o dactilógrafa

ty|po error de imprenta

t

Uu

ubiqui|tous omnipresente

ugly feo, desagradable
- **ug|li|ness** fealdad

ul|ti|mate último, primordial, fundamental
▸ **the ultimate in** lo último en

ul|ti|mate|ly finalmente, en resumidas cuentas, en última instancia

ultra|sound ecografía

ultra|vio|let ultravioleta

um|bili|cal cord cordón umbilical

um|brel|la paraguas, organización que aglutina numerosos grupos

um|pire árbitro *o* árbitra, arbitrar

un|able incapaz

un|ac|cep|table inaceptable

un-Ameri|can anti-estadounidense

unani|mous unánime
- **unani|mous|ly** por unanimidad

un|armed desarmado

un|ashamed sin vergüenza alguna, sin reparo alguno
- **un|asham|ed|ly** sin reparo alguno

un|avoid|able inevitable

un|aware sin darse cuenta

un|bal|anced forces fuerzas desequilibradas

un|bear|able insoportable
- **un|bear|ably** insoportablemente

un|beat|able inmejorable

un|beat|en invicto

un|be|liev|able increíble
- **un|be|liev|ably** increíblemente

un|born nonato, que aún no nace, feto

un|can|ny extraño, asombroso
- **un|can|ni|ly** asombrosamente

un|cer|tain inseguro
- **un|cer|tain|ly** con aire vacilante, incierto
▸ **in no uncertain terms** muy claramente, inequívocamente

un|cer|tain|ty incertidumbre

un|chal|lenged sin respuesta, indiscutible

un|changed igual, invariable

un|cle tío

un|clear poco claro

Uncle Sam tío Sam

un|com|fort|able incómodo
- **un|com|fort|ably** inquietantemente, desagradablemente

un|com|pro|mis|ing inflexible

un|con|di|tion|al incondicional
- **un|con|di|tion|al|ly** incondicionalmente

un|con|scious inconsciente
- **un|con|scious|ly** inconscientemente
- **un|con|scious|ness** inconsciencia

un|con|sti|tu|tion|al inconstitucional

un|con|ven|tion|al poco convencional

un|cool
▸ **be uncool** no estar en la onda

un|count noun nombre incontable

un|cov|er descubrir, destapar

un|de|ni|able innegable
- **un|de|ni|ably** innegablemente

un|der debajo, bajo, en, bajo

el mando de, bajo la tutela de, con, menor

under|brush maleza

under|class clase marginada

under|cov|er secreto

under|cur|rent trasfondo

under|cut vender más barato, rebajar los precios

under|dog el que tiene menos posibilidades

under|es|ti|mate subestimar

under|go sufrir, someterse

under|gradu|ate estudiante universitario *o* estudiante universitaria

under|ground subterráneo, clandestino

under|growth *también* **underbrush** maleza

under|hand *también* **underhanded** turbio, sin levantar el brazo por encima del hombro

under|line poner de relieve, subrayar

un|der|ly|ing oculto

under|mine debilitar, minar

under|neath debajo, bajo, en el fondo, tras, parte de abajo

under|pants calzoncillos, calzones

under|per|form *también* **under-perform** tener un rendimiento bajo

• **under|per|for|mance** bajo rendimiento

• **under|per|form|er** de bajo rendimiento

under|score poner de relieve, subrayar

under|shirt camiseta

under|stand entender, comprender

under|stand|able comprensible

• **under|stand|ably** comprensiblemente

under|stand|ing comprensión, entendimiento, acuerdo, comprensivo, entendido

under|state subestimar

under|state|ment declaración exageradamente modesta

un|der|stood *ver* understand

under|take encargarse, comprometerse

• **under|tak|ing** empresa

under|tak|er director *o* directora de funeraria, empleado *o* empleada de funeraria

un|der|took *ver* undertake

under|way en marcha

under|wear ropa interior

under|world bajo mundo

under|write asegurar, respaldar

un|dip|lo|mat|ic poco diplomático, descortés

• **un|dip|lo|mati|cal|ly** con poca diplomacia

undo abrir, desabrochar, anular, reparar

un|doubt|ed indudable

• **un|doubt|ed|ly** indudablemente

un|dress desvestir(se)

• **un|dressed** desvestido

un|due excesivo, demasiado

• **un|du|ly** excesivamente

un|easy inquieto, precario

• **un|easi|ly** nerviosamente, incómodamente

• **un|easi|ness** inquietud

un|em|ployed desempleado

▶ **the unemployed** los desempleados

un|em|ploy|ment desempleo, subsidio por desempleo

un|em|ploy|ment com|pen|sa|tion subsidio por desempleo, seguro de desempleo

un|em|ploy|ment line filas del desempleo

un|equaled inigualado

un|even disparejo, accidentado, entrecortado

u

un|ex|pec|ted inesperado
• **un|ex|pect|ed|ly**
inesperadamente

un|fair injusto • **un|fair|ly**
injustamente • **un|fair|ness**
injusticia

un|fit no apto, inadecuado,
fuera de forma

un|fold desenvolverse,
desdoblar

un|for|get|table inolvidable

un|for|tu|nate
desafortunado, inoportuno

un|for|tu|nate|ly
desgraciadamente

un|friend|ly hostil,
desagradable

un|gram|mati|cal
gramaticalmente incorrecto
• **un|gram|mati|cal|ly** con
agramaticalidad

un|hap|py desdichado,
desafortunado
• **un|hap|pi|ly** tristemente
• **un|hap|pi|ness** infelicidad,
descontento

un|healthy poco saludable,
enfermizo

un|heard of inexistente

uni|cel|lu|lar unicelular

un|iden|ti|fied desconocido

uni|fi|ca|tion unificación

uni|form uniforme
• **uni|form|ity**
uniformidad • **uni|form|ly**
uniformemente

uni|formed uniformado

uni|fy unificar • **uni|fied**
uniforme

uni|lat|er|al unilateral

un|in|forma|tive poco
revelador

un|in|stall desinstalar

un|ion sindicato, unión

unique único, excepcional,
exclusivo • **unique|ly**
excepcionalmente,
exclusivamente
• **unique|ness** singularidad

uni|son
▸ **in unison** al unísono

unit unidad
▸ **family unit** familia
nuclear (no extendida)

Uni|tar|ian unitario o
unitaria

unite unir

unit|ed unido, unificado

Unit|ed Na|tions Naciones
Unidas

Unit|ed States of Ameri|ca
Estados Unidos de América

unit frac|tion fracción
unitaria

unity unidad, unity

uni|ver|sal general
• **uni|ver|sal|ly**
mundialmente

uni|ver|sal gravi|ta|tion
gravitación universal

uni|verse universo

uni|ver|sity universidad

un|just injusto • **un|just|ly**
injustamente

un|known desconocido o
desconocida, incógnita
▸ **the unknown** lo
desconocido

un|lead|ed sin plomo,
combustible sin plomo

un|leash dar rienda suelta a

un|less si no, a menos que

un|li|censed no autorizado,
ilegal, tolerado, pirata, sin
registro

un|like diferente, distinto, a
diferencia de, no propio de

un|like|ly improbable,
remoto

un|load descargar

un|lock abrir (algo cerrado
con llave)

un|moved indiferente,
impasible

un|natu|ral poco natural,
poco normal, artificial,
forzado • **un|natu|ral|ly**
extrañamente,
anormalmente

un|nec|es|sary innecesario,
inútil, superfluo
• **un|nec|es|sari|ly**

innecesariamente
un|of|fi|cial extraoficial
● **un|of|fi|cial|ly** extraoficialmente
un|ortho|dox poco convencional, poco ortodoxo
un|pack desempacar, deshacer las maletas
un|pal|at|able desagradable
un|par|al|leled sin par, inigualado
un|pleas|ant desagradable, antipático ● **un|pleas|ant|ly** desagradablemente
un|plug desconectar, desenchufar
un|popu|lar impopular ● **un|popu|lar|ity** impopularidad
un|prec|edent|ed sin precedentes, inaudito
un|pre|dict|able impredecible ● **un|pre|dict|abil|ity** lo impredecible
un|pro|duc|tive improductivo
un|prof|it|able improductivo
un|pro|tect|ed desprotegido
un|pub|lished inédito
un|quali|fied no calificado, rotundo
un|ques|tion|able innegable ● **un|ques|tion|ably** indudablemente
un|rav|el desenmarañar, desenredar, desentrañar, aclarar, descifrar
un|re|al|is|tic poco realista, irreal
un|re|lent|ing tenaz, riguroso, implacable, constante
un|re|pent|ant impenitente
un|rest malestar, descontento, intranquilidad
un|ru|ly indisciplinado, ingobernable, rebelde
un|sat|is|fac|tory insatisfactorio, deficiente
un|satu|rat|ed

hydro|car|bon hidrocarburo insaturado
un|scathed indemne, ileso
un|set|tling inquietante, perturbador
un|sight|ly de aspecto feo
un|sports|man|like antideportivo
un|suc|cess|ful infructuoso, fallido ● **un|suc|cess|ful|ly** en vano, sin éxito
un|sure inseguro, indeciso
un|tie desatar, desamarrar, desanudar
un|til hasta, hasta que
un|treat|ed sin tratar, no tratado
un|usual raro, inusual ● **un|usu|al|ly** excepcionalmente
un|veil develar, descubrir, revelar
un|want|ed indeseado, no deseado
un|wieldy estorboso, inmanejable
un|will|ing mal dispuesto, que no está dispuesto a ● **un|will|ing|ly** de mala gana ● **un|will|ing|ness** renuencia
un|wind relajarse, desenrollar, desenredar
un|wit|ting involuntario, sin querer ● **un|wit|ting|ly** involuntariamente
un|zip abrir el cierre/la cremallera, bajar el cierre/la cremallera, descomprimir
up arriba, a lo largo de, por, hacia arriba, levantado, pasado, subir, aumentar, acelerar
▸ **be up to** corresponder a
▸ **(feel) up to** con ánimo para, capaz de
▸ **stand up** ponerse de pie
▸ **up against** contra
▸ **up and down** de arriba abajo, de un lado a otro
▸ **up and leave** irse abruptamente
▸ **up for** sujeto a

u

▸ **up to** hasta

up-and-coming ambicioso, emprendedor

up|beat optimista

up|bring|ing educación, crianza

up|com|ing cercano, próximo

up|date poner al día, información reciente

up|draft corriente ascendente

up front *también* **up-front** franco, por adelantado

up|grade mejorar, actualización

up|heav|al agitación

up|hill cuesta arriba, difícil, arduo

up|hold apoyar

up|hol|stery tapicería

up|keep mantenimiento

up|lift|ing alentador

upon encima de, sobre, en el momento de, al, tras, y ▸ **be upon someone** ser inminente

up|per de arriba, superior ▸ **the upper hand** ventaja

up|per class *también* **upper-class** clase privilegiada, privilegiado

upper|class|man varón estudiante de los últimos años de preparatoria o universidad

upper|class|woman mujer estudiante de los últimos años de preparatoria o universidad

up|per man|tle manto superior

up|right erguido, recto

up|ris|ing revuelta, revolución, alzamiento

up|roar alboroto, protesta, escándalo, conmoción

up|scale de muy buena calidad, caro

up|set trastornado, alterado, descompuesto, trastornar,

molestar • **up|set|ting** angustioso

up|side down *también* **upside-down** al revés, de cabeza

up|stairs hacia arriba, escaleras arriba, en un piso de arriba, el piso de arriba

up|start advenedizo, arribista

up|state en el norte, lejos de la ciudad capital, más arriba, más al norte

up|stream río arriba, contra la corriente

up|surge aumento repentino

up-to-date *también* **up to date** al día, muy moderno, bien informado

up|town hacia el norte, en el norte

up|turn repunte, mejora

up|ward ascendente, hacia arriba, al alza, en aumento, más de, mayor que

up|wards *ver* upward

up|wel|ling afloramiento, surgencia

ura|nium uranio

Ura|nus Urano

ur|ban urbano

urethra uretra

urge alentar, instar, impulso irrefrenable de hacer algo

ur|gent urgente • **ur|gen|cy** urgencia, apremio • **ur|gent|ly** urgentemente, apremiante, con tono apremiante

uri|nate orinar

urine orina

URL URL

us nosotros *o* nosotras, nos ▸ **one of us** uno de los nuestros

us|able usable, utilizable

us|age uso, modo de usarse, modo de uso

USB USB

use usar, utilizar, aprovecharse de, uso

U

▶ **use up** acabarse

▶ **in use** en uso

▶ **make use of** hacer uso de

▶ **be no use** no tener caso

used usado, de segunda mano

▶ **be used to** estar acostumbrado a

▶ **get used to** acostumbrarse a

use|ful útil • **use|ful|ly** útilmente • **use|ful|ness** utilidad

▶ **come in useful** ser útil, venir bien

use|less inservible, inútil, negado

user usuario o usuaria

U-shaped val|ley valle en U

ush|er hacer pasar a, acompañar, acomodador o acomodadora

usu|al habitual, común y corriente

▶ **as usual** como siempre, como es de esperarse

usu|al|ly generalmente

usurp usurpar

uten|sil utensilio

util|ity servicio, empresa de utilidad pública

util|ity pole poste de servicios públicos

uti|lize utilizar • **uti|li|za|tion** aprovechamiento

ut|most máximo, mayor

▶ **one's utmost** lo máximo

uto|pia utopía

ut|ter articular, pronunciar, total, absoluto

ut|ter|ance expresión, declaración

ut|ter|ly completamente

U-turn vuelta en U, giro de 180 grados

u

Vv

v. versus

va|can|cy vacante, cuarto disponible

va|cant desocupado, vacío, vacante, ausente, distraído
• **va|cant|ly** distraídamente

va|cant lot baldío

va|ca|tion vacaciones, pasar las vacaciones

va|ca|tion|er persona que está de vacaciones, vacacionista

vac|ci|nate vacunar
• **vac|ci|na|tion** vacunación

vac|cine vacuna

vacu|ole vacuola

vacuum vacío, pasar la aspiradora, aspirar

vacuum clean|er aspiradora

vague vago • **vague|ly** vagamente, ligeramente

vain vano, inútil, vanidoso, presumido • **vain|ly** en vano
▸ **in vain** en vano

vale|dic|to|ri|an alumno que pronuncia el discurso de despedida durante la ceremonia de graduación

va|lence elec|tron electrón de valencia

val|et park|ing servicio de estacionamiento de autos

val|id válido • **va|lid|ity** validez

vali|date validar
• **vali|da|tion** validación

val|ley valle

val|or valentía

valu|able valioso, de valor

valu|ables objetos de valor

value valor, valuar, apreciar, evaluar, valorar, tasar

value scale escala de valores

valve válvula

vam|pire vampiro

van camioneta, vagoneta

van|dal vándalo

van|dal|ism vandalismo

van|dal|ize dañar, estropear

va|nil|la vainilla

van|ish desaparecer

van|ish|ing point punto de (la) vista, punto de fuga

van|ity vanidad

va|por vapor

va|por|ize evaporar(se), vaporizar(se)
• **va|pori|za|tion** evaporación

va|por|iz|er vaporizador

vari|able variable
• **vari|abil|ity** variabilidad

vari|ation variación

var|ied variado

va|ri|ety variedad, variación

va|ri|ety store bazar

var|ious vario

var|sity equipo titular de una secundaria, colegio o universidad en un deporte en particular

vary variar, diferir

vas|cu|lar plant planta vascular

vas de|fe|rens conducto deferente

vase jarrón, florero

vast vasto

vau|de|ville vodevil

VCR grabadora de videocintas

vec|tor vector

veer virar, dar un viraje

veg|eta|bles verduras

veg|etar|ian vegetariano o vegetariana

veg|eta|tion vegetación

veg|eta|tive re|pro|duc|tion *también* **vegetative propagation** reproducción

V

asexual, reproducción vegetativa

veg|gie verduras

ve|hi|cle vehículo, medio

veil velo

vein vena

vel|vet terciopelo

ven|dor vendedor ambulante *o* vendedora ambulante

venge|ance venganza
▸ with a vengeance en sumo grado, de veras, con ganas

Venn dia|gram diagrama de Venn

vent ventilador, ventila, orificio de ventilación, falla volcánica (lava), fumarola (gases o vapores), ventilar, desahogar

ven|ti|late ventilar
• **ven|ti|la|tion** ventilación

ven|tri|cle ventrículo

ven|ture empresa, aventurarse

venue lugar

Ve|nus Venus

verb verbo

ver|bal verbal, oral
• **ver|bal|ly** verbalmente

verb phrase perífrasis verbal, frase verbal

ver|dict veredicto, opinión

verge
▸ on the verge of al borde de
▸ verge on rayar en

veri|fy verificar, confirmar, corroborar • **veri|fi|ca|tion** verificación

ver|sa|tile versátil, de usos múltiples • **ver|sa|til|ity** versatilidad

verse verso, estrofa, versículo

ver|sion versión

ver|sus versus, frente a, contra

ver|te|brate vertebrado

ver|ti|cal vertical, cortado a pico • **ver|ti|cal|ly** verticalmente

very muy, justo, hasta, precisamente
▸ not very no muy/mucho
▸ very much so muchísimo
▸ very well muy bien

vesi|cle vesícula

ves|sel navío, nave, buque

vest chaleco

ves|tig|ial struc|ture *también* **vestigial organ** órgano rudimentario

vet veterinario *o* veterinaria

vet|er|an veterano *o* veterana, ex combatiente

vet|eri|nar|ian veterinario *o* veterinaria

veto vetar, veto

vex irritar, molestar • **vexed** irritado • **vex|ing** irritante

via por, vía, a través de

vi|able viable • **vi|abil|ity** viabilidad

vi|brate vibrar • **vi|bra|tion** vibración

vice vicio

vice ver|sa viceversa

vi|cin|ity vecindad, inmediaciones, alrededores

vi|cious despiadado, cruel
• **vi|cious|ly** brutalmente, cruelmente • **vi|cious|ness** ferocidad

vic|tim víctima

vic|tim|ize tratar injustamente
• **vic|timi|za|tion** discriminación

vic|tor vencedor *o* vencedora

Vic|to|rian victoriano *o* victoriana, conservador, decimonónico

vic|to|ri|ous victorioso, vencedor, triunfante

vic|to|ry victoria

video video

video ar|cade sala recreativa (con videojuegos)

video game videojuego

video|tape *también* **video tape** cinta de video

vie rivalizar, competir

V

view opinión, punto de vista, visión, vista, considerar, ver
▸ **in view of** en vista de
▸ **on view** en exhibición
▸ **with a view to** con miras a, con el propósito de

view|er expectador *o* expectadora, televidente

view|point punto de vista

vig|or vigor, energía, vitalidad

vig|or|ous vigoroso
• **vig|or|ous|ly** vigorosamente

vil|la villa, casa de campo

vil|lage pueblo, aldea

vil|lag|er vecino *o* vecina, aldeano *o* aldeana

vil|lain villano *o* villana

vine vid, parra

vin|egar vinagre

vine|yard viñedo, viña

vin|tage vendimia, cosecha, añejo, clásico, antiguo

vi|nyl vinilo

vio|la viola

vio|late violar, profanar
• **vio|la|tion** violación, profanación

vio|lence violencia

vio|lent violento, intenso, agudo • **vio|lent|ly** violentamente, enérgicamente

vio|let violeta, violáceo, violado

vio|lin violín • **vio|lin|ist** violinista

VIP persona muy importante

vir|gin virgen • **vir|gin|ity** virginidad

vir|tual virtual • **vir|tu|al|ly** virtualmente

vir|tual re|al|ity realidad virtual

vir|tue virtud, ventaja
▸ **by virtue of** en virtud de

vir|tu|ous virtuoso
• **vir|tu|ous|ly** virtuosamente

vi|rus virus

visa visa

vis|cos|ity viscosidad

vis|ible visible, evidente
• **vis|ibly** visiblemente

vi|sion visión, vista

vis|it visitar, visita
▸ **visit with** visitar

vis|ita|tion rights derecho de visita

vis|it|ing hours horario de visitas

vis|it|ing pro|fes|sor profesor visitante *o* profesora visitante

vis|itor visitante

vis|ual visual • **visu|al|ly** visualmente

visu|al|ize imaginar

vis|ual lit|era|cy alfabetismo visual, comprensión visual

vis|ual meta|phor metáfora visual

vi|tal vital, esencial, fundamental • **vi|tal|ly** vitalmente

vita|min vitamina

viv|id vívido, vivo • **viv|id|ly** vívidamente, vivamente

vo|cabu|lary vocabulario, léxico

vo|cal enérgico, vocal, vocálico

vo|cal|ist cantante, vocalista

vo|cal pro|jec|tion proyección vocal

vo|cal qual|ity timbre vocálico

vo|cals letra, voz

vogue moda
▸ **in vogue** de moda

voice voz, expresar

void vacío, nulo, inválido, carente, desprovisto

vola|tile volátil, voluble

vol|ca|no volcán

volley|ball voleibol, volibol

volt voltio

vol|ume volumen

vol|un|tary voluntario, opcional • **vol|un|tar|ily**

voluntariamente, de beneficencia

vol|un|teer voluntario *o* voluntaria, ofrecerse, alistarse como voluntario
▸ **volunteer information** ofrecer información sin que sea solicitada

vom|it vomitar, vómito

vote voto, votación, derecho de voto, votar ● **vot|ing** votación ● **vot|er** votante

vouch|er vale

vow jurar, promesa solemne

vow|el vocal

voy|age viaje, travesía

vs. contra

vul|ner|able vulnerable ● **vul|ner|abil|ity** vulnerabilidad

V

Ww

wage salario, hacer

wag|on carro, carromato, carreta

waist cintura

wait aguardar, esperar
- **wait|ing** que espera, espera
  ▸ **can't wait/can hardly wait** no ver la hora de
  ▸ **wait around** esperar a, esperar para

wait|er mesero, camarero

wait|ress mesera, camarera

wait|staff meseros, camareros

wake despertar(se), estela, velorio, secuela, resultado

walk caminar, escoltar, acompañar, paseo, caminata, paso, marcha
- **walk|out** suspensión, paro de labores
  ▸ **walk off with** llevarse
  ▸ **walk out** abandonar

wall muro, pared, muralla

wall cloud muralla de nubes

wall|let cartera, billetera

wall|paper papel tapiz, imagen de fondo, empapelar

wal|nut nuez, nuez de Castilla

wan|der deambular, vagar, pasear, alejarse, dejar vagar la imaginación, distraerse, divagar, paseo

want querer, deber, buscar
- **want|ed** buscado
  ▸ **for want of** a falta de, por falta de

want ad anuncio clasificado

war guerra

ward sala
  ▸ **ward off** proteger(se)

ward|robe guardarropa, vestuario, armario, ropero

ware|house depósito, bodega, almacén

war|fare guerra, contienda, conflicto

warm tibio, templado, caliente, cálido, cariñoso, afectuoso, calentar, simpatizar
- **warm|ly** calurosamente, cariñosamente • **warm-up** ejercicio de calentamiento, calentarse
  ▸ **warm up** calentar(se), prepararse

warm-blooded de sangre caliente

warmth calor

warn advertir

warn|ing advertencia, aviso

war|rant justificar, orden

war|ri|or guerrero o guerrera

war|ship buque de guerra

war|time tiempo de guerra, de la guerra

wary cauteloso, precavido
- **wari|ly** cautelosamente

was ver be

wash lavar(se), bañar
  ▸ **be in the wash** estar algo sucio, lavándose o recién lavado
  ▸ **wash away** arrasar, llevarse
  ▸ **wash down with (a drink)** acompañar la comida con (un líquido)
  ▸ **wash up** lavarse
  ▸ **be washed up** ser traído, llevado o arrastrado por la corriente

wash|cloth toallita para lavarse, paño para lavarse

wash|er arandela, rondana, roldana, lavadora

wasn't = was not

waste desperdiciar, perder, gastar, desperdicio, pérdida,

desecho
▸ **waste away** consumirse
waste|basket cesto de papeles, papelera, basurero
watch observar, mirar, ver, tener cuidado
▸ **keep watch** hacer guardia, vigilar, alerta, reloj de pulsera, reloj de pulso, reloj de bolsillo
▸ **watch it** tener cuidado
▸ **watch for** o **watch out for** estar atento a
▸ **watch out** tener cuidado
wa|ter agua, regar, llenarse (los ojos) de lágrimas, llorar (los ojos), hacerse agua (la boca)
▸ **water down** diluir, suavizar, atenuar
wa|ter cool|er enfriador de agua, bebedero (de agua refrigerada)
wa|ter cy|cle ciclo del agua
wa|ter pow|er *también* **waterpower** energía hidráulica, fuerza hidráulica, energía hidroeléctrica
water|proof impermeable
water|spout tromba marina, manga, torbellino
wa|ter ta|ble nivel freático
wa|ter va|por vapor de agua
wa|ter vas|cu|lar sys|tem sistema acuovascular
wa|ter wave ola
waterwheel *también* **water wheel** rueda hidráulica, noria
wave agitar, saludar, hacer señas para que alguien se vaya, ondear, gesto, ola, oleada
wave height altura de las olas
wave|length longitud de onda, frecuencia
▸ **on the same wavelength** estar en sintonía
wave pe|ri|od período de onda

wave speed velocidad de onda
wavy ondulado
wax cera
wax pa|per papel encerado, papel de cera
way manera, modo, sentido, costumbre, hábito, paso, camino, dirección
▸ **a long way/quite a way** lejano, alejado, lejos
▸ **by the way** por cierto
▸ **can't have it both ways** tener que decidirse
▸ **every/any which way** en todos sentidos
▸ **get/have one's (own) way** salirse con la suya
▸ **give way to** dar paso
▸ **give way** ceder
▸ **in a way** en cierto sentido
▸ **get in the way** interponerse
▸ **make way** ceder el lugar
▸ **go out of one's way** hacer todo lo que se puede
▸ **keep/stay out of somebody's way** no interponerse
▸ **be out of the way** quitarse de encima
▸ **other way round** por el otro lado
▸ **right way up** boca arriba
▸ **way too (long/much etc.)** demasiado
way of life estilo de vida
we nosotros o nosotras
weak débil, pobre, poco convincente, aguado
• **weak|ly** débilmente
weak|en debilitar(se), flaquear
weak|ness debilidad
wealth riqueza, abundancia
wealthy rico, acaudalado, adinerado
▸ **the rich** los ricos
weap|on arma
weap|ons of mass de|struc|tion armas de destrucción masiva
wear usar, vestir, llevar,

desgastarse, ropa, uso, desgaste
▶ **wear away** desgastarse
▶ **wear down** erosionar, desgastar, cansar
▶ **wear off** pasar
▶ **wear out** agotarse, acabarse

wea|ry cansado, agotado, exhausto

weath|er clima, tiempo, erosionar(se), desgastar(se), capear, sobrellevar

weath|er fore|cast pronóstico del tiempo

weath|er|ing erosión

weath|er map mapa climatológico

weave tejer • **weav|er** tejedor o tejedora • **weav|ing** tejido
▶ **weave one's way** zigzaguear

web red, maraña, telaraña
▶ **the Web** la red

web|cam también **Webcam** cámara

web|log bitácora en la red, blog • **web|log|ger** que participa en blogs de internet • **web|log|ging** bitácora en línea

web|master administrador o administradora de un sitio de la red

web page también **Web page** página (de un sitio de internet), página web

web|site también **Web site**, **web site** sitio de internet, sitio web

wed|ding boda

wedge cuña, calza, calce, rebanada, tajada, calzar, meter, tapar

Wednes|day miércoles

weed mala hierba, maleza, escardar, deshierbar
▶ **weed out** eliminar

week semana
▶ **working week** semana laboral

▶ **during the week** entre semana

week|day día entre semana

week|end fin de semana

week|ly semanal, semanalmente, semanario

weep llorar

weigh pesar(se), sopesar
▶ **weigh down** agobiar

weight peso • **weights** pesas
▶ **lose weight** bajar de peso
▶ **gain/put on weight** subir de peso
▶ **pull one's weight** poner de su parte

weight train|ing hacer pesas

weird raro, extraño

wel|come dar la bienvenida, acoger, bienvenida, bienvenido, alegrarse
▶ **make welcome** acoger
▶ **you're welcome** de nada, no hay de qué

wel|fare bienestar, asistencia social, prestaciones sociales

well bueno, vaya, este, bien, mejor, mucho, bastante, pozo, brotar, manar
▶ **oh well** bueno
▶ **as well** también
▶ **as well as** tanto...como
▶ **be just as well** qué mejor
▶ **may/might as well** bien se podría

well-being bienestar

well-intentioned también **well intentioned** bienintencionado, que tiene buenas intenciones

well-known bien conocido

well-off adinerado

well-to-do adinerado

well-traveled que ha viajado mucho, que ha visto mucho mundo

went ver go

wept ver weep

were ver be

weren't = were not

west también **West** poniente,

W

oeste, viento poniente, Occidente

west|ern *también* **Western** occidental, novela/película de vaqueros, novela/película del oeste

west|ern|er *también* **Westerner** occidental

west|ward hacia el poniente, hacia el oeste, poniente, oeste

wet mojado, humedecer, lluvioso, fresco
  ▸ **wet oneself/the bed** orinarse, mojar (la cama)

wet|land tierra pantanosa, humedal

we've = we have

whale ballena

wharf muelle, embarcadero

what qué, lo que
  ▸ **what about...** qué tal ...
  ▸ **what if...** y si no ...

what|ev|er lo que, sin importar, independientemente de, no importa, sea lo que fuere

what's = what is o what has

what|so|ev|er en absoluto, absolutamente

wheat trigo

wheel rueda, volante, dirigir, conducir, enfilar

wheel|barrow carretilla

wheel|chair silla de ruedas

when cuándo, cuando, si

when|ever siempre que, cuando

where dónde, donde, en que

where|as mientras que

where|by conforme a

wher|ever dondequiera, en cualquier parte

wheth|er si, ya sea que

which cuál, qué, que, lo que, cuyo

while mientras, mientras que, aunque, rato, poco (tiempo)
  ▸ **while away** matar el tiempo, pasar el rato,

entretenerse

whip látigo, azotar, fustigar, batir ● **whip|ping** tunda, paliza, zurra
  ▸ **whip out** sacar rápidamente/a todo prisa
  ▸ **whip up** excitar

whisk llevar rápidamente, batir, batidor, batidora

whis|key whisky

whis|ky whisky

whis|per susurrar, murmurar, susurro, murmullo

whis|tle silbar, chiflar, pitar, aullar, silbato

whistle-blowing *también* **whistleblowing** denuncia

white blanco, clara (de huevo), blanco (del ojo)

white blood cell glóbulo blanco

white|cap cabrilla, borrego

white-collar *también* **white collar** oficinista, empleado de oficina

white dwarf enana blanca

White House Casa Blanca

white light luz blanca

White Pages sección blanca

whiz *también* **whizz** zumbar

whiz kid fenómeno, prodigio, niño prodigio

who quién, que

WHO OMS

who'd = who had o who would

who|ever quienquiera, quien uno quiera

whole todo, entero, totalidad, totalmente
  ▸ **as a whole** en conjunto, en general
  ▸ **on the whole** en general

whole note redonda, semibreve

whole|sale al por mayor, al mayoreo, general

whole|wheat *también* **whole wheat** de trigo entero, integral, pan integral,

W

harina de trigo entero, harina de trigo integral

who'll = who will o who shall

whol|ly totalmente, completamente

whom a quién, quién, quien

whoop|ing crane grulla americana

who's = who is o who has

whose cuyo, de quién

who've = who have

why por qué, vaya

wick|ed malvado, perverso, vil • **wickedness** iniquidad

wide ancho, amplio, ampliamente • **wide|ly** ampliamente
▸ **wider issues** cuestiones más importantes

wid|en ampliar, ensanchar, extender

wide|screen de pantalla ancha

wide|spread generalizado

wid|ow viuda

width ancho, anchura

wie|ner *también* **weenie**, **wienie** salchicha de Viena, salchicha de Frankfurt

wife esposa

wig peluca

wild salvaje, silvestre, montés, loco • **wild|ly** a rabiar, aventuradamente
▸ **wild guess** suposición aventurada
▸ **the wilds** región silvestre

wil|der|ness desierto, páramo, soledad

wild|life vida silvestre

wild|ly disparatadamente

will querer, desear, voluntad, deseo, intención, testamento

will|ing dispuesto • **willingly** con gusto • **willingness** disposición

win ganar, lograr, triunfo
▸ **win over** convencer

wind viento, energía eólica, dejar sin aliento, cortar la respiración, serpentear, enrollar, dar cuerda
▸ **wind down** reducir paulatinamente
▸ **wind up** poner fin a, concluir

wind chill fac|tor *también* **wind-chill factor**, **windchill factor** factor de sensación térmica

win|dow ventana, recuadro

win|dow shade visillo, cortinilla

wind|shield parabrisas

wind|shield wip|er limpiaparabrisas

wind|sock *también* **wind sock** manga cataviento, manga de viento, cono de viento

wind vane veleta

windy ventoso

wine vino

win|ery bodega, vinería

wing ala, alerón, bastidor

wink parpadear, guiñar el ojo, guiño

win|ner ganador o ganadora

win|ning ganador, encantador

win|ter invierno

wipe limpiar(se), limpieza, limpiada
▸ **wipe out** exterminar, aniquilar

wire alambre

wired nervioso

wire|less inalámbrico

wis|dom sabiduría, prudencia

wise sabio, prudente • **wise|ly** prudentemente

wish deseo, saludo, desear, querer

wit ingenio, agudeza

witch bruja o brujo

witch hunt caza de brujas

with con, de

with|draw retirar(se), sacar

with|draw|al retiro, abandono

with|drew *ver* withdraw

W

with|hold retener, ocultar

with|in dentro, en, adentro, a, antes de
▶ **within sight** a la vista

with|out sin

wit|ness testigo, presenciar, atestiguar

wit|ness stand estrado de los testigos

wit|ty ingenioso

wives ver wife

wiz|ard mago, brujo

WMD abreviatura de weapons of mass destruction

wolf lobo, devorar, engullir(se)

wom|an mujer

wom|en's room baño de damas, baño de mujeres

wom|en's shel|ter refugio para mujeres maltratadas

won ver win

won|der preguntarse, asombrarse, milagro, maravilla
▶ **no/little/small wonder** no ser de extrañar
▶ **work/do wonders** hacer maravillas

won|der|ful maravilloso, estupendo • **won|der|ful|ly** de maravilla

won't = will not

woo atraer

wood madera, bosque

wood|en de madera

wood|land bosque

woods|man también **woodman** leñador

wool lana

word palabra, expresar(se)
• **-worded** redactado
▶ **give your word** prometer
▶ **have a word with** hablar con, tener una conversación con
▶ **offer a word of (warning/advice/praise/thanks)** tener algo importante que decir

▶ **have the last word/the final word** decir la última palabra
▶ **in other words** en otras palabras
▶ **word for word** palabra por palabra
▶ **word of** información, noticias de

word pro|cess|ing también **word-processing** tratamiento de textos, procesamiento de textos

word rec|og|ni|tion reconocimiento de palabras

work trabajar, funcionar, surtir efecto, operar, manejar, manipular, trabajo, obra • **worked up** furioso
▶ **work your way somewhere** abrirse camino
▶ **work off** desahogarse
▶ **work out** encontrar, salir, resultar, hacer ejercicio, entrenar
▶ **work up** ponerse, reunir

work|day también **work day** jornada

work|er trabajador o trabajadora, obrero u obrera, operador u operadora

work|force fuerza laboral, potencial de mano de obra, personal, planta laboral

work|ing que trabaja, empleado, funcionamiento
▶ **working life** vida activa, vida laboral, vida de trabajo

work|ing class clase obrera, clase trabajadora, de clase obrera

work in|put carga de trabajo

work|out sesión de ejercicio

work out|put rendimiento

work|place también **work place** lugar de trabajo

work|shop taller

work|station también **work station** lugar de trabajo, estación de trabajo

work week semana laboral

W

world mundo, mundial
▶ **have the best of both worlds** tener todas las ventajas
▶ **the outside world** el mundo exterior
World Health Or|gani|za|tion OMS, Organización Mundial de la Salud
world war guerra mundial
world|wide en todo el mundo
World Wide Web la red mundial, Internet, WWW
worm gusano
worn *ver* wear, desgastado
worn out *también* worn-out desgastado, agotado, exhausto
wor|ri|some preocupante
wor|ry preocupar(se), preocupación ● **wor|ried** preocupado
worse peor
▶ **change for the worse** empeorar, cambiar para mal
wors|en empeorar
wor|ship adorar, venerar, rendir culto, culto
● **wor|ship|er** adorador *o* adoradora, devoto *o* devota
worst peor
▶ **the worst** lo peor
▶ **at (the) worst** en el peor de los casos
▶ **at one's worst** en su peor momento
worst-case el peor de los casos
worth
▶ **be worth** valer
▶ **worth (of)** por un valor de
▶ **be worth it** *o* **be worth somebody's while** valer la pena
worth|less sin (ningún) valor

worth|while que vale la pena
wor|thy digno
would forma modal para formar el potencial de los verbos
would-be supuesto, pretendido, aspirante
wouldn't = would not
would've = would have
wound *ver* wind, herida, herir
wrap envolver(se)
▶ **wrap up** abrigarse, dar por terminado
wrap|per envoltura
wreck destrozar, naufragio
wrench arrebatar, llave, llave de tuercas, torcer(se), dislocar(se)
wres|tle batallar, lidiar, luchar
wrin|kle arruga, arrugar(se), fruncir ● **wrin|kled** arrugado
wrist muñeca
write escribir, hacer, llenar
▶ **write down** anotar
▶ **write in** escribir
▶ **write into** incluir
▶ **write off** dar por perdido, descartar
▶ **write up** describir, redactar un informe
writ|er escritor *o* escritora, autor *o* autora
writ|ing escrito, estilo, escritura, letra, escribir
writ|ten *ver* write, escrito, tácito
wrong mal, malo, equivocado, incorrecto ● **wrong|ly** equivocadamente
▶ **go wrong** ir mal
▶ **in the wrong** obrar mal
wrote *ver* write
WWW WWW, World Wide Web, red de redes

Xx

X-rated sólo para adultos
X-ray *también* **x-ray** rayo-X, radiografía, hacer una radiografía, radiografiar
xy|lem xilema

Yy

yad|da *también* **yada** bla-bla-bla
y'all = you all
yam ñame, camote
yang yang
Yan|kee yanqui
yard yarda, patio, patio (ferrocarriles), taller (industrial), astillero (naval), jardín
yard|age medida en yardas, longitud en yardas
yard sale bazar casero, venta de garaje
yarn hilo, estambre
yawn bostezar, bostezo
yeah sí
year año
  ▸ **all year round** todo el año
  ▸ **financial/business year** año fiscal
  ▸ **school/academic year** año escolar/académico
yeast levadura
yell gritar, grito
yel|low amarillo
yel|low card tarjeta amarilla, tarjeta de amonestación
yen yen
yes sí
yes|ter|day ayer

yet todavía, aún, sin embargo
yield ceder, ceder el paso, producir
yin *también* **ying** yin
yip aullar, aullido
yo|gurt *también* **yoghurt** yogur, yogurt
yolk yema
you tú, usted(es), vos, te, lo, la, los, las, le, les, ti, usted(es)
young joven, tierno, cría, hijuelo
  ▸ **the young** los jóvenes
young|ster joven, niño *o* niña, chico *o* chica, muchacho *o* muchacha
your tu, su, tus, sus
yours tuyo, tuya, tuyos, tuyas, suyo, suyos, suya, suyas, de usted, de ustedes, atentamente
your|self tú mismo *o* tú misma, usted mismo *o* usted misma, ustedes mismos
youth juventud, joven
yuck *también* **yuk** fuchi, guácala, guácatelas
yucky asqueroso

ZZ

zero cero, nada, nulo

zeros of a function *también* **zeroes of a function** raíz de una función, cero de una función

zig|zag *también* **zig-zag** zigzag, zigzaguear

zinc zinc, cinc

zip code código postal

zip|per cierre (de cremallera), zíper

zone zona, dividir en zonas, zonificar • **zon|ing** zonificación

zoo zoológico

zoom ir como bólido, pasar volando
▶ **zoom in** acercar

zoo|plank|ton zooplancton

zuc|chi|ni calabacita, calabacín

zy|gote zigoto

Spanish-English

A

a: at, by, on, onto, to, within
a bordo: aboard, on board
a cambio de: in exchange for
a causa de: because of
a ciencia cierta: for certain
a condición de: on condition that
a corto plazo: in the short term
a costa de: at a/the cost of
a cuadros: check, checked
a de J.C.: BC
a diario: daily
a diferencia de: as opposed to, by contrast/ in contrast to, unlike
a distancia: at/from a distance
a distancia de la costa: offshore
a doble espacio: double-spaced
a escala: model
a escala federal: federally
a escala nacional: nationally, nationwide
a ese respecto: on that/ this score
a falta de: for want of, in the absence of
a favor: in favor
a favor de: for
a fin de cuentas: on balance
a final de cuentas: overall
a flote: afloat
a fondo: in-depth
a la inglesa: rare
a la larga: eventually, in the long run
a la manera de: like
a la mano: at hand, handy, on hand, ready
a la medida: made to order
a la mitad: halfway
a la moda: à la mode, cool, fashionable, fashionably, in
à la mode: à la mode
a la vanguardia: cutting edge
a la venta: on sale, on the market, out
a la vez: at the same time
a la vista: in/within sight, on sight, within sight
a la vuelta: around
a largo plazo: in the long term
a las brasas: charbroiled
a lo largo: along
a lo largo de: along, over, up
a lo lejos: beyond, far off
a mano: by hand
a manos llenas: freely
a más de: far
a más no poder: be (bored/worried/scared

etc.) stiff
a más tardar: at the latest
a medio: halfway
a menos que: otherwise, unless
a menudo: often
a merced de: at the mercy of
a mí: me
a mí misma: myself
a mí mismo: myself
a nivel: level
a nombre de: in somebody's name/in the name of somebody
a partir de: as, from
a pesar de: against, despite, in spite of, regardless of
a pesar de todo: against all odds
a petición de alguien: at somebody's request/ at the request of somebody
a pie: on foot
a plazos: by installments
a plena luz del día: in broad daylight
a poca distancia de: off
a primera vista: at first glance
a principios: earlier
a profundidad: intimately
a propósito: deliberate, incidentally, on purpose
a prueba de balas: bulletproof
a punta de pistola: at gunpoint
a punto: as good as, ready
a punto de: about, around/round the corner, near, on the brink of, on the point of
a qué distancia: how far
a quién: whom
a rabiar: wildly
a regañadientes: grudging, grudgingly
a reserva de: pending
a saber: namely
a sabiendas: knowingly
a salto de mata: flight
a salvo: safe
a salvo de: safe from
a sangre fría: in cold blood
a sí misma: themselves
a sí mismo: itself, themselves
a simple vista: to the naked eye
a solas: alone, solo
a solicitud: on demand, on request
a su debido tiempo: in due course
a su disposición: at one's disposal
a sueldo: paid
a tiempo: in/on time
a toda costa: at all costs
a toda mecha: lickety-split
a toda velocidad: flat out
a todas partes: around,

everywhere
a todo dar: neat
a todo vapor: flat out
a todos lados: everywhere
a través: across, through
a través de: from, through, via
a través de terceros: secondhand
a través del país: cross-country
a ultima hora: last minute
a últimas fechas: lately
a un lado: aside
a un tiempo: together
a veces: sometimes
a vencer o morir: do-or-die
A.M.: AM
a.m.: a.m.
A/C (aire acondicionado): a/c
abadía: abbey
abajo: below, beneath, down, downstairs
abalanzarse: charge, dive
abandonado: abandoned, neglected
abandonar: abandon, back out, desert, drop, drop out, give up, leave, leave behind, neglect, scrap, turn off, walk out
abandono: abandonment, desertion, neglect, withdrawal
abanicar(se): fan
abanico: fan
abanico aluvial: alluvial fan
abarcar: embrace, include, juggle, span
abarrotado: crowded, packed
abarrotar: jam
abarrotes: grocery
abastecedor: supplier
abastecedora: supplier
abastecer: supply
abastecerse: stock up
abatir: recline, shoot down, strike down
ABC: ABC's
abdomen: abdomen
abdominal: abdominal
abecedario: ABC's
abeja: bee
abejorro: bumblebee
abertura: gap, opening, slit
abiertamente: openly, outright
abierto: free, open, out
abigeo: rustler
abiótico: abiotic
abismo: gulf, split
ablandar: soften
abofetear: slap
abogacía: bar, law
abogada: advocate, attorney, barrister, counselor, defender, lawyer, solicitor
abogada de oficio: public defender

abogado: advocate, attorney, barrister, counselor, defender, lawyer, solicitor

abogado de oficio: public defender

abogar: defend

abogar por: advocate, champion

abolición: abolition

abolir: abolish, strike down

abolladura: dent

abollar: dent

abono: subscription

abordar: approach, attack, board, go about, tackle

aborto: abortion

aborto espontáneo: miscarriage

aborto no provocado: miscarriage

abotonar: button, do up

abrasión: abrasion

abrazadera: band, clamp

abrazar(se): embrace

abrazo: embrace, hug

abrevadero: trough

abreviar: abbreviate, shorten

abreviatura: abbreviation

abridor: opener

abrigar: nurse

abrigarse: wrap up

abrigo: coat, overcoat

abril: April

abrir(se): fragment, open, open out, open up, part, set up, start, start up, undo

abrir (algo cerrado con llave): unlock

abrir (mariscos): shuck

abrir el cierre/la cremallera: unzip

abrir la llave: run (water/faucet/bath)

abrir la puerta: answer the door

abrir las cartas: give the game away

abrir un hueco: blast

abrir un túnel: tunnel

abrirle al agua: run (water/faucet/bath)

abrirse camino: thread, to work your way somewhere

abrirse camino a: fight one's way to/through

abrirse de golpe: spring

abrirse paso: maneuver, thread

abrirse paso a empujones: barge into/through, push your way through

abrirse paso a golpes: smash

abrirse paso con dificultad: scramble

abrirse paso con los codos: barge into/through

abrirse paso entre: fight one's way to/through

abrochar(se): buckle, button, do up, fasten

abrocharse el cinturón: buckle up

abrogar: strike down

abrumado: overwhelmed

abrumador: overwhelming

abrumadoramente: overwhelmingly

abrumar: overcome, overwhelm

abrumar(se): swamp

abruptamente: abruptly, steeply

abrupto: abrupt, steep

absolutamente: a hundred percent/one hundred percent, absolutely, whatsoever

absoluto: absolute, complete, dead, implicit, utter

absolver: acquit, clear

absorbente: consuming

absorber: absorb, soak up

absorción: absorption, takeover

abstemia: teetotaler

abstemio: teetotaler

abstenerse: refrain

abstracto: abstract, nonobjective

absurdamente: absurdly

absurdo: absurd, irrational

abucheo: Bronx cheer

abuela: grandmother, grandparent

abuelita: grandma, granny

abuelito: granddad, grandpa

abuelo: grandfather, grandparent

abundancia: bundle, mass, wealth

abundante: abundant, ample, healthy, hearty, high, large, liberal

abundantemente: heartily

abundar: enlarge

aburrida: bore

aburrido: bore, bored, boring, dull, tedious, tired

aburrimiento: boredom

aburrir: bore

aburrirse: tire

abusar de: abuse

abusar sexualmente (de alguien): molest

abusivo: abusive

abuso: abuse

abuso de sustancias: substance abuse

acá: over here

acabado: finish, finished, over

acabado en punta: pointed

acabar(se): be out of something, complete, end, end up, finalize, finish, finish off, run

out, shake out, use up, wear out

acabar con: eliminate, kill

acabar de: have just, only just

academia: academy

académicamente: academically

académico: academic

acallar: crush

acaloradamente: heatedly

acalorado: heated

acampar: camp

acantilado: cliff

acaparar: corner, hog

acariciar: pet, stroke

acarrear: incur, transport

acarreo glacial: till

acaso: maybe

acatar: conform

acaudalado: wealthy

acceder: give in

acceder a: access

accesibilidad: accessibility

accesible: accessible

accesible (económicamente): affordable

acceso: access, approach, entry

accesorio: accessory, attachment, auxiliary, fitting

accesorios: accessory, fittings

accidentado: hilly, uneven

accidental: accidental

accidentalmente: accidentally, by accident

accidente: accident

accidente automovilístico: crack-up

accidente geográfico: landform

acción: act, action, deed, share, stock

acción afirmativa: affirmative action

acción creciente: rising action

acción refleja: reflex (action)

accionar un interruptor: flick a switch

acciones ordinarias: common stock

accionista: shareholder, stockholder

acechar: stalk

acedo: sour

aceitar: oil

aceite: oil

aceite de oliva: olive oil

aceituna: olive

aceitunado: olive

aceleración: acceleration

aceleración centrípeta: centripetal acceleration

aceleración negativa: negative acceleration

aceleración positiva: positive acceleration

acelerador: accelerator, gas pedal
acelerar: accelerate, rush, step on the gas, up
acelerarse: speed up
acento: accent, emphasis, stress
acentuar: stress
acepción: meaning
aceptabilidad: acceptability, adequacy
aceptable: acceptable, reasonable, respectable
aceptablemente: reasonably
aceptación: acceptance, embrace, recognition
aceptado: accepted
aceptar: accept, come around, come to terms with, consent, embrace, meet, take, take on
aceptar el reto: rise to the challenge
aceptar inmediatemente: jump at
acequible: accessible
acera: curb, sidewalk
acerca de: about, concerning
acercamiento: approach
acercar(se): approach, be closing on, come up, draw, edge, zoom in
acería: mill
acero: iron, steel
acero inoxidable: stainless steel
acertar algo: put one's finger on something
acertijo: puzzle, riddle
achú: achoo
acicatear: spur
acidez: acidity
ácido: acid, sharp, sour
ácido nucleico: nucleic acid
aclamación: acclaim
aclamar: acclaim, cheer
aclaración: clarification
aclarar: clarify, clear, illustrate, shed/throw/cast light on , sort out, straighten out, unravel
aclararse: fall/click/fit into place
aclararse la garganta: clear one's throat
aclimatación: acclimation
aclimatar(se): acclimate
acné: acne
acobardarse: chicken out
acogedor: cozy, homey
acoger: foster, greet, make welcome, receive, take in, welcome
acogida: reception
acolchado: padded
acolchar: quilting
acomodador: usher
acomodadora: usher
acomodar: fit in, put
acomodar en capas: layer

acompañamiento: side
acompañante: escort
acompañar: accompany, escort, go with, join, show, usher, walk
acompañar a alguien: keep somebody company
acompañar la comida con (un líquido): wash down with (a drink)
acondicionamiento del aire: air-conditioning
aconsejar: advise, counsel, preach, recommend
acontecimiento: development
acontecimiento importante: landmark
acontecimiento sin precedentes: first
acopio: stockpile
acoplarse: dock
acorazado: battleship
acordar: set
acordar de: remind
acordarse de: remember
acorde: chord
acorde perfecto: triad
acorralar: corner, corral, hunt down, keep/hold at bay, pen
acortar: cut down, shorten
acosador: bully, stalker
acosadora: bully, stalker
acosar: bully, hound, pester, stalk
acoso: bullying
acostarse: lie, lie down
acostarse temprano/tarde: have an early/late night
acostumbrarse a: get used to
acotamiento: shoulder
acre: acre
acrecentar: heighten
acreditación: proof
acreedor: creditor
acreedora: creditor
acribillar: pepper
acribillar a preguntas: grill
acrónimo: acronym
acta: certificate
actitud: attitude, manner, outlook
actitud para darse tono: show
activamente: actively
activar: activate
activarse: go off
actividad: activity, pursuit
actividad suplementaria: sideline
actividades: activity, movement
activista: activist
activo: active, alive
activos: asset
acto: act, deed
acto de sujetar algo con fuerza: grip
acto reflejo: reflex (action)

acto sexual: intercourse
actor: actor, performer
actriz: actor, actress, performer
actuación: acting
actual: contemporary, current, going, present
actualización: upgrade
actualizado: running
actualmente: currently, nowadays, today
actuar: act, behave, feature, perform, play
actuar como mediador: mediate
actuar de manera distinta: react
actuar por su propia cuenta: strike out
acuchillar: knife, slash, stab
acuclillarse: crouch
acudir a: turn
acudir en apoyo de: rally around
acudir en tropel: flock
acuerdo: accord, agreement, deal, settlement, treaty, understanding
acuerdo prenupcial: prenup, prenuptial agreement
acuífero: aquifer
acumulación: accumulation, build-up
acumular(se): accumulate, add up, collect, gather, gather up, heap, mount, pile up, run up
acunar: cradle
acuñación: minting
acuñar: coin, mint
acurrucarse: curl up
acusación: accusation, allegation, charge
acusada: accused, defendant
acusado: accused, defendant
acusar: accuse, level, point the finger at
acusar recibo de: acknowledge
acústica: acoustics
acústico: acoustic
ad hominem: ad hominem
adaptación: adaptation
adaptar(se): acclimate, adapt, adjust, settle in, tailor, take to
adecuadamente: appropriately, aptly, fittingly, properly, securely, suitably
adecuado: adequate, all right, appropriate, apt, fit, fitting, proper, right, suitable, suited
adecuado para: equal to
adelantado: ahead, ahead of/before one's time, fast, forward
adelantar: advance, be getting somewhere, bring forward, further

adelante: after you, ahead, forward, in front, onward
adelante de: ahead of
adelgazar: lose weight, slim down
ademán: gesture, motion
además: besides, furthermore, in addition, moreover, too
además de: apart from, aside from, on top of
además de eso: if nothing else
adenina: adenine
adentrarse: make inroads
adentro: in, indoor, indoors, inside, within
adentro de la tienda: in-store
aderezar: season
aderezo: dressing
adeudar: owe
adherirse: bond, stick
adhesivo: adhesive
adicción: addiction
adición: addition
adicional: additional, auxiliary, extra, fresh, further, spare, subsidiary
adicta: addicted
adictivo: addictive
adicto: addict, addicted
adinerado: wealthy, well-off, well-to-do
adiós: bye, goodbye
aditamentos: fittings, fixtures
aditivo: additive
adivinanza: puzzle, riddle
adivinar: guess
adjetivo: adjective
adjuntar: attach, enclose
administración: administration, management
Administración de la Seguridad y Salud Ocupacionales: OSHA
administración pública: civil service
administrador(a): administrator, manager
administrador(a) de un sitio de la red: webmaster
administrador(a) financiero: fund manager
administrar: administer, manage
administrativo: administrative, ministerial
admirable: admirable, impressive, remarkable
admirablemente: admirably, impressively
admiración: admiration
admirador: admirer, fan
admiradora: admirer, fan

admiradoras: fan base
admiradores: fan base
admirar: admire, look up to
admisible: acceptable
admisión: admission
admitir: acknowledge, admit, own up, stand up
ADN: DNA
ADN recombinante: recombinant DNA
adobo: pickle
adolescencia: adolescence, teen
adolescente: adolescent, teen, teenage, teenager
adolorido: painful, sore
adopción: adoption, embrace
adoptar: adopt, assimilate, assume, cultivate, embrace, take on
adoptar una actitud firme: make/take a stand
adorable: lovely
adoración: adoration
adorador: worshiper
adoradora: worshiper
adorar: adore, worship
adormecerse: doze off
adormecido: numb
adormilado: sleepy
adornar: decorate, grace, trim
adorno: decoration, trim
adquirir: acquire, gain, pick up, purchase, take on
adquirir propiedad accionaria: buy into
adquisición: acquisition, purchase, takeover
adrede: deliberate
aduana: customs
aducir: plead
adueñarse: take
adular: flatter
adulta: adult, grown-up
adulterar: doctor
adulto: adult, grown, grown-up, mature
advenedizo: upstart
adverbio: adverb
adversamente: adversely
adversario: opponent
adverso: adverse, ill
advertencia: advisory, caution, warning
advertir: caution, detect, warn
aéreo: aerial, airborne
aerobics: aerobics
aerófono: aerophone
aerolínea: airline
aeronave: aircraft
aeroplano: airplane
aeropuerto: airport
aerosol: spray
aerotransportado: airborne
afabilidad: friendliness
afanador: cleaner
afanadora: cleaner
afección: complaint, condition, disorder

afectado: artificial, stiff, theatrical
afectar: affect, bite, disrupt, erode, get, hit, impact, interfere with, make inroads, shake, strike, tell, touch
afecto: affection
afectuoso: caring, loving, warm
afeitada: shave
afelio: aphelion
aferrar(se): claw, cling, hang on, hold on
afianzar: clamp
afición: fondness
aficionada: amateur, enthusiast, fan, fanatic, lover
aficionado: amateur, enthusiast, fan, fanatic, fanatical, lover
aficionarse: take to
afídido: aphid
áfido: aphid
afijo: affix
afilado: sharp
afilar: sharpen
afiliación: affiliation, membership
afiliarse a: join
afiliarse con: affiliate
afinado/desafinado: in tune/out of tune
afinar: fine-tune, tune
afinidad: sympathy
afirmación: affirmation, assertion, claim, statement
afirmar: affirm, assert, claim, contend, maintain
aflicción: distress
afligido: distressed, pained
afligir: distress, trouble
aflojar: cough up, ease up, relax
aflojar(se): loosen
afloramiento: upwelling
aflujo: runoff
afortunadamente: fortunately, happily
afortunado: fortunate, lucky
afrenta: offense
africana: African
africano: African
afroamericana: African-American
afroamericano: African-American
afrocaribeña: African-Caribbean
afrocaribeño: African-Caribbean
afrontar: brave, cope
afuera: back, outdoors, outside
afuera de: outside
agachar: flattenbastid
agacharse: bend, crouch, duck, get down, hunker down
agallas: gut
agarrado: cheap
agarrar: grab, grasp, grip, rope in, seize, stab

agarrar algo: get/grab hold of (something)

agarrar con fuerza: clutch

agarrarla con: pick on

agarrarle la onda (a algo): get the hang of something

agarrotarse: seize up

agasajar: entertain

agasajarse: feast

agasajo: treat

agazaparse: crouch

agencia: agency, branch

agencia de cobro: collection agency

agencia de distribución de publicaciones: syndicate

agencia de impuestos interiores estadounidense: Internal Revenue Service

agencia de noticias: news agency

agencia de publicidad: ad agency

agencia de viajes: travel agency

agenda: calendar

agenda electrónica: PDA

agente: agent, officer

agente comercial: rep

agente de policía: constable, trooper

agente inmobiliario: real estate

agente legal: attorney

agente libre: free agent

agente secreto: operative

agentes del FBI: feds

agentes federales: feds

ágil: agile

agilidad: agility

agitación: ferment, fuss, trouble, turmoil, upheaval

agitadamente: excitedly

agitar: shake, wave

agitar(se): flap

agitarse: stir

aglomeración: crush

aglomerarse: crowd, swarm

agobiado: stricken

agobiar: burden, weigh down

agonía: agony

agonizante: dying

agosto: August

agotado: booked up/ fully booked/booked solid, depleted, drained, frazzled, weary, worn out

agotador: draining, exhausting, tiring

agotamiento: exhaustion

agotar: deplete, drain, exhaust, stretch

agotarse: be out of something, dry up, peter out, run out, sell out, wear out

agradable: delightful, enjoyable, pleasant, pleasing, sweetly

agradablemente: pleasantly, pleasingly

agradar: please

agradecer: appreciate, thank

agradecido: grateful, thankful

agradecimiento: appreciation, thank

agradecimientos: acknowledgment

agrandar: magnify

agrandar(se): enlarge

agravar: compound

agraviado: injured

agredir: assault, attack

agregar: add, add in, add on, insert, tack on

agresión: aggression, assault, attack, battery

agresivamente: aggressively

agresivo: aggressive, assertive

agriamente: sourly

agrícola: agricultural

agricultor: farmer

agricultora: farmer

agricultura: agriculture, farming

agrio: sour

agronomía: agriculture

agrupación: syndicate

agrupar: group, herd, lump together

agruparse: cluster, troop

agua: water

agua con hielo: ice water

agua de Seltz: seltzer

agua del subsuelo: groundwater

agua dulce: freshwater

agua fría: ice water

agua helada: ice water

agua mineral: club soda, mineral water, seltzer

agua salada: saltwater

agua subterránea: groundwater

aguacate: avocado

aguado: floppy, limp, thin, weak

aguamala: jellyfish, medusa

aguanieve: sleet

aguantar: bear, bear with, endure, hang on, hold out, put up with, sit through, stand, tolerate

aguantarse la risa: keep a straight face

aguardar: await, wait

aguardiente casero: moonshine

aguas artesianas: artesian spring

aguas del mar: seas

aguas freáticas: groundwater

aguas residuales: sewage

aguaviva: jellyfish

aguda: keen

agudeza: sharpness, wit

agudizar: intensify, sharpen

agudo: acute, high, violent

aguijón: sting

águila: eagle

aguja: needle, switch

aguja de tejer: needle

aguja hipodérmica: needle

agujerear: pierce

agujeta: lace, shoestring

ah: oh

ahí: over there, there

ahí está: there you go / there we are

ahí tiene: there you are/go

ahogar(se): choke, drown, smother, stall, suffocate

ahondar: deepen

ahondar en: expand on

ahora: next, now, on

ahora mismo: at once

ahorcar(se): hang

ahorrador: saver

ahorrar: conserve, save, save up

ahorrarle a alguien: save

ahorrativo: economical

ahorro: conservation, thrift

ahorros: savings

ahuecar las manos: cup one's hands

ahumar: smoke

ahuyentar: scare away/ off, shut out

airadamente: angrily

airado: angry

aire: air, tune

aire acondicionado: air-conditioning

airear: air

aislado: isolated, lonely

aislamiento: insulation, isolation

aislante: insulation, insulator

aislar: insulate, isolate

ajardinar: landscape

ajedrez: chess

ajeno: alien

ajetreado: busy

ajo: garlic

ajustadamente: tightly

ajustado: form-fitting, tight

ajustar: adjust, fine-tune, fit, grow into, tighten

ajustar cuentas pendientes: settle a score

ajustarse: conform

ajuste: adjustment

ajuste aproximativo: coarse adjustment

ajuste fino: fine adjustment

ajuste grueso: coarse adjustment

al: as, at, upon

al aire: on the air

al aire libre: in the open, out of doors, outdoor, outdoors

al alcance: within grasp

al alza: upward

al azar: at random,

randomly
al borde de: near, on the brink of, on the verge of
al carbón: charbroiled
al contrario: far from, on the contrary
al corriente: in touch, informed
al descenso: downward
al día: up-to-date
al este: east
al extranjero: abroad
al fin: at last/at long last
al fin y al cabo: after all
al final: finally, late
al frente: in front
al gusto de cada quien: at leisure/at somebody's leisure
al lado: side by side
al lado de: alongside, by
al lado derecho: right-hand
al margen: sideline
al máximo: to the full
al mayoreo: in bulk, wholesale
al menos: at least
al mismo nivel de: level with
al mismo tiempo: at once/all at once, in the process
al nombre de: by name/by the name of
al oriente: east
al pasar: passing
al por mayor: in bulk, wholesale
al principio: at first, early, first, initially, to begin with
al revés: backward, in reverse, inside out, over, upside down
al ritmo propio: at one's own pace
al rojo (vivo): red-hot
al sudeste: southeast
al sudoeste: southwest
al sur: south
al sureste: southeast
al suroeste: southwest
al tanto: in the know
al teléfono: on the phone, on the telephone
al unísono: in unison
al ver: at the sight of
al/del otro lado: over
ala: wing
ala derecha: right-wing
alabar: praise, talk up
alacena: cupboard
alambre: strand, wire
alambre de cobre: copper wire
alancear: spear
alardear: show off
alargar(se): drag out, spin out, stretch, stretch out
alarido: howl, scream
alarma: alarm
alarma contra incendio: fire alarm
alarmado: alarmed
alarmante: alarming, disturbing, frightening

alarmar: alarm
alba: dawn, sun-up, sunrise
albañil: builder
albaricoque: apricot
alberca: pool, swimming pool
albergar: accommodate, harbor, house
albor: dawning
alborear: dawn
alborotado: stoked
alborotador: rioter
alborotadora: rioter
alboroto: fuss, uproar
álbum: album
alcachofa: artichoke
alcalde: mayor
alcaldesa: mayor
alcance: extent, range, scope
alcantarilla: sewer
alcanzar(se): attain, catch up, follow, go around, grab, level, make, reach, run into, top out
alcanzar a reconocer: appreciate
alcanzar el nivel más alto: peak
alcohol: alcohol, liquor
alcohol para usos médicos: rubbing alcohol
alcohólica: alcoholic
alcohólico: alcoholic
alcoholismo: alcoholism
aldea: village
aldea de indios: pueblo
aldea global: global village
aldeana: villager
aldeano: villager
aleación: alloy
aleatorio: random
alegato: plea
alegrar: brighten
alegrarse: welcome
alegre: cheerful, good-humored, jolly, merry, sunny
alegremente: cheerfully, merrily
alegría: cheerfulness, joy
alejado: a long way/quite a way, alienated, apart, away, far off, lonesome, remote
alejamiento: alienation, departure
alejar(se): alienate, draw, drive away, frighten away, get away, go off (somewhere), keep back, move off, pull away, recede, wander
alelo: allele
alentador: cheering, encouraging, refreshing, uplifting
alentadoramente: encouragingly
alentar: cheer on, encourage, spur, urge
alergia: allergy
alérgico: allergic
alerón: fin, wing

alerta: alert, keep watch
alertar: alert
aleta: fin
aletear: flap
alfabético: alphabetical
alfabetismo visual: visual literacy
alfabeto: alphabet
alfarería: pottery
alféizar: sill
alfil: bishop
alfiler: pin
alfombra: carpet, rug
alga: seaweed
alga marina: seaweed
algas: algae
álgebra: algebra
algo: any, anything, element, kind of, little, something
algo (de): some
algo borroso: blur
algo como: anything like/close to
algo parecido a: anything like/close to
algo seguro: certainty
algodón: cotton, pad
algodón de azúcar: cotton candy
algoritmo: algorithm
alguacil: constable, sheriff
alguien: anybody, anyone, somebody, someone
algún: any, few, one, some
algún día: sometime
algún lado: anywhere
algún lugar: anyplace, someplace, somewhere
alguna: one, some
alguna parte: someplace, somewhere
alguna que otra vez: now and then/now and again/every now and then/every now and again, off and on
alguna vez: ever
algunas: some
alguno: any, certain, either, few, one, some
algunos: few, some
aliada: ally
aliado: allied, ally
aliados: friends
alianza: alliance, ring
alianza estratégica: joint venture
aliarse: ally
alicate(s): pliers
alienígena: alien
aliento: breath, encouragement
alimentación: feeding
alimentado: fueled
alimentar(se): feed, raise
alimentarse de: prey on
alimento: feeding, food
alimento básico: staple
alimento natural: natural food
alimentos: board
alineación: alignment
aliño: dressing
alisar: brush, smooth

alistarse: enlist, join up
alistarse como voluntario: volunteer
alistarse en: join
alistarse para enfrentarse: square off
alistarse para pelear: square off
alita: brownie
aliteración: alliteration
aliviado: relieved
aliviar: ease, release, relieve, soothe
alivio: release, relief
allá: over, there
allanamiento: raid
allanar: raid, smooth out
allegado: close
allí: over there, there
alma: soul
almacén: repository, store, warehouse
almacenaje: storage
almacenamiento: storage
almacenar: stockpile, store, store away
almeja: clam
almíbar: syrup
almidón: starch
almirante: admiral
almohada: pillow
almohadilla: pad
almuerzo: box lunch, lunch
alocado: mad
alojamiento: accommodation
alojar(se): accommodate, house, lodge, put up, sleep, stay
alpinismo: climbing
alpiste: birdseed
alquilado: charter
alquilar: charter, lease, rent
alquiler: lease, rent, rental
alrededor: around
alrededor de: about, circa, in the region of, some, somewhere
alrededores: scenery, vicinity
alta: discharge
alta fidelidad: high fidelity
alta presión: H
alta tecnología: high technology
altanero: proud
altavoz: bullhorn
alteración: alteration
alteración del orden público: disorderly conduct
alterado: upset
alterar: alter, doctor
alternar: alternate, socialize, stagger
alternar (el trabajo): job share
alternativa: alternative
alternativamente: alternately, alternatively
alternativo: alternately, alternative

alterno: alternate
altiplanicie: highlands
altitud: altitude, elevation
altitud: height
alto: aloud, high, highly, loud, tall
¡alto!: hold it!
alto horno: furnace
alto mando: brass
altoestrato: altostratus
altricial: altricial
altura: height, level
altura de las olas: wave height
alud de lodo: mudflow, mudslide
alud de rocas: rock fall
aludir: touch
alumbramiento: delivery
alumbrar: shine
aluminio: aluminum
alumna: alum, schoolgirl, student
alumnado: student body
alumno: alum, alumnus, pupil, schoolboy, student
aluvión: alluvium
aluvión glaciárico: till
alveolo: alveolus
alvéolo: socket
alza abrupta: jump
alzamiento: uprising
alzar: lift, raise
alzarse: revolt, rise up, stand
ama de casa: homemaker, housewife
amabilidad: kindness
amable: friendly, kind, kindly, neighborly, nice, sweet
amablemente: kindly, nicely
amado: beloved
amagar: threaten
amainar: die, let up
amalgama: composite
amalgamar(se): fuse
amamantar: feed
amanecer: break, dawn, sun-up, sunrise
amante: lover
amañar: fix, rig
amar: love
amargado: bitter, cynical, sour
amargamente: bitterly
amargar: sour
amargo: bitter
amargura: bitterness
amarillo: yellow
amarrar(se): bind, lace, lash, moor, rope, tie, tie up
amasar: knead
amazona: rider
ambición: ambition
ambicioso: ambitious, up-and-coming
ambiental: environmental
ambientalista: environmentalist
ambientalmente: environmentally
ambiente: atmosphere,

background, environment, surroundings
ambiguamente: ambiguously
ambiguo: ambiguous
ámbito: scene, scope, sphere
ambivalente: mixed
ambos: both
ambulancia: ambulance
ambulante: mobile
amenaza: threat
amenaza de bomba: scare
amenazador: threatening
amenazar: hang, loom, threaten
americana: American
americano: American
ameritar: merit
ametralladora: machine gun
amiba: amoeba
amiga: friend, girlfriend
amigable con el ambiente: eco-friendly
amígdala: tonsils
amigo: bud, friend, kiddo
amigos: friends
aminorar: ease up
aminorar la velocidad: slow, slow down
amish: Amish
amistad: friendship
amistoso: friendly, good-humored
amnios: amnion
amnistía: amnesty
amo: master
amoblar: furnish
amonestar: scold
amontonar(se): accumulate, bunch up, crowd, heap, pile, scramble, swarm
amor: darling, love, sweetheart
amor propio: self-esteem
amoratado: bruised
amorío: affair
amorosamente: lovingly
amoroso: loving, sweet
amortiguar: cushion, soften
amotinarse: riot
ampliación: enlargement, extension
ampliamente: amply, broadly, wide, widely
ampliar: elaborate, enlarge, extend, widen
ampliar las actividades: branch out
amplificar: magnify
amplio: broad, generous, large, spacious, wide
amplitud: amplitude
amplitud de la marea: tidal range
amueblado: furnished
amueblar: furnish
amuleto: charm
anaeróbico: anaerobic
anafase: anaphase
analfabeto: illiterate

analgésico: painkiller

análisis: analysis, exam, test

análisis de muestras de ADN: DNA fingerprinting

análisis detallado: breakdown

análisis dimensional: dimensional analysis

análisis literario: literary analysis

analista: analyst, forecaster

analizar: analyze, consider, look, talk through, test

análogo: analog

anaranjado: ginger, orange

anatomía: anatomy

anatómico: anatomical

ancestral: ancestral

ancho: broad, wide, width

ancho (amplitud, anchura) de banda: bandwidth

anchura: width

anciano: aged, elder, elderly, old

ancla: anchor

anclar: anchor

ándale: come on

andamiaje: scaffolding

andamio: scaffolding

andanada: round

andar: go, ride, run

andar a la caza de: chase

andar a la rebatiña: scramble

andar apresuradamente: tear

andar de gira: tour

andar de un lugar a otro: schlep

andar detrás de: chase

andar en bici: cycle

andar en bicicleta: cycle

andar en busca: chase

andar errado: be off base

andar pesado: shuffle

andén: platform

andrajos: rag

andrajoso: ratty

anécdota: anecdote, story

anegar: swamp

anegar(se): flood

anemia: anemia

anémico: anemic

anemómetro: anemometer

anestesia: anesthetic

anestesióloga: anesthesiologist

anestesiólogo: anesthesiologist

anestesista: anesthesiologist

anexar: attach, enclose

anexo: addition, attachment, extension

anfibio: amphibian

anfiteatro: amphitheater, balcony

anfitrión: host

anfitriona: host, hostess

ángel: angel

angiosperma: angiosperm

anglófona: anglophone

anglófono: anglophone

anglohablante: anglophone

angostarse: narrow

angosto: narrow

anguila: eel

ángulo: angle

ángulo recto: right angle

angustia: anguish, distress

angustiante: distressing

angustiar: distress

angustioso: upsetting

anhelar: desire, hunger, pine for

anhelo: desire

anidar: nest

anillo: ring

anillo anual: annual ring

animación: animation

animado: alive, bright, encouraged, high, lively

animador: animator, entertainer

animadora: animator, entertainer

animal: animal

animal de caza: game

animal de peluche: stuffed animal

animar(se): brighten, cheer on, cheer up, dare, encourage

ánimo: encouragement, morale

aniquilador: devastating

aniquilar: bring to its knees, wipe out

aniversario: anniversary

anochecer: dusk

anómalo: abnormal

anonadar: overwhelm

anónimamente: anonymously

anonimato: anonymity

anónimo: anonymous

anormalmente: abnormally, unnaturally

anotación: entry

anotado: down on paper

anotador: scorer

anotadora: scorer

anotar: log, mark down, note, note down, put down, score, take down, write down

anotarse: chalk up

anquilosado: stale

ansia: itch

ansiar: hunger

ansias: hunger

ansiedad: anxiety

ansiosamente: anxiously, eagerly

ansioso: anxious, eager, hungry, impatient, itchy

ante: before, in the face of

ante (sus/los/mis propios) ojos: before/in front of/under your eyes

ante todo: above all

antebrazo: forearm

antecedente: antecedent, background

antecedentes: history, track record

antecedentes penales: rap sheet

antecesor: predecessor

antena: antenna, mast

antena de satélite: satellite dish

antena parabólica: dish

anteojera: blinders

anteojos: eyeglasses, glasses

anteojos de sol: sunglasses

antepasado: ancestor

antepasado: ancestor

antepasado común: common ancestor

antepecho: sill

antera: anther

anterior: above, earlier, former, last, past, previous, prior

anteriormente: at one time, formerly

antes: before, earlier, formerly, once, previously, then

antes de: ahead of, by, prior to, within

antes de Jesucristo: BC

antes de nuestra era: BCE

antes que: rather

antes que nada: first of all, of all

anti-estadounidense: un-American

antibiótico: antibiotic

anticipado: advance

anticipar: advance, anticipate

anticiparse: further

anticipo: advance

anticlinal: anticline

anticoncepción: contraception

anticonceptivo: contraceptive

anticuado: dated, old-fashioned, outdated

anticuerpo: antibody

antideportivo: unsportsmanlike

antifaz: mask

antigüedad: antique

antiguo: ancient, former, old, one-time, vintage

antipático: unpleasant

antiséptico: antiseptic

antitranspirante: antiperspirant

antivirus: anti-virus

antojarse: feel like

antorcha: torch

antropóloga: anthropologist

antropología: anthropology

antropólogo: anthropologist

anual: annual

anualmente: annually

anudar: knot, tie, tie up

anulación: override

anular: cancel out, override, overturn, undo

anular (legal): reverse

anunciante: advertiser

anunciar: advertise, announce, declare, herald

anuncio: ad, advertisement, announcement

anuncio clasificado: want ad

anuncios clasificados: personals

añadir: add, insert, tack on

añejo: stale, vintage

año: year

año bisiesto: leap year

año escolar/académico: school/academic year

año fiscal: financial/ business year

año luz: light year

Año Nuevo: New Year's

añoranza: homesickness

añorar: be homesick for, long

apachurrar: crush

apagado: dull, faded, off, out

apagador: switch

apagar(se): blow out, cut out, die, fade, go off, peter out, put out, shut off, stub out, switch off, turn off

apagón: outage

apalear: batter

aparador: cupboard

aparato: appliance, device, gadget

aparato de Golgi: Golgi complex

aparato ortopédico: brace

aparato respiratorio: respiratory system

aparearse: mate

aparecer(se): appear, break out, emerge, feature, figure, pop up, turn up, show

aparejo de poleas: block and tackle

aparejos: tackle

aparentar: present, pretend

aparente: apparent, outward

aparentemente: apparently, outwardly

aparición: appearance

apariencia: appearance, exterior, look

apartado: isolated

apartar: avert, dodge, isolate, lay aside, move back, set aside

aparte: aside, separate

aparte de: aside from

aparte de eso: if nothing else

apartheid: apartheid

apasionadamente: passionately

apasionado: intense, passionate

apatía: inertia

apegado: attached

apego: attachment

apelación: appeal

apelar: appeal

apellido: surname

apenado: embarrassed

apenar: sorry

apenas: as few as, barely, faintly, hardly, just, lightly, mere, merely, only just, scarcely

apéndice: appendix

aperitivo: cocktail

apestar: reek, smell, stink

apetecer: feel like

apetito: appetite

apetitoso: tasty

apilar: heap, pile, stack

apilar(se): pile up

apiñado: squash

apiñar(se): pack, troop

apio: celery

aplanar(se): flatten

aplastar: crush, flatten, put down, squash

aplaudido: acclaimed

aplaudir: acclaim, applaud, clap

aplauso: acclaim, applause

aplazar: postpone

aplicación: application

aplicación de la ley: law enforcement

aplicar: apply, deal out

aplicar paulatinamente: phase in

apodar: dub, nickname

apoderarse: take hold, take over

apodo: nickname

apogeo: peak

apología: eulogy

apoquinar: pony up, shell out

aporrear: bash, batter

aportación: contribution, input

aportar: contribute, kick in

aposición: appositive

apósito: dressing

apostar: bet, gamble, stake, station

apóstrofe: apostrophe

apoyar(se): aid, back, back up, brace, lean, lend, prop, prop up, recline, rest, second, sponsor, subscribe, support, sustain, uphold

apoyar alguien: be behind somebody

apoyarse en: lean on

apoyo: aid, backing, backup, support

apoyo fraterno: fraternity

apoyo moral: moral support

apreciación: appreciation

apreciar: appreciate, prize, recognize, value

apreciar mucho: treasure

aprecio: esteem, favor

apremiante: urgently

apremiar: hurry

apremio: urgency

aprender(se): learn, pick up

aprendizaje: learning

apresuradamente: hastily

apresurado: hasty, rushed

apresurar(se): hurry, rush, scramble

apretadamente: tightly

apretado: stiff, tight

apretar: clutch, press, screw, squeeze

apretar las clavijas: clamp down

apretar(se): tighten

apretarse el cinturón: tighten one's belt

apretón: grasp, squeeze

apretón de manos: handshake

apretujar: crush, squash

aprieto: plight

aprobación: acceptance, approval, endorsement, sanction, sympathy

aprobado: pass

aprobar: approve, carry, enact, endorse, sanction, sympathize

apropiado: apt, clean, decent, proper, suited

aprovechamiento: exploitation, utilization

aprovechar: seize, seize on

aprovechar algo: take advantage of something

aprovechar(se) de la situación: get a free ride

aprovecharse de: cash in, exploit, milk, play on, use

aprovecharse de alguien: take advantage of someone

aprovisionamiento: provision

aprovisionar: supply

aprovisionarse: stock up

aproximadamente: approximately, around, in/of the order of something, roughly, somewhere

aproximado: approximate, rough, something like

aproximar: approximate

aptitud: bent

apuesta: bet, gamble, stake

apuestas: betting

apuntalar: shore up

apuntar: aim, mark down, point, put down, take aim, take down

apuntarse: chalk up

apuñalar: stab

apurar: hurry

apurarse: hurry, hurry along

apuro: hardship, plight

aquel: that

aquella: that

aquellas: those

aquello: that

aquellos: anybody, anyone, those

aquí: here, over here

arácnido: arachnid

arado: plow

arancel: tariff

arandela: washer

araña: spider

arañar: claw

arañar(se): graze, scratch

arañazo: scratch

arar: plow

árbitra: referee, umpire

arbitrar: judge, mediate, referee, umpire

arbitrariamente: arbitrarily

arbitrariedad: injustice

arbitrario: arbitrary

árbitro: referee, umpire

árbol: shaft, tree

árbol de Navidad: Christmas tree

árbol de Pascua: Christmas tree

arboleda: grove

arbusto: bush, shrub

arce: maple

archivar: file

archivo: archive, file

archivo de audio: podcast

archivos de computadora: PDF

arcilla: clay

arco: arch, bow

arco del proscenio: proscenium

arco iris: rainbow

arder: blaze, burn, itch, smart, smolder

arder (sin llamas): smolder

ardid: trap, trick

ardiendo: burning

ardiente: burning, strong

ardilla: squirrel

arduo: uphill

área: area, ground, region

área de descanso: rest area

área de reposo: rest area

área silvestre: bush

arena: sand

arenero: sandbox

arenoso: sandy

arete: earring

argot: slang

argüir: contend

argumentar: argue, contend

argumento: argument, contention, plot, plotline, point, proposition, thesis

argumento de autoridad: appeal to authority

argumento emocional: appeal to emotion, appeal to pathos

argumento racional: appeal to reason

argumentos a favor: case

argumentos en contra: case

árido: dryness

arista: arête

aristócrata: noble

aritmética: arithmetic

arma: ammunition, arm, gun, weapon

arma biológica: bioweapon

arma de fuego: firearm

arma para aturdir: stun gun

armada: navy

armado: armed

armadura: armor

armar: arm, assemble, put together, set up

armar caballero: knight

armario: closet, cupboard, wardrobe

armarse de valor: steel oneself

armas de destrucción masiva: weapons of mass destruction

armazón: frame, framework

armonía: harmony

armonizar: blend

ARN: RNA

aro: ring

arodillado: on one's knees

aroma: aroma, fragrance, scent

arpa: harp

arpón: spear

arponear: spear

arqueado: bowed

arquear: arch

arquebacteria: Archaebacteria

arqueóloga: archeologist

arqueología: archeology

arqueológico: archeological

arqueólogo: archeologist

arquetípico: archetypal

arquetipo: archetype

arquitecta: architect

arquitecto: architect

arquitectónico: architectural

arquitectura: architecture

arraigado: ingrained

arrancar: boot, exact, kick-start, pull, pull out, start, tear

arrancar bien: get off to a flying start

arrancar de/a: drag

arrancar el alma a alguien: break somebody's heart

arrancar(se): pull away, rip, tear away, tear off

arranque: burst, impulse

arrasar: level, wash away

arrastrar(se): crawl, drag, haul, pull, scrape, tow, trail, tug

arrastrar los pies: drag your feet, shuffle

arrastrar y soltar: drag and drop

arrear: drive

arrebatar: snatch, wrench

arreglado: settle

arreglar: adjust, arrange, fix, patch up, rig, sort out, square away, trim

arreglar cuentas: settle up

arreglar un jardín: landscape

arreglarse: settle down

arreglárselas: cope, fend, get by, manage, muddle through

arreglárselas sin: do without, go without

arreglo: accord, adjustment, arrangement, compromise, deal, fix, setup

arremeter contra: lash out

arremolinarse: mill around, roil

arrendador: landlord

arrendamiento: lease

arrendar: lease

arrepentimiento: regret

arrepentirse: regret

arrestar: arrest

arresto: arrest

arriar: herd

arriate: bed

arriba: above, high, on top, up

arriba de: above

arriba de ochenta: the eighties

arribista: upstart

arriesgadamente: dangerously

arriesgar: risk, stake

arriesgarse: dare, risk, take a chance, to take the plunge

arrimar: draw

arrimar el hombro: pitch in

arrodillarse: kneel

arrogancia: arrogance

arrogante: arrogant, proud, superior

arrojar: fling, hurl, pitch, throw, toss

arrojar chorros de agua: spray

arrojar con violencia: slap

arrojar luz: shed/throw/cast light on

arrojar vapor: steam

arrojar violentamente: slap

arrojarse: dive

arrojo: daring

arrollador: runaway

arrollar: overwhelm

arropar: tuck (someone) in

arrostrar: brave

arroyo: stream

arroz: rice

arruga: line, wrinkle

arrugado: wrinkled

arrugar(se): wrinkle
arruinar: bankrupt, destroy, mess up, ruin
arte: art
arte de acción: performance art
arte dramático: creative drama, theater
arte marcial: martial art
artefacto: device, gadget
arteria: artery
artesa: trough
artesanía: craft
articulación: articulation, joint
articular: utter
artículo: article, commodity, feature, item, paper, piece, story
artículo (de la materia de que se trate): notion
artículo de exportación: export
artículo definido: definite article
artículo determinado: definite article
artículo indefinido: indefinite article
artículos de confección: dry goods
artículos de opinión: op-ed
artículos o útiles de escritorio: stationery
artifice: architect
artificial: artificial, man-made, theatrical, unnatural
artificialmente: artificially
artificioso: theatrical
artillería: artillery
artilugio: gadget
artimaña: trap
artista: artist, entertainer
artístico: artistic
artrítico: arthritic
artritis: arthritis
arveja: snow pea
as: ace
asa: handle
asado: barbecue, cookout, roast
asador: barbecue
asaltante: mugger
asaltar: attack, hold up, mug, raid, rob, storm
asalto: assault, attack, mugging, raid, robbery, round
asamblea: assembly, gathering
asar: barbecue, roast
asar a la parrilla: grill
ascendente: upward
ascender: climb, graduate, promote, rise, spiral
ascender a: add up to
ascendiente: influence
ascensión: rise
ascenso: climb, elevation, promotion
ascensor: elevator
asediar: besiege, mob, stalk

asegurado: secure
aseguradora: insurer
asegurar(se): assure, ensure, fasten, get something straight, insure, lock up, make certain, make sure, secure, underwrite
asemejarse: parallel
asentamiento: settlement
asentar: settle
asentir con la cabeza: nod
asequible: accessible
aserradero (madera): mill
aserrar: saw
asertividad: assertiveness
asertivo: assertive
asesina: killer, murderer
asesinar: assassinate, murder
asesinar con crueldad: massacre
asesinato: assassination, murder, slaying
asesino: killer, murderer
asesor: consultant
asesor financiero: financial adviser
asesora: consultant
asesora financiera: financial adviser
asestar: deliver
aseverativo: declarative
asfixia: suffocation
asfixiar(se): choke, smother, suffocate
asfixiar con gas: gas
así: like that/this/so, so, such, thus
así mismo: likewise
así que: so
asiática: Asian
asiático: Asian
asidua: regular
asiduo: regular
asiento: saddle, seat
asignación: allocation
asignar: allocate, assign, attribute, cast, commit, draft, set
asignar a un puesto: post
asilo: asylum, home, institution
asimetría: asymmetry
asimétrico: asymmetrical
asimilación: assimilation
asimilar: absorb, assimilate, digest, take in
asimismo: likewise, too
asíntota: asymptote
asir: seize
asir algo: get/grab hold of (something)
asistencia: assistance, attendance, help
asistencia médica dirigida: managed care
asistencia pública: public assistance
asistencia social: welfare
asistenta: aide, attendant, helper

asistente: aide, assistant, attendant, attendee, deputy, helper
asistente de abogado: paralegal
asistir: assist, attend, help, see, sit in on
asistir en el parto: deliver
asma: asthma
asno: donkey
asociación: association, fraternity, league, partnership, society
asociación estudiantil masculina: fraternity
asociación libre: free association
Asociación Nacional de Baloncesto/Basketball: NBA
asociación o federación estudiantil: student council
asociada: member
asociada médica: physician's assistant
asociado: member
asociado médico: physician's assistant
asociar(se): associate
asociarse con: affiliate, team up
asolar: devastate
asoleado: sunburned
asomar: poke
asomarse algo vagamente: loom
asombrado: amazed, astonished
asombrar: amaze, astonish
asombrarse: wonder
asombrosamente: strikingly, stunningly, uncannily
asombroso: staggering, startling, striking, uncanny
aspecto: aspect, dimension, expression, exterior, face, light, look, point, side
aspecto físico: look
aspecto superficial: surface
aspereza: harshness, roughness
áspero: harsh, rough
aspersor: sprinkler
aspiración: aspiration
aspiradora: vacuum cleaner
aspirante: applicant, contender, would-be
aspirar: draw, inhale, suck, vacuum
aspirar a: aim
aspirina: aspirin
asqueroso: disgusting, filthy, gross, yucky
astenosfera: asthenosphere
astenósfera: asthenosphere
asterisco: asterisk
asteroide: asteroid
astigmatismo: astigmatism

astillero (naval): yard
astro: star
astróloga: astrologer
astrología: astrology
astrólogo: astrologer
astronauta: astronaut
astrónoma: astronomer
astronomía: astronomy
astrónomo: astronomer
asumir: assume, take on board, take up
asumir el control: take over
asunto: affair, business, concern, issue, matter, point, theme, topic
asustado: startled
asustar: frighten, frighten away, scare
atacante: attacker
atacar: assault, attack, lash out, strike, tackle
atacar salvajemente: savage
atacar verbalmente: lash out
ataque: attack, attempt, bout, fit, strike
ataque al corazón: heart attack
ataque cardíaco: heart attack
ataque de apoplejía: stroke
ataque de nervios: crack-up
ataque de risa: howl, hysterics
atar: attach, bind, lash, rope, tie, tie up
atardecer: sundown, sunset
atascado: stuck
atascamiento: traffic jam
atascar: choke
atascarse: seize up
ataúd: casket, coffin
atemorizar: frighten
atención: attention, focus
atención de la salud: health care
atender: attend, look after, mind, nurse, see, treat
atendiendo sólo a la palabra: honor system
atenerse a: stick to
atentado: attempted
atentamente: intently, sincerely, yours, yours faithfully
atento: alert, considerate, thoughtful
atenuar: dim, tone down, water down
aterrado: terrified
aterrador: frightening, terrifying
aterrar: terrify
aterrizaje: landing
aterrizar: land, touch down
aterrorizar: terrify, terrorize
atesorar: accumulate, treasure

atestar: stuff
atestiguar: witness
atiborrar: cram, fill
ático: attic
atinar: hit
atisbo: gleam
atlas: atlas
atleta: athlete
atlético: athletic, lean
atletismo: athletics
atmósfera: atmosphere
atmosférico: atmospheric
atómico: atomic
átomo: atom
atonal: atonal
atontado: numbed
atontar: numb
atorado: plugged
atorar(se): catch, jam, lodge, seize up, stuck
atormentado: plague
atormentar: torture
atornillar: bolt, screw
ATP: ATP
atracadero: dock
atracar: dock, land, moor
atracción: attraction
atractivo: amenity, attraction, attractive, attractiveness, desirable, lure, striking
atraer: appeal, attract, be a lightning rod for, court, draw, engage, invite, lure, seduce, target, woo
atraer la atención de alguien: catch someone's eye
atragantar(se): choke
atraído: attracted
atrapada: catch
atrapado: grip
atrapar: catch, catch up with, trap
atrás: back, behind
atrasado: backward and forward, behind, overdue, slow
atrasarse: lag, run late
atraso: late, lateness
atravesando: crosstown
atravesar(se): cross, go round, pass, span
atrayente: attractive
atreverse: dare, presume
atrevido: daring, off-color, snippy
atribuir: attribute, pin
atribuir a: put down to
atribuir el crédito: credit
atribulado: troubled
atributo: attribute, complement
atrincherar: barricade
atrocidad: atrocity
atropellar: run down, run over
atroz: miserable, terrible
aturdirse: reel
AU: AU
audacia: boldness, daring
audaz: bold, daring
audible: audible
audición: audition, hearing

audicionar: audition
audiencia: audience, hearing
audífono: earphone
audífonos: headphones
audio: audio
auditar: audit
auditor: auditor
auditora: auditor
auditoría: audit
auditorio: audience, auditorium
auge: boom
aula del curso: homeroom
aullar: howl, whistle, yip
aullido: howl, yip
aumentar: escalate, expand, gain, grow, heighten, increase, magnify, mount, raise, rise, step up, surge, swell, up
aumentar de volumen: rise
aumentar rápidamente: balloon, snowball
aumento: increase, magnification, raise, rise
aumento de precio: appreciation
aumento dramático: explosion
aumento repentino: surge, upsurge
aun: even
aún: even, still, yet
aun así: equally, even so
aun cuando: even
aún más: further, furthest
aun si: even
aunque: albeit, although, if, though, while
aurícula: atrium
auricular: receiver
auriculares: headphones
aurora: dawn
ausencia: absence
ausente: absent, absentee, distant, gone, vacant
ausente por enfermedad: out sick
australopithecus: Australopithecine
australopiteco: Australopithecine
autenticidad: authenticity
auténtico: authentic, full-blown, genuine, legitimate
auto: automobile
auto deportivo: sports car
autobiografía: autobiography
autobiográfico: autobiographical
autobús: bus, coach
autóctono: indigenous
autodeterminación: self-determination
autódromo: raceway
autoestudio: self-study
autofecundado: self-pollinating
autofertilizante: true-

breeding
autografiar: autograph
autógrafo: autograph
automática: automatic
automáticamente: automatically
automático: automatic, mechanical
automatizar: mechanize
automóvil: automobile
automovilista: motorist
autonomía: autonomy
autónomo: autonomous
autopista: freeway, thruway
autopolinizado: self-pollinating
autopsia: postmortem
autor: author, playwright, writer
autor intelectual: brain
autora: author, playwright, writer
autora intelectual: brain
autoridad: authority, influence, leadership
autoritario: authoritative
autorización: authority, authorization, clearance, license
autorizado: authoritative, licensed
autorizar: authorize, clear, license
autosuficiencia: self-sufficiency
autosuficiente: self-sufficient
auxiliar: aid, auxiliary, junior
auxiliar de vuelo: steward, stewardess
auxilio: aid, help, relief
Av.: avenue
avalancha: avalanche
avalúo: appraisal
avance: advance, development, march, move, movement, preview, progress
avance espectacular: quantum
avance publicitario: trailer
avances: trailer
avanzada: scout
avanzado: advanced
avanzar: advance, along, be getting somewhere, come on, go, move, progress
avanzar pesadamente: lumber
avanzar violentamente: surge
avaramente: greedily
avasallar: grind down
ave: bird
Ave.: avenue
ave de corral: fowl
avecinarse: brew, loom
avena: oatmeal, oats
avenida: avenue, parkway, strip
avenirse: conform
aventar(se): bundle somebody somewhere,

fling, knock, plunk, sweep, throw, toss
aventura: adventure, fling
aventuradamente: wildly
aventurado: risky
aventurar: hazard
aventurarse: go out on a limb, venture
aventurera: adventurer
aventurero: adventurer
avergonzado: ashamed, embarrassed
avergonzar: be/feel shy, embarrass, shame
avería: breakdown
averiar(se): break, break down
averiguación: inquiry
averiguar: find out, inquire, track down
aversión: dislike
aves: poultry
aves de corral: poultry
aviación: aviation
aviador: flyer
aviario: aviary
ávidamente: hungrily
avinagrado: sour
avión: aircraft, airplane, plane
avión a reacción: jet
avión de combate: fighter
avión de pasajeros: jetliner
avión, autobús o tren de enlace: shuttle
avíos: gear
avisar: give somebody notice, notice, tip off
aviso: heads-up, notice, warning
aviso de despido: pink slip
avispero: nest
axila: armpit
axioma: axiom
axón: axon
ayer: yesterday
ayuda: aid, assistance, help, relief, support
ayudante de mesero: bus boy
ayudante: helper
ayudante (de la policía): deputy
ayudante de enfermera: LPN
ayudante de enfermería: LPN
ayudante de maestro: teacher's aide
ayudar: aid, assist, be of help, help, help out, lend, support
ayudar a recordar: refresh one's memory
ayudar en el parto: deliver
ayunar: fast
ayuno: fast
ayuntamiento: council, township
azadón: hoe
azotar: batter, lash, slam, whip

azote: lash
azúcar: sugar
azúcar glas(é): confectioners' sugar
azúcar morena: brown sugar
azucarado: sweet
azucena: lily
azufre: sulfur
azul: blue
azul marino: navy
azulejo: tile
azuzar: egg on

B

babor: port
bacalao: cod
bachillerato: high school
bacteria: bacteria
bacteriano: bacterial
bacterias productoras de metano: methanogen
bádminton: badminton
bafle: speaker
bagatelas: small potatoes
baguette: loaf
bahía: bay
bailar: dance
bailarín: dancer
bailarina: dancer
baile: ball, dancing
baile de graduación: prom
baile de la escuela: prom
baile de salón: ballroom dancing
baile social: social dance
baja: casualty, discharge
baja presión: L
bajar: come down, dim, drop, duck, ebb, fall, go down, lower, mark down, turn down
bajar de las nubes: come back/down to earth
bajar de peso: lose weight
bajar el cierre/la cremallera: unzip
bajar el ritmo: ease up
bajar el sonido o el volumen: mute
bajo: bass, below, beneath, flat, gentle, low, low-rise, mute, poor, short, under, underneath
bajo control: in hand, under control
bajo el control: under one's control
bajo el mando de: under
bajo impacto: low-impact
bajo la tutela de: under
bajo los reflectores: glare
bajo mundo: underworld
bajo órdenes de: under orders
bajo rendimiento: underperformance
bajo techo: indoor, indoors
bajo y fornido: stocky
bala: ammunition, bullet
balacera: firing
balancear(se): bounce,

juggle, sway, swing
balanceo: swing
balanza: balance
balazo: shot
balbucear: babble, stammer
balcón: balcony
baldaquín: canopy
balde: pail
baldío: vacant lot
baldosa: tile
ballena: whale
ballena jorobada: humpback whale
ballet: ballet
balneario: seaside
balneario de aguas termales: spa
balón de futbol: football
balsa: raft
baluarte: stronghold
bambú: bamboo
banana: banana
banca: banking, bench
bancarrota: bankruptcy
banco: bank, stool
banco de alimentos: food bank
banco de esperma: sperm bank
banco de semen: sperm bank
banda: band, belt, boy band, gang, ring
banda ancha: broadband
banda ciudadana: citizens band
banda elástica: rubber band
banda sonora: soundtrack
bandada: flock
bandeja: platter, tray
bandeja de entrada: inbox
bandeja de salida: outbox
bandera: flag
bandera de Estados Unidos: Old Glory
banderín: flag
báner: banner ad
banquera: banker
banquero: banker
banqueta: curb, sidewalk
banquete: feast
banquillo de los acusados: dock
banquina: shoulder
bañadera: tub
bañado en sudor: sweating
bañador: swimsuit
bañar: dip, lap, smother, wash
bañar(se): bathe
bañarse: shower
bañarse con agua caliente: soak
bañera: bathtub, tub
baño: bath, bathroom, shower
baño (de tina): bath
baño con agua caliente: soak
baño de damas: women's room

baño de hombres: men's room
baño de mujeres: women's room
baños: bathroom, restroom
baqueta: stick
bar: bar
baraja: deck, playing card
barajar: shuffle
barata: sale
barato: cheap, cheaply, downscale, inexpensive
barba: beard
¡qué barbaridad!: fancy (that)!
barbero: barber
barbilla: chin
barbiquejo: guard
barboquejo: guard
barcaza: barge
barco: boat, ship
barco cisterna: tanker
barco de pasajeros: liner
barco portacontenedores: container ship
barman: bartender
barométrico: barometric
barómetro: barometer, bellwether
barra: bar, cash bar, loaf, rail, rod
barra de herramientas: toolbar
barra de labios: lipstick
barra de pesas: barbell
barra de trabajo: taskbar
barra deslizable: scroll bar
barra diagonal: forward slash
barra oblicua: forward slash
barranco: gulch, gully
barrer: sweep, sweep up
barrera: barrier
barriada: slum
barricada: barricade
barriga: belly, pot
barril: barrel, drum
barrio: barrio, neighborhood, quarter
barrio bajo: slum
barro: clay
barros: acne
basado en la biología: biologically
basalto: basalt
basar: base
basarse en: build on
báscula: scale
base: base, basis, footing, foundation, fundamentals, stand, substance
base de datos: database
base de los dedos del pie: ball
base del bateador: home plate
base del pulgar: ball
bases: grassroots
básicamente: essentially
básico: basic, elementary, skeleton, staple
básquetbol: basketball
bastante: a reasonable

amount of, enough, fairly, pretty, quite, quite a bit, reasonably, sufficient, well
bastar: do
bastardilla: italic
bastidor: wing
bastilla: cuff
bastión: stronghold
basto: club
bastón: cane, stick
bastón de dulce: candy cane
bastoncillo: rod
bastonera: drum majorette
basura: garbage, litter, refuse, trash
basurero: dumping, garbage can, garbage collector, garbage dump, garbage man, trash can, wastebasket
bata: robe, scrub
bata de laboratorio: lab apron
batalla: battle
batallar: wrestle
batallón: battalion
bate: bat
bateador: batsman, batter, slugger
bateadora: batter
batear: bat
batear de emergencia: pinch-hit
batería: battery
baterista: drummer
batidor: whisk
batidora: whisk
batir: beat, scramble, whip, whisk
batir las alas: flap
baúl: footlocker, trunk
baya: berry
bazar: fair, variety store
bazar casero: yard sale
bazar de cosas usadas: thrift shop
bebé: baby, infant
bebedero (de agua refrigerada): water cooler
bebedor: drinker
bebedor empedernido: drinker
bebedora: drinker
bebedora empedernida: drinker
beber: booze, drink
beberse: consume
bebida: beverage, booze, drinking, liquor
bebida alcohólica: alcohol, liquor
bebida espirituosa: liquor
bebidas alcohólicas: alcohol
beca: grant, scholarship
beige: beige
béisbol: baseball
beisbolista: ballplayer
bella: beauty
belleza: beauty
bello: beautiful, beauty
bemol: flat
bendecir: bless

bendición: blessing
beneficiar(se): benefit
beneficiarse con algo: profit from
beneficio: benefit, interest, payoff, profit
beneficio de la duda: benefit of the doubt
beneficio indirecto: spinoff
beneficioso: beneficial, helpful
benéfico: charitable
benevolente: charitable
bengala: flare
benigno: mildly
bentos: benthos
berenjena: eggplant
berrear: scream
besar: kiss
beso: kiss
besos: love/love from/all my love
bestia: animal
betabel: beet
betún: frosting, polish
bi-: twin
Biblia: Bible
bíblico: biblical
bibliografía: bibliography
bibliografía anotada: annotated bibliography
biblioteca: library
bibliotecaria: librarian
bibliotecario: librarian
bicentenario: bicentennial
bicho: bug
bicho raro: freak
bici: bike, cycle
bicicleta: bicycle, cycle
bicicleta de montaña: mountain bike
bicimoto: moped
bicla: bike, cycle
bidimensional: two-dimensional
bidireccional: two-way
bidón: drum
bien: all right, asset, fine, good, okay, okey dokey, right, securely, well
bien conocido: well-known
bien informado: up-to-date
bien que: albeit, though
bien raíz: real estate, real property
bien se podría: may/might as well
bienes: goods
bienestar: health, welfare, well-being
bienintencionado: well-intentioned
bienvenida: welcome
bienvenido: welcome
bifurcación: fork
bifurcarse: branch off, fork
bigote: mustache
bilé: lipstick
bilingüe: bilingual
billar: pool, pool hall
billete: fare, ticket
billete (de banco): bill

billetera: billfold, wallet
billón: trillion
bingo: bingo
binoculares: binoculars
binomio: binomial
biodegradable: biodegradable
biodiversidad: biodiversity
biógrafa: biographer
biografía: biography
biográfico: biographical
biógrafo: biographer
bióloga: biologist
biología: biology
biológico: biological
biólogo: biologist
bioma: biome
biomasa: biomass
biombo: screen
bioquímica: biochemist, biochemistry
bioquímico: biochemical, biochemist
biosfera: biosphere
biotecnología: biotechnology
biótico: biotic
bióxido de carbono: carbon dioxide
birlar: pinch
birrete: mortarboard
bisoño: raw
bit: bit
bitácora: log
bitácora en la red: weblog
bitácora en línea: weblogging
bizcocho: pound cake
bla-bla-bla: yadda
blackjack: blackjack
blanca: half note
blanco: butt, fair, target, white
blanco (del ojo): white
blanco y negro: black and white
blando: floppy, soft, tender
blanquear: bleach
blindado: armored
blindaje: armor
bloc de notas: pad
blog: blog, weblog
blogósfera: blogosphere
bloguear: blogging
bloguera: blogger
bloguero: blogger
bloque: bloc, block
bloque de concreto de cenizas: cinder block
bloque de falla: fault-block mountain
bloque fallado: fault-block mountain
bloquear: bar, block, blockade, jam, lock
bloqueo: blockade
blues de doce compases: twelve-bar blues
blusa: blouse, shirt, top
bobo: dumb, sappy
boca: mouth, muzzle
boca arriba: right way up
bocado: bit, nosh
bocanada: puff
bochorno: flush

bochornoso: close, sticky
bocina: speaker
boda: marriage, wedding
bodega: hold, store, warehouse, winery
bodegón: still life
bofetada: slap
bogar: row
boicot: boycott
boicotear: boycott
boicotec: boycott
boina: beret
bol: basin
bola: ball, tumor
bola de nieve: snowball
boleta: ticket
boleta de calificaciones: report card
boletería: box office
boletín: bulletin
boletín general: all-points bulletin
boleto: fare, ticket
boliche: bowling
bolillo: roll
bolita: marble
bolita de chicle: gumball
bollo: bun
bollo inglés: English muffin
bolos: bowling
bolsa: bag, pocket, pocketbook, pouch, purse
bolsa (de mano): handbag
bolsa (de valores): stock exchange
bolsa de aire: air sac
bolsa de dormir: sleeping bag
bolsa de sorpresas: grab bag
bolsa grande: tote bag
bolsa pequeña: pouch
bolsas de mano: carry-on
bolsillo: pocket
bolsita de dulces: goody bag
bolso: purse
bolsón: tote bag
bomba: bomb, pump
bomba (de excusado): plunger
bombardear: bomb, shell
bombardeo: bombing, shelling
bombardero: bomber
bombear: pump
bombera: firefighter
bombero: firefighter
bombilla: light bulb
bombín: derby
bonche: bunch
bondad: goodness
bondadoso: caring
bonificación: bonus
bonito: lovely, pretty, trim
bono: bond
bono del Tesoro: treasury bill
boquera: fever blister
boqui-:-mouthed
bordado: embroidery
bordar: stitch
borde: border, edge, rim
borde de la acera:

curbstone
borde de la banqueta: curbstone
borde del camino: roadside
bordear: border, skirt
borona: crumb
borracha: drunk
borracho: drunk
borrador: draft, eraser
borrar: blur, delete, erase, rub
borrego: lamb, sheep, whitecap
borroso: blurred, dim, fuzzy
bosque: forest, wood, woodland
bosque (ecuatorial o pluvial): rain forest
bosquejar: outline, sketch
bosquejo: outline, sketch
bostezar: yawn
bostezo: yawn
bota: boot
bota de goma: rubber boot
bota de hule: rubber boot
botadura: launch
botánica: botanist, botany
botánico: botanical, botanist
botar: bounce, chuck, ditch, dump, launch
botas vaqueras: cowboy boots
bote: boat, bounce, jar, tin
bote de basura: garbage can, trash can
bote de remos: rowboat
botella: bottle
botica: drugstore, pharmacy
botín: boot
botiquín: first aid kit
botón: button, pin
botón regulador: dial
botones: bellhop
boulevard: avenue
box: box spring, boxing
box lunch: box lunch
box spring: box spring
boxeador: boxer, fighter
boxeadora: boxer, fighter
boxear: box
boxeo: boxing
boxer: shorts
boy band: boy band
boya: buoy
bozal: muzzle
bra: bra
bracera: field hand
bracero: field hand
brackets: braces
bragueta: fly
bramar: roar
branquia: gill
brasier: bra
brassiere: bra
bravo: brave
bravucón: bully
bravucona: bully
bravuconería: saber-rattling
brazada: stroke

brazalete: band, bracelet
brazo: arm
brazo de gitano: jelly roll
break: break
breakdown: breakdown
brecha: gap
breve: brief
bridge: bridge
brigada: brigade, gang, squad
brillante: bright, brilliant, shiny
brillantemente: brilliantly
brillar: flash, shine, glow
brillar con luz tenue: glow
brillo: brightness, glitter, luster, polished, shine, sparkle
brincar: bounce, jump, leap, skip, spring
brincar de cojito: hop
brinco: leap, skip
brindar: drink to, toast
brindis: toast
brisa: breeze
británica: Briton
británico: British, Briton
brocha: brush, paintbrush
broche: barrette, brooch, button, clip, pin
brócoli: broccoli
broma: trick
¡Debes estar bromeando!: you're/ you must be/you've got to be joking
¡Estás bromeando!: you're/you must be/ you've got to be joking
bromear: fool around, joke, kid
bronce: bronze
bronceado: sunburned, suntan, tan, tanned
bronceador: suntan
broncearse: tan
bronces: brass
bronquios: bronchi
brotar: pour, well
brote: eruption, outbreak, shoot
bruja: witch
brujo: witch, wizard
brújula: compass, orientation
bruma: mist
brumoso: foggy, hazy
bruscamente: roughly, rudely
brusco: abrupt, rough
brutal: brutal
brutalmente: brutally, viciously
bruto: gross
bucal: oral
buceador: diver
buceadora: diver
bucear: dive
buceo: diving
bucle: curl
bucodental: oral
budín: pudding
budismo: Buddhism
budista: Buddhist

buen: fond
buen juicio: judgment
buen tirador: a good shot
buena forma física: fitness
buena suerte: good luck/ best of luck
buena voluntad: goodwill
buena tiradora: a good shot
buenas nuevas: good news
buenas tardes: good afternoon
bueno: all right, fine, fond, good, good guy, handsome, hello, nice, now, oh well, solid, well
bueno en: good at
bueno, está bien: fair enough
buenos modales: good manners
buey: ox
búfalo: buffalo
bufanda: scarf
buffet: buffet
búho: owl
bujía: spark plug
bulbo: bulb
bulbo raquídeo: medulla
bulla: racket
bullicio de rumores: buzz
bullicioso: lively
bullir: buzz
bullpen: bullpen
bulto: lump, tumor
búnker: bunker
buque: ship, vessel
buque de guerra: warship
buque cisterna: tanker
buque portacontenedores: container ship
burbuja: bubble
burbujear: bubble
burdo: clumsy, coarse, crude
burla: joke
burlar: cheat on
burlarse: make fun of, tease
burlarse de: mock
burlón: mocking
burocracia: bureaucracy, red tape
burócrata: bureaucrat
burocrático: bureaucratic
burro: donkey
buscado: wanted
buscador: hunter, seeker
buscadora: hunter, seeker
buscar: come for, court, fetch, hunt, look, look out for, look up, pick, prospect, pursue, rifle, search, seek, seek out, want
buscar algo: scout
buscar aprobación: lobby
buscar significado: read into
buscar(se): feel for
búsqueda: drive, exploration, hunt,

hunting, pursuit, quest, search
búsqueda del tesoro: scavenger hunt
búsqueda y rescate: search and rescue
busto: bust
butaca de platea: orchestra
buzo: diver
buzón: mailbox
byte: byte

C
C.P.: CPA
caballería: cavalry
caballeriza: stable
caballero: gentleman, knight
caballeroso: gentle
caballete: easel
caballito de mar: seahorse
caballito del diablo: dragonfly
caballo con arzones: pommel horse
caballo marino: seahorse
cabaña: cabin, hut
cabecear: head, nod off
cabecera: head, headwaters
cabecilla: leader
cabello: hair
caber: fit
cabeza: head, mind
cabildear: lobby
cabilderos: lobby
cabina: booth, cab, cabin, cockpit
cabina de mando: flight deck
cabina telefónica: phone booth
cable: cable, cord, lead, line
cables de arranque: jumper cables
cabo: cape
cabra: goat
cabrilla: whitecap
cabrito: kid
cabús: caboose
cacahuate: peanut
cacao en polvo: cocoa
cacería: hunt, hunting
cacerola: saucepan
cachar: catch
cacharro: clunker
cachetada: slap
cachete: cheek
cachetear: slap
cachiporra: blackjack
cacho: stub
cachorro: puppy
caco: thief
cactus: cactus
cactus erizo: hedgehog cactus
cada: each, either, every, individual
cada dos días/semanas/meses: every other day/week/month
cada quince días: every other day
cada tercer día: every

other day
cada uno: a/per head, each
cada vez más: increasingly, more and more
cadáver: corpse
cadena: chain, network, range
cadena alimentaria: food chain
cadena alimenticia: food chain
cadena de producción y distribución: supply chain
cadena independiente de televisión: PBS
cadena trófica: food chain
cadera: hip
caducar: expire, run out
caducifolio: deciduous
caer(se): come down, crash, crumble, descend, drop, fall, fall off, fall out, go down, land, sag, sink, slide, slip, throw, tip over, topple, tumble
caer bien: could do with
caer de golpe: flop
caer en desuso: die out
caer en el olvido: blow over
caer en la cuenta: click, dawn on
caer en la cuenta de: realize
caerle a alguien: hang
caerse de bruces: pitch
café: brown, café, coffee, java
café internet: Internet café
cafeína: caffeine
cafetera: kettle, pot
cafetería: cafeteria, coffee shop
caída: drop, fall, overthrow, tumble
caída de agua: falls
caída de la tarde: sundown
caída libre: free fall
caimán: alligator, gator
caja: box, carton, case, checkout, coffin
caja de ahorros: kitty
caja de Petri: Petri dish
caja de sorpresas: grab bag
caja de transmisión: gear
caja fuerte: safe
caja registradora: till
cajera: cashier, teller
cajero: cashier, teller
cajero automático: ATM
cajón: bin, coffin, drawer
cajuela: trunk
cal: lime
calabacín: zucchini
calabacita: zucchini
calabacita fresca: summer squash
calabaza: pumpkin
calabaza de Halloween:

jack-o'-lantern
calada: puff
calafateado: caulking
calafatear: caulk, caulking
calambre: cramp
calar: sink in
calcar: trace
calce: wedge
calcetín: sock
calcio: calcium
calcomanía: decal, sticker
calculado: calculated
calculadora: calculator
calcular: calculate, estimate, figure up, gauge, put at, reckon
cálculo: calculation, estimate, guess
caldeado: heated
caldera: caldera, furnace
caldo: soup, stock
calefacción solar pasiva: passive solar heating
calefactor: fire, heater
calendario: calendar, timeline
calentador: fire, heater
calentamiento global: global warming
calentamiento solar activo: active solar heating
calentar(se): heat, heat up, warm, warm-up, warm up
calentar en horno de microondas: microwave
calentón: fire, heater
calentura: fever, temperature
calidad: capacity, grade, quality, standard
calidad de asociado: membership
calidad de juguetón: playfulness
calidad de socio: membership
calidad de vida: quality of life
cálido: tender, warm
caliente: hot, warm
calificación: grade, mark, marking, qualification
calificación intermedia: plus
calificar: characterize, grade, label, mark, marking
caligrafía: script
cáliz: cup
calladamente: quietly
callado: quiet, silent
callar(se): keep (something) quiet, keep (something) to yourself, silence, shut up
calle: avenue, road, street
calle lateral: side street
Calle Mayor: Main Street
Calle Principal: Main Street
calle principal: main drag

callejero: stray
callejón: alley
callejón sin salida: dead end, no-win situation, standoff
callo de hacha: scallop
calma: calm
calmante: calming, soothing
calmar(se): calm, calm down, cool down, ease up, pull together, quiet, settle down, soothe
calor: heat, warmth
calor del sol: sunshine
calor específico: specific heat capacity
caloría: calorie
calorímetro: calorimeter
calumnia: smear
calumniar: libel
calurosamente: warmly
caluroso: hot
calvicie: baldness
calvo: bald
calza: wedge
calzar: wedge
calzoncillos: shorts, underpants
calzones: briefs, panties, underpants
cama: bed, box spring
Cámara: house
cámara: camera, chamber, webcam
cámara de seguridad: security camera
cámara digital: digital camera
cámara lenta: slow motion
camarera: bartender, stewardess, waitress
camarero: bartender, steward, waiter
camareros: waitstaff
camarón: shrimp
camarote: cabin
cambiar: barter, break, change, change over, remold, replace, reverse, revise, shift, swing, switch
cambiar de: change
cambiar de equipo: be traded
cambiar de idea: change one's tune
cambiar de lugar: transfer
(inter)cambiar de lugar: trade places with
cambiar de opinión: have a change of heart, change one's mind
cambiar de orden: rearrange
cambiar de parecer: change one's tune
cambiar para mal: change for the worse
cambiar(se): change, move, move in, swap
cambio: adjustment, change, move, shift, swap, swing, switch, transfer
cambio de estado:

change of state
cambio físico: physical change
cambio químico: chemical change
camello: camel
camellón: median strip
camilla: gurney
caminando: on foot
caminante: hiker
caminar: get around, walk
caminar con dificultad: limp
caminar con paso enérgico: stomp
caminar despreocupadamente: stroll
caminar fatigosamente: trek
caminar tranquilamente: stroll
caminata: hike, stroll, trek, walk
caminata rápida: power walking
camino: approach, course, lane, path, pathway, road, route, track, way
camino de entrada: drive, driveway
camino de peaje o cuota: turnpike
camino del éxito: high road
camino secundario: side road
camión cisterna: tanker
camión con remolque: tractor-trailer, trailer truck
camión con tráiler: tractor-trailer
camión de bomberos: fire engine, fire truck
camión de carga: truck
camión de la basura: garbage truck
camión de remolque: rig
camionera: trucker
camionero: trucker
camioneta: pickup, station wagon, truck, van
camioneta de reparto: panel truck
camisa: shirt
camiseta: T-shirt, undershirt
camiseta sin mangas: tank top
camisón: nightgown
camote: yam
campamento: camp, campsite
campamento de verano: summer camp
campamento militar: boot camp
campamento para remolques: trailer park
campana: bell
campanada: chime, stroke
campaña: campaign
campaña publicitaria: ad

campaign
campeón: champion
campeona: champion
campeonato: championship, title
cámper: recreational vehicle, RV, trailer
campesino: peasant
campestre: rural
camping: campground
campiña: countryside
campo: country, course, domain, field, front, land, park, realm, scope
campo de batalla: battlefield
campo de fuerza: force field
campo de fútbol/futbol: football field
campo de tiro: range
campo de trabajos forzados: labor camp
campo local: home field
campo magnético: magnetic field
campo traviesa: cross-country
campo visual: field
canal: canal, channel
canal de televisión: channel
canalizar: channel
canasta: basket, hamper
canasto: basket
cancelación: cancellation
cancelado: off
cancelar: call off, cancel, pull the plug
cancelarse: rain out
cáncer: cancer
canceroso: cancerous
cancha: course, court, field
cancha de fútbol/futbol: football field
canciller: chancellor
canción: song, tune
canción infantil: nursery rhyme
canción publicitaria: jingle
cancionero: songbook
candidata: candidate, nominee
candidato: candidate, nominee
canela: cinnamon
cañería: plumbing
cañería principal: mains
cangrejo: crab
cangrejo de río: crawfish
cangurera: fanny pack
canguro: kangaroo
canica: marble
canícula: dog days
canilla: faucet, spigot
canjeable: convertible
canjear: exchange, trade
canoa: canoe
canola: canola
cansado: tired, tiring, weary
cansancio: fatigue, tiredness
cansar: wear down
cansar(se): tire
cansarse: run out of

steam
cantante: singer, vocalist
cantante de rap: rapper
cantar: chant, crow, sing, talk
cantar a coro: sing along
cántico: chant
cantidad: amount, pool, quantity, sum
cantidad sustancial de: a lot of
cantinera: bartender
cantinero: bartender
canto: chant, singing, song
caña: cane
cañón: barrel, cannon, canyon
cañón (de un arma): muzzle
cañón de órgano: pipe
caos: chaos, mess
capa: cape, coat, covering, film, layer
capa de ozono: ozone layer
capacidad: capability, capacity, competence, fitness, power, talent
capacidad de persistencia: carrying capacity
capacitación: training
capacitado: fit
capacitar: qualify
capacitar(se): train
capataz: foreman
capaz: capable, talented
capaz de: (feel) up to, equal to
capear: weather
capilar: capillary
capilar linfático: lymph capillary
capilla: chapel
capital: capital
capital comercial: stock
capitalismo: capitalism
capitalista: capitalist
capitán: captain, skipper
capitán de fragata: commander
capitán de meseros: maitre d'
capitán/capitana de puerto: harbormaster
capitanear: captain, navigate
capitolio: capitol
capitulación: surrender
capitular: surrender
capítulo: chapter, episode, installment
caprichoso: fancy
cápsula: capsule
cápsula de Petri: Petri dish
captar: attract, catch on, click, engage, pick up
captura: capture
captura de datos: data entry
capturar: capture, hunt down, input, seize
capturar y enjuiciar: bring to justice
capucha: hood
capullo: bud

caqui: khaki
cara: face, front, head, side, surface
cara a cara: face to face
cara de enojo/ concentración: frown
caracol: cochlea, snail
carácter: character, moral fiber, nature, temper
característica: attribute, characteristic, feature, landmark, point, quality
característicamente: distinctively
características de la línea: line quality
característico: characteristic, distinctive, peculiar, typical
caracterización: characterization
caracterizar: characterize
¡caramba!: shucks
carámbano: icicle
caramelo: sweet
caramelo masticable: taffy
carátula: face
caravana: recreational vehicle, RV
¡caray!: shucks
carbohidrato: carbohydrate
carbón: coal
carbón (vegetal): charcoal
carbonatado: carbonated
carbono: carbon
carburador: carburetor
carburante: fuel
carcacha: clunker
carcajada: laughter
carcajearse: howl
cárcel: jail, prison
cárcel (local): jailhouse
cárcel abierta: minimum security prison
cárcel de puertas abiertas: minimum security prison
cardenal: cardinal
cardiaco: cardiac
carecer: lack
carencia: lack
carente: void
carente de valor: sour grapes
careta: mask
careta (de esgrima): helmet
carga: baggage, burden, charge, freight, load
carga de trabajo: work input
carga eléctrica: electrical charge
carga fiscal: taxation
cargado: heavy, live, loaded
cargado de electricidad: electric
cargador: longshoreman, magazine, mover
cargadora: mover

cargamento: cargo
cargar: bear, carry, charge, debit, lift, load
cargar con: schlep
cargar contra: charge
cargar (con) el muerto: be left holding the bag
cargo: office
cargo de oficial: commission
cargo extra: extra
cargo financiero: finance charge
caricatura: cartoon
caridad: charity
caries: decay
cariño: attachment, darling, dear, fondness, honey, sweetheart, TLC
cariñosamente: fondly, lovingly, warmly
cariñoso: fond, loving, tender, warm
carísimo: extravagant
caritativo: charitable
carnada: bait
carnal: bro
carnaval: carnival
carne: flesh, meat
carne de ave: poultry
carne de borrego/ carnero: mutton
carné de identidad: ID card, identification card, identity card
carne de res: beef
carnes frías: cold cuts, lunch meat
carnet de identidad: ID card, identification card, identity card
carnicera: butcher
carnicería: massacre, slaughter
carnicero: butcher
carnívora: carnivore
carnívoro: carnivore
caro: big-ticket, expensive, upscale
caro a: dear to
carpa: marquee
carpeta: binder, folder, portfolio
carpintera: carpenter
carpintero: carpenter
carraspear: to clear one's throat
carrera: career, dash, race, rally, run, sprint
carrera de motocicletas: speedway
carrera de obstáculos: hurdle
carrera de postas: relay
carrera de relevos: relay
carrera de velocidad: sprint
carreras: racing
carreta: cart, wagon
carrete: reel, spool
carretera: highway, road, route, Rte.
carretera de dos carriles separados: divided highway
carretera interestatal: interstate
carretilla: pushcart,

wheelbarrow
carril: lane, rail
carril de alta velocidad: fast lane
carriola: baby carriage
carrito: cart, pushcart, shopping cart
carrito del súper: shopping cart
carro: automobile, car, wagon
carro de bomberos: fire engine, fire truck
carro de carga: freight car
carro de la basura: garbage truck
carro deportivo: sports car
carro dormitorio: Pullman
carrocería: body
carromato: wagon
carroñero: scavenger
carruaje: carriage, coach
carta: card, chart, charter, letter, menu, playing card
carta adjunta: cover letter
carta de diamantes: diamond
cartas a una personalidad: fan mail
cartel: poster
cártel: cartel
cartera: billfold, letter carrier, purse, wallet
carterita de cerillos: matchbook
cartero: letter carrier, mailman
cartílago: cartilage
cartón: card, cardboard, carton, construction paper
cartucho: ammunition, cartridge
cartulina: card, construction paper
casa: home, house, household, place
casa (principal): ranch house
casa adosada: row house
Casa Blanca: White House
casa club: clubhouse
casa de campo: lodge, villa
casa de huéspedes: guest house
casa de la moneda: mint
casa de moneda: mint
casa de muñecas: dollhouse
casa de una planta: bungalow
casa de una sola planta: ranch house
casa dúplex: duplex
casa prefabricada: manufactured home
casa rodante: trailer
casado: married
casamiento: marriage
casar(se): marry, match
cascada: falls

cáscara: peel, shell, skin
cascarrabias: cranky
casco: helmet, hoof, hull
casero: garden-variety, homemade, landlord
casi: almost, hardly, near, nearly, next to
casi crudo: rare
casi todos: most
casilla: box
casilla de votación: polling place
casino: casino
casita de campo: cottage
caso: case, instance, point
cassette: cassette
casta: caste
castañetear: chatter
castigar: hammer, punish
castigo: detention, penalty, punishment
castigos corporales: corporal punishment
castillo: castle
casual: casual
casucha: hut
casucha del perro: doghouse
catalizar: catalyze
catalogar: label, stereotype
catálogo: catalog, schedule
catarata(s): falls
catarina: ladybug
catarro: cold
catarsis: catharsis
catástrofe: catastrophe, disaster
catastrófico: disastrous
cátcher: catcher
catear: search
cátedra: chair, lecture
catedral: cathedral
catedrática: lecturer, professor
catedrático: lecturer, professor
categoría: category, grade, league, rank, status
categóricamente: outright
categórico: emphatic, flat, outright, outspoken
catering: catering
católica: Catholic, Roman Catholic
catolicismo: Catholicism
católico: Catholic, Roman Catholic
católico romano: Roman Catholic
catorce: fourteen
catorceavo: fourteenth
caucho: rubber
caudal (volumétrico): discharge
causa: cause, reason
causa de muerte: killer
causalidad falsa: false causality
causar: cause, create, do, hold, inflict, move
causar buena/mala

impresión: make a good/bad impression
causar disturbios: riot
causar molestia: put out
causar un revuelo: make a splash
cautela: caution
cautelosamente: cautiously, warily
cauteloso: cautious, wary
cautiva: captive
cautivo: captive
cavar: dig
cavidad: cavity
cavilación: musing
cavilar: meditate, muse
caza: fighter, game, hunt, hunting
caza de brujas: witch hunt
cazador: hunter
cazadora: hunter
cazar: hunt, trap
cazuela: casserole
cc: cc
CD: CD
CD-ROM: CD-ROM
cebar: bait
cebo: bait
cebolla: onion
cebolla cambray: green onion, scallion
cebollín/ cebollino/ cebollita: green onion, scallion
ceder: bow, cave in, give, give way, recede, yield
ceder el lugar: make way
ceder el paso: yield
cédula de identidad: identity card
cefalea: headache
cefalotórax: cephalothorax
cegar: blind
ceguera: blind, blindness
ceja: eyebrow
celda: cell
celda de combustible: fuel cell
celebración: celebration, festival
celebrar: celebrate, hold
célebre: celebrated
celebridad: celebrity
celestial: celestial
celoma: coelom
celos: jealousy
celosamente: jealously
celoso: jealous
Celsius: Celsius
célula: cell
célula de combustible: fuel cell
célula de guarda: guard cell
célula electroquímica: fuel cell
célula eucariota: eukaryotic cell
célula fotoeléctrica: photocell
célula hija: daughter cell
célula madre: parent cell
célula oclusiva: guard cell
célula procariota:

prokaryotic cell
célula procariótica:
prokaryotic cell
célula sexual: sex cell
celular: cellphone,
cellular, cellular phone
celular (que también
toma fotografías):
camera phone
celular inteligente:
smart phone
cementerio: cemetery
cemento: cement,
mortar
cena: dinner, supper
cenar: dine
cenefa: border, fringe
ceniza: ash, cinder
censo: census
censurar: fault
centavo: cent, nickel,
penny
centenares: hundreds
centenario: centennial
centeno: rye
centésima parte:
hundredth
centésimo: hundredth
centígrados: Celsius
centilitro: centiliter
centímetro(s):
centimeters, cm
céntimo: nickel, penny
centrado en: centered
central: central
central eléctrica: power
plant, power station
centralmente: centrally
centrar(se) en: center
centrarse: center oneself
céntrico: centrally
centro: bureau, center,
core, focus, heart,
infield, middle,
midfielder, midtown
centro comercial: mall,
plaza, shopping center,
strip mall
centro de atención:
center
centro de atención
diurna para ancianos o
minusválidos: day care
centro de atención
telefónica: call center
centro de ayuda
(remota): help desk
centro de detención:
detention center
Centro de
Entrenamiento de
Oficiales de la Reserva:
ROTC
centro de la atención:
front and center
centro de la ciudad: city
center
centro de la tierra: inner
core
centro de readaptación
social para menores:
reform school
centro de salud: health
center
centro del campo:
midfield
centro del escenario:
center stage

centro electoral: polling
place
centro estudiantil:
student union
centro izquierda: left-
of-center
centro médico: health
center
centro vacacional: resort
centrocampista:
midfield
centrómero: centromere
centuria: century
ceñido: form-fitting,
snug, tight
ceño fruncido: frown
cepillada: brush
cepillar: brush, groom,
plane, shave off
cepillo: brush, plane
cepillo de dientes:
toothbrush
cera: polish, wax
cerámica: ceramic,
pottery
cerca: by, close by/at
hand, fence, near,
nearby
cerca de: circa, close to/
on, near, off
cercanía: approach,
closeness
cercano: close,
immediate, near,
nearby, upcoming
cercano a: toward
cercar: besiege, close in,
fence, ring, surround
cercenar: chop off
cerda: sow
cerdo: pig, pork
cereal: cereal
cereales: cereal
cerebelo: cerebellum
cerebro: brain, cerebrum,
mind
ceremonia: ceremony,
function
ceremoniosamente:
stiffly
ceremonioso: stiff
cereza: cherry
cerezo: cherry
cerilla: match
cerillo: bagger, match
cerillos de carterita:
matchbook
cero: nil, zero
cero (en tenis): love
cero absoluto: absolute
zero
cero de una función:
zeros of a function
cerrado: closed, narrow,
sharp, shut
cerradura: lock
cerrajera: locksmith
cerrajero: locksmith
cerrar(se): clamp, close,
close down, exit, fasten,
seal, shut, shut down
cerrar con barricadas:
barricade
cerrar con llave: lock
cerrar con un chasquido:
snap

cerrar con un golpe seco:
snap
cerrar de golpe: bang,
slam
cerrar el paso: box in
cerrar el sistema: log out
cerrar filas: close ranks
cerrojo: bolt, lock
certamen: tournament
certeza: assurance,
certainty, security
certificado: certificate
certificado de regalo:
gift certificate
cerveza: beer
cese al fuego: ceasefire
césped: lawn
cesta: basket
cesta de Venus: basket
sponge
cesto: basket, hamper
cesto de papeles:
wastebasket
CFC: CFC
CGI: CGI
chabacano: apricot
chafa: low-end
chal: shawl
chaleco: vest
chamaco: boy
chamarra: jacket
champaña: champagne
champú: shampoo
chance: chance
chancho: pig
chanchullo: fix
chancla: flip-flop,
slipper, thong
chancla de pata de gallo:
thong
chango: monkey
chantaje: blackmail
chantajear: blackmail
chantajista: blackmailer
chapa: badge, license
plate, lock
chapado: plated
chapalear: lap
chapaleo: lapping
chaparro: short
chaparrón: shower
chapas: plates
chapotear: splash
chapoteo: splash
chapurreado: broken
charco: pool, puddle
charla: bull session, chat,
chatter
charla digital: chat room
charlar: chat
charola: tray
charola metálica para
hornear: cookie sheet
chasquear: flick, pop
chasquido: flick, pop,
snap
chatarra: junk, scrap
chavo: guy
checar: make sure
chef: chef
chelo: cello
cheque: bank check,
check
cheque certificado:
certified check
cheque de caja: cashier's
check
cheque de viajero:

traveler's check
cheque en blanco: blank check
cheque inservible: bad check
cheque sin fondos: bad check
chica: youngster
chicana: Chicana
chicano: Chicano
chícharo: pea
chícharo (chino): snow pea
chichón: bump, lump
chicle: gum
chicloso: taffy
chico: boy, little, small, youngster
chiflado: insane, nuts (about something/somebody)
chiflar: whistle
chiíta: Shiite
chile: chili
chile con carne: chili, chili con carne
chile con frijoles: chili
chillido: cry, scream
chillón: loud
chimenea: chimney, fireplace, grate
chimpancé: chimpanzee
chinche: tack, thumbtack
chincheta: tack, thumbtack
chino: curl, curly, fuzzy
chipote: bump, lump
chiquero: pigpen
chiquito: tiny
chiripa: break
chirriar: grate, squeak
chirrido: squeak
chisme: gadget, gossip
chismear: gossip, schmooze
chismosa: gossip, rumormonger
chismoso: gossip, rumormonger
chispa: spark, sparkle
chispazo: flash
chispear: sparkle, sprinkle
chiste: joke
chistera: top hat
chistoso: funny
chivo: goat
chivo expiatorio: scapegoat
chocar: bump, clash, collide, crash, slam
chocar contra: run into
chocolate: chocolate, cocoa
chocolate amargo: dark chocolate
chocolate oscuro: dark chocolate
chocolate sin leche: dark chocolate
chocolatina: candy bar
chofer: driver
chompa: sweater
chongo: bun
choque: clash, collision, crash, impact, shock
chorrear: drip, streak
chorrito: squirt

chorro: fountain, jet
choza: hut, shack
chubasco: shower
chueco: crooked
chuleta: chop
chupar: suck
cianobacteria: cyanobacteria
cibercafé: Internet café
ciberespacio: cyberspace
cicatriz: scar
cicatrizar: heal
cicla: bike, cycle
ciclismo: cycling
ciclista: biker, cyclist, rider
ciclo: cycle
ciclo celular: cell cycle
ciclo de las rocas: rock cycle
ciclo del agua: hydrologic cycle, water cycle
ciclo hidrológico: hydrologic cycle
ciclón: cyclone
ciclopista: bike path
ciego: blind, mindless
cielo: heaven, sky
ciempiés: centipede
cien: hundred
cien por ciento: a hundred percent/one hundred percent
ciénaga: bog, marsh, swamp
ciencia: science
ciencia ficción: sci-fi, science fiction
ciencias biológicas: life science
ciencias de la Tierra: earth science
ciencias de la vida: life science
ciencias físicas: physical science
ciencias sociales: social science
cieno: silt
científica: scientist
científicamente: scientifically
científico: scientific, scientist
cientos: hundreds
cierre: catch, closing, closure, shutdown
cierre (de cremallera): zipper
cierta cantidad: so much/many
cierto: certain, positive, some, true
ciervo: deer
cifra: figure
cifrar: pin
cigarrillo: cigarette
cigarro: cigarette
cilantro: cilantro
cilindro: cylinder
cilio: cilia
cima: crest, peak, summit
cimientos: foundation
cinc: zinc
cinco: five
cincuenta: fifty
cincuentavo: fiftieth

cine: cinema, motion picture, movie, movie theater, theater
cinematográfico: cinematic
cinestético: kinesthetic
cínicamente: cynically
cínico: cynical
cinismo: cynicism
cinta: band, ribbon, tape
cinta adhesiva: duct tape, tape
cinta de llegada: tape
cinta de video: videotape
cinta métrica: tape measure
cintura: waist
cinturón: belt
cinturón de asteroides: asteroid belt
cinturón de Kuiper: Kuiper belt
cinturón de seguridad: seat belt
circo: circus
circo mediático: media circus
circuito: circuit
circuito cerrado: closed-circuit
circuito en paralelo: parallel circuit
circuito en serie: series circuit
circuito integrado: chip
circulación: circulation, traffic
circulación general: systemic circulation
circulación pulmonar: pulmonary circulation
circulación sistémica: systemic circulation
circular: circular, circulate, cruise, form letter, get around, memo
circulatorio: circulatory
círculo: circle
circuncidar: circumcise
circuncisión: circumcision
circunferencia: circumference
circunspección: restraint
circunstancia: circumstance, matter, picture
cirro: cirrus
ciruela: plum
ciruela pasa: prune
cirugía: surgery
cirugía de puente coronario: bypass
cirujana: surgeon
cirujano: surgeon
cisma: split
cita: appointment, date, engagement, quotation, quote
citar: cite, quote
citatorio: summons
citocinesis: cytokinesis
citoplasma: cytoplasm
citosina: cytosine
cítrico: citrus
ciudad: city, town
ciudad dormitorio:

bedroom
ciudad pequeña: Main Street
ciudad universitaria: campus
ciudadana: citizen, national
ciudadanía: citizenship
ciudadano: citizen, national
cívico: civic
civil: civil, civilian
civilización: civilization
civilizado: civilized
civismo: civics, civility
clamar: bay, clamor, cry out for, pop off
clan: clan
clandestino: underground
claqué: tap dance
clara (de huevo): white
claramente: brightly, clearly, distinctly, markedly
claridad: clarity, definition, light
clarificar: clarify
clarinete: clarinet
claro: anyway, clear, clearing, distinct, explicit, light, marked, obviously, of course, opening, pale, plain, sharp, thin, transparent
claro está: indeed
claro que no: not at all, of course not
clase: breed, class, lesson, sort
clase baja: lower class
clase dirigente: establishment
clase marginada: underclass
clase media: middle class
clase obrera: working class
clase privilegiada: upper class
clase trabajadora: working class
clásicamente: classically
clásico: classic, classical, derby, vintage
clasificación: classification, designation
clasificado: qualifier
clasificar(se): class, classify, fall into, file, place, qualify, rank, rate, sort
cláusula: clause
clavada: slam dunk
clavado: diving
clavar(se): dig, drive, glue, hammer, nail, plunge, stick, tack
clave: central, clef, code, crucial, key, password
clave contextual: context clue
clave de fa: bass clef
clave de sol: treble clef
clave dicotómica: dichotomous key

clavija: plug
clavo: clove, nail, pin
claxon: horn
clerecía: ministry
clérigo: Reverend
clero: clergy, ministry
click: click
cliente: client, customer, patron
clientela: practice
clima: climate, weather
clímax: climax
clínica: clinic
clínicamente: clinically
clínico: clinical
clip: clip, paper clip
clon: clone
clonar: clone
cloro: bleach
clorofila: chlorophyll
cloroplasto: chloroplast
clóset: closet, cupboard
club: club
club de golf: golf club
club estudiantil masculino: fraternity
club nocturno: nightclub
clustering: clustering
clutch: clutch
cm: cm
coacción: constraint
coalición: coalition
cobarde: coward
cobertizo: shed
cobertura: coverage, reporting
cobijas: cover
cobrador: collector, conductor
cobradora: collector, conductor
cobrar: cash, charge, claim, gain, gather
cobrar vida: come alive
cobrar(se): take its toll
cobre: copper
coca: coke
cocaína: cocaine
cocer: boil
cocer a fuego lento: stew
cocer al vapor: steam
coche: automobile, car, coach
coche de alquiler: taxi, taxicab
coche deportivo: sports car
cochecito: baby carriage
cochina: sow
cochino: filthy
cocido: done
cocina: cooking, cuisine, kitchen
cocinar: cook, cooking
cocinar al vapor: steam
cocinar en horno de microondas: microwave
cocinera: chef, cook
cocinero: chef, cook
cóclea: cochlea
coco: coconut
cocoa: cocoa
cocodrilo: crocodile, gator
coctel: cocktail
coctel de camarones: shrimp cocktail

COD: C.O.D.
codearse: rub shoulders/ elbows with someone
codicia: greed
codicioso: greedy
codificado con colores: color-coded
código: code
código abierto: open-source
código de zona: area code
código postal: zip code
codo: bend, cheap, elbow
codo con codo: alongside, side by side
codorniz: quail
coeficiente: coefficient
coeficiente intelectual: IQ
coestrella: costar
coevolución: coevolution
cofre: chest, hood
coger: scoop, seize, take
coger a alguien desprevenido: catch somebody off guard
coherente: consistent
cohete: rocket
cohete espacial: rocket
coincidencia: agreement, coincidence
coincidir: coincide
coincidir parcialmente: overlap
coito: intercourse
cojear: limp
cojera: limp
cojín: cushion
cojín del mouse: mouse pad
cojín del ratón: mouse pad
cojín para los pies: ottoman
cojo: lame
col: cabbage
col de Bruselas: brussels sprout
cola: line, tail
cola de caballo: ponytail
colaboración: collaboration
colaborador: collaborator
colaboradora: collaborator
colaborar: collaborate, contribute, help
coladera: colander
colador: colander
colapso: collapse
colar: strain
colcha: quilt
colchón: mattress
colear(se): fishtail
colección: assortment, collecting, collection, portfolio
coleccionar: collect
coleccionista: collector
colecita de Bruselas: sprout
colectivamente: collectively
colectivo: collective
colega: associate, colleague, fellow
colegial: schoolboy
colegiala: schoolgirl

colegiatura: tuition
colegio: college, school
colegio electoral: electoral college
colegio privado: public school
cólera: cholera, rage
colesterol: cholesterol
coleta: ponytail
colgador: hanger, peg
colgajo: flap
colgante: pendant
colgar: hang, hang up, perch, post, put up, ring, sag, suspend
coliflor: cauliflower
colilla: butt
colina: hill
colina de arena: sand dune
colisión: collision, impact
collar: collar, necklace, string
colmado: heaping
colmar de: heap, shower
colmena: nest
colmo: breaking point
colocado: set
colocar: fit, install, lay, place, plant, position, put, set, stack, stand
colocar (subrepticiamente): plant
colocar en bolsa: float
coloide: colloid
colon: colon
colona: colonist, settler
colonia: colony, community
colonial: colonial
colonialismo: colonialism
colonizador: colonist, pioneering
colonizadora: colonist, pioneering
colonizar: colonize
colono: colonist, settler
color: color
color aceituna: olive
color al óleo: oil paint
color caprichoso: arbitrary color
color carne: flesh-colored
color durazno: peach
color local: local color
color naranja: orange
color primario: primary color
color secundario: secondary color
colorado: dirty
colorear: color
colorido: color, colorful
colosal: heroic
columna: column
columna vertebral: backbone, spine
columnista: columnist
columpiar(se): swing
columpio: swing
coma: comma
comadreja: opossum
comadrona: midwife
comandante: commander, major
combate: battle, combat,

engagement, fight
combatir: battle, combat, fight, fight off
combativo: militant
combinación: blend, cocktail, combination, mix, permutation
combinación (de colores): color scheme
combinado: combined
combinar(se): combine, couple, integrate, match, mix
combustible: fuel
combustible fósil: fossil fuel
combustible sin plomo: unleaded
combustión: combustion
comedero: trough
comedero para pájaros: bird feeder
comedia: comedy, soap, soap opera, stand-up
comedia del arte: commedia dell'arte
comedor: canteen, dining room, lunchroom
comensalismo: commensalism
comentar: comment, remark
comentario: comment, commentary, dig, remark
comentario favorable: puff
comentario jugada a jugada: play-by-play
comentario medio en broma: tongue in cheek
comentario socarrón: crack
comentarios de la funda del CD: liner note
comentarista: commentator
comentarista de deportes: sportscaster
comenzar: begin, kick off, start
comenzar como: start out
comenzar con: start on
comenzar de nuevo: start over
comenzar por: start off
comer(se): consume, eat, eat away, eat into, feed, lunch, picnic
comercial: commercial, for-profit
comercializar: market
comercialmente: commercially
comerciante: dealer, merchandiser, merchant, shopkeeper, trader
comerciar: trade
comerciar en: deal
comercio: commerce, trade, trading
comestible: edible
comestibles: grocery
comestibles no perecederos: dry goods

cometa: comet, kite
cometa Halley: Halley's comet
cometer: commit
cometer un desliz: slip up
cometer un error: err
comezón: itch
cómic: comic book
cómica: comedian, comic
cómico: comedian, comic, comical, funny
comida: cooking, dinner, food, lunch, meal
comida en el campo: picnic
comida para llevar: takeout
comida preparada: takeout
comida rápida: fast food
comienzo: beginning, opening, outset, start
comillas: quotation marks, quotes
comiquísimo: hilarious
comisaría: police station, station house
comisión: commission
Comisión Controladora de Acciones y Valores: SEC
comisión investigadora: tribunal
comisionada: commissioner
comisionado: commissioner
comisionar: commission
comité: committee
comité de acción política: political action committee
como: after, as, for instance, like
cómo: how, however
¿Cómo?: sorry?
como consecuencia de: on the strength of
como de costumbre: typically
como de rayo: at lightning speed
como es característico: typically
como es de esperarse: as usual
como estarlo viendo: in one's mind's eye
como guste: as you please/whatever you please
como loco: crazily, like mad
como más: at most/at the most
¡cómo no!: by all means
como pez en el agua: in one's element
como por arte de magia: magically
como rayo: at lightning speed
como sea: however
como si: as, if
como siempre: as ever, as usual
como sigue: as follows
como tal: as such

cómo te atreves/se atreve/se atreven: how dare you
como último recurso: as a last resort
como una flecha: dart
cómoda: bureau
cómodamente: comfortably, snugly
comodidad: comfort, convenience
comodín: joker
comodino: NIMBY
cómodo: at ease, comfortable, convenient, snug
compactado: compacted
compacto: compact, dense
compadecer(se): feel for, sympathize, take pity on
compaginar: gel
compañera: colleague, companion, date, fellow, peer
compañera de candidatura: running mate
compañera de clase: classmate
compañera de equipo: teammate
compañera de trabajo: colleague
compañero: colleague, companion, date, fellow, peer
compañero de candidatura: running mate
compañero de clase: classmate
compañero de cuarto: roommate
compañero de equipo: teammate
compañía: company, corporation, firm, operation
compañía afiliada: affiliate
compañía de seguros: insurer
compañía de telecomunicaciones: carrier
compañía multinacional: multinational
comparable: comparable, matched, matching
comparación: comparison
comparado con: compared with/to, in proportion to
comparar: compare, contrast, match
comparar notas: compare notes
comparativo: comparatively
comparecer: appear
compartimento: compartment, stall
compartimiento: compartment, stall
compartir: share

compartir archivos: file-sharing
compás: bar, measure, meter, time
compás binario: duple meter
compás compuesto: compound meter
compás mixto: mixed meter
compás ternario: triple meter
compasión: compassion, sympathy
compatibilidad: compatibility
compatible: compatible
compensación: comp, compensation
compensar: balance, compensate, offset
competencia: competence, competition, contest, derby, tournament
competente: capability, competent
competentemente: capably, competently
competidor: competitor, contestant
competidora: competitor, contestant
competir: compete, contend, vie
competitivamente: competitively
competitividad: competitiveness
competitivo: competitive
compilar: compile
complacer: oblige, please
complacido: pleased
complaciente: fond, indulgent
complejidad: complexity, intricacy
complejo: complex, compound, elaborate, intricate, involved, sophisticated
complejo de viviendas: housing project
complejo habitacional: development
complementar: complement, supplement
complemento: complement, supplement
complemento directo: direct object
completamente: completely, entirely, fully, heartily, in full, thoroughly, utterly, wholly
completamente despierto: wide awake
completar: complete, supplement
completo: al., all-around, all-over, booked up/fully booked/booked solid, complete, full, full-length, thorough, total

complexión: build, constitutional
complicación: complication
complicado: complicated, elaborate
complicar: complicate, confuse
complicar(se) la existencia: fuss
cómplice: accessory
complot: plot
componente: component, constituent
componer(se): compose, heal
comportamiento: behavior
comportamiento aprendido: learned behavior
comportarse: act, behave, sound
composición: composition, essay, makeup
compositor: composer
compositora: composer
composta: compost
compostura: restraint
compra: acquisition, buy, purchase
comprado: store-bought
comprador: buyer, purchaser, shopper
compradora: buyer, purchaser, shopper
comprar: buy, fix, purchase, shop
comprar acciones de socios: buy out
comprar todo lo posible: buy up
comprar un seguro: insure
compras: shopping
compraventa por correo: mail order
comprender: embrace, grasp, make out, realize, sink in, sympathize, understand
comprender mal: misunderstand
comprensible: understandable
comprensiblemente: understandably
comprensión: comprehension, grasp, realization, understanding
comprensión visual: visual literacy
comprensivo: understanding
comprimido: caplet
comprobado: established
comprobar: check
comprometer: bind, compromise, pin down
comprometerse: pledge, undertake
comprometerse a: commit
comprometido: at stake,

engaged, involved, on board

compromiso: commitment, engagement, pledge

compuesto: composite, compound, double-barreled

compuesto covalente: covalent compound

compuesto iónico: ionic compound

compuesto orgánico: organic compound

computación: computing

computadora: computer

computadora central: mainframe

computadora de escritorio: desktop

computadora personal: personal computer

computadora portátil: laptop, notebook

computarizado: computerized

computarizar: computerize

común: common, crude, ordinary, popular, regular

común y corriente: garden-variety, usual

comunicación: communication

comunicaciones: communication

comunicado de prensa: news release

comunicar(se): communicate, inform, let somebody know, put through, reach

comunicativo: forthcoming

comunidad: community

comunismo: communism

comunista: communist

comunitario: communal

comúnmente: commonly

con: in, on, to, under, with

con actitud desafiante: defiantly

con agradecimiento: gratefully

con agramaticalidad: ungrammatically

con aire acondicionado: air-conditioned

con aire de culpabilidad: guiltily

con aire vacilante: uncertainly

con amabilidad: helpfully, neighborly

con ambages: roundabout

con ambigüedad: ambiguously

con ánimo para: (feel) up to

con anticipación: in advance

con aptitud: inclined

con aptitudes para la

música: musical

con arrogancia: arrogantly

con audacia: boldly

con bombo y platillo: hoopla

con cariño: fondly

con carrera: professional

con certeza: for certain

con clase: classy

con comprensión: sympathetically

con confianza: confidently, feel free

con confidencialidad: confidentially

con corrección: correctly

con corriente: live

con criterio selectivo: selectively

con cuidado: carefully, neatly, with ease

con delicadeza: delicately

con demasiada confianza: familiar

con desaprobación: disapprovingly

con desconcierto: blankly

con desesperación: badly

con destino a: bound for

con detenimiento: at length

con dinamismo: dynamically

con dotes artísticas: artistically

con dureza: hard

con el propósito de: in order to, with a view to

con el tiempo: eventually, in time

con empuje: go-ahead

con energía: energetically

con enojo: crossly

con ensimismamiento: distantly

con entusiasmo: enthusiastically, heartily, keenly

con envidia: jealously

con escarcha: frosty

con esfuerzo: with effort

con estabilidad: on an even keel

con estilo: classy

con excepción de: aside from, excluding

con facilidad: easily, with ease

con financiamiento: installment plan

con fines de lucro: for-profit

con firmeza: fast

con fluidez: fluently

con forma de: shaped

con franqueza: straight

con frecuencia: often

con ganas: with a vengeance

con gran alegría: delightedly

con gusto: gladly, happy, willingly

con honores: cum laude

con humildad: humbly

con humor: humorously

con impotencia: helplessly

con indignación: disgustedly

con indulgencia: indulgently

con información práctica: how-to

con justicia: justly

con la derecha: right-handed

con la esperanza de: in the hope of/that

con la inclinación: inclined

con las manos: with one's bare hands

con las manos vacías: empty-handed

con lentejuelas: sequined

con lo cual: thereby

con magnetismo: magnetic

con miras a: with a view to

con molde: cookie cutter

con mucha visión: keen

con mucho: by far

con muy poco dinero: on a shoestring

con muy pocos recursos: on a shoestring

con naturalidad: naturally

con optimismo: optimistically

con pericia: expertly

con poca diplomacia: undiplomatically

con pretensiones: self-righteousness

con pretexto de: in the name of something

con propiedad: properly

con qué frecuencia: how often

con recelo: dubiously

con receta: by prescription

con relación a: in relation to, relative to

con renuencia: grudging, reluctantly

con reservas: qualified

con respecto a: concerning, with respect to

con (buenos) resultados: to (good) effect

con rigidez: stiffly

con rodeos: roundabout

con rumbo a: bound for

con salvedad: qualified

con seguridad: for certain, safely, surely

con sencillez: simply, straightforwardly

con sensatez: sensibly

con sensibilidad: sensitively

con sentido: meaningful

con seriedad: earnestly

con severidad: severely

con sueño: sleepily

con suerte: hopefully, luckily

con tal que: as long as/ so long as

con tecnología de punto: state-of-the-art

con toda naturalidad: come naturally

con toda sinceridad: from the heart/from the bottom of one's heart

con toda tranquilidad: casually

con todo: all told, for all

con todo cariño: love/ love from/all my love

con todo respeto: with due respect

con tono apremiante: urgently

con trabajos: with effort

con tristeza: gloomily, sadly

con un lenguaje vulgar: dirty

con un olfato agudo: keen

con un solo/único propósito: single-minded

con vidrio: glazed

cóncavo: concave

concebir: conceive, devise, formulate

conceder: accord

concentración: concentration, rally

concentrado: concentrated, full, massed

concentrar(se): center oneself, concentrate, cluster, focus, mass, one's mind is on/have one's mind on, turn

concepción: conception

concepto: concept, idea

conceptual: conceptual

concernir: concern

concertar: arrange, broker

concesión: concession, franchise

concesiones mutuas: give and take

concha: shell

conchita: shell

conciencia: awareness, conscience, consciousness

conciencia fonémica: phonemic awareness

concientizar: educate

concienzudo: thorough

concierto: concert, concerto

conciso: brief

concluido: complete

concluir: close, conclude, finalize, finish, wind up

conclusión: conclusion, ending

conclusiones finales: closing argument

concordada: matching

concordar: agree, square

concretamente: specifically

concretar: fix, nail down

concreto: concrete, hard, particular

concreto asfáltico: blacktop

concurrencia: attendance

concursante: competitor, contestant

concurso: quiz

concurso de belleza: beauty pageant

concurso de horneado: bake-off

concurso de ortografía: spelling bee

condado: county, parish

conde: count

condecoración: medal

condena: condemnation, conviction

condenado: doomed

condenar: condemn, convict

condensación: condensation

condensar: condense

condensarse: condense

condescendiente: indulgent

condición: condition, qualification, status

condicional: conditional

condicionamiento: conditioning

condicionar: condition

condimentar: season

condimento: flavoring

condominio: condominium

condón: condom

conducción: conduct, conduction, leadership

conducir: conduct, drive, guide, lead, navigate, shepherd, steer, wheel

conducir bajo la influencia del alcohol: DUI, DWI

conducir ebrio: drunk driving

conducirse: conduct

conducta: behavior, conduct

conducta social: social behavior

conductismo: behaviorism

conductista: behaviorist

conducto: duct, pipeline, tube

conducto deferente: vas deferens

conductor(a): broadcaster, conductor, driver

conductor(a) de camión: trucker

conductor(a) ebrio: drunk driver

conectar: connect, link, plug in, tie

conectar(se): hook up

conejo: rabbit

conejo de cola de algodón: cottontail

conexión: connection

conexiones: connection

confabulado con: in league with

confabularse contra: gang up

confederación: confederation

conferencia: lecture

conferencia de prensa: news conference, press conference

conferenciante: lecturer

conferencista: lecturer

conferir: accord

conferir poder: empower

confesar: confess, cop to, own up

confesarse (culpable): plead guilty

confesión: confession

confesional: sectarian

confiable: reliable, solid, sound

confiablemente: reliably

confiado: assertive, assured

confianza: confidence, faith, familiarity, trust

confianza del consumidor: consumer confidence

confianza en sí mismo: self-confidence

confianzudamente: familiarly

confiar: look to, trust

confiar en: rely on

confiar en que alguien hará algo: trust someone to do something

confiar(le) a: trust someone with

confidencial: classified, confidential, inside

confidencialidad: confidentiality

confinado: confined

confinamiento: confinement

confinar: confine

confirmación: confirmation

confirmar: bear out, confirm, verify

conflicto: conflict, warfare

confluir: merge

conformación: shape

conformarse: make do

conformarse con: settle for

conforme: content

conforme a: according to, whereby

confort: comfort

confrontación: confrontation

confrontar: confront, tackle

confundido: confused, lost, mixed up, muddled, puzzled

confundir: cloud, confuse, mistake, mix up, muddle, muddle up, puzzle

confusión: confusion, scramble, turmoil

confuso: confused, confusing, fuzzy, mixed up
congelación: freezing
congelado: freezing, frozen
congelador: freezer
congeladora: freezer
congelamiento: freeze
congelar(se): freeze
congeniar: hit it off
congestionar: choke
congresista: congressman, congressperson, congresswoman
congreso: conference, Congress, congress, convention
congruente: congruent
conífera: conifer
conjeturar: speculate
conjunción: conjunction
conjuntamente: jointly
conjunto: band, ensemble, joint, outfit
conjunto deportivo: sweats
conllevar: carry
conmemoración: commemoration
conmemorar: commemorate
conmemorativo: memorial
conmoción: ferment, shock, shock wave, uproar
conmocionado: shocked
conmocionar: stun
conmovedor: moving
conmover(se): move
conmovido: moved, touched
connexion: link
cono: cone
cono de viento: windsock
cono volcánico: cinder cone
conocedor: knowledgeable
conocer(se): get to know, know, learn, meet, meet up
conocida: acquaintance
conocido: acquaintance, household, known, noted, renowned
conocimiento: acquaintance, insight, know-how, knowledge
conocimientos: expertise
conquistador: conqueror
conquistadora: conqueror
conquistar: conquer
consagrado: time-honored
consagrar: devote
consagrarse: dedicate
consanguíneo: own flesh and blood
consciente: aware, conscious
conscientemente: consciously
consecución:

achievement
consecuencia: aftermath, consequence, implication, outcome
consecuentemente: consequently
consecutivo: consecutive, running
conseguir: accomplish, achieve, attain, come by, drum up, enlist, fix up, gain, get, score
conseguir a: get/grab ahold of
conseguir algo: get hold of (something)
conseguir comunicarse: get through
conseguir con trabajos: scrape together
consejera: adviser, councilor, counselor, governor
consejera sentimental: advice columnist
consejero: adviser, councilor, counselor, governor
consejero sentimental: advice columnist
consejo: advice, board, counsel, hint
consejo municipal de vecinos: town meeting
consejo práctico: tip
consejos: guidance
consenso: consensus
consentidor: indulgent
consentimiento: consent, sanction
consentir(se): consent, fuss over, indulge, sanction, spoil
consentir en: agree to
conserje: janitor, superintendent
conservación: conservation
conservación de la energía: conservation of energy
conservación de la masa: conservation of mass
conservador: conservative, Victorian
conservadora: conservative
conservadoramente: conservatively
conservadurismo: conservatism
conservar: conserve, preserve, retain
considerable: considerable, fair, sizable, substantial
considerablemente: considerably, significantly, steeply
consideración: consideration, regard
consideradamente: thoughtfully
considerado: considerate, good, thoughtful
considerando:

considering
considerar: allow, class, consider, contemplate, debate, deem, deliberate, entertain, envisage, look into, perceive, rate, regard, see, take into account/ take account of, think, toy with, treat, view
considerar como: look on
considerarse: flatter
consigna: chant, slogan
consignar: state
consignas: chanting
consistente: consistent
consistir: consist
consola: consolation
consolar: comfort, console
consolidar: cement, consolidate
consomé: soup
consonante: consonant
consonante inicial: initial consonant
consorcio: consortium
conspiración: conspiracy, plot
conspirador: plotter
conspiradora: plotter
conspirar: plot, scheme
constancia: certificate, solidity
constante: consistent, constant, regular, steady, unrelenting
constantemente: constantly, continuously
constar: comprise, consist
constelación: constellation
consternación: dismay
consternado: dismayed
constitución: constitution
constitucional: constitutional
constituido legalmente: Incorporated
constituir: account for, constitute, form, make up
constitutivo: constituent
constituyente: constituent
construcción: building, construction, erection
construcción naval: shipbuilding
constructivo: constructive
construido: built
construir: build, construct, engineer, erect, put up
construir un jardín: landscape
consuelo: comfort, consolation
cónsul: minister
consulta: consultation, office
consultar: query, refer, see
consultar a: consult

consultar con: consult
consultivo: advisory
consultor: consultant
consultora: consultant
consultorio: office
consultorio (médico): doctor's office
consultorio dental: dentist's office
consultorio sentimental: advice column
consumado: accomplished, perfect
consumidor: consumer
consumidora: consumer
consumir: consume, run
consumirse: waste away
consumo: consumption, intake
contabilidad: accounting
contactar: contact
contacto: contact, touch
contado por un pajarito: on the grapevine
contador: accountant, counter
contador público titulado: certified public accountant
contadora: accountant
contadora pública titulada: certified public accountant
contagiar: infect, transmit
contagiarse: contract
contagiarse de: catch
contagioso: contagious, infectious
contaminación: contamination, pollution
contaminación sin origen determinado: nonpoint-source pollution
contaminación térmica: thermal pollution
contaminado: polluted
contaminante: pollutant
contaminante derivado: secondary pollutant
contaminante secundario: secondary pollutant
contaminar: contaminate, infect, pollute
contar: count, count up
contar con: bank on, count on, depend, reckon with, rely on, spare
contar uno por uno: count out
contemplación: contemplation
contemplar: contemplate, entertain, eye, look on
contemporáneo: contemporary
contender: run
contendiente: challenger
contenedor: container, holder
contener: contain, curb, hold, hold/keep

in check, include, restrain, stem, suppress
contenerse: hold back
contenido: content, subject matter
contenido emocional: expressive content
contentar: please
contento: content, glad, happy, high, pleased
contestador automático: answering machine
contestar: answer, reply, write/call back
contexto: context
contienda: contest, race, warfare
continental: continental
continente: continent, mainland
Continente Americano: Americas
contingente: contingent
continuación: follow-up
continuamente: all the time, continually, through
continuar: carry on, continue, follow through, go on
continuar con: pursue
continuar haciendo algo: keep doing something
continuo: continual, continuous
contra: against, crack, into, minus, up against, versus, vs.
contra la corriente: upstream
contra la ley: illegal
contra las reglas: illegal
contra reembolso: C.O.D.
contraatacar: counter
contrabajo: double bass
contrabandear: smuggle
contrabandista: smuggler
contrabando: smuggling
contracción: contraction
contracepción: contraception
contradecir: contradict
contradicción: contradiction
contradictorio: contradictory
contraer(se): catch, contract, come down with, get
contraer matrimonio: marry
contraer nupcias: marry
contrainterrogar: cross-examine
contrainterrogatorio: cross-examination
contraoferta: counteroffer
contraparte: counterpart
contrapeso: counterbalance
contrapunto: descant
contrario: contrary, opposite, reverse
contrario a: counter to
contrastar: contrast
contraste: contrast

contratar: contract, employ, engage, hire, sign, sign up, take on
contratiempo: setback, trouble
contratista: contractor
contrato: contract
contravención: breach
contraventana: shutter
contribución: contribution, taxation
contribución de impuestos: taxation
contribuir: chip in, contribute
contribuyente: taxpayer
contrincante: opponent
control: control, curb, grip, hold
control de crucero: cruise control
control de la ira: anger management
control de la natalidad: birth control
control de retroalimentación: feedback control
control remoto: remote control
controlado: controlled, under control
controlador: controller, driver
controladora: controller, driver
controlar(se): control
controlarse: get ahold of oneself
controversia: controversy
controvertido: controversial
contundente: decisive, emphatic
convección: convection
convencer: convince, get, induce, satisfy, win over
convencer de: persuade, talk into
convencido: convinced, strong
convención: convention
convención teatral: theatrical convention
convencional: conventional
convencionalismo: convention
convencionalmente: conventionally
conveniencia: convenience, desirability
conveniente: convenient, desirable, helpful, suitable
convenientemente: conveniently
convenio: accord, agreement, deal, settlement, treaty
convenir: pay, suit
convenir algo: have an interest in
convenir en: agree on
conversa: convert
conversación: chat,

conversation, talk
conversar: chat, talk
conversión: conversion, metamorphosis
conversión de energía: energy conversion
converso: convert
convertible: convertible
convertir(se): become, change, convert, evolve, make, transform, translate, turn
convertirse en realidad: realize
convicción: conviction, persuasion
convidar: treat
convincente: compelling, convincing, plausible
convincentemente: convincingly
convocar: call, convene, summon
convoy: convoy
conyugal: marital
cónyuge: spouse
cookie: cookie
cool: cool
cooperación: cooperation
cooperar: cooperate
cooperarse: chip in
cooperativa: collective
coordenada polar: polar coordinate
coordenadas: coordinates
coordinación: coordination
coordinado: coordinated
coordinador: coordinator
coordinadora: coordinator
coordinar: coordinate
copa: cup, drink, trophy
copia: copy
copiadora: copier, copy machine
copiar: copy, duplicate, imitate
copo de nieve: snowflake
coprotagonizar: costar
copyright: copyright
coque: coke
coqueta: flirt
coquetear: flirt
coqueteo: flirtation
coqueto: flirt
coraje: backbone, bravery, nerve
coral: chorale
Corán: Koran
corazón: core, heart
corbata: tie
corcovear: buck
cordel: string
cordero: lamb
cordial: friendly, hearty
cordiales saludos: Yours truly
cordillera: range
cordillera oceánica central: mid-ocean ridge
cordón: lace, shoestring
cordón umbilical: umbilical cord
cordura: sanity
córnea: cornea

cornear: gore
coro: choir, chorale, chorus
corona: corona, crown
coronar: cap, crown
coronel: colonel
coronilla: crown
corporación privada: privately held corporation
corporativo: corporate
corpúsculo (del espacio): planetesimal
corral: barnyard, bay, corral, pen
correa: belt, strap
correcaminos: roadrunner
corrección: correction, correctness
correccional: correctional
correctamente: correctly, right, truly
correctivo: correctional
correcto: correct, grammatical, proper, right
corrector: editor
corrector ortográfico: spell-checker
correctora: editor
corredor: aisle, broker, dealer, hall, jogger, runner
corredor de valores: stockbroker
corredora: dealer, jogger, runner
corredora de valores: stockbroker
corregir(se): correct, edit, heal, reform
corregir la ortografía: spell-check
correligionario: fellow
correo: e-mail, mail, post office
correo certificado: certified mail
correo electrónico: e-mail
correoso: tough
correr(se): circulate, draw, fire, flow, jog, jogging, kick out, race, run, running, rush, stream
correr con: meet
correr el riesgo: run a risk, take a chance
correr rápidamente: sprint
correr riesgos: be at risk
correspondencia: correspondence, mail
correspondencia electrónica no deseada: spam
corresponder: correspond, equate, go, repay
corresponder a: be up to
corresponderle: fall to
correspondiente: corresponding
corresponsal: correspondent

corriente: cheap, current, draft, running, tide
corriente ascendente: updraft
corriente costera longitudinal: longshore current
corriente (oceánica) de aguas profundas: deep current
corriente de convección: convection current
corriente de superficie: surface current
corriente descendente: downdraft
corriente en chorro: jet stream
corriente litoral: longshore current
corriente longitudinal de la costa: longshore current
corriente principal: mainstream
corriente superficial: surface current
corroborar: verify
corroer: eat away
corromper(se): corrupt
corrupción: corruption, pork barrel
corrupto: corrupt, pork barrel
cortada: cut
cortado: dead, sour
cortado a pico: vertical
cortadora de pasto: lawnmower
cortante: abrupt, cutting
cortar(se): carve, chop, chop down, clip, cut, cut off, hack, nick, pick, ring, shred, slit, split, sting
cortar al ras: crop
cortar en cubitos: dice
cortar en pedazos: cut up
cortar la respiración: wind
cortar por lo sano: nip in the bud
cortarse la comunicación: cut off
cortarse la línea: cut off
corte: court, cut, cutoff, nick, slash, slit, trim
corte de apelaciones: appeals court
corte de luz: outage
corte de pelo: haircut
corte de pelo estilo militar: buzz cut
corte superior: superior court
cortés: civil, courteous, gentle, polite
cortesía: courtesy, politeness
cortésmente: courteously, gently, politely
corteza: bark, crust
corteza inferior: lower mantle
corteza terrestre: crust
cortina: curtain
cortinero: curtain

rod, rail
cortinilla: window shade
corto: little, short, trailer
corto de: short of
corto de dinero: out of pocket
corto de vista: nearsighted
corto plazo: short run, short-term
cortos: shorts
corva: crook
cosa: matter, thing
cosa imprescindible: must
cosa segura: certainty
cosas: matter, stuff
cosecha: crop, harvest, vintage
cosechar: harvest
coseno: cosine
coser: sew, stitch
cosido: sewn
cosita: thing
cosmético: cosmetic
cosmología: cosmology
costa: coast, coastline, seaside, shore
costado: flank, side
costal: sack
costal (de boxeo): punching bag
costar: cost, price, set back
costear(se): finance
costero: coastal
costilla: chop, rib
costo: cost, price
costoso: big-ticket, costly
costra: crust
costumbre: custom, ritual, tradition, way
costura: seam, sewing
cota: contour line
cotidiano: day-to-day
cotiledón: cotyledon
cotización: quotation, quote
cotizar: quote
cotizar en bolsa: float
cotonete: cotton swab
cotorrear: chatter, schmooze
cotorreo: chatter
coyuntura feliz: break
CPT: certified public accountant
crac: crash
crack: crack, crash
cráneo: skull
cráter: crater
crayón: crayon
creación: construction, creation, formation, setting up
creador: author, creator, founder
creadora: author, creator, founder
crear: build, create, establish, form, found, set up, think up
creatividad: creativity
creativo: creative
crecer: grow, increase, mature, swell
crecer bien: flourish
crecer como hongo:

mushroom
crecer rápidamente: snowball
creciente: crescent
crecimiento: development, growth
credencial: card, ID card, identification card, identity card
credibilidad: credibility, plausibility
crédito: credit, credit hour, loan
credo: persuasion
creencia: belief, faith, persuasion
creer: believe, expect, feel, suppose, swallow, think
creer a: believe
creer que: should think
creíble: credible, plausible
creído: grand
crema: cream
crema ligera: light cream
crema para el sol: sunscreen
cremera: creamer
creo: I think
crepúsculo: dawn, sunset
cresa: maggot
crespo: fuzzy
cresta: arête, crest, ridge
cresta peñascosa: arête
cría: breeding, young
cría selectiva: selective breeding
criadero: kennel
criador: breeder
criadora: breeder
crianza: upbringing
crianza de animales: farming
criar: breed, bring up, nurture, raise, rear
criar animales: farm
criarse: grow up
criatura: creature, infant
cricket: cricket
crimen: crime, offense
criminal: criminal
crin: mane
crioclastia: ice wedging
críptico: obscure
críquet: cricket
crisálida: chrysalis
crisis: crisis, depression
crisis de identidad: identity crisis
crisis nerviosa: breakdown
crispar (los nervios): jar, get on somebody's nerves
cristal: crystal
cristal cortado: crystal
cristalino: lens
cristiana: Christian
cristianismo: Christianity
cristiano: Christian
criterio: criterion, judgment
criterios estéticos: aesthetic criteria
crítica: attack, critic, criticism, review,

reviewer
crítica arquetípica: archetypal criticism
crítica de arte: art criticism
crítica literaria: literary criticism
críticamente: critically
criticar: attack, criticize, fault, find fault, knock, level, take exception to something
criticar severamente: damn
crítico: critic, critical, reviewer
Cro-Magnon: Cro-Magnon
croissant: croissant
crol: crawl
Cromañón: Cro-Magnon
cromátide: chromatid
cromosfera: chromosphere
cromosoma sexual: sex chromosome
crónica: chronicle, commentary
crónicamente: chronically
crónico: chronic
cronología: timeline
cronometrar: time
cross-country: cross-country
cruce: crossing, crossroads
cruce de peatones: crosswalk
crucero: crossing, cruise, railroad crossing
crucial: crucial
crucigrama: crossword
crudamente: brutally, starkly
crudo: bleak, brutal, crude, raw
cruel: cruel, inhuman, mean, nasty, ruthless, vicious
crueldad: cruelty, ruthlessness
cruelmente: cruelly, viciously
crujido: crunch
crujiente: crisp
crujir: crunch, squeak
cruz: cross
cruza: cross
cruzamiento: crossing over
cruzar los dedos: cross one's fingers
cruzar velozmente: streak
cruzar(se): cross, fold
CST: CST
cuaderno (de notas): notebook
cuaderno para colorear: coloring book
cuadra: block, stable
cuadrado: sq., square
cuadragésimo: fortieth
cuadrante: dial
cuadrar: add up, fit in
cuadrilátero: ring
cuadrilla: gang

cuadro: frame, painting, picture, piece, plaid, square

cuadro al óleo: oil painting

cuadro de diálogo: dialog box

cuadro de honor: honor roll

cuadro vivo: tableau

cuádruple: quadruple, quadruplet

cuadruplicar: quadruple

cuádruplo: quadruple

cuaga: quagga

cuajar: gel, set

cuál: which

cualidad: attribute, quality

cualitativo: qualitative

cualquier: any, any old, anything, either

cualquiera: anybody, anyone, either

cuan largo es: full-length

cuando: as, when, whenever

cuándo: when

cuando menos: at least

cuando mucho: at best, at the latest, maximum

cuando pasa la tormenta: when the dust settles

cuando se tiene tiempo: at leisure/at somebody's leisure

cuando uno quiere: at leisure/at somebody's leisure

cuánta: how, many, much

cuántas: how, many, much

cuantioso: massive

cuánto: how, many, much

(unos) cuantos: handful

cuántos: how, many, much

cuarenta: forty

cuarentavo: fortieth

cuarentena: quarantine

cuarta parte: fourth, quarter

cuartel: barracks

cuartel general: headquarters

cuarteto: quartet

cuarto: bedroom, fourth, quarter, room

cuarto (de galón): quart

cuarto de baño: bathroom

cuarto de final: quarterfinal

cuarto de la tele: family room

cuarto de televisión: family room

cuarto disponible: vacancy

cuarto oscuro: darkroom

cuata: friend

cuate: buddy, dude, friend, pal

cuatrera: rustler

cuatrero: rustler

cuatro: four

cubeta: bucket, pail

cúbico: cubic

cubículo: carrel, cubicle, stall

cubierta: binding, cover, deck, hood, jacket

cubierta de cocina: countertop

cubierta de vuelo: flight deck

cubierto: plastered

cubierto de cicatrices: scarred

cubierto de escarcha: frosty

cubiertos: flatware

cubito para caldo: bouillon cube

cubo: bucket, cube, pail

cubo de basura: trash can

cubrir: blanket, bury, coat, cover, fall into, fill in, mask, span, swathe

cubrir con azúcar glaseada: frost

cubrir de: shower

cubrir(se) de neblina: mist

cubrirse: hedge, hedge one's bets

cucaracha: cockroach, roach

cuchara: scoop, spoon

cuchara para servir: tablespoon

cucharear: spoon

cucharilla: teaspoon

cucharita: teaspoon

cucharón: ladle, scoop

cuchilla: blade

cuchillada: slash

cuchillo: knife

cuclillas: squat

cuello: collar, neck, throat

cuello alto: turtleneck

cuello (de) tortuga: turtleneck

cuenca: basin, socket

cuenca (fluvial): drainage basin

cuenca abisal (oceánica): deep ocean basin

Cuenca del Pacífico: Pacific Rim

cuenco: basin

cuenta: account, bead, bill, check, count

cuenta corriente: checking account

cuenta de cheques: checking account

cuenta regresiva: countdown

cuentas: account

cuento: story, tale

cuento de hadas: fairy tale

cuerda: cord, line, rope, string

cuerda para/de saltar: jump rope, skip rope

cuerdas: string

cuerdo: sane

cuerno: croissant, horn

cuero crudo o sin curtir: rawhide

cuerpo: body, corps, flesh, frame

cuerpo de abogados: bar

cuerpo docente: faculty

cuerpo legislativo: legislature

cuervo: crow

cuesta: incline

cuesta arriba: uphill

cuesta continental: continental rise

cuestión: issue, matter, question

cuestión de: a case of

cuestionamiento: challenge

cuestionar: challenge

cuestionario: questionnaire

cuestiones más importantes: wider issues

cueva: cave

cuidado: care, TLC

¡cuidado!: heads up!, look out

cuidados intensivos: intensive care

cuidadosamente: carefully, thoughtfully

cuidadoso: careful, deliberately, thorough

cuidar: attend, care, mind, nurse

cuidar de: look after

cuidar la casa: house-sit

cuidar niños: babysit

culata: butt

culebra: snake

culebrón: soap, soap opera

culminar: climax

culminar en: lead up to

culpa: blame, fault, guilt

culpabilidad: guilt

culpable: guilty

culpar: accuse, blame, lay

cultivador: grower

cultivadora: grower

cultivar: cultivate, farm, grow, raise

cultivo: crop, cultivation, culture, farming

culto: educated, learned, worship

cultura: culture

cultural: cultural

culturalmente: culturally

cum laude: cum laude

cumbre: peak, summit, top

cumpleaños: birthday

cumplido: compliment

cumplimiento: enforcement, realization

cumplir: comply, conform, fulfill, go through with, keep, make good, meet, serve, turn

cumplir con: discharge, honor, live up to, stick to

cumplirse: realize

cúmulo: cumulus, mass

cúmulo abierto: open

cluster
cúmulo globular: globular cluster
cúmulonimbo: cumulonimbus
cuna: birthplace, cradle, crib
cuneta: curb
cuña: wedge
cuñada: sister-in-law
cuñado: brother-in-law
cuota: fee, quota, subscription, toll
cupón: coupon
cúpula: dome
cura: cure
curar: heal, treat
curar(se): cure, mend
curiosamente: curiously
curiosear: pry
curiosidad: curiosity
curioso: curious, funny, inquisitive, quaint
currículum vitae: résumé
curry: curry
cursi: kitsch
cursiva: italic
curso: course
curso de la vida: lifetime
curso de verano: summer school
cursor: cursor
curul: seat
curva: bend, curve
curva ascendente: spiral
curva de nivel: contour line, index contour
curvar: bend
curvatura: curvature
curvearse: curve
curvilíneo: curvilinear
curvo: curved
cúspide: top
custodia: custody
custodiar: guard, protect
custodio: guard
cutícula: cuticle
cuyo: which, whose
cybercafé: Internet café
cyberespacio: cyberspace

D

dactilógrafa: typist
dactilógrafo: typist
dádiva: handout
dado: dice, given
dado que: seeing as/that
daga: dagger
daim: dime
daltoniano: color-blind
daltónico: color-blind
daltonismo: color-blindness
dama: lady
dama de honor: bridesmaid, maid of honor, matron of honor
damas: checkers
danza: dancing
danza contemporánea: modern dance
danza jazz: jazz dance
danza moderna: modern dance
danza posmoderna: postmodern dance
dañar: damage, hurt, vandalize

dañino: damaging, harmful
daño: damage, harm, mischief
daños y perjuicios: damages
dar: award, bring, come on, deal, deliver, dish up, get, give, hand over, put out, throw
dar (con la mano): hand
dar (un anticipo): put down
dar a: back onto
dar a entender: be given to, imply, indicate, make out
dar a luz: give birth, have a baby
dar alaridos: howl, scream
dar aliento: encourage
dar cabida: accommodate
dar carpetazo: shelve
dar carta blanca: give free rein to
dar caza: hunt down
dar click: click
dar codazos: elbow
dar con: hit on, stumble across
dar con algo: put one's finger on something
dar consistencia: thicken
dar cuerda: wind
dar cuerpo: flesh out
dar de alta (hospital): discharge
dar de baja (ejército): discharge
dar de comer: feed
dar de mamar: feed
dar de sí: give
dar derecho: entitle
dar el biberón: feed
dar el papel de: cast
dar el paso: to take the plunge
dar el primer golpe a la pelota de golf: tee off
dar empleo: employ
dar empujones: shove
dar energía a: power
dar explicaciones: explain
dar flojera: can't be bothered
dar fruto: bear fruit
dar garrotazos: club
dar golpecitos: tap
dar golpes: bang, strike
dar hacia: look
dar igual: matter
dar indicios: indicate
dar inicio: open
dar instrucciones: instruct
dar la bienvenida: welcome
dar la hora: strike
dar la impresión: seem, sound, strike
dar la mamila: feed
dar la mano: shake hands
dar la propia opinión: speak out
dar la talla: make the grade

dar la vuelta: loop, skirt
dar largas: drag your feet, sit on, stall
dar las gracias: grace, thank
dar lástima: feel for
dar lengüetazos: lap
dar lugar a: give rise to
dar marcha atrás: back, back down, back out, reverse
dar muestras: show
dar origen a: give rise to
dar palmadas: smack
dar palmaditas: pat
dar parte de: report
dar paso: give way to
dar pasos: step
dar pereza: can't be bothered
dar permiso: let
dar poder: empower
dar por descontado: take for granted
dar por perdido: write off
dar por sentado: take for granted
dar por terminado: wrap up
dar prioridad: give priority
dar propina: tip
dar puñetazos: punch
dar rabia: make somebody sick
dar refugio: shelter
dar resultado: succeed
dar rienda suelta a: give free rein to, unleash
dar sabor: flavor
dar saltitos: hop
dar satisfacciones: make amends
dar sermones: lecture
dar servicio: service
dar sombra: shade, shadow
dar su aprobación: approve
dar testimonio: give evidence, testify
dar tono: tone
dar tormento: torture
dar trabajo: employ
dar trancazos a: belt
dar trompadas: punch
dar tumbos: bump, flounder
dar un aventón: give somebody a lift somewhere
dar un manotazo: smack
dar un "ride": give somebody a lift somewhere
dar un sermon: preach
dar un traspié: trip
dar un viraje: veer
dar una calada: puff
dar una capa o mano: coat
dar una fumada: puff
dar una impresión: come across
dar una lección de humildad: humble
dar una palmada: clap

dar una vuelta de campana: overturn

dar vergüenza: be/feel shy

dar virajes: flip-flop

dar vuelta: bend, round, spin, turn, turn over, twist

dar vuelta a: turn around

dar vueltas: circle, mill around, revolve

dar vueltas a: debate, turn over

dar zancadas: stride

dardo: dart

dari: Farsi

darle a uno la impresión: seem

darle clases a: coach

darle fuerzas a: build up

darle una lección a alguien: teach somebody a lesson

dar(se) masaje: massage

darse: flourish

darse a la fuga: flee

darse cuenta: find, hit

darse cuenta de: realize

darse el lujo de: afford

darse la gran vida: live it up

darse por satisfecho: call it quits

darse por vencido: give up

darse prisa: hurry, speed up

darse un festín: feast

darse un gusto: indulge

dar(se) vuelta: swing, turn

dar(le) vueltas a una idea: toy with

datación absoluta: absolute dating

datación relativa: relative dating

dátil: date

dato: data

datos: data, information

dC.: AD

de: by, from, in, made out of, of, off, on, than, with

de (edad): aged

de … a: through

de abajo: lower

de acceso prohibido: off limits

de acceso telefónico: dial-up

de acogida: foster

de actualidad: hot

de acuerdo: okay

de acuerdo con: according to, in agreement with, in keeping with, in/into line, on the basis of

de adentro: inside

de admisión: admission

de agua salada: saltwater

de ahí en adelante: thereafter

de al lado: next

de algún modo: somehow

de alguna manera: somehow

de alquiler: rental

de alta tecnología: high-tech

de alto impacto: high-impact

de ancho: across

de años atrás: long-standing

de arriba: overhead, top, upper

de arriba abajo: up and down

de aspecto feo: unsightly

de atrás: back

de atrás para adelante: back and forth, backward and forward

de baja calidad: low-end

de bajo rendimiento: underperformer

de beneficencia: charitable, voluntarily

de bolsillo: pocket

de buen carácter: good-natured

de buen grado: freely

de buen humor: good-humored, in a good humor

de buena fe: in good faith

de cabeza: upside down

de cada: out of

de cada día: day-to-day

de camino a: en route

de campamento: camping

de campo: field

de capa caída: at a low ebb

de cerca: close up

de cero: from scratch

de chiste: in fun

de ciertas maneras: -mannered

de cierto modo: like that/this/so

de cierto tamaño: -sized

de cierto tipo: such

de ciertos modales: -mannered

de clase baja: lower class

de clase media: middle class

de clase obrera: working class

de clóset: closet

de color: color, colored

de color subido: off-color

(tejido) de colores y dibujos vistosos: paisley

de conexión: onward

de confección: off the rack, ready-made

de conformidad con: in/into line

de corta estatura: short

de cuadros: check, checked, checkerboard

de cualquier forma: even so

de cualquier modo: anyhow, anyway, even so

de cuando en cuando: from time to time, now and then/now and again/every now and then/every now and

again, off and on

de cuerpo entero: full-length

de culto: cult

de cuota: toll

de (gran) demanda: in (great) demand

de dentro: inside

de derecha: right-wing

de día y de noche, toda la semana: 24-7

de diseño (exclusivo): designer

de distancia: apart

de dos cañones: double-barreled

de edad: old

de élite: elite

de ella: hers

de emergencia: emergency

de encargo: made to order

de enfrente: opposite

de enmedio: middle

de época: period

de escasez: lean

de escritorio: desktop

de estado: state

de exhibición: friendliness

de éxito: successful

de extremo a extremo: cross-country

de fibra óptica: fiber optics

de forma aceptable: acceptably

de forma definitva: positive

de forma espesa: thickly

de forma gruesa: thickly

de forma histérica: hysterically

de forma rudimentaria: crudely

de frente: face to face, head-on

de fuente fidedigna: reliably

de fuera del lugar: out-of-state

de funcionamiento: operational

de gabinete: ministerial

de gran clase: high-class

de gran envergadura: full-scale

de gran éxito: best-selling

de gran rendimiento energético: energy-efficient

de grava: graveled

de hecho: actually, in effect, in fact, indeed

de hierbas: herbal

de hoja caduca: deciduous

de hoja perenne: evergreen

de horror: horror

de hueso colorado: hard core

de ida: one-way, outward

de igual modo: by the same token, equally

de impuestos diferidos:

tax-deferred
de inmediato: fast, immediately, on the spot, right away, there and then/then and there
de interés: interesting
de interés actual: topical
de izquierda: left-wing
de la biología: biologically
de la ciudad: civic
de la Edad Media: medieval
de la guerra: wartime
de la marina: naval
de la misma manera: likewise
de la nada: nowhere
de la noche: at night
de la noche a la mañana: overnight
de la provincia: provincial
de la tercera edad: elderly
de la verde: marijuana
de lado: off-center
de larga distancia: long-distance
de largo normal: full-length
de largo plazo: long-range
de las agujas del reloj: clockwise
de libre acceso: on demand
de línea dura: hard-line
de lista de espera: standby
de lleno: fully
de lo alto: above
de lo contrario: else, otherwise
de lo que se trata: (question/point) at issue
de los mil diablos: doggone
de los padres: parental
de lujo: deluxe
de madera: wooden
de mal genio: ornery
de mal gusto: cheap, in bad/poor taste, tasteless
de mal humor: in a bad humor, moodily
de mala fama: notorious
de mala gana: unwillingly
de mala muerte: rinky-dink
de mala reputación: infamous
de manera alarmante: alarmingly, frighteningly
de manera ausente: absently
de manera característica: characteristically
de manera conmovedora: movingly

de manera crítica: critically
de manera cruel: nastily
de manera decepcionante: disappointingly
de manera efectiva: effectively
de manera eficiente: efficiently
de manera egoísta: selfishly
de manera experimental: experimentally
de manera hidropónica: hydroponically
de manera independiente: independently
de manera indignante: indignantly
de manera ineficiente: inefficiently
de manera intermitente: intermittently
de manera intrigante: intriguingly
de manera muy cómica: hilariously
de manera muy divertida o entretenida: amusingly
de manera natural: naturally
de manera ordinaria: coarsely
de manera parecida: similarly
de manera provisional: provisionally
de manera rara: oddly, strangely
de manera rentable: profitably
de manera romántica: romantically
de manera ronca: hoarsely
de manera sarcástica: sarcastically
de manera satisfactoria: satisfactorily
de manera selectiva: selectively
de manera sentimental: sentimentally
de manera simétrica: symmetrically
de manera similar/semejante: similarly
de manera temblorosa: shakily
de manera trágica: tragically
de maravilla: splendidly, wonderfully
de más: spare
de más alto grado: ranking
de más alto rango: senior
de matrimonio: double
de mayor jerarquía: ranking
de mayor venta: best-selling
de mediana edad: middle-aged
de memoria: by heart,

from memory
de menor calidad: second-class
de menor importancia: secondary
de mentalidad abierta: broad-minded
de mi/tu/su parte: on somebody's part
(cómico) de micrófono: stand-up
de miedo: scary
de moda: fashionable, in fashion, in vogue
de modo audible: audibly
de modo extraño: bizarrely
de modo extravagante: extravagantly
de modo interesante: interestingly
de modo que: therefore
de mucho mantenimiento: high-maintenance
de mujeres: female
de muy buena calidad: upscale
de muy mal gusto: sick
de nacimiento: natural
de nada: It's a pleasure/my pleasure, you're welcome
de ninguna manera: in the least, on no account
de no intromisión: hands-off
de nota: of note
de nueva cuenta: again
de nueve a cinco: nine-to-five
de nuevo: again, over
de obsequio: complimentary
de observación: observational
de oriente: eastern
de oro: golden
de otra parte: elsewhere
de pacotilla: cheap
de paga: subscription
de pantalla ancha: widescreen
de pasada: in passing
de perlas: peachy
de pie: on one's feet
de plano: flatly
de poca altura: low, low-rise
de poco peso: lightweight
de por vida: life
de posguerra: postwar
de posición acomodada: comfortably
de preferencia: ideally
de prestigio: established
de primer nivel: top-shelf
de primera: class act, crack, prime
de primera línea: major league
de primera mano: directly
de principio a fin: through
de probada calidad: tried
de pronto: all of a sudden

de puerta en puerta: (from) door to door

de puntos: dotted

de que se trate: in question

de quién: whose

de referencia: reference

de regimiento: regimental

de reojo: sideways

de repente: in a flash

de sabor intenso: full-flavored

de salida: outgoing

de sangre caliente: warm-blooded

de sangre fría: cold-blooded

de segunda: B-grade, downscale, minor league, second-class

de segunda mano: secondhand, used

de sentido único: one-way

de sexo femenino: female

de siempre: long-time

de sobra: plenty, spare

de soslayo: sideways

de sueño: sleepily

de suspenso: thriller

de talento: gifted

de tamaño natural: full-scale

de temporada: seasonal

de tener: given

de tiempo atrás: long-time

de tiempo completo: full-time

de tiempo en tiempo: from time to time

de todas formas: all the same/just the same, in any case

de todas maneras: equally

de todo tipo: miscellaneous, mixed

de todos los tiempos: all-time, of all time

de todos modos: anyway, even so, still

de tradición: established

de transición: transitional

de tránsito: in transit

de trigo entero: wholewheat

de triste memoria: infamous

de turno: on call

de último momento: last minute

de un lado a(l) otro: across, around, back and forth, from side to side, through, up and down

de un lado para otro: on the move

de un monomio: monomial

de un solo sentido: one-way

de un solo término: monomial

de una costa a (la) otra: coast-to-coast

de una manera empírica: empirically

de una u otra manera: somehow

de una vez por todas: once and for all

de uno: one's

de usos múltiples: versatile

de usted: yours

de ustedes: yours

de vacas flacas: lean

de valor: valuable

de vanguardia: state-of-the-art

de veras: all too/only too, big time, indeed, really, too, truly, with a vengeance

de verdad: for real, really

de vez en cuando: every now and then, every so often, now and then/now and again/every now and then/every now and again, off and on, once in a while

de vez en vez: every now and then, from time to time

de vida o muerte: do-or-die, life and/or death

de volada: lickety-split

deambular: wander

deán: dean

debajo: below, under, underneath

debate: debate

debe: debit

deber: duty, have got to, must, ought, owe, should, want

deber + inf.: be

deber de + inf.: be

debido: due

debido a: because of, owing to

débil: dim, faint, lame, muted, weak

debilidad: weakness

debilitar: undermine

debilitar(se): weaken

débilmente: dully, lamely, weakly

débito: debit

debut: debut

década: decade

decadencia: decay

decaer: decay, ebb, flag, peter out

decaído: at a low ebb

decano: dean

decenas: dozen

decenio: decade

decente: decent

decentemente: decently

decepción: disappointment

decepcionado: disappointed

decepcionante: disappointing

decepcionar: disappoint, let down

deceso: demise

decidido: determined,

go-ahead, intent, settle

decidido a: set on

decidir: choose, decide, elect, fix

decidir(se): decide on

decidirse: make up one's mind

decidirse por: go for, settle on

decimal: decimal

décimo: tenth

decimoctavo: eighteenth

decimocuarto: fourteenth

decimonónico: Victorian

decimonono: nineteenth

décimonoveno: nineteenth

décimoquinto: fifteenth

decimosegundo: twelfth

decimoséptimo: seventeenth

decimosexto: sixteenth

decimotercero: thirteenth

decir: break, mention, name, read, say, tell

¡no me digas!: indeed

¡y que lo digas!: you can say that again

decir a una voz: chorus

decir algo de alguien: speak of somebody

decir de todo: call somebody names

decir en serio: mean

decir la última palabra: have the last word/the final word

decir mentiras: lie

decir mucho de alguien: be to somebody's credit

decir todo: say it all

decirse a sí mismo: say to oneself

decisión: choice, decision, resolution

decisivamente: decisively

decisivo: decisive, definitive, instrumental

declaración: announcement, declaration, statement, testimony, utterance

declaración exageradamente modesta: understatement

declaración tergiversada: misstatement

declarado: full-scale

declarar: declare, designate, find, pronounce, testify

declarar culpable: convict

declarar en ruinas: condemn

declarar ilegal: outlaw

declararse (culpable o inocente): plead guilty/innocent

declararse a favor/en contra: come out for/against

declinación magnética: magnetic declination

declinar: decay, decline, recuse

declive: dip, incline, slant, tilt

declive continental: continental slope

decolorar: bleach

decolorar(se): fade

decoración: decoration

decorado: decorating, scenery

decorador: decorator

decoradora: decorator

decorar: decorate, trim

decorativo: decorative

decretar: decree

decreto: act, decree

dedicación: dedication

dedicado: dedicated, devoted, engaged

dedicar: devote, give over to, put, put in, spend

dedicar(se): dedicate

dedicarse: apply, engage

dedicarse a (la compraventa): deal

dedicarse a algo intensamente: throw oneself into something

dedicatoria: dedication, inscription

dedo: finger

dedo de pescado: fish stick

dedo del pie: toe

deducción: deduction

deducible: deductible

deducir: deduct, gather, infer

deducir(se): follow

defecto: defect, fault

defectuoso: defective

defender: champion, defend, plead, protect, stand for, stand up for, stick up for

defenderse: fight back

defensa: backcourt, bumper, defender, defense, fender, protection

defensa civil: civil defense

defensa propia: self-defense

defensivo: defensive

defensor: advocate, champion, defender, guardian, protector, supporter

defensora: advocate, champion, defender, guardian, protector, supporter

deficiencia: deficiency, minus

deficiente: unsatisfactory

déficit: deficit

déficit comercial: trade deficit

déficit de la balanza comercial: trade deficit

definición: by definition, definition

definir: decide, define, establish

definitiva: final, firm

definitivamente: absolutely, definitely, definitively

definitivo: definite, definitive, hard

deflación: deflation

deforestación: deforestation

deformación: deformation

deformar: distort

defraudar: deceive

degenerar: deteriorate, develop

deglutir: swallow

degustar: sample

dejar: drop, leave, let, put down, quit, set, turn off

dejar (un depósito): put down

dejar (un mal hábito): kick

dejar a un lado/dejar de lado: put to/on one side

dejar afuera: shut out

dejar algo atrás: grow out of

dejar atrás: clear, leave behind

dejar botado: lie around

dejar correr: run away with

dejar de: cease, stop

dejar de cumplir: default

dejar de hacer algo temporalmente: suspend

dejar de lado: lay aside, set aside, sidestep

dejar de poner atención: switch off

dejar de quedar: grow out of

dejar en libertad: free

dejar en remojo: soak

dejar entrar: let in

dejar estupefacto: stagger

dejar fuera: leave off, leave out

dejar helado: floor

dejar huérfano: orphan

dejar ir: part with

dejar las manos libres: give free rein to

dejar libre: free

dejar lisiado: disable

dejar marca: leave one's/a mark, make your/a mark

dejar marcado: leave one's/a mark, scar

dejar pasar: let in, miss out, pass up

dejar perplejo: stagger, stump, stun

dejar salir: let out

dejar sin aliento: wind

dejar tirado: lie around

dejar una marca: mark

dejar una sensación: feel

dejar vagar la imaginación: wander

dejar ver: reveal

dejar correr el agua: run (water/faucet/bath)

dejar(se) caer: drop, flop, plunk

dejarse crecer: grow

dejarse de hablar: be not speaking

dejarse llevar: get/be carried away

dejarse llevar por: run away with

dejo: hint

del ayuntamiento: civic

del campo: rural

del centro: downtown, midtown

del congreso: congressional

del día: topical

del este: east

del hogar: domestic

del lado de: on somebody's side

del mismo modo: alike

del mismo nivel: on a par with

del montón: indifferent

del norte: northern

del orden de: in/of the order of something

del sexo femenino: female

del sonido: sonic

del sudeste: southeast, southeastern

del sudoeste: southwest(ern)

del sur: south, southern

del sureste: southeast, southeastern

del suroeste: southwest(ern)

del todo: fully

delante: ahead

delante de: ahead of, before

delantera: striker

delantero: lineman, striker

delatar: betray, talk away

delatarse: give the game away

delegación: branch, delegation, mission

delegada: delegate

delegado: delegate

delegar: delegate

deleitar: take delight in/take a delight in

deleitarse: lap up

deleite: delight, relish

deletrear: spell

deletreo: spelling

delfín: dolphin

delgada franja de tierra: panhandle

delgadamente: thinly

delgado: fine, lean, slim, thin

deliberación: debate

deliberadamente: deliberately, pointedly

deliberado: conscious

deliberar: deliberate

delicadamente: delicately, finely, intricately

delicadeza: delicacy

delicado: delicate, intricate, sensitive, tricky

delicatessen: deli, delicatessen
deliciosamente: deliciously, delightfully
delicioso: delicious, delightful
delincuencia: delinquency
delincuencia callejera: street crime
delincuente: criminal, delinquent, offender
delincuente sexual: sex offender
delineador (de ojos): eyeliner
delinquir: offend
delito: crime, offense
delito grave: felony
delta: delta
demacrado: drawn
demanda: demand, suit
demandada: defendant
demandado: defendant
demandante: plaintiff, prosecutor
demandar: sue
demasiado: too, too much, undue, way too (long/much etc.)
demasiado tarde: too late
demente: insane
democracia: democracy
demócrata: democrat
democráticamente: democratically
democrático: democratic
demoler: bulldoze, knock down, pull down
demolición: demolition
demoler: demolish
demonios: on earth
demora: lag, late, lateness
demorar: delay, detain
demostración: demonstration, display, show
demostrar: demonstrate, establish, illustrate, prove, register, show
demostrar poder: flex one's muscles
dendrita: dendrite
denegación: denial
denegar: deny
denotar: indicate
densamente: densely
densidad: density
denso: dense
dentado: jagged
dentadura (postiza): dentures
dental: dental
dentífrico: toothpaste
dentista: dentist, doctor
dentro: in, indoor, indoors, inside, into, within
dentro de poco: before long, shortly
dentro de una tienda: in-store
dentro del plazo previsto: on target
denuncia: whistle-blowing
denunciar: denounce,

lodge, report
departamental: departmental
departamento: apartment, department, office, suite
departamento de bomberos: fire department
departamento de policía: police department
Departamento de Salud y Seguridad en el Trabajo: OSHA
departamento de urgencias: ER
dependencia: dependence, dependency
depender: depend, rest
depender de: hang on, lean on, rely on
dependienta: assistant, clerk, dependent
dependiente: assistant, clerk, dependent
deportación: deportation
deportar: deport
deporte: game, sport
deportes: athletics, phys ed, physical education
deportista: sportsman, sportswoman
deportivo: sporting
depositar: deposit, lay, put down
depósito: deposit, deposition, repository, storage, store, tank, warehouse
depósito de madera: lumberyard
depósito glacial: till
depósito para combustibles: bunker
depredador: consumer, predator
depresión: depression, slump, trough
depresión posparto: postpartum depression
depresión tropical: tropical depression
deprimente: depressing
deprimido: depressed, down, low
deprimir: depress, get down
depurador de gases: scrubber
derby: derby
derecha: right
derechista: right-wing, right-winger
derecho: entitlement, erect, law, right, right-handed, straight, toll
derecho de aduana: duty
derecho de paso: right of way
derecho de visita: visitation rights
derecho de voto: franchise, vote
derechos: copyright, fee
derechos civiles: civil

rights
derechos de autor: copyright
derechos humanos: human rights
deriva de los continentes: continental drift
derivar: derive, divert
dermatóloga: dermatologist
dermatología: dermatology
dermatólogo: dermatologist
dermis: dermis
derogar: strike down
derramar: shed
derramar(se): spill
derramarse: boil over, overflow
derrame cerebral: stroke
derrame de petróleo: slick
derrapar: skid
derrape: skid
derretido: melt
derretir(se): melt, thaw
derribar: break down, demolish, fell, knock down, push over, shoot down, tear down, topple
derrocamiento: overthrow
derrocar: bring down, overthrow, topple
derrochador: lavish
derrochar: lavish
derrota: defeat
derrota en cero: shutout
derrotar: beat, defeat, knock out
derrubio estratificado: stratified drift
derrumbamiento: landslide
derrumbarse: cave in, collapse, crash, crumble
derrumbe: collapse, landslide
desabotonar: open
desabrido: tasteless
desabrochar: open, undo
desacatar: defy
desaceleración: negative acceleration
desacreditado: discredited
desacreditar: discredit
desacuerdo: disagreement, dissent
desafiante: challenging, defiant
desafiar: challenge, dare, defy
desafilado: blunt
desafinado: flat
desafío: challenge, dare, defiance
desafortunado: unfortunate, unhappy
desagradable: messy, rude, sour, ugly, unfriendly, unpalatable, unpleasant

desagradablemente: uncomfortably, unpleasantly

desaguar: drain

desahogar: vent

desahogarse: work off

desairar: slight, snub

desaire: snub

desalentado: discouraged, dismayed, gloomy

desalentador: discouraging, gloomily, grim, negative

desalentar: discourage, put off

desaliento: discouragement, dismay, gloom

desalinización: desalination

desamarrar: untie

desanimado: dismayed, low

desanimar: discourage

desánimo: dismay

desanudar: untie

desaparecer: disappear, melt, vanish

desaparecido: missing

desaparecido en acción: MIA

desaparición: disappearance

desaprobar: disapprove, find fault, frown upon

desaprobatorio: disapproving

desaprovechar: miss out, throw away

desarmado: unarmed

desarmador: screwdriver

desarmar: dismantle, take apart

desarreglado: disheveled

desarreglar: mess up

desarrollado: advanced, developed, mature

desarrollar: evolve, flesh out, progress

desarrollar(se): break out, develop

desarrollarse: mature, move, set

desarrollo: development, evolution, progress

desarrollo habitacional: apartment complex

desasosiego: discomfort

desastre: disaster, mess

desastrosamente: disastrously

desastroso: disastrous, fatal

desatar: spark, trigger, untie

desatascador: plunger

desatender: neglect

desatino: nonsense

desatornillador: screwdriver

desautorizar: discredit

desayuno: breakfast

desayuno continental: continental breakfast

desbandada: stampede

desbaratar: take apart

desbastar: plane

desbordarse: overflow

descabellado: insane

descalificación: disqualification

descalificar: disqualify

descalzo: bare

descansado: lazy, rested

descansar: relax, rest

descansar con los pies en alto: put your feet up

descansillo: landing

descanso: break, landing, rest

descanso y esparcimiento: R&R

descapacitado: disabled

descapotable: convertible

descarado: outright

descarga: discharge

descarga eléctrica: electric shock, shock

descarga electrostática: electrostatic discharge

descargable: downloadable

descargado: flat

descargar: discharge, download, unload

descaro: nerve

descartar: brush aside, discount, dismiss, exclude, rule out, scrap, write off

descascarillado: chipped

descendencia: offspring

descendente: downward

descender: descend, dip, drop, fall, go down, slope

descenso: drop, fall

descentrado: off-center

descentralización: decentralization

descentralizar(se): decentralize

descifrar: break, crack, unravel

descodificar: decoding

descolgar: be off the hook

descomponedor: decomposer

descomponer(se): break, break down

descomponerse: decay, go, rot

descomposición: decay

descomposición química a la intemperie: chemical weathering

descompostura: breakdown

descomprimir: unzip

descompuesto: decayed, down, out of order, upset

desconcertado: blank

desconcertar: throw

desconectado: dead, offline

desconectar: disconnect, unplug

desconectarse: switch off

desconfiado: suspicious

desconfianza: mistrust, suspicion

desconfiar: not like the look of something/ somebody, not trust

desconfiar de: mistrust

desconocida: unknown

desconocido: outsider, unidentified, unknown

descontar: dock

descontento: unhappiness, unrest

descortés: undiplomatic

describir: depict, describe, write up

descripción: characterization, depiction, description, picture

descriptivo: descriptive

descuartizar: butcher

descubierto: naked

descubrimiento: discovery

descubrir: catch, catch sight of, discover, find, find out, get at, reveal, uncover, unveil

descubrir el pastel: give the game away

descuento: discount

descuidado: careless, sloppy

descuidar: neglect, overlook

descuido: carelessness, neglect, sloppiness

desde: from, since

desde cerca: at close quarters

desde cero: from scratch

desde el principio: from the get-go

desde el punto de vista arquitectónico: architecturally

desde el punto de vista de: in terms of

desde entonces: ever since

desde la perspectiva espacial: spatially

desde lejos: at/from a distance

desde luego: certainly, of course

desde luego que no: of course not

desde que: ever since

desdicha: misery

desdichado: miserable, unhappy

desdoblar: unfold

deseable: desirable

deseado: desired

desear: desire, hunger, look forward to, love, will, wish

desechable: disposable

desechar: discard, discount, dismiss, scrap

desecho: trash, waste

desechos: scraps

desembocadura: mouth

desembolsar: fork out, pay out

desempacar: unpack

desempañador: defogger

desempeñar(se): fill, fulfill, perform

desempeño: performance

desempleado: jobless, unemployed

desempleo: unemployment

desempolvar: dig out

desencadenar: spark, trigger

desenchufar: unplug

desenfocado: out of focus

desenfrenadamente: madly

desenfrenado: mad

desenfreno: abandon

desenfundar: draw

desenlace: denouement, denouement design, ending

desenmarañar: unravel

desenmascarar: expose

desenredar: unravel, unwind

desenrollar: unwind

desentonar: clash

desentrañar: unravel

desenvolverse: unfold

desenvuelto y seguro de sí mismo: smooth

deseo: desire, eagerness, hunger, will, wish

deseoso: hungry

desequilibrado: frantic

desequilibrio: imbalance

deserción: defection, desertion

desertar: defect, desert

desertor: defector, deserter

desertora: defector, deserter

desesperación: despair

desesperadamente: desperately, frantically

desesperado: desperate, frantic, hopeless

desesperanza: hopelessness

desesperar: despair

desestimación: dismissal

desestimar: dismiss, minimize

desfiladero: gorge

desfilar: parade

desfile: parade, show

desganado: low

desgarradura: tear

desgarrar: tear apart

desgastado: worn, worn out

desgastar: eat away, wear down

desgastar(se): weather

desgastarse: wear, wear away

desgaste: wear

desgaste mecánico: mechanical weathering

desglose: breakdown

desgracia: disgrace, ill, misery

desgraciadamente: unfortunately

desgraciado: miserable

deshacer(se): fall apart, go, take apart, strip, thaw

deshacer las maletas: unpack

deshacerse de: dispose of, get rid of, scrap, shake off, throw away

deshacerse en elogios por: rave about

deshielo: thaw

deshierbar: weed

deshonesto: crooked, dishonest, improper

deshonor: dishonor

deshonra: dishonor

deshonrar: disgrace, dishonor, shame

deshonrosamente: dishonorably

deshonroso: dishonorable

deshuesado: pitted

deshuesar: bone

desierto: barren, desert, deserted, wilderness

designación: appointment

designado: designated

designar: appoint, designate

desilusionar: let down

desinfectante: disinfectant

desinfectar: disinfect

desinflado: flat

desinstalar: uninstall

desintegración: disintegration

desintegrarse: crumble, disintegrate

desinteresado: selfless

deslindador: surveyor

deslindadora: surveyor

deslindar: survey

desliz: misstep, slip

deslizador: snowboarder

deslizadora: snowboarder

deslizamiento de tierra: landslide

deslizamiento lento: creep

deslizamiento masivo: mass movement

deslizar(se): slide, slip

deslizarse en la nieve en una tabla: snowboarding

deslizarse en trineo: sled

deslumbrar: glare

desmantelar: dismantle

desmañado: klutz

desmayar: black out

desmayarse: faint

desmedido: excessive

desmelenado: disheveled

desmentido: denial

desmentir: disprove

desmenuzar: shred

desmerecer: eclipse

desmontar: dismantle, take down

desmonte: clearance

desmoronamiento: collapse

desmoronar(se): crumble

desmoronarse: fall apart

desnudar(se): strip

desnudez: nakedness

desnudo: bare, naked

desobedecer: defy, disobey

desobediencia: disobedience

desocupado: empty, free, idle, vacant

desodorante: antiperspirant, deodorant

desolación: bleakness

desolado: bleak

desolador: bleak

desollar: skin

desorden: disorder, mess

desorden alimenticio: eating disorder

desorden bipolar: bipolar disorder

desordenado: littered, messy

desordenar: mess up, muss

desorientado: lost, mixed up

desorientar(se): lose one's bearings

desovar: lay

despachador: dispatcher

despachadora: dispatcher

despachar: dispatch, send off

despacho: dispatch, firm, practice

despampanante: stunning

desparramado: scattered

despatarrarse: sprawl

despedida: goodbye

despedida de soltera: bachelorette party

despedida de soltero: bachelor party

despedir(se): dismiss, excuse, fire, give off, give somebody notice, lay off, release, see off, send

despegar: blast off, off the ground, peel, take off

despegue: cleavage, takeoff

despeinar: muss

despejado: clear, crisp, fair

despejar el ambiente: clear the air

despeje: clearance

despellejar: skin

desperdiciar: throw away, waste

desperdicio: refuse, scrap, trash, waste

desperdigado: scattered

desperezarse: stretch

despertado: awoken

despertador: alarm, alarm clock

despertar: arouse, awaken, awakening, excite, stir

despertar(se): wake

despiadadamente: ruthlessly

despiadado: ruthless, vicious

despido: dismissal
despierto: awake
despilfarrar: squander
desplantador: trowel
desplazamiento: displacement, movement
desplazar: displace
desplazarse: cruise, get around
desplegable: drop-down menu
desplegar: deploy, open, open out
desplegar(se): fan out
despliegue: array, blaze, deployment, display, show
desplomarse: collapse, drop, flop, keel over, plunge, slump, tumble
desplome: plunge, slump
despojar: strip, strip away
despojarse de: shed
desportillar: chip
desposeído: deprived
despostillar: chip
despotricar: rave
desprecio: contempt, dismissal, slight
desprender(se): break off
desprendido: selfless
desprendimiento de rocas: rock fall
despreocupadamente: idly
despreocupado: carefree, casual
desprestigiar: discredit
desproporción: imbalance
desproporcionado a: out of proportion to
desprotegido: unprotected
desprovisto: void
después: after, afterward, beyond, later, since, then
después de: after, beyond, following
después de todo: after all
desquitarse: retaliate
destacado: leading, outstanding, prominent
destacar: excel, feature, highlight, shine, station
destapado: open
destapador: opener, plunger
destapar: uncover
destellar: flash, glitter, sparkle
destello: flash, sparkle
desternillarse (de risa): double over
destinado: destined
destinar: devote, earmark
destinataria: recipient
destinatario: recipient
destino: destination, destiny, fate
destitución: ouster, ousting

destreza: skill
destripar: gut
destrozar: blow, shatter, smash up, tear apart, tear down, wreck
destrozo: shattering
destrucción: destruction
destructivo: destructive
destruir: bring to its knees, destroy, gut, knock down, shred
desvalido: helpless, impotent
desván: attic
desvanecerse: disappearance, fade, melt, recede
desvariar: rave
desvelado: sleepless
desventaja: disadvantage, drawback, handicap, liability, minus, strike
desvergüenza: nerve
desvestido: undressed
desvestir(se): undress
desvestirse: strip
desviación: departure, detour
desviación estándar: standard deviation
desviación normal: standard deviation
desviación tipo: standard deviation
desviar: avert, divert
desviarse: curve, swerve
desvío: diversion
desvivirse: lavish
detalladamente: at length
detallado: close, detailed
detallar: detail
detalle: detail, touch
detalles: particulars
detalles (específicos): specifics
detección: detection, screening
detección a distancia: remote sensing
detectar: detect
detective: detective, investigator
detector de humo: smoke detector
detención: arrest, detention, standstill
detener: arrest, check, contain, detain, inhibit, keep
detener en tierra: ground
detener(se): come to rest, halt, pause, pull in, stop
detenida: detainee
detenidamente: closely
detenido: close, detainee, in custody
detergente: detergent
detergente para lavaplatos/ lavavajillas: dishwashing liquid
deteriorar: deteriorate
deterioro: decay, deterioration, erosion
determinación: decision, determination

determinado: determined, given
determinante: determiner
determinar: decide, determine, dictate, lay down, plot
determinar la antigüedad de: date
detestable: nasty
detonación: bang
deuda: debt, liability
deuda nacional: national debt
devaluación: devaluation
devaluar: devalue
devastación: devastation
devastado: shattered
devastador: devastating, shatter
devastar: devastate
develar: unveil
devengar: earn
devoción: devotion
devolución: refund, return
devolver: bounce, give back, put back, refund, restore, return, take back, throw up
devorar: wolf
devota: worshiper
devoto: devoted, worshiper
día: day, daytime
día de fiesta nacional: national holiday
día entre semana: weekday
día feriado: holiday
día y noche: around/ round the clock, day and night/night and day
diabetes: diabetes
diabética: diabetic
diabético: diabetic
diablo: devil
diablos: on earth
diablura: mischief
diafragma: diaphragm
diagnosticar: diagnose
diagnóstico: diagnosis
diagonal: diagonal, forward slash
diagonalmente: diagonally
diagrama: diagram
diagrama de flujo: flow chart
diagrama de Hertzsprung-Russell: Hertzsprung-Russell diagram
diagrama de Venn: Venn diagram
diagrama HR: Hertzsprung-Russell diagram
dialecto: dialect
diálogo: dialogue
diamante: diamond, infield
diámetro: diameter
diapositiva: slide
diariamente: daily
diario: daily, day-to-day, diary, everyday, journal,

newspaper, per diem
diario de navegación: log
diarrea: diarrhea
dibujar: draw
dibujo: drawing, tread
dibujo gestual: gesture drawing
dibujo perfilado: contour drawing
dicción: diction
diccionario: dictionary
dicho: saying
diciembre: December
dictado: dictation
dictador: dictator
dictadora: dictator
dictadura: dictatorship
dictar: deal out, dictate
dictar cátedra sobre: lecture
didáctico: instructive
diecinueve: nineteen
dieciocho: eighteen
dieciochoavo: eighteenth
dieciséis: sixteen
dieciseisavo: sixteenth
diecisiete: seventeen
diente: clove, tooth
diente de leche: baby tooth
diesel: diesel
diestro: right-handed, skillful
dieta: diet
diez: ten
difamar: libel, smear
difamatorio: libelous
diferencia: difference
diferencia potencial: potential difference
diferenciación: differentiation
diferenciar: differentiate
diferente: another matter/a different matter, different, separate, unlike
diferentemente: differently
diferir: contrast, differ, spread, table, vary
difícil: awkwardly, difficult, hard, heavy, labored, rough, tough, tricky, uphill
dificultad: difficulty
dificultad para respirar: breathlessness
dificultar: hamper, impede
difracción: diffraction
difundir: diffuse
difundir(se): spread
difunta: deceased
difunto: deceased, late
difusión: diffusion, spread
diga: hello
digerir: digest
digestión: digestion
digestivo: digestive
digital: digital
dígito: digit, figure
dignidad: dignity, self-respect
digno: fit, fitting, respectable, worthy

digno de admiración: impressive
digno de confianza: dependable
digno de nota: of note
digno de premio: prize
dígrafo: digraph
dilatación: dilation
dilema: dilemma
diluir: dilute, water down
diluviar: pour
dim sum: dim sum
dimensión: dimension
dimensiones: proportions
diminutivo: short
diminuto: minute, tiny
dinámica: dynamics
dinámico: dynamic
dinamismo: dynamism
dinastía: dynasty
dinero: fund, money
dinero en efectivo: cash
dinoflagelado: dinoflagellate
dinosaurio: dinosaur
diorama: diorama
Dios: God
dios: god
¡Dios mío!: goodness/my goodness, (good) heavens
diosa: goddess
diploma: diploma
diploma técnico de dos años: associate degree
diplomacia: diplomacy
diplomática: diplomat
diplomáticamente: diplomatically
diplomático: diplomat, diplomatic
dique: dam, levee
dirección: address, directing, direction, leadership, office, running, way
dirección cardinal: cardinal direction
Dirección de Alimentos y Medicinas: Food and Drug Administration
dirección IP: IP address
dirección lineal: line direction
direccional: turn signal
directamente: direct, directly, smack dab, straight
directiva: director, executive
directivo: director, officer
directo: close, direct, outspoken, straight
director: conductor, dean, director, manager, principal
director (de escuela): headmaster
director de funeraria: undertaker
director de escena: stage manager
director general: director general
director general de salud pública: surgeon general

directora: conductor, director, manager, principal
directora de funeraria: undertaker
directora general: director general
directora general de salud pública: surgeon general
directorio: directory
directriz: mandate
dirigente: leader
dirigir(se): address, aim, conduct, direct, head, lead, route, run, steer, target, wheel
dirigirse a: address, make for
dirigirse poco a poco: drift
disc-jockey: deejay, disc jockey, DJ
discapacitado: disabled
discar: dial
discernimiento: discrimination
disciplina: discipline
disciplinar: discipline
disciplinario: disciplinary
discípula: follower, pupil
discípulo: follower, pupil
disco: disk, record
disco (compacto): disk
disco compacto: compact disc
disco de larga duración: LP
disco de video: DVD
disco duro: hard disk, hard drive
disco flexible: floppy disk
discontinuar por etapas: phase out
Discontinuidad de Mohorovicic: Moho
discontinuo: broken, irregular
discordante: jarring
discordar: clash
discoteca: club, disco
discreción: discretion
discrepancia: disagreement
discrepar: conflict, differ, disagree, dissent
discrepar de: disagree
discretamente: discreetly
discreto: discreet, gentle
discriminación: discrimination, victimization
discriminar: discriminate
disculpa: apology
disculpar: excuse
disculparse: apologize, sorry
disculpe: excuse me, pardon
discurso: address, speech
discurso indirecto: reported speech
discusión: argument, contention, debate, discussion, fight
discutible: questionable

documentación

discutir: argue, debate, discuss, fight, talk, talk over

disecar: stuff

diseminar(se): disperse, spread

diseminarse por metástasis: metastasize

disensión: dissent

disentir: dissent

diseñador: designer, developer

diseñadora: designer, developer

diseñar: design, style

diseño: design

diseño correlacionado: correlational design

diseño descriptivo: descriptive design

diseño experimental: experimental design

diseño gráfico: graphics

disertación: dissertation, lecture

disfraces: dress-up

disfraz: mask

disfrazado: disguised, masked

disfrazar: mask

disfrazar(se): disguise

disfrutar: enjoy, indulge, take delight in/take a delight in

disfrutar de: enjoy

disgustado: sore

disgustar: dislike

disidente: dissenter, dissenting, dissident

disimulado: disguised

disimular: disguise, mask

disiparse: melt

dislexia: dyslexia

dislocar(se): wrench

disminución: decline, decrease, drop-off, reduction

disminuir: break, cut down, decline, decrease, diminish, ease, ease up, ebb, fall, flag, knock down, let up, mute, slow up, tail off, thin

disolución: dissolution

disolver: break up, disband, dissolve

disolver(se): thaw

disparador: trigger

disparar: blast, fire, let off, shoot, trigger

dispararse: jump, rocket, soar, spiral

disparatadamente: wildly

disparatar: rave

disparate: nonsense

disparejo: uneven

disparidad: clash

disparo: fire, round, shot

disparos: gunfire

dispersar: disband, split up

dispersar(se): disperse, spread out

disperso: scattered

disponer: lay out, provide

disponibilidad: availability

disponible: available, up for grabs

disposición: directive, disposal, provision, readiness, willingness

dispositivo: device

dispuesto: inclined, poised, ready, willing

disputa: contention, dispute

disputar: dispute

disqueta: floppy disk

disquete: floppy disk

distancia: distance, spacing, span

distancia vertical: contour interval

distanciado: distanced, estranged

distanciamiento: distance, estrangement

distanciar(se): alienate, distance, drive away, grow apart, step back

distante: distant, far off, remote, removed

distensión: loosening

distinción: distinction

distinguido: distinguished, select

distinguir(se): differentiate, discriminate, distinguish, make out, pick out, separate, single out, tell apart

distinguir el sabor de: taste

distinto: different, distinct, unlike

distorsión: distortion

distorsionado: distorted

distorsionar: distort

distraer: divert, put off, take one's mind off

distraerse: stray, wander

distraídamente: absent-mindedly, vacantly

distraído: absent-minded, vacant

distribución: distribution, spread

distribución binómica: binomial distribution

distribuidor: distributor

distribuidora: distributor

distribuir: distribute, market, spread

distrito: borough, district

distrito electoral: constituency

distrito escolar: school district

distrito segregado: township

disturbio: disorder, disturbance, riot, rioting, trouble

disuadir: deter, discourage, talk out of

divagar: stray, wander

diván: ottoman

diversamente: broadly

diversidad: diversity

diversificación: diversification

diversificar(se): branch out, diversify

diversión: amusement, fun, pleasure, recreation

diverso: broad, diverse, mixed

divertido: amused, amusing, fun, funny, humorous

divertir: amuse, entertain

divertirse mucho: have a ball

dividendo: dividend

dividido: divided, split

dividir(se): break up, carve up, divide, divide up, fork, sort, split, split up

dividir en dos: halve

dividir en zonas: zone

dividir por partes iguales: share out

divinamente: divinely

divinidad: divinity

divino: divine

divisa: crest

divisar: glimpse

divisas: currency, foreign exchange

división: divide, division, split

división celular: cell division

división en sílabas: syllabication

divisional: divisional

(línea) divisoria: divide

divorciada: divorcée

divorciado: divorcé, divorced

divorciar: divorce

divorciarse: divorce

divorcio: divorce

divulgación: release

divulgar: publicize, release

dobladillo: cuff

doblado: bent

doblar(se): bend, buckle, double over, dub, fold, fold up, give, lean, round, toll, turn

doble: double, dual, twice, twin

doble consonante: consonant doubling

doble crema: heavy cream

doble espacio: double spacing

doble hélice: double helix

doble sentido: two-way

doblez: fold

doce: twelve

doceavo: twelfth

docena: dozen

doctor: doctor, professor

doctor en filosofía: doctor of philosophy

doctora: doctor, professor

doctorado: doctorate, Ph.D.

doctrina: doctrine

doctrinal: doctrinal

documentación: documentation

documental: documentary

documentar: document

documento: document, paper

documento de identificación: ID card, identification card, identity card

dodecafónico: twelve-tone

dodo: dodo

dólar: buck, dollar

doler: ache, be in pain, hurt

dolor: ache, be in pain, grief, pain, suffering

dolor de cabeza: headache

dolorosamente: painfully

doloroso: painful

domado: tame

domar: tame

domesticado: tame

domesticar: tame

doméstico: domestic

domicilio principal: base

dominación: dominating, domination

dominante: dominant, dominating

dominar: dominate, hold sway, master

dominar una lengua: be fluent in a language

dominarse: get a grip

domingo: Sunday

dominio: command, domain, dominance

dominio de sí mismo: self-control

domo: dome

don: genius, gift

don nadie: nobody

dona: doughnut, scrunchie

donación: contribution, donation, endowment

donador: contributor, donor

donadora: contributor, donor

donante: contributor, donor

donar: donate, give

doncella: maiden

donde: where

dónde: where

dondequiera: anywhere, wherever

dorado: gilt, gold, golden

dormida: sleep

dormido: asleep

dormir: sleep

dormir para reponerse: sleep off

dormirse: drop off

dormitar: doze, nap

dormitorio: dormitory

dorsal: dorsal

dos: both, two

dos encuentros consecutivos: double-header

dos partes: AB

dos puntos: colon

dos terceras partes: two-thirds

dos tercios: two-thirds

dos veces: twice

dosel: canopy

dosis: dose

dosis excesiva: overdose

dotado de personal: staffed

dotar de personal: staff

Dr.: Dr.

dragar: drag

dragón: dragon

drama: drama

dramáticamente: dramatically

dramático: dramatic, theatrical, tragic

dramaturga: dramaturg, playwright

dramaturgo: dramaturg, playwright

drástico: dramatic, drastic

drenaje: drain, drainage

drenar: drain

droga: dope, drug

drogadicción: habit

drogadicta: drug addict

drogadicto: drug addict

drogar: dope, drug

DSL: DSL

dual: dual

dubitativamente: doubtfully

ducha: shower

ducharse: shower

ductilidad: ductility

ducto: pipeline

duda: doubt, hesitation, query, question

dudar: doubt, hesitate

dudar de: doubt, question

dudoso: doubtful, dubious, questionable

duende: leprechaun

dueña: owner, proprietor

dueño: landlord, master, owner, proprietor

dulce: candy, sweet

dulcemente: sweetly

dulzura: sweetness

duna: dune, sand dune

duodécimo: twelfth

duplicación: duplication

duplicado: duplicate

duplicar: duplicate

duplicar(se): double

durabilidad: durability

durable: durable, lasting

duración: duration, length, life

duradero: enduring, lasting, long-standing

duramente: harshly, sharply

durante: during, for, over, through, throughout

durante la noche: overnight

durar: last, run, span

durazno: peach

dureza: hardness, harshness, toughness

duro: hard, harsh, heavy, insensitive, sharp, stark, stiff, tough

E

e-mail: e-mail

ébola: Ebola

ebrio: drunk

echar(se): chase, eject, kick out, lie, pin, send, shut out, throw

echar a alguien de algún lugar: throw out

echar a alguien hacia algún lado: bundle somebody somewhere

echar a andar: set the wheels in motion

echar a perder: blow, flub, mess up, screw up, sour, spoil

echar brotes: sprout

echar de menos: long, miss

echar de repente: pop

echar el cerrojo: bolt

echar la mano: pitch in

echar llave: lock

echar luz: shed/throw/cast light on

echar mano de: fall back on

echar por tierra: demolish

echar raíz: take root

echar retoños: sprout

echar suertes: draw lots

echar un chorrito: squirt

echar un ojo: eye

echar un vistazo: cast your eyes/a look, glance, eye, look through, scan

echar un volado: draw lots, toss

echar una mano: help out

echar(se) a correr: flee

echarse a: burst into

echarse al hombro: carry (responsibilities/problems) on one's shoulders

echarse para atrás: back down, pull back

echarse un clavado: dive

echar(se) una carrera: race

ecléctico: eclectic

eclipsar: dwarf, eclipse

eclipse: eclipse

eclipse anular: annular eclipse

eclipse de luna: lunar eclipse

eclipse lunar: lunar eclipse

eclipse parcial: partial eclipse

eclipse solar: solar eclipse

eclipse total: total eclipse

eco: echo

ecografía: scan, ultrasound

ecógrafo: scanner

ecología: ecology

ecológicamente: ecologically

ecológico: ecological

ecologista: ecologist, environmentalist
economía: economics, economy, thrift
económicamente: economically
económico: economic, economical, inexpensive, low-end
economista: economist
economizador de trabajo: labor-saving
ecosistema: ecosystem
ectotérmico: ectotherm
ecuación: equation
ecuación de coordenadas polares: polar equation
ecuación lineal: linear equation
ecuación química: chemical equation
ecuador: equator
edad: age
edad de hielo: Ice Age
Edad de Piedra: Stone Age
edición: edition, publishing
edición de tapa blanda: paperback
edición en rústica: paperback
edificio: building, premise
edificio de departamentos: apartment building
edificio de oficinas: office building
edificio de poca altura: low-rise
edificio de varios pisos: multistory
edificio representativo: landmark
edificios municipales: civic center
editar: edit
editor: editor, publisher
editora: editor, publisher
editorial: editorial
edredón: comforter, quilt
educación: education, instruction, schooling, upbringing
educación continua: further education
educación en casa: home schooling
educación física: phys ed, physical education
educación para adultos: further education
educación superior: higher education
educado: civilized, educated
educador: educator
educadora: educator
educar(se): educate, nurture, raise
educativo: educational, instructive
edulcorante: sweetener
EEB: BSE
efectivamente: indeed, sure enough, truly

efectividad: effectiveness
efectivo: effective
efectivos: strength
efecto: effect, impact, impression
efecto colateral: side effect
efecto Coriolis: Coriolis effect
efecto invernadero: greenhouse effect
efecto secundario: side effect
efectos especiales: special effects
efectuar: effect
eficiencia: efficiency
eficiencia energética: energy efficiency
eficiente: efficient
EFL: EFL
ego: ego
egocéntrico: self-centered
egoísmo: self-interest, selfishness
egoísta: self-centered, selfish
egresada: graduate
egresado: graduate
eh: aw
¡eh!: hey
eje: axis, axle
ejecución: execution
ejecución de la ley: law enforcement
ejecutante: performer, player
ejecutar: execute, implement, perform, put (somebody) to death
ejecutiva: executive
ejecutivo: executive
ejemplar: copy
ejemplificar: illustrate
ejemplo: example, illustration, instance
ejercer: exercise, exert, practice
ejercer presión: strain
ejercicio: drill, exercise, practice
ejercicio de baile: dance study
ejercicio de calentamiento: warm-up
ejército: army, battery, military, troop
ejote: string bean
el: the
él: he, him, it
El Capitolio: The Capitol
el colmo: the last straw
el mío: mine, my own
él mismo: himself
el mundo exterior: the outside world
El niño: El Niño
el nombre del juego: the name of the game
el nuestro: ours, our own
el orden del universo: the (grand) scheme of things
el paso del tiempo: age
el peor de los casos:

worst-case
el piso de arriba: upstairs
el primero: former, top
el pro y contra: pros and cons
el que fuera: one-time
el que habla: speaker
el que sufre: sufferer
el siguiente: following
el suyo: his, his own, theirs, their own, yours, your own
el tanque: the pen
el tejido: knitting
el tuyo: yours, your own
el culpable: to blame
el que surfea: surfer
elaboración: making, manufacture
elaborado: elaborate
elaborar: belabor
elástico: elastic
elección: choice, election
elección primaria: primary
elecciones generales: general election
elector: constituent, elector
electora: constituent, elector
electorado: electorate
electoral: electoral
electores potenciales: constituency
eléctricamente: electrically
electricidad: electricity
electricidad dinámica: current electricity
electricidad estática: static
electricista: electrician
eléctrico: electric, electrical
electrizante: electric
electrochoque: shock
electrocución: electrocution
electrocutar(se): electrocute
electrodoméstico: appliance
electroimán: electromagnet
electrón: electron
electrón de valencia: valence electron
electrónica: electronics
electrónicamente: electronically
electrónico: electronic
elefante: elephant
elegancia: elegance
elegante: dress-up, elegant, fancy, graceful, spiffy, stylish, trim
elegantemente: elegantly, stylishly
elegibilidad: eligibility
elegible: eligible
elegir: choose, elect, pick
elemental: elementary
elemento: element, ingredient
elemento artístico: art element
elemento constitutivo:

constituent
elemento menor: trace gas
elementos artísticos: elements of art
elementos musicales: elements of music
elenco: cast
elevado: high
elevador: elevator
elevador de escalera: stairlift
elevar: boost, elevate, put up
elevar al cuadrado: square
elevarse: rise, soar
eliminación: disposal, elimination
eliminado: out
eliminar: cut out, delete, do away with, eliminate, weed out
eliminar paulatinamente: phase out
eliminatoria: qualifier
elipse: ellipse
élite: elite
ella: her, it, she
ella misma: herself
ellas: them, they
ellas mismas: themselves
ello: it
ellos: them, they
ellos mismos: themselves
elocuencia: eloquence
elocuente: eloquent, fluent
elocuentemente: eloquently
elogiar: compliment, eulogize
elogio: praise
elogioso: complimentary
eludir: dodge, duck, fend off, get around, sidestep, skirt
embadurnado: smeared
embadurnar: smear
embajada: embassy
embajador: ambassador
embajadora: ambassador
embalar: pack
embalse: reservoir
embarazada: pregnant
embarazo: pregnancy
embarazoso: embarrassing
embarcación: craft
embarcadero: jetty, wharf
embarcar(se): board, embark, ship
embarcarse en: launch into
embargo: embargo
embarque: shipment, shipping
embaucador: slick
embaucar: snow, trick
embestida: thrust
embestir: slam
embetunar: frost
emblema: crest
embolsarse: pocket, rake in
emboscada: ambush

emboscar: ambush
embotellamiento: backup, jam, traffic jam
embotellar: bottle, choke
embravecer: rage
embrión: embryo
embustera: cheater
embustero: cheater
embutido: lunch meat
emergencia: emergency
emerger: emerge, surface
emigración: emigration, migration
emigrar: emigrate, migrate
eminencia: eminence
eminente: eminent
emisión: emission, transmission
emisión deportiva: sportscast
emisión por televisión: telecast
emitir: air, cast, emit, issue, return, send
emitir acciones: float
emoción: emotion, excitement, thrill
emocionado: excited, stoked
emocional: emotional
emocionalmente: emotionally
emocionante: exciting, heart-stopping, impressive, thrilling
emocionar: excite, thrill
emotivo: emotional
empacado de carne: meatpacking
empacar: pack, package
empalagoso: icky
empañar(se): color, diminish, mist
empapado: soaked, soaking
empapado en sudor: sweating
empapar: soak
empapelar: decorate, paper, wallpaper
empaque: packaging
empaquetador: bagger
empaquetadora: bagger
emparedado: sandwich
emparejar: even out
emparentado: related
empastar: bind
empaste: filling
empatar: tie
empate: tie
empatía: empathy
empeine: liverwort
empeñado en: bent
empeñar: pawn
empeorar: change for the worse, worsen
empeorar(se): escalate
empequeñecer: dwarf
emperador: emperor
emperatriz: empress
empezar: begin, break into, break out, get down to, go about, initiate, start, take up
empezar a: become, get
empezar a gustar: grow on

empezar como: start out
empezar con: start on
empezar con el pie derecho: get off to a flying start
empezar de nuevo: start over
empezar por: start off
empinar el codo: booze
empinarse: rear
empírico: empirical
emplazamiento: siting
emplazar: cite, site
empleada: clerk, employee, staffer
empleada de funeraria: undertaker
empleado: clerk, employee, staffer, working
empleado de funeraria: undertaker
empleado de oficina: white-collar
empleador: employer
empleadora: employer
empleados: staff
emplear: employ
empleo: employment, job
empoderamiento: empowerment
empoderar: empower
empotrar: build
emprendedor: enterprising, go-ahead, up-and-coming
emprender: embark, fight, go about, launch, take up
emprenderla contra: turn on
empresa: business, enterprise, firm, operation, operator, undertaking, venture
empresa conjunta: joint venture
empresa cotizada en la bolsa: performer
empresa de utilidad pública: utility
empresa difícil: tall order
empresa punto com: dot-com
empresa que ofrece las mismas oportunidades: equal opportunity employer
empresaria: entrepreneur
empresarial: entrepreneurial
empresario: entrepreneur
empréstito: loan
empujar: press, push, shove, sweep, thrust
empujar con los codos: elbow
empuje: drive
empujón: push, shove, thrust
en: about, against, around, at, by, in, inside, into, on, to, under, within
en absoluto: any, at

all, in the slightest, whatsoever
en adelante: onward
en alta mar: at sea
en alto: high
en ángulo: at an angle
en ángulo recto: at right angles
en apenas: flat
en aplicación: in place
en aposición: appositive
en aprietos: in trouble
en asociación con: in association with
en aumento: increasingly, upward
en avión: by air
en bancarrota: bankrupt
en beneficio de: benefit
en blanco: blank
en blanco (noche): sleepless
en boga: in fashion
en breve: shortly
en bruto: gross
en buen estado: functional
en (buena) forma: in (good) shape
en buena parte: largely
en buenas manos: in safe hands, safe in someone's hands
en busca de: after, in search of, out to (do something)
en cada estación: seasonally
en calma: calmly
en cámara: on camera
en camino a: en route
en camino de: on course for
en carne viva: raw
en casa: at home, home
en caso de: in the event of
en caso de que: in the event that
en ciernes: in the making
en cierto modo: sort of
en cierto sentido: in a way
en comparación con: relative to
en común: in common
en conclusión: in conclusion
en confianza: in confidence
en conjunción con: in conjunction with
en conjunto: as a whole, overall
en consecuencia: consequently, in consequence/as a consequence
en contacto con: in contact with, in touch with
en contra: against
en contra de: against
en contra de nuestra voluntad: in spite of oneself
en contra de todo: against all odds

en contraposición a: as opposed to
en contrario: to the contrary
en crisis: depressed
en cualquier caso: in any case
en cualquier forma: anyhow
en cualquier momento: (at) any minute (now), any day/moment/time now, anytime
en cualquier parte: wherever
en cuanto: anytime, the moment
en cuanto a: as, as regards, regarding
en cuanto a eso: on that/this score
en cuatro patas: on all fours
en cuclillas: crouch
en cuestión: (question/point) at issue, in question
en curso: ongoing
en curva cerrada: sharp
en cuyo caso: in that/which case
en decadencia: in decline/on the decline
en declive: in decline/on the decline
en déficit: in deficit
en desacuerdo: at odds
en descubierto: in deficit
en desventaja: at a disadvantage
en detalle: fully, in detail, in full
en deuda: in debt, indebted
en diagonal: catty-corner
en días/semanas/meses alternos: every other day/week/month
en dificultades: in difficulty
en dirección de: toward
en dirección este: eastward
en directo: live
en disco: on record
en disminución: in decline/on the decline
en disputa: in dispute
en duda: in doubt
en efecto: effectively
en el acto: outright
en el aire: airborne
en el centro: downtown
en el extranjero: abroad, overseas
en el favor: in favor
en el fondo: at heart, for all intents and purposes, underneath
en el futuro: a long time/way off, in (the) future
en el haber de uno: under one's belt
en el ínterin: in the interim
en el interior: indoor, indoors, inside
en el lugar de: in

somebody's shoes
en el mar: at sea
en el mercado: on the market
en el momento: the minute, the moment
en el momento de: upon
en el norte: upstate, uptown
en el pellejo de: in somebody's shoes
en el peor de los casos: at (the) worst
en el poder: ruling
en el sentido de: in that
en el sentido de las agujas del reloj: clockwise
en el umbral de: on the threshold of
en ese caso: in that/which case
en esencia: essentially, in essence
en eso: there
en especie: in kind
en espera de: pending
en esta época: these days
en este momento: at the moment, just
en este preciso momento: right now
en este punto: here
en este sentido: in this respect
en este/ese sentido: to this/that effect
en estudio: under consideration
en exceso: to excess
en exceso de: over
en exhibición: on view
en exteriores: on location
en extinción: dying
en fase terminal: terminally
en favor de: for, toward
en favor de alguien: in somebody's favor
en fila: single file
en fila india: single file
en flor: flowering, in bloom, out
en foco: in focus
en forma: fit
en forma de caracol: spiral
en frente de: in front of
en funcionamiento: operational
en general: across the board, all in all, as a whole, at large, broadly, general, generally, in general, in the main, on the whole
en gran escala: large-scale
en gran medida: largely
en grande: large-scale
en guardia: on alert, on one's guard, on standby
en honor a: after
en honor de: for, in honor of
en igualdad de condiciones: on equal terms/on the same terms

en jefe: chief
en juego: at stake
en la actualidad: nowadays
en la bolsa: in the bag
en la cima: at its height
en la cumbre: at its height
en la cúspide: top
en la debida forma: accordingly
en la mañana: in the morning
en la miseria: penniless
en la onda: cool, funky, hip
en la periferia: fringe
en la práctica: in practice, practically
en las afueras: fringe
en las afueras de: outside
en las garras de alguien: in somebody's clutches
en las horas de menor demanda: off-peak
en las narices: under somebody's nose
en libertad: free, on the loose
en línea: on line, online
en lista de espera: standby
en litigio: in dispute
en llamas: in flames
en lo alto: high up
en lo esencial: essentially
en lo financiero: financially
en lo más hondo: in the depths
en lo más mínimo: in the least, in the slightest
en lo referente al funcionamiento: operationally
en locación: on location
en lontananza: distantly
en lugar de: in place of, in something's/somebody's place
en marcha: in motion, on the move, underway
en marcha atrás: reverse
en medio de: in the middle of, in the midst of
en medio de la nada: in the middle of nowhere
en medio: middle
en mi opinión: to my mind
en miniatura: in miniature, model
en movimiento: in motion, on the move
en muchos sentidos: in many respects
en ningún lugar: nowhere
en nombre de: in the name of something
en nombre de alguien: on somebody's behalf/on behalf of somebody
en números rojos: in the hole, in the red
en otra parte: elsewhere

en otras palabras: in other words
en otro lugar: elsewhere
en otro tiempo: once
en pañales: in its infancy
en paro: idle
en parte: in part, partly
en particular: in particular, particular
en persecución de: in pursuit of
en persona: himself, in person, in the flesh
en picada: tailspin
en plena marcha: in full swing
en pleno desarrollo: in full swing
en polvo: powdered
en posición de: position
en presencia de: in someone's presence
en primer lugar: first of all, in the first instance, in the first place
en primer término: for one thing, in the first instance
en principio: in principle
en privado: in private, privately
en pro de: in favor of, in the interest(s) of
en problemas: in trouble
en proceso: in progress, on
en proceso de: in the process of
en proceso de análisis: under consideration
en profundidad: in depth
en promedio: on average/on an average
en proporción: correspondingly
en público: in public
en puerta: on the horizon
en punto: o'clock, sharp
en que: where
en quiebra: bankrupt
en realidad: actual, in reality
en rebaja: on sale
en reconocimiento por: in recognition of
en relación con: as regards, in relation to, in/with regard to, regarding, relative to, toward, with/in reference to
en reserva: in reserve, in store
en resumen: in short, in summary
en resumidas cuentas: on balance, ultimately
en retrospectiva: in retrospect
en reversa: reverse
en riesgo: at stake
en ruinas: in ruins
en salmuera: pickled
en secreto: in secret
en segundo lugar: secondly
en sentido literal: at face value

en serio: earnest, for real, indeed, seriously
en servicio: operational
en servicio: in service
en sí: actual, itself
en silencio: silently
en síntesis: briefly, in summary
en sólo: flat
en su elemento: in one's element
en su (sano) juicio: rational
en su mayor parte: mostly
en su peor momento: at one's worst
en suma: in short
en sumo grado: with a vengeance
en tándem: in tandem
en teoría: in the abstract
en términos electorales: electorally
en términos generales: broadly
en toda la extensión de la palabra: full-blown
en todo: around
en todo caso: anyway, at any rate
en todo el mundo: worldwide
en todo el país: nationwide
en todos sentidos: every/any which way
en total: altogether, in all, in total
en tránsito: in transit
en tren: by rail
en trozos grandes: coarsely
en última instancia: ultimately
en un arranque: on impulse
en un futuro: in (the) future
en un futuro próximo: in the near future
en un piso de arriba: upstairs
en un principio: initially
en un sentido amplio: broadly
en uso: alive, in use
en vano: in vain, unsuccessfully, vainly
en venta: for sale, up for sale
en verdad: seriously
en vez de: instead of
en vías de desarrollo: developing
en vigor: effective, operative
en virtud de: by reason of, by virtue of
en vista de: in the light of, in view of
en vivo: live
en voz alta: aloud, out loud
en vuelta cerrada: sharply
en todas partes: everywhere

en todos lados: everywhere

en/fuera de la carrera: in the running/out of the running

enamoramiento: crush

enamorarse: fall in love

enamorarse de: fall for

enana blanca: white dwarf

enano: dwarf

enardecer(se): flare

encabezado: headline

encabezamiento: headline

encabezar: head, lead

encabritarse: rear

encajar: fit in

encaje: lace

encaminar: route

encantado: delighted

encantado de conocerlo/ conocerla: pleased to meet you

encantador: charming, delightful, lovely, sweet, winning

encantadoramente: charmingly

encantamiento: spell

encantar: charm

encantar a alguien: take somebody's fancy

encanto: appeal, charm, spell

encaramar: perch

encarar: brave, confront

encarcelamiento: imprisonment

encarcelar: imprison, lock up

encargada: attendant, groundskeeper, superintendent

encargado: attendant, groundskeeper, superintendent

encargar: send out for

encargarle: commission

encargarse: undertake

encargarse (de algo): handle

encargarse de: arrange, see

encargo: commission

encarnizado: bitter

encéfalo: brain

encefalopatía espongiforme bovina: BSE

encender(se): boot, come on, flare, go on, light, put on, set fire to , start, strike, switch on, turn on

encenderse la luz: light up

encendido: on

encerrar: imprison, lock away, pen, put, shut in

enchapado en oro: gilt

enchinar(se): curl

enchufar: plug in

enchufe: outlet, plug, socket

encía: gum

enciclopedia: encyclopedia

encima: into the bargain/in the bargain, on

encima (de): over

encima de: on top/on top of something, upon

encogerse: shrink

encogerse de hombros: shrug

encontrado: mixed

encontrar(se): come across, encounter, find, lie, link up, meet, meet up, strike, stumble across, track down, work out

¿se encuentra...?: Is ... there? (telephone)

encontrar a: get/grab ahold of

encontrar a alguien: get hold of (somebody)

encontrar defectos: fault

encontrar el camino: find one's way

encontrar el momento para: get around to

encontrar una mina de oro: strike paydirt

encontrarse con: run across, run into

encorvado: bowed

encorvarse: lean

encrespado: ruffled

encrucijada: crossroads

encuadernación: binding

encuadernar: bind

encubierto: masked

encuentro: encounter, meeting

encuesta: poll, survey

encuesta de opinión: opinion poll

encuesta de salida: exit poll

encuestar: survey

encurtido: pickle

encurtidos: pickle

enderezar: right

enderezar(se): straighten

enderezarse: sit up

endeudamiento: borrowing

endeudarse: get into debt

endibia: endive

endivia: endive

endocitosis: endocytosis

endocrino: endocrine

endoesqueleto: endoskeleton

endotérmico: endothermic

endotermo: endotherm

endulzado: sweet

endulzante artificial: sweetener

endurecer(se): harden

endurecimiento: hardening

enemiga: enemy

enemigo: enemy

energía: energy, power, vigor

energía acumulada: stored energy

energía almacenada: stored energy

energía cinética: kinetic energy

energía de activación: activation energy

energía de luz: light energy

energía eléctrica: electric power, electrical energy, electricity

energía eólica: wind energy

energía geotérmico: geothermal energy

energía hidráulica: water power

energía hidroeléctrica: hydropower, water power

energía mecánica: mechanical energy

energía nuclear: nuclear energy

energía potencial: potential energy, stored energy

energía potencial gravitacional: gravitational potential energy

energía química: chemical energy

energía sonora: sound energy

energía térmica: thermal energy

enérgicamente: briskly, dynamically, violently

enérgico: alive, emphatic, firm, hearty, strong, vocal

enero: January

enfadado: cross

enfado: anger, irritation

énfasis: emphasis, stress

enfáticamente: emphatically

enfático: emphatic

enferma alcohólica: alcoholic

enfermar: make somebody sick

enfermedad: disease, illness, infection, sickness, trouble

enfermedad de las vacas locas: BSE

enfermedad de transmisión sexual: sexually transmitted disease

enfermedad del beso: mono, mononucleosis

enfermera: nurse

enfermera especializada: nurse practitioner

enfermera titulada: registered nurse

enfermero: nurse

enfermero especializado: nurse practitioner

enfermero titulado: registered nurse

enfermizo: unhealthy

enfermo: ill, inmate, sick

enfermo alcohólico: alcoholic

enfilar: wheel

enfocado: in focus

enfocar(se): aim, focus
enfoque: approach, tack
enfrascarse: immerse
enfrentado: at odds
enfrentamiento: face-off
enfrentar: contend, cope, face, meet, pit, stand up to, tackle, take on
enfrentar(se): brave, encounter
enfrentarse: confront
enfrentarse a: come to grips with, contend
enfrente: opposite
enfrente de: opposite
enfriador de agua: water cooler
enfriamiento: chill
enfriar(se): chill, cool
enfurecer: anger, infuriate, rage
enfurecerse: see red
enganchar: hook
engancharse: hook up, snag
enganche: deposit
engañar: cheat on, deceive, fool, mislead, take in, trick
engaño: deceit, deception
engañosamente: misleadingly
engañoso: misleading
engarrotarse: seize up
engendrar: breed, father
englobar: lump together
engordar: put on weight
engorro: mischief
engrapadora: stapler
engrapar: staple
engrasar: grease
engrudo: paste
engullir(se): wolf
enharinar: coat
enhebrar: thread
enigma: puzzle, riddle
enjambrar: swarm
enjambre: swarm
enjardinar: landscape
enjoyado: bejeweled
enjuagar: rinse
enjuague: rinse
enjuiciar: prosecute
enlace: link, marriage
enlace covalente: covalent bond
enlace iónico: ionic bond
enlace metálico: metallic bond
enlace químico: chemical bond, chemical bonding
enlatar: can
enlazar: connect, link, loop
enlodar(se): muddy
enlutarse: mourn
enmarañado: shaggy
enmarañar: muddy
enmarañar(se): tangle
enmarcar: frame
enmascarado: masked
enmasillar: caulk
enmedio: middle
enmendar: amend
enmienda: amendment
enojado: angry, annoyed, cross

enojar: irritate
enojo: irritation
enorgullecerse: pride oneself
enorme: awful, enormous, huge, immense, jumbo, massive, tremendous
enormemente: enormously, hugely, massively, terribly
enrarecimiento: rarefaction
enredado: mixed up, muddled up
enredar: confuse, muddle, muddy
enredar(se): tangle
enriquecer: enrich
enriquecerse: thrive
enriquecimiento: enrichment
enrojecer: glow
enrolarse: enlist
enrollar(se): loop, roll, roll up, wind
enroscado: curly
enroscar: screw
enroscarse: curl up
ensalada: salad
ensalada de col: slaw
ensalada del chef: chef's salad
ensamblaje: assembly
ensamble: ensemble
ensanchar: widen
ensangrentado: bloody
ensartar: thread
ensayar: run through
ensayo: dry run, essay, rehearsal, run-through
ensayo general: dress rehearsal
ensayo y error: trial and error
ensenada: inlet
enseñanza: instruction, teaching
enseñanza del inglés como lengua extranjera: TEFL
enseñar: instruct, show, teach
enseñar sobre: lecture
ensillar: saddle
ensombrecer: shadow
ensuciar: dirty, litter
entablar: engage, file, strike up
entablar una demanda: sue
ente: being
entender: catch on, figure out, follow, get, make out, make sense of, see, sympathize, understand
entender mal: misread, misunderstand
entendido: understanding
entendimiento: understanding
entera libertad: a free hand
enterar: inform
enterarse: find out, learn

enternecedor: touching
entero: entire, intact, integer, whole
enterrar: bury
entidad: agency, entity
entonación: inflection
entonces: so, then
entorno: environment, surroundings
entrada: access, admission, cue, door, entrance, entry, input, lobby, mouth, receipt, ticket
entrada de datos: data entry
entrante: incoming
entrañas: insides
entrar: break into, come in, descend, enter, go into, march
entrar a montones en: pour
entrar a raudales: roll in, stream
entrar al sistema: log in
entrar en: access, get into, go into
entrar en conflicto: clash
entrar en decadencia: go into decline
entrar en detalles: elaborate
entrar en pánico: panic
entrar en razón: come to one's senses/bring somebody to their senses
entrar en vigor: take effect
entrar desordenadamente: pile into
entrar por la fuerza: break in, break into
entrar sin llamar: barge into/through
entrar tranquilamente: breeze in(to)
entre: among, between, in the midst of
entre bambalinas: backstage
entre bastidores: backstage, behind the scenes
entre facciones: factional
entre semana: during the week
entrecortadamente: breathlessly
entrecortado: uneven
entrega: delivery, installment, issue, presentation, surrender
entrega contra reembolso: cash on delivery
entrega inicial: deposit
entregar: deliver, hand in, issue, submit, turn over
entregarse: surrender
entrenador: coach, trainer
entrenadora: coach, trainer

entrenamiento: training

entrenar: coach, work out

entrenar(se): train

entrepierna: groin

entretanto: (in the) meantime, for the time being, in the interim, meanwhile

entretener: amuse, delay, entertain

entretenerse: busy oneself, mess around, putter, while away

entretenido: amusing, entertaining

entretenimiento: entertainment, recreation

entreverar: muddle

entrevista: interview

entrevistador: interviewer

entrevistadora: interviewer

entrevistar: interview

entrometerse: butt in, interfere, muscle in

entumecer: numb

entumecido: numb, stiff

entumecimiento: numbness

entusiasmado: enthusiastic, excited, taken

entusiasmar: encourage, thrill

entusiasmo: enthusiasm, excitement

entusiasta: enthusiast, enthusiastic

enumerar: list, recite

enunciativo: declarative

envasar: enclose, pack, package

envase: packaging, tub

envejecer: age

envejecimiento: aging

envenenamiento: poisoning

envenenar: poison

envergadura: span

enviada: envoy

enviada plenipotenciaria: envoy

enviado: envoy

enviado plenipotenciario: envoy

enviar: dispatch, forward, route, send

enviar mensajes electrónicos: message

enviar por barco: ship

enviar por correo: mail out

enviar por fax: fax

enviar spam: spam

enviar un mensaje de texto: text

enviar/mandar por correo: mail

enviar/mandar por correo electrónico: mail

envidia: envy, jealousy

envidiar: envy

envidiosamente:

enviously

envidioso: envious, jealous

envío: dispatch, shipment, shipping

envío de mensajes de texto: text messaging, texting

envoltura: wrapper

envolver: enclose, envelop, swathe

envolver(se): wrap

enzima: enzyme

epicentro: epicenter, focus

épico: epic

epidemia: epidemic

epidermis: epidermis

epidídimo: epididymis

episodio: episode

época: age, day, era, time

epopeya: epic

equilátero: equilateral

equilibrado: balanced

equilibrar: balance

equilibrio: balance, footing

equilibrio térmico: thermal equilibrium

equipaje: baggage, luggage

equipar: equip, fit out, outfit

equiparable: comparable

equiparar: equate, match

equipo: crew, equipment, gear, kit, outfit, squad, team

equipo de primeros auxilios: first aid kit

equipo para mantener la vida: life support

equitación: horseback riding, riding

equitativamente: evenly

equivalente: equivalent

equivaler: amount to, equate

equivocación: error, mistake

equivocadamente: mistakenly, wrongly

equivocado: erroneous, incorrect, misplaced, mistaken, wide of the mark, wrong

equivocarse: err

era: age, era

era cenozoica: Cenozoic era

era paleozoica: Paleozoic era

erecto: erect

erguido: erect, straight, upright

erigir: erect

erizado: ruffled

erosión: erosion, weathering

erosionar: wear down

erosionar(se): erode, weather

erótico: erotic

erradicación: eradication

erradicar: eradicate, root out, stamp out

errado: wide of the mark

errar: err, miss

erróneamente: erroneously

erróneo: erroneous, improper, inaccurate, incorrect

error: blooper, bug, error, flub, misperception, mistake

error de imprenta: typo

erudición: scholarship

erudita: scholar

erudito: learned, scholar

erupción: eruption, rash

eruptivo: extrusive

es decir: in short, namely, that is to say, that is/that is to say

es evidente: goes without saying

es mejor que: had better

es posible: possibly

es todo: that is that

esa: that

esas: those

esbelto: slim, trim

esbozar: sketch

esbozar con los labios: mouth

esbozo: sketch

escabeche: pickle

escabullir(se): sneak

escabullirse: scuttle

escala: layover, range, scale

escala de cinco notas: pentatonic scale

escala de valores: value scale

escala del tiempo geológico: geological time scale

escala diatónica: diatonic scale

escala pentatónica: pentatonic scale

escalar: climb, scale

escalera: ladder

escalera de mano: ladder

escalera eléctrica: escalator

escalera(s): stair

escaleras abajo: downstairs

escaleras arriba: upstairs

escalinata: staircase, stairway

escalofriante: creepy, hairy

escalofrío: chill, shiver

escalón: stair, step

escalonar: stagger

escama: scale

escandalizado: outraged, shocked

escandalizar: outrage

escandalizar(se): shock

escándalo: fuss, outrage, scandal, storm, uproar

escandalosamente: grossly, outrageously, shockingly

escandaloso: loud, outrageous, shocking

escáner: scanner

escaño: seat

escapar(se): break, escape, flee, get away, make off, run away escapársele a uno algo: miss

escape: escape, exhaust pipe, tailpipe

escarabajo: beetle

escarbar: dig

escarcha: frost

escardar: weed

escarpado: jagged, sheer, steep

escasamente: narrowly

escasear: be at a premium

escasear(se): be in short supply, thin

escasez: shortage

escaso: insufficient, light, little, narrow, scarce, short, slim

escena: scene, sketch

escenario: scenario, scene, setting, stage

escénico: theatrical

escenografía: scenery

escepticismo: disbelief

escéptico: cynical, skeptical

escindir(se): split

escisión: fragmentation, split

esclava: slave

esclavitud: slavery

esclavo: slave

esclerosis múltiple (EM): MS

esclusa: lock

escoba: broom

escocer: smart

escoger: choose, pick, select

escogido: select

escollo: stumbling block

escolta: escort

escoltado: under escort

escoltar: escort, walk

escombros: debris

esconder(se): hide

escondido: hidden, hiding

escopeta: shotgun

escopeta de aire comprimido: BB gun

escotilla: hatch

escribir: make a note/list, mark down, pen, put down, state, take down, type in, write, write in, writing

escribir a doble espacio: double-space

escribir a la carrera: dash off

escribir a máquina: type

escribir con letra de molde: print

escribir un prefacio: preface

escrito: writing, written

escrito a mano: handwritten

escrito difamatorio: libel

escritor: author, writer

escritor mercenario: hack

escritora: author, writer

escritora mercenaria: hack

escritorio: desk, desktop

escritura: deed, script, writing

escritura creativa: creative writing

escritura emocional: expressive writing

escroto: scrotum

escrúpulo (de conciencia): qualm

escrutar: scan

escuadrón: squadron, troop

escuchar: catch, hear, listen

escuchar a escondidas: eavesdrop, listen in

escuchar con imparcialidad: give a fair hearing

escudo: shield

escudriñar: peer, probe, scan

escuela: college, school

escuela (edificio): schoolhouse

escuela comunitaria: community college

escuela de gobierno: public school

escuela elemental: elementary school

escuela oficial: public school

escuela primaria: elementary school

escuela pública: public school

escuela religiosa: parochial school

escuela secundaria: junior high school

escuela semisuperior: junior college

escuela técnica: junior college

escueto: bare

escuincle: boy

escultura: sculpture

escultura aditiva: additive sculpture

escultura sustractiva: subtractive sculpture

escupir: spit

escurridor: colander

escurridora: colander

escurrimiento: runoff

escurrir: drain, drip, strain

escurrirse: duck out

ese: that

ese punto: there

esencia: essence, substance

esencial: bare-bones, essential, indispensable, of the essence, vital

esencialmente: essentially, in essence

esfera: dial, realm, sphere

esforzarse: endeavor, labor, strive

esfuerzo: effort, endeavor, exertion, stress

esfumarse: go down the drain

esgrima: fencing

esguince: strain

eslabón: link

eslogan: catchword

esmalte: enamel

esmerarse: take pains to

esmero: thoroughness

esmog: smog

esnob: snob

eso: so, that, thing

esos: those

espacial: spatial

espaciar: space

espacio: gap, room, space, tract

espacio aéreo: airspace

espacio exterior: outer space

espacio sideral: outer space

espacioso: spacious

espada: spade, sword

espadón: brass

espagueti: spaghetti

espalda: back

espantar: appall, frighten

espantosamente: appallingly, hideously

espantoso: appalling, dreadful, fearful, frightening, hideous, terrifying

esparcido: dotted, scattered

esparcimiento: recreation

esparcir(se): diffuse, filter, scatter, spray

espárrago: asparagus

espátula: palette knife

especia: spice

especiación: speciation

especial: particular, special

especialidad: field, specialty

especialista: consultant, specialist

especialización: specialization

especializado: skilled, specialized

especializarse: major, specialize

especialmente: especially, notably, specially

especie: breed, species

específicamente: specifically

especificar: specify

específico: particular, special, specific

espécimen: specimen

espectacular: dramatic, spectacular

espectacularmente: spectacularly

espectáculo: entertainment, exhibition, show, spectacle

espectáculo realista: reality show

espectador: spectator

espectro: spectrum

espectro electromagnético:

electromagnetic spectrum
especulación: speculation, theorizing
especulador: speculator
especuladora: speculator
especular: speculate, theorize
espejo: mirror
espeleóloga aficionada: spelunker
espeleólogo aficionado: spelunker
espeluznante: harrowing, shocking
espera: waiting
esperanza: hope
esperanzado: hopeful
esperanzador: encouraging, hopeful
esperar: await, expect, hang on, hold, hope, look to, wait
esperar (un bebé): be expecting
esperar a: wait around
esperar a que algo termine: sit out
esperar algo: be in for something
esperar con ansias: look forward to
esperar para: wait around
¡espere!: hold it!
esperma: sperm
espermatozoide: sperm
espesar(se): thicken
espeso: thickness
espía: agent, spy
espiar: eavesdrop, spy
espiar una conversación: listen in
espiga: ear, peg
espina dorsal: backbone
espinaca: spinach
espinal: spinal
espinilla: shin
espionaje: spying
espiral: curl, spiral
espíritu: heart, soul, spirit
espiritual: spiritual
espiritualidad: spirituality
espiritualmente: spiritually
espita: spigot
espléndidamente: brilliantly, lavishly
espléndido: glorious, lavish, magnificent, marvelous, splendid, superb
esplendor: blaze, brilliance
espolvorear: sprinkle
esponja: basket sponge, sponge
espontáneamente: spontaneously
espontáneo: hearty, spontaneous
esporofito: sporophyte
esporófito: sporophyte
esposa: spouse, wife
esposo: husband, spouse
espuma: surf

esqueje: cutting
esqueleto: skeleton
esquema: scheme
esquí: ski, skiing
esquiador: skier
esquiadora: skier
esquiar: ski
esquina: corner
esquivar: avoid, dodge, duck, fend off
esta: this
esta noche: tonight
está usted escuchando: this is (telephone/radio/television)
estabilidad: stability
estabilización: stabilization
estabilizar(se): stabilize
estabilizarse: level off
estable: settled, sound, stable
establecer: develop, draw, enter into, establish, found, institute, make, pitch, set, set down
establecer con certeza: nail down
establecer contacto: network
establecer lazos de unión: bond
establecer una distinción: draw/make a distinction
establecerse: set up, settle
establecerse en un nuevo lugar: relocate
establecido: established, set
establecimiento: establishment
establo: barn
estaca: stake
estación: season
estación de autobuses: station
estación de gasolina: gas station
estación de radio o canal de televisión: station
estación de trabajo: workstation
estación del año: season
estación del ferrocarril: station
estación espacial: space station
estación radiofónica especializada en comentarios, noticieros: talk radio
estacionado: parked
estacional: seasonal
estacionamiento: parking garage, parking lot
estacionar(se): park, parking, pull into, pull over
estacionario: static, stationary
estadio: arena, stadium
estadista: statesman
estadística(s): statistic
estadísticamente:

statistically
estadístico: statistical
Estado: state
estado: nation, province, state
estado de alarma: state of emergency
estado de alerta: alertness
estado de ánimo: spirit, state of mind
estado de cuenta: statement
estado de emergencia: state of emergency
estado de la materia: state of matter
estado malhechor: rogue state
Estados Unidos: the States
Estados Unidos de América: United States of America
estadounidense: American
estafa: con, swindle
estafador: cheater, swindler
estafadora: cheater, swindler
estafar: cheating, con, swindle
estallar: burst out, erupt, explode, flare, go up, pop
estallar de risa: howl
estallar en llamas: burst into flames
estallido: bang, burst, crack
estambre: stamen, yarn
estampa: trading card
estampar: printmaking
estampida: stampede
estampilla: stamp
estancado: holding pattern, stuck
estancar: stall
estancarse: grind to a halt
estancia: stay
estándar de vida: standard of living
estando: being
estaño: tin
estanque: pond, pool
estante: bookcase, rack, shelf
estaquilla: peg
estar: be, lie
estar a favor de: come down on, favor
estar a la altura: match, measure up, rise to the challenge
estar a la altura de: live up to
estar a la cabeza: head
estar a oscuras: be in the dark
estar a punto de: stop short of
estar a punto de estallar: bursting at the seams
estar acostumbrado a: be used to

estar aficionado: be fond

estar agachado: crouch

estar agotado: wear yourself/be worn to a frazzle

estar al día: keep track of

estar al mando de: command

estar algo sucio, lavándose o recién lavado: be in the wash

estar apretado: feel the pinch, squeeze

estar asustado: be frightened

estar atento: listen

estar atento a: look out for, watch for

estar autorizado para: be at liberty to

estar bajo: come under

estar bien encaminado: be on the right track

estar claro el día: be (day) light

estar de acuerdo: agree, go along with, subscribe

estar de frente: face

estar de luto por alguien: grieve

estar de mal humor: be in a mood

estar de pie: stand

estar de suerte: be in luck, luck out

estar dedicado a: be intended for

estar destinado a: be intended for, be meant for

estar destinado a algo: be bound to happen

estar discutiéndose: be under discussion

estar dispuesto: game

estar embarazada: have a baby

estar en alerta: stand by

estar en algún lugar: be in

estar en apuros: be in dire/desperate straits

estar en buenos términos: be friends

estar en cartelera: show

estar en contacto: touch

estar en desacuerdo: dissent

estar en desacuerdo con: disagree

estar en llamas: burn

estar en sintonía: be in step, on the same wavelength

estar en un aparador: be in a fishbowl

estar encadenado a algo: be chained to something

estar encariñado con alguien: be fond of someone

estar enojado con alguien: have it in for somebody

estar enterado: be in

the loop

estar equivocado: be off base

estar frente a: back onto

estar fuera de sí: be beside oneself

estar hablando por teléfono: be on the phone

estar hambriento: be hungry

estar harto: be finished

estar hecho polvo: wear yourself/be worn to a frazzle

estar hecho una fiera: do one's nut/go nuts

estar iluminado: be light

estar lleno de: be crawling with

estar loco: be out of one's mind

estar loco por: be mad about

estar los nervios de punta: on edge

estar mal visto: frown upon

estar maldito: be cursed

estar muerto de cansancio: wear yourself/be worn to a frazzle

estar obligado: owe

estar ocupado en: go about

estar parado: stand

estar presente: sit in on

estar previsto: be in the pipeline

estar proyectado: be in the pipeline

estar resentido: smart

estar sentado: sit

estar situado: lie

estar vivo: live

estas: these

estático: static

estatua: sculpture, statue

estatura: height

este: east, er, oh, this, well

estela: trail, wake

estenógrafa: stenographer

estenógrafo: stenographer

estéreo: stereo

estereofónico: stereo

estereotipo: stereotype

estéril: barren, infertile, sterile

esterilidad: sterility

esterilización: sterilization

esterilizar: sterilize

esteroide: steroid

estética: aesthetic, aesthetics, salon

estéticamente: aesthetically

estibador: longshoreman

estigmatizar: brand

estilo: format, kind, mode, stroke, style, writing

estilo de baile: dance

form

estilo de vida: lifestyle, mode, way of life

estilo directo: direct discourse

estilo indirecto: indirect discourse, indirect speech, reported speech

estima: esteem

estimación: estimate, favor

estimado: dear, estimate, estimated

Estimado Señor: sir

estimar: estimate, gauge, look on, put at, reckon, take stock

estimulante: stimulant, stimulating

estimular: boost, encourage, spur, stimulate

estímulo: boost, incentive, spur, stimulation, stimulus

estipendio: stipend

estipular: mandate, provide

estirado: tight

estiramiento: stretch

estirar(se): crane, loosen up, pull, stretch, stretch out

estivación: estivation

esto: this

esto y aquello: this and that/this, that, and the other

estofado: stew

estofar: stew

estolón: runner

estoma: stoma

estómago: stomach

estorboso: unwieldy

estornudar: sneeze

estornudo: sneeze

estos: these

estrado: bench, stand

estrado de los testigos: witness stand

estrambótico: fancy

estrangular: choke, strangle

estratagema: maneuver

estrategia: strategy, tack, tactic

estrategia de salida: exit strategy

estrategia retórica: rhetorical strategy

estrategias de agrupamiento: clustering

estratégicamente: strategically

estratégico: strategic

estratificación: stratification

estrato: layer, stratus

estratovolcán: composite volcano

estrechamente: closely, tightly

estrechar: deepen

estrecharse: narrow

estrechez: narrowness

estrecho: close, narrow, strait

estrella: star
estrella de David: Star of David
estrella de mar: sea star
estrella de neutrones: neutron star
estrella de secuencia principal: main-sequence star
estrella del cine: movie star
estremecer: rock
estremecerse: quake, tremble
estreno: premiere
estrépito: clangor, crash, roar, thunder
estresante: stressful
estribar: lie
estribillo: chorus, refrain
estribo: stirrup
estrictamente: purely, strictly, tightly
estricto: strict, tight, tough
estrofa: verse
estropajo: dishrag
estropear: hurt, mar, vandalize
estropear(se): break down
estructura: fabric, framework, makeup, organization, structure
estructura de barras para juegos infantiles: monkey bars
estructura de una canción: song form
estructura del baile: dance structure
estructura reticular del cristal: crystal lattice
estructurado: structured
estructural: structural
estructuralmente: structurally
estructurar: structure
estruendo: clangor, thunder
estuche: case
estudiantado: student body
estudiante: alum, alumnus, learner, schoolboy, schoolgirl, student
estudiante de medicina: medic
estudiante de posgrado: graduate student
estudiante universitaria: undergraduate
estudiante universitario: undergraduate
estudiar: learn, read up on, review, study
estudio: exam, review, studio, study
estudio de baile: dance study
estudios: schooling, studies
estudios clásicos: classics
estudiosa: scholar
estudioso: scholar
estufa: stove

estupefaciente: drug
estupendo: terrific, wonderful
estúpida: schmuck
estupidez: moonshine, stupidity
estúpido: foolish, schmuck, stupid
et: ampersand
etapa: leg, phase, stage
etc.: etc.
etcétera: and so on/and so forth, and the rest/all the rest of it, etc.
eternamente: eternally, forever
eternizarse (tiempo): drag
eterno: endless, eternal, perennial
ética: ethic
éticamente: ethically
ético: ethical
etimología: etymology
etiqueta: label, tag
etiqueta engomada: sticker
etiquetar: label, tag
etiquetar a: brand
étnicamente: ethnically
étnico: ethnic
eubacteria: eubacteria
eufemismo: euphemism
euforia: elation
eufórico: elated
euglena: euglena
euro: euro
eurodiputado: MEP
europea: European
europeo: European
evacuación: evacuation
evacuar: evacuate
evadir: fend off
evaluación: appraisal, assessment, estimate, evaluation
evaluar: assess, calculate, evaluate, gauge, take stock, value
evangelio: gospel
evaporación: evaporation, vaporization
evaporar(se): evaporate, vaporize
evento: event
evento exitoso: success story
evento más importante: highlight
evento para recaudar fondos: fundraiser
evidente: evident, manifest, marked, noticeable, obviously, patent, visible
evidentemente: evidently, patently
evitar: avert, avoid, bypass, get around, prevent, shrink away from, steer clear of, stop
evitar algo a alguien: spare
evocar: evoke
evolución: evolution, progress
evolución de las

especies: speciation
evolucionar: develop, evolve
ex: former
ex combatiente: veteran
exactamente: accurately, exactly, just, smack dab
exactitud: accuracy
exacto: accurate, exact, exactly, precise
exageración: exaggeration
exagerado: exaggerated, far-fetched
exagerar: exaggerate, overdo, to err on the side of
examen: exam, examination, quiz, review, test
examen médico: checkup
examen oral: oral
examinar: examine, explore, inspect, look, review, test
exasperante: infuriating
excavadora: backhoe
excavar: dig
excedente: surplus
exceder: exceed
exceder el límite de velocidad: speed
excederse: overdo
excedido de peso: overweight
excelencia: excellence
excelente: excellent, fine, golden, prime, sterling, superb
excelentemente: excellently
excéntrica: eccentric
excentricidad: eccentricity
excéntrico: eccentric
excepción: exception, odd one out
excepcional: exceptional, one-shot, unique
excepcionalmente: exceptionally, uniquely, unusually
excepto: but, except
excepto por: other than
excesivamente: excessively, unduly
excesivo: excess, excessive, undue
exceso: excess
exceso de velocidad: speeding
excitar: whip up
exclamación: gasp
exclamar: cry, exclaim
exclamativo: exclamatory
excluir: exclude
excluir por fases: phase out
exclusión: exclusion
exclusiva: scoop
exclusivamente: exclusively, uniquely
exclusivo: exclusive, unique
exculpar: acquit, clear, excuse
excursión: hike, outing, trip

excusado: toilet

excusado exterior: outhouse

exención: exemption

exención fiscal: tax break

exenciones para las personas físicas: personal exemption

exentar: excuse, exempt

exento: exempt

exento de: free of

exento de impuestos: tax-exempt

exhalar: exhale

exhaustivamente: comprehensively

exhaustivo: comprehensive, in-depth

exhausto: exhausted, weary, worn out

exhibición: display

exhibir: display, exhibit, lay out, parade

exigencia: claim, demand

exigente: demanding

exigir: call for, cry out for, demand

exiliada: exile

exiliado: exile

exiliar: exile

exilio: exile

eximir: release

eximirse: recuse

existencia: being, existence, life

existencias: stock, supply

existente: existing

existir: exist, prevail

éxito: achievement, blockbuster, hit, sensation, success, triumph

éxito de taquilla: sell-out

exitoso: successful

exluir: leave out

exocitosis: exocytosis

éxodo: drift

exoesqueleto: exoskeleton

exosfera: exosphere

exotérmico: exothermic

exóticamente: exotically

exótico: exotic

expandir(se): expand

expansión: expansion, sprawl

expansión del fondo del mar: sea-floor spreading

expansión del fondo oceánico: sea-floor spreading

expansión térmica: thermal expansion

expectador: viewer

expectadora: viewer

expectativa: expectation

expedición: dispatch, expedition, issue

expediente: file, paper trail

expediente judicial: filings

expedir: issue, send

expeditivo: brisk

experiencia: experience, expertise, taste

experiencia teatral: theatrical experience

experimentación: experimentation

experimentado: experienced

experimental: experimental

experimentar: experience, experiment, see, taste

experimento: experiment, trial

experimento controlado: controlled experiment

experta: authority, expert

experto: authority, expert, master, maven, practiced

expiatorio: sacrificial

expirar: breathe out

explicación: account, explanation

explicación (de símbolos, distancias, etcétera): map key

explicar: account for, elaborate, explain

explicar con detalle: spell out

explicativo: explanatory

explícitamente: explicitly

explícito: explicit

exploración: exploration

explorador: explorer

exploradora: explorer

explorar: explore, prospect

explosión: blast, explosion

explosivo: explosive

explotación: exploitation

explotación a tajo abierto: strip mining

explotador forestal: logger

explotar: blast, blow up, burst, explode, exploit, go off, mine, play on

exponer: exhibit, expose, lay out, set out, state, talk

exponer falsamente: misstate

exponer mal: misstate

exportación: export

exportador: exporter

exportadora: exporter

exportar: export

exposición: display, exhibition, exposure, fair, show, show and tell, talk

expresamente: expressly, specifically

expresar(se): express, formulate, phrase, put, voice, word

expresar ira: rage

expresarse bien o muy bien: articulate

expresarse con claridad: articulate

expresión: expression, grammar, language, utterance

expresión idiomática: idiom

expresión lineal: linear expression

expresión oral: delivery

expreso: express

express: express

expuesto: open

expulsar: chase, drive, eject, expel, oust, throw out

expulsar temporalmente: suspend

expulsión: ejection, expulsion

exquisitamente: exquisitely

exquisito: exquisite

éxtasis: ecstasy

extender(se): belabor, enlarge, extend, lie, open, open out, put out, span, sprawl, spread, stretch, stretch out, sweep, widen

extenderse sobre: straddle

extenderse por metástasis: metastasize

extendido: rife

extensamente: at length, extensively

extensión: extension, extent, tract

extensivamente: extensively

extensivo: extensive

extenso: extensive

extensor: extensor

exterior: exterior, external, foreign, outer, outside, overseas

exteriorizar: display

exterminar: kill off, wipe out

externamente: externally

externo: external, outside, outsider, outward

externo a: outside

extinción en masa: mass extinction

extinción masiva: mass extinction

extinguidor de incendios: fire extinguisher

extinguir: put out

extinguirse: die

extinto: extinct

extintor de incendios: fire extinguisher

extirpación: removal

extirpar: root out

extra: extra, on the side, premium

extracción: extraction

extracto: excerpt, extract

extradición: extradition

extraditar: extradite

extraer: draw, extract, mine, pull

extraer la raíz de un número: root extraction

extragrande: supersize

extraña: stranger

extrañamente: unnaturally

extrañar: long, miss, pine for

extranjera: alien, foreigner

extranjero: alien, foreign, foreigner, overseas

extraño: bizarre, curious, eccentric, foreign, funny, odd, outsider, quaint, strange, stranger, uncanny, weird

extraoficial: off the record, unofficial

extraoficialmente: unofficially

extraordinariamente: exceptionally, extraordinarily, outstandingly, remarkably

extraordinario: exceptional, extraordinary, formidable, outstanding, remarkable, tremendous

extrapolación: projection

extraterrestre: alien

extravagancia: extravagance

extravagante: extravagant, fancy, lavish

extravagantemente: extravagantly

extraviado: lost

extraviarse: stray

extremadamente: extra, extremely, impossibly, overwhelmingly

extremidad: limb

extremismo: extremism

extremista: extremist

extremo: edge, end, extreme, far, furthest, gross, tip

Extremo Oriente: Far East

extrovertido: extrovert, extroverted, outgoing

F

fábrica: factory

fábrica (algodón): mill

fábrica de cerveza: brewery

fábrica de rumores: rumor mill

fabricación: manufacture

fabricante: maker, manufacturer

fabricante de automotores: automaker

fabricar: brew, manufacture

fabricar en masa: mass-produce

fabricar en serie: mass-

produce

fabuloso: fabulous

facción: faction, feature

fachada: mask

fachada de una tienda: storefront

facial: facial

fácil: easy, ready, slam dunk, straightforward

fácil de mantener: low-maintenance

facilidad: ease

facilidades de pago: installment plan

facilitar: aid, ease, facilitate

fácilmente: easily, with ease

factor: coefficient, consideration, factor

factor de sensación térmica: wind chill factor

factor limitante: limiting factor

factura: bill, invoice

facturación: turnover

facturar: bill

facultad: faculty, power, school

facultar: authorize

faena: labor

Fahrenheit: Fahrenheit

faja: swathe

fajar(se): tuck, tuck in/into (something)

fajita: fajita

falda: skirt

faldón: flap

falla: breakdown, bug, failure, fault, miss

falla inversa: reverse fault

falla invertida: reverse fault

falla normal: normal fault

falla volcánica (lava): vent

fallar: backfire, fail, flounder, flub, founder, let down, miss

fallecer: pass away, pass on

fallecida: deceased, late

fallecido: deceased, late

fallecimiento: demise

fallido: unsuccessful

fallo: judgment, miss, ruling

falsa alarma: false alarm

falsamente: falsely

falsea: fake

falsedad: hollowness

falsificación: counterfeit, fake, forgery

falsificador: forger

falsificar: counterfeit, doctor, fake, forge

falso: counterfeit, empty, fake, false, hollow, mistaken, phony

falta: default, foul, lack, lacking

falta de ética profesional: misconduct

falta de vivienda:

homelessness

faltar: absent, away, default, lack, miss, to go

faltar a: dishonor

falto de: short of

falto de aliento: breathless

falto de naturalidad: self-conscious

fama: fame

familia: family, household

familia con hijastros: stepfamily

familia nuclear (no extendida): family unit

familia política: in-laws

familiar: conversational, familiar, own flesh and blood, survivor

familiaridad: familiarity

familiarizado: familiar

famoso: celebrated, famous, renowned

fanática: fan, fanatic, nut

fanático: fan, fanatic, fanatical, nut

fanfarronada: saber-rattling

fango: mud

fantasear: daydream, fantasize

fantasía: daydream, fantasy, imagination

fantasma: ghost

fantásticamente: fantastically

fantástico: fantastic

farándula: show business

faringe: pharynx

farmacéutico: pharmaceutical

farmacia: drugstore, pharmacy

faro: headlight

farol: lantern

farolear: strut

farsante: phony

fascículo: installment

fascinado: entranced

fascinante: fascinating, intriguing

fascinar(se): entrance, fascinate

fascinar a alguien: take somebody's fancy

fascismo: fascism

fascista: fascist

fase: phase

fastidiar: bug, tick off

fastidiar algo: screw up

fastidio: peeve, pest

fastidioso: troublesome

fatal: fatal

fatalidad: fatality

fatalmente: fatally

fatiga: fatigue

fatigado: tired

fatigoso: labored

fauces: jaw

faul: foul

favor: favor

favorable: favorable, sympathetic

favorecedores: friends
favorecer: favor, further, help, second
favorita: favorite
favoritismo: favoritism
favorito: bookmark, favorite, pet
fax: fax
FDA: FDA
fe: faith, trust
fealdad: ugliness
febrero: February
febril: furious
febrilmente: furiously
fecha: date
fecha de caducidad: expiration date
fecha de nacimiento: DOB
fecha límite: closing date, deadline
fecha tope: closing date
fechamiento relativo: relative dating
fechar: date
fécula: starch
fecundo: fertile
federación: federation, league
federal: federal
feldespato: feldspar
felicidad: happiness
felicidades: congratulations
felicitación: congratulation
felicitaciones: congratulations
felicitar: congratulate
felino: cat
feliz: content, happy, merry
felizmente: happily, mercifully
felpudo: mat
félsico: felsic
femenino: female, feminine
fémico (máfico): mafic
feminidad: femininity
feminista: feminist
fenómeno: freak, phenomenon, whiz kid
fenómeno de circo: freak
fenotipo: phenotype
feo: ugly
féretro: coffin
feria: carnival, fair
feria comercial: trade show
fermentación: fermentation
fermentar: ferment
ferocidad: viciousness
feromona: pheromone
feroz: fierce, furious
ferozmente: fiercely
ferretería: hardware
ferrocarril: railroad, train
ferrocarril metropolitano: subway
ferrocarril subterráneo: subway
ferry: ferry
fértile: fertile
fertilidad: fertility
fertilización: fertilization

fertilización externa: external fertilization
fertilización interna: internal fertilization
fertilizante: fertilizer
fertilizar: fertilize
festejar: feast
festín: feast
festival: festival
fétido: foul
feto: fetus, unborn
fiabilidad: reliability
fiambre: lunch meat
fiambres: cold cuts
fianza: bail
fiar(se): trust
fiasco: flop
fibra: backbone, fiber, pad
fibra de vidrio: fiberglass
fibra óptica: optical fiber
ficción: fiction
ficha: counter, token
fichar: sign
ficticio: fictional
fidedigno: authentic, authoritative, reliable
fideicomisaria: trustee
fideicomisario: trustee
fideicomiso: endowment, trust
fidelidad: allegiance, loyalty
fideo: noodle
fiduciaria: trustee
fiduciario: trustee
fiebre: fever, temperature
fiebre glandular: mono, mononucleosis
fiel: accurate, faithful, loyal
fieles: congregation
fielmente: faithfully
fieltro: felt
fiera: beast
fiero: fierce
fiesta: festival, party
fiesta de disfraces: costume party
fiesta del barrio: block party
fiesta patria: national holiday
fiestear: party
figura: face card, figure, force, shape
figura esquemática: stick figure
figurado: figurative
figurar(se): figure, imagine
figurativo: figurative
fijamente: steadily
fijar: anchor, fasten, fix, post, set, steady
fijar la mirada: gaze
fijarse: look
fijo: fixed, flat, secure, set, steady
fila: line, row
filas: ranks
filas del desempleo: unemployment line
fildeador: fielder
fildear: field
filete: filet, steak, thread
filial: affiliate, subsidiary
film: film

filmación: filming, shoot
filmar: film, shoot
filme: film
filo: edge, phylum
filón: seam, streak
filosofía: philosophy
filosóficamente: philosophically
filosófico: philosophical
filósofo: philosopher
filtración: leak
filtrar(se): filter, leak, soak
filtro: filter
filtro solar: sunscreen
filum: phylum
fin: end, extreme, finish, passing, purpose
fin de semana: weekend
final: bottom, end, ending, eventual, extreme, final, finish, playoff
finalizar: finalize
finalmente: at last/at long last, eventually, finally, ultimately
finamente: finely
financiación: finance, funding
financiamiento: finance, funding
financiar(se): finance, fund
financiero: financial
finanzas: finance
finca: farm
fingidamente: falsely
fingido: false, mocking
fingir: act, pretend
fingir ser: impersonate
fino: delicate, fine, thin
firma: signature, signing
firmar: autograph, sign
firmar (por algo): sign for
firmar con sus iniciales: initial
firmar sobre la línea punteada: sign on the dotted line
firme: fast, firm, steady, strong, tight, tough
firmemente: fast, firmly, solidly
fiscal: fiscal, prosecutor
fiscal de distrito: D.A., district attorney
fisgonear: pry
física: physicist, physics
físicamente: physically
físico: physical, physicist, physique
fisión binaria: binary fission
fisión nuclear: nuclear fission
fisioterapia: physical therapy
fitoplancton: phytoplankton
FIV: IVF
flácido: limp
flaco: skinny, thin
flacucho: skinny
flagelo: flagella
flagrante: glaring
flagrantemente: glaringly

flama: flame
flamante: brand-new
flamear: flare
flamenco: flamingo
flanco: flank
flanquear: flank
flaquear: flag, reel, weaken
flash: flash
flashazo: flash
flauta: flute
flauta dulce: recorder
flautista: flutist
flecha: arrow
fleco: bang, fringe
fleje: band
fletado: charter
fletar: charter
flete: freight
flexibilidad: flexibility
flexible: flexible, floppy, loose
flexión de brazos: push-up
flexor: flexor
flirtear: flirt
floema: phloem
flojear: goof off
flojera: laziness
flojo: idle, lazy, limp, loose
flopy: floppy disk
flor: bloom, blossom, flower
florecer: bloom, blossom, flourish, flower
floreciente: flourishing, healthy, prosperous
florecimiento: flowering
florería: florist
florero: vase
florido: flowering
florista: florist
floritura: embellishment
flota: fleet
flotador: float
flotar: float, swim
flotar en el aire: fly
flotilla: fleet
fluidamente: fluently
fluidez: fluency
fluido: fluent, fluid
fluir: flow
flujo: flow
fluorescente: fluorescent
fobia: phobia
foca: seal
foco: bulb, focus, light bulb
fogata: campfire, fire
fogonazo: flash
fólder: folder
folículo: follicle
folklor: folklore
folleto: booklet, brochure, flyer, leaflet, pamphlet
folleto informativo: handout
folleto publicitario enviado por correo: mailer
fomentar: encourage, foster, further, nurture, promote
fondear: dock
fondo: background, bottom, depth, floor,

fund
fondo común: pot
fondo de inversión: mutual fund
fondo de inversiones: trust
fondo de jubilación: retirement fund
fondo de retiro: retirement fund
fondos: fund, funding
fonema: phoneme
fonética: phonics
fonógrafo: record player
fonograma: phonogram
fontanera: plumber
fontanería: plumbing
fontanero: plumber
foráneo: out-of-state
forastero: out-of-state
forcejear: struggle
forjar: carve out, forge, shape
forma: fashion, form, shape
forma de vida: life, living
forma desarrollada: expanded form
formación: formation, parade, schooling
formal: dress-up, formal
formalidad: formality
formalmente: formally
formar(se): build, establish, form, get together, join, marshal, stand/wait in line
formar parte: make
formar parte de: sit
formar parte de algo: be in the loop
formas principales del verbo: principal parts
formatear: format
formato: format
formidable: awesome, tremendous
fórmula: formula, recipe
fórmula química: chemical formula
formulación: formulation
formular: formulate, phrase, pose
formulario: form
fornido: barrel-chested, stocky
foro: forum
forrar: line
forrarse con: rake in
forro: lining
fortalecer: beef up, reinforce, shore up, strengthen
fortalecer a: build up
fortaleza: strength
fortísimo: mighty
fortuito: casual, random
fortuna: fortune
forúnculo: boil
forzado: artificial, labored, unnatural
forzar: force, pick, prize, pry
forzar a: compel
fosa oceánica: ocean trench
fosa séptica: septic tank

fosa submarina: ocean trench
fosfolípido: phospholipid
fósforo: match
fósil: fossil
foto: photo, snap, snapshot
fotocelda: photocell
fotocélula: photocell
fotocopia: photocopy
fotocopiadora: photocopier
fotocopiar: photocopy
fotógrafa: photographer
fotografía: photograph, photography, picture, shot
fotografiar: photograph
fotográfico: photographic
fotógrafo: photographer
fotorreceptor: photoreceptor
fotorreceptora: photoreceptor
fotosfera: photosphere
fotosíntesis: photosynthesis
fototropismo: phototropism
fotovoltaico: photovoltaic
FPS: SPF
fracasado: broken
fracasar: backfire, break down, collapse, fail, fall flat, founder, strike out
fracasar estrepitosamente: flop
fracaso: collapse, failure, flop
fracción: fraction
fracción unitaria: unit fraction
fraccionamiento: development
fraccionamiento cerrado: gated community
fractura: break, fracture
fractura por fatiga: stress fracture
fracturar(se): break, fracture
fragancia: fragrance, scent
fragante: fragrant
frágil: delicate, fragile
fragilidad: fragility
fragmentación: fragmentation
fragmentar(se): fragment
fragmento: extract, fragment, snatch
fragor: thunder
fraguar: forge, set
frambuesa: raspberry
francamente: bluntly, frankly, openly, straight, straightforwardly
franco: blunt, direct, frank, off duty, open, straightforward, up front
franja: belt, strip, swathe

franqueo: postage
franqueza: bluntness, directness, frankness, outspokenness
franquicia: concession, franchise
frasco: flask, jar
frasco para conservas: mason jar
frase: expression, phrase
frase adjetival: adjective phrase
frase adverbial: adverb phrase
frase hecha: phrase
frase verbal: phrasal verb, verb phrase
fraseo: phrasing
fraternidad: fraternity
fraude: fraud, rigging
fraude organizado: racket
fraudulentamente: dishonestly, fraudulently
fraudulento: dishonest, fraudulent
freak: freak
frecuencia: frequency, wavelength
frecuente: frequent
frecuentemente: frequently, often, oftentimes
fregadero (cocina): sink
fregador: dishrag
fregar: scrub
fregón: dishrag
freír: fry
frenar: brake, check, curb, rein in
frenético: frantic, furious
freno: brake
freno de emergencia: emergency brake
freno de mano: emergency brake
frenos: braces
frente: forehead, front
frente a: before, in front of, off, opposite, versus
frente a la costa: offshore
frente interno: home front
fresa: preppy, strawberry
fresca: fresh
fresco: cool, fresh, refreshed, sassy, wet
frescura: nerve
fresno: ash
frialdad: coldness
fríamente: coldly, coolly
fricción: friction, rubdown
friega: rubdown
frijol: bean, kidney bean
frijol carita: black-eyed pea
frijol de soya: soybean
frijol pinto: pinto bean
frijoles refritos: refried beans
frío: brisk, chilly, clinical, cold, cool, crisp
frito de los dos lados: over easy
frívolo: light
frontal: head-on

frontalmente: head-on
frontera: border, boundary, frontier
frontera de placas tectónicas: plate boundary
frotar(se): rub
fructífero: productive
fructificar: bear fruit
frugalidad: thrift
fruición: relish
fruncir: purse, wrinkle
fruncir el ceño: frown
fruncir el entrecejo: frown
fruslería: small potatoes
frustración: frustration
frustrado: frustrated
frustrante: frustrating
frustrar: defeat, foil
frustrar(se): frustrate
fruta: fruit
fruto: fruit
fuchi: yuck
fuego: fever blister, fire
fuego amigo: friendly fire
fuegos artificiales: fireworks
fuegos de artificio: fireworks
fuegos pirotécnicos: fireworks
fuente: fountain, platter, source, spring
fuente de energía: energy source
fuente de los medios: media source
fuente energética: energy source
fuente luminosa: light source
fuente mediática: media source
fuente puntual de la contaminación: point-source pollution
fuera: away, off, out, outside
fuera de: beyond, out of, outside, outta
fuera de casa: away
fuera de circulación: out of action
fuera de condición: out of shape
fuera de control: get out of hand, out of control
fuera de duda: beyond doubt
fuera de foco: out of focus
fuera de forma: unfit
fuera de la vista: out of sight
fuera de las horas pico: off-peak
fuera de línea: offline
fuera de lo normal: out of the ordinary
fuera de servicio: out of service
fuereño: out-of-state
fuerte: firm, fort, hard, heavy, high, loud, powerful, strong, tight, tough

fuertemente: loudly, strongly
fuerza: force, intensity, power, pull, strength, strong
fuerza aérea: air force
fuerza ascensional: lift
fuerza de esfuerzo: effort force
fuerza de flotación: buoyant force
fuerza eléctrica: electric force
fuerza hidráulica: water power
fuerza hidroeléctrica: hydropower
fuerza laboral: labor, labor force, workforce
fuerza neta: net force
fuerzas armadas: armed forces, service
fuerzas del orden: police force
fuerzas desequilibradas: unbalanced forces
fuerzas equilibradas: balanced forces
fuga: escape, flight, fugue, leak
fugado: on the run
fugarse: escape, run off
fugaz: brief
fugazmente: briefly
fugitiva: fugitive
fugitivo: fugitive, runaway
fulcro: fulcrum
fulgor: luster
fumada: puff
fumador: smoker
fumadora: smoker
fumar: puff, smoke, smoking
fumarola (gases o vapores): vent
fumigar: crop dusting
función: function, performance, role
función cuadrática: quadratic function
función exponencial: exponential function
funcional: functional
funcionamiento: behavior, operation, working
funcionar: function, operate, run, work
funcionar bien: be in working order, go strong
funcionar también como: double
funcionaria: incumbent, official, staffer
funcionaria pública: civil servant
funcionario: incumbent, official, staffer
funcionario público: civil servant
funda: slipcover
fundación: foundation, founding
fundador: founder
fundadora: founder
fundamentado:

informed
fundamental: basic, cardinal, critical, fundamental, ultimate, vital
fundamentalismo: fundamentalism
fundamentalista: fundamentalist
fundamentalmente: basically, fundamentally
fundamentar: ground
fundamento: footing, foundation, fundamentals, substance
fundamentos: essential
fundar: found
fundido: molten
fundir(se): cast, fuse, go, melt, thaw
funeral: funeral
funeraria: funeral home, funeral parlor
funesto: deadly, tragic
funicular: cable car
furgón: baggage car
furgón de cola: caboose
furia: fury
furibundo: furious
furiosamente: furiously
furioso: frantic, furious, mad, worked up
furor: fury
fuselaje: body
fusible: fuse
fusión: fusion, melting, merger
fusionar(se): fuse, meld, merge, press together
fustigar: whip
futbol: football
fútbol: football, soccer
futbol americano: football
fútbol americano: football
futbol soccer: football
fútil: idle
futuro: forthcoming, future

G

gabinete: cabinet
gafas: goggles
gafete: tag
gajo: cutting
galán: boyfriend
galaxia: galaxy
galaxia elíptica: elliptical galaxy
galaxia espiral: spiral galaxy
galaxia irregular: irregular galaxy
galería: balcony, gallery, pit
gallardete: pennant
galleta: cookie, cracker
galleta de harina de trigo integral: graham cracker
galleta salada: saltine
galletita: cookie
gallina: hen
gallo: rooster
gallon: braid

galón: gallon
gama: range, spectrum, spread
gametofito: gametophyte
ganadería: livestock
ganado: cattle, livestock
ganado con dificultad: hard-earned
ganador: recipient, winner, winning
ganadora: recipient, winner
ganancia: bonus, gain, profit
ganancias: proceeds
ganar: beat, buy, clinch, come in, earn, gain, get in, make, net, win
ganar sin conceder puntos en contra: shut out
ganar terreno: gain ground
ganarle a alguien con sus propias armas: beat somebody at their own game
ganarse: earn
gancho: hanger, hook, peg
ganga: bargain
ganglio: ganglion
gángster: gangster
ganso: goose
garage: garage
garaje: garage
garantía: assurance, guarantee, security
garantizar: guarantee, secure
garganta: throat
garlopa: plane
garra: claw
garrotero: bus boy
garrotte: club
gas: gas
gas inerte: noble gas
gas invernadero: greenhouse gas
gas natural: natural gas
gas noble: noble gas
gas pimienta: pepper spray
gas raro: noble gas
gasear: gas
gaseoso: carbonated
gases: exhaust
gasohol: gasohol
gasolina: gas, gasoline
gasolinera: gas station
gastado: bald, shabby
gastar(se): blow, fork out, play, spend, waste
gasto: expenditure, expense
gastos de envío: delivery charge, postage
gástrico: digestive
gatear: crawl
gatillo: trigger
gatito: kitten, kitty
gato: cat, jack, tic-tac-toe
gaviota: seagull
gay: gay
GED: GED
gel: gel
gel de baño: shower gel

gelatina: gelatin
gélido: bitter
gelifracción: ice wedging
gema: stone
gemela: twin
gemelo: twin
gemelos: binoculars
gemido: groan, moan
gemir: groan, moan
gen: gene
generación: generation
generador: generator
generador de electricidad: electric generator
generador de energía eléctrica: electric generator
general: blanket, general, generic, overall, universal, wholesale
generalización: generalization
generalizado: broadly, general, mass, popular, widespread
generalizar: generalize
generalmente: generally, usually
generar: generate, open up
genérico: generic
género: gender, genre, sort
género humano: mankind
generosamente: generously, nobly
generosidad: generosity, heart
generoso: generous, handsome, lavish, liberal
genética: genetics
genéticamente: genetically
genético: genetic
genialidad: genius
genio: genius, temper
genocidio: genocide
genotipo: genotype
gente: crowd, folk, people, public
gentío: crowd
genuino: authentic, genuine, pure, true
geoestacionario: geostationary
geografía: geography
geográficamente: geographically
geográfico: geographical
geóloga: geologist
geología: geology
geológico: geological
geólogo: geologist
geometría: geometry
gerencia: management
gerente: manager
germen: germ, seed
germinación: germination
germinar: germinate
gestación: gestation period
gesto: gesture, motion, wave

gesto ceremonioso: flourish

GI: GI

gigabyte: gigabyte

gigante: giant, monster

gigante gaseoso: gas giant

gigante roja: red giant

gigantesco: giant, gigantic

gimnasia: gym

gimnasio: gym, gymnasium

gimnosperma: gymnosperm

ginecóloga: ob/gyn

ginecología: ob/gyn

ginecólogo: ob/gyn

gira: tour

girar: revolve, rotate, spin, swing, turn

girar en torno a: revolve around

girasol: sunflower

giro: rotation, spin, turn, twist

giro de 180 grados: U-turn

giro postal: money order

giroscopio: gyro, gyroscope

gis: chalk

glaciación: Ice Age

glacial: glacial

glaciar: glacier

glamoroso: glamorous

glamour: glamour

glándula: gland

glándula mamaria: mammary glands

glándula sudorípara: sweat gland

global: global, overall

globalmente: globally

globo: balloon, fly ball, globe

globo aerostático: balloon

globo ocular: eyeball

globo terráqueo: globe

glóbulo blanco: white blood cell

glóbulo rojo: red blood cell

gloria: glory

glorioso: gloriously

glosa: anecdotal scripting

glucosa: glucose

gnomo: leprechaun

go kart: go-cart

gobernador: governor

gobernadora: governor

gobernante: ruler

gobernar: govern, rule, steer

gobierno: government

gobierno local: local government

goggles: goggles

gol: goal

gol de campo: field goal

golf: golf, golfing

golfista: golfer

golfo: gulf

golondrina: swallow

golpe: bang, blow up, bump, hit, knock, poke, rap, stroke, swing

golpe de estado: coup

golpe de nocaut: knockout

golpe de remo: stroke

golpe maestro: coup

golpear(se): bang, bash, beat, beat up, bump, hammer, hit, knock, pound, slam, smash, stab, strike

golpear (la pelota): putt

golpear con algo: swipe

golpearse un dedo del pie: stub

golpecitos: tap

golpes: knocking

golpetear: drum, rap

golpeteo: rap

golpiza: beating

goma: eraser, rubber, tire

goma de borrar: eraser

gong: gong

gorda: fatso

gordinflón: fatso, pudgy

gordinflona: fatso

gordo: fat, fatso, stout, thick

gordura: fatness

gorila: gorilla

gorila de montaña: mountain gorilla

gorra: cap

gorra de béisbol: baseball cap

gorrión: sparrow

gorro: bonnet

gospel: gospel

gota: bead, drip, drop

gota de lluvia: raindrop

gotear: drip, leak

gotero: drip

gotita: droplet

gozar: enjoy

GPS: GPS

grabación: recording

grabadora de discos de video: DVD burner

grabadora de videocintas: VCR

grabadora portátil: boom box

grabar: carve, printmaking, record

grabar (en cinta): tape

gracia: grace, spark

gracias: thank you

gracias a: thanks to, through

gracias a Dios: thank God

gracias al cielo: thank God

graciosamente: gracefully

gracioso: funny, humorous

gradería: bleachers

grado: degree, grade, pitch

grado (militar): rank

graduación: graduation

graduada: grad, graduate

graduado: grad, graduate, graduated

gradual: gradual

gradualmente: gradually

graduarse: graduate

gráfica: chart, graph

gráfica circular: pie chart

gráfica de barras: bar graph, histogram

gráfica de caja: box plot

gráfica de datos: data table

gráfica de dispersión: scatterplot

gráfica lineal: line graph

gráficamente: graphically

gráficas: graphics

gráfico: chart, graphic

gráfico circular: pie chart

grafiti: graffiti

gramática: grammar

gramatical: grammatical

gramaticalmente incorrecto: ungrammatical

gramo: gram

gramófono: record player

gran: grand, high, keen

gran almacén: department store

gran avance: breakthrough

gran cantidad: host, mass, score

gran esfuerzo: labor

gran espectáculo: spectacular

gran liga: major league

gran medida: measure

gran número: load

gran preocupación: alarm

gran slam: grand slam

grande: big, enormous, grand, great, large, long

grandeza: greatness

grandísimo: immense, massive

granero: barn

granizo: hail

granja: farm

granjera: farmer

granjero: farmer

grano: bean, grain

granola: granola

grapa: staple

grasa: fat, grease

graso: fatty

grasoso: fatty, rich

gratificante: rewarding

gratis: free, free of charge

gratitud: gratitude, thank

gratuitamente: free of charge, toll-free

gratuito: toll-free

gravable: taxable

gravamen: levy

gravar: tax

grave: deep, grave, large, severe

gravedad: gravity, severity

gravedad específica: specific gravity

gravedad superficial: surface gravity

gravemente: badly, dangerously, gravely, severely

gravitación universal: universal gravitation

gravitacional: gravitational

gravitropismo: gravitropism

gremio: guild, labor union

grieta: crevasse

grifo: faucet

grillo: cricket

gripa: flu

gripe: flu

gripe aviar: bird flu

gris: gray

gritar: call, cry, cry out, scream, shout, shout out, yell

gritería: shouting

grito: cry, scream, shout, yell

groseramente: rudely

grosería: rudeness

grosero: abusive, coarse, rude

grosor: thickness

grúa: crane

grueso: bulk, fat, thick

grulla: crane

grulla americana: whooping crane

grunge: grunge

gruñir: babble

grupito: gang

grupo: batch, class, cluster, crowd, gang, group, lot, network, party, pool

grupo de ataque y armas especiales: SWAT team

grupo de control: control

grupo de pesión: lobby

grupo de reseña literaria: book group

grupo de sondeo: focus group

grupo de votantes: constituency

grupo táctico: SWAT team

guácala: yuck

guacarearse: throw up

guácatelas: yuck

guajolote: turkey

guanina: guanine

guante: glove

guapísimo: gorgeous

guapo: good-looking, handsome

guardacostas: Coast Guard

guardaespaldas: bodyguard, escort

guardar: away, harbor, hold, keep, put aside, put away, save, store, store away, tuck away

guardar bajo llave: lock, lock away

guardar rencor a: hold against

guardar silencio: keep (something) quiet

guardarropa: wardrobe

guardarropa(s): coat check, coatroom

guardería (de perros): kennel

guardia: guard, keeper

guardia de la prisión: corrections officer

guardia marina/ guardiamarina: midshipman

guarida: stomping ground

guarismo: figure

guarnición: on the side, side

guarura: escort

gubernamental: governmental

guerra: war, warfare

guerra civil: civil war

guerra mundial: world war

guerra santa: holy war

guerrera: warrior

guerrero: warrior

guerrillera: guerrilla

guerrillero: guerrilla

gueto: ghetto

guía: directory, guide, leader, runner

guía de turistas: tour guide

guía práctica sobre algún tema: tutorial

guiar: guide, lead

guijarro: pebble

guiñar el ojo: wink

guiño: wink

guión: dash, hyphen, screenplay, script

guisante: pea

guisar: cook

guisar a fuego lento: stew

guiso: casserole

guitarra: guitar

guitarrista: guitarist

gusano: maggot, worm

gusano del corazón: heartworm

gustar: like, love

gustar a alguien: take somebody's fancy

gustar mucho (algo): love

gustarle mucho algo a uno: be fond of something

gusto: enthusiasm, favor, fondness, interest, kick, pleasure, taste, treat

gustosamente: gladly

H

haba: fava bean

haber: be, contain, have, occur

haber acabado: be finished

haber detrás de: lie behind

haber llegado: be in

haber luz: be (day)light

haber sido: become

haber sol: be (day)light

haber/no haber existencias: be in stock/out of stock

habérselas con: to be reckoned with

hábil: able, skilled, skillful, slick

habilidad: ability, skill

habilidad de hacer algo difícil: knack

habilidades para trabajar en equipo: partner and group skills

habilidoso: skillful

habilitar: qualify

hábilmente: ably, skillfully

habitación: room

habitaciones: suite

habitante: citizen, inhabitant, resident

habitantes: locals

habitar: inhabit, live

hábitat: habitat

hábitat pelágico: pelagic environment

hábito: habit, way

habitual: regular, usual

habla: speech

habla por sí mismo/solo: speaks for itself

hablado: spoken

hablante: speaker

hablar: speak, talk

hablar con: have a word with

hablar con brusquedad: snap

hablar con descaro: sass

hablar con fluidez una lengua: be fluent in a language

hablar de algo con entusiasmo: rave about

hablar de alguien: speak of somebody

hablar entre dientes: mutter

hablar irrespetuosamente: sass

hablar mal: knock

hablar mal de: run down

hablar más fuerte: speak up

hablar por los codos: chatter

hace: ago

hace un rato: just now

hacer: be, do, get, give, make, put together, realize, render, run, stage, take, wage, write

hacer (planes): lay

hacer a un lado: blow off, cast aside

hacer acopio: stockpile, store up

hacer acordarse a: remind

hacer alarde: show off

hacer algo a hurtadillas: sneak

hacer algo con disimulo: sneak

hacer aprobar: push through

hacer bola de: roll

hacer bosquejos: sketch

hacer buenas migas: hook up

hacer burbujas: bubble

hacer caer: oust

hacer campaña: campaign

hacer caso: listen

hacer caso omiso de: fly

in the face of, shrug off

hacer causa común: band together

hacer click: click

hacer cola: stand/wait in line

hacer colchas: quilting

hacer como si nada: think nothing of

hacer con cuidado: craft

hacer coro: sing along

hacer correr el agua: run (water/faucet/bath)

hacer cortes: score

hacer cosquillas: tickle

hacer crecer: build up

hacer creer: be given to, fool

hacer crisis: come to a head/bring something to a head

hacer cumplir: enforce

hacer daño: harm

hacer de árbitro: referee

hacer de maestro: emcee

hacer de mediador: mediate

hacer dieta: diet

hacer doble clic: double-click

hacer efecto: take effect

hacer ejercicio: exercise, work out

hacer el jardín: garden

hacer énfasis: emphasize

hacer enojar: tee off

hacer entender: put across

hacer entender algo: drive/hammer something home

hacer entrega de: present

hacer erupción: erupt

hacer estallar: let off, trigger

hacer explotar: set off

hacer falta: be in need of

hacer falta algo: miss

hacer fiestas: fuss over

hacer frente: confront, meet, stand up to

hacer frente a: brave

hacer fuego: fire

hacer funcionar: drive

hacer gestos: gesture

hacer grabados: printmaking

hacer guardia: keep watch

hacer hincapié: emphasize, stress

hacer historia: make history

hacer huelga: strike

hacer juego: match

hacer justicia: do justice

hacer la comida: cooking

hacer la prueba de carretera: test drive

hacer la raya: part

hacer la vista gorda: bend/stretch the rules, turn a blind eye

hacer las compras: shop

hacer las maletas: packing

hacer las paces: patch up

hacer las veces: function

hacer las veces de: act

hacer malabares: juggle

hacer maravillas: work/do wonders

hacer marchar: march

hacer más estricto: tighten

hacer más grave: deepen

hacer mejoras: improve

hacer mella: dent

hacer memoria: think back

hacer menos denso: thin

hacer muecas: screw

hacer obedecer: enforce

hacer observaciones: remark

hacer olvidar: live down

hacer participar: draw in

hacer pasar a: usher

hacer pasar por: pass off as

hacer pasar vergüenza: embarrass

hacer payasadas: clown

hacer pedazos: smash

hacer pesas: weight training

hacer planes: plan

hacer posible: enable

hacer preguntas: fire questions, question

hacer presupuestos: budget

hacer propuestas a: approach

hacer público: publicize

hacer quebrar: bankrupt

hacer realidad: fulfill

hacer referencia a: refer to

hacer reflexionar: give food for thought

hacer respetar: enforce

hacer responsable a alguien: pass the buck

hacer retroceder: turn back

hacer saber: let it be known, let somebody know

hacer salir: flush

hacer senderismo: trek

hacer sentir: feel

hacer señales con una luz: flash

hacer señas: gesture, signal

hacer señas para que alguien se vaya: wave

hacer snowboard: snowboarding

hacer sonar: set off

hacer su mejor esfuerzo: give something your best shot

hacer sufrir: hurt

hacer surgir: open up

hacer tictac: tick

hacer todo lo posible: go to great lengths

hacer todo lo que se puede: go out of one's way

hacer trampa: cheat, cheating

hacer trenzas: braid

hacer tropezar: trip

hacer trueque: barter

hacer un agujero: bore

hacer un boicot: boycott

hacer un cargo: debit

hacer un crucero: cruise

hacer un diagrama: diagram

hacer un gran esfuerzo: exert

hacer un gran esfuerzo para: strain

hacer un índice: index

hacer un lavado de estómago: have one's stomach pumped

hacer un llamado: call on

hacer un llamamiento: appeal

hacer un moño: tie

hacer un nudo: tie

hacer un pedido: place an order

hacer un resumen: summarize

hacer un total de: total

hacer un túnel: tunnel

hacer un viaje: travel

hacer una apología: eulogize

hacer una audición: audition

hacer una auditoría: audit

hacer una bocina con las manos: cup one's hands

hacer una copia: back up

hacer una curva: curve

hacer una distinción: draw/make a distinction

hacer una gira: tour

hacer una limpia de: root out

hacer una limpieza concienzuda: clean out

hacer una lista: list

hacer una muesca: nick

hacer una parada breve: stop off

hacer una pausa: break, pause, stop

hacer una pregunta a: put a question to (somebody)

hacer una radiografía: X-ray

hacer una redada de: round up

hacer una reverencia: bow

hacer una visita: pay a visit

hacer una visita corta: call

hacer uso de: apply, draw on, make use of

hacer venir: call out

hacer(se) añicos: smash

hacer(se) daño: hurt

hacer(se) entender: get across

hacerle eco a: chime in

hacerle señas a: hail

hacer(se) para atrás: hang back

hacerse a la mar: set sail

hacerse a un lado: move up, stand aside/back, step down

hacerse aceptar: impose

hacerse agua (la boca): water

hacerse añicos: shatter

hacerse cargo: take over

hacerse cargo de: charge, take on

hacerse de: earn

hacerse de fama: make a name for oneself/make one's name

hacerse de un nombre: make a name for oneself/make one's name

hacerse eco: echo

hacerse el hábito: be in the habit of/get into the habit of/make a habit of

hacerse el payaso: clown

hacerse el tonto: fool around

hacerse evidente: manifest

hacerse guaje: fool around

hacerse ilusiones: daydream

hacerse independiente: strike out

hacerse largo (película, espectáculo, tiempo): drag

hacerse nudos: knot

hacerse para atrás: stand aside/back

hacerse pasar: disguise, impersonate, pose

hacerse público: get out

hacerse realidad: realize

hacerse responsable: claim

hacerse tontos: kid

hacer(se) valer: assert

hacha: ax

hacia: across, at, toward

hacia abajo: downward

hacia adelante: forward, onward

hacia adentro: inwardly

hacia afuera: off, out, outward

hacia arriba: up, upstairs, upward

hacia atrás: backward

hacia el este: eastward

hacia el exterior: outward

hacia el norte: uptown

hacia el oeste: westward

hacia el poniente: westward

hacia la izquierda: left

hacia un lado: over

hacienda: farm

hackear: hack, hacking

hacker: hacker

hada: fairy

halagar: flatter

halagüeño: rosy

halcón: hawk

hálito: breath

hall: lobby

hallar: find

hallazgo: find, finding

Halloween: Halloween

halófila: halophile

halógeno: halogen

hamaca: swing

hambre: hunger, starvation

hambruna: famine

hamburguesa: burger, hamburger, patty

haragán: idle

harapos: rag

hardware: hardware

harina: flour

harina de otro costal: a different story

harina de trigo entero: wholewheat

harina de trigo integral: wholewheat

harina que no necesita levadura: self-rising flour

hartarse de: gorge

harto: fed up

harto de: sick of

hasta: actually, as, how far, not least, onto, till, to, until, up to, very

hasta ahora: since, so far

hasta cierto punto: so much/many, to a certain extent, up to a point

hasta dónde: how far

hasta donde se sabe: to (the best of) somebody's knowledge

hasta el copete: fed up

hasta el gorro: fed up

hasta el momento: so far, to date

hasta entonces: previously

hasta este momento: for the moment, so far

hasta la coronilla de: sick of

hasta la fecha: to date

hasta nuevo aviso: until further notice

hasta que: until

hasta qué punto: how far

hato: herd

hay mucho en juego: high-stakes

hazaña: deed, exploit, feat

HDTV: HDTV

hebilla: buckle

hebra: strand, thread

hechizo: spell

hecho: act, deed, fact, made

hecho a mano: handmade

hecho con levadura: leavened

hecho erróneo: misstatement

hecho polvo: frazzled

hecho por el hombre: man-made

hecho real: fact

hecho un lío: muddled

hechura: making

hechura de uno: of one's own making

hedor: reek

helada: frost

heladera: fridge

helado: freezing, frosty, frozen, ice cream, iced

helarse: freeze

hélice: helix, propeller

helicóptero: helicopter

help desk: help desk

hematología: hematology

hembra: cow, female

hemisferio: hemisphere

heno: hay

hepática: liverwort

heraldo: herald

herbívoro: herbivore, herbivorous

heredar: come into, inherit, leave, take after

heredera: heir

heredero: heir

herencia: heredity, legacy

herida: injury, wound

herido: casualty, hurt, injured

herir: dent, injure, wound

herir profundamente: sting

herir(se): hurt

hermana: sister

hermandad: fraternity

hermano: brother, sibling

hermético: close-mouthed

hermosamente: nicely, prettily

hermoso: beautiful

hermosura: beauty

hernia: rupture

herniar(se): rupture

héroe: hero

heroicamente: heroically

heroico: epic, heroic

heroína: hero, heroin, heroine

herramienta: gear, implement, instrument, tool

herramienta de búsqueda: search engine

herrar: shoe

herrumbrarse: rust

herrumbre: rust

hervir: boil, swarm

hervir a fuego lento: simmer

heterodoxo: off-center

heterogéneo: heterogeneous, miscellaneous

heterosexual: heterosexual

heterosexualidad: heterosexuality

hexágono: hexagon

hiato sísmico: seismic gap

hibernación: hibernation

hibernar: hibernate

híbrido: hybrid

hidrocarburo: hydrocarbon

hidrocarburo insaturado: unsaturated

hydrocarbon

hidrocarburo saturado: saturated hydrocarbon

hidroelectricidad: hydroelectricity

hidroeléctrico: hydroelectric

hidrógeno: hydrogen

hidroponia: hydroponics

hidroponía: hydroponics

hidropónico: hydroponic

hielo: ice

hielo seco: dry ice

hierba: herb

hierro: iron

hígado: liver

higo: fig

hija: child, daughter

hijo: child, son

hijuelo: young

hilacho: lint

hilar: spin

hilera: row

hilo: thread, yarn

hilo dental: thong

himno: anthem

hincar: drive, plunge, sink

hincarse: kneel

hinchado: swollen

hinchar(se): balloon, inflate, swell

hindú: Hindu

hipersónico: hypersonic

hipervínculo: hyperlink

hipocampo: seahorse

hipotálamo: hypothalamus

hipoteca: mortgage

hipotecar: mortgage

hipotermia: exposure

hipótesis de la falla: gap hypothesis

hipotético: theoretical

hiriente: cutting, stinging

hirviendo: boiling

hispano: Hispanic

histeria: hysterics

histéricamente: hysterically

histérico: hysterical

histerismo: hysterics

histograma: histogram

historia: history, story, tale

historia oral: oral history

historiador: historian

historiadora: historian

historial: history, track record

históricamente: historically

histórico: historic, historical

histriónico: theatrical

hito: landmark, mark

hobby: hobby

hocico: muzzle

hockey: field hockey, hockey

hockey sobre pasto: field hockey

hogar: fireplace, home, household

hogar de convalecencia: assisted living

hogareña: homebody

hogareño: homebody

hogaza: loaf

hoguera: campfire, fire

hoja: blade, leaf, page, panel, sheet

hojalata: tin

hoja: pane

hojear: flick, flip, glance, leaf through, rifle

hojuelas de avena: oatmeal

hola: hey, hi, howdy

holgadamente: comfortably

holgado: loose

holgazán: lazy

hombre: male, man

hombre de estado: statesman

hombre de Neanderthal: Neanderthal

hombre de negocios: businessman, promoter

hombro: shoulder

home: home plate

homenaje: tribute

homeostasis: homeostasis

homeostático: homeostatic

homicida: killer

homicidio: killing

homínido: hominid

Homo sapiens: homo sapiens

homofobia: homophobia

homofóbico: homophobic

homófono: homophone

homogéneo: smooth

homógrafo: homograph

homólogo: homologous

homosexual: gay, homosexual

homosexualidad: homosexuality

honda: slingshot

hondo: deep

hondonada: gully, hollow

honestamente: honestly

honestidad: honesty

honesto: genuine, honest

hongo: fungus, mushroom

honor: honor

honorarios: fee

honrar: honor

hooligan: punk

hora: hour, time

hora de comer: lunchtime

hora (media) de Greenwich: GMT

hora de la comida: lunchtime

hora del tránsito pesado: rush hour

hora pico: rush hour

horario: schedule, timetable

horario de clases: class schedule

horario (hora) de verano: daylight saving time

horario de visitas: visiting hours

horario flexible: flextime

horca: fork

horizontal: horizontal, level

horizontalmente: horizontally

horizonte: horizon, skyline

hormiga: ant

hormiguear: tickle

hormiguero: nest

hormona: hormone

hormonal: hormonal

hornada: batch

hornear: bake, baking

horno: furnace, oven

horno de microondas: microwave

horqueta: fork

horrendo: hideous

horrible: awful, dreadful, fearful, hideous, horrible, nasty

horriblemente: horribly

horripilante: nasty

horror: dread, horror

horrorizado: shocked

horrorizar: dread, horrify

horroroso: hideous, horrifying, shocking, terrifying

hospedaje: accommodation

hospedar(se): accommodate, lodge

hospital: hospital

hospital general: general hospital

hospitalidad: hospitality

hostería: inn

hostil: cool, hostile, unfriendly

hostilidad: hostility

hostilidades: hostilities

hot dog: hot dog

hotcake: pancake

hotel: hotel, inn

hotel campestre: lodge

hoy: today

hoy en día: nowadays, today

hoyo: green, hole

hoyo negro: black hole

html: HTML

hueco: empty, gap, hollow

huelga: strike

huelguista: striker

huella: footprint, impression, scar, track, trail

huella digital: fingerprint

huérfana: orphan

huérfano: orphan

huerta: orchard

huerto: orchard, patch

hueso: bone, pit

hueso compacto: compact bone

hueso esponjoso: spongy bone

hueso reticulado: spongy bone

huésped: guest, host, lodger

huevo: egg

huida: escape, flight

huir: flee, run away, run off

hule: rubber

hule espuma: sponge

humanidad: humanity, mankind

humanidades: liberal arts

humanitario: humanitarian

humano: human

humear: smoke

humedad: dampness, humidity, moisture

humedad relativa: relative humidity

humedal: wetland

humedecer: wet

húmedo: damp, humid, moist, sticky

humildad: humility

humilde: humble

humillación: humiliation

humillado: humiliated

humillante: humiliating

humillar: humiliate, put down

humo: smoke

humo de terceros: secondhand smoke

humor: humor, mood, temper

humus: humus

hundido: hollow

hundir(se): dip, go down, go under, plunge, sink, swamp

huracán: hurricane

huraño: timid

hurgar: root

hurto: theft

hurto en una tienda: shoplifting

husmear: pry

I

iceberg: iceberg

ID: ID

idea: guide, idea, image, indication, notion, perception, picture, thinking, thought

idea brillante: brainstorm

idea central: main idea

idea principal: theme, topic sentence

ideal: ideal

idealista: idealistic

idealmente: ideally

idear: devise, dream up, formulate, think, think up

ideas políticas: politics

idea falsa: misperception

idénticamente: identically

idéntico: identical

identidad: identity

identidad propia: self

identificación: ID, ID card, identification, identification card, identity card, paper

identificación personal: identity card

identificador de llamadas: caller ID

identificar: equate, name

identificar(se): identify

ideología: ideology

ideológicamente: ideologically

ideológico: ideological

idilio: romance

idiófono: idiophone

idioma: language, tongue

idiota: fool, idiot

idoneidad: suitability

iglesia: church

ígneo: igneous

ignorancia: ignorance

ignorante: ignorant

ignorar: fly in the face of, ignore

igual: alike, equal, evenly, identical, level, peer, same, unchanged

igual que: like

igualar: tie

igualador: leveler

igualar: equal, tie

igualdad: equality

iguales: all

igualmente: equally

ilegal: illegal, unlicensed

ilegalmente: illegally

ilegítimo: illegitimate

ileso: unscathed

ilimitado: infinite

iluminación: light, lighting

iluminar: light

iluminarse: light up

iluminársele: brighten

ilusión: illusion

ilusionarse: daydream

ilustración: illustration, plate

ilustrado: learned

ilustrar: illustrate, show

ilustre: eminent

IM: IM, instant message

imagen: image, perception, picture

imagen corporal: body image

imagen de fondo: wallpaper

imagen de sí mismo: self-image

imagen en espejo: reflection

imaginación: imagination

imaginado: supposed

imaginar(se): envisage, envision, figure, imagine, picture, presume, pretend, see, suppose, think, think up, visualize

imaginario: imaginary

¡imagínate!: fancy (that)!

imaginativamente: imaginatively

imaginativo: imaginative

imán: magnet

imantar: magnetize

imbécil: idiot, jerk, sucker

IMC: BMI

imitación: fake, impression

imitador: imitator

imitar: ape, imitate, impersonate

impaciencia: impatience, itch

impaciente: eager, impatient, itchy, restless

impacientemente: impatiently

impactante: eye-popping

impactar: impact, impress

impactarse: reel

impacto: impact, shock

impar: odd

imparcial: color-blind

impasible: unmoved

impedido: handicapped

impedimento: handicap, stumbling block

impedir: forbid, impede, inhibit, keep, prevent, rule out

impenetrable: impenetrable

impenitente: unrepentant

impensable: out of the question

imperial: imperial

imperialismo: imperialism

imperialista: imperialist

imperio: empire

impermeable: slicker, waterproof

impersonal: impersonal

impertinencia: back talk

implacable: unrelenting

implementación: implementation

implementar: implement

implemento: implement

implicación: implication

implicado: involved

implícitamente: implicitly

implícito: implicit

imponente: imposing, impressive

imponer(se): assert, command, deal out, dictate, impose, inflict, lay down, levy

imponer contribuciones: tax

imponer una multa: fine

impopular: unpopular

impopularidad: unpopularity

importación: import, importation

importador: importer

importadora: importer

importancia: emphasis, importance, significance

importante: high, important, large, leading, meaningful, prominent, relevant, significant, substantial

importar: care, import, matter, mind

imposibilidad: impossibility

imposibilitar: rule out

imposible: impossible, out of the question
imposición: imposition
impostor: fraud, phony
impostora: fraud
impotencia: impotence
impotente: helpless, impotent
impráctico: impractical
impreciso: indefinite
impredecible: unpredictable
imprenta: press, printer, printing
imprescindible: indispensable
impresión: feeling, illusion, impression, shock, sound
impresionado: impressed, shocked
impresionante: awesome, heart-stopping, imposing, impressive, tremendous
impresionar: impress, shake, shock, strike
impreso como prueba: in black and white
impresora: printer
impresos: literature, matter
imprimir: print, print out
imprimir en: print
improbable: a long shot, unlikely
improductivo: unproductive, unprofitable
impropiamente: improperly
impropio: improper, off-color
improvisación: improvisation
improvisado: off the cuff
improvisar: improvise
imprudentemente: rashly
impuesto: duty, levy, tax
impuesto predial: property tax
impuesto sobre la propiedad inmobiliaria: property tax
impuesto sobre la renta: income tax
impugnar: contest
impulsar: encourage, promote, push
impulsar a: drive
impulsivamente: impulsively, on the spur of the moment
impulsivo: impulsive
impulso: impulse, momentum, pulse, push
impulso irrefrenable de hacer algo: urge
impulsor: driving, propeller
imputación: allegation
imputar: attribute
in: hip, in
inaceptable: out of the question, unacceptable

inactividad: inactivity
inactivo: idle, inactive
inadaptada: misfit
inadaptado: misfit
inadecuadamente: inadequately
inadecuado: improper, inadequate, inappropriate, unfit
inadmisible: irregular
inalámbrico: wireless
inalcanzable: sour grapes
inapelable: final
inaudito: unprecedented
inauguración: opening
inaugural: maiden
inaugurar: open
Inc.: Inc.
incapacidad: disability, inability
incapacitado: disabled
incapaz: incapable, ineffectual, unable
incendiar: set fire to
incendiarse: catch fire, go up
incendio: blaze, fire
incendio provocado: arson
incentivo: carrot, incentive
incentivo fiscal: tax incentive
incertidumbre: suspense, uncertainty
incesante: relentless
incesantemente: relentlessly
incesto: incest
incidental: incidental
incidente: incident
incierto: hazy, indefinite, uncertainly
incineración: incineration
incinerar: incinerate
incisivo: incisor
inciso: bullet point
incitar: egg on, move, prompt
inclinación: slant, slope, tilt, trend
inclinado: loaded, sloping
inclinar(se): bend, bow, incline, lean, slant, slope, tilt, tip
inclinarse por: be partial to
incluido: including, not least
incluir: come complete with, embrace, feature, include, incorporate, write into
inclusive: even
incluso: even, including
incógnita: unknown
incomestible: inedible
incomible: inedible
incómodamente: uneasily
incomodidad: discomfort
incómodo: awkward, awkwardly, bumpy, embarrassing, ill at ease, uncomfortable
incompetencia: incompetence

incompetente: inadequate, incapable, incompetent, inefficient
incompleto: incomplete
incomprendido: misunderstood
incomprensible: impenetrable
inconcluso: incomplete
incondicional: implicit, unconditional
incondicionalmente: implicitly, no strings/ no strings attached, unconditionally
inconfundible: distinct
inconsciencia: unconsciousness
inconsciente: senseless, subconscious, unconscious
inconscientemente: subconsciously, unconsciously
inconstitucional: unconstitutional
incontable: countless
incontrolable: hysterical
inconveniencia: trouble
inconveniente: drawback, inconvenient, snag
incorporar: build
incorporar algo: incorporate
incorporarse: sit up
Incorporated: Incorporated
incorrectamente: incorrectly
incorrecto: improper, inaccurate, incorrect, out, wrong
incorregible: incurable
incredulidad: disbelief
increíble: amazing, bodacious, incredible, tremendous, unbelievable
increíblemente: amazingly, incredibly, unbelievably
incrementar(se): elevate, heighten, hike, increase, mark up, put up, raise
incremento: gain, increase
incremento repentino: surge
incriminar: accuse, frame
incrustación: filling
incrustar: grind
inculcar: impress
inculpar: charge
incumplimiento: default
incumplir: dishonor
incurable: incurable
incurablemente: incurably
incurrir en: incur
incurrir en mora: default
indagación: inquiry
indebidamente: improperly
indebido: improper
indecencia: indecency

indecente: indecent

indeciso: tentative, unsure

indecorosamente: indecently

indecoroso: dishonorable, improper, indecent

indefensión: helplessness

indefinidamente: indefinitely

indefinido: indefinite

indemne: unscathed

indemnización: award, comp, compensation

indemnizar: compensate

independencia: independence

independiente: independent

independientemente: regardless, whatever

indeseado: unwanted

indeterminado: indefinite

indexar: index

indicación: cue, direction

indicado: right

indicador: indicator, mark, measure

indicar: indicate, point, show, suggest, tell

indicar con la mano: motion

indicar con un gesto: motion

indicar el camino: direct

indicativo: suggestive

índice: coefficient, content, index, rating

índice analítico: index

índice de masa corporal: body mass index

índice de natalidad: birth rate

índice de precios al consumidor: Consumer Price Index

índice de siniestralidad: toll

índice de Sörensen: pH

indicio: gauge, indication, trace

indicio falso: red herring

indiferencia: indifference

indiferente: indifferent, unmoved

indiferentemente: indifferently

indígena: indigenous

indigente: penniless

indigestión: indigestion

indigesto: rich

indignación: disgust, outrage

indignado: disgusted, indignant, shocked

indignar: disgust, outrage

indignar(se): shock

indirecta: dig, hint

indirectamente: indirectly

indirecto: indirect, roundabout

indisciplinado: unruly

indiscutible

unchallenged

indispensable: essential, indispensable

indispuesto: ill

individual: individual, single

individualmente: individually

individuo: individual

índole: nature

inducir: induce, influence, prompt

inducir a error: mislead

indudable: undoubted

indudablemente: undoubtedly, unquestionably

indulgencia: indulgence

indulgencia consigo mismo: self-indulgence

indulgente: forgiving, indulgent, soft

indulgente consigo mismo: self-indulgent

indultar: pardon

indulto: pardon

industria: industry, sector

industria textil: textiles

industrial: industrial, industrialist

industrialista: industrialist

industrialización: industrialization

industrializado: industrial

industrializar(se): industrialize

inédito: unpublished

ineficazmente: ineffectually

ineficiencia: inefficiency

ineficiente: inefficient

ineludible: inevitable

ineptitud: inability, inadequacy

inepto: incompetent

inequívocamente: in no uncertain terms

inequívoco: clear-cut

inercia: inertia

inerme: impotent

inescrutable: impenetrable

inesperadamente: unexpectedly

inesperado: freak, sudden, unexpected

inestabilidad: instability

inevitabilidad: inevitability

inevitable: inevitable, unavoidable

inevitablemente: inevitably

inexactitud: inaccuracy, misstatement

inexacto: inaccurate

inexistente: unheard of

inexperto: inexperienced, raw

infame: infamous

infancia: childhood, infancy

infante de marina: marine

infantería: infantry

infantil: childish

infección: bug, infection

infección en la garganta: strep

infeccioso: infectious

infectar: infect

infecundo: infertile

infelicidad: misery, unhappiness

infeliz: miserable

inferior: bottom, inferior, lesser, lower

inferioridad: inferiority

infernal: doggone

infértil: infertile

infertilidad: infertility

infidelidad: infidelity

infierno: hell

infiltración: infiltration, penetration

infiltrar(se): infiltrate

infiltrarse: penetrate

infinitamente: infinitely

infinitivo: infinitive

infinito: endless, infinite, infinity

inflable: inflatable

inflación: inflation

inflamación: inflammation

inflamación de garganta: strep

inflamación estreptocócica: strep

inflamado: swollen

inflamarse: swell

inflar(se): blow up, inflate, pump up, swell

inflexible: tough, uncompromising

inflexión: inflection

infligir: inflict

influencia: bearing, influence, leverage, muscle

influenciar: influence, sway

influir: color, influence, inspire, play a part/play a role, sway, touch

influir: make a difference

influyente: influential

información: info, information, intelligence, literature, word of

información introducida: input

información reciente: update

informado: in touch with, informed

informal: casual, informal, relaxed

informalmente: casually, informally

informar: break, educate, fill in, inform, let somebody know, report

informarse: inquire

informativo: informative

informe: account, paper, report

informe presidencial (en los Estados Unidos): State of the Union

infortunio: ill
infracción: breach, infraction, offense
infraestructura: infrastructure
infrarrojo: infrared
infringir: breach, break
infringir la ley: offend
infructuoso: unsuccessful
infundir: command, strike
infundir respeto: assert
infusión: brew
ingeniera: engineer
ingeniería: engineering
ingeniería genética: genetic engineering
ingeniero: engineer
ingenio: wit
ingenioso: clever, neat, slick, witty
ingenuamente: naively
ingenuidad: naiveté
ingenuo: naive
ingerir: swallow
ingestión: intake
ingle: groin
inglés: English
inglés como lengua extranjera: EFL
inglés estadounidense común: standard American English
ingobernable: unruly
ingrediente: ingredient
ingresar: enter
ingreso: entrance, entry, income, receipt, revenue, revenue stream
ingreso de datos: data entry
ingresos: earnings, means
inhalación: inhalation
inhalar: inhale
inherente: inherent
inhibición: inhibition
inhibidor: inhibitor
inhibir(se): inhibit, hold back
inhumano: inhuman
iniciación: initiation
inicial: initial, opening
inicialar: initial
inicialmente: initially
iniciar: begin, enter into, initiate, launch, open
iniciarse: start
iniciativa: enterprise, initiative
inicio: beginning, initiation, start
inigualado: unequaled, unparalleled
iniquidad: wickedness
injuria: insult
injurioso: libelous
injustamente: unfairly, unjustly
injusticia: injustice, unfairness
injusto: unfair, unjust
inmaduro: immature
inmanejable: unwieldy
inmanente: inherent

inmediaciones: vicinity
inmediatamente: at once, fast, immediately, readily, right away, straight
inmediato: immediate, instant, prompt
inmejorable: unbeatable
inmenso: immense, infinite, overwhelming
inmerso: immersed
inmigración: immigration
inmigrante: immigrant
inminente: imminent, impending
inmiscuirse: interfere
inmobiliaria: real estate
inmoral: immoral
inmoralidad: misconduct
inmóvil: stationary
inmovilizar: boot, freeze, lock, pin
inmueble: property, real property
inmune: immune
inmunidad: freedom, immunity
inmunización: immunization
inmunizar: immunize
inmunodeficiencia: immunodeficiency
inn: inn
innato: born, natural
innecesariamente: pointlessly, unnecessarily
innecesario: unnecessary
innegable: undeniable, unquestionable
innegablemente: undeniably
innovación: innovation
innovador: innovative, pioneering
inocencia: innocence
inocente: innocent
inocentemente: innocently
inocuo para el ambiente: eco-friendly
inocuo para la capa de ozono: ozone-friendly
inodoro: bowl, odorless, toilet
inofensivo: harmless
inolvidable: unforgettable
inoportuno: inappropriate, inconvenient, unfortunate
inorgánico: nonliving
input: input
inquietante: disturbing, troubling, unsettling
inquietantemente: uncomfortably
inquietar(se): concern, fuss, rattle, trouble
inquieto: concerned, rattled, restless, uneasy
inquietud: concern, discomfort, restlessness, uneasiness
inquilina: lodger,

occupant, tenant
inquilino: lodger, occupant, tenant
inquirir: inquire, query
inquisitivo: inquisitive
insaciable: insatiable
insatisfactorio: unsatisfactory
inscribir(se): enroll, enter, register
inscripción: enrollment, inscription
insecticida: insecticide
insecto: insect
insecto nocivo: pest
inseguridad: insecurity
inseguro: insecure, uncertain, unsure
insensatez: foolishness, insanity
insensato: foolish, insane, mindless
insensibilidad: insensitivity
insensible: indifferent, insensitive
inseparable: inseparable
inserción: insertion
insertar: insert, sandwich
inservible: useless
insignificancia: insignificance
insignificante: insignificant, little, petty, small
insinuación: hint, suggestion
insinuar: hint, imply, intimate, suggest
insípido: bland, flavorless, tame, tasteless
insistencia: insistence, persuasion
insistente: insistent
insistentemente: insistently
insistir: insist, persist, press
insistir en: harp on
insólito: freak
insomnio: insomnia, sleeplessness
insoportable: impossible, unbearable
insoportablemente: unbearably
inspección: examination, inspection, survey
inspeccionar: inspect, supervise
inspector: inspector, superintendent
inspector general de sanidad: surgeon general
inspectora: inspector, superintendent
inspectora general de sanidad: surgeon general
inspiración: inspiration
inspiración súbita: brainstorm
inspirador: inspiring
inspirar: breathe in, inspire, command,

model
inspirarse en: draw on
instalación: facility,
installation,
installation art
instalaciones:
accommodation
instalar: fit, fix, install,
lay
instalar con tornillos:
screw
instantánea: snap,
snapshot
instantáneamente:
instantly, outright
instantáneo: instant
instante: instant,
minute, moment
instar: urge
instintivamente:
instinctively
instintivo: instinctive
instinto: instinct
institución: institution
institución de
beneficencia: charity
institución escolar o
universitaria pública:
state school
instituir: institute
instituto: bureau,
institute
instrucción: instruction,
mandate
instructivo: informative,
instructive
instructor: instructor,
trainer
instructora: instructor,
trainer
instruir: instruct
instruirse: learn
instrumental:
instrumental
instrumentar:
implement
instrumento: gadget,
implement,
instrument, means
medium, puppet, tool
instrumento de cuerda:
chordophone
instrumento musical:
musical instrument
insuficiencia: inadequacy
insuficiente: inadequate,
insufficient
insuficientemente:
insufficiently
insufriblemente:
irritatingly
insulina: insulin
insulso: bland
insultado: insulted
insultante: insulting
insultar: call somebody
names, curse, insult,
swear
insulto: curse, insult,
offense
insultos: abuse
insurrección:
insurrection
intacto: intact
integración: absorption,
assimilation,
integration
integrado: integrated

integral: all-over, brown,
wholewheat
íntegramente: in full
integrantes: lineup
integrar(se): absorb,
assimilate, integrate,
join
integridad: integrity
íntegro: intact, of
integrity
intelecto: brain, intellect
intelectualmente:
intellectually
inteligencia: brain,
cleverness, intellect,
intelligence
inteligente: bright,
clever, intellectual,
intelligent, perceptive,
rational
inteligentemente:
cleverly, intelligently
intelectual: intellectual
intención: intention,
meaning, will
intencional: deliberate
intencionalmente: on
purpose
intensamente: heavily,
intensely, intensively
intensidad: intensity,
strength
intensificación:
escalation
intensificar(se): escalate,
intensify
intensivo: intensive
intensivo en mano de
obra: labor-intensive
intenso: concentrated,
deep, full, heavy, high,
intense, intensive,
loud, profound, violent
intentado: attempted
intentar: attempt,
endeavor, seek, try
intentar conseguir: try
intentar dar un golpe:
swing
intento: attempt, bid,
endeavor, go, intent,
stab, try
intento de agarrar: grab
intento de calcular algo:
guess
interacción: interaction
interactividad:
interactivity
interactivo: interactive
interactuar: interact
intercalar: sandwich
intercambiar: exchange,
swap, switch, trade
intercambio: exchange,
swap
intercambio de gases:
gas exchange
intercepción:
interception
interceptar: intercept
intercolegial:
intercollegiate
interés: concern, focus,
interest, stake
interés propio: self-
interest
interesado: interested
interesante: attractive,

colorful, interesting
interesar(se): interest,
concern, follow
interestatal: interstate
interfase: interface
interfaz: interface
Interfaz Gráfica de
Usuario: GUI
interferencia:
interference, jamming,
static
interferir: interfere
interino: acting, interim
interior: inner, inside,
interior, overhead
interior de un país:
inland
intermediario:
middleman
intermedio:
break, interlude,
intermediate, medium
interminable: drawn-
out, endless, running
interminablemente:
endlessly
intermitente:
intermittent
internacional:
international
internacionalmente:
internationally
internado: internship,
residency, residential
internado privado:
public school
internamente: internally
internar: commit, intern,
put
internar(se): check in
Internet: Internet, net,
World Wide Web
internista: internist
interno: inmate, inner,
inside, intern, internal,
inward
interponer: lodge
interponerse: get in
the way
interpretación:
interpretation, layer
interpretar: interpret
interpretar mal: misread,
misunderstand
intérprete: interpreter,
performer
intérprete de música rap:
rapper
interpreter: perform
interrogador: questioner
interrogadora:
questioner
interrogar: question,
quiz
interrogar a: put a
question to (somebody)
interrogatorio: grilling,
questioning
interrumpir: break,
cut, halt, interrupt,
punctuate
interrumpir(se)
bruscamente: cut/
stop short
interrumpirse la
comunicación: cut off
interrupción:
breakdown,

interruption, interval
interruptor: knob, switch
intervalo: gap, interlude, interval, lag, range, slot
intervalo aumentado: augmented interval
intervalo disminuido: diminished interval
intervención: intervention, tap
intervención quirúrgica: surgery
intervenir: intervene, move in, operate, step in, tap
intestinal: intestinal
intestino: bowel, gut, intestine
íntimamente: intimately, privately
intimidación: intimidation
intimidado: cowed, intimidated
intimidar: cow, intimidate
intimidatorio: intimidating
íntimo: inner, intimate, private
íntimo y agradable: cozy
intitulado: entitlement
intolerable: impossible
intolerante: impatient, narrow
intramuros: intramural
intranet: intranet
intranquilidad: unrest
intransitivo: intransitive
intrascendente: irrelevant
intratable: ornery
intravenoso: intravenous
intriga: intrigue, racket
intrigado: intrigued
intrigar: intrigue, scheme
intrincado: intricate
intrínsecamente: inherently
intrínseco: inherent
introducción: introduction, opening
introducir: bring in, enter, input, insert, introduce
introducir paulatinamente: phase in
introducirse: break into, penetrate
intromisión: interference, invasion
intuición: instinct, intuition
intuir: sense
inundación: flood, flooding
inundación repentina: flash flood
inundar(se): flood, swamp
inusitado: freak
inusual: unusual
inútil: incapable, ineffectual, pointless, unnecessary, useless, vain

inutilizar: disable
invadir: come over, descend, invade
inválida: invalid
invalidar: override, overturn
invalidez: disability
inválido: disabled, invalid, lame, null and void, void
invaluable: invaluable
invariable: static, unchanged
invariablemente: invariably
invasión: invasion
invasor: invader
invasora: invader
invención: invention
inventar: invent, make up, manufacture, think up
inventario: inventory, schedule, supply
invento: invention
inventor: inventor
inventora: inventor
invernadero: greenhouse
invernar: hibernate
inversión: holding, investment, retrograde
inversión magnética: magnetic reversal
inversionista: investor
inverso: reverse
invertebrado: invertebrate
invertir: invert, invest, put, reverse
investigación: inquiry, investigation, probe, research
investigador: investigator, researcher
investigadora: investigator, researcher
investigar: check out, check up, do one's homework, inquire, investigate, probe, read up on, research, trace
investir: invest
invicto: unbeaten
invierno: winter
invisibilidad: invisibility
invisible: invisible
invitación: invitation, invite
invitada: guest
invitada de honor: guest of honor
invitado: guest
invitado de honor: guest of honor
invitar: ask, comp, entertain, invite, treat
invocación: invocation
involucrado: concerned, involved
involucrar: draw in, involve
involuntariamente: involuntarily, unwittingly
involuntario: involuntary, unwitting
inyección: injection, shot
inyectar(se): inject

ión: ion
IPC: Consumer Price Index, CPI
IQ: IQ
ir(se): attend, clear out, come, come along, depart, draw, get away, get out, go, go around, go away, head, leave, march, pull out, run
ir a buscar: pick up
ir a contracorriente: go against the grain
ir acompañado de: go with
ir al fondo de: get to the bottom of
ir bien: grow into
ir bien/mal: do well/badly
ir como bólido: zoom
ir con alguien: see
ir con tiempo: run late
ir contra: go against the grain
ir de aquí para allá: fuss
ir de caminata: hike, hiking
ir de compras: shop
ir de excursión: hike
ir de juerga: party
ir (tomado) de la mano: hand in hand
ir de luna de miel: honeymoon
ir de prisa: hurry along
ir de... a: range from... to
ir demasiado lejos: go too far
ir en aumento: be on the increase
ir en auxilio de: go to somebody's rescue/come to somebody's rescue
ir en busca de: explore
ir en contra de: go against
ir en reversa: back up
ir en trineo: sled
ir en tropel: flock
ir hacia: head
ir mal: go wrong
ir pegado a: hug
ir por: fetch, go after, retrieve
ir rápidamente: hop
ir sin rumbo fijo: drift
ir y venir: shuttle
ir/venir en auxilio de alguien: come/go to someone's aid
ira: anger, fury, rage
iremos: we shall go
iris: iris
irle bien/mal: fare well/badly
ironía: irony
irónicamente: ironically
irónico: ironic
irracional: irrational
irracionalidad: irrationality
irracionalmente: irrationally
irrazonable: irrational
irreal: unrealistic
irreflexivo: rash

irregular: irregular, spotty
irregularidad: irregularity
irregularmente: irregularly
irrelevancia: irrelevant
irrelevante: irrelevant
irresistible: irresistible
irresistiblemente: irresistibly
irresponsabilidad: irresponsibility
irresponsable: irresponsible
irresponsablemente: irresponsibly
irreversible: irreversible
irrevocable: irreversible
irrigación: irrigation
irrigar: irrigate
irritación: irritation, itching
irritado: annoyed, irritated, itchy, vexed
irritante: annoying, irritating, vexing
irritar: grate, irritate, provoke, vex
irritarse con facilidad: have a short temper
irrumpir: swarm
irrumpir en: burst
IRS: Internal Revenue Service
irse a la quiebra: to go broke
irse a las nubes: go through the roof
irse a pique: plunge and leave
irse al caño: go down the drain
irse al traste: come to grief
irse con cuidado: tread
irse corriendo: dash off
irse de bruces: pitch
irse sin: leave behind
irse sobre: go for
írsele a uno algo: miss
isla: island, isle
islam: Islam
islámico: Islamic
islamismo: Islam
isobara: isobar
isótopo: isotope
IT: information technology
itálica: italic
itálico: italic
itinerario: timetable
IV: IV
Ivy League: Ivy League
izquierda: left, left-hand, left-wing
izquierdista: left-wing
izquierdo: left

J

jabón: soap
jade: jade
jadear: gasp, puff
jalar: flush, pull, tug
jalar la cadena: flush
jalarle al baño: flush
jaleo: racket, ruckus
jalón: pull, tug
jamás: ever
jamón: ham
jaqueca: migraine
jarabe: syrup
jaranera: reveler
jaranero: reveler
jardín: garden, yard
jardín de niños: kindergarten
jardinear: garden
jardinería: gardening
jardinero: gardener
jardines: grounds
jarra: pitcher
jarrón: vase
jaula: cage
jauría: pack
jazz: jazz
jeans: jeans
jefa: chief, employer, head, superior
jefa de cocina: chef
jefa de estado: head of state
jefa del estado mayor: chief of staff
jefatura de policía: headquarters
jefe: boss, chef, chief, chief of staff, employer, head, leader, master, superior
jefe de bomberos: marshal
jefe de comedor: maitre d'
jefe de estado: head of state
jefe de policía: marshal
jeque: sheikh
jengibre: ginger
jerarquía: hierarchy
jerárquico: hierarchical
jerga: slang
jerga jive: jive
jersey: sweater
jet: jet
jinete: jockey, rider
jingle: jingle
jirafa: giraffe
jitomate: tomato
jive: jive
jonrón: home run
jonrón con las bases llenas: grand slam
jornada: workday
jornalera: field hand
jornalero: field hand
joroba: hump
jota: jack
joven: juvenile, young, youngster, youth
jovial: good-humored, jolly
joya: jewel
joyera: jeweler
joyería: jeweler, jewelry
joyero: jeweler
Juan N: John Doe
Juana N: Jane Doe
jubilación: retirement
jubilado: retired, retiree
jubilarse: retire
júbilo: joy
judía: Jew
judía pinta: pinto bean
judicatura: judiciary

judicial: judicial
judío: Jew, Jewish
juego: ball game, gambling, game, gaming, hand, kit, match, play, puzzle, scrimmage, suite
juego de azar: game
juego de béisbol: ball game
juego de exhibición: exhibition game
juego de pelota: ball game
juego dramático infantil: dramatic play
juego teatral: theatrical game
juegos olímpicos: Olympic Games
juerga: bash
juerguista: reveler
jueves: Thursday
juez: judge, justice, magistrate
jueza: magistrate
jugada: ball game, move
jugador: player
jugador de béisbol: ballplayer
jugador de bolos o petanca: bowler
jugador de fútbol: soccer player
jugador más valioso: MVP
jugadora: player
jugadora de béisbol: ballplayer
jugadora de bolos o petanca: bowler
jugadora de fútbol: soccer player
jugadora más valiosa: MVP
jugar: fiddle, play
jugar a: play, play at, shoot
jugar con: play, toy with
jugar contra: play
jugar para tratar de igualar a: play catch-up
jugar un papel: play a part
jugar una carrera: race
jugar(se): stake
jugarreta: trick
jugársela: gamble
jugo: juice
jugo de naranja: OJ
jugoso: juicy
juguete: toy
juguetear: fiddle, play around, toy with
juguetón: playful
juguetonamente: playfully
juicio: estimate, hearing, lawsuit, suit, trial
juicio nulo: mistrial
julio: joule, July
jumbo jet: jumbo
jumper: jumper
junio: June
junta: consultation, joint, meeting
junta de educación: school board

juntar a duras penas: scrape together

juntar(se): associate, gather, gather up, get together, meet, mix, pool

junto: together

junto a: alongside, beside, by, next to

junto con: along with, alongside, in association with, together with

juntos: together

Júpiter: Jupiter

jurado: jury

jurado de acusación: grand jury

jurado en desacuerdo: hung

juramentar: swear in

juramento: oath

jurar: swear, vow

jurídico: legal

justa: tournament

justamente: just

justicia: fairness, justice

justificación: justification, legitimacy

justificadamente: legitimately

justificado: justified, legitimate

justificar(se): excuse, explain away, justify, warrant

justo: dead, fair, just, right, very

justo a tiempo: in the nick of time

justo ahora: right now

justo después: right after

juvenil: teen

juventud: youth

juzgado: courthouse, tribunal

juzgar: deem, gauge, judge, try

K

kabuki: Kabuki

karate: karate

KB: KB

Kb: Kb

kg: kg

kilo: kilo

kilobit: Kb, kilobit

kilobits por segundo: Kbps

kilobyte: KB, kilobyte

kilocaloría: kilocalorie

kilogramo: kg, kilogram

kilometraje: mileage

kilómetro: kilometer, km

kilovatio: kW

kinesiología: physical therapy

kiosko: kiosk

kiwi: kiwi, kiwi fruit

kurda: Kurd

kurdo: Kurd, Kurdish

KW: kW

L

la: her, it, the

la culpable: to blame

La Gran Mancha Roja: Great Red Spot

la mayor: most

la mayor parte: most, much

la mayoría: most

la mitad de las veces: as often as not

la que habla: speaker

la que surfea: surfer

la Quinta Enmienda: Fifth Amendment

la red: the Web

la red mundial: World Wide Web

la Reserva Federal: the Fed

la tarde: p.m.

la suya: hers, her own, theirs, their own, yours, your own

la Tierra: earth

lab: lab

labanotación: labanotation

labial: lipstick

labio: lip

labo: lab

laboratorio: lab, laboratory

labranza: farming

lacio: straight

lacra: curse

lácteo: dairy

ladear(se): lean, tilt

ladera: face, side, slope

lado: face, side

ladrar: bark

ladrido: bark

ladrillo: brick

ladrillo de cenizas: cinder block

ladrón: robber, shoplifter, thief

ladrón de casas: burglar

ladrona: robber, shoplifter, thief

ladrona de casas: burglar

lagartija: lizard, push-up

lagarto: gator, lizard

lago: lake

lágrima: drip, tear

laico: lay, secular

lamedura: lick

lamentable: miserable, sorry

lamentar: mourn, regret, sorry

lamento: moan

lamer: lap, lick

lamida: lick

lámina: plate, sheet, trading card

lámina bimetálica: bimetallic strip

lámpara: lamp

lámpara de pie: floor lamp

lámpara fluorescente: fluorescent light

lana: coat, wool

langosta: lobster

lanza: spear

lanzacohetes: launch vehicle

lanzador: launcher, pitcher

lanzadora: pitcher

lanzamiento: dropping, launch, shot, throw

lanzar(se): bowl, dash, fling, hurl, launch, pitch, release, send, shoot, throw, toss

lanzar rápidamente: dart

lanzarse en: launch into

lanzarse en paracaídas: parachute

lap: laptop

lápiz: pencil

lápiz de labios: lipstick

lapso: lag, length, slot, space, span, time

laptop: laptop

larga distancia: long-distance

largarse: butt out, clear out, skedaddle

largo: full-length, length, lengthy, long

laringe: larynx

larva: larva, maggot

las: the, them, you

las afueras: outskirts

las bellas artes: art

las cosas: the going

las dos y media: half past two

las más de las veces: as often as not

las olimpiadas: the Olympics

las otras: (the) others

láser: laser

Lasik: Lasik

last night: anoche

lástima: pity, sympathy

lastimado: hurt

lastimar: harm, injure

lastimar(se): hurt

lastimarse: bruise

lastimeramente: pathetically

lastimoso: sorry

lata: bore, can, chore, pest, tin

lateral: side

latido: beat

latigazo: lash

látigo: whip

Latina: Latina

latino: Hispanic, Latino

latinoamericano: Latin American

latir: beat

latir apresuradamente: race

latir con fuerza: pound

latitud: latitude

latón: brass

lava: lava

lavabo: basin

lavabo (baño): sink

lavadora: washer

lavamanos (baño): sink

lavandería: laundry

lavandería automática pública: laundromat

lavaplatos: dishwasher

lavaplatos (cocina): sink

lavar el cabello con shampoo: shampoo

lavar el estómago: have one's stomach pumped

lavar en seco: dry-clean

lavar(se): bathe, wash, wash up

lavarse las manos de alguien/algo: wash one's hands of somebody/something
lavavajillas: dishwasher
lawn bowling: lawn bowling
laxitud: latitude
lazada: loop
lazo: attachment, bow, loop
lazo de union: bond
le: her, him, it, them, you
leal: loyal
lealmente: loyally
lealtad: allegiance, loyalty
lección: lesson
lección de humildad: humbling
leche: milk
leche descremada: skim milk, two-percent milk
leche desnatada: skim milk
lechería: dairy
lechero: dairy
lecho: bed
lechuza: owl
lector: reader
lectora: reader
lectura: read, reading
lectura sin preparación: cold reading
leer: read, run through
leer en voz alta: read out
leer mal: misread
legado: endowment, estate, heritage, legacy
legal: legal, legitimate
legalidad: legality
legalizar: authorize
legalmente: legally
legendario: epic, legendary
leggings: leggings
legislación: legislation
legislador: lawmaker
legisladora: lawmaker
legislativo: legislative
legislatura: legislature
legítima defensa: self-defense
legítimamente: legitimately, rightfully
legitimidad: justice, legitimacy
legítimo: authentic, genuine, legitimate, rightful
lego: lay
lejano: a long way/quite a way, distant, far, far off, faraway
Lejano Oriente: Far East
lejísimos: farthest, miles (away)
lejos: a long way/quite a way, away, far
lejos de: away, far from
lejos de la ciudad capital: upstate
lema: slogan
lengua: language, tongue
lengua persa: Farsi
lenguaje: language, tongue
lenguaje hablado: speech

lenguaje obsceno: foul language
(mover) lentamente: inch
lente: lens
lente cóncavo: concave lens
lente convexa: convex lens
lente de contacto: contact lens
lenteja: lentil
lentes: eyeglasses, glasses
lentes de sol: sunglasses
lentitud: slowness
lento: slow
lento pero seguro: slowly but surely
leña: log
leñador: logger, lumberman, woodsman
león: lion
león de montaña: mountain lion
leotardos: leggings
les: them, you
lesbiana: lesbian
lesión: battery, injury
lesionado: injured
lesionar: injure
letal: deadly, lethal
letargo estival: estivation
letra: handwriting, letter, lyric, script, vocals, writing
letras: art
letrero: inscription, notice, sign
levadura: yeast
levantado: up
levantamiento: insurrection, revolt, survey
levantar(se): clear, elevate, erect, get back on one's feet, get up, get/rise to one's feet, lift, pick up, put up, raise, rise, rise up, scoop, scoop up, stir up
levantar cargos: press charges
levantar el ánimo: cheer
levantar la ceja/las cejas: raise an eyebrow
leve: subtle
leventar acta: take minutes
lexema: base word
léxico: vocabulary
ley: act, law, statute
ley de Boyle: Boyle's law
ley de Gay-Lussac: Charles's law
ley de la reflexión de la luz: law of reflection
ley de Pascal: Pascal's principle
ley de periodicidad: periodic law
ley de prescripción: statute of limitations
ley mordaza: gag rule
leyenda: legend
leyes: law

liado: mixed up
libar: suck
libelo: libel
libélula: dragonfly
liberación: discharge, liberation, release
liberado: liberated
liberador: liberating
liberal: liberal
liberalización: liberalization
liberalizar: liberalize
liberalmente: liberally
liberar(se): discharge, free, liberate, release, let go of
libertad: freedom, latitude, liberty
libertad de expresión: free speech, freedom of speech
libertar: liberate
libra: lb., pound
libra esterlina: pound
libramiento: bypass
librar(se): be off the hook, get off, rid
librarse de: get out of
libras esterlinas: sterling
libre: free, up for grabs
libre comercio: free trade
libre de: free of
libre de impuestos: tax-free
libre de servicio: off duty
libremente: freely
librería: bookstore
librero: bookcase
libreta: book
libro: book
libro (de contabilidad): book
libro de cocina: cookbook
libro de pasta dura: hardcover
libro de recetas: cookbook
libro de texto: textbook
libro para colorear: coloring book
licencia: authority, license
licencia de manejo: driver's license
licencia de matrimonio: marriage license
licencia matrimonial: marriage license
licencia para casarse: marriage license
licencia poética: poetic license
licenciada: grad, graduate, lawyer
licenciado: grad, graduate, lawyer
liceo: high school
licitar: tender
lícito: permissible
licorería: liquor store
líder: leader
liderazgo: leadership
lidiar: wrestle
lidiar con: contend
lienzo: canvas
liga: elastic, league, rubber band, scrunchie
liga mayor: major (league)

liga menor: minor (league)

Liga Nacional de Fútbol: NFL

Liga Nacional de Hockey sobre hielo: NHL

ligar(se): hook up

ligeramente: lightly, marginally, mildly, slightly, vaguely

ligereza: lightness

ligero: faint, light, lightweight, mild, short, slight, subtle

lijar: sand

lima: file

limar(se): file

limitación: constraint, limitation, qualification, restraint

limitado: confined, limited

limitante: limiting

limitar(se): confine, keep down, keep to, limit, restrict

limitar con: border

límite: boundary, breaking point, ceiling, cutoff, frontier, limit, line

límite convergente: convergent boundary

límite de crédito: credit limit

límite de transformación: transform boundary

límite de velocidad: speed limit

límite del estado: state line

límite divergente: divergent boundary

límites: bounds

limo: silt

limón: lemon

limón (verde): lime

limonada: lemonade

limosnera: beggar

limosnero: beggar

limpiada: wipe

limpiador: cleaner

limpiadora: cleaner

limpiamente: fairly

limpianieve: snowplow

limpiaparabrisas: windshield wiper

limpiar: bus, clean, cleanse, clear, mop up

limpiar (pescado): gut

limpiar a conciencia: clean up

limpiar con una esponja: sponge

limpiar concienzudamente: clean up

limpiar en seco: dry-clean

limpiar y arreglar: preen

limpiar y ordenar: clear out

limpiar(se): wipe

limpieza: cleaning, wipe

limpieza completa: spring-cleaning

limpieza y arreglado: preening

limpio: clean, clear

linchar: lynch

lindamente: prettily

lindar con: border

linde: boundary

lindero: boundary

lindo: beautiful, cute, lovely, pretty, sweet

línea: line, streak

línea aérea: airline, carrier

línea cronológica: timeline

línea de armado: assembly line

línea de crédito: credit line, line of credit

línea de ensamblaje: assembly line

línea de faul: foul line

línea de llegada: finish line

línea de montaje: assembly line

línea de negocio: line

línea de rompimiento de las olas: breaker zone

línea de scrimmage: line of scrimmage

línea de tiempo: timeline

línea divisoria: line

línea lateral: lateral line system, sideline

linfa: lymph

linfocito: lymphocyte

linguine: linguine

lingüística: linguistics

lingüístico: linguistic

link: link

lino: linen

linterna: flash, flashlight, lantern

lío: muddle

lípidos: lipid

liquidación: closeout

liquidar: settle

líquido: fluid, liquid, runny

líquido para lavaplatos/ lavavajillas: dishwashing liquid

lírico: lyric

lirio: lily

lisiado: disabled

liso: bald, plain, smooth

lisosoma: lysosome

lista: list, register, roll, schedule, stripe

lista de casos: docket

lista de correo: listserv

lista de personajes importantes: A-list

listado: striped

listo: clever, done, on standby, poised, prepared, ready, smart

listo para: prepared for, set to

listón: ribbon

listserv: listserv

literalmente: literally

literario: literary

literatura: literature

litigio: dispute, lawsuit

litoral: littoral zone

litosfera: lithosphere

litósfera: lithosphere

litro: liter

liviano: light, slight

llaga: sore

llama: flame

llamada: call

llamada a cobro revertido: collect call

llamada por cobrar: collect call

llamada telefónica: phone call

llamado: plea, so-called

llamado a filas: draft

llamar: call, call in, call up, catch, dub, get back to, name, rap, recall, summon, term

llamar a filas: call up, draft

llamar la atención a alguien: take somebody's fancy

llamar la atención de alguien: catch someone's eye

llamar por cobrar: call collect

llamar por radio: radio

llamar por teléfono: phone, telephone

llamativo: boldness, loud

llamativo y elegante: sassy

llamear: flare

llana: trowel

llano: flat, flatlands

llanta: spare tire, tire

llanta de refacción: spare tire

llantita: spare tire

llanto: cry, crying

llanura: flatlands, plain, prairie

llave: faucet, key, spigot, wrench

llave de encendido: switch

llave de tuercas: wrench

llegada: arrival, coming, entrance

llegar: arrive, carry, come, come in, get at, reach, set in

llegar a: draw, get on to, run into, stand at

llegar a estar: get

llegar a la conclusión: conclude

llegar a montones: pour

llegar a saber: hear of

llegar a ser: get

llegar a su fin: draw to an end/draw to a close

llegar a un arreglo: compromise

llegar al final del recorrido: terminate

llegar de nuevo: come around

llegar/salir en cantidades grandes: pour

llenador: filling

llenar(se): complete, fill, fill in, fill out, fill up, fulfill, line, load, pour out, write

llenar el tanque: refuel

llenarse (los ojos) de

lágrimas: water

lleno: crowded, filled, full, littered, loaded, sell-out

lleno completo: capacity crowd

lleno de: pitted

lleno de baches: bumpy

lleno de energía: energetic

llevar: bear, bring, carry, drive, drop, enter, escort, feed, ferry, give somebody a lift somewhere, go into, keep, lead, march, pipe, run, show, steer, take, wear

llevar a: bring forth, drive

llevar a alguien: see

llevar a cabo: accomplish, carry out, conduct, effect, execute, fulfill, go through with, hold, perform

llevar consigo: take/bring along with you

llevar en los brazos: hug

llevar gradualmente a: lead up to

llevar la cuenta: keep count

llevar la delantera: lead

llevar las de perder: things/the odds are stacked against

llevar luto: mourn

llevar rápidamente: rush, whisk

llevar sobre las espaldas: carry (responsibilities/problems) on one's shoulders

llevar tiempo: to take time

llevar un lunch al trabajo o a la escuela: brown-bag

llevarse: take away, walk off with, wash away

llevarse a: raise

llevarse a cabo: go ahead

llevarse bien: get along

llorar: cry, mourn, weep

llorar (los ojos): water

llorar a alguien: grieve

lloroso: runny

llover: rain

llovizna: drizzle

lloviznar: drizzle, sprinkle

lluvia: rain, shower

lluvia ácida: acid rain

lluvia radiactiva: fallout

lluvioso: rainy, wet

lo: him, it, the, you

lo absurdo: absurdity

lo anterior: above

lo básico: essential

lo bueno: beauty

lo comprado: purchase

lo contrario: opposite

lo delicado: sensitive subject/issue

lo desconocido: the unknown

lo escrito permanece: in

black and white

lo esencial: essential, substance

lo ideal: ideally

lo imposible: impossible

lo impredecible: unpredictability

lo imprevisto: suddenness

lo inevitable: inevitable

lo más: most

lo más alto: high, the height of, top

lo más importante: high priority, the issue

lo más lejos: farthest

lo más rápidamente: flat out

lo más temprano: earliest

lo máximo: blast, one's utmost

lo mejor: best, the pick, top

lo menos: least

lo mínimo: least

lo mismo: likewise, the same

lo nocivo: evil

lo normal: average

lo peor: hell, the worst

lo posible: the possible

lo positivo: positive

lo primero: first, first/last thing, former

lo probable: likely

lo programado: schedule

lo que: what, whatever, which

lo que es más: what is more

lo que le plazca: as you please/whatever you please

lo que pasó: incident

lo que queda: last, left

lo que quiera: as you please/whatever you please

lo que sea: anything

lo que sigue: following

lo que sobra: left

lo recomendable: ideally

lo repugnante: nastiness

lo sagrado: sacredness

lo siguiente: following

lo sobrenatural: the supernaural

lo tarde: lateness

lo último: first/last thing, last

lo último en: the ultimate in

lo único que: nothing but

lobo: wolf

lóbulo: lobe

lóbulo de la oreja: earlobe

loca: crazy

local: home, local

localizar: locate, trace, track down

localmente: locally

locamente: insanely

loco: crazy, insane, mad, nuts, wild

loco por: crazy about

locomotor: locomotor

locomotora: engine,

locomotive

locomotriz: locomotor

locución idiomática: idiom

locura: insanity, madness

locutor: broadcaster, newscaster

locutora: broadcaster, newscaster

lodo: mud

lodoso: muddy

loes: loess

loess: loess

logaritmo: logarithm

lógica: logic, logical

lógicamente: logically

lógico: logical

logística: logistics

logo: logo

logotipo: logo

logrado: slick

lograr: accomplish, achieve, attain, effect, fight off, gain, get, make, make it, pull off, score, succeed, win

lograr comunicarse: get through

lograr decir una palabra: get a word in edgewise

lograr el éxito merecido: come into one's/its own

lograr llegar: make it

logro: accomplishment, achievement, attainment, success

LOL: LOL

lombriz (de tierra): earthworm

lona: canvas

lona impermeabilizada: tarp

longitud: length

longitud de onda: wavelength

longitud en yardas: yardage

lonja: spare tire

loquero: shrink

loquita: kook

loquito: kook

lord: lord

los: the, them, you

los alrededores: outskirts

los ancianos: the aged, the old

los anteriores: above

los astros: the/one's stars

los (años) cincuenta: the fifties

los (años) cuarenta: the forties

los demás: (the) others, else

los desempleados: the unemployed

los enfermos: the sick

los heridos: the injured

los incondicionales: the faithful

los ingleses: the English

los jóvenes: the young

los juegos olímpicos: the Olympics

los (años) noventa: the

nineties
los obreros: shop floor
los (años) ochenta: the eighties
los otros: (the) others
los pobres: the poor
los que no tienen hogar: the homeless
los ricos: the rich
los seis reinos orgánicos: six kingdoms
los (años) sesenta: the sixties
los (años) setenta: the seventies
los (años) treinta: the thirties
los (años) veinte: the twenties
loseta: tile
lote: crop, lot
lotería: bingo, lottery
low-end: low-end
loza: china, tile
LP: LP
lubricante: lubricant
luces altas: brights, high beams
lucha: battle, fight, fighting, push, struggle
luchador: fighter
luchadora: fighter
luchar: battle, fight, labor, push, struggle, wrestle
luchar por: pursue
luchar por la vida: fight for one's life
lucrativo: for-profit, lucrative, profitable
luego: then
lugar: ground, place, point, room, site, space, spot, venue
lugar alguno: anyplace
lugar común: garden-variety, platitude
lugar de interés: sight
lugar de nacimiento: birthplace
lugar de trabajo: workplace, workstation
lugar favorito: haunt
lugar predilecto: stomping ground
lugarteniente de la gobernadora: lieutenant governor
lugarteniente del gobernador: lieutenant governor
lúgubre: grim
lujo: luxury
lujoso: fancy, luxury
lumbre: fire
luminosidad: lightness
luminoso: bright
luna: moon
luna de miel: honeymoon
lunar: beauty mark, lunar
lunares: polka dots
lunch: box lunch, brown-bag
lunes: Monday
lustrar: polish
lustre: luster
luterana: Lutheran

luterano: Lutheran
luz: light
luz artificial: artificial light
luz blanca: white light
luz de día: daylight
luz de (la) luna: moonlight
luz del día: sunlight
luz del sol: sunlight, sunshine
luz natural: daylight, natural light
luz solar: sunlight
luz verde: go-ahead

M

m/s, metros por segundo: m/s
m/s², metros por segundo cuadrado: m/s/s
ma: mom
macana: nightstick
macareo: tidal bore
macarrones con queso: macaroni and cheese
machacar: drum into
machacar acerca de: harp on
machaqueo: drumbeat
macho: buck, bull, macho, male
machucón: boo-boo
macroeconomía: macroeconomics
macroeconómico: macroeconomic
madera: lumber, smarts, wood
madera de construcción: timber
maderería: lumberyard
maderero: logger
madrastra: stepmother
madre: mother, parent
madre patria: mother country
madre soltera: single parent
madrina: attendant
madrina de boda: matron of honor
madurar: grow up, mature, ripen
madurez: manhood, maturity, middle age
maduro: mature, middle-aged, ripe
maestra: teacher
maestra auxiliar: teaching assistant
maestra de ceremonias: emcee
maestra particular: tutor
maestra suplente: sub, substitute teacher
maestro: master, teacher, tutor
maestro auxiliar: teaching assistant
maestro de ceremonias: emcee
maestro particular: tutor
maestro suplente: sub, substitute teacher
mafia: Mafia
maga: magician

magia: magic
mágico: magic, magical
magma: magma
magnético: magnetic
magnetizar: magnetize
magníficamente: finely, gloriously, magnificently, superbly
magnificencia: magnificence
magnífico: beautiful, fine, glorious, gorgeous, magnificent, shining, splendid, superb
magnitud: -sized
magnitud absoluta: absolute magnitude
magnitud aparente: apparent magnitude
mago: magician, wizard
magro: lean
maicena: cornstarch
maíz: corn
majestad: majesty
majestuosamente: majestically
majestuosidad: majesty
majestuoso: grand, majestic
mal: bad, bad off, badly, foul, ill, illness, poor, wrong
mal comportamiento: misbehavior
mal dispuesto: unwilling
mal humor: moodiness
mal momento: senior moment
mal necesario: necessary evil
mal olor: stink
mal rato: a rough ride
mal tirador: a bad shot
mala conducta: misbehavior, misconduct
mala hierba: weed
mala interpretación: misreading
mala pasada: a raw deal
mala suerte: bad luck
mala tiradora: a bad shot
malabarismo: juggling
malabarista: juggler
malagua: medusa
malas nuevas: bad news
maldad: meanness, mischief, spite
maldecir: curse, swear
maldición: curse
maldito: doggone
maleabilidad: malleability
maleable: malleable
malecón: boardwalk, jetty
maleducado: ignorant, rude
malestar: discomfort, unrest
maleta: baggage, suitcase
maletas: luggage
maletero: porter, trunk
maleza: scrub, underbrush, undergrowth, weed

malgastar: throw away

malhumorado: bad-tempered

maligno: malignant

malinterpretar: misread

malísimo: terrible

malla de baño: swimsuit

mallas: leggings

mallones: leggings

malo: bad, foul, ill, lame, low, mean, wrong

malvado: evil, wicked

mama: breast

mamá: mama, mom, momma

mamario: mammary

mambo: mambo

mameluco: overall

mami: mommy

mamífera: mammal

mamífero: mammal

mamífero placentado: placental mammal

mamífero placentario: placental mammal

mamografía: mammography

mampara: screen

manada: herd

manantial: fountain, spring

manar: flow, well

manatí: manatee

mancha: mark, smear, spot, stain

mancha solar: sunspot

manchado: stained

manchar: stain

mandado: errand

mandar: command, dispatch, forward, instruct, send, send off, send out

mandar a la cárcel: jail

mandar a por: send out for

mandar de acá para allá: order around

mandar en avión: fly

mandar hacer: have something done

mandar llamar: summon

mandar mensajes instantáneos: instant messaging

mandar por: send for, send out for

mandar por fax: fax

mandar por mensajería: courier

mandar un correo electrónico: e-mail

mandar un e-mail: e-mail

mandar un mensaje instantáneo: instant message

mandato: directive, mandate

mandíbula inferior: mandible

mandíbulas: jaw

mando: command, leadership

mandonear: boss

manecilla: hand

manejar: drive, handle, man, operate, work

manejo: driving, handling

manera: fashion, manner, means, style, way

manera de expresarse: turn of phrase

manga: arm, sleeve, waterspout

manga catavientos: windsock

manga de viento: windsock

mango: handle

manguera: hose

maní: peanut

manicomio: institution

manifestación: demonstration, expression, march, protest, rally

manifestante: demonstrator, marcher, protester

manifestar: declare, display

manifestarse: demonstrate

manifiestamente: manifestly, nakedly

manifiesto: manifest, manifesto, naked

manija: handle

maniobra: maneuver

maniobra dilatoria: filibuster

maniobrar: maneuver

manipulación: manipulation

manipular: handle, man, manipulate, operate, rig, work

manipular indebidamente: tamper

mano: coat, hand

mano de mortero: pestle

mano de obra: labor, labor force

manos libres: hands-free

manotazo: smack, swipe

mansión: mansion

manta: blanket

manta contra incendios: fire blanket

manteca: shortening

mantel individual: mat

mantelito: mat

mantener(se): carry on, hang on, hold, hold down, keep, keep up, maintain, provide for, stay, sustain

mantener a alguien como empleado: keep someone on

mantener a raya: keep/ hold at bay

mantener bajo: keep down

mantener correspondencia: correspond

mantener la calma: keep one's head

mantener la ventaja: hold on

mantener ojos abiertos:

keep your eyes open, keep an eye out

mantenerse a flote: buoy

mantenerse al margen: stand by, take a back seat

mantenerse al ritmo: keep pace

mantenerse firme: put one's foot down, stand firm, stand one's ground/hold one's ground, stick to one's guns

mantenimiento: maintenance, upkeep

mantequilla: butter, shortening

manto: blanket, mantle

manto superior: upper mantle

mantón: shawl

manual: manual

manualmente: manually

manufactura: manufacture, manufacturing

manufacturar: manufacture

manuscrito: handwritten, manuscript

manzana: apple, block

manzana acaramelada: candy apple

mañana: morning, tomorrow

mapa: chart, map

mapa climatológico: weather map

mapa en relieve: relief map

mapa topográfico: topographic map

maqueta: kit, maquette, model

maquillaje: makeup

máquina: engine, machine

máquina compuesta: compound machine

máquina corazón-pulmón: life support

máquina de búsqueda: search engine

máquina de escribir: typewriter

máquina de movimiento perpetuo: perpetual motion machine

máquina ideal: ideal machine

máquina simple: simple machine

máquina térmica: heat engine

maquinal: mechanical

maquinaria: machine, machinery

maquinaria pesada: plant

mar: sea

maraña: jungle, tangle, web

maratón: marathon

maratónico: marathon

maravilla: sunflower, wonder

maravillosamente: beautifully, marvelously

maravilloso: great, magical, marvelous, wonderful

marca: brand, check mark, impression, make, mark, record, scar

marca de fábrica: trademark

marca dinámica: dynamic marking

marca libre: store brand

marca registrada: trademark

marcado: marked, stark, steep

marcador: bookmark, highlighter, marker, score

marcar(se): bookmark, brand, check, dial, leave one's/a mark, mark, punch in, say, scar, score, tag

marcar (con hierro candente): brand

marcar posiciones: blocking

marcha: march, walk

marchar: march

marchar a: go forth

marchar bien: go strong

marcial: martial

marco: frame, framework

marco de referencia: framework

marea: tide

marea alta: high tide

marea baja: ebb, low tide

marea muerta: neap tide

marea negra: slick

marea viva: spring tide

mareado: carsick, dizzy, faintly

mareo: dizziness

mares: seas

marfil: ivory

margarina: shortening

margen: fringe, margin, room

margen continental: continental margin

mariachi: mariachi

marido: husband

mariguana: marijuana

marihuana: marijuana

marijuana: marijuana

marina de guerra: navy

marinar(se): marinate

marinero: sailor

marines: marine

marino: marine, offshore

marioneta: puppet

mariposa: butterfly

mariquita: ladybug

mariscal de campo: quarterback

marisco: seafood, shellfish

marisma: marsh

marital: marital, spousal

marítimo: marine, maritime

mármol: marble

marquesina: marquee

marrana: sow

marsupial: marsupial

Marte: Mars

martes: Tuesday

martillo: hammer

martillo neumático: jackhammer

marxismo: Marxism

marxista: Marxist

marzo: March

más: added, best, better, else, further, more, most, most of all, plus

más adelante: further, later

más al norte: upstate

más allá: beyond, further

más alto: peak

más arriba: upstate

más bajo: low

más bien: instead of, rather

más bien que: rather

más de: more than, over, plus, upward

más lejano: furthest

más lejos: farther, further

más o menos: fairly, give or take, or so, something like

más que: better, in excess of, more than, only

más que eso: if nothing else

más que suficiente: plenty

más reciente: latest

más tarde: later

más temprano: earlier

más vale que: had better

más y más: more and more

masa: bank, batter, bulk, dough, mass, pastry, tumor

masa atómica: atomic mass

masa continental: land mass

masa de aire: air mass

masa fermentada: sourdough

masacrar: massacre, slaughter

masacre: massacre

masaje: massage, rubdown

masajear(se): massage

mascada: scarf

máscara: face mask, mascara, mask

mascarilla: face mask, mask

mascota: pet

masculinidad: masculinity

masculino: male, masculine

mascullar: mutter

masivo: mass, massive

masticar: chew

masticar haciendo ruido: crunch

mástil: mast

mata: shrub

matanza: massacre, slaughter

matar: kill, kill off, put down, slaughter

matar a tiros: gun down

matar el tiempo: while away

matar en la cámara de gases: gas

matar en masa: massacre

mate: dull, matte

matemática: mathematician

matemáticamente: mathematically

matemáticas: math, mathematics

matemático: mathematical, mathematician

materia: credit hour, material, matter, subject, topic

materia gris: gray matter

materia principal: major

material: material

material impreso: matter

material para cercas: fencing

material piroclástico: pyroclastic material

materiales: material

materialmente: materially

maternal: maternal

maternidad: maternity

materno: maternal, native

matiné: matinee

matiz: shade

matiz estilístico: stylistic nuance

matorral: scrub

matrícula: tuition

matrimonial: double

matrimonio: marriage

matriz escalar: scalar matrix

máximo: at most/at the most, maximum, top, utmost

mayo: May

mayonesa: mayonnaise

mayor: elder, eldest, grown-up, major, senior, utmost

mayor parte: bulk

mayor que: upward

mayoría: majority

mayormente: largely

mayúscula: capital

mazo: deck

mazorca: ear

me: me

mecánica: mechanic

mecánicamente: mechanically, mindlessly

mecánico: mechanic, mechanical, mindless

mecanismo: mechanic, mechanism

mecanismo de defensa: defense mechanism

mecanismo elemental: simple machine

mecanización: mechanization

mecanizar: mechanize

mecanógrafa: typist
mecanografía: typing
mecanografiar: type
mecanógrafo: typist
mecenas: patron
mecer(se): rock
mecerse: sway
mechar: slash
mechón: lock
medalla: medal
Medalla de Honor: Medal of Honor
medalla de oro: gold medal
medallista: medalist
médano: sand dune
media: half, mean, sock, stocking
media hora: half-hour
media luna: crescent
mediación: mediation
mediador: mediator
mediadora: mediator
medialuna: croissant
mediana: median, median strip
mediana edad: middle age
mediano: medium, moderate
mediano plazo: medium term
medianoche: midnight
mediante: by means of
mediar: mediate
medias: pantyhose
médica: doctor, medic, physician, practitioner
médica de cabecera: GP
médica familiar: GP
médica forense: medical examiner
médica interna: resident
medicación: medication, medicine
médicamente: medically
medicamento: drug, medication, medicine
medicina: medication, medicine
médico: doctor, medic, medical, physician, practitioner
médico de cabecera: GP
médico familiar: GP
médico forense: medical examiner
médico interno: resident
medida: action, measurement
medida en yardas: yardage
medidas: provisions
medidas enérgicas: crackdown
medidor: gauge, meter
medieval: medieval
medio: facility, half, means, medium, middle, midfielder, vehicle
medio ambiente: environment
medio ambiente béntico: benthic environment
medio litro: pint
medio mal: funny
Medio Oriente: Middle

East
medio plano: middle ground
medio tiempo: halftime, part-time
medio/mediocampista: midfield
mediocre: indifferent, inferior, mediocre
mediocridad: mediocrity
mediodía: noon, noontime
medios: means
medios de comunicación: media
medios de comunicación (de masas): mass media
medios de vida: living
medios electrónicos: electronic media
medir(se): gauge, measure, size up, survey
medir el tiempo: time
meditabundo: thoughtful
meditación: meditation
meditar: deliberate, meditate, think
médium: psychic
médula: medulla
médula espinal: spinal cord
médula oblonga: medulla
medusa: jellyfish, medusa
megabyte: megabyte
megatienda: big-box
meiosis: meiosis
mejilla: cheek
mejillón: mussel
mejor: best, better, prime, top, well
mejor momento: best
mejora: enhancement, improvement, pickup, upturn
mejorar(se): be on the mend, enhance, improve, raise, refine, upgrade
melanina: melanin
melena: mane
melodía: melody, ringtone, tune
melodioso: sweet
melón: melon
membrana celular: cell membrane
membranófono: membranophone
memorable: memorable
memorándum: memo
memoria: memory
memoria sensorial: sense memory
memorias: memoirs
memorizar: learn, memorize
mención honorífica: honorable mention
mencionar: cite, mention
mendiga: beggar, panhandler
mendigar: beg, panhandle

mendigo: beggar, panhandler
menear: stir
menearse: bob
menisco: meniscus
menonita: Mennonite
menopausia: menopause
menopáusico: menopausal
menor: junior, least, lesser, minor, minor league, petty, under
menor de edad: minor
menorá: menorah
menos: but, least, less, lesser, minus
menos aún: let alone
menos de: less than
menos importante: minor
menos que: less than
menospreciar: devalue, look down on, talk down
mensaje: mail, message
mensaje de texto: text, text message
mensaje instantáneo: IM, instant message
mensajera: courier, page
mensajería instantánea: instant messaging
mensajero: courier, messenger, page
menso: dingbat
menstruación: menstruation
menstruar: menstruate
mensual: monthly
mensualidad: allowance
mensualmente: monthly
menta: mint
mental: mental
mentalmente: mentally
mente: head, mind
mentir: lie
mentira: lie
mentiras: lying
mentón: chin
mentor: mentor
mentora: mentor
menú: menu
menudo: petite, tiny
mercadería: merchandise
mercado: market
mercado bursátil: stock market
mercado de divisas: foreign exchange
mercado de valores: stock market
mercado laboral: labor market
mercadotecnia: marketing
mercancía: commodity, merchandise
mercante: merchant
merced a: thanks to, through
Mercurio: Mercury
mercurio: mercury
merecer: deserve, merit
meridional: southern
merienda: supper
mérito: credit, merit
mermar: tail off

mermelada: jam, jelly
mero: mere
mes: month
mesa: mesa, table
mesa de trabajo: bench
mesada: allowance
mescolanza: mixture
mesera: server, waitress
mesero: server, waiter
meseros: waitstaff
meseta: mesa
Mesías: Messiah
mesosfera: mesosphere
mesozoico: Mesozoic era
meta: aim, finish line, goal, mark
metabolismo: metabolism
metadona: methadone
metafase: metaphase
metáfora: metaphor
metáfora visual: visual metaphor
metafóricamente: figuratively
metafórico: figurative
metal: metal
metal alcalino: alkali metal
metal de tierra alcalina: alkaline-earth metal
metales: brass
metaloide: metalloid
metamórfico: metamorphic
metamorfosis: metamorphosis
metanol: methanol
metedura de pata: snafu
meteoroide: meteoroid
meteorología: meteorology
meter(se): break in, dig, dip, drop, get into, go in, grind, insert, place, poke, score, slot, squeeze, stick, stuff, tuck, tuck in/into (something), wedge
meter a fuerza: force
meter a la cárcel: imprison
meter a presión: jam
meter de contrabando: smuggle
meter en la cárcel: imprison
meter en líos: land in (a bad situation)
meter en problemas: land in (a bad situation)
meter la mano: reach
meter la pata: flub
meterse algo en la cabeza: get something into one's head
meterse con: mess around, pick on
meterse por la fuerza: muscle in
meticulosidad: thoroughness
metida de pata: boo-boo, flub
metido: stuck
metódicamente: methodically
metódico: methodical,

systematic
método: method, system
método científico: scientific method
metraje: footage
métrico: metric
metro: meter, metro, subway, tape measure
metropolitano: metro, metropolitan
metros por segundo: meters per second
mezcla: blend, composition, cross, meld, mix, mixture
mezcla heterogénea: heterogeneous mixture
mezcla homogénea: homogeneous mixture
mezclado: mixed, mixed up
mezclar(se): blend, combine, integrate, meld, mix
mezclilla: denim
mezquindad: pettiness
mezquino: petty, sleazy
mezquita: mosque
mezzanine: mezzanine
mi: my
mí: me
mí/mío: mine
micótico: fungal
microbio: germ
microcircuito: microchip
microclima: microclimate
microeconomía: microeconomics
microeconómico: microeconomic
microelemento: trace gas
microfibra: microfiber
micrófono: microphone
microorganismo: microorganism
microscópico: microscopic
microscopio: microscope
microscopio compuesto: compound light microscope
microscopio de electrones: electron microscope
microscopio electrónico: electron microscope
miedo: fear, fright
miedoso: fearful
miel: honey
miembro: fellow, limb, member
miembro de un grupo: insider
miembro del jurado: juror
miembro del parlamento: Member of Parliament
miembro fundador: founding member
miembro veterano: holdover
miembros de la iglesia: congregation
mientras: (in the) meantime, in the process, while

mientras más … más: the more … the
mientras que: whereas, while
mientras tanto: (in the) meantime, meanwhile
miércoles: Wednesday
miga: crumb
migaja: crumb
migración: immigration, migration
migraña: migraine
migrar: migrate
mil: thousand
mil dólares o mil libras: grand
mil millones: billion
milagro: miracle, wonder
milagroso: miracle
miles: thousands
miles de millones: billions
milicia: militia
miligramo: milligram
miligramo (mg): mg
mililitro: ml
milímetro: millimeter, mm
militancia: militancy
militante: campaigner, militant
militar: military, serviceman
militarmente: militarily
milla: mile
millas por hora: mph
millón: million
millonaria: millionaire
millonario: millionaire
millonésimo: millionth
mimar: fuss over, indulge
mimbre: cane
mina: lead, mine, pit
mina a tajo abierto: strip mine
minar: undermine
minera: miner
mineral: mineral, ore
mineral sin silicatos: nonsilicate mineral
minería: mining
minero: miner
miniatura: miniature
minibús: minibus
mínima: minimum
minimalismo: minimalism
mínimamente: minimally, minutely
mínimo: low, marginal, minimal, minimum, skeleton, slight
ministerial: ministerial
ministerio: department, ministry, office
ministra: minister, secretary
ministra de hacienda/ economía: chancellor
Ministra de Relaciones Exteriores: Secretary of State
ministro: minister, secretary
ministro de hacienda/ economía: chancellor
Ministro de Relaciones Exteriores: Secretary of State

minivan: minivan
minoría: minority
minorista: merchandiser, retail, retailer
minstrel show: minstrel show
minuciosamente: elaborately
minucioso: thorough
minúsculo: tiny
minusválido: disabled
minuta: minute
minuto: minute
minuto luz: light minute
miocardio: heart
miope: far-sighted, near-sighted
mira: look
¡mira nada más!: fancy (that)!
mirada: eye, glance, look, stare
mirada fija: gaze
mirada furiosa: glare
mirada penetrante: gaze
mirar: look, stare, watch
mirar a hurtadillas: peek
mirar atrás: look back
mirar con: regard
mirar detenidamente: peer
mirar fijamente: gaze
mirar furiosamente: glare
mirar los toros desde la barrera: sit on the fence
misa: mass
miscelánea: general store
miserablemente: miserably
miseria: misery
misil: missile, rocket
misión: mission, task
misionera: missionary
misionero: missionary
mismo: equal, identical, itself, same
misterio: mystery, puzzle, riddle
misteriosamente: darkly, mysteriously
misterioso: mysterious, mystery
mitad: half, half note
mitad de un período: midterm
mítico: mythical
mitigar: subdue
mito: legend, myth
mitocondria: mitochondrion
mitología: mythology
mitológico: mythological
mitosis: mitosis
mixto: coed, heterogeneous, miscellaneous
mixto: mixed
mixtura: mix, mixture
mL: ml
ml: ml
mm: mm
mmm: er
moción: motion
moda: fashion, vogue
moda pasajera: fad
modelaje: modeling
modelar: model, mold

modelo: model
modelo a escala: scale
modelo climático: station model
modelo de conducta: role model
modelo meteorológico: station model
moderación: moderation
moderada: moderate
moderadamente: moderately, modestly
moderado: gentle, moderate, modest, restrained
moderar: moderate, qualify, restrain, soften, tone down
modernización: modernization
modernizar: modernize
moderno: cool, modern
modestamente: modestly
modestia: modesty
modesto: humble, modest
modificación: modification
modificado genéticamente: genetically-modified
modificador: modifier
modificar: modify, reform
modismo: idiom
modo: manner, mode, way
modo de usarse: usage
modo de uso: usage
modo de vida: mode
modo subjuntivo: subjunctive
modulación: inflection
módulo de maniobra y mando: command module
módulo lunar: lunar module
mofle: exhaust pipe
moho: mold
mojado: wet
mojar: dip
mojar (la cama): wet oneself/the bed
molde: mold
molde para galletas: cookie cutter
molde para pastel: cake pan
moldear: mold, shape
molécula: molecule
moler: grind
molestar: annoy, bother, disturb, irritate, pester, spite, tee off, tick off, trouble, upset, vex
molestarse: bother
molestia: annoyance, bother, irritation
molesto: tiresome
molido: ground
molino: mill
momento: instant, minute, moment, momentum, point, time
momentum: momentum

monarca: monarch
monarquía: monarchy
monasterio: monastery
moneda: coin, currency
monedas: change
monedas de plata: silver
monedero: pocketbook
monetario: monetary
monitor: monitor
monja: nun
monje: monk
mono: ape, cute, monkey, sweet
monocromático: monochromatic
monolítico: monolithic
monólogo: monologue
monomio: monomial
mononucleosis: mono, mononucleosis
monopolio: monopoly
monopolizar: corner, monopolize
monoteísmo: monotheism
monoteístas: monotheistic
monotonía: dullness
monótono: monotonous
monotrema: monotreme
monóxido de carbono: carbon monoxide
moño: bow
monstruo: freak, monster
monstruosidad: atrocity
monstruoso: hideous
monta: riding
montado: mounted
montaje: assemblage
montaña: mountain
montaña de plegamiento: folded mountain
montaña submarina: seamount
montañismo: climbing
montar: horseback riding, install, mount, put on, ride, set, stage, start, start up
montar en cólera: fly into
monte: bush, mount
montés: wild
montículo: hump, mound
monto: sum
montón: batch, bunch, crop, gob, heap, mass, mound, mountain, pile, stack, swarm
montón de: a lot of
montón de cosas varias: grab bag
montones: heaps, hundreds, thousands
montones de: masses of
montura: saddle
monumental: formidable, monumental
monumento: memorial, monument
monzón: monsoon
mora: default
morado: purple
moral: moral

moraleja: moral
moralidad: moral, morality
moralmente: morally
morboso: sick
mordaz: dryness, pointed
mordazmente: dryly
morder: bite
morderse los labios/la lengua: bite one's lip/tongue
mordida: bite, payoff
mordido: bitten
mordisquear: chew
morena: glacial drift, moraine
morena estratificada: stratified drift
moretón: bruise
moribundo: dying
morir(se): die
morir(se) de hambre: starve
morir(se) por la falta de: be starved of
morirse (de la risa): double over
morirse de hambre: be starving
morona: crumb
morralla: change
morrena: till
mortal: deadly, fatal, lethal, mortal
mortalidad: mortality
mortalmente: mortally
mortero: mortar
mortífero: deadly, lethal
mosaico: mosaic, tile
mosca: fly
mosquito: mosquito
mostaza: mustard
mostrador: counter, desk
mostrar: bare, display, exhibit, illustrate, manifest, produce, show
mostrarse más hábil que: outmaneuver
mota: marijuana
mote: nickname
motel: motel
motivación: motivation
motivado: motivated
motivar: motivate
motivo: cause, motive, reason
moto: bike, cycle
motocicleta: cycle, motorcycle
motociclista: biker, rider
motor: engine, motor
motor de combustión externa: external combustion engine
motor de combustión interna: internal combustion engine
motor de reacción: jet engine
motor térmico: heat engine
motorizado: motor
mouse: mouse
mousepad: mouse pad
mousse: mousse
mover(se): drive, get going, jog, move, push, shift, stir
mover (bruscamente): jerk
mover (repentinamente): jerk
mover como apuñalando: stab
moverse rápidamente: leap
moverse sigilosamente: creep
movible: moving
movida: move
móvil: mobile, moving
movilidad: mobility
movilización: mobilization
movilizar(se): mobilize
movimiento: motion, move, movement, traffic, turnover
movimiento axial: axial movement
movimiento paulatino del terreno: creep
movimiento rápido: dive
movimiento rígido: rigid motion
mozo de cuadra: groom
MP3: MP3
mph: mph
mucama: maid
mucha: many
muchacha: girl, youngster
muchacha bonita: chick
muchacho: boy, youngster
muchacho que cuida niños: babysitter
muchas: many
muchas gracias: thank you very much
muchedumbre: crowd
muchísimo: big time, terribly, very much so
mucho: a great deal of, a load of, a lot of, a mass of, ample, every, far, long, many, masses of, much, plenty, strongly, well
mucho gusto de conocerlo/conocerla: pleased to meet you
mucho menos: let alone
mucho tiempo: long
muchos: heaps, many
mucosa: mucus
muda (piel, pelo, plumaje): molting
mudanza: move
mudanza/cambio de opinión: move
mudar: move, shed
mudar/cambiar de opinión: move
mudarse: move in, move out
mudo: dumb, mute
muebles: furniture
muelle: dock, jetty, wharf
muerte: death, passing
muerto: dead, fatality, pooped
muerto de: to death
muesca: nick
muestra: display, mark, sample, sign, specimen
muestra de: testimony
muestra gratis: goody bag
mugre: dirt, grunge
mugroso: filthy, grungy
mujer: female, woman
mujer de negocios: businesswoman, promoter
mujer policía: policewoman
muladar: dumping
multa: fine, penalty, ticket
multar: fine
multicelular: multicellular
multicolor: multicolored
multifamiliar: apartment complex
multilateral: multilateral
multimedia: multimedia
multimillonaria: billionaire
multimillonario: billionaire
multinacional: multinational
múltiple: multiple
multiplicación: multiplication
multiplicador: multiplier
multiplicar: multiply
múltiplo: multiple
multitud: battery, crowd, flock, swarm
multiuso: multipurpose
multivitamínico: multivitamin
mundano: sophisticated
mundial: world
mundialmente: universally
mundo: globe, world
mundo del espectáculo: show business
mundo real: real world
munición: ammunition
municiones: munitions
municipal: civic, municipal
municipalidad: township
municipio: borough, township
muñeca: doll, wrist
muñeco: doll
mural: mural
muralla: wall
muralla de nubes: wall cloud
murciélago: bat
murmullo: babble, murmur, mutter, whisper
murmullos: muttering
murmurar: murmur, whisper
muro: wall
muscular: muscular
músculo: muscle
músculo cardiaco: cardiac muscle
músculo esquelético: skeletal muscle
músculo involuntario: smooth muscle
músculo liso: smooth

muscle

musculoso: lean, muscular

museo: museum, repository

musgo: moss

música: music, musician, player

música country: country and western, country music

música folklórica: folk

música instrumental: instrumental

música popular: folk, pop

música punk: punk

música serial: serial music

música soul: soul

musical: musical

musicalidad: musicality

musicalmente: musically

músico: musician, player

muslo: thigh

musulmán: Muslim

musulmana: Muslim

mutágeno: mutagen

mutualismo: mutualism

mutuamente: each

mutuamente excluyente: mutually exclusive

mutuo: mutual

muy: awfully, greatly, mighty, quite, too, very

muy a mano: convenient

muy bien: nicely, very well

muy de cuando en cuando: few and far between

muy de vez en cuando: few and far between

muy difícil: hard going

muy lejano: a long time/ way off

muy rara vez: few and far between

N

nabo de Suecia: rutabaga

nacer: born, dawn

naciente: headwaters

nacimiento: birth

nación: nation

nacional: domestic, federal, national

nacionalidad: nationality

nacionalismo: nationalism

nacionalista: nationalist

Naciones Unidas: United Nations

nada: any, anything, nil, none, nothing, zero

nada más que: no/ nothing other than

nadador: swimmer

nadadora: swimmer

nadar: swim

nadie: anybody, anyone, no one, nobody

nado: swim, swimming

naipe: playing card

nalga: buttock

nana: nanny

naranja: orange

narciso: daffodil

nariz: nose

narración: narrative

narrar: tell

narrativa: fiction

nata: skin

natación: swim, swimming

natal: native

natilla: custard, pudding

nato: born, natural

natural: natural

naturaleza: nature, quality

naturaleza humana: human nature

naturaleza muerta: still life

naturalidad: naturalness

naturalmente: naturally

naufragio: wreck

nauseabundo: foul

náuseas: sickness

náutico: maritime

navaja para rasurarse: razor

naval: naval

nave: craft, vessel

nave espacial: spacecraft, spaceship

navegación: navigation

navegador: browser

navegar: navigate, sail, surfing

navegar a vela: sail

navegar entre canales: channel-surfing

Navidad: Christmas

navío: vessel

NBA: NBA

Neanderthal: Neanderthal

nébeda: catnip

neblina: fog, mist

nebulosa: nebula

nebulosa solar: solar nebula

nebuloso: foggy

necesariamente: necessarily

necesario: necessary

necesidad: necessity, need, requirement

necesitado: in need

necesitar: be in need of, need, require, take

necia: idiot

necio: idiot

néctar: nectar

necton: nekton

negación: negative

negado: useless

negando con la cabeza: with a shake of the head

negar(se): deny, refuse

negar con la cabeza: shake one's head

negativa: refusal

negativamente: negatively

negativismo: negativity

negativo: ill, negative

negligencia: neglect

negligencia profesional: malpractice

negociación: bargain, dispute, negotiation

negociar: bargaining,

hammer out, negotiate

negocio: business, concern, trade, transaction

negocios: interest

negra: quarter note

negro: black

nena: babe, baby

nene: babe, baby

Neptuno: Neptune

nervio: nerve

nervio óptico: optic nerve

nerviosamente: nervously, restlessly, uneasily

nerviosismo: nervousness

nervioso: anxious, nervous, restless, wired

net: net

netamente: neatly

neto: net

neumático: tire

neurona: neuron

neurona motora: motor neuron

neurona sensorial: sensory neuron

neutral: neutral

neutralidad: neutrality

neutro: neutral

neutrón: neutron

nevado: snowy

nevar: snow

nevera: refrigerator

newton: newton

ni: either, neither, nor

ni con mucho: not nearly, nowhere near

ni en sueños: would not dream of

ni falta hace decirlo: goes without saying

ni hablar de: never mind

ni mucho menos: far from

ni por asomo: nowhere near

ni siquiera cerca: nowhere near/not anywhere near

ni uno ni otro: neither

ni…ni: either

nido: nest

niebla: fog

nieta: grandchild, granddaughter

nieto: grandchild, grandson

nieve: ice cream, sherbet, snow

nimbo: nimbus

nimio: petty

ningún lugar: anywhere

ninguna: neither, no, none

ninguno: any, either, neither, no, none

niña: child, girl, kid, youngster

niña guía exploradora: brownie

niñera: babysitter, nanny

niñez: childhood, infancy

niño: boy, child, kid, youngster

niño prodigio: whiz kid

níquel: nickel

nítidamente: sharply
nitidez: sharpness
nítido: sharp
nitrato: nitrate
nitrógeno: nitrogen
nivel: league, level
nivel de vida: standard of living
nivel del mar: sea level
nivel freático: water table
nivelador: leveler
nivelarse: level off
no: no, not
No.: No.
no hay de qué: It's a pleasure/my pleasure, you're welcome
no importa: anyway, it doesn't matter, whatever
no más: no longer/any longer
no obstante: albeit, nevertheless, nonetheless
no poder: cannot
no transgénicos: GM-free
no tratado: untreated
noble: lord, noble
nocaut: knockout
noche: night, nite
noche de brujas: Halloween
noche y día: day and night/night and day
Nochebuena: Christmas Eve
noción: conception, idea
noctívago: nocturnal
nocturno: nocturnal, overnight
nódulo linfático: lymph node
nogal americano: hickory
nómada: nomad, nomadic
nómade: nomad
nombramiento: appointment, commission, nomination
nombrar: appoint, call, elect, name, nominate
nombre: first name, name, noun
nombre contable: count noun, countable noun
nombre de pila: first name
nombre del archivo: filename
nombre incontable: uncount noun
nombre propio: proper noun
nomenclatura binómica: binomial nomenclature
nómina: payroll
nómina de socios: membership
nominación: nomination
nominal: nominal
nominalmente: nominally
nominar: nominate
non: odd
nonagésimo: ninetieth

nonato: unborn
noquear: knock out
noreste: northeast, northeastern
nordeste: northeast, northeastern
noria: waterwheel
norma: norm, rule
norma de conducta: standard
normal: normal, ordinary, regular, standard
normalizar: standardize
normalmente: normally
norte: north
norte geográfico: true north
norte verdadero: true north
norteño: northerner
nos: ourselves, us
nos vemos: see you
nosotras: us, we
nosotros: us, we
nosotros (mismos): ourselves
nostalgia: longing
nota: mark, note
nota a pie de página: footnote
nota al margen: anecdotal scripting
nota al pie: footnote
nota de pie de página: footnote
nota necrológica: obituary
notable: impressive, marked, notable, of note, outstanding
notación: notation
notación científica: scientific notation
notar: detect, note, notice, spot
notas: handout
noticia: news, report, story
noticiario (formal): newscast
noticias: news
noticias de: word of
noticiero (informal): newscast
notificación: notification
notificar: notify
notoriamente: notoriously
notorio: notorious
novata: freshman, novice, rookie
novatada: hazing
novato: freshman, inexperienced, novice, raw, rookie
novedad: innovation, release
novedoso: novel
novela: novel
novela de misterio: mystery
novela de suspenso: mystery
novela romántica: romance
novela rosa: romance
novela de vaqueros:

western
novela del oeste: western
novelista: novelist
noveno: ninth
noventa: ninety
novia: bride, fiancée, girlfriend
noviembre: November
novio: boyfriend, bridegroom, fiancé, groom, lover
nube: cloud, puff
nube de electrones: electron cloud
Nube de Oort: Oort cloud
nublado: cloudy
nublar: cloud
nuclear: nuclear
núcleo: core, heart
núcleo externo: outer core
nucleótido: nucleotide
nudillo de la mano: knuckle
nudo: knot
nuera: daughter-in-law
nuestro: our, ours
nueva: news
nueve: nine
nuevo: brand-new, fresh, new
nuez: nut, walnut
nuez de Castilla: walnut
nulo: nil, null and void, void, zero
numerar: number
número: -sized, figure, issue, number, schtick
número atómico: atomic number
número complejo: complex number
número de la Seguridad Social: Social Security number
número de masa: mass number
número de muertos: death toll
número de placa: license number
número de víctimas: death toll, toll
número entero: integer
número irracional: irrational number
número másico: mass number
número primo: prime
número racional: rational number
número real: real number
numeroso: numerous
nunca: ever, never
nunca jamás: never ever
nupcial: bridal, marital
nupcias: marriage
nutrición: nutrition
nutriente: nutrient
nutritivo: nutritious

Ñ
ñame: yam

O
o: either, else, or
o…o: either, else

olvidadizo

oasis: oasis

obedecer: obey

obejtivo de gran aumento: high power lens

obertura: opening

obesidad: obesity

obeso: fat, obese

obispo: bishop

obituario: obituary

objeción: objection

objetar: object, take exception to something

objetivamente: in perspective, objectively

objetividad: objectivity

objetivo: end, idea, objective, objective lens, purpose, target

objeto: aim, artifact, item, object, target

objeto curioso: curiosity

objeto de oro: gold

objeto directo: direct object

objeto indirecto: indirect object

objeto perdido: lost and found

objetos de cerámica: ceramics

objetos de valor: valuables

objetos de vidrio: glass

objetos perdidos: lost and found

objetos salvados: salvage

obligación: duty, obligation

obligar: bind, force, make, oblige, push, require

obligar a: compel, drive

obligar a alguien a hacer algo: bully somebody into something

obligatorio: binding, compulsory

obra: piece, play, work

obra de teatro: theater

obra dramática: drama

obra en construcción: site

obra maestra: masterpiece

obra suya: of one's own making

obrar mal: be in the wrong

obras viales: roadwork

obrera: laborer, worker

obrero: blue-collar, laborer, worker

obsceno: indecent

obscuridad: blackness

obscuro: black

obsequiar: treat

obsequio: gift, treat

observación: observation, point, remark, scrutiny, surveillance

observador: observer

observadora: observer

observancia: observance

observar: eye, look, monitor, observe, remark, watch

obsesión: obsession

obsesionado: obsessed

obsesionar(se): obsess

obstaculizar: impede

obstáculo: bar, hurdle, obstacle, speed bump, stumbling block

obstinación: stubbornness

obstinadamente: stubbornly

obstinado: insistent, stubborn

obstinarse: insist

obstruccionismo: filibuster

obstruido: plugged

obstruir: clog

obtener: acquire, derive, drum up, elicit, get, obtain, score

obtener una victoria: triumph

obturador: shutter

obviamente: clearly, obviously

obvio: distinct, obvious

ocasión: occasion, time

ocasional: casual, occasional, odd

ocasionalmente: occasionally

ocasionar: give rise to, produce

occidental: western, westerner

Occidente: west

océano: ocean, sea

oceanografía: oceanography

ochenta: eighty

ochentavo: eightieth

ocho: eight, figure eight

ocio: pleasure

ociosamente: idly

ocioso: idle

ocre: beige

octagésimo: eightieth

octava: eighth note

octava parte: eighth

octavo: eighth

octubre: October

ocular: eyepiece

ocultamiento: concealment, suppression

ocultar: conceal, cover up, disguise, hide, hold back, keep, mask, screen, suppress, sweep under the carpet/rug, tuck away, withhold

ocultar micrófonos: bug

oculto: hidden, underlying

ocupación: occupation

ocupado: busy, busy signal, occupied

ocupante: occupant

ocupar(se): eat into, fill, line, occupy, take

ocupar un lugar sin derecho: squat

ocuparse de: deal with, handle, look after, man, see about, see to

ocurrente: funny

ocurrir(se): come about,

cross one's mind, happen, occur, think

odiar: hate

odio: hate, hatred

odisea: odyssey

odómetro: odometer

oeste: west, westward

ofenderse: take offense

ofendido: hurt, injured, offended

ofensa: insult, offense, slight

ofensiva: offense, offensive

ofensivo: offensive

oferta: bid, offer, offering, proposal, proposition

ofender: insult, offend

oficial: officer, official

oficial de policía: police officer

oficialmente: officially

oficina: bureau, office

oficina central: headquarters, HQ

oficina de atención al público: front office

oficina que da a la calle: storefront

oficinista: clerk, white-collar

oficio religioso: service

ofrecer: bid, host

ofrecer servicios: cater

ofrecer un servicio: hire out

ofrecer una disculpa: apologize

ofrecer(se): offer

ofrecerse: volunteer

ofrecimiento: offer

ofrezca: obo

ofuscar: blind, cloud

oh: aw

oído: ear, hearing

¡oiga!: hey

oír: hear, listen, tune in

oír de: hear from

oír razones: listen

oírse: sound

ojal: buttonhole, eye

ojeada: look

ojear: glance

ojera: bag

o.o: eye

ojo compuesto: compound eye

ojo morado: black eye

ola: water wave, wave

oleada: glow, wave

oleaje: surf, swell

óleo: oil paint, oil painting

oler: reek, scent, smell, sniff

oler a: smack

olfatear: scent, sniff

olfato: smell

oligoelemento: trace gas

olimpiadas: Olympic Games

olímpico: Olympic

olivo: olive

olla: kettle, pot

olor: odor, scent, smell

olor corporal: body odor

olvidadizo: forgetful

olvidar(se): forget, leave, omit

omelet: omelet

omitir: cut, miss, omit, skip

omnipresente: ubiquitous

omnívora: omnivore

omnívoro: omnivore, omnivorous

OMS: WHO, World Health Organization

once: eleven

once de septiembre: nine-eleven

onceavo: eleventh

onda: wave

onda (primaria): P wave

onda de radio: radio wave

onda de superficie: surface wave

onda electromagnética: electromagnetic wave

onda estacionaria: standing wave

onda expansiva: shock wave

onda longitudinal: longitudinal wave

onda radioeléctrica: radio wave

onda S: S-wave

onda sonora: sound wave

onda superficial: surface wave

onda transversa: transverse wave

ondear: flap, fly, wave

ondulado: wavy

ondularse: curl

onomatopeya: onomatopoeia

onza: ounce, oz.

opacar: dull

opaco: dull, low

opción: option

opción a la compra de acciones: stock option

opcional: optional, voluntary

ópera: opera

operación: operation, surgery, transaction

operador: operator, worker

operador de bolsa: trader

operadora: operator, worker

operadora de bolsa: trader

operar: operate, run, work

operaria: operative, operator

operario: operative, operator

operístico: operatic

opinar: feel

opinión: contention, feeling, idea, judgment, opinion, point, point of view, sentiment, thought, verdict, view

opino: I think

oponente: opponent

oponer(se): fight back, oppose, put up

oporto: port

oportunidad: break, chance, opening, opportunity, scope, shot, timing

oportunidades iguales: equal opportunity

oportuno: convenient, ripe

oposición: opposition

opositor: opponent

opositora: opponent

oprimir: punch

optar: choose, opt

optar por: go for

optar por no hacer algo: opt out

optativo: elective

optimismo: optimism

optimista: hopeful, optimist, optimistic, positive, upbeat

opuesto: opposed, opposite, reverse

opuesto a: hostile

oración: clause, prayer, sentence

oración adjetiva: relative clause

oración compuesta: compound

oración de relativo: relative clause

oración principal: main clause

oración subordinada: subordinate clause

orador: speaker

oradora: speaker

oral: oral, verbal

oralmente: orally

oratorio: oratorio

órbita: orbit

órbita retrógrada: retrograde orbit

orbitar: orbit

orden: command, directive, instruction, mandate, order, sequence, warrant

orden del día: agenda

orden ejecutiva: executive order

orden mordaza: gag order

orden público: law and order

orden restrictiva: restraining order

ordenado: neat, settled

ordenador: computer

ordenar: boss, command, instruct, order, sort, straighten, straighten up

ordeña: milking

ordeñar: milk

ordinario: coarse, crude, mediocre

oreja: ear

orfanatorio: institution

orgánicamente: organically

orgánico: organic, organizational

organismo: organism

organismo transgénico: GMO

organista: organist

organización: business, fraternity, organization, setup

Organización Mundial de la Salud: World Health Organization

organizado: organized

organizador: organizer, steward

organizadora: organizer, stewardess

organizar: get together, line up, marshal, organize, put on, sort, throw

organizativo: organizational

órgano: organ

órgano de cañones: pipe organ

órgano de tubos: pipe organ

órgano rudimentario: vestigial structure

órgano sensorio: receptor

órganos internos: insides

orgánulo: organelle

orgullo: pride

orgullosamente: proudly

orgulloso: proud

orientación: counseling, guidance, orientation

orientado: oriented

orientador: counselor

orientador vocacional: guidance counselor

orientadora: counselor

orientadora vocacional: guidance counselor

oriental: eastern, oriental

orientar(se): counsel, gear, gear up, find one's way, get/find one's bearings

oriente: east

Oriente Medio: Middle East

orificio de ventilación: vent

origen: germ, origin, source

original: colorful, funky, manuscript, original

originalidad: originality

originalmente: originally

originario de: native

originarse: originate

orilla: bank, edge, shore

orilla del camino: roadside

orilla del lago: lakefront

orín: rust

orina: urine

orinar: urinate

orinarse: wet oneself/ the bed

oriol: oriole

oro: gold

oropéndola: oriole

orquesta: orchestra

orquesta sinfónica: symphony orchestra

orquestal: orchestral

ortodoxo: orthodox

ortografía: orthography, spelling
ortopédico: orthopedic
ortopedista: orthopedic
oruga: caterpillar
osadía: daring
osado: daring
osar: dare
oscilación: swing
oscilar: swing
oscuramente: darkly
oscuridad: darkness, obscurity
oscuro: dark, obscure
óseo: skeletal
oso: bear
ostentosamente: expensively
ostinato: ostinato
ostión: oyster
ostra: oyster
otomana: ottoman
otoño: autumn, fall
otorgar: accord, award, give, grant
otorgar un permiso: license
otorgar una licencia: license
otra: other
otra cosa: another matter/a different matter, else
otra parte: else, somewhere
otra vez: again, over
otro: another, fresh, further, other
otro asunto: another matter/a different matter
otro cantar: a different story
otro lugar: else
otro tanto: likewise
ovación: acclaim, cheer
ovacionar: cheer
oval: oval
ovalado: oval
óvalo: oval
oveja: sheep
overol: coveralls, overall
óvulo: egg, ovule
oxidarse: rust
óxido: rust
oxígeno: oxygen
oye: say
¡oye!: doh, hey
oyente: listener
ozono: ozone

P

pa: pop
pabellón de los condenados a muerte: death row
PAC: PAC
paciencia: patience
paciente: patient
pacientemente: patiently
pacíficamente: peacefully
pacífico: peaceful
pacto: pact
padecer: suffer
padecimiento: illness
padrastro: stepfather

padre: father, parent
padre soltero: single parent
padres: folks
padrino: attendant
padrino de bodas: best man
padrón: register, registration, roll
paga: pay
pagano: pagan
pagar: pay, pay back, pay up, pony up, repay, settle
pagar a plazos: spread
pagar dividendos: pay dividends
pagar la cuenta: check out
pagar la fianza: make bail
pagar por adelantado: pre-pay
pagaré: promissory note
página: page
página (de un sitio de internet): web page
página web: web page
pago: payment, repayment
pago contra entrega: C.O.D.
pago inicial: deposit
país: country, land, nation
paisaje: landscape, scenery
paisajismo: landscaping
Paisley: paisley
paja: straw
pajarera: aviary
pájaro: bird
pajita: straw
pala: blade, scoop, shovel, spade
palabra: language, word
palabra clave: keyword
palabra de uso frecuente: high-frequency word
palabra por palabra: word for word
palacio: palace
paladar: roof
paladín: champion
palanca de velocidades: gearshift, stick shift
palangana: basin
palco: box
palco de platea: orchestra
palear: shovel
paleontóloga: paleontologist
paleontología: paleontology
paleontólogo: paleontologist
palestra: arena
paleta: blade, paddle, palette knife, trowel
pálidamente: dully
pálido: dull, light, pale
palillo: stick
palito de pescado: fish stick
paliza: whipping
palma: palm

palmada: pat
palmearse: smack
palmera: palm
palo: stick
palo de golf: club, golf club
paloma: pigeon
palomita: check mark
palomitas: popcorn
palote: rolling pin
palpar: feel, feel for, finger
palpitar: beat
pan: bread
pan comido: cakewalk
pan de centeno: rye
pan francés: French toast
pan integral: wholewheat
pan tostado: toast
panadera: baker
panadería: bakery
panadero: baker
pancarta: banner
panceta: bacon
pancito: roll
panda: giant panda, panda
panda gigante: giant panda
pandereta: tambourine
pandero: tambourine
pandilla: band, gang
pandillera: gangster
pandillero: gangster
panecillo: popover
panel: panel
panel solar: solar collector
panelista: panelist
Pangaea: Pangaea
pánico: panic
panorama: landscape, outlook, scenery
panquecito: muffin
panqueque: muffin
pantalla: desktop, front, screen
pantalla de plasma: plasma screen
pantalón: trousers
pantalones: pants, trousers
pantalones cargo: cargo pants
pantalones cortos: shorts
pantalones de peto: overall
pantano: bog, marsh, swamp
panteón: cemetery
pantomima: pantomime
pants: sweats
pantufla: slipper
panza: belly
pañal: diaper
paño para lavarse: washcloth
pañuelo: handkerchief
pañuelo desechable: tissue
papa: potato, potato chip
papá: dad, father
papalote: kite
paparazzi: paparazzi
papás: folks
papas a la francesa:

French fries, fries
papas fritas: chips, French fries, fries
papel: line, paper, part, role
papel aluminio: foil
papel confort: toilet paper
papel de baño: toilet paper
papel de cera: wax paper
papel de china: tissue
papel de seda: tissue
papel destacado: high profile
papel encerado: wax paper
papel higiénico: toilet paper
papel periódico: newspaper
papel principal: lead
papel sanitario: toilet paper
papel tapiz: wallpaper
papeleo: red tape
papeleo burocrático: paperwork
papelera: wastebasket
papeleta: ticket
papelito habla: in black and white
papi: daddy
papila gustativa: taste bud
papito: daddy
paquete: bundle, mailer, pack, package, packet, parcel, pkg.
paquete postal: parcel post
par: couple, even, pair, peer
para: for, in order to, to
para (la hora): of
para bien: for the better
para llevar: to go
para que: so
para siempre: for good, forever
parabrisas: windshield
paracaídas: parachute
parada: layover, save, stand, stop
parada de descanso: rest area, rest stop
parada de taxi: cab stand
parada de taxis: taxi stand
paradero: stop
paradero de camiones: truck stop
paradero de taxis: taxi stand
parado: idle, on one's feet
parafrasear: paraphrase
paráfrasis: paraphrase
paraguas: umbrella
paraíso: heaven, paradise
paralaje: parallax
paralelismo: parallel
paralelismo sintáctico: parallelism
paralelo: parallel
paralización: standstill
paralización del tráfico: gridlock
paralizado: paralyzed

paralizar: paralyze
paralizarse: freeze, seize up
paramecio: paramecium
parámetro: framework
páramo: wilderness
parar(se): break, check, cut out, get up, get/rise to one's feet, halt, let up, pull up, stand, stay
parar a alguien en seco: stop somebody dead
parar el gol: save
parar repentinamente: break off
pararrayos: lightning rod
pararse en dos patas: rear
parásita: parasitic
parasitismo: parasitism
parásito: consumer, parasite, parasitic
parcela: patch, plot
parchar: patch
parche: patch
parcial: biased, partial
parcialidad: bias
parcialmente: partially
¿te parece?: okay
parecer: appear, approximate, come over, find, look, resemble, seem, sound, strike, take after
parecer adecuado: see fit
parecer apropriado: see fit
parecer conveniente: see fit
parecerle a uno: should think
parecido: resemblance, similar, similarity
pared: wall
pared celular: cell wall
pared colgante: hanging wall
pared de la célula: cell wall
pared interior: lining
pareja: couple, date, mate, partner
parejo: even, level
paréntesis: interlude
pariente: next of kin, own flesh and blood, relation, relative
pariente de: related
parientes políticos: in-laws
parir: give birth
parlamentaria: Member of Parliament
parlamentario: Member of Parliament, parliamentary
parlamento: parliament
parlotear: babble, chatter
parlotero: chatter
paro: shutdown
paro carbonero: chickadee
paro de labores: walkout
parpadear: blink, wink
parpadeo: blink
párpado: eyelid
parque: park

parque de diversiones: amusement park
parque industrial: industrial park
parra: vine
párrafo: paragraph
parranda: bash
parrandera: reveler
parrandero: reveler
parrilla: grill
parrilla superior del horno: broiler
parrillada: barbecue, cookout
parroquia: parish
parte: element, line, part, party, piece, portion, proportion, quota, section, segment, share, side, slice
parte acusadora: prosecution
parte de: part and parcel
partera: midwife
participación: involvement, part, participation
participante: attendee, competitor, entry, participant
participar: enter into, feature, fight, get into, participate, take part
participar en: be in on, join, join in
participio: participle
partícula: particle
partícula alfa: alpha particle
partícula beta: beta particle
particular: particular, private
particularmente: especially, notably, particularly, specially
partida: departure, departures
partida decisiva: playoff
partidaria: supporter, sympathizer
partidario: partisan, supporter, sympathizer
partidarios: friends
partido: match, party, scrimmage
partido de desquite: rematch
partido de práctica: scrimmage
partido de revancha: rematch
partir(se): break off, crack, depart, set off, split
partir en dos: halve
partitura: score
parto: delivery, labor
pasa: raisin
pasadas: after, past
pasado: last, past, up
pasado de moda: dated, old-fashioned, outdated
pasado meridiano: p.m.
pasador: bobby pin, catch, clip

pasaje: fare, passage
pasajera: passenger
pasajero: passenger, passing
pasamontañas: balaclava
pasando: past
pasante de maestro: teaching assistant
pasaporte: passport
pasar: be traded, drop by, drop in, elapse, give away, go by, go past, move, pass, run, screen, show, slip, spend, transfer, wear off
pasar a: get on to, stop by
pasar a duras penas: scrape through
pasar a la historia: go down in history
pasar a máquina: type up
pasar a mejor vida: pass away
pasar a ver: call on
pasar apenas: scrape through
pasar apuros: be in dire/ desperate straits
pasar como rayo: flash
pasar de mano en mano: change hands
pasar de moda: date
pasar de panzazo: scrape through
pasar el rato: hang out, while away
pasar estrecheces: feel the pinch
pasar fuera cierto tiempo: stay out
pasar haciendo mucho ruido: thunder past
pasar hambre: go hungry, starve
pasar información: tip off
pasar la aspiradora: vacuum
pasar la bolita: pass the buck
pasar la comunicación: put through
pasar la cuenta: bill
pasar las vacaciones: vacation
pasar por: call for, go round
pasar por alto: miss, overlook, pass over
pasar por encima de: override
pasar un buen rato: have a ball
pasar una etapa: grow out of
pasar volando: flash, zoom
pasarla bien: have a ball
pasarle factura a: invoice
pasar(se) por la cabeza: cross one's mind
pasarse de la raya: go too far
pasarse la embriaguez: sober up
pasatiempo: hobby, pursuit

pascal: pascal
Pascua: Easter
pase: pass
pase de abordar: boarding pass
pase usted: after you
pasear(se): pace, wander
paseo: drive, ride, stroll, walk, wander
pasillo: aisle, hall, hallway, landing, passage
pasión: passion
pasiva: passive
pasivamente: passively
pasivo: debit, liability, passive
paso: access, footstep, move, pace, passage, passing, step, walk, way
paso a desnivel: overpass
paso a nivel: railroad crossing
(mover) paso a paso: inch, step by step
paso de tortuga: crawl
paso elevado: overpass
paso en falso: misstep
paso superior: overpass
pasta: pasta, paste
pasta blanda: softcover
pasta de dientes: toothpaste
pasta dentífrica: toothpaste
pastar: graze
pastel: cake, pie
pastel de chocolate y nueces: brownie
pastel de frutas: shortcake
pastel de queso: cheesecake
pastelera: baker
pastelería: bakery
pastelero: baker
pastilla: tablet
pastilla de menta: mint
pastizal: grassland
pasto: grass, lawn
pastor: minister, shepherd
pastor alemán: German shepherd
pastora: minister, shepherd
pastura: pasture
pata: leg, paw
patada: kick, kickoff, shot
patada a botepronto: drop kick
patada inicial: kickoff
patalear: kick
pateador: kicker
pateadora: kicker
patear: kick, shoot, stamp
patentar: patent
patente: apparent, manifest, patent
paternal: paternal
paternidad: parenthood
patéticamente: pathetically
patético: pathetic
patillas: sideburns
patín: runner

patinador: skater
patinadora: skater
patinaje: skating
patinar: skate, skid
patinazo: skid
patines de hielo: ice skates
patines de ruedas: roller skates
patines en línea: in-line skates
patio: barnyard, courtyard, yard
patio (ferrocarriles): yard
patio de recreo: playground
patio trasero: backyard
pato: duck
patria: homeland
patrimonio: heritage
patriota: patriot, patriotic
patriotismo: patriotism
patrocinador: backer, patron, sponsor
patrocinadora: backer, patron, sponsor
patrocinar: sponsor
patrocinio: sponsorship
patrón: employer, master, pattern, skipper
patrón de movimiento: movement pattern
patrona: employer, skipper
patrulla: patrol
patrulla de reconocimiento: scout
patrullar: patrol, police
patrullero: patrolman
pausa: break, pause, truce
pausadamente: deliberately
pauta: guideline, indication
pava: kettle
pavimentar: pave
pavimento: pavement
pavo: turkey
pavonearse: strut
pay: pie
payasa: clown
payasear: clown
payaso: clown
paz: peace
PBS: PBS
PC: BTW
PC (computadora personal): PC
PDF: PDF
peaje: toll
peatón: pedestrian
peatona: pedestrian
peca: sunspot
pecado: sin
pecador: sinner
pecar: sin
pecar de: to err on the side of
pecera: fishbowl
pecho: breast, chest
pechuga: breast
pectoral: pectoral
peculiar: peculiar
peculiarmente: peculiarly

pedacito: chip, scrap
pedagoga: educator
pedagogo: educator
pedal: pedal
pedalear: pedal
pedazo: chunk, gob, length, piece
pedestal: stand
pedestre: pedestrian
pediatra: pediatrician
pedido: order
pedir: ask, hit up, order, press, seek, send for, send off for
pedir a gritos: cry out for
pedir identificación: card
pedir prestado: borrow
pedir un permiso: take off
pegado: form-fitting, plastered, tight
pegajoso: icky, sticky
pegamento: adhesive, glue
pegar: attach, bash, catch, cement, fasten, knock, paste, stick, tack on
pegar con cinta adhesiva: tape
pegar(se): flatten, glue
pegársele a alguien: tag along
peinar: comb, style
peine: comb
pelaje: coat, fur
pelar: peel, shell
pelar (verduras): shuck
peldaño: stair
pelea: fight, quarrel
pelea a puñetazos: fistfight
peleador: fighter
peleadora: fighter
pelear(se): battle, fall out, fight, quarrel
pelear (por algo): scramble
peliagudo: nasty, tough, tricky
película: feature, film, motion picture, movie, picture
película adherente: plastic wrap
película de vaqueros: western
película del oeste: western
película para mujeres: chick flick
peligro: danger, distress, hazard, threat
peligrosamente: dangerously
peligroso: dangerous, risky, rough
pelirrojo: ginger, red
pellejo: hide
pellizcar: pinch
pellizco: pinch
pelo: coat, fur, hair, pile, strand
pelo absorbente o radical: root hair
pelota: ball
pelota de futbol: football
peluca: wig

peludo: hairy
peluquera: barber
peluquero: barber
pelusa: lint
pena: embarrassment, grief, penalty, pity, shame
pena capital: capital punishment
penal: criminal, penalty
penalti: penalty
penalty: penalty
pendiente: earring, grade, incline, outstanding, pending, slope
pendiente resbaladiza: slippery slope
péndulo: swing
pene: penis
penetración: penetration
penetrante: strong
penetrar: break through, penetrate, surge
península: peninsula
penitenciaría: penitentiary
penosamente: distressingly, embarrassingly
penoso: bitter, sticky, troublesome
pensamiento: thinking, thought
pensar: contemplate, envisage, feel, guess, puzzle, reason, reflect, see, think, think over
pensar de: make of
pensar detenidamente: think through
pensar en: be on one's mind, give thought/attention (to), intend, plan on, think in terms of
pensar sobre: feel
pensativo: thoughtful
pensión: kennel, pension, rooming house
pensión alimenticia: maintenance
pensión completa: room and board
pensión para el mantenimiento de los hijos: child support
Pentágono: Pentagon
pentagrama: staff
penumbra: gloom
peñasco: rock
peñón: rock
peón: laborer, pawn
peón de campo: field hand
peor: worse, worst
pepino: cucumber
pequeña empresa: small business
pequeña escala: small-scale
pequeño: fine, insignificant, little, petite, small
pera: pear
percatarse: find, see
percentil: percentile

percepción: perception
perceptible: audible, noticeable
perceptiblemente: noticeably
percha: roost
percibir: perceive
percusión: percussion
perdedor: loser
perdedora: loser
perder(se): go, lose, lose one's way, miss, shed, stray, waste
perder color o intensidad: fade
perder contacto: lose touch
perder de las manos: slip from one's grasp
perder de vista: lose sight of
perder el conocimiento: pass out
perder el control de: bobble
perder el equilibrio: topple
perder el rastro: lose track of
perder el sueño: lose sleep
perder la cabeza: lose one's head
perder la calma: lose one's head
perder la compostura: break down
perder la conciencia: lose consciousness
perder la cuenta: lose count
perder la esperanza: despair
perder la paciencia: lose one's temper
perder los estribos: lose one's temper
perder pie: flounder
perderse uno algo: miss
perdición: downfall
pérdida: loss, waste
perdido: lost, missing, stray
perdido de vista: long-lost
perdón: excuse me, forgiveness
¿Perdón?: pardon, sorry?
perdonar(se): forgive, let off
perdurable: lasting
perdurar: endure, remain
peregrino: pilgrim
perejil: parsley
perenne: perennial
perezosamente: lazily
perezoso: idle, lazy
perfección: perfection
perfeccionar(se): improve, perfect, polish, refine
perfectamente: perfectly
perfecto: perfect, thorough
perfil: profile
perforadora: punch
perforar: bore, drill, pierce, punch

performance: gig
perfume: perfume, scent
pericia: expertise
perico: parrot
periferia: suburb
perífrasis verbal: verb phrase
perihelio: perihelion
perilla: knob
perímetro: perimeter
periódicamente: periodically
periódico: journal, newspaper, paper, periodical
periódico amarillista: tabloid
periódico sensacionalista: tabloid
periodismo: journalism
periodista: journalist
periodo: era, period, span, time
período: period, spell, stretch, term
periodo de atención: span
periodo de descanso: downtime
periodo de gestación: gestation period
período de onda: wave period
período de revolución: period of revolution
período de rotación: period of rotation
periodo generacional generation time
periodo glaciar: Ice Age
perita: surveyor
peritaje: survey
perito: surveyor
perjudicar: count against, damage, prejudice
perjudicarse: suffer
perjudicial: damaging
perla: pearl
permafrost: permafrost
permanecer: remain, stay on
permanencia: permanence
permanente: permanent
permanentemente: chronically, forever, permanently
permeabilidad: permeability
permeable: permeable
permisible: permissible
permiso: authority, leave, license, permission, permit
permiso para conducir: driver's license, learner's permit
permitir: allow, enable, permit
permitir(se): let
permutación: permutation
pernera: leg
perno: pin
pero: but, only
perplejo: staggered,

stunned
perra: bitch
perrera: doghouse
perrito: puppy
perro: dog
persecución: chase, persecution
perseguidor: persecutor, pursuer
perseguidora: persecutor, pursuer
perseguir: chase, dog, follow, haunt, persecute, pursue, stalk
perseguir y atrapar: chase down
perseverar: stick with
persiana: blind, shade
persistencia: persistence
persistente: persistent, stubborn
persistentemente: persistently, stubbornly
persistir: insist, linger, persist, remain
persona: individual, person, self, soul
persona a cargo: dependent
personaje: character, figure
personaje estereotipado: stock character
personal: household, individual, personal, personnel, staff, workforce
personalidad: figure, force, personality, self
personalmente: in person, personally
personas: people
personificación: itself
perspectiva: perspective, prospect, scenario, standpoint
perspectiva aérea: aerial perspective, atmospheric perspective
perspectiva angular: two-point perspective
perspectiva con un solo punto de fuga: one-point perspective
perspectiva de dos conjuntos: two-point perspective
perspectiva lineal: linear perspective
perspicacia: perception
perspicaz: perceptive, quick study, sharp
persuadir: get, induce, influence, talk into
persuadir de: persuade
persuasión: persuasion
persuasivo: compelling
pertenecer: belong
pertenencias: belongings
perturbación: disruption, disturbance
perturbación tropical: tropical disturbance
perturbado: disturbed
perturbador: disturbing, unsettling

perturbadoramente: disturbingly
perturbar: disrupt, disturb
perverso: wicked
pesadamente: heavily
pesadilla: nightmare
pesado: heavy, rich, tiresome
pesar: regret, sorrow
pesar(se): weigh
pesas: weights
pesca: fishing
pescado: fish
pescado capeado con papas fritas: fish and chips
pescador: fisherman
pescar: fish
pésimo: miserable, rotten
peso: heaviness, load, weight
peso específico: specific gravity
peso ligero: lightweight
peso pesado: heavyweight
pestaña: eyelash, lash
peste: reek
peste (bubónica): plague
pesticida: pesticide
pestillo: catch
petaca: suitcase
pétalo: petal
petanca (inglesa): bowling
petición: petition, plea, request
petirrojo: robin
petrificado: numb
petróleo: kerosene, oil, petroleum
petróleo crudo: crude oil
(barco) petrolero: tanker
pez: fish
pez dorado: goldfish
pez gordo: heavyweight
pezuña: hoof
piadoso: saintly
pianista: pianist
piano: piano
picada: tailspin
picante: spicy
picar(se): bait, bite, chop up, cut up, itch, mince, punch, smart, sting, tickle
picar en cubitos: dice
pícaro: dirty
picazón: itch
pichón: pigeon
pick-up: truck
picnic: picnic
picnic al lado de un coche: tailgate party
pico: beak
pico piramidal: horn
picor: itch
picoso: hot
pie: bottom, cue, foot
piedad: mercy
piedra: rock, stone
piedra (preciosa): stone
piedra angular: keystone
piedra caliza: chalk
piedrita: pebble
piel: coat, fur, hide,

leather, skin

pieles: fur

piercing: piercing

pierna: leg

pieza: item, part, piece, track

pieza en exposición: exhibit

pieza simple: simple machine

pigmento: pigment

pijama: pajamas

pila: battery, heap, pile, stack

pilar: pillar

pilates: Pilates

píldora: pill

pileta: pool, sink, swimming pool

pillar: loot

pillo: crook

pilotar: pilot

pilotear: pilot

piloto: pilot

pimentero: pepper shaker

pimentón: pepper

pimienta: pepper

pimiento: pepper

pimiento dulce: bell pepper

pincel: brush, paintbrush

pinchar: pierce, spear

pingüino: penguin

pino: pine

pinta: pint

pintalabios: lipstick

pintar: color, color in, decorate, paint, painting

pintar su raya: draw the line

pintor: painter

pintora: painter

pintoresco: colorful, old world, quaint, scenic

pintura: paint, picture

pintura abstracta: abstract

pintura al óleo: oil paint, oil painting

pintura de labios: lipstick

pinza(s): pliers

piña: cone, pineapple

piojo: cootie, louse

pionera: pioneering

pionero: pioneering

pipa: pipe

piquete: bite, sting

pirámide: pyramid

pirámide energética: energy pyramid

pirata: pirate, pirated, unlicensed

piratear: pirate

pisada: footprint, track

pisar: press, step, tread

pisar el acelerador: step on the gas

piscina: pool, swimming pool

piso: floor, level, story, suite

pisotear: stamp, stomp

pista: clue, lead, track

pista de aterrizaje: runway

pista de carreras:

raceway

pista falsa: red herring

pista para carreras de motocicletas: speedway

pistilo: pistil

pistola: pistol

pistolera: gangster

pistolero: gangster, gunman

pitar: whistle

pitazo: tip-off

pítcher: pitcher

pits: pits (auto racing)

piyama: pajamas, pjs

piyamada: slumber party

pizarra: chalkboard, slate

pizarrón: board, chalkboard

pizca: dash, grain, ounce, pinch, scrap

pizza: pizza

placa: badge, license plate, plate

placa tectónica: tectonic plate

placas: plates

placenta: placenta

placentero: enjoyable

placer: delight, enjoyment, pleasure

plaga: pest, plague

plan: agenda, plan, schedule, scheme, strategy

plan de estudios: curriculum

plan de jubilación: retirement plan

plan de pagos: installment plan

plan de retiro: retirement plan

plancha: iron, push-up

plancha bimetálica: bimetallic strip

planchado: ironing

planchar: iron, press

plancton: plankton

planeador: glider

planear: engineer, line up, map out, plan, plan on, soar

planeta: planet

planeta enano: dwarf planet

planeta similar a la Tierra: terrestrial planet

planeta terrestre, telúrico o rocoso: terrestrial planet

planetario: planetary

planicie: plain

planificación: planning

planificador: planner

planificadora: planner

planificar: map out

planimetría: survey

planisferio: map

plano: flat, level, plan, plane

plano abisal: abyssal plain

plano inclinado: inclined plane

planta: plant, sole

planta baja: first floor

planta de producción: shop floor

planta de tratamiento de aguas residuales: sewage treatment plant

planta laboral: workforce

planta sin sistema vascular: nonvascular plant

planta vascular: vascular plant

planta verde: green plant

plantación: plantation

plantar: plant, sow

plantar de: planting

plantar en maceta: pot

plantear: bring up, lay out, pose, set

plaqueta: platelet

plástico: plastic

plástico adherente: plastic wrap

plata: silver

plataforma: bay, dock, platform, rig

plataforma continental: continental shelf

plataforma de lanzamiento: launch pad

plataforma petrolífera: oil platform

plátano: banana

platea: mezzanine, orchestra

plateado: silver

platería: silver

plática: chat, lecture, talk

platicar: chat, schmooze, talk

platina: slide, stage

platito para la taza: saucer

plato: course, dish, plate

plato de ensalada: side salad

plato rápido: short-order

platón: platter

plausible: credible

playa: beach, seaside

playera: T-shirt, top

plaza: market, plaza, square

plaza fuerte: stronghold

plazo: deadline, time

plebiscito: referendum

plegable: folding

plegar(se): fold, fold up

pleito: lawsuit

pleito a puñetazos: fistfight

plenamente: acutely

plenitud: fullness, prime

pleno: fulfilling, full

pliegue: crook, fold

pliegue monoclinal: monocline

pliegue sinclinal: syncline

plisado: pleated

plomera: plumber

plomería: plumbing

plomero: plumber

plomo: lead

pluma: feather, pen

pluma de contorno: contour feather

plumón: down, down

feather
plural: plural
pluricelular:
multicellular
Plutón: Pluto
población: population,
town
poblar: people
pobre: bad off, lame,
penniless, poor, weak
pobremente: poorly
pobreza: poverty
pocas veces: rarely
pocilga: pigpen
poco: few, light, lightly,
little, short
poco (tiempo): while
poco apropiado:
inappropriate
poco asado: rare
poco atractivo: plain
poco claro: unclear
poco convencional: off-
center, unconventional,
unorthodox
poco conveniente:
inconvenient
poco convincente: weak
poco costoso:
inexpensive
poco después: shortly
after
poco diplomático:
undiplomatic
poco importante: minor
poco natural: unnatural
poco normal: unnatural
poco ortodoxo:
unorthodox
poco práctico:
impractical
poco profundo: shallow
poco realista: unrealistic
poco revelador:
uninformative
poco saludable:
unhealthy
poco serio: lightweight
podadora de pasto:
lawnmower
podar: prune
podcast: podcast
poder(se): be able to, can,
force, get, leverage,
may, might, power
poder (manejar una
situación): handle
poder ganar: stand
to gain
poder legislativo:
legislature
poder más que: to get the
better of
poder más que uno:
catch up with
poderío: might
poderosamente:
powerfully
poderoso: mighty,
powerful
podía: could
podíamos: could
podían: could
podías: could
podómetro: pedometer
podría: could
podríamos: could

podrían: could
podrías: could
podrido: rotten
poema: poem, rhyme
poema sinfónico: tone
poem
poesía: poetry
poeta: poet
poetisa: poet
polar: polar
polea: pulley
polea fija: fixed pulley
polea móvil: movable
pulley
polémico:
confrontational,
controversial
poli: cop
policía: officer, police,
police force, policeman
policía de caminos:
highway patrol
policía de élite: SWAT
team
policía estatal: state
trooper
policía montada:
mounted police
policías: police
poliéster: polyester
polilla: moth
polinización: pollination
polinizar: pollinate
polinomio: polynomial
polio: polio
poliomielitis: polio
pólipo: polyp
poliqueto tubícola: tube
worm
política: policy, politics
política sanitaria: health
care
políticamente: politically
político: political,
politician
póliza de seguro: policy
pollo: chick, chicken
polluelo: chick
polo: pole
polo magnético:
magnetic pole
polvareda: dust
polvo: dust, powder
polvoriento: dusty
pompa: ceremony, luxury
ponchado: flat
ponchar(se): strike out
ponche: punch
ponderado: balanced
ponderar: gauge, ponder
ponencia: paper
poner(se): get, fit, go
down, lay, lodge, place,
play, post, pull, put,
put on, raise, set, sink,
stand, tune, turn, twist,
work up
poner (huevos): lay
poner (un apodo):
nickname
poner a enfriar: chill
poner a hervir: boil
poner a la venta: market
poner a prueba: pilot, put
to the test, try out
poner a punto: fine-tune
poner al corriente: fill in
poner al día: brief, update

poner altanto: put
somebody in the
picture
poner atención: beware
poner changuitos: cross
one's fingers
poner con cuchara:
spoon
poner de relieve:
spotlight, underline,
underscore
poner de su parte: pull
one's weight
poner droga: dope
poner el ejemplo: set an
example
poner el grito en el cielo:
hit the roof/go through
the roof
poner en circulación:
release
poner en duda:
challenge, question
poner en duda algo: cast
doubt on something
poner en escena: stage
poner en libertad: free,
release
poner en libertad
(prisión): discharge
poner en marcha: set the
wheels in motion
poner en peligro: breach,
endanger, expose
poner en práctica:
implement, put into
action, put into practice
poner en reversa: back
poner en riesgo:
endanger, threaten
poner en su lugar: put
(somebody) in their
place
poner en tela de juicio:
challenge, question
poner en un índice: index
poner énfasis:
emphasize, stress
poner fin a: put a stop to,
terminate, wind up
poner fuera de combate:
knock out
poner furioso: infuriate
poner gasolina: refuel
poner los nervios
de punta: get on
somebody's nerves
poner los pies en la
tierra: come back/
down to earth
poner mala cara: make/
pull a face
poner nervioso: rattle
poner objeción: object
poner precio: pricing
poner remedio: cure
poner sobre aviso: alert,
tip off
poner sus iniciales:
initial
poner término a:
terminate
poner un bozal: muzzle
poner un límite: draw
the line
poner una etiqueta: label
poner una marca: mark
poner una multa: fine

poner una señal: mark
poner una zancadilla: trip
poner(se) en fila: line up
ponerse (algo de ropa): get into
ponerse a: get down to, settle down
ponerse a dieta: diet
ponerse a disposición: oblige
ponerse a la altura: measure up
ponerse al día: catch up
ponerse colorado: flush
ponerse cómodo: settle oneself, sit back
ponerse de moda: catch on, come in
ponerse de parte de: come down on, side
ponerse de pie: get/rise to one's feet, rise, stand, stand up
ponerse el cinturón: buckle up
ponerse elegante: dress up
ponerse en blanco: go blank
ponerse en contacto (con): contact
ponerse en contacto con: get/grab ahold of
ponerse en cuclillas: hunker down, squat
ponerse en el piso: get down
ponerse furioso: see red
ponerse hecho una furia: fly into
ponerse o sentarse a horcajadas: straddle
ponerse rojo: flush
ponerse severo: clamp down
pongamos que: for the sake of argument
poniente: west, westward
pony: pony
pop: pop
popote: straw
popular: folk, hot, in (great) demand, popular
popularidad: popularity
poquito: a bit of a, minute
por: a, an, at, because, by, for, from, in, out of, per, through, times (multiplication), up, via
por accidente: accidental, by accident
por adelantado: up front
por ahí: by
por año: per annum
por aquí: around
por así decir: so to speak
por cabeza: a/per head
por casualidad: by chance, luckily
por ciento: percent
por cierto: by the way, incidentally
por completo: fully
por consiguiente:

therefore, thus
por cuenta propia: on someone's account
por cuenta y riesgo propios: at one's own risk
por debajo de: below
por dentro: inwardly
por derecho: by rights
por derecho propio: in one's own right
por día: per diem
¡por Dios!: (good) heavens
por ejemplo: e.g., for example, for instance, like, say
por el bien de: for the sake of
por el contrario: by contrast/in contrast/in contrast to
por el momento: at present, at the moment, for the time being
por el otro lado: other way round
por encargo: made to order
por encima: high, overhead, superficial
por encima (de): above, over
por escrito: down on paper
por eso: so, thus
por falta de: for want of
por favor: please
¡por favor!: honestly
por fibra óptica: fiber optics
por fin: at last/at long last, finally
por fortuna: fortunately, mercifully
por invitación: invitational
por la misma razón: by the same token
por lo demás: otherwise
por lo general: as a rule, in the main
por lo menos: at least, easily
por lo pronto: (in the) meantime
por lo tanto: hence, therefore, thus
por medio de: by means of
por menor: retail
por mi parte: for my part, myself
por miedo de: for fear of
por mucho: by far
por necesidad: of necessity
por no decir: if not
por no decir más: to say the least
por omisión: by default
por otra parte: furthermore, then
por persona: a/per head
por principio: on principle
por qué: why
por regla general: as

a rule
por satélite: satellite
por separado: separately
por si fuera poco: to add insult to injury
por si las dudas: in case/just in case
por sí mismo: for its/their own sake
por sí solo: in isolation, itself, of its own accord
por siempre: forever
por sobre: over
por su naturaleza: by its nature
por suerte: fortunately, luckily
por supuesto: by all means, certainly, of course
por supuesto que no: of course not
por todas partes: everywhere
por todo: throughout
por todos lados: everywhere, throughout
por tradición: traditionally
por último: finally
por un impulso: on impulse
por un valor de: worth (of)
por una parte: on the one hand
por una vez siquiera: for once
por unanimidad: unanimously
por vía intravenosa: intravenously
por vía secreta: on the grapevine
porcelana: china, porcelain
porcentaje: percentage, proportion
porche: porch
porción: patch, portion, section, serving
pormenores: particulars
porosidad: porosity
poroso: porous
poroto: bean
porque: as, because, cuz, in that, since
porquería: crud, garbage, trash
porra: nightstick
portaaviones: carrier
portada: cover
portaequipaje: luggage rack
portaequipajes: luggage rack
portafolios: briefcase
portaobjetos: slide, stage
portar: carry
portarse: behave
portarse bien: behave
portátil: portable
portavoz: herald, spokesman, spokesperson, spokeswoman
porte: presence

portera: goalie, goalkeeper, superintendent
portería: goal
portero: goalie, goalkeeper, superintendent
portón: gate
porvenir: future
posada: inn
posar: pose
posarse: perch, roost
posdata: P.S.
pose: pose
poseedor: holder
poseer: own, possess
posesión: possession
posesividad: possessiveness
posesivo: possessive
posibilidad: chance, likelihood, possibility, potential, prospect, scope
posibilidades de algo: fighting chance
posible: likely, possible, prospective
posiblemente: maybe, possibly, potentially
posición: location, position, posture, setting, stance
posición corporal: body position
posición del actor: actor's position
posición fetal: fetal position
positivamente: positively
positivo: positive
posponer: delay, hold off, postpone, put back, put off, table
posponer algo: put something on hold
posposición: postponement
possible: potential
postal: postcard
poste: pole, post
poste de la portería: goalpost
poste de servicios públicos: utility pole
poste de teléfonos: telephone pole
póster: poster
postergar: put off
posterior: later
posteriormente: subsequently
postigo: shutter
postizo: false
postor: bidder
postración: collapse
postre: dessert, sweet
postulación: nomination
postular: nominate
postura: line, posture, stance
potable: potable
potear: putt
potencia: potency, power, strength
potencia de entrada: input force

potencia de salida: output force
potencial: potential, prospective
potencial de hidrógeno: pH
potencial de mano de obra: workforce
potencialmente: potentially
potente: potent, powerful
potentemente: powerfully
potrero: field
pozo: pit, pot, shaft, well
pozo artesiano: artesian spring
PPO: PPO
PR: public relations
práctica: practice
prácticamente: for all intents and purposes, just about, next to, practically
practicante: practicing
practicar: go in for, practice
practicar rappel: rappel
práctico: convenient, functional, handy, practical
pradera: grassland, prairie
prado: lawn, pasture
precámbrico: Precambrian
precario: shaky, uneasy
precaución: caution, precaution
precavido: wary
precedente: precedent
preceder: lead up to, precede
preciado: precious, treasured
precio: charge, price
precio de lista: sticker price
precioso: darling, precious
precipicio: cliff
precipitación: precipitation
precipitación pluvial: rainfall
precipitado: rash, rushed
precipitar(se): dive, plunge, rush
precisamente: precisely, very
precisar: pin down
precisión: precision
preciso: accurate, express, fine, precise
precocial: precocial
precocido: ready-made
precursor: herald, pioneer
precursora: herald, pioneer
predecesor: predecessor
predecesora: predecessor
predecible: predictable
predecir: anticipate, forecast, predict
predestinado: doomed
predicar: preach

predicción: prediction
predilección: preference
predisponer: incline, prejudice
predispuesto: biased
predominante: prevailing
predominar: dominate
preestablecido: default
preestreno: preview
prefacio: preface
preferencia: like, preference
preferible: preferable
preferiblemente: preferably
preferido: of choice
preferir: favor, prefer, would just as soon
preferir hacer: would rather do
prefijo: prefix
pregunta: inquiry, question
preguntar(se): ask, fire questions, inquire, muse, question, quiz, wonder
preguntar (por): ask, query
preguntara: put a question to (somebody)
preguntas frecuentes: FAQ
preguntón: inquisitive
prejuicio: prejudice
preliminar: preliminary
prematuramente: prematurely
prematuro: premature
premédico: premed
premiado: prize
premiar: reward
premio: award, prize, reward
Premio Pulitzer: Pulitzer Prize
premisa: premise
premura: hurry
prenda: article
prenda de vestir: garment
prendas combinables: separates (clothing)
prendedor: brooch, pin
prender: light, put on, start, switch on, turn on
prender con alfileres: pin
prender fuego: set fire to
prenderse: light up
prensa: press
prensar: crush
preocupación: care, concern, consideration, headache, worry
preocupado: afraid, anxious, bothered, troubled, worried
preocupante: puzzling, worrisome
preocupar: alarm, bother, burden, trouble
preocupar(se): bother, care, fuss, worry
prepa: senior high school
prepagar: pre-pay
preparación:

preparation, preparedness, readiness

preparado: mix, poised, prepared, ready, ready-made

preparado para: prepared for

preparador: trainer

preparador físico: trainer

preparadora: trainer

preparadora física: trainer

preparar: brew, coach, equip, gear, groom, lay, lay out, prep, prepare, prime, put together

preparar comida: cook

preparar el terreno para: lead up to

preparar la comida: cooking

preparar para: prepare for

preparar(se): brace, get, train

prepararse: do one's homework, gear up, ready, warm up

preparativo: arrangement

preparativos: build-up, preparation

preparatoria: high school, senior high school

preposición: preposition

presa: convict, dam, detainee, prey, reservoir

presagiar: herald, promise

présbite: far-sighted

prescindir de: do without

prescribir: prescribe

prescripción: Rx

presencia: exposure, presence

presenciar: witness

presentación: packaging, presentation

presentaciones: introductions

presentador: anchor, emcee, host, newscaster

presentadora: anchor, emcee, host, newscaster

presentar(se): arise, come forward, develop, emcee, exhibit, file, forward, host, introduce, present, produce, put forward, report, represent, run, show, submit

presentar ante: go before

presentar con parcialidad: slant

presentar la renuncia: hand/give in one's notice

presentar respetos: pay one's respects

presentar una demanda: petition

presentar una petición: petition

presentarse a una prueba: try out for

presente: gift, present

presentimiento: instinct

preservación: preservation

preservar: conserve, preserve

preservativo: condom

presidencia: chair, presidency

presidencial: presidential

presidenta: chair, chairperson, chairwoman

presidenta de la corte: chief justice

presidenta del tribunal: chief justice

presidenta municipal: mayor

presidente: chair, chairman, chairperson, chief justice, mayor, president, speaker

presidiaria: convict

presidiario: convict

presidir: chair, preside

presión: press, pressure, strain

presión arterial: blood pressure

presión atmosférica: atmospheric pressure

presión del aire: air pressure

presión del grupo: peer pressure

presionado: pressured

presionar: lobby, press, pressure, punch, push

preso: convict, detainee, inmate

prestación: benefit

prestaciones sociales: welfare

prestado: on loan

prestamista: lender

préstamo: lending, loan

préstamo estudiantil: student loan

préstamo puente: bridge loan

prestar: lend, loan, pay

prestar atención: give thought/attention (to), listen, pay attention, take notice

prestar juramento: swear in

prestar testimonio: testify

prestarse a: be (a) party to

prestataria: borrower

prestatario: borrower

prestigiado: eminent

prestigio: face, prestige

prestigioso: eminent, prestigious

presumiblemente: presumably

presumido: snob, vain

presumir: boast, presume, show off, suppose

presunción: boast

presunto: supposed

presupuestar: budget, quote

presupuesto: budget, budgeting, quotation, quote

presurizado: pressurized

pretemporada: preseason

pretencioso: self-righteous

pretender: allege

pretendido: would-be

pretexto: excuse

prevalecer: hold sway, prevail

prevención: prevention

prevenido: alert

prevenir: avert, guard against, tip off

prever: anticipate, forecast, foresee, provide for

previa cita: by appointment

previamente: previously

previo: advance, earlier, previous, prior

previo al juego o al partido: pregame

previsibilidad: predictability

previsible: predictable

previsiblemente: predictably

previsión: forecast

previsiones: provisions

prima: bonus, cousin, premium, raw, reward

primaria: primary

primate: ape, primate

primavera: spring

primer: first

primer actor: lead, leading man

primer balcón: mezzanine

primer meridiano: prime meridian

primer ministro: premier, prime minister

primera: top

primera actriz: lead, leading lady

Primera Dama: First Lady

primera escena: opening

primera línea: front line

primera ministra: premier, prime minister

primera ministro: premier, prime minister

primera plana: front-page

primero: early, first, initial, opening, premier

primeros auxilios: first aid

primicia: scoop

primitivo: primitive

primo: cousin

primordial: overriding, primary, ultimate

primordialmente: primarily

princesa: princess

principal: central, chief,

downstage, first, leading, main, prime, principal

principal contaminante: primary pollutant

principalmente: largely, mainly, mostly

príncipe: prince

principianta: beginner, novice

principiante: beginner, novice

principiar: initiate

principio: beginning, fundamentals, head, launch, outset, principle, source, start

principio alfabético: alphabetic principle

Principio de Arquímedes: Archimedes' principle

principio de Bernoulli: Bernoulli's principle

principios: principle

principios de composición: principles of composition

principios de diseño: principles of design

prioridad: priority

prioritario: high priority

prisa: hurry, rush, scramble

prisión: lock-up, prison

prisión de baja seguridad: minimum security prison

prisión perpetua: life

prisionera: prisoner

prisionero: prisoner

prisma: prism

privacía: privacy

privacidad: privacy

privación: deprivation, hardship

privado: private

privar: deprive, rob

privar de comida: starve

privatización: privatization

privatizar: privatize

privilegiado: privileged, upper class

privilegiar: favor

privilegio: privilege

proa: nose

probabilidad: likelihood, odds

probable: likely

probablemente: likely, presumably, probably

probadita: glimpse

probado: approved

probar(se): attempt, prove, road test, sample, taste, test, try, try on, try out

probar suerte: try your hand

probeta: test tube

problema: headache, issue, matter, problem, trouble

problema del sistema: catch

problemático: troublesome

proceder: proceed

procedimiento: procedure

procedimiento debido: due process

procesador: processor

procesamiento: processing

procesamiento de textos: word processing

procesar: process, prosecute, try

procesión: procession

proceso: lawsuit, process, prosecution, trial

proclamar: herald, proclaim

proclive: inclined, prone

procrear: breed

procurador: attorney, solicitor

procurador general: D.A., district attorney

procuradora: attorney, solicitor

procuradora general: D.A., district attorney

procurar: try

prodigar(se): heap

prodigio: whiz kid

prodigioso: marvelous

producción: output, production

producido en serie: mass-produced

producir: breed, bring forth, earn, generate, induce, net, produce, yield

producir en masa: mass-produce

producir en serie: mass-produce

producir explosiones: backfire

producir intensivamente: pump out

productividad: productivity

productivo: productive

producto: commodity, product

producto agrícola: produce

producto de marca (registrada): brand-name product

producto defectuoso: reject

producto químico: chemically

productor: producer

productora: producer

productos: goods

productos farmacéuticos: pharmaceuticals

productos importados: imports

productos textiles: textiles

proeza: exploit, feat

profanación: violation

profanar: violate

profase: prophase

profesión: profession

profesional:

occupational, pro

profesionalismo: professionalism

profesionalmente: professionally

profesor: professor, teacher

profesor adjunto: associate professor

profesor asistente: assistant professor

profesor auxiliar: instructor

profesor universitario: lecturer, professor

profesor visitante: visiting professor

profesora: professor, teacher

profesora adjunta: associate professor

profesora asistente: assistant professor

profesora auxiliar: instructor

profesora universitaria: professor

profesora visitante: visiting professor

profesorado: faculty

professional: professional

profeta: prophet

profundamente: deeply, keenly, profoundly, with all one's heart

profundamente dormido: fast asleep, sound asleep

profundidad: depth

profundizar: deepen

profundo: deep, depth, heavy, intense, intimate, profound, sound

profusamente: freely

progenie: offspring

progenitor: father

programa: broadcast, program, schedule, scheme, show, timeline

programa de telerrealidad: reality show

programa de una materia: curriculum

programa especial: feature

programación: planning, programming

programador: programmer

programadora: programmer

programar: plan, program, schedule, time

programas de extensión universitaria: further education

progresar: develop, progress

progresión aritmética: arithmetic sequence

progresión armónica: harmonic progression

progresista: progressive

progresivamente:

progressively
progresivo: progressive
progreso: advance, progress, stride
prohibición: ban, embargo, prohibition
prohibida la entrada: no entry
prohibido: forbidden
prohibir: ban, bar, forbid, outlaw, prohibit
proliferación: proliferation, rash
proliferar: proliferate
prologar: preface
prolongado: lengthy, long, prolonged
promediar: average
promedio: average, GPA, grade point average, mean
promesa: promise
promesa solemne: vow
prometedor: promising
prometer: give your word, pledge, promise, show promise, swear
prometer solemnemente: swear
prometida: fiancée
prometido: fiancé
prominencia: prominence
prominente: ace, prominent
prominentemente: prominently
promoción: class, endorsement, promotion
promoción intensa: hype
promocional: promotional
promocionar: advocate, endorse, push
promocionar intensamente: hype
promotor: promoter
promotor inmobiliario: developer
promotora: promoter
promotora inmobiliaria: developer
promover: foster, plug, promote
promulgación: enactment
promulgar: enact
pronombre: pronoun
pronombre indefinido: indefinite pronoun
pronombre personal: personal pronoun
pronombre reflexivo: reflexive pronoun
pronombre relativo: relative pronoun
pronosticar: forecast, see
pronóstico: forecast, projection
pronóstico del tiempo: weather forecast
prontamente: promptly
pronto: prompt, soon, speedy
pronunciación: pronunciation
pronunciar: deliver, utter

pronunciar (un discurso): speak
pronunciar un sermón: preach
pronunciar(e): pronounce
propaganda: propaganda, publicity
propagarse: travel
propenso: apt, prone
propenso a: liable to
propiamente: by rights
propicio: ripe
propiedad: estate, ownership, property
propiedad característica: characteristic property
propiedad física: physical property
propiedad intelectual: intellectual property
propiedad química: chemical property
propietaria: owner, proprietor
propietario: landlord, owner, proprietor
propina: tip
propinar: deliver
propio: own, proper
proponer(se): aim, forward, intend, make a point of, propose, put forward, set out, suggest
proponer matrimonio: propose
proporción: proportion, ratio
proporcional: proportional
proporcionar: furnish, lend, provide, supply
proporciones: proportions
proposición: proposition
propósito: intention, meaning, object, purpose, resolution
propuesta: approach, paper, proposal, proposition, suggestion, tender
propulsión: thrust
propulsión total: four-wheel drive
propulsor: propeller
prorratear: prorate
prórroga: OT
prosa: prose
proscenio: downstage, proscenium
proseguir: continue, pursue
prosimio: prosimian
prosperar: flourish, thrive
prosperidad: health, prosperity
próspero: flourishing, prosperous, successful
prostituta: prostitute
protagonista: hero, heroine, lead, leading role, player
protagonizar: star
protección: conservation, defense, protection

protector: protective, protector
protector solar: sunscreen
protectora: protector
proteger(se): guard, hedge, mother, protect, secure, shelter, shield, ward off
proteína: protein
prótesis dental: dentures
protesta: protest, uproar
protestante: Protestant
protestar: moan, protest
protista: Protista
protisto: protist
protoctista: Protista
protón: proton
prototipo: prototype
protozoario: protozoan
protozoo: protozoan
protuberancia: lump, ridge
provecho: interest, mileage
provechosamente: profitably
provechoso: lucrative
proveedor: supplier
proveedor de servicios: service provider
proveedor de servicios de internet: ISP
proveedora: supplier
proveer: feed, furnish, provide, supply
proveer de algo: fit out
provenir: stem
proverbio: proverb
provincia: Main Street, province
provincial: provincial
provinciano: provincial
provisión: provision, store
provisional: interim, provisional, temporary, tentative
provisiones: supply
provocar: bait, bring, bring about, bring forth, create, draw, elicit, generate, induce, lead, prompt, provoke, roust, spark, stir up, trigger
provocar rechazo: put off
(queso) provolone: provolone
próximo: close, coming, forthcoming, next, toward, upcoming
proyección: projection, screening
proyección acimutal: azimuthal projection
proyección cónica: conic projection
proyección de/conforme a Mercator: Mercator projection
proyección vocal: vocal projection
proyectar(se): cast, project, screen, show
proyectil: missile, shell
proyecto: enterprise, project, scheme

proyecto de ley: bill
Proyecto del Genoma Humano: Human Genome Project
prudencia: wisdom
prudente: cautious, wise
prudentemente: wisely
prueba: attempt, audition, evidence, exhibit, go, proof, road test, taste, test, trial, try
prueba de: testimony
prueba de aptitud: placement test
prueba de carretera: road test, test drive
prurito: itch
pseudópodo: pseudopod
psicoanalista: analyst
psicóloga: psychologist
psicología: psychology
psicología en reversa: reverse psychology
psicológicamente: psychologically
psicológico: psychological
psicólogo: psychologist
psicoterapeuta: psychotherapist
psicoterapia: psychotherapy
psicrómetro: psychrometer
psíquico: psychic
pteridosperma: seed fern
púa: tooth
publicación: publication
publicación periódica: periodical
públicamente: publicly
publicar(se): issue, print, publish, put out
publicidad: advertising, exposure, plug, publicity
publicitario: promotional
público: (out) in the open, audience, public
puchero: stew
pude haber: could have
pudiera: could
pudiéramos: could
pudieran: could
pudieras: could
pudieron haber: could have
pudimos haber: could have
pudiste haber: could have
pudo haber: could have
pudrirse: decay, rot
pueblerino: provincial, small town
pueblo: people, town, village
puente: bridge
puente aéreo: airlift
puerca: sow
puerco: hog, pig, pork
pueril: childish
puerta: door, gate, threshold
puerta de embarque: gate
puerto: dock, harbor, port
puerto aéreo: airport

pues: then
puesta de sol: sundown
puesta del sol: sunset
puesto: booth, position, post, stall, stand
puesto de elección popular: public office
puesto público: public office
púgil: fighter
pugilista: boxer
pugnar: bid
pujar: bid
pulcritud: neatness
pulcro: trim
pulgada: inch
pulgar: thumb
pulido: polished, slick
pulir: polish, refine
pullman: Pullman
pulmón: lung
pulóver: sweater
pulpa: flesh
pulpo: octopus
pulsación: pulse
pulsar: pulsar
pulsera: bracelet
pulso: pulse
pulular: swarm
puma: cougar, mountain lion
punching bag: punching bag
punk: punk
punta: end, lead, point, spike, tip
puntada: stitch
puntal: prop, strut
punteado: dotted
puntera: leader
puntería: aim
puntero: leader
puntiagudo: pointed
punto: dot, item, mark, period, point, stitch
punto caliente: hot button, hot spot
punto de apoyo: fulcrum
punto de condensación: condensation point, dew point
punto de congelación: freezing point
punto de ebullición: boiling point
punto de fuga: vanishing point
punto de fusión: melting point
punto de partida: tee
punto de referencia: mark, reference point
punto de rocío: dew point
punto de saturación: dew point
punto de sutura: stitch
punto de vista: contention, point of view, standpoint, vanishing point, view, viewpoint
punto decimal: decimal point, point
punto muerto: gridlock, neutral
punto porcentual: percentage point

punto y coma: semicolon
puntos cardinales: points of the compass
puntuación: punctuation, score
puntual: punctual
puntualmente: promptly, punctually
punzada: stab, stitch
puñado: handful
puñal: dagger
puñetazo: punch
puño: cuff, fist
pupila: pupil
pura verdad: gospel
pureza: purity
purificador: cleaner
puro: bald, cigar, pure, sheer
púrpura: purple
putrefacción: rot
putter: putter

Q

quántum: quantum
quarterback: quarterback
quasar: quasar
que: than, that, which, who
qué: what, which
qué bien: great
qué mejor: be just as well
qué pena: I'm sorry (to hear that)
qué tal … how/what about …
qué tan: how
qué tan lejos: how far
qué tan seguido: how often
quebradero de cabeza: headache
quebrado: broke
quebrantar: breach, dishonor
quebrar(se): break, crack, collapse, crash, go bust, go under, snap
quedar(se): linger, remain, settle, stay, stay behind, stay in, stay put, stick around
quedar bien: fit, go
quedar bien algo: suit
quedar deshecho: go to pieces
quedar en: arrange
quedar inválido: cripple
quedar lisiado: cripple
quedar reducido a cenizas: burn down
quedarlo algo: take (a size in shoes/clothes)
quedarse a la zaga: fall behind
quedarse atrás: be left behind, lag
quedarse dormido: doze off, drift off, drop off, fall asleep, nod off
quedarse en vela: sit up
quedarse inmóvil: freeze
quedarse levantado: stay up
quedarse mirando: gaze
quedarse varado: be stranded

queja: complaint, moan
quejarse: complain, moan, protest
quejido: moan
quema: burn
quemado por el sol: sunburned
quemador: burner
quemador de CDs: CD burner, CD writer
quemadura: burn
quemar(se): be on fire, burn, incinerate
quemazón: burning
querellante: prosecutor
querer: aim, care, like, love, want, will, wish
querer (hacer): intend
querer algo: feel like
querer decir: get at, mean
querer llegar: get at
querida: darling, dear
querido: beloved, darling, dear, lover, sweetheart
queroseno: kerosene
queso: cheese
queso mozzarella: mozzarella
queso ricota: ricotta
quicio: doorway
quiebra: bankruptcy
quien: those, whom
quién: who, whom
quien uno quiera: whoever
quienes: those
quienquiera: whoever
quieto: still
quijada: jaw
quilate: karat
química: chemist, chemistry
química farmacéutica: pharmacy
químicamente: chemically
químico: chemical, chemist
quince: fifteen, fifteenth
quinceavo: fifteenth
quincenal: biweekly
quincuagésimo: fiftieth
quinesiología: physical therapy
quinto: fifth
quíntuple: quintuplet
quirófano: operating room, surgery
quirúrgicamente: surgically
quirúrgico: surgical
quisquilloso: persnickety
quitamanchas: cleaner
quitanieve: snowplow
quitar: flick, move, sweep, take, take down
quitar la ropa de: strip
quitarse: remove, slip, take off
quitarse de encima: be out of the way
quitarse la ropa: strip off
quizá(s): may, maybe, perhaps

R
rabia: rage
rabino: rabbi

racha: bout
racial: racial
racialmente: racially
racimo: bunch
ración: serving
racional: rational
racionalidad: rationality
racionalizado: streamlined
racionalizar: streamline
racionalmente: rationally
racismo: racism
racista: racist
radar: radar
radiación: radiation
radiación del fondo cósmico: cosmic background radiation
radiantemente: brightly
radical: drastic, extremist, radical, seismic
radicalmente: drastically, radically
radicar: lie
radio: radio, radius
radio digital: digital radio
radioactividad: radioactivity
radioactivo: radioactive
radioescucha: listener
radiofaro de respuesta: transponder
radiografía: X-ray
radiografiar: X-ray
radiorreceptor: radio telescope
radiotelescopio: radio telescope
raíces: root system
raíces fibrosas: fibrous root
raído: ratty
rail: rail
raíz: root, root word
raíz cuadrada: square root
raíz de una función: zeros of a function
raíz primaria: taproot
rajadura: crack
rajarse: chicken out
rallador: grater
rallar: grate
rally: scavenger
ralo: scraggly
rama: branch, stick
ramillete: bouquet
ramo: bouquet, bunch
rampa: ramp
rana: frog
ranchera: farmer
ranchero: farmer
rancho: estate, farm, ranch
rancio: stale
ranura: groove, slot
rap: rap
rápida y enérgicamente: briskly
rápidamente: fast, quickly, rapidly, swiftly
rapidez: quickness, rapidity, speed, swiftness
rapidísimo: lickety-split

rápido: express, fast, quick, rapid, rapid-fire, speedy, swift
rápido y enérgico: brisk
raqueta: racket
rara: misfit
rara vez: seldom
raramente: rarely
rarefacción: rarefaction
rareza: strangeness
raro: bizarre, freak, funny, misfit, odd, peculiar, rare, rarely, strange, unusual, weird
rascacielos: skyscraper
rascar(se): scrape, scratch
rasgadura: rip, slit
rasgar: rip, tear, tear up
rasgarse: split
rasgo: feature, streak, trait
rasgo distintivo: feature
rasguñar(se): scratch
rasguño: graze, nick, scratch
raspar(se): scrape
rasparse: graze
rastrear: comb, scent, trace, track, trail
rastrillar: rake
rastrillo: rake
rastrillo para rasurarse: razor
rastro: scent, trail
rasurada: shave
rasuradora: razor, shaver
rasurar(se): shave
rasurarse: shaving
rata: rat
rata canguro: kangaroo rat
ratera: thief
ratero: thief
ratificación: ratification
ratificar: ratify
rato: minute, time, while
ratón: mouse
ratonera: nest
ratos de ocio: leisure
ratos libres: spare time
raudal: flood
raya: line, part, pinstripe, stripe
rayado: striped
rayar: scrape
rayar en: verge on
rayo: lightning, ray, shaft, spoke
rayo (de luz): beam
rayo láser: laser
rayo-X: X-ray
rayos del sol: sunshine
rayos gamma: gamma rays
rayos solares: sunshine
raza: breed, race
razón: argument, cause, ground, reason
razonable: logical, rational, reasonable
razonablemente: plausibly, reasonably
razonar: reason
razonar con: reason with

RCP: CPR
reabastecer: refuel
reabastecimiento de combustible: refueling
reacción: reaction, response
reacción de descomposición: decomposition reaction
reacción de desplazamiento: single-replacement reaction
reacción de doble substitución: double-replacement reaction
reacción de reemplazo simple: single-replacement reaction
reacción de síntesis: synthesis reaction
reacción instintiva: gut reaction
reacción química: chemical reaction
reacción violenta: backlash
reacción visceral: gut reaction
reaccionar: react
reacio: reluctant
reactivación: recovery
reactivar: revive
reactivo: reactant
reactor nuclear: reactor
reafirmar: bolster
real: actual, real, royal, true
realeza: royalty
realidad: real world, reality, truth
realidad virtual: virtual reality
realista: authentic, realistic
realistamente: realistically
realizar: execute, fulfill, mount
realizarse: come true
realmente: genuinely, real, really
realzar: enhance
reanimar: revive
reanudación: resumption
reanudar: resume
reasumir: resume
reata para/de saltar: skip rope
rebaja: discount
rebajar: knock down, knock off, mark down, put down
rebajar drásticamente: slash
rebajar los precios: undercut
rebajarse: descend
rebanada: slice, wedge
rebanar: slice
rebaño: flock, herd
rebasar: cut across, pass, surpass
rebatiña: scramble
rebatir: disprove, dispute, refute
rebelarse: rebel, revolt,

rise up
rebelde: defiant, rebel, unruly
rebeldía: defiance
rebelión: insurrection, rebellion
rebosante de: overflow
rebosar: spill
rebotar: bounce, rebound
recado: errand, message
recalcar: emphasize, impress
recalentar: heat up
recámara: bedroom, magazine
recamarera: maid
recargo: extra
recaudación: collection
recaudación de fondos: fund-raising
recaudador: collector
recaudador de fondos: fundraiser
recaudadora: collector
recaudadora de fondos: fundraiser
recaudar: collect, levy, raise
recelar: suspect
recelar de: mistrust
recelo: mistrust, suspicion
recepción: front desk, function, receipt, reception
recepcionista: receptionist
receptivo: sympathetic
receptor: catcher, receiver, receptor, recipient
receptora: catcher, recipient
recesión: recession
recesivo: recessive
receta: formula, prescription, recipe, Rx
recetar: prescribe
recetario: cookbook
rechazar: fight off, nix, refuse, reject, repel, throw out, turn away, turn down
rechazo: refusal, rejection, revolt
rechinar: squeak
rechoncho: pudgy, squat
recibidor: hallway
recibir: come in, earn, get, greet, meet, pick up, receive
recibir invitados: entertain
recibir una herencia: inherit
recibirse: qualify
recibo: receipt, sales slip
reciclar: recycle
recién: freshly, newly
recién llegada: arrival
recién llegado: arrival, newcomer
reciente: fresh, recent
recientemente: lately, newly, recently
recipiente: container
recital: reading
recitar: recite, reel off

recitar monótonamente: chant
reclamación: claim
reclamar: claim
reclamo: claim
reclinar(se): recline
recluir: intern
reclusa: convict
recluso: convict, inmate
recluta: recruit
reclutamiento: recruiting, recruitment
reclutar: draft, induct, recruit
recobrar: recover, regain
recobrar la compostura: pull together
recobrar la conciencia: regain consciousness
recobrarse: recuperate
recoger: clear away, clear up, collect, fetch, gather, gather up, lift, meet, pick, pick up, scoop up
recoger con rastrillo: rake
recogida: pickup
recolección de equipaje: baggage claim
recolectar: collect
recolector: collector
recolectora: collector
recomendación: recommendation, reference
recomendado: recommended
recomendar: recommend
recompensa: reward
recompensar: reward
reconciliación: reconciliation
reconciliar(se): make up, reconcile
reconocer: acknowledge, appreciate, concede, credit, grant, identify, own up, pick out, recognize, survey
reconocer el terreno: scout
reconocimiento: acknowledgment, admission, appreciation, recognition
reconocimiento de palabras: word recognition
reconsiderar: reevaluate, revise
reconstruir: piece together, rebuild
reconvenir: scold
recopilación: collection
récord: bumper, record
recordar: bring back, come back, look back, recall, remember, reminisce, think back
recordar a: remind
recordatorio: prompting, reminder
recorrer: cover, tour
recorrer con la vista: scan

recorrido: circuit, round, tour

recortar: cut, cut back, cut out, trim

recortarse: outline

recorte: cut, trim

recostar(se): recline

recreación: pursuit

recreativo: recreational

recreo: break

recrudecer: intensify

recrudecer(se): flare

recta: line drive

rectángulo: box, rectangle

rectificar: rectify, right

rectilíneo: rectilinear

rectitude: rightness

recto: straight, upright

rector: chancellor

rector (de escuela): headmaster

rectora: chancellor

recuadro: window

recubierto: plated

recubrir: line

recuerdo: memory, souvenir

recuperación: payback, reclamation, recovery, recuperation, retrieval, return

recuperación de la deformación elástica: elastic rebound

recuperación de recursos: resource recovery

recuperar(se): get back, get back on one's feet, get over, pull through, rally, reclaim, recover, recuperate, regain

recuperar la posesión de: repossess

recuperar los costos: break even

recurrente: intermittent

recurrir: recur, resort

recurrir a: draw on, fall back on, turn

recurso: resource

recurso energético: energy resource

recursos: funding, means

recursos naturales: natural resources

recursos no renovables: non-renewable resources

red: net, network, ring, web

red cristalina: crystal lattice

red de cadenas alimenticias: food web

red de redes: WWW

red de suministro: mains

red interna: intranet

redacción: grammar

redactado: -worded

redactar: draw up, pen, phrase

redactar un borrador de: draft

redactar un informe: write up

redil: pen

redituable: cost-effective, profitable

redituar: bring in

redoblar: step up

redomado: perfect

redonda: whole note

redondear: round

redondo: round

reducción: cut, depletion, drop, lowering, narrowing, reduction, rollback

reducción del nivel intelectual: dumbing down

reducido: confined

reducir(se): blunt, cut, cut down, deplete, depress, diminish, downgrade, drop, ease, erode, knock off, lower, mark down, narrow, narrow down, reduce, scale back/down, shrink, shorten

reducir a: reduce to

reducir a la mitad: halve

reducir al mínimo: minimize

reducir el personal: slim down

reducir paulatinamente: wind down

reducirse a: come down to

redundante: redundant

reelección: reelection

reelegir: reelect

reembolsar: refund, reimburse

reembolso: refund, reimbursement

reemplazar: fill in, replace

reemplazo: replacement

reencuentro: reunion

reenviar: forward

reestrenar: revive

reestreno: revival

reestructuración: restructuring

reestructurar: restructure

refacción: spare, spare part

refectorio: lunchroom

referencia: reference, referral

referendo: referendum

referéndum: referendum

referente a la política: politically

réferi: referee

referir: refer

referirse: touch

referirse a: refer to

refinación: refining

refinamiento: refinement

refinar: refine

refinería: refinery

reflector: spotlight

reflejar: catch, project

reflejar(se): mirror, reflect

reflejo: reaction, reflection, reflex

reflexión: reflection, thought

reflexionar: look back, meditate, muse, puzzle, reason, reflect, think

reflujo: ebb

reforma: reform

reformado: reformed

reformador: reformer

reformadora: reformer

reformar: reform

reformar(se): reform

reformatorio: correctional facility, reform school

reforzar: beef up, reinforce

refracción: refraction

refractar(se): refract

refractario: pan

refrán: proverb

refrenar: curb

refrenarse: refrain

refrendar: defend, endorse

refrescante: refreshing

refrescantemente: refreshingly

refrescar: refresh

refrescarse: cool off

refresco: soda pop, soft drink

refresco de cola: cola

refri: fridge

refriega: struggle

refrigerador: fridge, refrigerator

refrigerio: box lunch, snack

refuerzo: backing, reinforcement

refugiada: refugee

refugiado: refugee

refugiarse: shelter

refugio: cover, haven, refuge, safe haven, sanctuary, shelter

refugio para mujeres maltratadas: women's shelter

refutar: contest, disprove, dispute, refute

regadera: shower

regadera de Filipinas: basket sponge

regado: scattered

regalar: give away

regalías: royalty

regalo: gift, present, treat

regañar: scold, tell off

regar: hose, irrigate, water

regatear: bargain

regazo: lap

reggae: reggae

régimen: regime

régimen (alimenticio): diet

régimen terapéutico: treatment

regimiento: regiment

región: belt, region, territory

región baja: small of one's back

región silvestre: the wilds

región tropical: tropical zone

regional: regional

regir: govern

registrado: licensed

registrar: chart, check, enter, log, raid, record, search, take in

registrar(se): check in, register

registrarse: sign in

registro: raid, record, register, registration

registro de procedimientos: docket

registro fósil: fossil record

regla: regulation, rule, ruler

reglamentar: regulate

reglamentario: statutory

reglamento: bylaw, regulation

reglas impresas en un examen: rubric

regordete: squat

regresar: come back, get back, give back, go back, return, take back, turn back

regresar a: go back to

regresar la llamada: call back

regreso: return

regulador: regulator, regulatory

reguladora: regulator

regular: even, indifferent, regular, regulate

regularidad: consistency, regularity

regularmente: evenly, regularly, steadily

rehabilitación: rehabilitation, reinstatement

rehabilitar: rehabilitate, reinstate

rehén: hostage

rehuir: shrink away from, shy away from

rehusar: decline, refuse

reina: queen, ruler

reinar: reign

reiniciar: reboot

reinicio: reboot

reino: kingdom, reign

reino animal: Animalia

reinstalar: reinstall

reír(se): laugh

reír(se) a carcajadas: roar

reírse de: laugh off, make fun of, razz

reírse nerviosamente: giggle

reiterado: repeated

reiterar: reiterate

reivindicación: claim

reivindicar: claim, reclaim

reivindicar un derecho: stake a claim

reja: gate

rejilla de Punnett:

Punnett square

relación: attachment, connection, dealings, link, list, partnership, relation, relationship, tie

relación con: association

relación de los colores: color relationship

relación laboral: labor relations

relación superficie-volumen: surface-to-volume ratio

relacionado: allied, connected, related

relacionar(se): connect, hook up, interact, link, relate, tie

relaciones públicas: public relations

relaciones sexuales: intercourse

relajado: cool, lazy

relajamiento: relaxation

relajante: relaxing

relajar(se): chill out, loosen, loosen up, lounge, relax, unwind

relajo: scramble

relámpago: lightning

relativamente: comparatively, relatively

relativo: comparative, relative

relato: narrative, story, tale

relato inexacto: misstatement

relegar: relegate

relevancia: relevance

relevante: relevant

relevar: relieve

relieve: relief

religión: religion

religioso: religious, Reverend

rellano: landing

rellenar: complete, fill, stuff

relleno: dressing, filling, stuffing

relleno sanitario: garbage dump, landfill

reloj: clock

reloj biológico: biological clock

reloj de bolsillo: keep watch

reloj de pulsera: keep watch

reloj de pulso: keep watch

reloj despertador: alarm, alarm clock

remar: row

rematar: auction

remate: auction

remates: junk

rembolsar: refund

rembolso: refund

remedar: imitate

remediar(se): cure, heal, remedy

remedio: medication, medicine, remedy

rememorar: reminisce

remendar: mend

remesa: delivery

remitente: mailer, sender

remitir: forward, refer, send

remo: oar, paddle, rowing

remoción: removal

remojar: soak

remolacha: beet

remolcador: tug

remolcar: tow

remolque: trailer

remontar el vuelo: soar

remontarse: date back, further

remordimiento: regret

remoto: distant, far off, faraway, remote, unlikely

remover: remove, stir

renacimiento: renaissance

renacuajo: tadpole

renco: lame

rencor: grudge

rendición: submission, surrender

rendido: frazzled

rendija: crack

rendimiento: performance, return, work output

rendimiento mecánico: mechanical advantage

rendir culto: worship

rendir frutos: pay dividends

rendir homenaje a: salute

rendirse: give in, surrender

rengo: lame

renombrado: renowned

renombre: rating

renovación: refurbishment, renewal, renovation, revival, turnover

renovar: refurbish, renew, renovate

renta: rent, rental

rentabilidad: profitability

rentable: economically, profitable

rentar: lease, rent

renuencia: reluctance, unwillingness

renuente: reluctant, resistant

renuncia: resignation, surrender

renunciar: abandon, give up, resign, step down, surrender

renunciar a: drop

reñido: close

reñir: quarrel, scold

reo: convict

reorganización: rearrangement, reorganization

reorganizar: rearrange, reorganize

reparación: repair, satisfaction

reparar: fix, repair, undo

repartir: deal, dish out,

distribute, give/hand out, hand out
reparto: cast, issue
reparto de periódicos: paper route
repasar: brush up on, review, run through
repaso: review
repatriación: repatriation
repatriar: repatriate
repentinamente: suddenly
repentino: sharp, snap, sudden
repercusión: impact, implication
repetición: duplicate, recurrence, repeat, repetition, replay
repetición instantánea: instant replay
repetidamente: repeatedly
repetido: repeated
repetir(se): drum into, duplicate, echo, recur, repeat, replay
repetir como perico: parrot
repetir una y otra vez: chant
repicar: ring
repique: ring
repiquetear: ring
repleto: jammed
repleto de: overflow
réplica: retort
replicar: retort
repollito de Bruselas: sprout
reponer: reply, revive
reponerse: be on the mend, pull through, rally
reportajes: reporting
reportera: reporter
reportero: reporter
reposapiés: ottoman
reposición: revival
repostar: refuel
repostería: pastry
repreguntar: cross-examine
reprender: scold
represa: dam, reservoir
representación: image, performance, representation
representación teatral: theater
representante: agent, rep, representative
representante comercial: rep
representar: account for, constitute, depict, enactment, make up, portray, represent, stage
representar un papel: play
representarse: picture
representativo: representative, typical
represión: crushing, suppression
reprimir: fight back,

suppress
reprobar: fail, flunk
reproducción: reproduction
reproducción asexual: asexual reproduction, vegetative reproduction
reproducción sexual: sexual reproduction
reproducción vegetativa: vegetative reproduction
reproducir(se): play back, reproduce
reproductor de CDs: CD player
reproductor de MP3: MP3 player
reproductor portátil: boom box
reptil: reptile
república: republic
republicano: republican
repuesto: spare, spare part
repugnancia: disgust
repugnante: awful, disgusting, foul, nasty
repugnar: repel
repulsado: repelled
repulsivo: creepy
repuntar: pick up
repunte: pickup, upturn
reputación: character, rating, reputation
requerimiento: call
requerir: call for, demand, require
requesón: ricotta
requisito: qualification, requirement
res: livestock
resaca: surf
resaltar: stand out
resarcir: compensate
resbaladilla: slide
resbaladizo: slippery
resbalar: slip
resbaloso: slippery
rescatador: rescuer
rescatar: rescue, salvage
rescate: bailout, reclamation, rescuer, salvage
rescoldo: cinder
resentimiento: bad feeling/ill feeling, resentment
resentir: resent
resentirse: suffer
reseña: chronicle, résumé, review, sketch
reseñar: chronicle, review, sketch
reserva: preserve, qualification, reservation, reserve, reservoir, secrecy, spare, stock, store
Reserva Federal: Federal Reserve
reservación: reservation
reservado: booth, reserved
reservar: book, give over to, put aside, reserve, set aside
reservas: stockpile

reserve: standby
resfriado: cold
resfriarse: catch (a) cold
resfrío: cold
resguardo: protection
resguardo marítimo: Coast Guard
residencia: dormitory, residence, residency
residencia de estudiantes: residence hall
residencia para enfermos desahuciados: hospice
residencial: residential
residente: resident
residente extranjero: resident alien
residir en: be in residence
residuos: refuse
resignación: resignation
resignado: reconciled, resigned
resignarse: reconcile, resign
resistencia: element, resistance, strength
resistencia al avance: drag
resistente: hardy, resistant, stout, tough
resistir(se): bear, fight off, resist, stand, stand up to
resollar: sniff
resolución: decision, decisiveness, resolution, resolve, ruling, single-mindedness
resolver: conquer, get over, iron out, mandate, meet, resolve, settle, solve, sort out
resolver el problema: do the trick
resonancia: resonance
resonar: echo
resoplar: puff
resorte: spring
resortera: slingshot
respaldar: back, back up, endorse, underwrite
respaldar alguien: be behind somebody
respaldo: back, backing, backup, support
respectable: respectable
respectivamente: respectively
respecto a: as
respecto de: as regards, in proportion to, regarding, with/in reference to
respetabilidad: respectability
respetable: decent
respetado: respected
respetar: keep to, look up to, respect
respeto: regard, respect
respeto por sí mismo: self-respect
respiración: breath, breathing, gas exchange, respiration

respiración celular: cellular respiration

respirador artificial: life support

respirar: breathe, draw

respirar con dificultad: gasp

respiratorio: respiratory

respiro: truce

resplandecer: blaze, gleam, glow

resplandor: glare, glow

responder: reply, respond, write/call back

responder a: acknowledge, deal with

responder por: answer for

respondón: sassy

responsabilidad: accountability, commitment, fault, liability, responsibility, trust

responsable: liable, responsible, sound

responsable ante: accountable

responsablemente: responsibly

respuesta: answer, reply

resquebrajar: crack

resta: subtraction

restablecer: rebuild, restore

restablecerse: recuperate

restablecimiento: recovery, restoration

restante: remaining

restar: deduct, subtract, take away

restar importancia a: play down, talk down

restauración: restoration

restaurante: restaurant

restaurar: renovate, restore

restituir: reinstate, restore

resto: holdover, remainder, rest

restos: remains, scraps

restos de animales muertos en las carreteras: roadkill

restregada: scrub

restregar: rub, scrub

restricción: constraint, limitation, restraint, restriction

restringir(se): confine

restringido: limited, out of bounds, restricted

restringir: limit, restrict, tighten

resuello: gasp, sniff

resueltamente: decisively

resuelto: decisive, determined, intent, single-minded

resultado: finding, outcome, output, product, result, tribute, wake

resultado benéfico: spinoff

resultar: find, prove, result, turn out, work out

resultar cierto: come true

resultar electo: get in

resultar ser/estar: turn out

resumen: excerpt, résumé, summary

resumen de noticias: headline

resumir: condense, sketch, sum up, summarize

retacado: bursting at the seams

retador: challenging

retar: challenge, dare, defy

retardador: inhibitor

retardar: slow down

retener: defend, withhold

retículo cristalino: crystal lattice

retículo endoplásmico: endoplasmic reticulum

retina: retina

retirada: retreat

retirado: gone

retirar: draw, remove

retirar la palabra: be not speaking

retirar(se): bow out, move off, pull back, retreat, stand down withdraw

retiro: retreat, withdrawal

reto: challenge, dare

retocar: refurbish

retoñar: sprout

retoño: shoot

retorcer: twist

retorcido: twisted

retórica: rhetoric

retornar: return

retorno: comeback, return

retractarse: take back

retransmitir: relay

retrasar: delay, hold up, put back, set back

retraso: delay, lag, late

retratar: picture, portray

retrato: portrait

retrete: toilet

retroalimentación: feedback

retroceder: back away, back off, further, recede, shrink, step back

retumbar: boom, echo

reunión: consultation, gathering, meeting, reunion

reunión de apoyo: pep rally

reunión informativa: briefing

reunir(se): assemble, collect, convene, gather, gather up, get together, link up, marshal, meet, put together, round up, summon work up

reunirse con: see

reutilización: reuse

reutilizar: reuse

revaluación: reevaluation

revelación: disclosure, exposure, revelation

revelador: revealing

revelar: betray, come/ bring to light, develop, disclose, give away, reveal show, unveil

revelarse: come out, emerge

revendedor: scalper

revendedora: scalper

reventar(se): burst, pop, rupture

reverencia: bow

revertir: revert

revestimiento: lining

revisar: edit, go over, inspect, look through, review, revise, service, survey

revisión: check, review, revision

revisión médica: checkup

revisor: conductor, editor inspector

revisora: conductor, editor inspector

revista: journal, mag, magazine, periodical

revivir: bring back

revocar: lift, overturn

revocar (legal): reverse

revoltije: mess

revoltoso: rambunctious

revolución: revolution, uprising

revolucionaria: revolutionary

revolucionario: revolutionary

revolver: mix up, scramble, shuffle, stir

revólver: revolver

revolverse: roil, shuffle

revuelco: stir

revuelta: revolt, uprising

revuelto: scrambled

rey: king, ruler

rezagarse: fall behind, lag, leave behind

rezar: pray

rezos: prayer

riachuelo: stream

ribera: bank, shore

ribera del lago: lakefront

ribete: trim

ribosoma: ribosome

rico: flavorful, high, nice, rich, wealthy

ridículo: ridiculous

riel: rail, runner, track

rienda: rein

riesgo: danger, gamble, hazard, liability, risk, threat

riesgoso: risky

rifarse: draw lots

rifle: rifle

rigidamente: stiffly

rigidez: rigidity, stiffness

rígido: rigid, stiff

rigor: thoroughness

rigurosamente: rigidly, rigorously, strictly

riguroso: rigid, rigorous, strict, thorough, tight, unrelenting
rima: rhyme
rimar: rhyme
rímel: mascara
rincón: corner
ring: ring
rinoceronte negro: black rhino
riña: quarrel
riñón: kidney
río: river
río arriba: upstream
riqueza: riches, richness, treasure, wealth
risa: laugh
risa nerviosa: giggle
risotada: laughter
ritmo: beat, pace, pacing, rate, rhythm
ritmo circadiano: circadian rhythm
rito: rite
ritual: ritual
rival: challenger, opponent, rival
rivalidad: rivalry
rivalizar: rival, vie
rizado: curly, fuzzy
rizarse: curl
rizo: curl
rizoide: rhizoid, root hair
rizoma: rhizome, root hair
robado: stolen
robar: burglarize, loot, rob, take
robar en tiendas: shoplift
robar(se): steal
roble: oak
robo: break-in, burglary, robbery, stealing, theft
robo de identidad: identity theft
robot: robot
robusto: healthy, robust, sturdy
roca: boulder, rock
roca de dislocación: fault block
roca lamelar: foliated rock
roce: run-in
rociador: sprinkler
rociar: lace, spray, sprinkle
rocío: spray
rock: rock
rodaje: shoot
rodar: film, roll, shoot, taxi
rodear: envelop, ring, round, surround
rodearse: surround
rodeo: detour, roundup
rodilla: knee
rodillo: roller, rolling pin
roedor: rodent
roer: eat away
rogar: beg
rojo: flushed, red
roldana: washer
rollo: reel, roll
ROM: ROM
romana: Roman
romance: romance
romano: Roman

romántica: romantic
romanticismo: romance
romántico: romantic
rombo: diamond, rhombus
romper: breach, bust, rip, smash, tear up
romper el corazón a alguien: break somebody's heart
romper el hervor: bring to a boil
romper el hielo: break the ice
romper en pedazos: rip up
romper filas: break rank
romper(se): break, break off, rupture, snap, split
romperse (el cascarón): hatch
rompimiento: breach, break, breakdown, breakup
roncar: snore
roncha: rash
ronco: hoarse
ronda: round
ronda eliminatoria: round
rondana: washer
rondar: haunt
rondó: rondo
ronquido: snore
ropa: clothes, clothing, garment, gear, wear
ropa de cama: bedding
ropa heredada: hand-me-down
ropa interior: underwear
ropa lavada: laundry
ropa para lavar: laundry
ropero: wardrobe
rosa: pink, rose
rosado: pink
rosca: thread
rosquilla: doughnut
rostizar: broil
rostro: face
rotación: rotation
rotación prógrada: prograde rotation
rotación retrógrada: retrograde rotation
rotar(se): rotate
rottweiler (raza de perros): rottweiler
rotulador: highlighter
rotular: label
rótulo: label, tag
rotundamente: outright
rotundo: emphatic, flat, outright, unqualified
rotura: rupture, tear
round: round
rozar: brush, graze, scrape
RR.PP.: PR
rubia: blonde
rubio: blonde, fair
rubor: flush, glow
ruborizarse: flush
rúbrica: rubric
rudimentario: crude, primitive
rueca: spinning wheel
rueda: wheel
rueda de la fortuna: Ferris wheel
rueda de prensa: news conference
rueda de recambio: spare tire
rueda de repuesto: spare tire
rueda hidráulica: waterwheel
rugby: rugby
rugido: roar
rugiente: raging
rugir: rage, roar
ruido: noise, rattle, roar, sound
ruido del baño al jalarle: flush
ruidosamente: noisily
ruidoso: noisy
ruin: sleazy
ruina: collapse, downfall, ruin
rumbo: course
rumor: rumor
ruptura: breakup, rupture
rural: rural
rústica: softcover
ruta: route
ruta de navegación: lane
rutabaga: rutabaga
rutina: routine
rutinariamente: routinely
rutinario: routine

S

sábado: Saturday
sabana: savanna
sábana: sheet
sabedor: informed
sabelotodo: know-it-all
saber: find out, know, learn, scholarship, taste, tell
saber de: hear from
saber defenderse: hold one's own
saber perder: be a good loser
saberse: get out
sabia: scholar
sabiduría: wisdom
sabio: learned, scholar, wise
sabiondo: smart aleck
sable: saber
sabor: flavor, taste
saborearse: relish
saborizante: flavoring
sabroso: flavorful, juicy, nice, tasty
sabueso: hound
sacacorcho: corkscrew
sacacorchos: corkscrew
sacar: bring out, drag out, draw, eject, extract, get, publish, put out, remove, run off, score, serve, stick out, take out, take/get out, withdraw
sacar a la luz: come/bring to light
sacar a relucir: bring out, highlight
sacar adelante: make a go of

sacar brillo: polish
sacar con cuchara: scoop
sacar de apuros: bail out
sacar de onda: blindside
sacar de quicio: get on somebody's nerves
sacar el aire: breathe out
sacar el mayor provecho: make the most of something
sacar la vuelta a: duck
sacar provecho de: profit from
sacar rápidamente/a todo prisa: whip out
sacar ventaja: edge out, lap
sacarle algo a alguien: pry something out of somebody
sacarle jugo al dinero: (get your) money's worth
sacarle la vuelta a: get around
sacerdote: preacher, priest, Reverend
saco de dormir: sleeping bag
saco deportivo: sport coat, sport jacket
saco informal: sport coat, sport jacket
sacrificar: put down, put to sleep, sacrifice, slaughter
sacrificio: sacrifice
sacudida: beat, flick, jerk, shake
sacudir: brush, buffet, flick, rock, shake, toss
sacudir el polvo: dust
safari: safari
sagrado: holy, sacred
sal: salt
sala: chamber, hall, living room, room, ward
sala de espera: lounge
sala de estar: lounge
sala de estudio: study hall
sala de justica: courtroom
sala de operaciones: operating room, surgery
sala de recuperación: recovery room
sala de restablecimiento: recovery room
sala de urgencias: emergency room
sala recreativa (con videojuegos): video arcade
salado: salted, salty
salamandra: salamander
salar: salt
salario: salary, wage
salchicha: sausage
salchicha de Frankfurt: wiener
salchicha de Viena: wiener
saldar cuentas: settle a score
saldo: balance

salero: salt shaker
sales de baño: bath salts
salida: departure, departures, emergence, exit, outlet, output, sailing
salida del sol: sun-up, sunrise
saliente: outgoing
salinidad: salinity
salir(se): break, clear, come out, depart, emerge, exit, flow, get off, go, go out, leave, pull out, rise, set off, set out, sprout, turn off, work out
salir a: go forth
salir a borbotones: pour
salir a chorros: squirt
salir a la luz: come out, come/bring to light
salir a la superficie: surface
salir adelante: make a go of
salir bien/mal: do well/ badly
salir con: date
salir con vida: survive
salir corriendo: dash off, make off
salir de: burst
salir de vacaciones: get away
salir del cascarón (las crías): hatch
salir del sistema: log out
salir desordenadamente: pile out of
salir disparado: bolt, shoot
salir el tiro por la culata: rebound
salir en desbandada: stampede
salir ganando: gain
salir perdiendo: lose out
salir/entrar bramando de cólera: storm
salir(se) de control: get out of hand
salirse con la suya: get away with, get/have one's (own) way
saliva: saliva, spit
salmón: salmon
salón: hall, lounge
salón de belleza: beauty shop, salon
salón de clases: classroom
salpicado: dotted, pitted
salpicadura: splash
salpicar: splash, splatter
salpicar con: pepper
salpicar de: pepper
salpullido: rash
salsa: sauce
salsa (de frutas o verduras): relish
salsa (espesa): dip
salsa (hecha con el jugo de la carne asada): gravy
salsa de soya: soy sauce
salsa rusa: Russian dressing

salsa tártara: tartar sauce
saltación: saltation
saltar(se): bound, jump, leap, skip, spring
saltar con un pie: hop
saltar en un pie: hop
saltar la cuerda: skip, skipping
saltar la reata: skip
saltito: hop
salto: jump, leap, skip
salto con un pie: hop
salud: bless you, health
saludable: healthy, sound
saludablemente: healthily
saludar: greet, salute, wave
saludar con (un gesto de) la cabeza: nod
saludo: greeting, hello, salute, wish
saludos: (give) regards
salvación: salvation
salvaguarda: safeguard
salvaguardar: safeguard
salvaje: savage, wild
salvajemente: savagely
salvar: bridge, salvage, save
salvar la vida: survive
salvarse: escape
salvarse de: get out of
salvarse de milagro: have a narrow escape
salvavidas: life preserver
salvedad: qualification
salvo: except
salvo por: apart from, aside from, but for
sanar: heal
sanción: punishment
sancionar: discipline, punish
sanciones: sanctions
sandalias: sandal
sandez: moonshine
sándwich: sandwich, sub
sándwich de carne guisada en salsa: sloppy joe
sangrado: bleeding
sangrar: bleed
sangre: blood
sangre coagulada: gore
sangre nueva: new/ fresh/young blood
sangría: drain
sangriento: bloody
sanitario: sanitary
sanitarios: restroom
sano: healthy, sound
sano y salvo: in one piece
santo: saint
santuario: sanctuary
saque: serve
saqueador: looter
saqueador: looter
saquear: loot
saqueo: looting
sarampión: measles
sarcástico: sarcastic
sargassum: sargassum
sargento: sergeant
sargento mayor: sergeant major

sarpullido: rash
sarta: stream
sartén: frying pan, pan
sasafrás: sassafras
sastra: tailor
sastre: tailor
satélite: satellite
satélites meteorológicos geoestacionarios: GOES
satín: satin
sátira: satire
satisfacción: fulfillment, gratification, satisfaction
satisfacción con el empleo: job satisfaction
satisfacer: fulfill, gratify, meet, satisfy
satisfactoriamente: successfully
satisfactorio: gratifying, satisfactory, satisfying
satisfecho: content, fulfilled, full, proud, satisfied
saturar(se): flood
Saturno: Saturn
sazonado: flavored
sazonador: flavoring
sazonar: flavor, season
scatterplot: scatterplot
sci-fi: sci-fi
score: score
scroll bar: scroll bar
se him, himself, her, herself, it, itself, them, themselves, you, yourself, yourselves
se dice: rumour/legend/ tradition has it, they say
se lo tiene bien merecido: serve somebody right
se reduce a: boil down to
se supone: be supposed to
se supone que: be meant to
sea lo que fuere: whatever
SEC: SEC
secadora: dryer
secar(se): dry, dry out, dry up, mop up
secar con toalla: towel
secarse: dry up
secarse la frente: mop one's forehead
sección: section, segment
sección blanca: White Pages
seco: dried, dry
secoya: sequoia
secreción: discharge
secretamente: secretly
secretaria: minister, secretary
secretaría: department, ministry
secretaria de admisiones: registrar
Secretaria de Estado: Secretary of State
secretaria de hacienda/ economía: chancellor
secretario: chancellor,

minister, secretary
secretario de admisiones: registrar
Secretario de Estado: Secretary of State
secreto: classified, hidden, secrecy, secret, undercover
secta: cult, sect
sectario: sectarian
sector: industry, section, sector, segment
sector público: public sector
secuela: aftermath, sequel, wake
secuencia: footage, sequence, succession, thread
secuencia de pasos de baile: dance sequence
secuencia geométrica: geometric sequence
secuestrador: kidnapper
secuestradora: kidnapper
secuestrar: kidnap, seize
secuestro: kidnapping
secular: secular
secundar: go along with, second
secundaria: secondary
secundario: incidental, marginal, secondary, subsidiary
sed: thirst
seda: silk
sedán: sedan
sede: host
sediento: thirsty
sedimentario: sedimentary
sedimento: deposit, deposition, sediment
seducción: seduction
seducir: lure, seduce
seglar: lay, secular
segmento: segment
segmento de baile: dance phrase
segmento de danza: dance phrase
segregación racial: apartheid
seguido: running, solid
seguido de: followed by
seguidor: follower, supporter
seguidora: follower, supporter
seguidos: in a row
seguimiento: follow-up
seguir: continue, follow, forge, go on, keep, tail, take, trail
seguir adelante: forge ahead, get on, go ahead, keep going, proceed, push ahead, push on
seguir adelante con algo: follow through
seguir de cerca: monitor, shadow
seguir el ejemplo de alguien: follow someone's example
seguir en vigor: stand
seguir la corriente:

humor
seguir la pista: trace, trail
seguir la pista de: be on the trail of
seguir los pasos de alguien: follow in somebody's footsteps
seguir siendo cierto: hold true
seguir(le) la pista: track
según: according to
según parece: by the look of/by the looks of
según se dice: reportedly
según se informa: reportedly
segunda enseñanza: secondary
segunda mano: secondhand
segundas (productos): seconds
segundo: deputy, latter, second
segundo mejor: next best
seguramente: surely
seguridad: certainty, reassurance, safety, security
seguridad de funcionamiento: reliability
seguridad nacional: national security
seguridad social: Social Security
seguro: certain, certainly, confident, for sure, insurance, positive, safe, secure, sure
seguro de desempleo: unemployment compensation
seguro de sí mismo: self-confident
seguro de uno mismo: sure of oneself
seguro y fácil ganador: shoo-in
seis: six
selección: array, choice, extract, selection
selección natural: natural selection
seleccionar: pick, select
selectivo: selective
selecto: choice, elite, select
sellar: seal
sello: seal, stamp
sello hermético: seal
selva: forest, jungle
selva (tropical): rain forest
semáforo: stoplight
semana: week
semana laboral: work week, working week
semanal: weekly
semanalmente: weekly
semanario: weekly
sembradío: field
sembrar: farm, plant, sow
semejante: alike, analogous, similar
semejanza: similarity
semen: sperm

semental: stud
semestral: semiannual
semestre: semester
semibreve: whole note
semiconductor:
  semiconductor
semifinal: semifinal
semilla: seed
semillero: nursery
seminario: seminar
semínima: quarter note
semítico: Semitic
senado: Senate
senador: senator
senadora: senator
sencillo: one-way, plain,
  single, straightforward
senda: trail
sendero: lane, path,
  pathway, track, trail
senil: senile
senilidad: senility
seno: breast, sine, trough
sensación: feel, feeling,
  sensation, sense
sensacional: sensational
sensacionalmente:
  sensationally
sensatez:
  reasonableness, sanity,
  sense
sensatamente:
  reasonably
sensato: sane, sensible,
  sound
sensibilidad: sensation,
  sensitivity
sensible: sensitive,
  tender
sensor: sensor
sensorial: sensory
sensual: sexy
sentar cabeza: settle
  down
sentar las bases: lay
sentar un parámetro: set
  an example
sentar(se): seat, sit, take
  a seat
sentarse en el borde de
  algo: perch
sentencia: decree,
  sentence
sentenciado: doomed
sentenciar: sentence
sentido: meaning, point,
  sense, way
sentido común: common
  sense, sense
sentido del humor: sense
  of humor
sentido moral: moral
sentimental:
  sentimental
sentimentalismo:
  sentiment,
  sentimentality
sentimiento: feeling,
  sentiment
sentimientos de afecto:
  affection
sentir: feel, get, sense,
  touch
sentir afecto: feeling
sentir cosquillas: tickle
sentir lástima por:
  feel for
sentir nostalgia por: be

homesick for
sentir pena por: feel
  sorry for
sentir temor: fear
sentir(lo): sorry
sentir(se): feel
sentirse a gusto: take to
sentirse desairado: be/
  feel slighted
sentirse ofendido: be/
  feel slighted, take
  offense
sentirse perdido: be at
  a loss
seña: gesture
señal: cue, impression,
  mark, sign, signal
señalador: bookmark
señalar: gesture,
  indicate, mark, point
  out, single out
señalar (con el dedo):
  point
señalar con el dedo:
  point the finger at
señalar con la cabeza:
  nod
señor: gentleman, lord,
  master, mister, sir
señor (Sr.): Mr.
señora: lady, ma'am,
  madam
señora (Sra.): Mrs., Ms.
señorita: Miss
señorita (Srta.): Ms.
señuelo: lure
sépalo: sepal
separación: gap, parting,
  separation
separado: apart,
  estranged, separate,
  separated
separar(se): break up,
  cut off, detach, divide,
  isolate, part, pull away,
  separate, separate out,
  sort out, space, split up,
  tear apart
separatismo: separatism
separatista: separatist
septiembre: September
séptima parte: seventh
séptimo: seventh
septuagésimo:
  seventieth
sequedad: dryness
sequía: drought
ser: be, being, make
ser aceptado: get into
ser aclamado: hail
ser admitido: get into
ser afectado: suffer
ser aficionado a algo: be
  fond of something
ser amigos: be friends
ser apropiado: suit
ser capaz de: be able to
ser compatible: gel
ser complaciente:
  indulge
ser cuestión de: come
  down to
ser culpable: at fault
ser de ayuda: be of
  assistance
ser de día: be (day)light
ser decisivo para: be the
  making of

ser derrotado: lose
ser desfavorables las
  circunstancias para:
  things/the odds are
  stacked against
ser despiadado: play
  hardball
ser diferente: change,
  differ
ser digno rival: matched
ser distinto: differ
ser dueño de: own
ser el colmo: take the
  cake
ser el maestro: emcee
ser el padre: father
ser el primero en
  desarrollar: pioneer
ser el que manda: call
  the shots
ser electo: get in
ser evidente: be in
  evidence
ser hora de: be about
  time
ser humano: human
  being
ser igual: match
ser inconfundible algo:
  there's no mistaking
ser indulgente con
  alguien: make
  allowances for
  somebody
ser inminente: be upon
  someone
ser irritable: have a short
  temper
ser la sede de: host
ser libre de: be at
  liberty to
ser los últimos/primeros
  en la lista: be at the
  bottom/top of the pile
ser más numeroso:
  outnumber
ser miembro de: have a
  seat on
ser mucho más alto que:
  tower over
ser muy fácil: be nothing
  to it
ser muy reservado: keep
  to yourself
ser noticia: hit/grab the
  headlines
ser notorio: be in
  evidence
ser nuevo para: be news
  to (somebody)
ser objeto de: come in
  for, receive
ser para: be intended for,
  be meant for
ser pareja de: partner
ser parte de: be in on
ser posible: may
ser prioritario: take/have
  priority
ser producto de: spring,
  stem
ser publicado: be in print
ser razonable / sensato:
  make sense
ser responsable de:
  charge
ser seleccionado: letter
ser socio: belong

ser suficiente: do
ser sujeto de: liable for
ser traído, llevado o arrastrado por la corriente: be washed up
ser un cambio: change
ser útil: be of assistance, be of help, come in useful
será anunciado: TBA
sereno: poised
serial: serial
seriamente: seriously, soberly
serie: catalog, chain, serial, series, succession, train
serie de preguntas: quiz
seriedad: seriousness
serio: earnest, grave, serious, severe, sober, solid
serle desconocido algo a alguien: be a stranger to something
sermón: lecture, sermon
sermonear: lecture, scold
serpentear: curl, snake, wind
serpiente: snake
serrucho: saw
servicial: helpful
servicio: serve, service, tour of duty, utility
servicio activo: active duty
servicio al cliente: customer service
servicio civil: civil service
servicio comunitario: community service
servicio costanero: Coast Guard
servicio de estacionamiento de autos: valet parking
servicio de guardería infantil: day care
servicio de información telefónica: directory assistance
servicio diplomático: foreign service
servicio exterior: foreign service
servicio financiero: financial services
servicio para automovilistas: drive-through
servicio público: civil service
Servicio Secreto: Secret Service
servicio secreto: secret service
servicios: restroom
servicios de inteligencia: secret service
servicios médicos exclusivos para un grupo específico: health maintenance organization, HMO
servicios sociales: social services
servidor: server

servidor público: civil servant
servidora pública: civil servant
servidumbre: right of way
servilleta: napkin
servir(se): dish up, help, pour, serve, serve up, tip
servir (con cucharón): ladle
servir en bandeja de plata: hand on a platter
sesenta: sixty
sesgar(se): slant
sesgo: slant
sesión: hearing, session
sesión de contactos rápidos: speed dating
sesión de ejercicio: workout
sesión de entrenamiento: scrimmage
sesión de fotos: photo shoot
sesionar: sit
sesos: brain
set: set
setenta: seventy
seto: hedge
seudópodo: pseudopod
severamente: bitterly, sternly
severidad: rigidity, sharpness
severo: bitter, severe, sharp, stern
sexagésimo: sixtieth
sexismo: sexism
sexista: sexist
sexo: gender, sex
sexo opuesto: opposite sex
sexo seguro: safe sex
sexto: sixth
sexual: sexual
sexualidad: sexuality
sexualmente: sexually
sexy: foxy, sexy
shampoo: shampoo
short: shorts
shortcake: shortcake
shorts: cutoffs
si: if, when, whether
sí: sure, yeah, yes
si acaso/por si acaso: in case/just in case
si bien: though
si es que: if
si me preguntas a mí: if you ask me
sí mismas: themselves
sí mismo: oneself
sí mismos: themselves
si no: else, or, unless
si no es: if not
si quieres: if you like
si quieres saber: if you ask me
si uno debe hacer algo: if one must
si/do mayor: major key
sicóloga: psychologist
sicología: psychology
sicológico: psychological
sicólogo: psychologist
sicoterapia:

psychotherapy
SIDA: AIDS
sidra: cider, hard cider
siembra: planting
siempre: all the time, always, forever
siempre que: as long as/so long as, provided, whenever
siempre verde: evergreen
siempre y cuando: provided
sien: temple
siendo: being
sierra: range, saw, sierra
sierra eléctrica: buzzsaw
siesta: nap, sleep
siete: seven
sigilo: secrecy
sigla: acronym
siglo: century
significado: meaning, sense
significar: mean, spell, stand for
significativamente: meaningfully, significantly
significativo: important, meaningful, significant
signo: mark, sign
signo de admiración: exclamation point
signo de interrogación: question mark
signo de puntuación: punctuation mark
siguiente: as follows, following, next
sij: Sikh
sílaba: syllable
sílaba absurda: nonsense syllable
silabeo: syllabication
silbar: whistle
silbato: whistle
silenciar: silence
silencio: quietness, silence
silenciosamente: quietly, silently
silencioso: silent
silicato: silicate mineral
sílice: silica
silicio: silicon
silicona: silicone
silla: chair
silla de montar: saddle
silla de playa: beach chair
silla de ruedas: wheelchair
silla para jardín: lawn chair
sillar de clave: keystone
sillón: armchair, sofa
sillón reclinable: recliner
silueta: figure
silvestre: wild
silvicultura: forestry
simbiosis: symbiosis
simbólicamente: symbolically
simbólico: symbolic, token
simbolismo: symbolism
símbolo: symbol
símbolo de

radioactividad: radioactive symbol

simetría bilateral: bilateral symmetry

simetría radial: radial symmetry

simétrico: symmetrical

simiente: seed

similar: matching, similar

similar a: like

similitud: similarity

simio: ape

simpático: friendly

simpatizante: sympathizer

simpatizar: sympathize, warm

simple: mere, plain, simple

simple decoración: eye candy

simplemente: just, merely, plainly, simply

simplificación: simplification

simplificado: simplified

simplificar: dumb down, simplify

simulacro: drill, dry run

simulado: mocking

simulador: fraud

simuladora: fraud

simular: fake

simultáneamente: simultaneously, together

simultáneo: simultaneous

sin: free of, minus, without

sin aliento: out of breath

sin apretar: loosely

sin ayuda: single-handed

sin boleto: ticketless

sin ceremonias: informal

sin cohesion: loosely

sin comparación: second to none

sin complicaciones: easygoing

sin condición: no strings/ no strings attached

sin contratiempos: smooth

sin costo: free

sin cuidado: carelessly

sin darse cuenta: unaware

sin demora: on the spot, promptly

sin deudas: afloat

sin dificultad: readily

sin duda: certainly, no doubt, sure thing

sin duda alguna: definitely, without (a) doubt

sin embargo: however, nevertheless, nonetheless, on the other hand, yet

sin esperanzas: hopeless, hopelessly

sin éxito: unsuccessfully

sin experiencia: inexperienced

sin falta: without fail

sin fines de lucro: nonprofit

sin fines lucrativos: nonprofit

sin foliación: nonfoliated

sin fuerza: limply

sin futuro: dead-end

sin grumos: smooth

sin hogar: homeless

sin importancia: idle, insignificant, little

sin importar: however, no matter what, whatever

sin inconvenientes: clear

sin interrupción: on end

sin levantar el brazo por encima del hombro: underhand

sin mezcla: pure

sin necesidad de receta: nonprescription

sin obstáculos: clear

sin par: second to none, unparalleled

sin parar: on end, solid

sin peligro: safe

sin pensarlo: on the spur of the moment

sin plomo: unleaded

sin poder dormir: sleepless

sin porvenir: dead-end

sin precedentes: all-time, unprecedented

sin prejuicios: color-blind

sin problema: with ease

sin problemas: smooth

sin querer: by accident, unwitting

sin receta: nonprescription

sin recursos: helpless

sin registro: unlicensed

sin reparo alguno: unashamed, unashamedly

sin respuesta: unchallenged

sin restricciones: freely

sin rigidez: loosely

sin rodeos: baldly

sin sabor: flavorless

sin semilla: seedless

sin sentido: meaningless, mindless, pointless, senseless

sin sentido del humor: humorless

sin tacha: clean

sin tomar: be off something

sin trabajo: idle

sin tratar: untreated

sin usar: be off something

sin (ningún) valor: worthless

sin vergüenza alguna: unashamed

sin viento: calmly

sinagoga: synagogue

sinceramente: sincerely, truly

sinceridad: openness, sincerity

sincero: frank, genuine, hearty, open, sincere

s'nclina : syncline

s'ncopa: syncopation

sincronización: timing

sindicato: labor union, union

sindico: receiver, trustee

síndrome: syndrome

síndrome de Down: Down's syndrome

sinfonía: symphony

singular: singular

singularidad: uniqueness

siniestro: sinister

sinónimo: synonym

síntesis: summary

sintético: man-made, synthetic

sintetizar: sum up, summarize

síntoma: symptom

sintonizador: dial

sintonizar: tune, tune in

sinvergüenza: crook

síquico: psychic

Sir: sir

sirena: siren

sirope: syrup

sirvienta: maid, servant

sirviente: servant

sísmico: seismic

sismo: quake

sismógrafo: seismograph

sismograma: seismogram

sismóloga: seismologist

sismología: seismology

sismólogo: seismologist

sistema: facility, order, regime, setup, system

sistema (de órganos): tract

sistema acuovascular: water vascular system

sistema cardiovascular: cardiovascular system

sistema cerrado: closed system

sistema circulatorio abierto: open circulatory system

sistema circulatorio cerrado: closed circulatory system

sistema de coordenadas: coordinate system

sistema de órganos: organ system

sistema de posicionamiento global: global positioning system

sistema inmune: immune system

sistema inmunitario: immune system

sistema integumentario: integumentary system

sistema intravenoso: IV

sistema judicial: justice system

sistema linfático: lymphatic system

sistema métrico decimal: metric system

sistema muscular: muscular system

sistema nervioso: nervous system

sistema nervioso central: central nervous system
sistema nervioso periférico: peripheral nervous system
sistema operativo: OS
sistema periódico de los elementos: periodic table
sistema respiratorio: respiratory system
sistema solar: solar system
sistema tegumentario: integumentary system
sistemáticamente: consistently, systematically
sistemático: regular, systematic
sistémico: systemic
sitiar: besiege
sitio: siege, site, space, stand
sitio de internet: website
sitio de taxis: taxi stand
sitio web: website
situación: business, matter, picture, scene, situation
situación peligrosa: plight
situación trágica: tragedy
situado: located, situated
situar(se): lie, locate, put
situar la escena: set the scene/stage for
sketch: schtick
smartphone: smart phone
snowboard: snowboard
snowboarder: snowboarder
sobaco: armpit
sobajar(se): run down
soberana: ruler, sovereign
soberanía: sovereignty
soberano: ruler, sovereign
soberbio: glorious, superb
sobornar: bribe
soborno: bribe, payoff
sobrante: excess, surplus
sobrar: spare
sobras: scraps
sobre: about, above, against, envelope, into, mailer, on, on top, over, upon
sobre aviso: on alert
sobre la pista de: onto
sobre pedido: made to order
sobre todo: especially, largely
sobrecargo: steward, stewardess
sobrecoger: overtake
sobredosis: overdose
sobrellevar: cope, weather
sobrenatural: supernatural
sobrenombre: nickname

sobrentendido: implicit
sobrepasar: surpass
sobrepoblación: overpopulation
sobreponer: overlap
sobreponerse: rise above
sobreprecio: extra
sobresaliente: A-student, summa cum laude
sobresalir: excel
sobresaltar: jump, startle
sobresaltarse: start
sobresalto: start
sobretodo: overcoat
sobrevivencia: survival
sobreviviente: survivor
sobrevivir: come through, get through, survive
sobriamente: soberly
sobrina: niece
sobrino: nephew
sobrio: sober
soccer: football
socia: member, partner
socia fundadora: charter member
sociable: outgoing, sociable
social: social
socialismo: socialism
socialista: socialist
socializar: socialize
socialmente: socially
sociedad: partnership, society
sociedad de ahorro y préstamo: savings and loan
socio: member, partner
socio capitalista: silent partner
socio fundador: charter member
socióloga: sociologist
sociología: sociology
sociológico: sociological
sociólogo: sociologist
socorrer: help
socorro: help
sodio: sodium
sofá: couch, sofa
sofisticado: sophisticated
sofocar(se): put down, smother, suffocate
software: software
soga: rope
sol: head, sun
solamente: just, nothing but, only, simply
solar: lot, plot, plaza
soldado: soldier
soldado de caballería: trooper
soldado estadounidense: GI
soldado rasa: private
soldado raso: private
soldados: troop
soldar: heal
soleado: sunny
soledad: loneliness, wilderness
solemne: solemn
solemnemente: solemnly
solemnidad: solemnity

soler: tend
solfeo: solfege
solicitado: in (great) demand
solicitar: apply, ask, put in, request, take out
solicitud: application, request
sólidamente: solidly, strongly, sturdily
solidaridad: solidarity
solidez: solidity
sólido: firm, massive, solid, sound, stout, strong
solista: solo
(lombriz) solitaria: tapeworm
solitario: lone, lonely, lonesome, solitaire
sollozar: sob
sollozo: sobbing
solo: alone, by oneself, in isolation, lonely, on one's own, single, single-handed, solo
sólo: alone, but, just, only
sólo para adultos: X-rated
sólo parte de la historia: only part of the story/ not the whole story
sólo superado por: second only to
solsticio: solstice
soltar: cough up, drop, free, release, shell out, to let go of somebody/ something
soltarse: break loose, fall off
soltera: bachelorette
soltero: bachelor, single
solubilidad: solubility
soluble: soluble
solución: resolution, solution
solución saturada: saturated solution
solucionar: cure
soluto: solute
solvente: afloat
sombra: shade, shadow
sombra clara de ojos: highlighter
sombra de ojos: eye shadow
sombrero: bonnet, hat
sombrero de copa: top hat
sombrero de fieltro de ala ancha: fedora
sombrío: bleak, dark, gloomy, grim
someter: put through, subdue, subject
someter a juicio: try
someter a revisión médica: screen
someter a una prueba de carretera: road test
someterse: conform, submit, undergo
somnoliento: sleepy
sonaja: rattle
sonajero: rattle
sonar: blow, buzz, chime, dream, read, ring,

suegro

sound
sonar constantemente: ringing off the hook
sonar la hora: strike
sonarse: blow
sonata-allegro: sonata-allegro form
sonda espacial: space probe
sondear: explore, sound out, survey
sondeo: exploration, poll, survey
sondeo de opinión: opinion poll
sónico: sonic
sonido: audio, ring, sound
sonreír: grin, smile
sonreír radiante: beam
sonrisa: grin, smile
sonrojarse: blush, flush
sonrojo: blush, flush
sonrosado: rosy
soñar: fantasize
soñar con: dream of (somebody/something)
soñar despierto: daydream
soñoliento: sleepy
sopa: soup
sopesar: balance, weigh
soplar: blow
soplar(se): blow
soplo de aire fresco: breath of fresh air
soportar: bear, endure, put up with, stand, stick it out, support, tolerate
soporte: prop, support
sor: sister
sorber: sip
sorbo: sip
sordera: deafness
sórdido: sleazy
sordo: deaf, dull
sorprendente: astonishing, startling, striking, surprising
sorprendentemente: astonishingly, surprisingly
sorprender: spring, surprise
sorprendido: surprised
sorpresa: surprise
sorpresa causada por el precio de algo: sticker shock
sortear: get around, toss
sortija: ring
soso: dull, flavorless
sospecha: suspicion
sospechar: suspect
sospechosa: suspect
sospechosamente: dubiously, suspiciously
sospechoso: questionable, suspect, suspicious
sostén: bra, support
sostener(se): allege, carry through, contend, maintain, provide for, support, sustain
sostener en equilibrio: balance

sostener(se): support
sostenible: sustainable
sostenido: sharp
sótano: basement
soul: soul, soul music
soul food: soul food
soul music: soul music
souvenir: souvenir
soy: this is (telephone/radio/television)
soya: soy
spa: spa
spaghetti: spaghetti
spam: spam
spammer: spammer
squash: squash
statu quo: status quo
su: his, their, your
su seguro servidor: Yours truly
su Señoría: your/his/her honor
su(s): its
su/sus: her
suave: gentle, mild, smooth, soft
suavemente: gently, smoothly, softly
suavidad: gentleness, smoothness, softness
suavizar: qualify, smooth over, water down
subalterna: subordinate
subalterno: junior, subordinate
subasta: auction
subastar: auction, auction off
subcampeón: runner-up
subconsciente: subconscious
subcultura: subculture
súbdita: subject
súbdito: subject
subespecie: subspecies
subestimar: devalue, underestimate, understate
subida: climb
subido: deep
subíndice: subscript
subir: climb, elevate, gain, go up, hike, mark up, mount, post, rise, turn up, up
subir (la marea): come in
subir de peso: gain/put on weight
subir de precio: appreciate
subir de tono: rise
subir la ceja/las cejas: raise an eyebrow
subir repentinamente: jump
subírsele: go to one's head
subírsele a la cabeza: go to one's head
súbitamente: sharply
súbito: sharp, sudden
subjetivamente: subjectively
subjetividad: subjectivity
subjetivo: subjective
subjuntivo: subjunctive
sublevación: revolt
sublevarse: revolt

sublimación: sublimation
submarino: sub, submarine
subordinación: subordination
subordinada: subordinate
subordinado: inferior, subordinate
subordinar: subordinate
subrayar: emphasize, impress, stress, underline, underscore
subrepticiamente: creep
subscribir: sign
subsecuente: subsequent
subsidiado: subsidized
subsidiar: subsidize
subsidiaria: subsidiary
subsidiario: subsidiary
subsidio: grant, subsidy
subsidio por desempleo: unemployment, unemployment compensation
subsiguiente: subsequent
subsistir: remain
substancia: substance
substancia química: chemically
substituir: pinch-hit, stand in
substituta: stand-in
substituto: replacement, stand-in
subte: subway
subterráneo: subterranean, underground
subtexto: subtext
subtítulo: caption
subtropical: subtropical
suburbano: suburban
suburbio: suburb
suburbios: 'burbs
succionar: suck
sucedáneo: substitute
sucede que: as it happens
suceder: come about, go on, happen, have something happen, succeed
sucesión: string, succession, train
sucesión ecológica: ecological succession
sucesivo: successive
suceso: development, event
sucesor: successor
sucesora: successor
sucesos de actualidad: current events
suciedad: dirt
sucio: dirty, filthy, messy
sucio y descuidado: messy
sucursal: branch
sudadera: sweatshirt
sudar: sweat
sudeste: southeast
sudoeste: southwest, southwestern
sudor: sweat, sweating
suegra: mother-in-law
suegro: father-in-law

suela: sole
sueldo: paycheck, salary
suelo: earth, floor, ground, soil
suelo natal: birthplace
suelto: free, loose, stray
suena convincente/hueco: ring true/ring hollow
sueño: dream, sleep
suerte: fate, fortune, luck
suertudo: fortunate, lucky
suéter: jumper, sweater
suficiente: enough, sufficient
suficientemente: adequately, enough, sufficiently
sufijo: suffix
sufragar: meet
sufragio: franchise
sufragista: suffragist
sufrimiento: misery, suffering
sufrir: nurse, see, suffer, sustain, undergo
sufrir dolores atroces: rack
sufrir por la falta de: be starved of
sufrir un ataque de nervios: crack up
sufrir un colapso: collapse
sufrir una crisis nerviosa: crack
sugerencia: suggestion, tip
sugerente: suggestive
sugerir: imply, let, prompt, propose, signal, suggest
suicida: suicidal
suicidio: suicide
suite: suite
sujetador: bra
sujetapapeles: paper clip
sujetar(se): brace, clamp, fasten, hold, steady
sujetar (con un clip): clip
sujetar con cinta adhesiva: tape
sujetar con correa: strap
sujeto: subject
sujeto a: subject to, up for
sujeto a disponibilidad: standby
sujeto de: subject to
suma: addition, sum
sumamente: acutely, highly, mighty, supremely
sumar: add, add up, amount, figure up, total
sumergir(se): dive, immerse, submerge, swamp
suministrar: supply
sumir en: reduce to
sumir(se): throw
sumisión: submission
summa cum laude: summa cum laude
suni: Sunni
sunita: Sunni
suntuosidad: luxury

suntuoso: lavish, luxury
super: supermarket
súper: bang-up, super
Super Bowl: Super Bowl
Super Tazón: Super Bowl
superar: beyond, conquer, get over, improve, iron out, outdo, overcome, rise above, surpass
superar en número: outnumber
superávit: surplus
supercarretera: superhighway
supercarretera de la información: superhighway
supercelda: supercell
superficial: cosmetic, light, lightweight, shallow, superficial
superficialidad: superficiality
superficialmente: superficially
superficie: surface
superficie forestal: forest land
superfluo: redundant, unnecessary
supergigante: supergiant
superintendente: superintendent
superior: senior, superior, top, upper
superioridad: advantage, superiority
superlativo: superlative
supermercado: supermarket
supernova: supernova
superponer: overlap
superposición: overlap
superpotencia: superpower
supersónico: supersonic
superstición: superstition
supersticioso: superstitious
supertienda: big-box
supervisar: oversee, police, ride herd on, supervise
supervisión: supervision
supervisor: marshal, supervisor
supervisora: marshal, supervisor
supervivencia: survival
suplantación: impersonation
suplementario: extra
suplemento: supplement
suplente: acting, alternately, sub, substitute, surrogate
súplica: appeal, plea
suplicar: beg, plead
suplicio: ordeal, torture
suponer: assume, imagine, presume, reckon, suppose, think
supongo: I guess
suposición: assumption
suposición aventurada:

wild guess
supremo: supreme
supresión: suppression
suprimir: ax, cut out, delete, lift, suppress
supuestamente: allegedly, supposedly
supuesto: so-called, supposed, would-be
sur: south
sur geográfico: true south
sur verdadero: true south
surcar: streak
sureña: southern, Southerner
sureño: southern, Southerner
sureste: southeast
surf: surf
surfear: surf, surfing
surgencia: upwelling
surgir: arise, come up, crop up, develop, emerge, grow up, spring up
suroeste: southwest, southwestern
surtido: selection, supply
surtidor: fountain
surtir: furnish
surtir efecto: do the trick, kick in, work
susceptibilidad: sensitivity
susceptible: liable, sensitive
susceptible de: liable to
suscitar: arouse, bring forth, elicit, provoke
suscribir: subscribe
suscribirse: subscribe
suscripción: subscription
suscriptor: subscriber
suscriptora: subscriber
suspender: abandon, call, suspend
suspender (a un empleado): lay off
suspenderse: rain out
suspense: suspense
suspensión: abandonment, suspension, walkout
suspenso: suspense
suspicaz: suspicious
suspirar: gasp, sigh
suspirar por: pine for
suspiro: gasp, sigh
sustancia: substance
sustancia bioquímica: biochemical
sustancial: considerable, substantial
sustancialmente: substantially
sustantivo: noun
sustantivo contable: count noun, countable noun
sustentabilidad: sustainability
sustentable: sustainable
sustentar: support
sustento: keep, living
sustitución: substitution
sustituir: fill in, pinch-hit, substitute

sustituta: substitute

sustituto: foster, substitute, surrogate

susto: fright, scare, shock

sustraer: subtract

susurrar: murmur, whisper

susurrar algo: say something under one's breath

susurro: murmur, whisper

sutil: fine, subtle

sutilmente: delicately, subtly

suturar: stitch

suya: hers, its, theirs, yours

suyas: theirs, yours

suyo: his, its, theirs, yours

suyos: theirs, yours

switch: switch

Sylvilagus: cottontail

T

t-shirt: T-shirt

tabaco: tobacco

taberna: inn

tabla: board, table

tabla de contenidos: contents

tabla de picar: cutting board

tabla para deslizarse en la nieve: snowboard

tabla periódica de los elementos: periodic table

tableado: pleated

tablero: backboard, board, panel

tablero de ajedrez: checkerboard

tablero de anuncios: bulletin board, message board

tablero de damas: checkerboard

tablero de instrumentos: dashboard

tableta: bar, tablet

tabloide: tabloid

taburete: stool

tacaño: cheap

tachar: cross out

tachar de: brand

tache: cross

tacho de basura: trash can

tachón: stud

tachonado de joyas: bejeweled

tachuela: tack, thumbtack

tácito: implicit, written

tacleada: tackle

taclear: tackle

taco: burrito, cue, heel

tacón: heel

táctica: tack, tactic

tácticamente: tactically

táctico: tactical

tacto: feel, touch

tai chi: tai chi

taiga: taiga

tajada: wedge

tajar: slash

tajo: slash

tal: such, such and such

tal vez: maybe, perhaps

tal...que: such

talacha: grind, grunt work, legwork

taladradora: drill

taladrar: bore, drill

taladro: drill

talar: cut down, fell

talento: brilliance, gift, talent

talento innato: natural talent

talentoso: gifted, talented

talla: -sized

tallada: scrub

tallar: carve, scrub

taller: garage, shop floor, workshop

taller (industrial): yard

tallo: stalk, stem

talón: heel, stub

talonario: book

talud: bank

tamaño: proportion, size

tambalearse: flounder, reel, stagger, topple

también: also, as well, besides, so, too

tambor: drum, drummer, snare drum

tambor mayor: drum major

tamborilear: drum, tap

tamborileo: tap

tampoco: either, neither, nor

tan: so, such, that

tan ... como: as, every bit as

tan ... como sea posible: as ... as possible

tan pronto como: as soon as, the minute

tan sólo: only

tan... como para: so

tan/tanto... que: so

tanda: batch

tándem: tandem

tañer: toll

tanga: thong

tanque: cylinder, tank

tanque de combustible externo: external fuel tank

tanque de gasolina: gas tank

tantear: sound out

tanto: much, such

tanto ... como: as well as, both, not so much

tap: tap dance

tapa: binding, cap, cover, lid, top

tapadera: lid

tapado: blocked, plugged

tapadura: filling

tapar: block, cover up, cut out, obscure, plug, screen, wedge

tapete: mat, rug

tapete pequeño: throw rug

tapetí: cottontail

tapiar: board up

tapicería: upholstery

tapizar: paper

tapón: fuse, plug, stopper, top

taquigrafía: stenographer

taquigrafía: shorthand

taquígrafo: stenographer

taquilla: box office

tararear: hum

tardanza: lateness

tardar en irse: linger

tarde: afternoon, evening, late

tardío: late

tarea: assignment, homework, job, task

tareas domésticas: housework

tarifa: rate

tarima: deck

tarjeta: card

tarjeta (de banda magnética): swipe card

tarjeta amarilla: yellow card

tarjeta bancaria: bank card

tarjeta de amonestación: yellow card

tarjeta de crédito: bank card, charge card, credit card

tarjeta de débito: debit card

tarjeta de embarque: boarding pass

tarjeta de felicitación: greeting card

tarjeta de memoria: memory card

tarjeta de red: network card

tarjeta para raspar: scratch card

tarjeta que funciona como llave electrónica: key card

tarjeta roja: red card

tarjeta sim: SIM card

tarjeta telefónica: phonecard

tarrina: tub

tarro: mug

tarta de queso: cheesecake

tartamudear: stammer, stutter

tartamudeo: stammering, stutter, stuttering

tasa: rate

tasa de natalidad: birth rate

tasar: value

tatuaje: tattoo

tatuar: tattoo

taxi: cab, taxi, taxicab

taxonomía: taxonomy

taza: bowl, cup, toilet

tazón: bowl

te: you

té: tea

te lo juro: honest

té verde: green tea

teatral: theatrical

teatralmente: theatrically

teatro: creative drama, theater

teatro convencional:

formal theater

teatro de lectura: reader's theater

teatro de marionetas: puppetry

teatro de títeres: puppetry

teatro del absurdo: theater of the absurd

teatro épico: epic theater

teatro griego: Greek theater

teatro informal: informal theater

teatro isabelino: Elizabethan theater

teatro musical: musical theater

teatro no/nō: Noh

techo: ceiling, roof

tecla: key

teclado: keyboard

teclear: punch in, type

técnica: technician, technique

técnica mixta: mixed media

técnicamente: technically

técnico: technical, technician

tecnología: technology

tecnología de la información: information technology

tecnológicamente: technologically

tecnológico: technological

tecolote: owl

tectónica de placas: plate tectonics

tediosamente: tediously

tedioso: tedious, tiresome

tee: tee

teja de pizarra: slate

tejado: roof

tejano-mexicano: Tejano

tejedor: weaver

tejedora: weaver

tejemanejes: goings-on

tejer: knit, spin, weave

tejido: tissue, weaving

tejido conjuntivo: connective tissue

tejido de punto: jersey

tejido epitelial: epithelial tissue

tejido muscular: muscle tissue

tejido nervioso: nervous tissue

tela: cloth, fabric, material

tela de algodón especial para camisas: oxford

tela vaquera: denim

telar: loom

telaraña: web

tele: TV

telecomunicación: telecommunications

teleférico: cable car, tram

telefonear: phone, telephone

teléfono: phone,

telephone

teléfono celular: cellphone, cellular phone

teléfono celular versátil: smart phone

teléfono móvil: cellphone, cellular phone

telenovela: soap, soap opera

telerrealidad: reality TV

telescopio: telescope

telescopio de refracción: refracting telescope

televidente: viewer

televisar: televise

televisión: set, television, TV

televisión de circuito cerrado: CCTV

televisión digital: digital television

televisión oficial: public television

televisión realista: reality TV

televisor: television

televisor digital: digital television

telofase: telophase

telón: curtain

tema: issue, item, subject, subject matter, theme, thread, topic, topic sentence, track

tema y variación: theme and variation

temblar: quake, shiver, tremble

temblor: earthquake

temblor (de tierra): quake

tembloroso: shaky

temer: dread, fear, scared

temer que: be afraid (that)

temerario: daring

temeroso: fearful

temor: fear, scare

témpano de hielo: iceberg

temperamental: moody

temperatura: fever, temperature

tempestad: storm

tempestuoso: stormy

templado: warm

temple: spirit

templo: temple

temporada: run, season

temporada de rebajas: sale

temporal: temporary

temporalmente: temporarily

temprano: early

tenaz: persistent, stiff, unrelenting

tendencia: orientation, tendency, trend

tendencia a: liable to

tendencioso: biased, loaded

tender: hang out

tender a: tend

tender la mano: hold out

tender un puente: bridge

tender una trampa: trap

tendera: grocer, shopkeeper, storekeeper

tenderete: stall

tendero: grocer, shopkeeper, storekeeper

tendido de sol: bleachers

tendón: tendon

tenedor: fork

tener: be, contain, have, have got, hold, own

tener a raya: hold/keep in check

tener acceso a: access

tener admiradores: have a following

tener algo en las piernas: have something on one's knees

tener algo importante que decir: offer a word of (warning/advice/ praise/thanks)

tener algo/mucho a su favor: have something/a lot going for you

tener apenas lo suficiente para vivir: make ends meet

tener arreglado: down

tener bajo la manga: have up one's sleeve

tener buenas relaciones con: be on good terms with

tener cabida: accommodate

tener calentura: run/ have a temperature

tener calor: hot

tener cariño por: love

tener comezón: itch, tickle

tener como protagonista: star

tener confianza: trust

tener cuidado: beware, watch, watch it, watch out

tener cupo para: seat

tener debilidad por: be partial to

tener debilidad por algo: be a sucker for something

tener derecho: entitle

tener disponible: spare

tener dolor: hurt

tener dominio de una lengua: be fluent in a language

tener dudas o reservas: be dubious

tener el control: in control

tener el control de: be on top of/get on top of

tener el potencial para: have the makings of

tener en buen concepto: think

tener en claro: be clear about

tener en cuenta: bear/ keep in mind, take into

consideration

tener en la cabeza: be on one's mind

tener en las manos: be in one's grasp

tener en mente: bear/keep in mind

tener en total: number

tener entendido: gather

tener entradas: recede

tener espacio para: sleep

tener éxito: come off, make the grade, succeed, thrive

tener fe ciega en algo: swear by something

tener fiebre: run/have a temperature

tener fuerzas para: bring

tener ganas: feel like

tener ganas de vomitar: feel sick

tener hambre: be hungry

tener interés en: follow

tener invitados: entertain

tener la culpa: at fault

tener la impresión: be under the impression

tener la intención: mean

tener la intención de: have every intention of

tener la libertad de: be at liberty to

tener la mente puesta en: one's mind is on/have one's mind on

tener la oportunidad de: stand a chance of

tener la sensación: get

tener la última palabra: call the shots

tener la vista puesta en: set one's sights on

tener las probabilidades en contra: things/the odds are stacked against

tener los nervios de punta: on edge

tener los ojos puestos en algo: have your eye on something

tener lugar: take place

tener luz: be light

tener mal genio: have a short temper

tener miedo: be afraid, frightened, scared

tener náuseas: feel sick

tener o tomar en cuenta: reckon with

tener paciencia: bear with

tener permiso para: be at liberty to

tener por delante: lie

tener precio de: price

tener presente: bear/keep in mind

tener problemas con alguien: run/fall foul of someone

tener que: gotta, have got to, must

tener que decidirse: can't have it both ways

tener que enfrentar:

come up against

tener que hacer algo: have to do

tener que suceder: be bound to happen

tener que ver: play a part/play a role

tener que ver con: have a hand in something, have/be to do with

tener razón: be right, correct

tener razón en algo: have a point

tener relaciones sexuales: have sex

tener seguidores: have a following

tener sentido: make sense

tener sospechas: suspect

tener su residencia en: be in residence

tener suerte: be in luck, be lucky

tener temperatura: run/have a temperature

tener tendencias: tend

tener terror: dread

tener todas las ventajas: have the best of both worlds

tener un beneficio: have something to show for something

tener un día libre: have a day off

tener un éxito tras otro: go from strength to strength

tener un gran concepto de: think highly of

tener un papel en: come into

tener un pie en un lugar y el otro en otra parte: straddle

tener un rendimiento bajo: underperform

tener un segundo empleo: moonlight

tener una actitud abierta: have an open mind

tener una conversación con: have a word with

tener una opinión: hold an opinion

tener una posición: stand

tener una postura: stand

tener validez: run

tener vista a: overlook

tener voz y voto: have a say

tener/querer su audiencia: have/want one's day in court

tenia: tapeworm

teniente: lieutenant

tenis: sneaker, tennis

teñir: color, dye

tensar: tighten

tensar(se): tense

tensión: stress, tension

tensión arterial: blood pressure

tensión superficial: surface tension

tenso: tense

tentación: lure, temptation

tentado: tempted

tentador: tempting

tentar: finger, lure, tempt, touch

tentativa: attempt, endeavor, try

tentempié: nosh, snack

tenue: dim, faint

tenuemente: dimly

teorema binomio: binomial theorem

teoría: theory

teoría celular: cell theory

teoría de la gran explosión: big bang theory

teoría de los colores: color theory

teoría del big bang: big bang theory

teórica: theorist

teóricamente: in theory

teórico: theoretical, theorist

teorizar: theorize

terapeuta: therapist

terapia: therapy, treatment

terapia física: physical therapy

terapia intensiva: intensive care

terápsido: therapsid

Tercer Mundo: Third World

tercera parte: third

tercero: third

terceto: trio

tercio: third

terciopelo: velvet

terco: stubborn

tergiversar: twist

térmico: thermal

terminación: completion, termination

terminado: complete, done, finish, over, through (with something)

terminal: terminal

terminante: flat

terminar: close, complete, end, finalize, finish, get through

terminar de pagar: pay off

terminar en: end up

terminar(se): finish off, terminate

término: term

termita: termite

termo: flask

termoclina: thermocline

termocupla: thermocouple

termómetro: thermometer

termomotor: heat engine

termopar: thermocouple

termosfera: thermosphere

terna: trio

terno: suit

ternura: tenderness

terraza: terrace
terremoto: earthquake, quake
terreno: country, domain, ground, land, lot, plot, realm, territory
terreno aluvial: flood plain
terreno de aluvión: flood plain
terreno de juego: field
terreno forestal: forest land
terrible: dreadful
terriblemente: dreadfully, shockingly
territorial: territorial
territorio: territory
territorio continental: mainland
territorio personal: stomping ground
terror: dread, terror
terrorismo: terrorism
terrorista: bomber, terrorist
terso: smooth
tertulia digital: chat room
tesis: dissertation, thesis
tesorera: treasurer
tesorero: treasurer
tesoro: treasure
testamento: will
testículo: testis
testificar: testify
testigo: witness
testigo experto: expert witness
testigo ocular: eyewitness
testigo presencial: eyewitness
testimonio: testimony
tetera: pot, teakettle, teapot
tétrico: gloomy
Tex-Mex (tejano-mexicano): Tex-Mex
texto: print, text
textura: texture
tez: complexion
TI: information technology
ti: you
tía: aunt, dame
tianguis: market
tibio: warm
tiburón: shark
tictac: tick, ticking
tiempo: length, time, weather
tiempo (en deportes): half
tiempo aire: exposure
tiempo completo: full-time
tiempo de guerra: wartime
tiempo de inactividad: downtime
tiempo libre: leisure, spare time
tiempo muerto: downtime
tiempo suplementario: OT

tiempo verbal: tense
tienda: outlet, shop, store, tent
tienda de abarrotes: general store, grocer, grocery
tienda de comida para llevar: takeout
tienda de departamentos: department store
tienda de descuento: discount store
tienda de vinos y licores: liquor store
tienda que da a la calle: storefront
tiernamente: tenderly
tierno: gentle, sweet, tender, young
Tierra: globe
tierra: dirt, earth, ground, home, land
tierra adentro: inland
tierra comunal aledaña a una población: common
tierra firme: mainland
tierra negra: loam
tierra pantanosa: wetland
Tierra Santa: Holy Land
tierras altas: highlands
tieso: stiff
tifón: typhoon
tigre: tiger
tigre de Siberia: Siberian tiger
tigre siberiano: Siberian tiger
tijera: scissors
tijeras: scissors
tijeras de podar: pruning shears
tildar de: brand
timador: swindler
timadora: swindler
timar: cheating, con, rip off, swindle
timbrazo: ring
timbre: bell, stamp, timbre
timbre vocálico: vocal quality
tímidamente: shyly, timidly
timidez: shyness, timidity
tímido: self-conscious, shy, timid
timina: thymine
timo: swindle, thymus
timón: steering wheel
tímpano: eardrum
tina: bathtub, tub
tinglado: racket
tinta: ink
tinte: dye
tinterillo: pencil pusher
tintinear: jingle
tintorería: cleaner
tío: uncle
tío Sam: Uncle Sam
tip: hint, tip
típicamente: peculiarly, typically
típico: typical
tipo: character, form,

guy, individual, kind, sort, type
tipo de cambio: exchange rate
tipo de salchicha ahumada: bologna
tipo Ivy League: Ivy League
tira: strap, strip
tirada: circulation, throw
tiradero: dumping, garbage dump, litter
tiradores: suspenders
tirante: tight
tirantes: suspenders
tirar: chuck, drop, dump, pull, shoot, throw, throw away, toss
tirar basura: litter
tirar de: tug
tirar la toalla: throw in the towel
tirarse al agua: dive
tiritar: shiver
tiro: shot, throw
tirón: tug
tiroteo: shooting
tiroteo desde un vehículo en movimiento: drive-by
títere: pawn, puppet
titulado: entitlement
titular: incumbent
titularse: qualify
título: degree, title
tiza: chalk
tlacuache: opossum
to be orphaned: quedar huérfano
toalla: towel
toalla sanitaria: sanitary napkin
toallita para lavarse: washcloth
tobillo: ankle
tobogán: slide
tocada: gig
tocadiscos: record player
tocador: dresser
tocar(se): bunt, disturb, feel, finger, knock, meet, play, sound, toll, touch
tocar con la pata: paw
tocar la bola: bunt
tocarle: fall to
tocino: bacon
tocón: stump
todavía: even, on, still, yet
todavía más: further, furthest
todo: all, all-over, entire, every, everything, full, full-blown, quite, whole
todo el año: all year round
todo el mundo: everybody, everyone
todo el tiempo: all along, all the time, throughout
todo en uno: all-in-one, rolled into one
todos: everybody, everyone
todos los días: daily

tofu: tofu

toga: gown, robe

toldo: marquee

tolerado: unlicensed

tolerante: liberal

tolerar: endure, stand for, stomach, take, tolerate

toma: shot

toma de conciencia: reality check

toma del poder político: takeover

toma por asalto: storming

toma y daca: give and take

tomacorriente: outlet, socket

tomando: on (a drug)

tomar: catch, drink, get, have, hold, seize, snatch, take

tomar a alguien como rehén: take/hold somebody hostage

tomar a broma: laugh off

tomar aire: breathe in

tomar algo a pecho: take something to heart

tomar algo en consideración: make allowances for something

tomar aliento: take heart

tomar caminos distintos: go their separate ways

tomar (las cosas) con filosofía: be philosophical

tomar distancia: step back

tomar el pelo: razz

tomar en consideración: allow for, consider, take into account/take account of, take into consideration

tomar en cuenta: assuming, factor in, take into consideration

tomar en serio: take seriously

tomar forma: germinate, shape up

tomar la iniciativa: take the initiative

tomar la ofensiva: go on the offensive

tomar la temperatura: take someone's temperature

tomar las cosas con calma: take it easy

tomar las huellas digitales: take fingerprints

tomar medidas: act, take measures

tomar medidas drásticas: clamp down

tomar medidas enérgicas contra: crack down

tomar nota: log, take note

tomar parte: take part

tomar partido por: side

tomar por asalto: storm, take something by storm

tomar posesión: installation

tomar prestado: borrow

tomar prisionero: take/ hold captive

tomar represalias: retaliate

tomar tiempo: to take time

tomar un atajo: cut

tomar una sobredosis: overdose

tomar/beber a sorbos: sip

tomar/coger algo con delicadeza: cup something in one's hands

tomarla contra: gang up

tomarlo con calma: take it easy

tomarse la molestia: take the trouble

tomarse las cosas con calma: slow down, take something in one's stride

tomárselo con calma: take it easy

tomar(se) su tiempo: to take your time

tomate: tomato

tómelo o déjelo: take it or leave it

tonada: tune

tonalidad: tonality

tonel: barrel

tonelada: ton

tonelada (métrica): metric ton

tonificar: tone

tono: key, pitch, shade, tone

tono de discado: dial tone

tono de marcar: dial tone

tono menor: minor key

tonta: fool

tontamente: foolishly, stupidly

tontear: fool around

tontería: moonshine, nonsense, silliness, stupidity

tonterías: baloney

tonto: dingbat, dumb, fool, foolish, silly, stupid

top: top

toparse: encounter

toparse con: bump into, run across

tope: ceiling, speed bump, top

tópico: platitude, ready-made, topic

topógrafa: surveyor

topografía kárstica: karst topography

topógrafo: surveyor

toque: electric shock, finish, touch

toque de bola: bunt

toque de queda: curfew

toque final: the finishing touch

Torá: Torah

tórax: breast, chest, thorax

torbellino: rush, waterspout

torcedura: strain

torcer(se): bend, buckle, curve, strain, twist, wrench

torcer el gesto: screw

torcerse en espiral: spiral

torcido: bent, crooked

tordo norteamericano: robin

tormenta: firestorm, storm

tormenta de nieve: blizzard

tormenta eléctrica: thunderstorm

tormenta tropical: tropical storm

tormento: torture

tormentoso: stormy

tornado: tornado

torneo: tournament

torneo de atletismo: track meet

tornillo: bolt, screw

toro: bull

toronja: grapefruit

torpe: awkward, clumsy, klutz, labored, slowpoke

torpemente: awkwardly, clumsily

torpeza: clumsiness

torre: tower

torrija: French toast

torrente: flash flood, rush, stream

tortilla de huevo: omelet

tortitas: cakes

tortuga: tortoise, turtle

tortuga boba: loggerhead turtle

tortuga marina: sea turtle

tortuga mordedora: loggerhead turtle

tortura: torture

torturar: torture

tos: cough, coughing

toser: cough

tostada: toast

tostador: toaster

tostar: brown, toast

total: complete, dead, full, implicit, total, utter

totalidad: whole

totalmente: a hundred percent, one hundred percent, altogether, entirely, fully, quite, totally, whole, wholly

totopos: nachos

tour: tour

tóxico: toxic

toxicómana: drug addict

toxicomanía: substance abuse

toxicómano: drug addict

TQM: love, love from/all my love

trabajador(a): laborer, worker

trabajador(a) agrícola: laborer

trabajador(a) de la industria automotriz: autoworker

trabajador(a) extranjero: migrant

trabajador(a) independiente: self-employed

trabajador(a) itinerante: hobo

trabajador(a) social: social worker

trabajadores: labor, labor force

trabajar: clerk, work

trabajar con las manos: labor

trabajar de/como disc-jockey: deejay

trabajar en conjunto: pull together

trabajar en el jardín: garden

trabajar incansablemente: labor

trabajar la tierra: farm

trabajitos: odd jobs

trabajo: assignment, duty, employment, essay, job, occupation, project, work

trabajo comunitario: community service

trabajo de campo: legwork

trabajo de esclavos: slave labor

trabajo duro: labor

trabajo en equipo: teamwork

trabajo pesado: grunt work

trabajo preliminar: legwork

trabajo social: social work

trabajos forzados: hard labor

trabajoso: labored

trabar amistad: make friends

trabar(se): jam

tracalear: rip off

tracción integral: four-wheel drive

tracto: tract

tractor: tractor

tradición: folklore, tradition

tradicional: conventional, time-honored, traditional

tradicionalismo: conservatism

traducción: translation

traducir: translate

traducirse en: mean

traductor: translator

traductora: translator

traer: bring, bring along, fetch, get

traficante: trafficker

traficar con: traffic

tráfico: traffic, trafficking

tragar(se): fall for, swallow

tragedia: tragedy

trágico: tragic

trago: booze, drink, swallow

tragón de gasolina: gas guzzler

traición: sell-out

traicionar: betray

tráiler: trailer

tráiler park: trailer park

traje: costume, dress, outfit, suit

traje de baño: swimsuit

traje espacial: space suit

traje sastre: pantsuit, suit

trama: dramatic structure, plot, plotline

trama alimentaria: food web

tramar: cook up, engineer, hatch, scheme

trámites burocráticos: red tape

tramo: flight, leg, length, stretch

tramoyistas: stage crew

trampa: trap

trampa de arena: bunker, sand trap

tramposa: cheat, cheater

tramposo: cheat, cheater

trancazo: belt

tranquilamente: calmly, coolly, peacefully, quietly

tranquilidad: calm, quietness, stillness

tranquilizar(se): cool down, quiet, reassure, relieve, soothe, steady oneself

tranquilo: calm, cool, peaceful, quiet, soothing, still

transa: swindle

transacción: transaction

transar: swindle

transbordador: ferry, shuttle

transbordador espacial: shuttle, space shuttle

transbordar: change

transcontinental: coast-to-coast

transcripción: transcript

transcurrir: elapse, go on

transferencia: transfer

transferencia de créditos: credit transfer

transferir: hand over, transfer

transfigurar: transform

transformación: transformation

transformar: change into, transform

transformarse: evolve

transgénico: GM

transgresión: infraction

transición: transition

transitivo: transitive

tránsito: traffic, transit

transitorio: provisional

translúcido: translucent, transparent

traslucir: give away

transmisión: airing, broadcasting, transmission

transmisión de velocidad: gear

transmisión en las cuatro ruedas: four-wheel drive

transmisión por televisión: telecast

transmisor: transmitter

transmitir(se): air, beam, broadcast, convey, forward, hand down, transmit

transmitir por radio: radio

transmitir por repetidor: relay

transparencia: slide

transparente: clear, transparent

transpiración: transpiration

transpirar: sweat

transpondedor: transponder

transportado por aire: airborne

transportar: ferry, take, transport

transportar con dificultad: cart

transportar por aire: airlift

transporte: transit, transportation

transporte activo: active transport

transporte pasivo: passive transport

transporte público: mass transit, public transportation

transportista: trucker

transversal: transversal

tranvía: streetcar, tram

trapeador: mop

trapear: mop

trapo: cloth, rag

tráquea: trachea

traquetear: rattle

traqueteo: rattle

tras: after, onto, underneath, upon

tras bastidores: behind the scenes

tras las rejas: behind bars

trasatlántico: ocean-going

trascendental: definitive

trascender: cut across

trasero: back, behind, butt, rear

trasfondo: subtext, undercurrent

traslación: translation

trasladar(se): move on, relocate, transfer, transplant

traslado: relocation, transfer

traslapar: overlap

traslape: overlap

traslucir: betray

traspapelado: missing

traspaso: transfer

trasplantar: transplant

trasplante: transplant

trastornado: disturbed, upset

trastornar: upset

trastorno: trouble

trastorno alimenticio: eating disorder

trastorno de la alimentación: eating disorder

trasvasable: downloadable

trasvasar: download

tratado: treaty

tratamiento: course, therapy, title, treatment

tratamiento de textos: word processing

tratamiento severo o injusto: a raw deal

tratar: attempt, concern, seek, take up, treat, try

tratar con: deal with

tratar con mano dura: come down on

tratar de: deal with

tratar de contener: fight

tratar de morder: snap

tratar de no pensar en: block out

tratar injustamente: victimize

tratar por encima: touch

tratar sobre: show

trato: bargain, deal, dealings, treatment

trauma: trauma

traveler's check: traveler's check

travesía: crossing, voyage

travestí/travestí: in drag

travesura: mischief

traviesa: handful

travieso: handful, naughty

trayectoria: fortune

trayectoria del proyectil: projectile motion

trazar: chart, map out, plot

trazo: stroke

trazo rápido: flick

trébol: clover, cloverleaf, club

trece: thirteen

treceavo: thirteenth

trecho: leg, stretch

tregua: truce

treinta: thirty

tremendamente: awfully, tremendously

tremendo: tremendous

tren: train, tram

tren de vida: lifestyle

tren subterráneo: metro

trencita: cornrow

trenza: braid, pigtail

trenzar: braid

trepar: climb, scramble

tres: three

tres cuartas partes: three-quarters

tres cuartos: three-quarters

tres en línea: tic-tac-toe

tres partes: ABA

treta: trick

triada: triad

triangular: triangular

triángulo: triangle

triángulo rectángulo: right triangle

tribal: tribal

tribu: tribe

tribuna: stand

tribunal: court, courtroom, tribunal

tribunal de apelaciones: appellate court, Court of Appeals

tribunal de causas de poca monta: small claims court

tribunal de distrito: district court

tribunal superior: superior court

tributación: taxation

tributario: tributary

tributo: tribute

tricolor: tricolor

tridimensional: three-dimensional

trigésimo: thirtieth

trigo: wheat

trimestral: quarterly

trimestralmente: quarterly

trimestre: quarter, term, trimester

trineo: bobsled, sled

trino: song

trío: trio

tripas: gut

triple: triple

triplicar(se): triple

tripulación: crew

tripulado: manned

triste: bleak, lonely, lonesome, sad

tristemente: bleakly, sadly, unhappily

tristeza: sadness

triturador: garbage disposal

trituradora: garbage disposal

triturar: crunch, crush

triunfador: successful

triunfante: victorious

triunfar: triumph

triunfo: achievement, success, triumph, win

trivial: petty

trocito: chip

trofeo: cup, trophy

tromba marina: waterspout

trombón: trombone

trompa: trunk

trompa de Falopio: fallopian tube

trompada: punch

trompeta: trumpet

tronar: flunk, thunder

tronco: body, log, trunk

trono: throne

tropa: troop

tropas: troop

tropel: flock

tropezar: stub, stumble

tropezar con: run into, stumble across

tropezar(se): trip

tropezarse con: run across, run up against

tropical: tropical

tropismo: tropism

troposfera: troposphere

tropósfera: troposphere

troquelar: stamp

trozo: chunk, fragment, lump, piece, slip

truco: trick

trueno: boom, clap, thunder

tsunami: tsunami

tu: your

tú: you

tú misma: yourself

tú mismo: yourself

tuberculosis: TB

tubería: pipe, plumbing

tubería principal: mains

tubo: pipe, tube

tubo de ensayo: test tube

tubo de escape: tailpipe

tubo de órgano: pipe

tubo fluorescente: fluorescent light

túbulo seminífero: seminiferous tubule

tuerca: nut

tumba: grave

tumbar: break down, push over

tumbar a tiros: gun down

tumbarse: lie down

tumbona: beach chair

tumor: growth, tumor

tumulto: crush

tunda: whipping

tundra: tundra

túnel: tunnel

túnica: tunic

turba: mob, peat

turbina: turbine

turbio: cloudy, underhand

turismo: tourism

turista: tourist, traveler

turnar(se): rotate, take turns

turno: go, rotation, shift, turn

turno de noche: graveyard shift

turno nocturno: graveyard shift

tus: your

tutor: guardian

tutora: guardian

tuya: yours

tuyas: yours

tuyo: yours

tuyos: yours

U

ubicación: location

ubicado: set

ubicar: trace

ubicar(se): locate

UE: EU

ufano: proud

úlcera (por decúbito): bedsore

últimamente: lately

último: bottom, final, last, latest, latter, latter, ultimate

último modelo: state-of-the-art

último suspiro: last gasp
último toque: the finishing touch
últimos momentos: last gasp
ultrajar: outrage
ultraje: outrage
ultravioleta: ultraviolet
umbral: doorstep, threshold
un: a, an, one, some
un cachito: a bit
un desastre: hopeless
un pedacito: a bit
un poco: a bit
un poco (de): some
un poquito: (for) a bit, a bit
un tanto: somewhat
una: a, an, one, some
una vez: once
una vez que: once
una y otra vez: again/ time and again
unánime: unanimous
unas: some
uña: fingernail, nail
undécimo: eleventh
únicamente: purely, solely
unicelular: unicellular
único: isolated, one-of-a-kind, one-time, only, sole, unique
unidad: unit, unity
unidad astronómica: astronomical unit, AU
unidad de disco: disk drive, drive
unidad de disco portátil: flash drive
unidad de masa atómica: amu, atomic mass unit
unidad no normalizada: nonstandard unit
unido: united
unificación: unification
unificado: united
unificar: unify
uniformación: standardization
uniformado: uniformed
uniformar: standardize
uniforme: even, gear, unified, uniform
uniforme de faena: fatigue
uniformemente: uniformly
uniformidad: uniformity
unilateral: unilateral
unión: link, union
unión de crédito: credit union
Unión Europea: European Union
unir: bind, join, link, meld, straddle, unite
unir con cinta adhesiva: tape
unir en matrimonio: marry
unir fuerzas: join forces
unir los pedazos de: piece together
unir(se): band together, hook up, merge, pull together

unirse (en apoyo de): rally
unirse a: join in
unirse con: team up
unitaria: Unitarian
unitario: Unitarian
unity: unity
universidad: college, school, university
universidad pública: state university
universitario: collegiate
universo: universe
uno: one, some
uno a otro: each
uno al otro: one another
uno con otro: together
uno de los dos: one or other
uno de los nuestros: one of us
uno mismo: oneself
uno o dos: one or two
uno que otro: odd
uno u otro: one or other
uno y otro: either
unos: some
unos cuantos: few
untar: spread
untar mantequilla: butter
uranio: uranium
Urano: Uranus
urbanismo: city planning, planning
urbanismo funcional: smart growth
urbanismo orgánico: smart growth
urbanización: development
urbanizado: built-up, developed
urbano: urban
uretra: urethra
urgencia: urgency
urgencias: emergency room, ER
urgente: immediate, urgent
urgentemente: urgently
URL: URL
urna: poll
usable: usable
usado: pre-owned, secondhand, used
usar: employ, run, take, use, wear
USB: flash drive, USB
uso: usage, use, wear
uso de fondos obtenidos en préstamo: deficit spending
usted misma: yourself
usted mismo: yourself
usted(es): you
ustedes mismos: yourselves
usuaria: user
usuario: user
usuario final: end user
usurpar: usurp
utensilio: implement, instrument, tool, utensil
utensilio para hacer palomitas: popper

útil: helpful, useful
utilería: prop
utilidad: profit, usefulness
utilizable: usable
utilización: exploitation
utilizar: employ, use, utilize
útilmente: usefully
utopía: utopia
uva: grape

V

vaca: cow, pot
vacaciones: vacation
vacacionista: vacationer
vacante: opening, vacancy, vacant
vaciar(se): discharge, empty, pour, tip
vaciar y limpiar: clean out
vacilante: tentative
vacilantemente: tentatively
vacilar: hesitate, hover
vacilar a: razz
vacío: bare, blank, emptiness, empty, vacant, vacuum, void
vacuna: vaccine
vacunación: vaccination
vacunar: immunize, vaccinate
vacuno: dairy
vacuola: vacuole
vagabunda: hobo
vagabundo: hobo
vagamente: dimly, distantly, vaguely
vagar: roam, wander
vago: dim, hazy, indefinite, vague
vagón: car, carriage, coach
vagón de carga: freight car
vagón de equipaje: baggage car
vagoneta: van
vainilla: vanilla
vaivén: backward and forward, swing
vale: coupon, voucher
valenciana: cuff
valentía: bravery, valor
valer: be worth
valer la pena: be worth it/somebody's while, pay off
valerosamente: bravely
valeroso: brave
valerse por sí mismo: fend
válgame Dios: goodness/ my goodness
validación: validation
validar: validate
validez: validity
válido: legitimate, true, valid
valiente: brave, courageous, nervy
valija: suitcase
valioso: important, valuable
valla: barrier, fence
vallas: hurdle

valle: valley
valle en U: U-shaped valley
valle pendiente: hanging valley
valle producto de una fisura o grieta en la superficie de la tierra: rift valley
valor: backbone, bravery, courage, nerve, value
valor absoluto: absolute value
valor medio: median
valor nominal: face value
valor pH: pH
valoración: estimate
valorar: gauge, value
valores de producción: production values
valores familiares: family values
valores tradicionales: family values
valuar: value
válvula: valve
válvula de escape: outlet
vamos: come on, now
¿nos vamos?: shall we go?
vamos a ver: let me/ let's see
vampiro: vampire
vandalismo: vandalism
vándalo: punk, vandal
vanidad: vanity
vanidoso: vain
vano: hollow, pointless, vain
vapor: steam, vapor
vapor de agua: water vapor
vaporizador: vaporizer
vaporizar(se): vaporize
vaquero: cowboy
vara: stick
variabilidad: variability
variable: variable
variable aleatoria: random variable
variación: variation, variety
variado: diverse, miscellaneous, varied
variante: permutation
variar: vary
variar de... a: range from... to
variedad: brew, choice, range, variety
varilla: rod
vario: number, various
varios: several
varón: male
varonil: masculine
vaso: drink, glass
vaso (de precipitados): beaker
vaso capilar: lymphatic vessel
vasto: large, vast
vaya: oh, well, why
vecina: neighbor, villager
vecindad: vicinity
vecindario: neighborhood
vecino: neighbor, neighboring, resident, villager

vecinos del lugar: locals
vector: vector
vedar: ban
vegetación: vegetation
vegetal: plant
vegetales: Plantae
vegetariana: vegetarian
vegetariano: vegetarian
vehemente: intensely
vehículo: vehicle
vehículo con tracción en las cuatro ruedas: SUV
vehículo de recreo: recreational vehicle, RV
vehículo todo terreno: SUV
veinte: twenty
vejiga natatoria: swim bladder
vela: candle, sail
velar: sit up
velear: sail
veleo: sailing
velero: sailboat
veleta: wind vane
vello: hair
velo: veil
velocidad: gear, rate, speed
velocidad de llegada: terminal velocity
velocidad de onda: wave speed
velocidad final: terminal velocity
velocidad promedio: average speed
velocidad resultante: resultant velocity
velorio: wake
veloz: fast, quick, rapid-fire, swift
velozmente: fast
vena: vein
venado: deer
vencedor: victor, victorious
vencedora: victor
vencer: beat, conquer, defeat, overcome, run out, terminate
vencido: due, overdue
venda: bandage
vendaje: bandage, dressing
vendar: bandage
vendaval: gale
vendedor: clerk, sales clerk, salesman, seller, trader
vendedor ambulante: vendor
vendedora: clerk, sales clerk, seller, trader
vendedora ambulante: vendor
vender: be traded, fetch, get, market
vender al por menor: retail
vender ilegalmente: push
vender más barato: undercut
vender(se): sell
venderse todo: sell out
vendimia: vintage
veneno: poison

venenoso: poisonous
venerar: worship
vengar za: retaliation, revenge, vengeance
vengarse): avenge
vengarse: retaliate
venidero: ahead
venir: come, come around
venir bien: come in useful, suit
venir de lo profundo de uno: go run deep
venirse abajo: crumble, fall apart
venirse encima: come at
venta: sale
venta de artículos donados con fines caritativos: rummage sale
venta de garage: garage sale
venta de garaje: yard sale
ventaja: advantage, edge, merit, plus, the upper hand, virtue
ventana: window
ventas: business
ventas por teléfono: telemarketing
ventila: vent
ventilación: ventilation
ventilador: fan, vent
ventilar: air, vent, ventilate
ventisquero: drift
ventosa: sucker
ventoso: windy
ventrículo: ventricle
Venus: Venus
ver: look, look around, see, sight, tune in, view, watch
ver las cosas color de rosa: look through rose-colored glasses
ver venir: be in/within sight
veracidad: truth
verano: summer, summer school
verbal: verbal
verbalmente: verbally
verbo: verb
verbo auxiliar: auxiliary verb
verbo reflexivo: reflexive verb
verdad: right, truth
verdaderamente: real
verdadero: full-blown, genuine, proper, real, true
verde: green
verdor: greenness
verdugo: executioner
verduras: vegetables, veggie
vereda: trail
veredicto: verdict
vergonzoso: disgusting, dishonorable, guilty
vergüenza: disgrace, embarrassment, shame
verificación: check, verification
verificar: check, make sure, verify

verosímil: authentic, credible, plausible
versátil: versatile
versatilidad: versatility
verse: meet, reflect, show
verse envuelto en: catch up
verse recompensado: (get your) money's worth
vérselas con: to be reckoned with
versículo: verse
versión: version
versión de las cosas: side of the story
versión del director: director's cut
versión impresa: text
verso: verse
versus: v., versus
vertebrado: vertebrate
vertedero: dumping, landfill
verter: pour, tip
vertical: sheer, vertical
verticalista: top-down
verticalmente: vertically
vertido: dumping
vertiginoso: dizzying
vesícula: vesicle
vestíbulo: hall, lobby
vestido: clothed, dress, dressed
vestido de baño: swimsuit
vestido de gala: gown
vestigio: holdover, trace
vestir: wear
vestir informalmente: dress down
vestir(se): dress
vestirse elegante: dress up
vestuario: wardrobe
veta: grain, streak
vetar: veto
vetear: streak
veterana: veteran
veterano: veteran
veterinaria: doctor, vet, veterinarian
veterinario: doctor, vet, veterinarian
veto: veto
vez: time
vía: rail, railroad, route, track, via
vía de acceso: on-ramp
vía de salida: off-ramp
vía férrea: track
vía intravenosa: IV
Vía Láctea: Milky Way
viabilidad: viability
viabilidad (financiera): affordability
viable: credible, viable
viajante: traveler
viajar: get around, journey, ride, tour, travel
viajar en avión: flying
viajar en jet: jet
viaje: journey, tour, travel, trip, voyage
viaje de estudio: field trip
viaje de ida y vuelta: round trip

viaje largo y cansado: long haul
viaje redondo: round trip
viajera: tourist, traveler
viajero: tourist, traveler
vías respiratorias: respiratory system
vibración: vibration
vibrar: tremble, vibrate
vice-: deputy
vicegobernador: lieutenant governor
vicegobernadora: lieutenant governor
viceversa: vice versa
viciado (aire): stuffy
vicio: vice
vicisitudes: fortune
víctima: casualty, victim
víctima mortal: fatality
victoria: triumph, victory
victoria arrolladora: landslide
victoriana: Victorian
victoriano: Victorian
victorioso: victorious
vid: vine
vida: being, life, lifetime, sweetheart
vida activa: working life
vida cotidiana: daily life
vida de casado: marriage
vida de trabajo: working life
vida laboral: working life
vida media: half-life
vida privada: private life
vida silvestre: wildlife
video: video
videojuego: video game
vidriado: glazed
vidrio: glass
vidrioso: glazed
vieja: dame
viejo: aged, old, old-timer, stale
viento: wind
viento alisio: trade wind
viento polar de levante: polar easterlies
viento poniente: west
vientre: belly
viernes: Friday
viernes informal: casual Friday
viga: beam
vigente: alive, current, in force
vigésimo: twentieth
vigilancia: surveillance
vigilante: alert, guard, marshal
vigilar: guard, keep watch, keep your eyes open, keep an eye out, police, ride herd on, supervise
vigor: vigor
vigorosamente: vigorously
vigoroso: boldness, lively, vigorous
VIH: HIV
VIH positivo/negativo: HIV positive/negative
vil: cheap, sleazy, wicked

villa: villa
villana: villain
villano: villain
vinagre: vinegar
vincular: link, peg, tie
vínculo: attachment, bond, link, tie
vinería: winery
vinilo: vinyl
vino: wine
viña: vineyard
viñedo: vineyard
viola: viola
violáceo: violet
violación: breach, infraction, rape, violation
violación (cometida durante una cita): date rape
violado: violet
violador: rapist
violadora: rapist
violar: breach, break, rape, violate
violencia: violence
violencia vial: road rage
violentamente: fiercely, violently
violento: fierce, high, stormy, violent
violeta: purple, violet
violín: fiddle, violin
violinista: violinist
violoncelista: cellist
violoncelo: cello
violonchelo: cello
viraje: swing
viraje brusco: swerve
virar: swing, veer
virar bruscamente: swerve
virgen: virgin
virginidad: virginity
virtual: virtual
virtualmente: virtually
virtud: strength, virtue
virtuosamente: virtuously
virtuoso: virtuous
virus: virus
virus ébola: Ebola
visa: visa
vísceras: gut, insides
viscosidad: viscosity
visible: visible
visiblemente: visibly
visillo: window shade
visión: perspective, view, vision
visita: call, caller, hit, visit
visita a lugares de interés: sightseeing
visitante: away, tourist, visitor
visitar: look up, see, tour, visit, visit with
vislumbrar: glimpse
víspera: eve
vista: aspect, eyesight, hearing, landscape, sight, view, vision
vistazo: glimpse, look, peek, scan
visto bueno: go-ahead
vistoso: colorful
visual: visual

visualmente: visually
vital: vital
vitalidad: life, vigor
vitalmente: vitally
vitamina: vitamin
vitorear: acclaim, cheer
vitrina: cabinet
viuda: widow
vivacidad: liveliness
vivamente: brightly, vividly
vivaz: lively
víveres: supply
vivero: nursery
vívidamente: dynamically, vividly
vívido: vivid
vivienda subvencionada: public housing
viviendas: housing
vivir: live
vivir a costa de otros: sponge off (others)
vivir a tope: live in the fast lane
vivir al día: live hand to mouth
vivir con: live on
vivir de: live off (somebody)
vivir desahogadamente: live in comfort
vivir en: inhabit
vivo: alive, bright, live, vivid
vocabulario: language, vocabulary
vocal: vocal, vowel
vocálico: vocal
vocalista: vocalist
vocera: spokesperson, spokeswoman
vocero: spokesman, spokesperson
vociferar: pop off, scream
vodevil: vaudeville
volado: crapshoot, lottery, toss
volador: flying
volantazo: swerve
volante: flyer, steering wheel, wheel
volar: blast, flight, fly
volar con el viento: blow
volar en círculo: circle
volar en espiral: spiral
volatería: poultry
volátil: volatile
volcán: volcano
volcán cónico: composite volcano
volcán en escudo: shield volcano
volcánico: extrusive
volcar(se): flip, overturn, tip over, turn over
voleibol: volleyball
volibol: volleyball
voltear(se): flip, invert
voltio: volt
voluble: moody, volatile
volumen: volume
voluntad: will
voluntaria: volunteer
voluntariamente: freely, of one's own accord, voluntarily
voluntario: voluntary,

voluntario
voluta: spiral
volver(se): come back, get back to, go, go back, grow, return, revert, turn, turn against, turn back, twist
volver a arreglar o disponer: rearrange
volver a dictar: rewrite
volver a dividir en distritos: redistricting
volver a estar de moda: come back
volver a evaluar: reevaluate
volver a hacer: do over
volver a jugar: replay
volver a llamar: ring
volver a ocurrir: recur
volver a poner: replace
volver a ponerse en contacto: get back to
volver a redactar: rewrite
volver a utilizar: reuse
volver a visitar: revisit
volver en sí: come around, come to
volver enseguida: be right there/back
volver loco: be mad about, drive mad
volver(se) algo borroso: blur
volverse contra: turn on
volverse pesado (conversación, trabajo): drag
vomitar: barf, be sick, throw up, vomit
vómito: vomit
voraz: omnivorous
vos: you
votación: ballot, poll, vote, voting
votante: voter
votante indeciso: swing voter
votar: vote
voto: vote
voto indeciso: swing vote
voz: vocals, voice
voz activa: active voice
voz y presencia: projection
vuelo: flight
vuelo corto: hop
vuelta: comeback, dash, lap, loop, return, ride, round, spin, turn
vuelta corriendo: jog
vuelta en U: U-turn
vulgar: crude, tasteless
vulgarmente: crudely
vulnerabilidad: vulnerability
vulnerable: vulnerable

W

whisky: whiskey, whisky
World Wide Web: WWW
WWW: World Wide Web, WWW

X

xilema: xylem

Y

y: and, upon
¿Y?: so (what)?
¿Y qué?: so (what)?
y si no ...: what if ...
y tantos, y tantas: odd
ya: (at) any minute (now), already, now
ya era hora: overdue
ya no: any, more/longer, anymore
ya no decir para: never mind
ya no... más (tiempo): any more/longer
ya que: in that
ya sea que: whether
ya veremos: I'll/we'll see
yacimiento: deposit, field
yacimiento petrolífero: oilfield
yang: yang
yanqui: Yankee
yarda: yard
yegua: mare
yelmo: helmet
yema: yolk
yen: yen
yerba: herb, marijuana
yerno: son-in-law
yin: yin
yo: ego, I
yo misma: myself
yo mismo: myself
yogur: yogurt
yogurt: yogurt

Z

zahúrda: pigpen
zambullirse: dive, plunge
zanahoria: carrot
zancada: stride
zanja: ditch
zapatilla de deporte: sneaker
zapatilla escotada: pump
zapato: shoe
zapato de estilo Oxford: oxford
zapatos con tacón de aguja: spike heels
zarandear: buffet
zarcillo: earring
zarigüeya: opossum
zarpar: sail, set sail
zigoto: zygote
zigzag: zigzag
zigzaguear: weave one's way, zigzag
zinc: zinc
zíper: zipper
zona: region, zone
zona cero: ground zero
zona de actores: acting area
zona de agua superficial: open-water zone
zona de aguas profundas: deep-water zone
zona de alimentos: food court
zona de convección: convective zone
zona de radiación: radiative zone

zona de sombra: shadow zone

zona industrial: industrial park

zona pelágica: pelagic environment

zona polar: polar zone

zona templada: temperate zone

zona tropical: tropical

zonas urbanas deprimidas: inner city

zonificación: zoning

zonificar: zone

zoológico: zoo

zooplancton: zooplankton

zorro: fox

zozobrar: founder

zueco: clog

zumaque venenoso: poison oak

zumbar: buzz, hum, roar, whiz

zumbido: buzz, hum

zurcir: mend

zurdo: lefty

zurra: whipping